Healing the Traumatized Self

The Norton Series on Interpersonal Neurobiology
Louis Cozolino, PhD, Series Editor
Allan N. Schore, PhD, Series Editor (2007–2014)
Daniel J. Siegel, MD, Founding Editor

The field of mental health is in a tremendously exciting period of growth and conceptual reorganization. Independent findings from a variety of scientific endeavors are converging in an interdisciplinary view of the mind and mental well-being. An interpersonal neurobiology of human development enables us to understand that the structure and function of the mind and brain are shaped by experiences, especially those involving emotional relationships.

The Norton Series on Interpersonal Neurobiology provides cutting-edge, multidisciplinary views that further our understanding of the complex neurobiology of the human mind. By drawing on a wide range of traditionally independent fields of research—such as neurobiology, genetics, memory, attachment, complex systems, anthropology, and evolutionary psychology—these texts offer mental health professionals a review and synthesis of scientific findings often inaccessible to clinicians. The books advance our understanding of human experience by finding the unity of knowledge, or consilience, that emerges with the translation of findings from numerous domains of study into a common language and conceptual framework. The series integrates the best of modern science with the healing art of psychotherapy.

Healing the Traumatized Self

Consciousness, Neuroscience,

Treatment

Paul Frewen
Ruth Lanius

W. W. Norton & Company

New York • London

Cover Art: "Creation I," was painted by Ms. Tanaz Javan in 2007. Ms. Javan completed a Masters in Neuroscience as supervised by Professor Frewen.

Select artwork contributions by Graham M. Howell, Bev A., K. Shaw, Leisanne Sylvester-Jarvis, and Teresa Kinney (PTSD Survivor). Used with Permission.

For information about permission to reproduce selections
from this book, write to Permissions, W. W. Norton & Company, Inc.,
500 Fifth Avenue, New York, NY 10110

For information about special discounts for bulk
purchases, please contact W. W. Norton Special Sales at
specialsales@wwnorton.com or 800-233-4830

Manufacturing by Courier Westford
Production manager: Leeann Graham

Library of Congress Cataloging-in-Publication Data

Frewen, Paul, author.
 Healing the traumatized self : consciousness, neuroscience, treatment / Paul Frewen and Ruth Lanius. — First edition.
     p. ; cm. — (The Norton series on interpersonal neurobiology)
 Includes bibliographical references and index.
 ISBN 978-0-393-70551-5 (hardcover : alk. paper)
 I. Lanius, Ruth A., 1968– , author. II. Title. III. Series: Norton series on interpersonal neurobiology.
 [DNLM: 1. Stress Disorders, Traumatic—therapy—Case Reports.
 2. Adaptation, Psychological—Case Reports. 3. Cognition.
 4. Dissociative Disorders—therapy—Case Reports. WM 172.5]
 RC552.P67
 616.85'210651—dc23
                          2014036987

ISBN: 978-0-393-70551-5

W. W. Norton & Company, Inc., 500 Fifth Avenue, New York, NY 10110
www.wwnorton.com

W. W. Norton & Company, Ltd., Castle House, 75/76 Wells Street, London
W1T 3QT

2 3 4 5 6 7 8 9 0

To our patients,

who will always and forever

be our teachers

Contents

Foreword

by David Spiegel, MD

HEALING THE TRAUMATIZED SELF is an important clinical and scientific challenge that is met admirably by Frewen and Lanius with their ability to integrate compassion and neuroscience, psychotherapy and traumatology, heart and mind. Trauma, as they so vividly portray, is a dehumanizing experience, one in which those subjected to it are reduced to the status of objects, the victim of someone else's rage, nature's indifference, misfortune or misadventure. It involves being plunged into a state of helplessness and, as the authors note, dissociation can be a powerful means of maintaining mental control at a time when physical control is lost (Spiegel and Cardena 1991). Dissociation, the dis-integration of consciousness, memory, emotion, and somatic experience, can buffer the experience of trauma—a rape survivor said, "I heard someone screaming and realized it was me"—but it can also provide a template for traumatized living and self-misunderstanding that inhibits recovery. Frewen and Lanius, through decades of careful clinical and scientific experience, describe the problem and put forward a method for effectively treating it.

There is growing recognition of how intertwined trauma and dissociation are. The new Fifth Edition of the Diagnostic and Statistical Manual of Mental Disorders (APA 2013) placed the Dissociative Disorders adjacent to the Trauma and Stressor-Related Disorders purposely to underscore this. Furthermore, included in it is a new Dissociative Subtype of Post-Traumatic Stress Disorder (PTSD), defined by having all of the new PTSD symptoms plus depersonalization and/or derealization (Lanius, Brand et al., 2012). This change was based upon three categories of data. The first was the work of Lanius and colleagues showing with functional neuroimaging that a subgroup of those with PTSD respond to traumatic imagery with hyperactivity of the frontal cortex and limbic inhibition, just the opposite of the typical hyperarousal symptoms that are accompanied by hypofrontality and limbic activation (Lanius, Vermetten et al., 2010). Second, latent class analysis of datasets of PTSD symptoms show a relatively distinct subgroup with extra dissociative symptoms, beyond the flashbacks, amnesia, and numbing that are more typical (Wolf, Lunney et al., 2012; Wolf, Miller et al. 2012). Third, recent epidemiological data show that those with PTSD and depersonalization/derealization have more severe early life histories of trauma and abuse and are more prone to suicide (Stein, Koenen et al., 2012). This multi-pronged empirical foundation underscores the fact that the role of dissociation in trauma is scientifically established, not just theoretically advocated. We can be of most help to our patients when we deeply understand them and what they are going through. Diagnosing and treating dissociation does not mean accepting the patient's view of self and the world any more than working with someone with schizophrenia means believing his or her delusions. The proper stance is what the well-known interpersonal psychiatrist Harry Stack Sullivan called "participant observation" (Sullivan 1953). You form a real and meaningful relationship with your patient, but never get so close that you cannot step back and observe—it is both connection and evaluation. Frewen and Lanius wisely describe dissociative consciousness in a way that allows clinicians to meet such patients where they are and gently lead them, using the power of the therapeutic relationship, toward integration, incorporating their dissociated past into their more comprehensive present and future. They build upon trauma-focused psychotherapies that emphasize the importance of graded exposure to trauma-related memories (Foa, Davidson et al. 1999; Schnurr, Lunney et al., 2009). However, such exposure-based psychotherapies can be less effective for those with predominantly dissociative symptoms, who may simply be re-traumatized during re-exposure, so they draw upon current trends in phase-oriented psychotherapy for trauma survivors (Cloitre, Courtois et al., 2011; Resick, Suvak et al., 2012) with its emphasis on stabilization, careful working through of trauma-related material, and relapse prevention. They refer to important work on the power of mentalization in helping those with relationship and affective instability (Bateman and Fonagy 1999).

This book shows how far we have come from the time when Freud interpreted incest memories as childhood fantasies (Freud 1953), although in one brilliant paper, "Remembering, Repeating and Working Through" (Freud 1953), Freud anticipated much that has followed in the psychotherapy of traumatic experiences, using the working through of trauma-related transference issues as the focus. Psychotherapeutic examination and working through of trauma involves grief work as well, acknowledging, bearing, and putting into perspective our limitations and losses in order to free our psyches to engage in new relationships and aspects of life, as Lindemann described in his remarkable essay on the aftermath of the tragic Coconut Grove nightclub fire in Boston (Lindemann 1944(94)). Frewen and Lanius show that we have also moved beyond (Dalenberg, Brand et al., 2012) more recent false claims that trauma and dissociation are linked because those who dissociate are "fantasy-prone" (Giesbrecht, Lynn et al., 2008). Those with dissociation suffer from too much reality, not too little.

Healing the Traumatized Self presents a complex, problem-focused psychotherapy grounded in the evolution of modern psychotherapy and psychological science. It is clearly and thoughtfully written. It will help both psychotherapists and trauma survivors collect themselves and emerge stronger.

References

APA (2013). *Diagnostic and Statistical Manual of Mental Disorders, Fifth Edition (DSM-5)*. Washington, D.C., American Psychiatric Publishing.

Bateman, A. and P. Fonagy (1999). "Effectiveness of partial hospitalization in the treatment of borderline personality disorder: A randomized controlled trial." *American Journal of Psychiatry, 156,* 1563–1569.

Cloitre, M., C. A. Courtois, et al. (2011). "Treatment of complex PTSD: results of the ISTSS expert clinician survey on best practices." *Journal of traumatic stress, 24*(6), 615–627.

Dalenberg, C. J., B. L. Brand, et al., (2012). "Evaluation of the evidence for the trauma and fantasy models of dissociation." *Psychological bulletin, 138*(3), 550–588.

Foa, E. B., J. R. T. Davidson, et al. (1999). "Treatment of Posttraumatic Stress Disorder." *Journal of Clinical Psychiatry, 50*(Supplement 16), 4–69.

Freud, S. (1953). *Thee essays on the theory of sexuality.*

Giesbrecht, T., S. J. Lynn, et al., (2008). "Cognitive processes in dissociation: an analysis of core theoretical assumptions." *Psychological bulletin, 134*(5), 617–647.

Lanius, R. A., B. Brand, et al., (2012). "The dissociative subtype of posttraumatic stress disorder: rationale, clinical and neurobiological evidence, and implications." *Depression and anxiety, 29*(8), 701–708.

Lanius, R. A., E. Vermetten, et al., (2010). "Emotion modulation in PTSD: Clinical and neurobiological evidence for a dissociative subtype." *The American journal of psychiatry, 167*(6), 640–647.

Lindemann, E. (1944(94)). "Symptomatology and management of acute grief." *Am J Psychiatry, 151*(6 Suppl), 155–160.

Resick, P. A., M. K. Suvak, et al., (2012). "The Impact of Dissociation on Ptsd Treatment with Cognitive Processing Therapy." *Depression and Anxiety.*

Schnurr, P. P., C. A. Lunney, et al., (2009). "Sexual function outcomes in women treated for posttraumatic stress disorder." *Journal of women's health, 18*(10), 1549–1557.

Spiegel, D. and E. Cardena (1991). "Disintegrated experience: the dissociative disorders revisited." *Journal of Abnormal Psychology, 100*(3), 366–378.

Stein, D. J., K. C. Koenen, et al. (2012). "Dissociation in Posttraumatic Stress Disorder: Evidence from the World Mental Health Surveys." *Biological psychiatry.*

Sullivan, H. S. (1953). *The Interpersonal Theory of Psychiatry.* New York, W.W. Norton.

Wolf, E. J., C. A. Lunney, et al., (2012). "The Dissociative Subtype of Ptsd: A Replication and Extension." *Depression and Anxiety.*

Wolf, E. J., M. W. Miller, et al., (2012). "A Latent Class Analysis of Dissociation and Posttraumatic Stress Disorder: Evidence for a Dissociative SubtypeLatent Class Analysis of Dissociation and PTSD." *Archives of General Psychiatry, 69*(7), 698–705.

Foreword

by Bessel van der Kolk, MD

What do you see when you look in the mirror? What do you feel in your body when you check in with yourself? What we see and what we notice is to a large degree the long-term outcome of the relationships we had with our caregivers, particularly during the first few years of our lives. Children are intensely social from the start; they are captivated by faces and voices. From birth they are exquisitely sensitive to facial expression, posture, tone of voice, physiological changes, and tempo of movement. This inborn capacity for attunement—for being able to match their inner experience with that of those around them—is an evolutionary product essential to the survival of our species.

Children are also programmed to choose one particular adult (or, at most, a few) with whom their natural communication system develops. This creates a deep attachment bond, and children show who their principal attachment figure is by crying when they go away and delighting when they return. From this intimate give-and-take, children learn that other people have feelings and thoughts that may be different from their own. It is through secure attachment that children gradually develop the self-awareness, empathy, impulse control, and self-motivation to help them become contributing members of their families and, eventually, participants of the larger social culture.

Neuroscience research has affirmed that our brains and our sense of self are molded by our interactions with others. Those early interactions shape what we see when we look around and sense what is going on inside of ourselves. Our early relationships lay down the inner maps of the world around us and who we are. We are biologically primed to share our pleasures with each other, and to respond to distress by seeking comfort from people we trust. We learn to regulate our feelings by being soothed by someone who rocks us when we cry, feeds us when we're hungry, or covers us with a blanket when we're cold.

These also are exactly the qualities that are painfully missing in the patients we see at The Trauma Center in Boston, and that Paul Frewen and

Ruth Lanius have made such monumental contributions in helping us to understand and treat. If no one has ever looked at you with loving eyes, broken out in a smile when they see you, or rushed to help when you were distressed (instead saying, "Stop crying, or I'll give you something to cry about!"), you are prone to develop a disorganized and scattered relationship with yourself. You are forced to discover alternative ways of taking care of yourself. When nobody helps take care of you, you are likely to try anything to bring relief—drugs, alcohol, binge eating, cutting, or simply shutting down and giving up.

If nobody has ever seen you for who you are, valued you as a special person, or made sure that you were okay, how can you ever open your heart to yourself or others? Is it possible to create a different set of expectations and learn to envision new possibilities when you have no idea what it feels like to be cherished? These are some of the questions that Frewen and Lanius have encountered in the course of their clinical practice and researched with the help of state-of-the-art technology.

The authors blend a special combination of skills that mark all great innovators in psychology and psychiatry: frequent and in-depth exposure to patients (in their case, patients who struggle with the long-term effects of trauma, abandonment, and neglect), combined with expertise in cutting-edge scientific methodology. This combination is rare. The vast majority of researchers only see patients who are participants in their research studies—research subjects who check off long lists of predetermined questions—and very few clinicians possess the necessary research skills and technical expertise to scientifically explore the questions they confront in their practices every day.

Frewen and Lanius began with the realization that their traumatized patients did not seek psychiatric help because of classical PTSD symptoms—such as intrusions, avoidance, and hyperarousal—but because they could not feel safe with other human beings, or even with themselves. They were unable to negotiate the ordinary give-and-take of relationships, including relationships with their therapists. Even engaging with their doctors often only aggravated their profoundly damaged sense of self, and therapy sometimes did more harm than good.

As clinicians, Frewen and Lanius were constantly confronted with intriguing questions rarely mentioned in textbooks. For example, patients who mentioned that they didn't recognize themselves when they looked in a mirror; or who reported feeling like they were floating above the scene when they were physically intimate; or patients who hit their kids. Others mentioned that they felt no sensations in large swaths of their bodies, and felt no emotional connection with their own children. Others woke up with cuts and burns all over their bodies, with no memory of how they occurred. Frewen and Lanius soon understood that these patients were only trying to make themselves feel better in the best way they know how. However, these hallmark symptoms of not recognizing yourself and not being aware of major aspects of self-experience are rarely mentioned in textbooks on depression or anxiety, and rarely in treatment manuals for PTSD.

Some scientists think of traumatic stress as a malfunction of the brain's fear circuitry. However, Frewen and Lanius realized that the reason their patients were chronically overwhelmed was not simply because they were terrified, but because their brains had changed as a result of their terrifying experiences. This phenomenon was observed as far back as 1893, when Sigmund Freud and Joseph Breuer observed that trauma does not simply act as a releasing agent for symptoms. Rather, the memory of the trauma acts like a foreign body, which, long after its entry, continues to be an agent at work.[1] Like a splinter that causes an infection, the body's response to the foreign object becomes the problem, more than the object itself.[2]

In a series of brilliant scientific articles and books, neuroscientist Antonio Damasio has clarified the relationship between body states, emotions, and survival. He starts by pointing out the deep divide between our conscious thinking and the sensory life of our bodies. As he poetically explains:

> Sometimes we use our minds not to discover facts, but to hide them. . . . One of the things the screen hides most effectively is the body, our own body, by which I mean the ins of it, its interiors. Like a veil thrown over the skin to secure its modesty, the screen partially removes from the mind the inner states of the body, those that constitute the flow of life as it wanders in the journey of each day.[3]

Building on the century-old work of William James, Damasio argues that the core of our self-awareness rests on the physical sensations that convey the inner states of the body:

> [P]rimordial feelings provide a direct experience of one's own living body, wordless, unadorned, and connected to nothing but sheer existence. These primordial feelings reflect the current state of the body along varied dimensions, . . . along the scale that ranges from pleasure to pain, and they originate at the level of the brain stem rather than the cerebral cortex. All feelings of emotion are complex musical variations on primordial feelings.[4]

Our sensory world takes shape even before we are born. In the womb, we feel amniotic fluid against our skin, we hear the faint sounds of rushing blood and a digestive tract at work, we pitch and roll with our mothers' movements. After birth, our physical sensations define our relationship with ourselves and our surroundings. We start off *being* our wetness, hunger, satiation, and sleepiness. A cacophony of incomprehensible sounds and images presses in on our pristine nervous system. Even after we acquire consciousness and language, our bodily sensing system provides crucial feedback on how we are doing. Its constant hum communicates changes in our viscera and in the muscles of our face, torso, and extremities that signal pain and comfort, as well as urges such as hunger and sexual arousal.

The job of the brain is to constantly monitor and evaluate what is going on within and around us. These evaluations are transmitted by chemical messages in the bloodstream and electrical messages in our nerves, causing subtle or intense changes throughout the body and brain. These shifts usually occur entirely without conscious input or awareness; the subcortical regions of the brain are remarkably efficient in regulating our breathing, heartbeat, digestion, hormone secretion, and immune system. However, these systems can become overwhelmed if we are challenged by ongoing threat, or even the perception of threat. This accounts for the wide array of physical problems researchers have documented in traumatized people.

Yet, our conscious self also plays a vital role in maintaining our inner equilibrium. We need to register and act on our physical sensations to keep our bodies safe. Realizing we're cold moves us to put on a sweater; feeling hungry or spacey tells us our blood sugar is low and spurs us to get a snack; or, the pressure of a full bladder sends us to the bathroom. All of the brain structures that register background feelings are located near areas that control basic housekeeping functions, such as breathing, appetite, elimination, and sleep/wake cycles. As Damasio writes, "This is because the consequences of having emotion and attention are entirely related to the fundamental business of managing life within the organism. It is not possible to manage life and maintain homeostatic balance without data on the current state of the organism's body."[4] Damasio calls these housekeeping areas of the brain the "proto-self," because they create the "wordless knowledge" that underlies our conscious sense of self.

In 2000, Damasio and his colleagues published an article in one of the world's foremost scientific publications,[5] which showed that reliving a strong negative emotion causes significant changes in the brain areas that receive nerve signals from the muscles, gut, and skin. These areas are crucial for regulating basic bodily functions. Recalling an emotional event from the past causes us to actually re-experience the visceral sensations that we felt on the original occasion. Each emotion produced a characteristic pattern, distinct from the others. For example, a particular part of the brainstem was "active in sadness and anger, but not in happiness or fear." We acknowledge their involvement every time we use one of the common expressions that link strong emotions with the body: *You make me sick; It made my skin crawl; I was all choked up; My heart sank; He makes me bristle.*

The elementary self-system in the brainstem and limbic system is massively activated when people are faced with annihilation. This results in an overwhelming sense of fear and terror that is accompanied by intense physiological arousal. To people who are reliving a trauma, nothing makes sense; they are trapped in a life-or-death situation—in a state of paralyzing fear or blind rage. Mind and body are constantly aroused, as if they are in imminent danger. They startle in response to the slightest noises and are frustrated by small irritations. Their sleep is chronically disturbed, and food often loses its sensual pleasures. This, in turn, can trigger desperate attempts to shut those feelings down by freezing and dissociation.[6]

Abuse, trauma, and neglect interfere with the proper functioning of brain areas that manage and interpret those experiences, such as the medial prefrontal cortex, the anterior cingulate, the parietal cortex, the thalamus, precuneus, and posterior cingulate, just to name a few. A robust sense of self depends on a healthy and dynamic interplay among these areas. One of the robust findings in the neuroscience of early abuse and neglect is that kids who have to manage their feelings all by themselves learn to exclude their inner experience from self-awareness, and hence are prevented from developing such a robust sense of self.

In a brilliant research study, Ruth Lanius and her colleagues[7,8] showed that in an attempt to cope, chronically traumatized patients had learned to shut down the brain areas that transmit the visceral feelings and emotions that accompany and define terror. That probably helped them to not be completely overwhelmed, but at a price. In everyday life, those same brain areas are responsible for registering the emotions and sensations that form the foundation of our sense of who we are. In other words, adapting to feeling chronically ignored and unseen deadens the capacity to feel fully alive. This explains why so many traumatized people lose their sense of purpose and direction; their relationship with their inner reality is impaired. How can you make decisions, or put any plan into action, if you can't define what you want or what the sensations in your body—the basis of all emotions—are trying to tell you?

If patients with histories of trauma and neglect suffer from extreme disconnections from their bodies, how can we help? The professional training of most psychologists, psychiatrists, and other mental health clinicians focuses on understanding and insight, and largely ignores the relevance of the living, breathing body, the foundation of our selves. Understanding where impulses to cut, space out, or gorge and vomit come from make little difference; healing needs to reconfigure our patients' relationships with themselves, with the underlying physical organism.

Antonio Damasio said, "Consciousness was invented so that we could know life,"[3] but what if it is unbearable to face the reality of what is going on? You try to shut yourself down, ignore what is happening, and dull your consciousness. In this book Frewen and Lanius have organized the extremely complex and hitherto unsystematized effects of trauma in the context of serious disruptions in attachment relationships into four dimensions: distortions in the consciousness of 1) time, 2) thought, 3) body, and 4) emotion. All of these trauma-related altered states of consciousness (TRASC) are reflected in changes in brain function, and all of them have their origins in making overwhelming experiences of abuse, abandonment, and trauma more tolerable. In other words, they all started as psychological escape mechanisms where physical escape was impossible. Frewen and Lanius also propose a methodology for studying, assessing, and treating TRASC in trauma survivors, which they call *neurophenomenology*. This methodology integrates the study of an individuals' first-person experience with objective neurophysiological measures. But that is not where they stop. As clinicians they also have access to marvelously detailed reports of their patients' subjective experiences, their response to interventions, and their mental and artistic products, both in words and in pictures.

Owning Your Life

How do people regain control when their brains are stuck in a fight for survival? If what goes on deep inside our brains dictates how we feel, and if our body sensations are orchestrated by subcortical (subconscious) brain structures, how much control can we actually have?

"Agency" is the technical term for being in charge of your life—knowing where you stand, knowing that you have a say in what happens to you, knowing that you have some ability to shape your circumstances. Agency starts with being aware of our subtle sensory, body-based feelings. The greater our awareness, the greater our potential to control our lives. Knowing *what* we feel is the first step to knowing *why* we feel that way. If we are aware of the constant changes in our inner and outer environment, we can mobilize to manage them. But we can't do this unless our watchtower, the medial prefrontal cortex (MPFC), learns to observe what is going on inside us. This is why mindfulness practice, which strengthens the MPFC, is a cornerstone of recovery from trauma.

Without therapy, the trauma that came from outside continues to live inside the survivor. The price of avoiding awareness of sensations related to terror and helplessness is losing awareness of oneself and surrendering the capacity for any kind of sensory pleasure. However, traumatized people chronically feel unsafe inside their bodies. The past is alive in the form of gnawing interior discomfort. Their bodies are constantly bombarded by visceral warning signs and, in an attempt to control these processes, they often become expert at ignoring their gut feelings and the numbing awareness of what is played out inside. They learn to hide from their selves. "Scared stiff" and "frozen in fear" (collapsing and going numb) describe precisely what terror and trauma feel like. These descriptors are their visceral foundation. The experience of fear derives from primitive responses to threat, where escape is thwarted in some way. Trauma sufferers will be kept hostage to fear until that visceral experience changes.

Suppressing feelings may make it possible to take care of business, but at a price. These trauma survivors learned to shut down their emotions and, as a result, they no longer recognize what they are feeling. Paul Frewen performed a series of brain scans of people with PTSD who suffered from alexithymia. One of the participants told him, "I don't know what I feel; it's like my head and body aren't connected. I'm living in a tunnel, a fog, no matter what happens it's the same reaction—numbness, nothing. Having a bubble bath and being burned or raped are the same feeling. My brain doesn't feel." Frewen and Lanius found that the more people were out of touch with their feelings, the less activity they had in the self-sensing areas of the brain.[9]

Because traumatized people have trouble sensing what is going on in their bodies, they respond to stress by becoming "spaced out" or numb, or react with excessive anger and impulsivity. However they react, they can't really tell what is upsetting them. People with alexithymia can only get better by learning to recognize the relationship between their physical sensations and their emotions, much as colorblind people enter the world of color by learning to distinguish and appreciate shades of grey.

A Goal for Recovery: Befriending the Body

The neuroscience of selfhood and agency validates the kinds of somatic therapies that our colleagues Peter Levine and Pat Ogden have developed. In essence, the aim is threefold:

- to evoke the sensory information that is blocked and frozen by trauma
- to help patients befriend (rather than suppress) the energies released by that inner experience
- to complete the self-preserving physical actions that were thwarted when they were trapped, restrained, or immobilized by terror.

Trauma victims cannot recover until they become familiar with, and befriend, the sensations in their bodies. Being scared means that you live in a body that is always on guard. Angry people live in angry bodies. The bodies of child abuse victims are always tense and defensive until they find a way to relax and feel safe. In order to change, people need to become aware of their sensations and the way that their bodies interact with the world around them. Physical self-awareness is the first step in releasing the tyranny of the past.

Noticing sensations for the first time can be quite distressing. It may precipitate flashbacks in which patients curl up or assume defensive postures. These are somatic re-enactments of the undigested trauma. Images and physical sensations may deluge patients at this point, and the therapist must be familiar with ways to stem torrents of sensation and emotion. Some school teachers, nurses, police officers, and yoga instructors are very skilled at soothing terror reactions because they are confronted almost daily with out-of-control or painfully disorganized people.

All too often, however, drugs such as SSRIs (Prozac, Xyprexa, Seroquel, and others) are substituted for teaching people the skills to deal with such distressing physical reactions. Of course, medications only blunt sensations and do nothing to resolve them or transform them from toxic agents into allies. The mind needs to be re-educated to feel physical sensations, and the body needs to be helped to tolerate and enjoy the comforts of touch. With practice, they can learn to connect their physical sensations to psychological events and slowly become reconnected with themselves.

References

1. Freud, S. & Breuer, M. (1896). *Physical Mechanism of Hysterical Phenomena*.
2. van der Kolk, B. (in press). *The Body Keeps the Score: Mind, Brain, and Body in the Healing of Traumatic Stress.* New York: Viking Press.
3. Damasio, A. (2012). *Self Comes to Mind: Constructing the Conscious Brain.* New York: Vintage.
4. Damasio, A. (2000). *The Feeling of What Happens: Body and Emotion in the Making of Consciousness*. New York: Mariner, p. 256.
5. Damasio, A., et al. (2000). Subcortical and cortical brain activity during the feeling of self-generated emotions. Nature Neuroscience, 3, 1049-1056.
6. Nijenhuis, E. R. S., Van der Hart, O., Steele, K., 2002. The emerging psychobiology of trauma-related dissociation and dissociative disorders, in: D'haenen, H. A. H., Den Boer, J. A., Willner, P. (Eds.), Biological Psychiatry, Vol. 2. Wiley, West Sussex, pp. 1079–1098.
7. Bluhm, R.L., ...Lanius, R.A. (2009). Alterations in default network connectivity in post-traumatic stress disorder related to early-life trauma. Journal of Psychiatry and Neuroscience, 34, 187-194.
8. Lanius, R.A., et al. (2005). Functional connectivity of dissociative responses in posttraumatic stress disorder: A functional magnetic resonance imaging investigation. Biological Psychiatry, 15, 873-884.

9. Frewen, P.A., Lanius, R.A., et al. (2008). Clinical and Neural Correlates of Alexithymia in PTSD. *Journal of Abnormal Psychology*, 117, 171-181.

Preface

The Prison-House of the Traumatized Self

"Our normal waking consciousness, rational consciousness as we call it, is but one special type of consciousness, whilst all about it, parted from it by the filmiest of screens, there lie potential forms of consciousness entirely different. . . . We may go through life without suspecting their existence; but apply the requisite stimulus, and at a touch they are there in all their completeness, definite types of mentality which probably somewhere have their field of application and adaptation. No account of the universe in its totality can be final which leaves these other forms of consciousness quite disregarded."

—William James (1902/2002, pp. 373–374)

THIS CELEBRATED PASSAGE FROM William James, who is by many accounts the founding father of philosophical psychology and the psychological study of altered states of consciousness, describes his conviction that "normal waking consciousness" represents but a fraction of the range of potential modes of subjective awareness available to us. Worth emphasizing for present purposes are three points. First, James distinguishes between a "normal waking" or "rational" form of consciousness and various other forms of consciousness. These other forms of consciousness are thus, by definition, not considered "normal," and are nowadays typically referred to as "altered states of consciousness" (e.g., Vaitl et al., 2005). Second, James described altered states of consciousness as potentiated by specific psychophysiological conditions: "apply the requisite stimulus, and at a touch they are there in all their completeness." Third, James suspected that our capacity to experience altered states of consciousness is likely *purposeful*. In other words, he assumed that altered states of consciousness probably serve some yet unknown adaptive function, thus referring to them as "definite types of mentality which probably somewhere have their field of application and adaptation."

The passage above was taken from James's famous treatise on the *Varieties of Religious Experience*. In that text, his focus was on positive, spiritual states of mind that might be loosely labeled ecstatic, transcendent, and/or mystical in nature. Nevertheless, James also examined the sometimes frightening and melancholic character of religious experiences. Moreover, James held that the examination of psychopathology was key to understanding the structure and functions of human subjectivity. Therefore, in *Varieties* James also called for us to "address ourselves to the unpleasant task of hearing what the sick souls . . . have to say of the secrets of their prison-house, their own peculiar form of consciousness" (p. 136).

Answering that call, in the present text we address the imprisoned states of mind of the severely psychologically traumatized person. We describe how overwhelming experiences, including extreme acts of violence, torture, and abuse, often occurring in or preceded by a developmental context of serious disruption in attachment relationships between a child and his or her early caregivers, can alter four dimensions of consciousness in trauma survivors: the consciousness of (1) time, (2) thought, (3) body, and (4) emotion. It has been suggested that the principal function of these trauma-related altered states of consciousness (TRASC) may be to make the survival of overwhelming experiences more tolerable, that is, to afford mental escape when physical escape is not possible. However, the persistence of TRASC in the long-term aftermath of trauma is typically regarded as a marker of psychopathology. We also recommend a methodology for studying, assessing, and treating TRASC in trauma survivors: *neurophenomenology*. This methodology integrates the study of an individual's first-person experience with objective neurophysiological measures. Finally, we present some of the more severe case examples of TRASC that we have encountered in our research and clinical practices with traumatized persons throughout the text.

We begin in Chapter 1 by introducing a theoretical model for classifying the symptomatology of posttraumatic stress along dissociative-altered versus non-dissociative-normal forms of four dimensions of consciousness. The four dimensions of consciousness to which our model refers are the dimensions of (1) *time* (i.e., the span of time and the tenses of present, past, and future); (2) *thought* (i.e., the story-like narrative structure of verbal thought as incorporating content, perspective, and plot); (3) *body* (i.e., the embodied sense of having, consciously being in, and belonging to a body); and (4) *emotion* (the affective experience of emotional feelings). This four-dimensional model (which we refer to as a "4-D model") classifies symptoms of posttraumatic stress as either intrinsically dissociative in nature or not, reflecting the four dimensions either in the form of trauma-related altered states of consciousness (TRASC) or normal waking consciousness (NWC), respectively. The 4-D model also considers the processes through which TRASC develop within the context of exposure to psychological trauma.

In Chapter 2 we overview the methodological approach that we recommend for the systematic study of psychologically traumatized forms of consciousness, namely, *neurophenomenology*. In brief, *neurophenomenology* integrates the systematic investigation of moment-to-moment first-person subjective experience with neurophysiological recordings as dual interactive and integrative means for systematically describing the structure, processes, and function of human consciousness. For example, people may be encouraged to elaborate, moment by moment, on their first-person experience of remembering or reliving a traumatic event while neurophysiological measurements are recorded; interpretation of the psychological significance of the neurophysiological measures would then take into consideration people's first-person experiential accounts of the memory.

The neurophenomenological examination of consciousness in its normal and abnormal forms, as impacted by severe stress, should bring into clearer view the other side of James's "filmiest of screens," wherein we posit the nature of the subjectivity experienced by the chronically traumatized person is often to be found. However, we explicitly note as a limitation that the neurophysiological measures we discuss and associate with phenomenology in this text are in nearly all cases limited to neuroimaging. In other words, studies conducted at genetic, molecular, neuroendocrine, and neuroimmunological levels of analysis receive little to no attention herein. This is partly based on the fact that neuroimaging represents the research methodology with which we have the most personal expertise. More substantively, however, given that neurophenomenology seeks to investigate the intercausality between *moment-to-moment* first-person subjective experience with neurophysiological recordings, coupled with the fact that measures of *moment-to-moment* changes in molecular and neurochemical markers are largely unavailable in humans, empirical investigations at these levels of neurobiological analysis are yet to be conducted.

Chapters 3–6 describe the symptomatology of posttraumatic stress as it relates to normal versus altered forms of the consciousness of time (Chapter 3), thought (Chapter 4), body (Chapter 5), and emotion (Chapter 6). Finally, in Chapter 7 we consider the process of trauma recovery from dissociative trauma-related altered states of consciousness (TRASC) through to healthy, integrated senses of self as it takes place in trauma-focused psychotherapy. Note further that we include an Appendix that provides further clinical examples of TRASC of time, thought, body, and emotion in response to interviews we conducted with trauma survivors. We emphasize that these clinical examples represent relatively severe and prototypic cases.

Throughout this text we argue that both the treating clinician and researcher alike should distinguish between two general forms of consciousness that frequently present clinically within persons with trauma-related disorders: (1) states of distress that are not intrinsically *dissociative*, as such, by parsimony, presumed to maintain normal waking consciousness (NWC); and (2) states of distress that are quintessentially *dissociative* in nature, representing as such trauma-related altered states of consciousness (TRASC). It may be that distress presenting in the form of NWC versus TRASC represents *qualitatively* or *categorically* distinct forms of distress, thus differing *in kind* in the philosophical sense. As such, the two states may well be parted by what James called the "filmiest of screens." Nevertheless, at present we do not wish to rule out the theoretical possibility that these states differ more subtly, only in degree. In any case, the major thesis of this text is that theory, research, and clinical observations collected to date support the validity of distinguishing between dissociative and non-dissociative presentations of distress, only the former defined by TRASC.

James (1902/2002) noted further on in the *Varieties*:

> Insane conditions have this advantage, that they isolate special factors of the mental life, and enable us to inspect them unmasked by their more usual surroundings. They play the part in mental anatomy which the scalpel and the microscope play in the anatomy of the body. To understand a thing rightly we need to see it both out of its environment and in it, and to have acquaintance with the whole range of its variations. (p. 30)

Accordingly, we argue for the relevance of a theoretical synthesis of psychotraumatology with developments in the field of consciousness studies as a means of understanding not only normal but also altered states of consciousness. In addition, we suggest the value of the neurophenomenology paradigm as a methodological approach to understanding the effects of complex trauma.

In summary, we have argued that the neurophenomenology paradigm in consciousness studies provides a useful methodological framework for researching the effects of psychological trauma; in turn, trauma-related psychopathology provides an excellent model for further understanding human consciousness and subjective experience and its abnormalities as prompted by extreme life stress. Indeed our collective clinical and research experience working with trauma survivors suggests that the psychological phenomena of peritraumatic and posttraumatic stress represent powerful theoretical, empirical, and clinical paradigms for studying the complexities of human subjective experience in both the form of normal waking consciousness (NWC) and trauma-related altered states of consciousness (TRASC). In effect, we suggest that experiences of severe psychological trauma can act as James's "requisite stimulus" for the un-veiling of altered states of consciousness: "at a touch, they are revealed in all their completeness." Moreover, we strongly suggest that the clinical significance of psychological trauma cannot be rightly understood without understanding the effects traumatic events can have on altering normal waking states of consciousness. Following James: "No account of [psychological trauma] in its totality can be final which leaves these other forms of consciousness quite disregarded."

Acknowledgements

THE IDEA FOR THIS text began with an invitation from Allan Schore to contribute a volume on trauma and dissociation to the Norton Series in Interpersonal Neurobiology. Shortly thereafter we attended a think-tank following Bessel Van der Kolk's annual trauma conference in Boston 2009. This meeting inspired us to consider trauma-related dissociation from a dimensional and neurophenomenological perspective, ultimately culminating in the present work.

We are indebted to all of our colleagues and collaborators for their mentoring, teaching and research. A special thanks to Robyn Bluhm, Jim Hopper, Clare Pain, and Mischa Tursich for their comments on earlier drafts of this text. We would also like to express our gratitude toward our students who have always challenged our thinking and helped us grow as clinician scientists.

Franziska Unholzer, Carolin Steuwe, and Mischa Tursich participated in a number of the phenomenological interviews transcribed herein. Suzy Southwell, Stephanie Nevill, and Julia MacKinley assisted with scheduling and transcriptions of interviews. We are particularly indebted to Erica Lundberg and Nancy Mazza for their outstanding administrative support. A special thank you to Tanaz Javan, who is the author of the cover art.

We would also like to thank all Norton staff for their tireless support and patience with us throughout the writing and publishing process. We are especially grateful to Deborah Malmud for her encouragement and confidence in us as authors.

We would like to express our deepest gratitude to our families and friends for their patience and support throughout the writing process. Paul Frewen would like to acknowledge the love and support of his wife Kim, his children Nathan, Kaylin, Liam and Mya, his parents, and the rest of his family. Ruth Lanius would like to acknowledge the love and support of her husband Derm and the rest of her family.

Above all, we would like to thank all of the individuals who, through dialogue, their artwork and poetry, have shared with us their lived experiences of human suffering, perseverance, and resilience. Their stories have been the primary inspiration for this work.

We hope that theory, clinical research and practice in the fields of trauma and dissociation continues to grow, deepen, and mature. If we are to truly understand how recovery and healing of a traumatized self takes place, we believe that a disciplined integration of studies from consciousness, neuroscience, and treatment will be required.

We still have much to learn.

Paul Frewen and Ruth Lanius

Healing the Traumatized Self

CHAPTER 1

The Varieties of Posttraumatic Experience

A Four-Dimensional Model

"Extreme states induced by stress and trauma are robustly different on state-defining variables (i.e., dissociated) from normal states of consciousness. The more severe the trauma, at least on certain indices, the greater the likelihood that an individual will be driven into an altered state of consciousness. Chronic or repetitive trauma leads to a greater number of altered states, which coevolve with time."

—Frank Putnam (1996, p. 176)[1]

Case 1: A Traumatized Self: Distress Associated with Normal Waking Consciousness

"Kaylin" is a middle-aged married woman with three young children, two from a previous marriage. She is currently working and attending college part-time. She describes her current (second) husband, the father of her third child, as loving and supportive.

Kaylin was raised in an emotionally cold, strict, and rigidly religious home. Her father was emotionally and physically abusive, whereas her mother was withdrawn and emotionally unsupportive. Kaylin was repeatedly sexually abused at a young age by a member of her church. She married relatively young, moving continents. In her new country of residence, not knowing how to speak the national language, Kaylin was socially isolated. Furthermore, her first husband was an alcoholic and extremely emotionally and physically abusive. She sought help from her parents but was told by her father that "you made your bed, now you have to sleep in it." Shortly after bearing her second child, she separated and returned to Canada. Her former husband attempted to kidnap the children; fortunately, they were recovered without harm, and he was criminally charged. She then legally divorced him, upon which her father informed her that she was now doomed to hell. Kaylin then became involved in a series of abusive relationships, in the most significant of which she received repeated death threats, including at knife point, should she attempt to end the relationship. Ultimately she found a safe partner and remarried; as previously noted, her current husband is supportive.

Kaylin frequently experiences intrusive memories of her past traumas in the form of thoughts, feelings, and images. She reports not having slept a night in decades without a nightmare. Her dreams either directly replay her traumatic memories or involve her fleeing some indescribable danger, screaming for help but never being heard. Her dreams also frequently include themes of helplessness and abandonment. She exhibits tonic symptoms of hyperarousal, although at other times she experiences chronic dysphoric feelings of being rejected and unworthy. She notes being unable to view herself positively, finding compliments and affection in interpersonal relationships threatening and invalidating, and viewing herself as chronically undeserving of others' compassion and friendship. Asked to describe herself in words, she has reported that she does not like herself and that she morally sees herself as a bad person. These negative views of herself have been the most resistant to change in psychotherapy, whether through cognitive, emotion-focused, or mindfulness-based approaches.

Kaylin has not, however, reported or exhibited any clear signs of severe dissociation or trauma-related altered states of consciousness (TRASC). She denies experiencing flashbacks of her traumatic events. In other words, although her traumatic memories are intrusive, upsetting, and the cause of significant distress and avoidance behavior, she has never reported being so significantly absorbed in a traumatic memory that she has partially or fully lost awareness of her current environment, or has had the illusory experience that the memory is happening again in the present tense. Neither has she reported any of a number of prototypic dissociative disturbances of identity. In other words, although generally disliking herself morally and physically (i.e., body shape), she fully recognizes herself in mirrors, and reports knowing *who she is*. She also denies experiencing voices within her head, and reports that she has never had an out-of-body experience (i.e., depersonalization). Furthermore, she has never experienced significant distortions of her body schema such as the impression that her body, or part of it, feels as if not her own.

Kaylin experiences many difficult emotions, vacillating from fear to anger to guilt to shame. Nevertheless, she is usually aware of her feelings; specifically, if she were asked what she is feeling, she would not be expected to experience a marked sense of *not knowing*, or *not being able to know*. Moreover, she recognizes her feelings as her own and, upon reflection, including within psychotherapy, she is usually able to identify the causes or "triggers" of her emotional responses. By contrast, she has never reported the experience of emotional responses that seem "*not to be her own*," affective reactions that emerge seemingly without any known context whatsoever. Neither has she reported feeling so completely numb as to effectively lose all bodily sensation or feel as if she is already dead or "has no feelings."

Case 2: Another Traumatized Self: Distress Associated with Trauma-Related Altered States of Consciousness

"Mya" is a middle-aged woman who married young but has since been divorced for several years. She is currently in training to become a social worker. As a child, her father was emotionally cold but was not physically or sexually abusive. He was frequently absent from the home, whether due to work or related to his alcoholism. Her mother was self-absorbed and also often absent as a caregiver. Mya left home as a teenager, became involved in street drugs, and was repeatedly sexually abused by adult males within the context of drug taking.

Being raised within a politically hostile country wherein she was an ethnic minority with privileged social status, Mya experienced first-hand sociopolitical and community acts of violence from a young age. For example, on more than one occasion she was chased and threatened by individuals carrying stabbing weapons within the context of ethnic and sociopolitically based uprisings. She was also physically threatened on a personal level many times and was once abducted and held captive for several days. As a young adult, Mya became addicted to crack cocaine. She was trafficked sexually by controlling her access to addictive drugs. She has since been abstinent for more than 5 years.

Like Kaylin, Mya also frequently experiences intrusive memories and nightmares of past traumas and chronic symptoms of hyperarousal. Moreover, she also feels undeserving of positive feelings, particularly the love of another human being. In contrast to Kaylin, however, Mya frequently exhibits manifest signs of dissociation and TRASC. For example, she regularly experiences prototypic flashbacks of traumatic events. During such episodes she effectively loses full conscious awareness of her current surroundings and experiences altered perceptions, such as hearing and seeing things from the past event, and may speak to or move in context with such impressions (e.g., clench her fists or raise her hands as if to block her face from a threat). She further endorses several classic signs of identity disturbance: for example, avoiding and not recognizing herself in mirrors (more specifically, reporting that she "logically knows that that *must be me*, but things not looking right, and not feeling like it is"). Mya has also reported hearing voices within her head, most often those of her parents or past abusers. She also frequently has *out-of-body experiences*, for example, the perception that she is looking down at herself from above, particularly during times of distress.

Mya also reports frequently experiencing other prototypic distortions of her body schema, which have emerged in the context of psychotherapy during the practice of mindfulness meditations (e.g., "body-scan" exercises), such as the impression that her hands seem as if they are not attached to her arms. Not only does she experience cardinal signs of emotional dysregulation, she also often reports being totally unaware of what she is feeling, as well as feeling so completely numb that she experiences herself as not being able to feel "anything." Moreover, she has often reported feeling so little control over certain emotional reactions, particularly over anger/rage responses, that her experience of such reactions seems to her as if they are "not her own." Indeed upon becoming angry, she has reported that it is like she is *no longer herself*: "It's like I'm not there anymore—everything just goes red, and nobody's home."

These cases illustrate how traumatic experience can lead to two distinct subtypes of chronic posttraumatic adaptation: an *intrinsically* dissociative presentation, involving the experience of *trauma-related altered states of consciousness* (TRASC), and a presentation that lacks blatantly dissociative elements, involving clinically significant distress but presumed otherwise *normal waking consciousness* (NWC). As illustrated in the case of Kaylin, the first clinical presentation involves a posttraumatic symptomatology that, although distressing, severe, chronic, and disabling, is nevertheless not obviously, or at least *intrinsically*, dissociative in nature. In comparison, as exemplified by Mya, other cases are prominently dissociative, involving cardinal signs of TRASC. In Mya's case, these include alterations in her sense of time as she confuses past with present through dissociative flashbacks, alterations in the structure and process of her thought as exemplified by her hearing inner voices, alterations in her sense of her body as exemplified by depersonalization, and alterations in her affective experience, including her feelings of marked emotional numbness and her disidentification with the experience of anger.

In this text we introduce an argument for distinguishing between intrinsically dissociative versus otherwise presumed nondissociative presentations of posttraumatic stress. We propose a testable theoretical framework, which we refer to as a "4-D model," for classifying the symptomatology of posttraumatic distress into intrinsically dissociative versus nondissociative variants on the basis of four phenomenological dimensions of consciousness, whether presenting in the form of normal waking consciousness (NWC) or as trauma-related altered states of consciousness (TRASC). The four dimensions of consciousness to which the 4-D model refers are a person's awareness of (1) time, (2) thought, (3) body, and (4) emotions.

We also describe a process model through which TRASC may develop via attempted emotion regulation in the context of repeated and particularly developmental trauma exposure. We begin by briefly reviewing contemporary psychological theories and research concerning the construct of dissociation, and how our own framework fits in, focusing particularly on current understandings of TRASC.

Dissociating "Dissociation" from "Dissociation": Disintegration–Compartmentalization versus Detachment–Altered States of Consciousness

Significant progress has been made in recent years regarding our understanding of the descriptive symptomatology, underlying psychobiological processes, typically traumatogenic etiology, and effective treatment of trauma-related dissociation and dissociative disorders (e.g., reviews by Boon, Steele, & van der Hart, 2011; Brand, Lanius, Vermetten, Loewenstein, & Spiegel, 2012; Chu, 2011; Courtois & Ford, 2009; Dalenberg et al., 2012; Dell & O'Neil, 2009; Forgash & Copeley, 2007; Howell, 2005; Kluft, 2013; Meares, 2012; Paivio & Pascual-Leone, 2010; Silberg, in press; Sinason, 2011; Ross & Halpern, 2009; Spiegel et al., 2011, 2013; van der Hart, Nijenhuis, & Steele, 2006; Vermetten, Dorahy, & Spiegel, 2007; Wieland, 2011). Notwithstanding such progress, contemporary scholars have often lamented that, within both clinical and academic discourse, what different authors are referring to when using the term *dissociation* continues to vary widely, leading to much unnecessary confusion and disagreement in the field.

As one relatively recent, influential attempt at remedying the problem of multiple definitions for *dissociation*, Holmes and colleagues (Holmes et al., 2005) systematically reviewed a number of eminent theoretician's definitions of the term and noted that elements of their definitions could be reliably categorized into one of two sets that they labeled, following Allen (2001) and others (e.g., Putnam, 1997), as "compartmentalization" and "detachment." Holmes et al. (2005) also noted that factor analyses of endorsement rates of survey items from the Dissociative Experiences Scale (DES; Bernstein & Putnam, 1986), the most often used self-report measure of dissociative symptoms, tend to support this conceptual distinction. Specifically, endorsement rates of DES items have tended to differ between a subset seemingly assessing the experience of amnestic episodes, regarded as exemplary of the result of compartmentalization by Holmes et al., and another group of items seemingly assessing the experience of depersonalization–derealization, regarded by Holmes et al. as the result of detachment. As such, compartmentalization and detachment were identified by their characteristic sets of observable symptoms as amenable to self-report assessment and current diagnostic practices (e.g., conversion disorder vs. depersonalization disorder, respectively; Holmes et al., 2005).

Nevertheless, rather than differing merely as observable symptoms as assessed by self-report or clinical interview, we emphasize that compartmentalization and detachment also purportedly differ as semidistinct psychological *processes*. In terms of phenomenology, Holmes et al. (2005) defined detachment as an "altered state of consciousness characterized by a sense of separation (or "detachment") from certain aspects of everyday experience, be it their body (as in out-of-body experiences), their sense of self (as in depersonalization), or the external world (as in derealization)" (Holmes et al., 2005, p. 4). Brown (2006, p. 12) further elaborated upon this definition, extending it to "emotional experiences (as in emotional numbing)" as well. Although this definition plainly emphasizes phenomenology, Holmes et al. reference Sierra and Berrios's (1998) model of hyperinhibition of emotional arousal as a process mechanism potentially mediating experiences of detachment. In addition, Holmes et al. defined compartmentalization phenomena in the first case via process terminology as "a deficit in the ability to deliberately control processes or actions that would normally be amenable to such control" (Holmes et al., p. 7).

Falling generally within the rubric of what Holmes et al. (2005) would call *compartmentalization*, arguably the current dominant theoretical paradigm in the dissociative field is to define *dissociation* as a disintegration within or across one or more aspects of psychological functioning, including but not limited to identity, memory, perception, emotion, and motoric behavior. Note here again that dissociation is defined as a psychological process that gives rise to identifiable symptoms. Put simply, from this *process* point of view, dissociation is operative when, "in essence, aspects of psychobiological functioning that should be associated, coordinated, and/or linked are not" (Spiegel et al., 2011, p. 826). Thus, dissociation, defined as such, refers to a process through which psychological functions that normally operate together are thought to instead perform relatively independently; the effect, as such, may be to divide and fragment conscious experience rather than to integrate and unify it.

Dell has emphasized that the chief phenomenological outcome of dissociative processes, as such, is the experience of intrusions into one's primary sense of self, as associated with normal waking consciousness, by various phenomena commonly associated with altered states of consciousness (e.g., Dell 2006a, 2009a, 2009b). From this point of view, it is important to point out that the experience of dissociative intrusions into one's self-experience requires a person first to experience a sense of self as the background against which dissociative intrusions present:

> The experiential locus of pathological dissociation is the self—specifically, the conscious self. *Only the conscious self can experience and notice dissociative intrusions into executive functioning and sense of self.* No self, no intrusions. . . . In short, pathological dissociative

symptoms are ontologically grounded in a conscious self that feels, recognizes, and knows its own experiences. Only the self can sense the involuntary, ego-alien quality and inherent weirdness of pathological dissociative experiences. And only the self can be bothered and confused by those experiences. (Dell, 2009a, p. 233, emphasis in original)

It is further important to note that from this theoretical vantage, *dissociation* refers to a process or mechanism that is relatively *domain general* in its application to particular contents; indeed some scholars have explicitly emphasized that dissociative processes potentially apply to any and all psychological functions. For example, Dell (2009a) further explicitly asserts "that *the domain of dissociative psychopathology is all of human experience.* There is no human experience that is immune to invasion by the symptoms of pathological dissociation. Pathological dissociation can (and often does) affect seeing, hearing, smelling, tasting, touching, emoting, wanting, dreaming, intending, expecting, knowing, believing, recognizing, remembering, and so on" (Dell, 2009a, p. 228, emphasis in original).

This point notwithstanding, consistent with Holmes et al.'s (2005) emphasis in defining compartmentalization as "a deficit in the ability to deliberately control processes or actions that would normally be amenable to such control" (Holmes et al., p. 7), a particularly distressing variant of disintegrated or compartmentalized functions entails the perceived separation of will from action, that is, the dissociative compartmentalization of perceived agency. In other words, a person may experience a lack of normally expected conscious volitional control over his or her cognitive and behavioral–motor functions, with actions thus performed seemingly beyond the person's own will. For example, a traumatized client described taking very high (though fortunately nonlethal) doses of prescription medications "against her will." Specifically, despite her best intentions, she has frequently found that she cannot stop consuming the medication, the experience akin to her thoughts and actions seeming to be under dual control. Another traumatized client has described the experience of being without volitional control to stop acts of self-mutilation, which may, upon subsequent reflection, be understood as motivated by self-loathing and as epitomizing an act of aggression toward herself.

In comparison, excessive inhibition or suppression of anger at any sign of social confrontation, or a perceived dyscontrol over explosive acts of aggression and violence, are also frequently observed in complexly traumatized persons. As one example, an individual exhibited an inability to move her hand; upon later reflection she discovered this inability to be linked to a fear of involuntarily making a fist and attacking someone misperceived as a former perpetrator of her past abuse (her mother, in this case). Fortunately, perceived volitional control over action can be increased with psychotherapy. For example, a traumatized person reported that with long-term psychotherapy she began to actually feel that she exerted voluntary control over her own actions, albeit from a depersonalized perspective. Specifically, she describes that she is now better able to willfully direct her actions, but only from the point of view of seeing herself as if standing behind her own body.

In comparison with the notion of dissociation as involving a disintegration or compartmentalization of psychological functions, and falling primarily within the constellation of experiences that Holmes et al. (2005) named "detachment," scholars often also utilize the term *dissociation* to refer to the experience of altered states of consciousness. Although acknowledging that dissociative processes potentially apply to the entirety of human conscious experience, an identifiable set or *domain* of psychological phenomena (Cardeña, 1994) is thus commonly referred to as evidence of the operation of dissociative processes, exemplary among which include experiences of depersonalization and derealization, flashbacks, trance states, marked absorption, and identity confusion or alteration. Arguably what these experiences share in common, first and foremost, is that they each represent an identifiable alteration from a state of normal waking consciousness (NWC). Indeed Cardeña (1994, p. 23) characterized such dissociative states as "qualitative departures from one's ordinary modes of experiencing, wherein an unusual disconnection or disengagement from the self and/or the surroundings occurs as a central aspect of experience." Following Cardeña's (1994) description, the term *altered states of consciousness* refers to characteristic deviations from the normal way people tend to perceive themselves, others, and the world around them (e.g., Spiegel & Cardeña, 1991). In effect, such a rendering of the dissociation construct serves to be somewhat less domain general, highlighting particular forms of altered states of consciousness as prototypical outcomes inferred to be the result of the presence of dissociative processes.

It has been acknowledged, however, that the aforementioned cataloguing of dissociative phenomena arguably continues to remain rather heterogeneous. Reinforcing such a contention, factor analyses of symptom questionnaires support the thesis that dissociative experiences involving altered states of consciousness have a multifactorial structure; that is, different forms or dimensions of altered states of consciousness can be experienced more or less independently. For example, Dell's (2006b) Multidimensional Inventory of Dissociation (MID) is a highly regarded psychometric instrument specifically designed to provide a comprehensive, content-valid assessment of the more commonly observed experiences of persons with dissociative identity disorder, many of which represent prototypic descriptions of altered states of consciousness (e.g., depersonalization, derealization, posttraumatic flashbacks, and trance states, collectively described previously by Dell [2001] as instances of "pervasive dissociation"). Dell's findings that specific kinds of alterations in consciousness can be distinguished not only conceptually but further in terms of correlations between rates of symptom (item) endorsement (e.g., Dell, 2006b; Dell & Lawson, 2009) provide strong grounds for suggesting that the notion of dissociative "detachment" may itself be, at the same time, overly heterogeneous (in its stated referents), as well as overly noninclusive (in the experiences that it fails to encompass), relative to the varied kinds of alterations in consciousness often experienced by highly traumatized persons. Briere and colleagues, through their research with another multifactorial dissociation scale, the Multiscale Dissociation Inventory, also identified strong grounds for distinguishing between different kinds of dissociative experience (Briere, Weathers, & Runtz, 2005).

It should also be noted that some authors prefer to reserve the term *dissociation* for experiences or behaviors that emanate from different parts of a divided personality structure, suggesting that identity alteration should be both necessary and sufficient as a definition for dissociative phenomena (Nijenhuis & van der Hart, 2011). Following van der Hart, Nijenhuis, and Steele's (2006) structural theory of dissociation, a model that considers the spectrum of dissociative disorders in terms of increasing division and multiplicity within an individual's first-person experience of agency and selfhood, Steele and colleagues also proposed that dissociative disintegration of experience and identity alteration, on the one hand, and alterations in consciousness, on the other, represent related but distinctive psychological phenomena (Steele, Dorahy, van der Hart, & Nijenhuis, 2009). They pointed out that, although frequently co-occurring and confounded within any specific moment, "in theory it is simple to distinguish between the symptoms of structural dissociation and pathological fields and levels of conscious awareness: the former involves a division of the personality and the latter does not" (Steele et al., 2009, p. 160).

Furthermore, Steele and colleagues (2009) pointedly asserted that alterations in consciousness, in most though not all cases, represent clear instances of psychopathology. Therefore they disagreed with theories that place altered states of consciousness on the "normal" end of a single continuum, with pathological structural divisions of the personality at the other side. They further pointed out that, although those who exhibit structural division of the personality commonly exhibit altered states of consciousness, only relatively few individuals who experience altered states of consciousness also exhibit structural divisions of the personality. To clarify the distinction, Steele and colleagues preferred to reserve the terms *dissociation* and *dissociative* for instances of structural division of the personality, with *altered states of consciousness* instead referred to simply as such (see also Nijenhuis & van der Hart, 2011). Steel and colleagues called for further investigation of the psychological and neurobiological underpinnings of both pathological alterations in consciousness and structural division of the personality.

Trauma-Related Dissociative Processing:
A (Non)-Self-Referential Processing Model

The preceding brief overview of recent research into dissociation taxonomy substantiates extant theories as variably emphasizing the processes and observed symptomatology (i.e., outcomes) of disintegration–compartmentalization, detachment–altered states of consciousness, and identity alteration (altered self-reference) as more or less central to understanding the construct of dissociation. However, current multifactorial models of dissociation, although seeking to understand the underlying psychological processes *mediating* dissociative symptoms, with relatively few exceptions remain descriptive in nature, being limited to classification systems and definitions (e.g., see Beere, 1995, 2009; Brown, 2002, 2004, 2006; Dell, 2009b). In other words, most models neglect to discern the explanatory means and mediating pathways through which dissociative processes are enacted, and particularly how traumatic experiences, known to be a strong causal risk factor for the development of dissociative disorders (Dalenberg et al., 2012), act to bring about dissociation. Thus most current classification models of dissociation attempt to categorize apples as apples (e.g., disintegration–compartmentalization), and oranges as oranges (e.g., detachment–altered states of consciousness), but often fall short of explicating specifically *how* such experiences come about, and in particular how traumatic experiences give rise to the varying phenomena that fall under the domain of dissociation. We sketch our current way of thinking about the processes underlying trauma-related dissociation in the schematic of Figure 1.1 (also in color insert). We make clear that this framework is shared only as a testable hypothesis for future research rather than results that are already empirically substantiated or in any way theoretical givens.

The model in Figure 1.1 is perhaps most easily explicated with reference to a real-world example, for instance, a woman being raped by a man. As would be exemplary of normal waking consciousness (NWC), the model suggests that life events, including traumatic events, are normally encoded self-referentially, that is, via first-person perspective, labeled as Pathway A in Figure 1.1. In its most elementary (and somewhat colloquial) sense, self-referential processing (SRP), entailing first-person perspective, adds to what would otherwise be entirely impersonal sensory experiences a "tag" that effactually says: "This is happening to me." Thus, within NWC, the woman being raped would be fully self-referentially aware that the rape is happening to *her*; due to the intrinsic filtering of consciousness

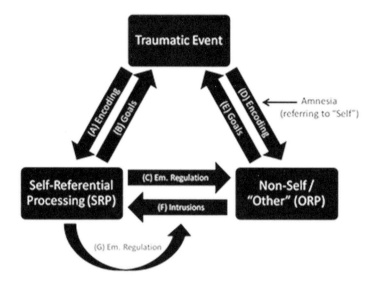

FIGURE 1.1. A (Non) Self Referential Processing Model of Dissociation.

Boxes at left and arrows A, B, C, and G denote potentially nondissociative processes and normal waking consciousness (NWC), whereas boxes at right and arrows D, E, and F denote intrinsically dissociative processes (trauma-related altered states of consciousness [TRASC]).

through SRP, she would be intrinsically aware that it is *she* who is being raped, rather than somebody else.

In comparison, Pathway B in Figure 1.1 is intended simply to note that previously encoded representations associated with SRP, for most psychologically healthy persons, will normally be adaptive for the most part, generally motivating goals that increase pleasure and avoid pain. As such, following Pathway B would suggest the obvious: that most people will be motivated to avoid being raped and, if possible, SRP will prompt active emotion regulation and coping: for example, attempted physical escape, akin to a fight-or-flight response, easily identifiable both behaviorally as well as through peripheral outputs of the autonomic nervous system (ANS), such as increased heart-rate, respiration, and muscle tone.

Although we have depicted both Pathways A and B as entailing SRP, it is important to note that we assume that both pathways vary as to the extent to which they are consciously versus unconsciously-automatically mediated, emphasizing cortical versus subcortical neural processes, respectively. It further serves to be noted that the chronically traumatized person who has come to believe him- or herself to be intrinsically "bad" and to view self in markedly negative terms (e.g., as "rejected," "unlovable," "despicable," "disgusting," "disgraceful"; Frewen et al., 2011b) may be more prone simply to assimilate the experience of traumatic events via SRP (Pathway A) without considering any accompanying defensive recourse (Pathway B). For example, a traumatized woman may believe that she is inherently deserving of abuse as punishment and that the traumatic event of rape is wholly her fault, obviating any motivation for her to follow Pathway B in the service of emotion regulation during traumatic events. Such a response, akin to learned helplessness, may be associated with different autonomic outputs—for example, a less significant increase or even a decrease in peritraumatic heart rate (e.g., Schauer & Elbert, 2010). In fact, scholars have noted that many trauma survivors appear at times even to seek out their further traumatization through various self-destructive reenactments and revictimizations, perhaps akin in certain respects to a form of addiction (e.g., Briere & Runtz, 1987, 1993; Chu, 2011; Courtois, 2004; Myrick, Brand, & Putnam, 2013; van der Kolk, 1989).

Assuming, however, that escape is a salient motivation but is not physically possible, Pathway C in Figure 1.1 suggests that SRP will naturally prompt other behaviorally more passive and *internal* coping responses, increasingly referred to in the contemporary affective neuroscience literature as instances of "emotion regulation" (Diekhof, Geier, Falkai, & Gruber, 2011; Ochsner & Gross, 2005; Ochsner, Bunge, Gross, & Gabrieli, 2002). Cardinal examples of emotion regulation—suppression, distraction, repression, decentering, and cognitive reappraisal (Aldao, Nolen-Hoeksema, & Schweizer, 2010)—are typically understood to be (and accordingly studied as) top-down (centrally mediated) emotion regulation processes (e.g., Ochsner & Gross, 2005), notwithstanding the acknowledgment by researchers that bottom-up (automatic, non-/less-conscious) emotion regulatory processing also frequently takes place (Gyurak, Gross, & Etkin, 2011; Mauss, Bunge, & Gross, 2007). Particularly as influenced by Gross and colleagues' research (e.g., Gross, 1998, 2002, 2013, in press), contemporary theorizing tends to suggest that, at least within the context of common and mild everyday stressors (e.g., late for an appointment, minor argument with a friend, burnt toast), certain emotion regulation strategies (e.g., cognitive reappraisal) are typically more effective in reducing negative affect and psychophysiological arousal than are other ones (e.g., suppression). Accordingly, affective neuroscience research has been decidedly biased toward the examination of cognitive reappraisal processes relative to other forms of emotion regulation (Diekhof et al., 2011; Ochsner & Gross, 2005). Nevertheless, it is important to point out that, in the context of more severe stressors such as rape, the relative adaptiveness of particular emotion regulation strategies over others may be decidedly less compelling.

Returning to our example of the traumatic event of rape, as illustrated by real-life quotations collected verbatim from sexual assault victims we have treated, rape victims often attempt various emotion regulation strategies either during or shortly after the rape: for example, trying to "make myself not feel it, shutting myself off" (i.e., suppression); "looking away, trying to focus on something else" (distraction); "trying to erase it from my mind, to forget that it happened" (repression); or "distancing myself, sort of like taking myself out of what's happening" (decentering). From the perspective of the present process framework, each of these emotion regulation strategies is understood implicitly to have the net effect of diminishing the self-referential emotional salience of the traumatic event. In other words, such emotion regulation strategies, each representing direct and variably conscious attempts at momentarily altering one's normal waking consciousness (NWC) and sense of self, serve to render the experience less immediately self-relevant in nature or affectively salient. The outcome may be akin to translating the traumatic experience into one that is less self-referential in nature, or closer to what we term "*non*-self-referential processing," taking place in the narrative perspective of third person (e.g., "Rape is [not] happening" in comparison with "I am being raped").

Note, by contrast, that the kinds of examples typically given as definitions of "cognitive reappraisal"—specifically, attempts at interpreting negative events and aversive stimuli in a less negative or even positive way—would decidedly be less applicable (and indeed inherently maladaptive) in the traumatic context of rape. In other words, any encouragement of a person to attempt to construe a traumatic experience such as rape as somehow not negative or even positive would be highly morally suspect. In fact, we do not believe it would naturally occur to any generally psychologically healthy person to consider this approach, although it is certainly true that an abuser may attempt to influence such an appraisal of the event in his victim (e.g., telling her that she likes or desires the assault).

Does cognitive reappraisal simply not apply as an emotion regulation strategy in instances of more severe psychological trauma? We believe there is at least one derivation of cognitive reappraisal that the woman might attempt: the *cognitive reappraisal of identity alteration*. To our knowledge, this particular theoretical application of cognitive reappraisal has not been made explicitly in the trauma literature. As noted earlier, the emotion regulation strategies of suppression, distraction, repression, and decentering were regarded as *implicitly* lessening the self-referential nature of the rape. By contrast, however, via a process of identity alteration, the woman might *explicitly* reappraise the situation as non-self-referential, imaginatively construing the event as one that is not happening to her, but is instead happening to someone else. As such, her reappraisal explicitly discounts the self-referential nature of the traumatic event, translating it into one involving "other-referential processing" (e.g., Frewen & Lundberg, 2012). For example, in the words of one trauma survivor: "I made it that it was happening to someone else."

In this regard identity alteration, via an extension of the methodology of simple cognitive reappraisal, stands out relative to other emotion regulation strategies in being explicitly (rather than only implicitly) *non*-self-referential in nature, not only in outcome but in process as well. Indeed, the extension of cognitive reappraisal to identity alteration, specifically in its initial instantiations, necessitates the formative and creative imagining of an "other," a process decidedly absent in the other forms of emotion regulation listed (represented in Figure 1.1 by the right lower box's denotation as non-self-referential processing or as "other-referential processing").

Importantly, the potential significance of such a translation from first- to second/third-person perspective in orienting toward traumatic events should not be underestimated, with several studies revealing distinct neurophysiological changes associated with such attentional manipulations that are further associated with subjective changes in affect. The first of such studies was conducted by Ruby and Decety (2001), who required participants to imagine themselves performing an action on certain experimental trials (first-person perspective; e.g., "I am pouring coffee into a mug"), while imagining another person performing the same action during other trials (third-person perspective; e.g., "He is pouring coffee into a mug"). Ruby and Decety found that taking a first-person perspective more greatly recruited responses within the left inferior parietal lobe, posterior insula, and bilateral post-central gyrus, whereas taking a third-person perspective more greatly recruited responses in the posterior cingulate cortex, precuneus, and right medial frontal pole.

A subsequent study by the same authors compared the neural correlates of imagining, given the same emotional situation, how one would respond oneself as compared with how one's mother would likely respond (e.g., "You are late for an important appointment" [first-person perspective] vs. "Your mother is late for an important appointment" [third-person perspective]). The results again showed that the medial frontopolar cortex was preferentially activated during *third*-person perspective, as was the right inferior parietal lobe and left temporal pole (Ruby & Decety, 2004). Several studies have since examined the neural correlates of manipulating narrative perspective as involving momentarily taking the experiential point of view of another person. Distinct from the earlier studies emphasizing response within the medial prefrontal cortex (mPFC) and anterior cingulate, a meta-analysis performed by van Overwalle (2009) found that, taking a region-of-interest approach, manipulation of agency perspective in studies of action intentionality preferentially recruit response within the left temporoparietal junction, with studies also commonly finding greater response within the right temporoparietal junction and bilateral lateral prefrontal cortex.

A meta-analysis by Qin and Northoff (2011a, 2011b) also found that considering another person's perspective during social-cognitive tasks, in comparison with taking the first-person perspective, tends to more commonly evoke response within the right temporoparietal junction, posterior cingulate cortex, and precuneus. Providing that response within the mPFC is commonly associated with both SRP (e.g., Northoff et al., 2006) and fear inhibition (e.g., Pitman et al., 2012), altering information processing from within the anterior midline cortex preferentially through posterior parietal regions medially or laterally, as well as to the bilateral lateral frontal cortex, strongly suggests that differential cognitive–affective mechanisms of processing are taking place in first- versus third-person perspective.

Reinders and colleagues have cleverly applied similar experimental paradigms to studies of traumatic memory recall in individuals with dissociative identity disorder. Specifically, Reinders and colleagues compared the neural correlates of exposure to and imagery of a trauma script from a first-person ("autonoetic") perspective, wherein the trauma memory was remembered as an autiobiographical event, to a third-person perspective wherein the trauma script was not considered the participant's own memory. Their studies showed that only in first-person perspective did recall prompt autonomic arousal, as evidenced in increased heart rate and skin conductance responses. Moreover, in their first study, taking a first-person perspective was associated with greater response within the left insula and left parietal operculum, whereas the third-person perspective was associated with greater response in the right superior frontal cortex, bilateral middle frontal gyrus, and bilateral temporoparietal junction (Reinders et al., 2003). In a replication and extension study, first-person perspective was associated with greater response within the bilateral amygdala, caudate, and left insula, whereas the third-person perspective was associated with greater response within the dorsomedial prefrontal cortex (dmPFC), anterior and posterior cingulate cortex, precuneus, parahippocampal gyrus, and left and right temporoparietal junctions, among other regions (Reinders et al., 2006). Finally, Reinders, Willemsen, Vos, den Boer, and Nijenhuis (2012) demonstrated that neural responses occurring within persons with dissociative identity disorder could be differentiated from those occurring in simulating control groups who varied in trait levels of fantasy proneness; between-group differences were observed within the precuneus, the left insula, and the left amygdala, among other regions. Neuroimaging case studies of cued alterations in first-person perspective among persons with dissociative disorders have also been conducted (e.g., Savoy, Frederick, Keuroghlian, & Wolk, 2012; Tsai, Condie, Wu, & Chang, 1999).

It should be noted that, to the extent that repeated exposure to traumatic stressors continuously overwhelms the coping resources associated with primary SRP, and secondary self-identity states are repeatedly and habitually invoked as cognitive reappraisals as means of coping, it is commonly held within the dissociation literature that an individual may develop increasingly complex "self-like" representations, referring to alter identities that are accompanied by multiple independent first-person per-spectives (Nijenhuis, 2013; Nijenhuis & van der Hart, 2011; van der Hart et al., 2006). In this way, a person may orient to events, *in the first case*, not through primary SRP but rather directly through non-self/other-refer-ential processing (Pathway D in Figure 1.1). Within this framework, refer-ring to the primary sense of self (left lower box in Figure 1.1), amnestic episodes are accounted for as periods during which an individual occu-pies the first-person perspective of an alternate identity state (Dell, 2009a, 2009b; Nijenhuis, 2013; Nijenhuis & van der Hart, 2011). Moreover, a person in such circumstances can be expected to experience marked dis-sonance, discord, and confusion when the goals of primary and alternate first-person perspectives conflict (Pathways B and E in Figure 1.1).

The extent to which emotion regulation strategies as a whole are affected by dissociative processes deserves consideration. We may note that emotion regulation strategies, in all cases, represent attempts to alter or "dissociate" from some previously dominant reactions or conscious experiences. In effect, the task of emotion regulation is to experientially "take a step back" and, at least in part, to "remove oneself" from one's current way of experiencing oneself and one's immediate environment in a less distressing direction. Indeed the analogy of "taking a step back," as enacting an experience of greater subjective distance or detachment between oneself and an emotional stimulus or event, is particularly direct in the case of the emotion regulation strategy that has been labeled "decen-tering" in recent literature (e.g., Ayduk & Kross, 2010; Fresco, Segal, Buis, & Kennedy, 2007; Fresco, Moore, et al., 2007; Kross, 2009). Indeed in a previous paper we noted that instructions given to participants to decen-ter and distance themselves from mild electric shocks and the viewing of saddening films in neuroimaging experiments are strikingly similar to the phenomenology of (at least mild) states of dissociative detachment (Fre-wen & Lanius, 2006a, 2006b):

> Subjects were instructed to reappraise the stimuli by taking a *dis-tance* from these stimuli, that is, to become a *detached observer*. . . .
> To do so, each subject was told to mentally imagine herself in a mov-ie theatre, watching herself reacting emotionally on the big screen and then feeling *dissociated*, that is, like if the person seen on the screen *was not related to her anymore*. (Lévesque et al., 2003, p. 362, emphasis added; see also Kalisch et al., 2005)

In fact, we believe that decentering, distancing, and detachment are outcomes affected to varying degrees by all emotion regulation strate-gies. Such strategies are entirely healthy, normative ways of managing and tolerating everyday distress, so long as one does not step back "too far, too often." In cases of the latter, however, the repeated and progressively habitualized enactment of increasingly marked forms of detachment in the service of emotion regulation may result in automatizing such strategies, lessening the extent to which they are experienced as being directed by conscious executive control. As noted previously, a participant's perceived level of conscious executive control over the deployment of emotion regulation strategies indeed varies (Gyurak et al., 2011; Mauss et al., 2007). Whereas at times participants perceive themselves as having actively *chosen* or *effected* an emotion regulation strategy (e.g., "I made myself go away," which we would attribute to traversing Pathway C in Figure 1.1), at other times the response seems to be more automatic, with participants describing the experience as if it were simply *happening to* them (e.g., "I started going away . . . ").

From the point of view of the notion of "compartmentalization" (Holmes et al., 2005), one might prefer to reserve designation of a dissociative process to instances such as the latter example—that is, one seemingly involving a perceived lack of willful agency and conscious executive control over action and experience. Such cases might be properly represented by following Pathway D in Figure 1.1; that is, a "direct route" to non-self-referential processing. Consonant with such an interpretation, Dell (2009b) noted, in comparing Freudian repression to Janetian dissociation, that repression exemplifies an emotion regulation strategy fully available to normal waking consciousness (NWC; Pathway C in Figure 1.1). In comparison, he described Janetian dissociation as *intrinsically* representing a dissociative process as inherently involuntary, occurring beyond a person's willful control.

The trauma survivor can be said to have been resilient in instances in which the emotion regulation strategies of suppression, distraction, repression, decentering, and cognitive reappraisal are fully effective in adaptively reducing the distress associated with a limited number of trauma occurrences. Referring again to an instance of rape, in such circumstances the horrible event can be said to be finally over with the woman only passing through Pathways A, B, and C of Figure 1.1. However, we believe that the terrorizing and shaming nature of certain repeated traumatic experiences alters SRP itself through repeated encoding (repetition of Pathway A), and coupled with the progressively more automated rehearsal of alterations in one's consciousness as a means of coping with them (Pathways C and D), serve to create an increasingly chronically traumatized self-state. Consistent with Dell's (2006a, 2009a, 2009b) emphasis on the phenomenology of dissociation as an intrusion into a person's (primary) sense of self, such an altered state of self would be experienced as progressively more frequent intrusions into normal waking consciousness (NWC) by trauma-related altered states of consciousness (TRASC), prompted by trauma reminders or ongoing traumatic events (Pathway F). Moreover, in more severe cases, the increasing establishment of a new baseline may occur, characterized by abnormal SRP; that is, by a sense of self that is chronically altered from the principles of NWC and infused with TRASC (Pathway D). Such a repeatedly traumatized individual may chronically orient toward herself, others, and the world around her with an increasingly altered sense of time, thought, body, and emotions. Furthermore, the increasingly disturbing nature of such a person's lived experience may lead her to engage in further attempts at altering her conscious states (Pathway G in Figure 1.1). After failing at using healthy forms of emotion regulation, the alternative attempts often take the form of intrinsically dysfunctional and maladaptive secondary emotion regulation strategies—for example, alcoholism, other forms of substance abuse, harming others, self-harm, alternate forms of self-abuse (e.g., unnecessary risk taking), and self-punishment. The unfortunate outcome of these secondary emotion regulation strategies is often to increase rather than decrease the individual's growing tendency toward dissociation and the experience of TRASC.

A Dissociative Subtype of Posttraumatic Stress Disorder

Among others, we proposed distinguishing a dissociative subtype of posttraumatic stress disorder (PTSD) as a means of recognizing the prominently dissociative symptomatology of certain cases of PTSD, at present defined solely by the presence, versus absence, of experiences of depersonalization or derealization (Bremner, 1999; Ginzburg et al., 2006; Lanius, Vermetten, et al., 2010; Lanius, Brand, Vermetten, Frewen, & Spiegel, 2012; Stein et al., 2013; Steuwe, Lanius, & Frewen, 2012; Wolf, Lunney, et al., 2012; Wolf, Miller, et al., 2012). That proposal was recently incorporated into the fifth edition of the *Diagnostic and Statistical Manual for Psychiatric Disorders* (DSM-5; American Psychiatric Association, 2013). The dissociative subtype of PTSD thus recognizes the clinical significance of differentiating between individuals with PTSD who exhibit (vs. who fail to show) prominent signs of derealization (altered perception of the environment and other people; e.g., experiencing others as if they are not real or the world as "dream-like" or "foggy") and depersonalization (altered perception of the bodily self; e.g., out-of-body experiences).

The term *derealization* refers explicitly to the feeling or perception that the world is not real, or involves related experiences of the external environment seeming dreamlike, foggy, lifeless, or visually distorted (American Psychiatric Association, 2013; World Health Organization, 2003). For example, when arriving at the hospital office where she has been seen for trauma-focused psychotherapy for several months, one individual with PTSD reported: "It feels like I don't know this place. I mean, I *know* where I am. But it doesn't seem real—it feels different, strange." Another trauma survivor, despite intact cognitive function, repeatedly has questioned "Is this place real? Am I real?" In comparison, the term *deperson-*

alization is often used interchangeably with out-of-body experiences in psychiatric discourse. Nevertheless, it should be recognized that the definition of depersonalization has a considerably broader application. Specifically, depersonalization has been defined to include experiences of being an outside observer of the happenings of one's own mind or body as may be exemplified by perceptual alterations, altered sense of time, emotional or physical numbing, or alterations in sense of self (American Psychiatric Association, 2013). Further, a person may complain of "being distant or 'not really here.' For example . . . that their emotions, feelings, or experience of the inner self are detached, strange, not their own, or unpleasantly lost, or that their emotions or movements seem as if they belong to someone else" (World Health Organization, 1993, p. 110). For example, one traumatized person described depersonalization this way: "It feels like I'm behind my eyes, or sometimes it feels like I'm beside myself. I can see my body, I can see what it's doing, but it's not me. It's not connected."

The notion that there might be a dissociative subtype of PTSD first arose to us when we were studying the brain bases of traumatic memory recall using the traumatic script-driven imagery method in patients with chronic PTSD. This method involves listening to an audio recording recounting what happened during a past personal trauma event (Pitman et al., 1987). Our original hypothesis was that traumatized persons with PTSD would invariably reexperience the traumatic event with a concomitant increase in hyperarousal, as evidenced by elevated heart rate, as had previously been found by several researchers (reviewed by Pole, 2007). However, the first participant we studied responded very differently than we had expected when hearing her personalized trauma script. Instead, her heart rate *decreased* from baseline by about four beats per minute during the script. Moreover, when the participant was later interviewed about her experience of the script-driven imagery procedure, she reported that, rather than reexperiencing the traumatic event: "It was too hard to go back there. I became disconnected from my body and was watching myself from above. It was like I was in a dream."

It therefore became clear to us that depersonalization–derealization responses should be taken into account in the traumatic script-driven imagery research design. Accordingly, we revised our study objectives to compare the neurophysiological correlates of the already well-recognized trauma reexperiencing response with the latter depersonalization–derealization response. Findings of the study ultimately showed that whereas approximately 70% of traumatized persons with PTSD whom we tested exhibited the reexperiencing response, usually together with an increase in heart rate, the remaining 30% of individuals reported prototypic symptoms of depersonalization–derealization, and either failed to exhibit a significantly elevated heart rate or exhibited a deceleration of heart rate, relative to baseline, when exposed to the auditory recounting of past personal traumatic life events (reviewed in Lanius, Bluhm, Lanius, & Pain, 2006).

Moreover, functional neuroimaging data showed that the brain bases of these seemingly qualitatively distinctive phenomenological and cardiovascular responses also differed. Relative to healthy trauma-exposed persons, those reporting the reexperiencing response exhibited, among other findings, a decreased response in the mPFC and adjacent perigenual anterior cingulate cortex (pACC)—regions of the brain known to be involved in SRP and emotion regulation, the latter including inhibition of response within the amygdala, a region of the brain known to be involved in fear responding (e.g., reviewed by Pitman et al., 2012). In contrast, those reporting the depersonalization–derealization response exhibited *increased* response within the mPFC and pACC, interpreted as consistent with Sierra and Berrios's (1998) predictions that such a response might be associated with hyperinhibition of limbic centers such as the amygdala, an effect we later termed *overmodulation* of emotional responsiveness (for review, see Lanius, Vermetten, et al., 2010).

Evidence collected and systematized since that time has tended to validate these early clinical impressions. In fact, the argument that PTSD and dissociative symptoms often co-occur should by now be regarded as well established. For example, Carlson and colleagues' meta-analysis of 17 studies showed that approximately 50% of the variance between PTSD and dissociative symptoms is shared (mean $r = .71$; Carlson, Dalenberg, & McDade-Montez, 2012). We also recently demonstrated that if researchers include derealization and depersonalization among the PTSD symptoms subjected to factor analysis, the fit of factor-analytic models of PTSD symptoms is maximized when depersonalization and derealization symptoms represent a unique dimension that is permitted to correlate with other PTSD symptom factors (Steuwe, Lanius, & Frewen, 2012). In comparison, fit is poorer when symptoms are conceived of as loading directly on other PTSD symptom factors. We argued that the latter would have been more consistent with dissociative symptoms being redundant with or "accounted for" by the other PTSD symptom factors. Moreover, a model that posited the dissociation factor as being uncorrelated with the PTSD symptom dimensions also exhibited poor fit, demonstrating that the more PTSD symptoms an individual experiences, the more dissociative symptoms he or she is also likely to endorse. These findings substantiate dissociative experiences as frequently occurring among the correlated symptom dimensions of traumatized persons with PTSD. In addition, there is strong evidence for an association between clinical dissociation and exposure to traumatic stress (e.g., reviewed by Dalenberg et al., 2012).

We suggest further that recognizing a dissociative subtype of PTSD affords a more parsimonious clinical description and diagnosis in comparison with the practice of diagnosing PTSD comorbid with an independent depersonalization disorder. Specifically, the dissociative subtype of PTSD inherently recognizes the traumatogenic etiology of a person's experience of depersonalization and derealization, whereas the comorbidity model does not (cf. Carlson & Dalenberg, 2012). Indeed a number of experts point out that depersonalization disorder, in contrast with other dissociative disorders, has not been strongly causally associated with trauma exposure (e.g., reviews by Dell, 2009b; Simeon & Abugel, 2006). In addition to including trauma exposure as a general etiological factor, the dissociative subtype of PTSD at least implicitly recognizes that a person's experiences of depersonalization and derealization are often prompted directly by exposure to cues of past traumas, for example, as demonstrated in our research participants' response to the traumatic script-driven imagery paradigm reviewed previously (e.g., Frewen & Lanius, 2006a, 2006b; Lanius et al., 2006; Lanius, Vermetten, et al., 2010).

It is important to point out that the argument for recognizing a dissociative subtype emphasizes that, although many individuals with PTSD exhibit depersonalization and derealization symptoms, *not all do*, and that distinguishing people with PTSD who *do* experience dissociation from those who do not is clinically important. In fact, a series of latent class analyses of relatively large samples suggests that among individuals with PTSD, perhaps only approximately 12–15% of men and 25–30% of women endorse clinically significant dissociative symptoms of derealization and depersonalization (Stein et al., 2013; Steuwe, Lanius, & Frewen, 2012; Wolf, Lunney, et al., 2012; Wolf, Miller, et al., 2012).

In the largest study conducted to date ($N = 25,018$), the dissociative subtype was observed in 14% of individuals with PTSD and was associated with childhood adversities, severe role impairment, and suicidality (Stein et al., 2013). Moreover, the association between PTSD and dissociative symptoms is recognized as *not* equally bidirectional. Whereas most individuals who report experiencing significant dissociative symptoms also report experiencing PTSD symptoms, most individuals with PTSD symptoms evidently do *not* experience clinically significant levels of dissociation. For example, in Waelde, Silvern and Fairbank's (2005) study of 316 trauma-exposed male veterans, 76 of whom had a PTSD diagnosis and 30 of whom exhibited pathological signs of dissociation (as identified by the DES–Taxon; Waller & Ross, 1997), 80% (24/30) with clinically significant dissociative symptoms met criteria for the PTSD diagnosis, whereas only 33% (30/76) of individuals with PTSD reported pathological signs of dissociation.

In sum, not only relatively large clinical samples but additionally much larger-scale international epidemiological evidence (Stein et al., 2013) suggests that, when measured dimensionally, symptoms of PTSD and dissociation often correlate strongly. However, when measured categorically (present or absent), although dissociative symptoms are often present in individuals with PTSD, the number of cases nevertheless represents a minority within the total PTSD population, probably somewhere between one in every seven to one in every three cases (i.e., ≈ 15–33%; Stein et al., 2013; Steuwe, Lanius, & Frewen, 2012; Waelde et al., 2005; Wolf, Lunney, et al., 2012; Wolf, Miller, et al., 2012).

It should be noted in this context, however, that the prevalence of dissociative symptoms in PTSD samples is likely to vary in terms of how *dissociation* is itself defined and measured. For example, following Wolf, Miller, et al. (2012), in our own study of the prevalence of the dissociative subtype (Steuwe, Lanius, & Frewen, 2012) we excluded from measurement what we consider to be relatively nonspecific and comparably less clinically significant dissociative experiences of reduced awareness of one's surroundings (e.g., "being in a daze," general "spaciness"). We consider the phenomenology of such experiences to be too similar to instances of the general confusion associated with nondissociative PTSD (and indeed many other affective and anxiety disorders) to clearly demarcate a "subtype" within the PTSD population. Moreover, it is important to acknowledge that such experiences as "being in a daze" and feeling "spacey" are themselves not inherently pathological or obviously indicative of trauma-related altered states of consciousness (TRASC). Instead, several scholars consider such experiences to be exemplary of "normative dissociation"—experiences that occur dimensionally within the general population, as well as experiences that are not necessarily associated with marked psychopathology (e.g., Butler, 2004, 2006; Dalenberg & Paulson, 2009; Dell, 2009b). We suggest that the clinical significance of distinguishing a dissociative subtype rests on its specificity from nondissociative presentations as involving marked, obvious departures from normal waking consciousness (NWC) into TRASC. Accordingly, we would not advocate for the inclusion of various instances of "normative dissociation" as being diagnostic of a dissociative subtype of PTSD.

Psychophysiological studies have tended to provide tentative support for the validity of differentiating between individuals with PTSD who do, versus do not, exhibit prominent dissociative states and traits such as depersonalization or derealization. Specifically, in contrast to the modal heart rate increases in response to stress and trauma reminders that are found in many individuals with PTSD (Pole, 2007), signifying not only sympathetic arousal but also significant downregulation of parasympathetic activity (e.g., Hopper, Spinazzola, Simpson, & van der Kolk, 2006; Sack, Hopper, & Lamprecht, 2004), the majority of studies of state (Lanius et al., 2005, 2002) and trait (Bonanno, Noll, Putnam, O'Neill, & Trickett, 2003; Koopman et al., 2004; Sierra et al., 2002; Sierra, Senior, Phillips, & David, 2006; Simeon, Yehuda, Knutelska, & Schmeidler, 2008) dissociation demonstrated *decreased* heart rate and skin conductance reactivity during experimental stress provocation. Hauschildt, Peters, Moritz, and Jelinek (2011) also observed lowered heart rate variability in participants while they watched videos depicting traumatic material as predicted by both trait and state dissociation.

Scholars have remarked that psychophysiological signs of dissociation can be understood in the context of animal predator–prey models of threat processing. Neuroimaging studies of mechanisms underlying dissociative responses have also provided further insight into the lack of elevated cardiovascular response often observed in individuals with high levels of dissociation, attributed to increased top-down control (or *overmodulation*) of limbic regions in the brain (Frewen & Lanius, 2006a, 2006b; Hopper, Frewen, Sack, Lanius, & van der Kolk, 2007; Lanius et al., 2002, 2012; Lanius, Vermetten, et al., 2010; Lanius et al., 2005; Sierra & Berrios, 1998). For example, dissociative states are frequently accompanied by reduced pain sensitivity as induced by trauma reminders, which were found to be associated with increased mid-cingulate and insular response among individuals with borderline personality disorder comorbid with PTSD (Ludäscher et al., 2010). In addition, dissociative traits predicted reduced response within the right amygdala during simultaneous trauma memory recall and pain processing in individuals with PTSD alone (Mickleborough et al., 2011). Time will tell whether these early observations concerning conjoint differential experiential and neurophysiological responses to stress withstand the tests of further scientific replication and scrutiny.

Making Depersonalization More Personal: An Expanded Definition

Whereas psychiatric definitions for depersonalization have been, in practice, largely synonymous with partial or full out-of-body experiences, an expansion of the definition of depersonalization was proposed (Spiegel et al., 2011, 2013) and incorporated into DSM-5 (American Psychiatric Association, 2013). In addition to recognizing out-of-body experiences as symptomatic of depersonalization disorder, added experiences of feeling like one is in a dream, a sense of the unreality or absence of a self, perceptual alterations, emotional or physical numbing, and a distorted sense of time were considered indicative of depersonalization phenomena (Spiegel et al., 2011, 2013). As an example, one research participant has described the experience of depersonalization this way:

> "Everything feels weird. It's hard to describe. It feels like I have to remind myself who I am . . . I live in a dream. It feels like I'm trapped in a random body. I don't know who I am. I don't remember myself before I had depersonalization."

This expanded definition, effectively treating the various listed phenomena as instances of a common experience, is consistent with current assessment practices. Indeed psychometric surveys of peritraumatic (e.g.,

Marmar, Weiss, & Metzler, 1997) and state dissociation (e.g., Bremner et al., 1998) typically measure a heterogeneous set of experiences. These include experiencing a distorted sense of time, the experience of perceptual alterations, feeling that one is physically separated from one's body, that one is not real, or feeling emotionally and physically numb. The fact that such surveys often exhibit high internal consistency or a unifactorial structure suggests that these experiences are more or less representative instances of a common psychological phenomenon. Nevertheless, these psychometric scales were not purposely designed to uncover distinctions between potentially different kinds of state dissociation, because only a single or a very small number of test items is dedicated to measuring each of the varied phenomenological experiences. Accordingly, this makes it very difficult to disambiguate these more specific psychological phenomena from each other independently of measurement error.

We personally consider the expansion of the depersonalization concept suggested by Spiegel et al. (2011, 2013) and incorporated into the current diagnostic system to be theoretically attractive because it may increase the explanatory power and clinical significance of depersonalization phenomena. Furthermore, the revised diagnostic criteria may encourage increased attention to the prevalence of trauma-related altered states of consciousness (TRASC) in complexly traumatized persons, with the suggested listing of exemplar symptoms highly representative of the typical psychological phenomena observed in clinical practice. Nevertheless, we also believe that content validity of the listing would be better achieved if the assessment was purposefully organized around experiential dimensions that are centrally recognized within the interdisciplinary field of consciousness studies and, in particular, the phenomenology of consciousness.

Dissociative Dimensions: Trauma-Related Altered States of Consciousness

As studied in largely normal, healthy populations, global, qualitative indicators of the conscious state include distinctions between task-focused versus non-task-focused attention and feelings of relative alertness versus drowsiness. In dimensional models, however, altered states of consciousness are classified along a finite number of axes. For example, Vaitl et al. (2005) differentiated altered from normal states of consciousness according to the following four phenomenological characteristics: (1) level of arousal activation (referring to an organism's readiness to interact with the physical and social environment); (2) span of awareness (can be narrow and focused vs. broad and extended); (3) the extent of self-awareness (the degree to which the self is a prominent focus within awareness); and (4) sensory dynamics (perceived intensity of physical sensations, e.g., the brightness of colors and loudness of sounds).

As defined by Vaitl and colleagues (2005), level of *activation* may vary from high arousal and agitation to low arousal and relaxation or inertia. Of course, lowering activation beyond a certain threshold eventually becomes incompatible with awareness of the external environment (as in deep sleep or anesthesia). Referring to traumatized persons with dissociative disorders, these individuals can exhibit, curiously, very high activation/arousal as well as very low activation/arousal at different times and under different circumstances, with extremely low levels of activation and arousal sometimes referred to as *dissociative stupor* or *dissociative catatonia* (Schauer & Elbert, 2010).

Awareness span ranges from narrow and focused (e.g., watching the flicker of a candle flame) to broad and extended (e.g., standing by the ocean, simultaneously aware of the sound of the waves, the sight of the seagulls flying overhead, and a cool breeze against one's cheek). Traumatized, highly dissociative persons can sometimes present in hyperfocused states, hypervigilant and acutely attuned toward particular aspects of their external environment that might represent potential signs of threat. Nevertheless, paradoxically here again traumatized persons are known just as well to exhibit characteristically opposite patterns of behavior at other times and in other contexts, such as a nonresponse even to the most focal stimuli, including aversive nociceptive (painful) stimulation.

Whereas *awareness span* refers to attention to things external to the self, extent of *self-awareness* refers to the degree to which the self is a prominent focus within awareness. For example, while watching a film or reading a novel, one may become so absorbed or immersed in it that one experiences a relative "loss of self-awareness." In comparison, while public speaking, one may experience a high degree of self-awareness, being anxiously concerned about what impression one is making. A more extreme example of loss of self-awareness would include a dissociative individual not recognizing him- or herself in the mirror, a phenomenon indeed frequently observed in severely dissociative individuals (e.g., Bernstein & Putnam, 1986; Frewen et al., 2011b).

Finally, *sensory dynamics* simply refer to the subjectively perceived intensity of physical sensations such as the brightness of colors or the loudness of sounds. Whereas traumatized, dissociative persons sometimes present as if hypersensitive to certain sounds or to the brightness of light within a room, they equally often report just the opposite—for example, that sounds are perceived as generally muffled, hollow, or distant, or that the world is "grayed-out" or unclear, such as if it were being viewed through a sheet of glass or a thin veneer of fog (Bernstein & Putnam, 1986).

Vaitl et al. (2005) noted that, in addition to direct physiological means such as via the ingestion of psychoactive substances, several robust psychological methods and environmental manipulations for inducing altered states of consciousness are scientifically validated. These include both sensory deprivation and sensory overload. During *sensory deprivation*, external sensory input is minimized, such as when one is physically confined to a restricted space (thus limiting movement) and deprived of visual, auditory, and tactile stimulation. Vaitl et al. reviewed evidence to suggest that doing so can significantly alter physiological function as measured by blood and plasma levels of epinephrine, norepinephrine, beta-endorphin, and stress hormones. In comparison, *sensory overload* characterizes an environment in which sensory stimulation is maximized to the point of being highly unpleasant and intrusive (e.g., repetitive flashing lights, loud and screeching sounds or yelling).

Although not directly addressed by Vaitl et al.'s (2005) review, certain traumatic events exemplify rather clear instances of sensory deprivation or sensory overload. For example, traumatic events that involve prolonged physical confinement or serious neglect (e.g., denial of basic food and clothing) appear to constitute forms of sensory deprivation. In comparison, other traumatic events appear to constitute forms of sensory overload, such as observing firsthand, being the object of, or forced participation in extreme acts of violence; repeatedly being the object of directed abuse, threatening, and torment; and being the subject of other dehumanizing and sadistic forms of human cruelty and degradation. Accordingly, following Vaitl et al.'s theory, traumatic events should, as such, constitute potential modulators of consciousness in humans. We suggest further that, when an individual is repeatedly exposed to such events over a prolonged period, particularly early in development before the patterns of adult normal waking consciousness (NWC) are securely established, altered forms of consciousness may become more sensitized, stable, and trait-like.

Steele and colleagues (2009) discuss two dimensions in their description of the basis of altered states of consciousness in traumatized persons. The first is "field of consciousness," defined as "the quantity of internal and external stimuli held in conscious awareness at a given time" (p. 157). This concept seems to overlap with the concept of "span of awareness" as described by Vaitl et al. (2005). The second dimension discussed by Steele et al. is "level of consciousness," which is intended to refer to qualitatively different types of mental functioning. Specifically, Steele and colleagues list as examples sleep versus deep relaxation, drowsiness, stupor, coma, and depersonalization–derealization. It is clear that such states as waking relaxation, sleep stages, and coma have been qualitatively distinguished within neurology, not only in terms of phenomenology but also objectively such as via signature profiles on the electroencephalogram (EEG). It also seems reasonable to describe these as *levels*, but as such the distinction between them suggests a quantitative rather than qualitative or categorical one (e.g., ratio of beta to alpha, theta, and delta rhythms on the EEG). Our reading of Steele et al.'s use of "level of consciousness" thus suggests conceptual overlap with the concept of arousal/activation as described by Vaitl et al. (2005). We therefore interpret Steele et al.'s concept of "level of consciousness" to represent a quantitative rather than qualitative variable. However, we find it less fitting that depersonalization and derealization should be referred to necessarily as "low levels" of consciousness. In particular, it is not necessarily clear what depersonalization and derealization have immediately in common with such states as sleep, deep relaxation, drowsiness, stupor, or coma. It should also be noted that in certain spiritual, mystical, and mind–body practices and traditions (e.g., meditation), states of depersonalization are highly sought after and valued as *higher*, rather than lower, states of consciousness.

Nevertheless, we fully agree with what we infer to be Steele and colleagues' (2009) principal argument, that is, to assert the theoretical validity and clinical utility of differentiating between normal and altered states of consciousness in traumatized persons. In agreement with Steele and colleagues' analysis, we would suggest that the latter include, but are not restricted to, depersonalization and derealization. Accordingly, we suggest that there is a need to look for an alternative classification scheme that is more encompassing and integrative than the conceptual grouping implied by "levels of consciousness."

A Four-Dimensional Model of the Traumatized Self

Fortunately, besides the *quantitative* concepts of level of arousal/activation, span of awareness, extent of self-awareness, and sensory dynamics (Vaitl et al., 2005), phenomenologists recognize a number of additional *qualitative* dimensions through which conscious experiences can be classified. Representative of the greater literature, Thompson and Zahavi's (2007) framework, for example, differentiates four qualitative dimensions through which the character of particular subjective experiences can be classified: (1) *temporality* (time sense); (2) *narrative* (the story-like nature of thought as incorporating content, perspective, and structure); (3) *embodiment* (sense of having and consciously being in and belonging to a body); and (4) *affect* (the experience of emotional feelings). For the sake of greater simplicity, we refer to the same four dimensions as the consciousness of (1) time, (2) thought, (3) body, and (4) emotion, respectively.

Although we do not propose that these four dimensions necessarily represent a comprehensive list of all dimensions of phenomenology that are likely relevant to psychotraumatology, we do take the theoretical position that these dimensions go far in explaining much of the symptomatology reported by individuals who have been chronically exposed to severe traumatic stress. We therefore describe each of the dimensions in greater detail here. We also describe our own classification model for trauma-related symptomatology as based on these four dimensions. Specifically, our model differentiates trauma-related symptoms into normal waking conscious (NWC) forms, versus forms of trauma-related altered states of consciousness (TRASC) referring to the dimensions of time, thought, the body, and emotion. A fifth dimension described by Thompson and Zahavi, *intersubjectivity*, relates to the interpersonal experience of another person. Although our 4-D model does not include this dimension directly, in the final chapter of this text we discuss the process of psychotherapy for trauma as an intersubjective practice through which TRASC can begin to be normalized and the sense of self of the trauma survivor healed and restored.

Simply stated, the fundamental principle of the 4-D model for classifying trauma-related symptomatology is that *the presenting symptoms of traumatized persons can be classified as either forms of normal waking consciousness (NWC) or trauma-related altered states of consciousness (TRASC) referring to the dimensions of time, thought, body, and emotion.*[1] Figure 1.2 (also in color insert) visually depicts how the 4-D model classifies trauma-related symptomatology within each of the four dimensions of consciousness of time, thought, body, and emotion in their NWC versus TRASC forms.

In the lower half of Figure 1.2, the dimensions are defined in their normal waking conscious (NWC) form as varied symptoms of elevated post-traumatic distress. This symptomatology represents the readily familiar and relatively nonspecific signs of general distress, negative cognition and affect, and interpersonal maladjustment apparent in most clinical presentations of PTSD as currently diagnosed in psychiatry and clinical psychology; such symptomatology greatly overlaps with other affective and anxiety disorders as well. The 4-D model explicitly asserts that the presence of these signs and symptoms of distress in traumatized persons is not intrinsically constitutive of the presence of trauma-related altered states of consciousness (TRASC). As such, in the absence of clear evidence of other dissociative processes as being involved in the expression of such

---

[1]Although we review both clinical and neurophenomenological studies to support the validity of each of the four dimensions, we emphasize that the basis upon which we differentiate them from each other is, at the present time, a purely conceptual and pragmatic one. Thus for simplicity and clarity of exposition we describe the theoretical and clinical significance of each TRASC *individually*. Nevertheless, in terms of statistical modeling, we are open to future empirical findings that might suggest the collapse of any of the four dimensions distinguished herein, as well as alternative conceptual schemas that might suggest distinguishing higher-order factors on the basis of multiple combinations of the four dimensions; indeed we discuss a number of possible permutations of the presenting dimensions that have frequently emerged in our own research and clinical observations throughout this text.

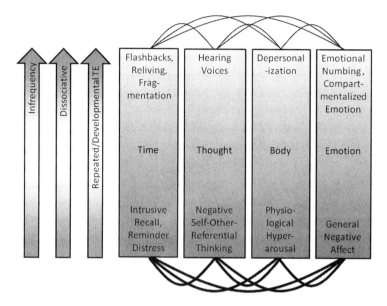

FIGURE 1.2. The 4-D Model of the Traumatized Self.

Boxes and lines at bottom denote potentially nondissociative processes and normal waking consciousness (NWC), whereas boxes and lines
at top denote *intrinsically* dissociative processes (trauma-related altered
states of consciousness [TRASC]). TE = trauma exposure.

experiences, this symptomatology, by parsimony, should be assumed to
be forms of general distress part and parcel of NWC.

In contrast, the same four dimensions are presented in the upper half
of Figure 1.2 in the form of what we regard to be trauma-related altered
states of consciousness (TRASC). We suggest that these are the signs and
symptoms of a dissociative subtype of posttraumatic symptomatology that
is more phenomenologically disturbed and complex. Nevertheless, we
have drawn the background shading of the dimensions as blending into
one another to represent that it is presently not known whether the difference between the normal waking conscious (NWC) and TRASC forms
is a qualitative (categorical) or only quantitative (dimensional) one. Moreover, it is important to point out that traumatized persons can experience
both sets of symptoms, that is, both NWC distress and TRASC, at different times and in different circumstances, as often promoted by perceived
external stress. We wish to make explicit note that experiences of TRASC
as described herein are *not* taken to be psychotic in nature. Finally, we

also contend that symptoms of TRASC can be experienced within or outside the context of accompanying identity alteration as occurs in people with dissociative identity disorder, and thus that they are not necessarily diagnostic of the latter. Indeed we suggest that such states are transdiagnostic, often experienced by individuals with other trauma-related disorders (e.g., borderline personality disorder), and accordingly serve to extend the notion of a dissociative subtype not only to PTSD but other trauma-related disorders as well.

The 4-D model includes four ancillary hypotheses that are also depicted in Figure 1.2. Two of these hypotheses are based on the basic concept of the existence of a state of "normal waking consciousness" (NWC) as generally accepted within the philosophy and psychology of consciousness studies. First, if one defines NWC as the typical and expected psychological state of human beings, in terms of simple frequency or prevalence, and as further consistent with research reviewed previously concerning the minority status of the dissociative subtype of PTSD relative to nondissociative cases of PTSD, it follows that that the four dimensions of consciousness specified by the 4-D model will be observed less frequently as trauma-related altered states of consciousness (TRASC) than as NWC forms of distress. Accordingly, we depicted this hypothesis in Figure 1.2 by including an arrow that is *increasing* in *infrequency* from bottom (nondissociative presentation; NWC) to top (dissociative presentation; TRASC).

Second, and further consistent with the basic concept and existence of a state of normal waking consciousness (NWC), we hypothesize that, if one defines NWC as the absence of altered states of consciousness, the presence of any two dimensions of normal, nondissociative distress will more often co-occur in moment-to-moment real time than the presence of any two dimensions of trauma-related altered states of consciousness (TRASC). We depicted this hypothesis in Figure 1.2 via the boldness of the arcs associating the four dimensions in NWC form (bolder) versus TRASC form (less bold). In summary, within any given moment, we hypothesize that symptom endorsements will be less strongly correlated among the dissociative TRASC than among the nondissociative NWC symptom dimensions. Note that this is akin to such dimensions of experience being more "compartmentalized" in TRASC than in their NWC form. We emphasize, however, that this hypothesis applies most strongly when the dimensions are measured in *real time*, that is, as discrete, time-limited, moment-to-moment phenomenological states.

In comparison, as assessed in terms of traits (e.g., frequency within last week/month/longer), the difference in strength between these correlations is likely to be less significant. Indeed, although we maintain that some trauma survivors will present with only a single or subset dimension(s) of the four dimensions of TRASC, therein emphasizing the clinical significance of distinguishing between them, clinical observations also suggest that, particularly in highly dissociative persons, trait co-occurrences among the four dimensions of TRASC are often found, providing that such individuals are sufficiently capable of self-awareness and self-monitoring of their occurrence.[2]

A third ancillary hypothesis of the 4-D model is that the four dimensions of consciousness, as measured in the form of trauma-related altered states of consciousness (TRASC), although being distinct *in concept* from the measurement of dissociation as a disintegration or compartmentalization of psychological functions (e.g., Holmes et al., 2005; Steele et al., 2009), will nevertheless be empirically observed more often in individuals who also experience dissociative disintegration or compartmentalization of psychological functions. This hypothesis was portrayed in Figure 1.2 by including an arrow labeled *dissociative* that is increasing from bottom (nondissociative presentation; normal waking consciousness [NWC]) to top (dissociative presentation; TRASC). It is important to be clear that this is *not* to say that dissociation measures will not correlate with forms of distress considered to be NWC in nature, but rather only to say that those without any other clear signs of dissociative symptomatology will likely only rarely (if at all) endorse experiences of TRASC. As such, symptoms of TRASC are hypothesized to be more *specific* indicators of dissociative processes. In comparison, symptoms of distress associated with NWC are hypothesized to be more *sensitive* to trauma-related disorders as a whole—that is, to groups of traumatized persons inclusive of those exhibiting nondissociative clinical symptoms as well as those demonstrating intrinsically dissociative symptoms.

Finally, theorists have long suspected, and empirical studies increasingly demonstrate, that the etiology of posttraumatic dissociation often

---

[2]Why do we hypothesize that the dimensions will be more correlated when reflecting NWC than TRASC? The answer becomes clear if one recognizes that any given discrete state of NWC is effectively defined as a form across *all* dimensions. In other words, NWC is defined as normal experience of time (i.e., regular speed, forward direction, and continuous, as well as clear differentiation between present, past, and future); normal experience of thought (i.e., first-person perspective); normal experience of the body (i.e., embodied experience); and normal experience of emotion (i.e., normal range of emotional experience). In comparison, consciousness is defined as altered if *any* of the dimensions is abnormal; in other words, one does not require that all or even multiple dimensions are abnormal for consciousness to be considered altered as a whole, but rather only that at least a single dimension is altered. It should be noted, however, that in persons with severe dissociative disorders, alterations in multiple dimensions of consciousness often co-occur at the state as well as trait level. Thus, this principal does *not* assert that the four dimensions will be uncorrelated in their TRASC form at the state or trait levels, but rather only that the correlations observed between the four dimensions are hypothesized to be lower in magnitude in their TRASC than NWC forms, on average. Again, whereas within NWC one simultaneously experiences a normal sense of time, thought, one's body, and emotion by definition, a TRASC is defined by the presence of one altered dimension, at minimum.

involves experiences of repeated traumatization, often developmental in origin. That is, posttraumatic dissociation often requires repeated trauma exposure, particularly at an early age of onset, when a child's brain is naturally more open to alterations in normal waking consciousness (NWC) taking place, such as normally exhibited in children during developmentally appropriate imaginary play. For this reason, the fourth ancillary hypothesis of the 4-D model is depicted as an arrow in Figure1.2, labeled *Developmental TE* (trauma exposure), which is increasing from bottom (nondissociative presentation; NWC) to top (dissociative presentation; trauma-related altered state of consciousness [TRASC]). We explicitly suggest that this hypothesis again refers to one of differential sensitivity versus specificity rather than only one relating to simple correlation. Specifically, we hypothesize that whereas forms of distress associated with NWC will have greater *sensitivity* to trauma exposure, forms of distress associated with TRASC will have greater *specificity*, particularly for repeated and developmental exposure. Theoretical and empirical background supporting this fourth hypothesis is elaborated upon further in the next section.

Neurodevelopment of a Traumatized Self

Normal waking consciousness (NWC)—that is, an experience of time as nonrepetitious, experiences of thought that are limited to the first-person perspective, an experience of oneself as embodied, and experiences that are motivated and colored by a healthy range of emotions—can be considered a reality orientation that is crystallized over the course of childhood and adolescent development within the context of empathic social learning experiences with caregivers, siblings, and peers. However, NWC may fail to fully develop in the presence of neglectful or impoverished caregiving or experiences that chronically threaten the safety and security of the child. Teicher and others, for example, have shown that not only physical and sexual maltreatment but also verbal and emotional abuse and neglect can have serious consequences for the developing child's sense of self, resulting in an increased likelihood of anxious, depressive, and dissociative symptomatology through adulthood (e.g., Teicher, Samson, Polcari, & McGreenery, 2006).

Research suggests that the sense of self or identity characteristic of adulthood is yet to emerge in the young child or even in the adolescent, partially as a consequence of developmental trajectories in structural and functional development of the brain, including in the medial prefrontal and posterior cortices, temporoparietal cortices, and temporal pole (reviewed by Pfeifer & Peake, 2012). For example, studies have found that cortical thickness in medial prefrontal regions increases significantly toward maturity over years 8–10, following both an inferior-to-superior and an anterior-to-posterior progression, accompanied by age-related increases in functional response during self–other referential processing tasks in the anteromedial versus dorsomedial prefrontal cortex between childhood/adolescence to adulthood (Pfeifer & Peake, 2012; Shaw et al., 2008). Cortical thickness in other brain regions of particular interest to self-development, such as medial posterior structures, may follow a superior-to-inferior and posterior-to-anterior progression over years 8–11, whereas cortical thickness in other brain regions may reach maturation levels earlier (e.g., approximately 9 years of age in the temporoparietal junction, approximately 1 year earlier in the left, relative to the right, hemisphere) or later (e.g., up to approximately 13 years of age in the dorsal anterior cingulate cortex, and up to 18 years in the insula) (Pfeifer & Peake, 2012; Shaw et al., 2008).

Researchers have demonstrated that early trauma exposure, perhaps especially as occurring chronically within the context of attachment relationships, can alter neurodevelopment presumably through experience-dependent (plastic) maturational processes (e.g., Perry, Pollard, Blakley, Baker, & Vigilante, 1995). Schore (2012) provides extensive reviews of this literature, wherein he notes that childhood abuse and neglect can have marked consequences for the developing child's affect regulation and sense of self. De Bellis and colleagues, for example, have conducted numerous investigations of cortical thickness in pediatric maltreatment-related PTSD in brain regions of putative interest to PTSD symptomatology. Among other findings, De Bellis and colleagues have observed maltreated youth to have lower total prefrontal and corpus callosum volumes (De Bellis & Keshavan, 2003), lower cerebellar volume (De Bellis & Kuchibhatia, 2006), larger hippocampal volume (particularly white matter; Tupler & De Bellis, 2006), larger superior temporal gyrus volumes (particularly within the right hemisphere; De Bellis et al., 2002), and larger pituitary volumes (in pubertal and postpubertal adolescents only; Thomas & De Bellis, 2004).

Moreover, Anderson, Teicher, and colleagues demonstrated that exposure to child abuse may differentially affect neurodevelopment at regionally specific critical periods of brain maturation (Andersen et al., 2008). Teicher's research group's work is particularly significant for having demonstrated that the neurodevelopmental effects of maltreatment may be somewhat distinctive across different types of trauma exposure, including experiences less often studied, such as witnessing intimate partner violence (e.g., affecting the inferior longitudinal fasciculus, a fiber tract connecting occipital and temporal cortices that is thought to be the primary visual–limbic pathway subserving emotional, learning, and memory processes specific to vision; Choi, Jeong, Polcari, Rohan, & Teicher, 2012) and being victim to harsh corporal punishment (e.g., affecting dopaminergic pathways, such as resting metabolism in the caudate and the putamen; Sheu, Polcari, Anderson, & Teicher, 2010).

Several studies have investigated the development of normal reality orientation and sense of self in children in association with their fantasy and imaginary play. For example, presented with emotional scenarios inclusive or exclusive of fantastical elements (e.g., monsters) and asked to indicate which stories "could happen in real life," 3-year-olds are less able than are 5-year-olds to discern reality from unreality, an effect that was only weakly correlated with age-based differences in general intelligence. In fact, research suggests that reality orientation has not reached adult levels even by age 7 or 8 (Martarelli & Mast, 2013). In addition, children at least up to age 5 exhibit an emotional response bias favoring the believability of fantastical stories that are neutral or happy in valence over those displaying characters' fear or anger (e.g., Carrick & Quas, 2006; Carrick & Ramirez, 2012; Harris, 2000; Samuels & Taylor, 1994). The brain bases of the development of reality orientation across childhood are important foci for future study.

Researchers have found that reality orientation can frequently develop along an altered path in children who have been maltreated from an early age. For example, Carrick, Quas, and Lyon (2010) found that, in comparison with nonmaltreated children, 3- to 5-year-olds who were abused or neglected, as substantiated by social services, were more likely to believe that fearful stories inclusive of fantastical elements (e.g., frightening giants, fire-breathing dragons) "could happen in real life." In fact, they were also more likely to believe that fearful stories devoid of fantastical elements could happen, perhaps directly as a result of their increased personal exposure to similarly frightening experiences (Carrick et al., 2010).

Research suggests that children who experience stronger emotional reactions to fantasy stories that are fearful or angry in nature are also those most likely to reject such stories as ones that "could happen in real life" (Carrick & Quas, 2006; Carrick & Ramirez, 2012; Samuels & Taylor, 1994). The latter findings have been interpreted as the utilization of an effective emotion regulation strategy: Children may attempt to regulate their negative emotional responses to fears of the paranormal by willfully rejecting them as real. Indeed, researchers have noted that caregivers often explicitly educate their children to regulate their negative emotions by rejecting the basis of their children's fears in reality (e.g., "Don't worry, it's only a dream"; "It's only a movie"; "It's only in your imagination"; "It's not real").

It is possible that trauma survivors use reappraisal and other emotion regulation strategies peritraumatically toward a similar end, as described by the (non)-self-referential processing model of dissociation we introduced earlier. For example, to cope with sexual abuse perpetrated by a school teacher occurring at age 8, one trauma survivor we interviewed noted: "It was like I made it happen to someone else. So it was less real, like it wasn't really happening anymore. So I didn't have to feel it." Another example was provided by Mya, introduced at the beginning of the chapter, who indicated that she frequently "dissociates" when required to tell the story of her past traumatic experiences such as during diagnostic interviews for PTSD:

> "I dissociate to tell it . . . that's a conscious decision. I take myself—
> my insides, my *ego*, or whatever you want to call it—and put it there
> (*motions to the side of herself*). And then *this* talks (*motions to the
> body*). And [after the telling is done], I can bring it [i.e., her "self"]
> back in, for lack of a better way of explaining it. Because that part is
> the part that will feel the shame, that's the part that will not be able
> to talk about it."

Relative to the typical adult, whose ability to modulate his or her consciousness is commonly considered to be less flexible, the child's increased capacity for and tendency toward fantasy and imaginary play, coupled with his or her less crystallized sense of self, may predispose him or her to utilize alterations in consciousness as a coping mechanism when faced with traumatic events, particularly when physical escape is not possible. Dalenberg et al. (2012) reviewed evidence suggesting that early trauma exposure is a strong risk factor for dissociative processes, including, but not limited to, the use of fantasy as an avoidance-based coping strategy during traumatic experiences. By contrast, they found no support for an alternative model that conceptualized fantasy proneness as a cause of false memories of traumatic events. Normal across-person variation in innate tendencies toward dissociation and alterations in consciousness, such as indexed by individual differences in trait hypnotizability, may also present as a vulnerability factor for the development of clinical levels of dissociation in the context of repeated trauma exposure, forming a diathesis–stress model (Butler, Duran, Jasiukaitis, Koopman, & Spiegel, 1996; Dell, 2009b). Researchers have often noted parallels between experiences of posttraumatic symptomatology and alterations in consciousness observed in the context of hypnosis, including their physiological expression within the brain and body (e.g., Spiegel & Vermetten, 1994; Vermetten & Bremner, 2004).

As an exemplar study of the longitudinal, intergenerational effects of childhood sexual abuse (CSA) on psychobiological functioning, Putnam and Trickett (1987, 1993) assessed children and adolescents (ages 6–16), with and without child protective services documented and family-perpetrated CSA histories, in addition to both the current or former caregivers (usually the mothers) of these children and adolescents. The study was also conducted longitudinally, ultimately allowing data collection of the children's own offspring; thus by the study's end data were collected from three generations. Initial outcomes showing increased dissociation in the CSA sample (Putnam, Helmers, & Trickett, 1993) have been reliable across longitudinal investigations, alongside a plethora of additional mental health outcomes that include not only psychiatric disorders (e.g., depression and substance abuse disorders; Noll, Tricket, Harris, & Putnam, 2009) but also increased risk for several other adverse psychological and interpersonal sequelae, including unusual, risky, and sexualized behaviors; being revictimized; self-harm; suicidal ideation; compromised cognitive performance; and risk outcomes on measures of psychobiological development and health (e.g., risk for obesity and accelerated pubertal development; reviewed by Trickett, Noll, & Putnam, 2011). Moreover, children of CSA mothers, among other findings, showed more anxious attachments to their mothers (Kwako, Noll, Putnam, & Trickett, 2010) and were more likely to be neglected, as substantiated by child protective services (Noll et al., 2009). Whereas Putnam and Trickett's research focused on the longitudinal outcomes of CSA, additional well-conducted longitudinal studies of predictors of dissociative symptomatology have also shown that, independent of direct abuse, quality of the early mother–child relationship (i.e., maternal emotional availability) is predictive of the development of dissociation in predominantly at-risk samples (Dutra, Bureau, Holmes, Lyubchik, & Lyons-Ruth, 2009; Ogawa, Sroufe, Weinfield, Carlson, & Egeland, 1997).

In sum, prior research studies provide the background for hypothesizing that trauma-related altered states of consciousness (TRASC), as specified by the 4-D model, are most likely to be seen in persons who have been traumatized or seriously emotionally neglected in attachment relationships from a young age—that is, those who have experienced events likely to perturb the regular (neuro)development of a child's sense of self, reality orientation, and progression toward adult forms of normal waking consciousness (NWC).

Four Dimensions of Consciousness Affected by Psychological Trauma

Having now introduced the fundamental structure of the 4-D model, we now turn to a brief initial introduction to its elements, that is, the four dimensions of consciousness of: (1) time, (2) thought, (3) body, and (4) emotion. Chapters 3–6 describe each dimension in greater detail, including analyses of clinical phenomenology, neuroscience, and clinical case examples; the present introductory descriptions are, by contrast, necessarily brief. However, as an initial means of grounding the present introduction in the current dissociation literature, we note survey items selected from the DES (Bernstein & Putnam, 1986) that, upon face validity, appear to well represent each of the four dimensions of consciousness to which the 4-D model refers. Given that, as noted previously, the DES represents the most often used self-report survey of dissociative symptomatology, the reader should note that the kinds of trauma-related altered states of consciousness (TRASC) specified by the 4-D model are well represented in the extant theory and measurement approaches of the dissociation field.

Dimension 1: Consciousness of Time (Temporality)

Phenomenologists describe the *temporality* dimension of consciousness as characterizing the ebb and flow of consciousness across time. There are at least three principles governing properties that characterize the consciousness of time as it is normally experienced: (1) speed, (2) direction, and (3) continuity.

The principle governing the first property, *speed*, clarifies that normal consciousness has a characteristic subjective *velocity*. The principle describes how long the experience of "right now" or "the present" seems to be, as inherently contrasted with both a subjective past and future. How long do humans typically consider "now" to be? Studies in cognitive neuroscience estimate that what is usually considered part of the "now" experience in humans expands over approximately 2–3 seconds (e.g., reviews by Pöppel, 1997, 2004, 2009). In other words, outside of a 2- to 3-second window, events in time are perceived as in the past or yet to come.

The principle for the second property of *direction* denotes that in normal states of consciousness, time is perceived as forward moving. Stated simply, time doesn't backtrack or repeat itself; it only moves forward.

Finally, the principle for the third property of *continuity* clarifies that consciousness is normally experienced as continuous, with the current moment or "now" seamlessly transitioning into the next. In other words, normally we have the experience of this moment directly and seamlessly flowing into the next moment. Other than in the case of sleep, we do not experience abrupt transitions or blank spots in between the present moment and the next one.

Our argument, however, is that in the case of all three principles, traumatic events have the power to modulate the fundamental character of the consciousness of time, both during the occurrence of a traumatic event (i.e., peritraumatically) and in the long-term aftermath (i.e., posttraumatically). In regard to the principle of speed, during states of especially high or low arousal, as frequently occurs during both traumatic events themselves and their recall (i.e., reexperiencing symptoms), individuals often report an alteration in their subjective perception of the passage of time. Specifically, time is frequently reported as seemingly moving more slowly or faster than is felt to be regular or "normal."

In regard to the principles of direction and continuity, the consciousness of time also becomes altered during the experience of flashbacks, during which individuals report that the past (i.e., a memory) intrudes so fully on their present consciousness that they lose experiential contact with their present environments; the traumatic memory is effectively experienced as though it were being *relived*. People often report that they feel like they are truly "back there" when experiencing a flashback, as if it were happening again in the here and now. For example, one may reexperience a childhood traumatic memory so vividly that one's subjective sense of self seems to temporarily regress to a prior state of being, as the adult experiences him- or herself as childlike and small. An exemplar item selected from the DES that is consistent with such a state of trauma-related altered state of consciousness (TRASC) is: "Some people have the experience of sometimes remembering a past event so vividly that they feel as if they were reliving that event." Chapter 3 reviews the literature on the effects of trauma on the consciousness of time in greater detail.

Dimension 2: Consciousness of Thought (Narrative)

Phenomenologists have noted the typically "story-like" structural organization of human consciousness, which has been described as a *narrative* dimension of consciousness. In particular, like a story, our own thoughts generally include content, plot (structural organization), and narrator.

Philosophers have long noted that consciousness is inherently directed toward some object of attention. In this way, consciousness is always considered to be "about something"— it necessarily has *content*. In philosophy, this is referred to as the property of *intentionality*. In simple terms, consciousness is intrinsically *referential*: It is not reasonable to consider one being conscious or aware if not being conscious *of* or aware *of* something, whether this be a sensation, image, thought, or action. In general, a distinction is often made between our awareness of things outside ourselves (exteroception) and *self*-consciousness, the latter referring to both internal feelings and sensations (interoception) and verbalized thoughts (introspection). For our purposes, narrative consciousness only refers to the consciousness of verbalized thoughts.

In Chapter 4 we discuss how traumatic life events frequently transform the content of the consciousness of thought. Most straightforwardly, traumatic events frequently cause consciousness to be unwillingly directed toward particular contents or objects, specifically those symbolizing the themes of past traumatic events. Thus, the traumatized person frequently experiences intrusive thoughts and memories of the past, and often acts upon his or her environment in stereotyped ways that further symbolize the influence of his or her life history (e.g., with anger, violence, self-harm, or excessive risk-taking).

Not only do our experiences have *content*, but the content is normally arranged in a coherent way. In other words, things are *happening* in our experience, and the order in which such happenings occur—the *course* of our ongoing experience—can be regarded as the ongoing plot of the story. Also referring to the continuity of consciousness, we review studies showing that both the memories of traumatic events as well as one's awareness of present events can be altered by psychological trauma. Specifically, traumatized persons often report that their experience seems disjointed and discontinuous; they may describe experiencing both current events and the memory of past traumatic events in fragments, sometimes interspersed by blank spells (amnestic episodes).

Finally, every story has a narrative perspective, whether in the first, second, or third person. Phenomenology reveals that consciousness is normally experienced from the perspective of *first person*. Taking a first-person perspective toward our thoughts is akin to the experience of owning our thoughts—they are *our* thoughts. The first-person perspective provides an experiential basis for accurate self–other differentiation: If you and I witness the same event (e.g., a hot air balloon taking off), I nevertheless do not mistake whose experience I'm having—the hot air balloon I'm seeing is *my* experience of the liftoff, not yours. Our experience of the event may be similar, for the most part, but I will not normally confuse the fact that the experience I am having is *mine* and not *yours*. Indeed, by definition, it can only be my experience when I say, "I see the hot air balloon taking off." Notice, in this way, how the notion of being a "self" partly emanates: It is assumed that the sense of self has, as part of its fundamental basis, a first-person orientation culminating in ownership of thoughts, feelings, sensations, and actions, referred to by our process model described earlier as *self-referential processing* (SRP; Northoff et al., 2006).

In Chapter 4 we review findings showing that the thoughts of traumatized persons are frequently experienced, not from the first-person perspective, as is normal, but instead from the *second*-person perspective, akin to experiencing thoughts as the voices of others within one's head. As such, thoughts are personified as voices emanating from internalized others. For example, individuals may actually *hear* a past abusive parent's voice inside their head, commenting upon or directing their thoughts, feelings, and actions (e.g., actually hearing the voice of one's mother saying "You are so stupid, don't do that!" inside one's head). We review how this experience is phenomenologically different from simply being aware of a *thought* concerning what a parent's likely opinion would be about a particular presenting circumstance (e.g., "Mother would think I'm stupid if I did this"). An item from the DES that refers to such phenomena states: "Some people sometimes find that they hear voices inside their head which tell them to do things or comment on things that they are doing." Chapter 4 reviews the literature on the effects of trauma on the consciousness of thought.

Dimension 3: Consciousness of the Body (Embodiment)

The *embodied* nature of consciousness clarifies the spatially situated nature of subjectivity. Phenomenologists agree that the normal character of consciousness seems as though to emanate from a particular point in physical space, that is, within the physical body and typically within the head. In other words, it normally seems to us that the point of origin for our thoughts is somewhere in the vicinity of our bodies and, at least in modernized cultures, specifically within the head. Moreover, the *form* of thought may somehow reflect and be constrained by the physical organization of the human body. So, imagining myself at a particular time and place, or moving, I naturally imagine a human body in these physical positions—I do not naturally envision myself in some other bodily (or non-bodily) form. Again, the normal physical embodiment of thought probably mediates, at least partially, the sense that we *own* our thoughts, referring our experience to a physical being that in turn facilitates the experience of being or having a "self."

Documented by neurologists, psychiatrists, and psychologists alike, the concept of an "out-of-body experience" effectively describes a situation in which thought and experience seem to originate from a location fully outside the physical body, often accompanied by seeing the physical body at a point below, beside, or in front of the experienced physical position of the self. Whereas hearing voices may be akin to experiencing thoughts in second-person perspective, states of disembodiment may be more like experiencing one's bodily self in *third*-person perspective, wherein bodily experience is decentered and disowned. For example, when grasping an object such as a coffee mug, instead of having the experience of "I am holding this," a person might have the experience of something akin to "This thing is being held." The latter experience is more devoid of self-ownership and represents a mild form of disembodiment, with full-body out-of-body experiences, of course, being a more extreme version.

In addition to frequently experiencing full out-of-body states, traumatized persons often report conversion-like symptoms that we consider in this text to be forms of *partial disembodiment*. In these partially disembodied states, the self is perceived as residing within the physical body, but the body, or at least part of it, is experienced as foreign or strange. Referring to the previous example regarding the experience of grasping an object without the accompanying perception that "I am doing so," it may seem to one that "these are not my hands" or "someone else is holding this"; the experience may also be accompanied by analgesia or insensitivity to touch (subjectively if not objectively) in the disowned body part. Furthermore, traumatized persons may perceive their body, as a whole, to be foreign or strange, even to the extent that their accompanying movement is uncoordinated, slowed, labored, or "robotic" as a result.

Finally, perceptual experiences referring to the body may also be altered. For example, some traumatized persons' experience of looking at themselves in mirrors is appreciably altered in some way. They may report, although knowing *logically* that the image they see is their own, that it nevertheless may not *feel* like it is. Exemplar items collected from the DES that seem to be representative of trauma-related altered states of consciousness (TRASC) in reference to the body include "Some people sometimes have the experience of looking in a mirror and not recognizing themselves" and "Some people sometimes have the experience of feeling that their body does not seem to belong to them." We review the literature on the effects of trauma on the consciousness of the body in Chapter 5.

Dimension 4: Consciousness of Emotion (Affect)

Phenomenologists recognize that consciousness typically includes a *valence* or emotion dimension—that is, one's experience can be described, typically unambiguously, as pleasant or unpleasant—as well as an *arousal* dimension as either intense or only mild and relatively neutral. Beyond these two dimensions, the affective dimension of consciousness clarifies the more complex nature of distinct emotional feelings. It is not controversial that many traumatized people interchangeably exhibit signs of both increased and decreased arousal that are typically negative in valence; for example, feelings of fear, anxiety, guilt, and shame. However, it is important to point out that, when emotional states are particularly intense, the sense of self may be briefly altered such that individuals experience themselves as if they were "someone else." In our clinical experience this type of alteration most often occurs during attacks of anger; in the words of one trauma survivor: "When I get really mad, I'm not there anymore." An example from the DES that may partly describe such phenomena is the experience of persons sometimes finding "that in one situation they may act so differently compared to another situation that they feel almost as if they were two different people."

Additionally, we suggest that in their more extreme form, signs of emotional numbing suggest the intrinsic presence of a trauma-related altered state of consciousness (TRASC) in relation to emotion. In marked states of emotional numbing and "affective shutdown," we consider a person to be essentially experiencing an "emotionless" state that we view to be outside the boundaries of normal waking consciousness (NWC) wherein core affective states are largely considered to be continuously present (Russell, 1980, 2003, 2005, 2009; Russell & Carroll, 1999). We also discuss the compartmentalized experience of emotions across discrete senses of self as a dissociative process. In discussing disturbances of emotionality in trauma-related disorders we consider several additional affective presentations, specifically social emotions (e.g., guilt and shame), dyscontrol of anger, anhedonia (i.e., the inability to experience positive affect), and alexithymia (i.e., the inability to identify and label emotional states). Chapter 6 reviews the literature on the effects of trauma on the consciousness of emotion.

Summary: A Four-Dimensional Model of the Traumatized Self

The fundamental hypothesis of this text is that there are at least two distinctive varieties of peritraumatic and posttraumatic experience to be found across complexly traumatized persons. One of these, which we might call "nondissociative distress," was exemplified by the case of Kaylin described at the beginning of this chapter, and can be fully expressed without traversing the boundaries of normal waking consciousness (NWC). Kaylin's clinical description, as distressed and symptomatic as she is, is nevertheless reflective of a nondissociative NWC form of distress, negative affect, and interpersonal maladjustment. In comparison, we have argued that clinical presentations such as that of Mya, clearly involving trauma-related altered states of consciousness (TRASC), demarcate *intrinsically* dissociative presentations of posttraumatic psychopathology. Our 4-D model describes posttraumatic symptomatology in NWC versus TRASC form along the four phenomenological dimensions of time, thought, body, and emotion (Figure 1.2). Under conditions of extreme and prolonged trauma, we hypothesize that people can experience a significant dissociation from the NWC of the external and internal reality of themselves, others, and the world around them—specifically, a TRASC. It needs to be noted that although TRASC can sometimes be adaptive in the survival of ongoing traumatic experience, as delineated by the process model overviewed in Figure 1.1, the repeatedly traumatized person may also experience an inability to return to NWC once the trauma has ended. Individuals who have experienced chronic traumatization may therefore be left without (1) the capacity to consciously live in the true present and experience a continuous sense of time that is separated from ongoing flashbacks of a traumatic past; (2) the ability to communicate their trauma in a coherent narrative from a first person perspective; (3) a sense of possessing, consciously being in, and belonging to a body and related interoceptive awareness; and (4) the healthy experience of emotional feelings, instead perceiving themselves as vacillating between states of hyperarousal and emotion dysregulation to being chronically "emotionless," having lost all sense of feeling.

We thus take the theoretical position that the intricately knitted fabric of normal waking consciousness (NWC), the ties of time, thought, body and emotion that bind NWC together—are often unraveled by repeated exposure to psychological trauma. In fact, in marked cases of chronic, repeated, and particularly developmental trauma, trauma-related altered states of consciousness (TRASC) may come to represent the basic thread of the traumatized person's everyday life, as reviewed in the process model of Figure 1.1. Chapters 3–6 examine in greater detail how the consciousness of time, thought, body, and emotion can present clinically, within complexly traumatized persons, either as relatively normal forms of distress (NWC) or alternatively in the form of intrinsically dissociative states

(TRASC). We also review what is so far known concerning the neurobiological bases of each dimension of consciousness in NWC versus TRASC forms in traumatized persons primarily through neuroimaging studies. Finally, Chapter 7 examines the healing of the traumatized self through the intersubjective practice of psychotherapy. Now let us consider Chapter 2, which describes the combined clinical–experimental methodology we recommend as best suited to the assessment and study of TRASC in survivors of psychological trauma: *neurophenomenology*.

CHAPTER 2

What Is It Like?

Neurophenomenology as a Methodology for Psychotraumatology

"[Regarding the neuro-]scientific study of consciousness . . . no piece-meal empirical correlates, nor purely theoretical principles, will re-ally help us at this stage. We need to turn to a systematic exploration of the only link between mind and consciousness that seems both obvious and natural: the structure of human experience itself."

—Francisco Varela (1996, p. 330)[1]

WHAT IS IT LIKE to be trapped within the prison-house of consciousness of the traumatized self? Our interviews with and clinical observations of survivors suggest that the complexly traumatized person often experiences him- or herself as imprisoned, hopeless, and resigned to a life devoid of any form of freedom. In fact, the idea of personal freedom is a foreign concept for many trauma survivors. They often report experiencing themselves as lost, disoriented, and helpless. They feel as if perpetually in the dark and without warmth. They often report feeling experientially detached from others, perceiving themselves as distant, far away, and unreachable. Their experience is often described as if an impenetrable wall or iron bars separate them from other people and the world around them. Within an empty cell, they experience themselves as faceless, nameless, silenced, and forgotten. At times they may even feel inhuman or that they have ceased to exist. They frequently feel abandoned, insignificant, alone, and undeserving of normal human contact. They report that experiencing emotions has become futile, and their emotional states no longer lead to action. A disconnection from bodily feelings and emotions often ensues; they report feeling emotionally numb or in some cases as if already

[1]Originally published in Varela, F. J. (1996). "Neurophenomenology: A method-ological remedy for the hard problem," *Journal of Consciousness Studies, 3*(4), pp. 330-49. Used with permission of Imprint Academic.

dead. The capacity for joy, pleasure, triumph, and all sense of curiosity has ceased to exist. A painting by trauma survivor "Gregory" depicts what it can feel like to be held captive within trauma-related altered states of consciousness (TRASC), the prison-house of the traumatized self. Fittingly, Gregory titled his painting "Let me out!" (Figure 2.1, also in color insert).

The following poem by "Kim" also describes what it can be like to experience TRASC and to feel imprisoned within a traumatized self. Kim's poem describes a state of utter isolation, desperation, helplessness, abandonment, and despair. She is alone in the darkness of her anguish and suffering; words do not begin to express the extent of her inner pain and agony. With time she becomes accustomed to the darkness; there is a sense of *belonging* to it and deserving it—it becomes all she knows. Nevertheless, by the end of the poem we are lifted up into the light of the presence and aid of caring and compassionate others. The poem ends with tremendous resilience, inspiration, and hope with Kim embracing and finding comfort in "the light," feeling a part of "the darkness" no longer:

FIGURE 2.1. Gregory's Artwork (2006): "Let Me Out!" Used with permission.

Imagine being taken captive and thrown down into a deep, dark cavernous hole. The hole is over 1,000 feet deep and its walls are damp and slippery. It is very, very, cold.

Initially you begin to scream, praying that someone will hear you. You scream yourself hoarse, until finally you stop, realizing that there is no one there to listen.

Out of frustration you throw yourself at the walls, clawing desperately, trying to get a foothold, but gaining no ground.

The light from above becomes only a tiny beacon, beckoning you. It taunts you and dares you to try to escape. After some time you collapse into a heap, weighted down with utter exhaustion. You curl into a ball, dreaming of the light that you once loved and now yearn for.

More time passes—maybe hours, maybe even days, and you grow accustomed to that darkness. Your eyes have adjusted and the darkness brings familiarity and comfort. You forget what it is to live in the light and believe you have always belonged in the darkness.

Then one day you hear a noise: at first indiscernible, then incredibly—voices! Someone is there!

The cave is suddenly flooded with light and in an instant your world has drastically changed. You scurry into the corner, shielding your face. You fear the floodlight and view it as a threat, a very terrifying force to be feared and hidden from. It burns your eyes. You cannot see and you cannot respond to those calling your name. You yearn for the very darkness you have been conditioned to.

The people searching for you see into the cave and see you struggling. They dim the light and the cave becomes like twilight—not quite light and yet not dark. You dare to open your eyes, hesitantly at first. You blink your eyes allowing them to compensate for the sudden change in light. Finally you can see. You can see the cave for what it really is: your private, horrific prison. The walls are cold and slimy. They are covered with your blood, the blood of your sweat and your tears. Suddenly you want out of the prison. More than anything in the world you want life. And so you call out, and you are heard. The workers bring you up slowly and with each inch that you are raised, you begin to tolerate the light. Little by little, bit by bit you discover you were meant to live in the light—never in darkness—and you fight to hang on.

Finally you are at the top totally in the light and it is a comfort.

I want to be in that light.

In our view, first-person accounts of TRASC, such as exemplified by Gregory's painting and Kim's poetry, must always be one of the cornerstones of psychotraumatology. It is only by listening openly to the lived stories of trauma survivors that we can begin to understand the often cavernous, enslaved nature of the traumatized self, and we can begin to appreciate how threatening and arduous it can be to even envision, let alone attain, a new sense of oneself as safe, in control, accepted, self-compassionate, curious, joyful, and triumphant.

This chapter, accordingly, introduces *phenomenology*, a philosophical–psychological approach to knowledge acquisition that places participants' first-person descriptions of their lived experience as the primary basis for our understanding of the nature of consciousness. Phenomenology also seeks to teach and train participants to become better describers of their experience. In this respect the practice of phenomenology may have therapeutic potential as well, improving self-reflection, mentalizing, and empathy, and enhancing mindful awareness of the moment-to-moment senses of time, thought, body, and emotion.

Neurophenomenology, the branch of phenomenology that addresses mind–body–brain correlation and mutual causation, involves examining both first-person subjective experience and third-person objective brain–body functions simultaneously so as to understand both better. For example, participants' self-reported experience may be surveyed as the activity of their central and autonomic nervous systems is measured via neuro-imaging, EEG, neuroendocrine, or peripheral psychophysiological measures. We suggest that neurophenomenology, in particular, provides an especially strong methodological paradigm for consciousness studies and psychotraumatology.

The phenomenological question to which we return to over and over again throughout this text is *"What is it like?"* to experience life through the eyes of the traumatized self. We also ask the *neuro*phenomenological question *"What is the brain–mind and body like?"* when traumatized persons experience TRASC. These questions, and the methodologies we believe are best equipped to answer them, are the subject of the present chapter.

Phenomenology and Consciousness Studies:
Describing *"What It Is Like"*

Philosopher of science and consciousness researcher Thomas Nagel (1974) famously observed that for an organism to be conscious, there must be "something that it must be like to *be* that organism—that it must be like *for* the organism" (p. 436). In other words, Nagel noted that for an organism to have consciousness, there must be some subjective way the world appears from the organism's experiential point of view.

Phenomenology is the science and philosophical practice of investigating consciousness from the first-person perspective of the organism that purportedly *is* conscious. Phenomenology is the study of conscious experience through the collection and analysis of first-person accounts of "what it is like" to *have* particular experiences. It is one of the methods of inquiry used in both philosophical and psychological studies, and has its theoretical roots primarily in the work of philosopher Edmund Husserl (1900/1901). The practice of phenomenology as a research methodology essentially involves systematically collecting first-person experience-based descriptions of what something happening "is like" from the person's own point of view. Thus phenomenology involves the study of what something "is like" from the perspective of the person *to whom* the "something" is happening. In simple terms, it asks a person who is having some experience to describe it. Importantly, however, the description must be given in a way that is based solely on his or her experience as it is arising in the *present tense*, that is, as it is happening at the time that it is occurring, moment by moment.

Phenomenology takes individuals' *immediate* experience, free of assumptions or theory concerning its interpretation or cause, as the primary foundation for knowledge about consciousness. Although the data acquired is first-person subjective, it is held that commonalities will emerge among the reports of different people who have similar sorts of experiences. In this way, phenomenology seeks to reductively describe the structural underpinnings of conscious experience common *across* individuals, which phenomenologists refer to as *intersubjective invariants* (e.g., Depraz, Varela, & Vermersch, 2003; Lutz & Thompson, 2003). These invariants include the structural "background" of experience against which the foreground of emerging stimuli present themselves.

As a methodology, the disciplined practice of phenomenology further seeks to develop the capacity of a research participant to be reflectively aware of, and then to subsequently describe, his or her own experience. It is assumed that the typical layperson lacks the skill necessary to describe his or her experience well enough to provide sufficient data for a deep understanding of consciousness. Accordingly, phenomenology seeks to improve upon the limits of the untrained participant's experiential access to his or her own conscious states through various forms of training (e.g., Ginsburg, 2005). Sometimes this requires encouraging a slightly detached observational stance toward one's experience. For example, to describe the experience of hearing internal voices, a person can be encouraged to passively "listen to" the content of his or her inner dialogue and then describe the nature, content, and location of any voice(s) that may be heard.

The discipline of phenomenology is similar to Eastern mindfulness meditation practices in its goal of developing the untrained person's ability to experientially access his or her own conscious states. Both disciplines involve the development of an interested, open, nonevaluative and receptive form of awareness. Within the mindfulness literature, this form of awareness is often referred to as "bare attention" and "beginner's mind" (e.g., Wallace & Shapiro, 2006; Wallace, 2007; see also the phenomenological concepts of "epoche" and "phenomenological reduction"; e.g., Depraz

et al., 2003; Lutz & Thompson, 2003). Achieving this form of bare awareness requires the ability to momentarily set aside or "bracket" one's "natural
attitude" toward lived experiences—for example, thinking that "I shouldn't
be thinking or feeling this way." Only then is a pristine experiential description able to emerge unadulterated by preconceived notions. In addition,
both disciplines subsequently encourage practitioners to describe the experiences that arise for them in a way that is as faithful to the original lived
experiences as possible.

Phenomenology is considered to be distinct from introspection. *Introspection* is an active, reflective, and interpretive approach to experience
that involves searching for an answer to a particular question about one's
consciousness. In comparison, phenomenological practice, like mindfulness meditation, involves a passive, receptive, and simply descriptive
attentional stance: "You go from 'looking for something' to 'letting something come to you' and 'letting something be revealed.' . . . You move from
the sort of active intentionality that looks for the [subjective] interior to a
'passive' acceptance, a letting-arrive" (Depraz et al., 2003, pp. 31, 37). It
should be noted, however, that both phenomenology and introspection
are defined differently by different authors, and therefore it is not always
easy, or practically useful, to distinguish between them (Bayne, 2004; den
Boer, Reinders, & Glas, 2008).

In general, limitations of cognitive introspection as a basis for objective psychological knowledge have been acknowledged for more than a
century. Innovations in phenomenological methods, however, seek to
improve upon the reliability of self-reports of conscious experience (e.g.,
Hurlburt & Heavey, 2001). For example, the *descriptive experience-sampling* method, developed by Hurlburt and colleagues, requires participants to respond to beepers programmed to occur at random as they
navigate their natural environments and everyday lives. At the "moment
of the beeps," participants are asked to describe in open form what they
were experiencing. Researchers also interview participants further within
24 hours about what occurred at each sampled moment to arrive at a
more detailed understanding of the experience (e.g., Hurlbert, 2011;
Hurlburt & Akhter, 2006; Hurlburt & Heavey, 2006). This phenomenological method has provided insights into the nature of the experience of
emotional feelings, such as the frequency with which emotional experiences are accompanied by bodily sensations, and the degree to which they
are simple versus mixed and complex, and clear versus vague (for review,
see Heavey, Hurlbut, & Lefforge, 2012). Fortunately, similar longitudinal, experience-sampling methodologies are also beginning to be utilized
in psychotraumatology. For example, Suvak and colleagues showed that
changes in intrusive recollections and avoidance since trauma occurrence
were strongly correlated prospectively across five intermittent time points
(separated by approximately 3 months) in survivors of rape or robbery
(Suvak, Walling, Iverson, Taft, & Resick, 2009).

Phenomenology and the 4-D Model

Table 2.1 provides examples from various standardized psychological surveys that characterize the kinds of phenomenological experiences described by the 4-D model in Chapter 1, that is, the TRASC of time, thought, body, and emotion. The examples of survey items included in Table 2.1 were collected from questionnaires that are commonly used clinically and in research as measures of dissociation. Based simply on face validity, these survey items, taken from recognized measures of dissociation, exemplify alterations in the four dimensions of consciousness specified by the 4-D model. In turn, such items suggest the dissociative character of the altered dimensions of consciousness described by the 4-D model.

TABLE 2.1.

Face Validity of Sample Items from Dissociation Questionnaires Seemingly Measuring TRASC of Time, Thought, Body, and Emotion

Time	Sample Items(s)
P-DEQ	"Sense of time changing—things happening in slow motion."
	"There were moments when I felt uncertain about where I was or what time it was."
CADSS	"Do things seem to be moving in slow motion?,"
	"Have you spaced out, or in some other way lost track of what is going on during this experience?"
RSDI	"Did you feel as though the event was reoccurring, like you were reliving it?"
DES	"Some people have the experience of sometimes remembering a past event so vividly that they feel as if they were reliving the event."
MID	"Reliving a traumatic event so vividly that you totally lose contact with where you actually are (that is, you think that you are 'back there and then')."
	"Feeling like time slows down or stops."

(Continued)

TABLE 2.1.

(Continued)

Thought	Sample Items(s)
CADSS	"Do you feel like there are different parts of yourself which do not fit together?"
	"Do you feel like you have more than one identity?"
DES	"Some people sometimes find that they hear voices inside their head which tell them to do things or comment on things that they are doing."
MID	"Hearing voices in your head that argue or converse with one another."
	"Hearing a voice in your head that tries to tell you what to do / wants you to hurt yourself / wants you to die, etc."
	"Hearing a voice in your head and, at the same time, seeing an image of that 'person' or of that voice."
	"Hearing a voice in your head that calls you names (e.g., wimp, stupid, no good, worthless, failure, liar, whore, slut, bitch, etc.)."
MDI	"Feeling like there was more than one person inside of you."
	"Having different people inside of you with different names."
	"Different people taking charge inside of your mind."

Body	Sample Item(s)
P-DEQ	"Feeling as though a spectator watching what was happening to me, as if floating above the scene, observing it as an outsider, . . . feeling disconnected from my own body."
CADSS	"Do you feel as if you are looking at things from outside of your body?"
	"Does your sense of your own body feel changed: for instance, does your own body feel unusually large or unusually small?"
RSDI	"Did you feel disconnected from your body?"
	"Did you feel like you were a spectator watching what was happening to you, like an observer or outsider?"

(Continued)

TABLE 2.1.

(Continued)

Body	Sample Item(s)
DES	"Some people sometimes have the experience of feeling as though they are standing next to themselves or watching themselves do something, and they actually see themselves as though they were looking at another person."
	"Some people have the experience of looking in a mirror and not recognizing themselves."
	"Some people sometimes have the experience of feeling that their body does not seem to belong to them."
MID	"Standing outside of your body, watching yourself as if you were another person."
	"Looking in the mirror and seeing someone other than yourself."
	"Feeling that part of your body is disconnected (detached) from the rest of your body."
	"Your body suddenly feeling as if it isn't really yours."
MDI	"Your body feeling like it was someone else's, or that you don't belong in your body."
	"Your hands or feet not feeling connected to the rest of your body."
	"Feeling outside of yourself."

Emotion	Sample Item(s)
CADSS	"Do you have some experience that separates you from what is happening? For instance, do you feel as if you are in a movie or a play, or as if you are a robot?"
	"Do people seem motionless, dead, or mechanical?"
	"Does it seem as if you are looking at the world through a fog, so that people and objects appear far away and unclear?"
DES	"Some people find that they sometimes are able to ignore pain."

(*Continued*)

TABLE 2.1.

(Continued)

Emotion	Sample Item(s)
MID	"Having an emotion (for example, fear, sadness, anger, happiness) that doesn't feel like it is 'yours.'"
	"Very strong feelings (for example, fear, or anger, or emotional pain and hurt) that suddenly go away."
MDI	"Knowing you must be upset, but not being able to feel it."
	"Not having any emotions or feelings at a time when you should have been upset."
	"Not being able to feel emotions."
	"Feeling frozen inside, without feelings."

Note. Certain highly similar items were combined and/or may have been altered slightly for the sake of brevity. CADSS = Clinician Administered Dissociative States Scale (Reprinted from *Journal of Traumatic Stress*, J. Douglas Bremner, John H. Krystal, Frank W. Putnam, Steven M. Southwick, Charles Marmar, Dennis S. Charney, and Carolyn M. Mazure, "Measurement of dissociative states with the Clinician-Administered Dissociative States Scale (CADSS)," pp. 125–136, June 2005, with permission from John Wiley and Sons. Copyright © 1998 International Society for Traumatic Stress Studies.); MDI = Multiscale Dissociation Inventory (Used with permission of John Briere. Items are from a copyrighted psychological test. Do not use without permission of the author (see johnbriere.com).); MID = Multidimensional Inventory of Dissociation (Used with permission of Paul F. Dell.); P-DEQ = Peritraumatic Dissociative Experiences Questionnaire (Republished with permission of Guilford Press, from "Assessing psychological trauma and posttraumatic stress disorder," J.P. Wilson and C.R. Marmar, 2004; permission conveyed through Copyright Clearance Center, Inc.); RSDI = Responses to Script-Driven Imagery Scale; TRASC = trauma-related altered states of consciousness (Republished with permission of Plenum Publishers, from "The Responses to Script-Driven Imagery Scale (RSDI): Assessment of State Posttraumatic Symptoms for Psychobiological and Treatment Research," Volume 29, Issue 4, James W. Hopper, Paul A. Frewen, Martin Sack, Ruth A. Lanius, Bessel A. van der Kolk, 2007; permission conveyed through Copyright Clearance Center, Inc.); DES (Bernstein, E.M., & Putnam, F.W. (1986). Development, reliability, and validity of a dissociation scale. *Journal of Nervous and Mental Disease, 174*(12), 727–735.).

In Chapter 1 we provided sample items describing the dimensions of the 4-D model as collected from the Dissociative Experiences Survey (DES; Bernstein & Putnam, 1986). However, the DES is not the only self-report survey of dissociative experiences in which the four dimensions of TRASC are described. An analysis of two established multifactorial measures of dissociative symptomatology, the Multiscale Dissociation Inventory (MDI; Briere, 2002; Briere, Weathers, & Runtz, 2005) and the Multidimensional Inventory of Dissociation (MID; Dell, 2006b), suggests that these measures also contain repeated reference to the four dimensions of TRASC specified by the 4-D model.

For example, in the case of the TRASC of *time*, the MID assesses the experience of "reliving a traumatic event so vividly that you totally lose contact with where you actually are (that is, you think that you are 'back there and then')." The experience described by this item, the essence of the trauma memory flashback, is described by the 4-D model as a TRASC of time, and considered phenomenologically distinct, as such, from forms of intrusive trauma memory recall and reminder distress that do not include a strong feeling of reliving (see Chapter 3).

In the case of the TRASC of thought, the MID assesses the experience of "feeling like there was more than one person inside of you," and the MID includes the phenomenon of "hearing a voice in your head that calls you names (e.g., wimp, stupid, no good, worthless, failure, liar, whore, slut, bitch, etc.)." The experience of voice hearing is also described by the 4-D model as a TRASC, in this case referring to the consciousness of (verbal) thought. Specifically, the 4-D model differentiates the experience of voice hearing, which it characterizes as thoughts taking the form of second-person perspective (e.g., hearing an audible inner voice saying "You are dirty, you are disgusting"), to be distinct from the experience of thoughts that occur in the NWC form of first-person perspective (e.g., having the thought, "I'm dirty, I'm disgusting") (see Chapter 4).

Regarding the case of TRASC of the *body*, the MID describes an experience of "your body feeling like it was someone else's, or that you don't belong in your body" and "your hands or feet not feeling connected to the rest of your body." The MID describes the experience of "standing outside of your body, watching yourself as if you were another person" and "feeling that part of your body is disconnected (detached) from the rest of your body." Such full or partial out-of-body experiences, respectively, which often occur during times of intense distress, are described by the 4-D model as a TRASC of embodiment, and differentiated as such from body-situated forms of anxiety and distress (e.g., panic attacks, feeling tense or jittery) (see Chapter 5).

Finally, the MDI assesses the experience of "not being able to feel emotions" and "feeling frozen inside, without feelings." These phenomenological descriptions seem to characterize an encapsulated form of emotionality, specifically, experiences of physical and emotional numbness that, in severe form, are considered by the 4-D model as a TRASC of emotion. In their extreme, the 4-D model differentiates marked states of emotional numbing from NWC forms of affective consciousness, including most forms of general emotional distress (e.g., fear, anxiety, guilt, shame) (see Chapter 6). A number of additional examples of phenomenological experiences that would be coded by the 4-D model as examples of dissociative TRASC are included in Table 2.1 as taken from other well-validated psychometric measures of dissociative states and traits.[1]

In summary, phenomenology is a philosophical and psychological method for describing the nature of consciousness. Phenomenology involves training participants in the elaborative description of their experience, and then collecting their subjective, first-person experiential reports, usually in an open-ended manner, about "what it is like" to *be* conscious of various stimuli and events. Questionnaires have also assessed the frequency of various familiar *kinds* of experiences reported by traumatized persons, and a content analysis of dissociation questionnaires, as shown in Table 2.1, suggests that these frequently involve TRASC of time, thought, body, and emotions, as consistent with the 4-D model. In comparison with phenomenology, neuroscience involves the objective measurement of neurophysiological processes as a way to understand the basis of consciousness. Might there be a way to integrate phenomenology and neuroscience in our study of traumatized senses of self?

Neurophenomenology and the Study of Consciousness: Describing *"What It Is Like"* in Both Mind and Brain–Body

Neurophenomenology is appropriately regarded as the subdiscipline or branch of phenomenological studies particularly directed toward understanding mind–brain–body correlation and causation (den Boer et al., 2008; Laughlin, McManus, & d'Aquili, 1992; Lutz, Lachaux, Martinerie, & Varela, 2002; Lutz & Thompson, 2003; Northoff & Heinzel, 2006; Petitot, Varela, Pachoud, & Roy, 1999; Varela, 1996, 1997, 1999; Varela & Shear, 1999). Neurophenomenology combines the disciplined examination of experience via first-person methods with neurophysiological recording. Self-reports of subjective phenomenal experience inform the analysis of neurophysiological markers, such as by the post hoc partitioning of a continuous neurophysiological recording within time segments so as to refer to transitions between subjective experiences "X and "Y."

For example, in what is often touted as the first study to explicitly follow the neurophenomenological method, Lutz and colleagues (2002) trained four men to relate in detail their experience of viewing autostereograms (an image designed to create the visual illusion of a three-dimensional scene from a two-dimensional image). Repeated training resulted in each research participant developing a regular number of discrete categories

---

[1]The measures included in Table 2.1 are intended to be representative of the measures often used in the scientific literature and clinical practice, but should by no means be considered a comprehensive list.

of experience that Lutz and colleagues referred to as *phenomenological clusters*. Specifically, the experimental protocol required participants to view a fixation screen on which they expected that an autostereogram would be presented. They then verbally related their preparatory state for the target stimulus for each trial, reporting phenomenological clusters that differentiated between states of "steady readiness" versus "fragmented readiness" versus "spontaneous unreadiness" versus "self-induced unreadiness." These states subsequently served to guide the analysis of neural dynamics measured in response to each trial via the EEG. Lutz et al. found that gamma-band energy in frontal electrodes increased and slower frequencies (8–16 Hz) decreased preceding stimulus onset, and synchrony across posterior electrodes increased during stimulus presentation, when the participant reported being in a state of readiness as compared with unreadiness at the time of stimulus onset. The findings therefore demonstrated the utility of using subjective reports to guide the analysis of objective data concerning brain functions.

Neurophenomenologists are interested in examining bidirectional causality and mutual constraints between phenomenological descriptions of consciousness and attendant objective neurophysiological measurements (Varela, 1996). The assumption of *bidirectional causality* means that experience and neurophysiology are intercausal; experience causes neurophysiological change, and neurophysiology causes experiential change. The principal of *mutual constraints* can be illustrated by analogy to a coin: What one knows from one side of the coin (e.g., "heads") serves to reduce the number of ways that one can interpret what can potentially be observed on the other side of the coin (i.e., "since it is heads on this side of the coin, the other side must be tails"). Applying the principle of mutual constraints to neurophenomenology, one assumes that, for any given experiential report one has acquired, one can expect only a finite number of potential interpretations of the neurophysiological correlates, and vice versa. Case examples may help to illustrate how a neurophenomenological approach to assessment can enrich our clinical understanding of the nature of consciousness within traumatized persons.

Case 1: Same Event, Different Experience—A Case Study of Reexperiencing

As previously described in Lanius, Hopper, and Menon (2003), a married couple was trapped in their car during a serious motor vehicle accident caused by fog. The accident occurred on a major highway, involved over 100 vehicles, and resulted in a numerous deaths and serious injuries. The couple crashed into the car in front of them, which they could not see due to the fog. Although neither sustained serious physical injuries, both were trapped in their vehicle for several minutes and feared that they would die. During this time they repeatedly heard the screams of an adolescent who could not get out of her burning car in front of them. The young girl was begging for someone to save her. The couple ultimately witnessed this young girl burn to death.

When interviewed later, the husband described that during this event he had felt intensely anxious and that his primary focus involved thinking about how to free himself and his wife from their vehicle. In contrast, the wife reported being "in shock, frozen, and numb." In fact, she reported that, beyond being physically immobilized within the car, she was equally psychologically incapable of moving; she noted that were it not for the directed coping of her husband, she would not have been able to escape from the car.

Four weeks after the accident, the husband and wife continued to be haunted by the memory of the accident. Both reported experiencing visual and auditory flashbacks of the accident and had frequent nightmares about it. Both also reported having difficulty sleeping, increased irritability, and hypervigilance. Additionally, they each experienced difficulty functioning at work due to lack of concentration, and they each avoided driving and other reminders of the accident. Both the husband and wife met diagnostic criteria for PTSD as assessed by structured clinical interview.

Whereas the husband denied any past psychiatric history, the wife had experienced a postpartum depression after the birth of her first child. In terms of early psychosocial history, the husband described his childhood as relatively unremarkable. In comparison, the wife experienced a number of difficulties during her childhood and adolescence. Specifically, her mother had a long-standing history of panic disorder and experienced frequent panic attacks, which were frightening experiences for her when she was a child. She remembered frequently "shutting down" for fear that her mother would die during one of the panic attacks. In addition, her father died when she was 9 years of age. She described this loss as causing her to feel unsafe because, due to her mother's anxiety and instability, she believed that she no longer had a caregiver with whom she felt secure.

To examine the neurophysiological bases for their PTSD symptoms, the couple agreed to participate in a functional magnetic resonance imaging (fMRI) experiment during which they would listen to an audio script that recounted some of their experiences during the accident. Although they had experienced the same traumatic event, the couple exhibited very different experiential and neurophysiological responses to the audio scripts. For both, the experiences they had while remembering the trauma in the scanner were similar to the reactions they had at the actual time of the accident. In response to hearing the audio script detailing the events of the accident, the husband reported feeling intense anxiety and emotional arousal, and that his thoughts were focused on actively finding a way for him and his wife to escape. By contrast, the wife reported feeling "numb," "frozen," and "in shock" while she listened to the script. Thus, the couple had different phenomenological responses both to the accident and to the script that they heard during the experiment.

The couple also exhibited very different neurophysiological responses during the neuroimaging session (see Figure 2.2). During recall of the traumatic event, the husband's heart rate increased by 13 beats per minute, and he showed an increase in blood oxygenation level dependent (BOLD) response within the anterior frontal and anterior cingulate cortex, middle temporal cortex (including the right amygdala), the left thalamus, and areas of the parietal and occipital lobes. Increased response within the temporal lobes and amygdala may be consistent with increased emotional hyperarousal, whereas frontocingulate response may be consistent with effortful coping and emotion regulation (e.g., escape planning). In contrast, the wife's heart rate did not change and, relative to baseline, she exhibited increases in the BOLD signal only within the occipital lobe

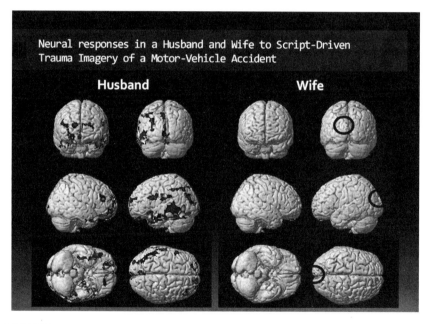

FIGURE 2.2. Neural Responses in a Husband and Wife to Script-Driven Trauma Imagery of a Motor Vehicle Accident.

The husband experienced a fear response motivating escape-related coping, associated with response in several brain regions, including the frontocingulate cortices, right ventrolateral prefrontal cortex, and right amygdala. The wife experienced a numbing/shutdown response associated only with response within visual cortex. See Lanius, Hopper, and Menon (2003) for further description.

(Brodmann areas 18 and 19). The lack of distributed neural response to the script, in contrast with baseline, may be consistent with her reported experiences of feeling "numb" and "frozen."

The couple received individual psychological treatment for PTSD consisting primarily of exposure-based therapy to reminders of the accident. Within 6 months the husband no longer met criteria for PTSD. In comparison, the wife continued to exhibit clinically significant levels of PTSD symptoms, despite receiving the same treatment approach. She also reported that intrusive recollections of her past childhood memories of feeling "numbed out and frozen" in response to her mother's panic attacks, as well as the loss of her father, had increased in frequency. As a result, she often required therapeutic assistance with affect regulation and grounding skills. Without this she reported that she felt herself "shutting down" within the session, feeling frozen, numb, and losing connection with the present, as if she were "back there at the place of the accident," or experiencing herself as if again a young child, scared and alone. This case is reported in greater detail in Lanius, Hopper, et al. (2003).

The significance of this case is that it directly illustrates the importance of ascertaining first-person experiential descriptions as means of understanding the psychological significance of neurophysiological recordings. Without the co-collection of extensive, open-ended phenomenological reports, the two brain scans and psychophysiological recordings would have simply looked very different, and we might have wondered about the reliability of the experimental procedure. By contrast, recognizing the different ways in which the partners responded experientially to the event provided further rationale for grouping the analysis of PTSD patients by the characteristics of their subjective response to traumatic reminders rather than by diagnosis alone (Frewen & Lanius, 2006a, 2006b; Lanius et al., 2006). The latter was instrumental in the later design of studies that examined differential response patterns to traumatic reminders in individuals with chronic PTSD (e.g., Hopper, Frewen, van der Kolk, & Lanius, 2007), eventually culminating in proposals for recognizing a dissociative subtype of PTSD (e.g., Lanius, Vermetten, et al., 2010; Lanius et al., 2012).

More generally, however, the differing phenomenological accounts of traumatic reexperiencing observed reinforced the idea that considering all persons with PTSD as if they were homogeneous cases sampled from a single population might prevent the appreciation of the heterogeneity of neurophenomenological responses to traumatic reminders (see Lanius et al., 2006; Foa, Riggs, & Gershuny, 1995). It was primarily through the use of neurophenomenology as a research methodology that such differentiations were originally ascertained. Moreover, although this case used standard post hoc fMRI subtraction analyses based on an experimental paradigm, technological advances making possible functional neuroimaging analysis in real time may facilitate moment-to-moment assessment of spontaneous changes in the BOLD signal, which can then be assessed for phenomenological significance or self-regulation (e.g., de Charms, 2008; LaConte, 2011; Weiskopf, 2012).

Case 2: A Tell-Tale Heart—Case Study of Reexperiencing

Heart-rate variability (HRV), as measured at rest, is generally regarded as a measure of parasympathetic tone regulated by the vagus nerve. It is often measured in terms of respiratory sinus arrhythmia (RSA); that is, the degree to which heart rate transiently increases and decreases with inhalation and exhalation, respectively. Low HRV is a risk factor for all-cause mortality and various specific cardiovascular disorders. Increasingly, higher HRV has also been broadly implicated in psychological health, including trait positive affect and psychological flexibility (Appelhans & Luecken, 2006; Ode, Hilmert, Desiree, & Robinson, 2010; Oveis et al., 2009). By contrast, low RSA, whether measured at rest (e.g., Cohen et al., 1997, 2000; Hopper et al., 2006), in response to trauma reminders (e.g., Cohen et al., 2000; Sack et al., 2004), in response to general emotional or experimental lab stressors (e.g., Hauschildt et al., 2011; Hughes, Dennis, & Beckham, 2007; Keary, Hughes, & Palmieri, 2009), and even in response to pleasant stimuli (Arditi-Babchuk, Feldman, & Gilboa-Schechtman, 2009), has been observed in traumatized persons as a function of increasing posttraumatic stress. Research has also demonstrated the potential efficacy of biofeedback training of HRV in persons with PTSD and comorbid substance abuse problems (Zucker, Samuelson, Muench, Greenberg, & Gevirtz, 2012) and depersonalization disorder (indirectly, via biofeedback training of skin conductance responses; Schoenberg, Sierra, & David, 2012). Accordingly, biofeedback training aimed at increasing HRV has been used not only as an intervention for cardiorespiratory disorders but also adjunctively as an intervention for affective disorders, including PTSD (review by Wheat & Larkin, 2010).

In this context, Kaylin, introduced at the beginning of Chapter 1, suddenly began to exhibit low HRV during only her second session of HRV biofeedback, following a lengthy period of relatively high HRV, illustrated on the feedback screen by a hand beginning to emit a blue-red "aura" rather than one of green hue (see Figure 2.3). Noticing this, the clinician cued the client back to an awareness of her breathing, and she was able to self-regulate her neurophysiological state, resuming a state of higher HRV. Upon debriefing, at the end of the biofeedback session, Kaylin noted that when the visual feedback stimulus was blue, she had unknowingly become "lost in bad thoughts from the past." Furthermore, this internal experience was not evident to the clinician in terms of Kaylin's external behavior; she was oriented toward the feedback screen and otherwise

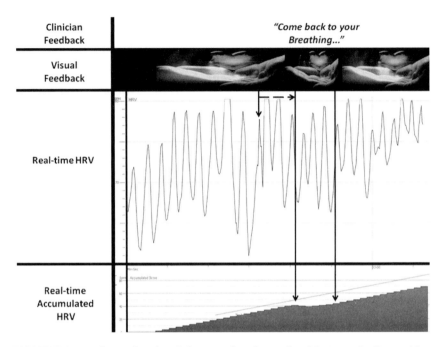

FIGURE 2.3.   Case Study of Onset of an Intrusive Memory Indicated by Transiently Low Heart-Rate Variability (HRV) during Biofeedback Training.

Heart rate (HR) was recorded by plethysmograph from the left earlobe (emWave2; www.heartmath.com), and respiratory rate (RR) was inferred from a visual pacing stimulus; conjunction between HR and presumed RR was calculated as a measure of HRV (i.e., respiratory sinus arrythymia). As indicated by visual feedback, a green "aura" emitting from an open hand indicated periods of a high rate of accumulating HRV (left and right "hands holding heart" in visual feedback panel), whereas a blue-red aura indicated a lower rate (middle "hands holding heart" in visual feedback panel). The solid downward arrow in real-time HRV panel indicates the physiological marker of the beginning of a period of lower accumulated HRV. It was later noted by the client that this neurophysiological state, in time, was associated with the onset of a trauma intrusion. Neither the client nor the clinician (through the client's outward behavior) were otherwise aware of the onset of the trauma intrusion in the client. The dashed rightward arrow indicates the lag in time (approximately 20 seconds) before this neurophenomenological event was represented in the visual stimulus feedback (based on accumulated HRV), also indicated by the long downward arrows. Shortly after the onset of visual feedback, to which the client did not respond, the clinician verbally cued the client back to an awareness of her breathing, and she was able to let go of the intrusion and return to a higher rate of accumulated HRV. She later noted that, had the trauma intrusion occurred under normal circumstances, she would have likely only "come to" after 10–20 minutes or longer, and have found herself in a state of utter confusion and significant distress that, in turn, would typically last hours longer.

apparently breathing normally. As such, it was only the neurophysiological measure—in this case Kaylin's HRV signal—that provided the indicator of a significant change in her phenomenological state (see Figure 2.3 for further description). The case illustrates how a neurophenomenological approach might guide the moment-to-moment assessment of the psychological and physiological states of traumatized persons; brief changes in neurophysiological measures might prompt phenomenological assessment, and vice versa. Indeed such a process is useful particularly in biofeedback-assisted psychotherapy.

Case 3: EEG Neurofeedback and Reembodying a Self—a Case Study of Depersonalization

A middle-age woman, "Suzy," reported being chronically prone to states of depersonalization, first occurring in her adolescence when she was repeatedly gang-raped from the ages of 11–13. The chronic and high severity of her dissociative symptomatology was also evident through administration of standardized self-report instruments (MDI and DES; see Table 2.1). Suzy volunteered to take part in a neuroimaging study of resting-state neural networks before and after a single session of neurofeedback training (reduction of alpha amplitude) (Kluetsch et al., 2014; Ros et al., 2013). At the time of the study she had been receiving trauma-focused psychotherapy for her posttraumatic stress and dissociative symptoms, with linear gains though without full resolution for nearly a decade.

Upon exiting the fMRI scanning session before the neurofeedback training session, Suzy reported experiencing a marked sense of depersonalization manifested behaviorally in a slowing of her speech as well as pronounced cognitive slowing. Suzy reported experiencing her hands and feet as if detached from her body as well as feeling like she was "in a dream." Although Suzy often experienced disembodied states, the present acute manifestation was particularly severe.

A 3-minute EEG recording was promptly collected on site with Suzy's eyes open prior to the neurofeedback session, and her results were compared with a normative database. Relative to norms, an overall increase in spectral power was observed over frontal, bilateral temporal, and midline central, parietal, and occipital electrodes, particularly within the theta (4–8 Hz) and alpha (8–12 Hz) frequency bands. High beta (18–25 Hz) activity was also elevated, specifically at left prefrontal and right frontal sites (see Figure 2.4). (Note that the aforementioned aspects of this case are also described in Lanius, Kluetsch, Bluhm, Ros, and Frewen, 2014). Irregular (primarily increased) theta activity, in particular, had been previously established as characteristic of dissociative disorders and hypnosis

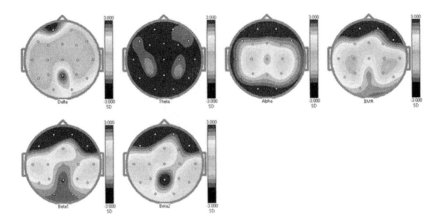

FIGURE 2.4. Topograms of EEG Power Spectra during an Experience of Depersonalization in Suzy.

Significance probability topographic scalp maps for the statistical comparison of Suzy's qEEG with corresponding spectra parameters from a normative database including multi-channel EEG recordings from 500 healthy adults, ages 18 to 60 years. The maps shown represent the level of deviation (Z scores) of the absolute EEG power (uV2) of the individual spectra from the mean value computed for the reference group of healthy subjects of the same age (Kropotov, 2008). The shading indicates the mean Z scores for absolute EEG power (uV2) differences for each of the six frequency bands: delta (1.5–4 Hz), theta (4–8 Hz), alpha (8–12 Hz), SMR (12–15 Hz), beta 1 (15–18 Hz), beta 2 (18–25 Hz); scales are presented at the right of each map. Although 2-tailed tests were conducted, darker shading in all cases indicates increases relative to norms. Frontal regions are at the top and occipital regions are at the bottom of each map. The left hemisphere is on the left.

(e.g., review by Spiegel & Vermetten, 1994), depersonalization phenomena secondary to temporal lobe epilepsy (e.g., review by Lambert, Sierra, Phillips, & David, 2002), and even of individual differences in dissociative traits within college students (Giesbrecht, Jongen, Smulders, & Merckelbach, 2006)—although state dissociation was negatively correlated with theta activity in a recent study of a diagnostically heterogeneous sample of psychiatric patients (Krüger, Bartel, & Fletcher, 2011).

Given the preponderance of slow wave activity, Suzy was subsequently invited to begin an experimental trial of adjunctive EEG neurofeedback therapy that took place over multiple sessions, primarily aimed at reducing alpha amplitudes recorded from the midline parietal lobe. We had previously shown that this particular experimental EEG intervention could modulate neural networks associated with self-referential processing (SRP) and salience detection in healthy individuals within a single session (Ros et al., 2013); as such it was thought that downregulation of the alpha rhythm might further be relevant to the symptomatology experienced by Suzy. Neurofeedback consisted of Suzy's attempting to cause a computer to emit auditory beeps contingent on her reducing her alpha amplitudes from baseline. Visual feedback was also provided, often of an arcade game-like nature, such that focused visual attention and a sense of willful action were encouraged.

The results of adjunctive neurofeedback therapy in Suzy's case were nothing short of striking. Within only four brief sessions scheduled over less than 2 months, Suzy reported experiencing a full normalization of her depersonalized states. In session, she described this experience as follows:

> "I was disconnected until I had that experience. I knew I had become completely associated, I was completely integrated, and it was a really physical experience. I became quite light-headed and very dizzy, and I knew that if I stood up, I would fall, so I just sat where I was, put my head down for a bit and after a few minutes it was like, 'OK, things are very real all of a sudden.' It felt like the sounds I was hearing were much louder. So at that point I am fully 100% in my body, and I am not sure that that had ever existed since childhood. I came in and it was a very physical experience of an integration of body, mind, and spirit and everything coming together—it was a very physical sensation for me."

Suzy's reduction in depersonalization has been sustained for 2 years, and her life has changed significantly as a result. Suzy is now able to work full-time as a teacher and has been able to develop, for the first time in her life, a social circle she can trust. Suzy also began to contemplate getting involved in an intimate relationship—something that she never dared to think about before. She is now also able to experience pleasure in a way that she never used to be able to do. She relates this to the fact that she no longer fears that "If I feel good, something bad will happen." Interestingly, these subjective alterations are also apparent behaviorally and somatically; for example, Suzy walks with greater buoyancy and exhibits a much more upright posture when both seated and standing. Moreover, Suzy's clinical improvements have been associated with sustained, clinically significant reductions of her waking alpha and theta rhythms, as assessed by periodic follow-up EEG sessions. Suzy has completed the final recovery phase of her psychotherapy and as of this writing was recently discharged from treatment.

One can conclude little about the treatment efficacy of this particular neurofeedback intervention from the results of only a single case; therefore, ongoing studies in our laboratory are continuing to examine the efficacy of this type of neurofeedback training. Nevertheless, the case of Suzy does illustrate how a serendipitous neurophenomenological assessment might serve to guide treatment innovation. Specifically, assessment of objective neurophysiological markers, as prompted by report of particular spontaneous phenomenological experiences, might then suggest novel therapeutic targets.

Neurophenomenology of Trauma-Related Altered States of Consciousness

It has been suggested, seemingly with a certain hope, that perhaps "someday a biomarker (or combination of biomarkers) may be the gold standard for PTSD diagnosis against which the accuracy of subjective measures will be judged" (Pitman et al., 2012, p. 783). However, we believe that a much greater aspiration exists for psychotraumatology, perhaps excepting in contexts where there are obvious concerns of secondary gain (and consequently wherein subjective reports of participants might be considered suspect). Specifically, following the neurophenomenological principle of *mutual constraints*, we believe that measures of subjective experience and objective neurobiomarkers, rather than being pitted against each other as if in conflict, or held in unequal regard, must instead be integrated and synthesized in our clinical descriptions of traumatized persons. If we are ever to fully comprehend the nature of the traumatized self, we believe that a deeper analysis, incorporating both subjective and objective measures, will be necessary. Indeed, consistent with Dell's (2006a, 2009a) analysis, markers of dissociation are inherently difficult to verify objectively alone (e.g., behaviorally and neurobiologically), and an accompanying analysis of traumatized persons' moment-to-moment subjective experience seems of the utmost importance to a scientifically valid psychotraumatology.

From the point of view of neurophenomenology, it is unfortunate that very few studies have directly compared the neurophysiological markers of NWC distress relative to TRASC in persons with trauma-related disorders. In support of neurophenomenology as a methodological framework for psychotraumatology, Figure 2.5 details the results of 10 representative neuroimaging studies that have investigated the neural correlates of dissociative TRASC in response to recall of traumatic memories (Hopper et al., 2007; Lanius et al., 2002; Reinders et al., 2006), viewing of emotional pictures (Phillips et al., 2001), an emotional memory task (Medford et al., 2006), pain processing (Ludäscher et al., 2010; Mickleborough et al., 2011), visual

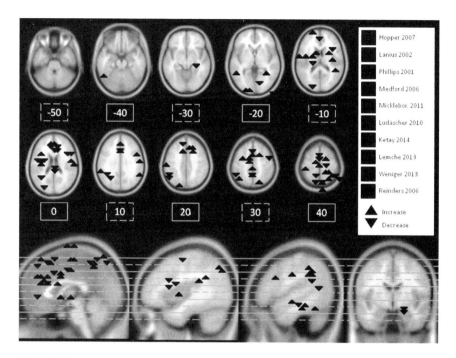

FIGURE 2.5. Neurophenomenology of Dissociative TRASC revealed by summary results from 10 representative functional neuroimaging studies.

Legend lists studies by first author and date of publication. Arrows indicate whether a decrease or increase in neural response was observed relative to various control conditions or correlated measures. Results for sagital midline slice includes findings for $-13 < x < +13$mm. Results plotted on other sagital slices reflect right hemisphere only for $35 < x < 45$mm (showing insula) and $45 < x < 55$mm. Coronal slice is plotted for $-12 < y < -4$mm.

self-recognition (Ketay et al., 2014), viewing of others' facial expressions (Lemche et al., 2013), and directed movement (Weniger et al., 2013).

Perusal of Figure 2.5 indicates that in the neuroimaging paradigms studied to date, dissociative symptoms are most reliably associated with altered response within cortical midline structures associated with self-referential processing (SRP) (including the medial prefrontal cortex, anterior cingulate cortex, posterior cingulate cortex, and precuneus; Northoff et al., 2006), but have also been associated with response in the bilateral insula, known to be associated with awareness of affective responses, and the right parietal cortex, associated with both the embodiment of consciousness and social cognition (e.g., van Overwalle, 2009). We review the results of these studies and others in greater detail in the context of our discussion of each of the four dimensions of consciousness specified by the 4-D model in Chapters 3–6. It is also important to note that most neuroimaging studies have examined the upper cortical mantle only; TRASC, however, may well have their primary bases within lower brain structures, and future neuroimaging studies should better take this into account (Schore, 2003a, 2003b).

It is important to point out that the common method used in neuroimaging studies of trauma and dissociative symptoms is *not* explicitly neurophenomenological. In comparison, most studies simply collect questionnaire ratings relating to the frequency of a list of expected subjective experiences, rather than measuring individuals' immediate experience in an open way, free of assumptions or theory concerning its eventual interpretation or description. Moreover, to date, researchers have largely considered the subjective experiences measured in studies as face valid. That is to say that researchers have not taken it upon themselves to assist participants in developing their capacities for exteroceptive, interoceptive, and phenomenal self-awareness prior to collection of subjective reports. Accordingly, when we refer to studies of phenomenology in traumatized persons throughout this text, we are largely referring to predetermined questionnaire ratings, such as those in Table 2.1, rather than the open measurement of subjective experience. We look forward to future studies that might more fully take up the neurophemenological approach, including pretraining of participants to improve the quality and depth of their phenomenological reports, and with some of the measures of conscious subjectivity collected emerging from the data themselves rather than being preordained by extant theory.

Psychotraumatology as a Paradigm for Consciousness Studies . . . and Vice Versa

Why do different people have different responses to what, on the surface, seem like similar traumatic events? Is there a link between differences in phenomenology and differences in neurophysiological response? Should different patterns of phenomenological and neurophysiological response be recognized within the diagnosis of trauma-related psychiatric disorders?

Our collective clinical and research experience working with trauma survivors suggests that the phenomena of peritraumatic and posttraumatic stress represent powerful theoretical, empirical, and clinical paradigms for studying human consciousness in both normal and altered forms. As such, we argue that the study of psychotraumatology should have as one of its primary theoretical bases the neuroscience of consciousness studies, following the neurophenomenological method.

Accordingly, a primary objective of this text is to begin to integrate the previously disparate fields of psychotraumatology and consciousness studies. Specifically, we suggest that the fields of psychotraumatology and consciousness studies each stand to be significantly enriched by their resulting synthesis. On the one hand, we assert that the field of consciousness studies, and particularly the discipline of neurophenomenology, provides both a tested research and clinical methodology, as well as a number of theoretical concepts, that will be useful in furthering our understanding of the experiences and symptomatology of traumatized persons. On the other hand, the study of severely traumatized persons, particularly in regard to the comparison of individuals presenting with relatively simple versus more complex clinical presentations involving TRASC, provides an opportunity to examine the breadth of current theories of human consciousness. Consciousness researchers and philosophers who follow the neurophenomenological method have often been interested in investigating the symptomatology of other psychiatric and neurological disorders, particularly schizophrenia and various forms of neurovegetative state, as means to ascertain the breadth of their theories. However, consciousness researchers have only very rarely paid much attention to the often equally complex forms of psychopathology suffered by severely traumatized people. It is therefore our opinion that the examination of complexly traumatized persons provides a natural model for understanding both NWC as well as its susceptibility to alteration in response to extreme life experiences (i.e., TRASC).

On this basis, the foregoing chapters overview what, according to contemporary neurophenomenologists (e.g., Thompson & Zahavi, 2007), represent four of the defining dimensions of consciousness: our experience of time, thought, our bodies, and emotion. We describe how the dimensions can present in traumatized persons, whether as states exemplary of NWC or as intrinsically dissociative TRASC. We also discuss how alterations in each of the dimensions of consciousness can be adaptive during the traumatic event. However, the focus of this text is on how the persistence of TRASC in the long-term aftermath of trauma is often associated with the presence of psychopathology.

CHAPTER 3

Consciousness of Time

When the "Now" Slows Down, and
When "Then" Becomes Now

"Mental time travel allows one, as an 'owner' of episodic memory ('self'), through the medium of autonoetic awareness, to remember one's own previous experiences, as well as to 'think about' one's own possible future experiences. . . . The essence of episodic memory lies in the conjunction of three concepts—self, autonoetic awareness, and subjective time."

—Endel Tulving (2005, p. 9)[1]

T HE PRESENT CHAPTER ON the consciousness of time includes a discussion of what is phenomenologically known about the human subjective sense of the passage of time, and how this may be relevant to an understanding of response to psychological trauma. Figure 3.1 highlights the dimension of time within the 4-D model. In brief, normally we have the experience of a "present tense," that is, that we exist within a "now" that is qualitatively distinct from our past and future. We also normally experience time as continuously moving, and as unidirectionally forward in its movement.

In this chapter we examine ways in which the consciousness of time can be significantly altered by the experience of psychological trauma. We review the results of research demonstrating that both during traumatic events and during flashbacks of past traumas, people's acute sense of the span of the subjective "now" can be altered. We also discuss the phenomenology of flashbacks as defined by experiencing past events as if they were *in the present*. Flashbacks thus represent a marked confusion of the normally strong sense that the present and the relatively distant past

[1]*The Missing Link in Cognition* edited by Herbert S. Terrace and Janet Metcalfe (2005) Ch. 1 'Episodic Memory and Autonoesis: Uniquely Human?' pp. 3–56, 53 words from p. 9. By permission of Oxford University Press, USA.

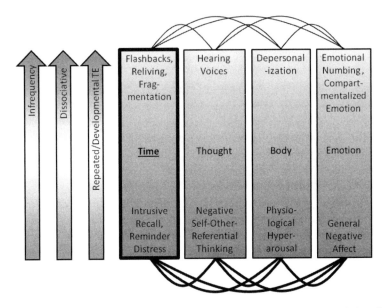

FIGURE 3.1. The 4-D Model of the Traumatized Self Highlighting NWC Distress versus TRASC of Time. TE = trauma exposure.

are qualitatively distinct. We argue that flashbacks, the sense of *reliving* traumatic events, represent trauma-related altered states of consciousness (TRASC). We suggest that flashbacks are qualitatively different from intrusively *remembering* past traumatic events, and from experiencing distress at trauma reminders, while nevertheless maintaining awareness of the present environment (i.e., that one is not *in* the past).

It should also be noted that traumatized persons frequently experience a subjective "loss of time" altogether. Lost time is evidenced by, on the one hand, markedly discontinuous memory for distal life events (i.e., psychogenic amnesia, e.g., for specific past traumatic events or whole developmental periods), and on the other hand, more recent events and ongoing experience (e.g., traumatized persons frequently find themselves in places without remembering how they got there, or why they are there). Whether the psychological mechanisms underlying such phenomena are distinct or overlapping is not presently known. However, discussion of the phenomenology of "lost time" as in amnesia and state switching is beyond the scope of the present chapter. (For further discussion of this topic, see Anderson et al., 2004; Brand et al., 2009; Reinders et al., 2003, 2006; Staniloiu & Markowitsch, 2010; Staniloiu, Markowitsch, & Brand, 2010.)

Our principal argument in this chapter is that forms of distress wherein the normal patterns of waking temporal consciousness are maintained (time span, continuity, and distinctness between past and present) should be distinguished from those wherein the sense of temporal consciousness is altered (time dilation, discontinuous time, and the sense of reliving, i.e., flashbacks). Using clinical examples, we also overview forms of psychological grounding and mindfulness practices that can help normalize the TRASC of time.

"Now" as a Length: A Neurophenomenological Approach

"The time in which episodic memory operates is the same in which all physical and biological events occur–physical time. But the time in which remembered events occur is different. We can call it subjective time. It is related to but not identical with physical time."

—Endel Tulving (2005, p. 16)

Our normal consciousness of time includes at least two attributes that might, at first, seem to be in contradiction. On the one hand, we experience the past, present, and future as qualitatively distinct and nonoverlapping: "That was then and this is now." On a narrower scale, however, we feel that time is continuous. Rather than being experienced as a disjointed series of discrete and fragmented moments, our lives seem to us to seamlessly transition between the immediate past, present, and anticipated future. Our immediate experience effectively encompasses a portion of the past, with a pinch of the predicted future mixed in. Tulving (2002a) termed our sense of time "chronesthesia" and phenomenologists often describe our sense of current time as a "specious present" or a window of "nowness" (e.g., James, 1890; Thompson & Zahavi, 2007). Our consciousness of time as being simultaneously discrete and continuous is thus reconciled by defining the present moment in terms of a certain *length*.

But how long *is* the subjective present? How long does a human "now" seem to last? The results of a number of experiments in cognitive neuroscience converge in findings that the human sense of the present usually spans between approximately 2 and 3 seconds (see reviews by Pöppel, 1997, 2004, 2009). In particular, the duration of events (e.g., the sounding of a tone or the presentation of a picture) that is somewhere between 2 and 3 seconds can be accurately determined (e.g., "Press the button to indicate the approximate length of the tone, the first button press representing the start and the second button press representing the stop"). By contrast, events shorter than 2 seconds tend to be overestimated, whereas events longer than 3 seconds tend to be underestimated.

This set of results is commonly interpreted to suggest that a window of 2–3 seconds represents for humans the basic building block of conscious time: Our brains create a span of "now" that is too short to accurately capture the length of briefer events (e.g., 1.5 seconds), resulting in our experiencing them as "a bit longer than they really were." In comparison, our experience of longer events (e.g., 5 seconds) may be akin to something like *x*-number full moment(s) plus/minus a part of another one. This imprecision in mental representation may cause us to make a greater number of mistakes when recalling the duration over which such events take place.

Numerous other experiments confirm the 2- to 3-second estimate of the subjective "now" (e.g., event groupings and temporal reversals such as binocular rivalry). For example, a metronome sounding up to every 2–3 seconds gives the impression of a continuous set of independent beats, whereas if the clicks are separated much longer than this, we experience each as if unto its own—they are too separated in time to seem part of a common composition. Regarding temporal reversals, if one presents a vase carved to reveal two faces directed toward each other against a background, the perception of the vase versus the two faces alternates at about a 2- to 3-second interval (though with variability). The experience is suggestive of the neurocognitive apparatus checking whether anything new or worth attending to has happened approximately every 2–3 seconds. Intriguingly, the 2- to 3-second span of time also approximates both the limiting interval for the acquirement and retention of information into working memory and the syllablistic pace of common social verbal discourse: in essence, if you talk too fast, I won't be able to follow you, but if you talk too slowly, I'll become bored (see reviews by Pöppel, 1997, 2004, 2009). In summary, Pöppel (2009) writes:

> It can be concluded that temporal integration in the range of 2–3 seconds represents a general principle of the neurocognitive machinery. This universal integration process is automatic and pre-semantic, i.e. it is not determined by what is processed, but it creates a temporal window within which conscious activities can be implemented. Owing to the omnipresence of this phenomenon, it can also be used as a pragmatic definition of the subjective present, which is characterized by the phenomenal impression of 'nowness.' Temporal integration in the range of 2–3 seconds defines, however, also singular STOBCON [states of being conscious]. Thus, this temporal window provides a logistical basis for conscious representation, a working platform for our phenomenal present. (p. 1893)

Of particular interest to traumatic stress studies are the results of an array of recent experiments that show that the phenomenology of temporal perception covaries with the phenomenology of affect (e.g., see reviews by Droit-Volet & Meck, 2007; Noulhiane, Mella, Samson, Ragot, & Pouthas, 2007; Smith, McIver, Di Nella, & Crease, 2011). The time-dilating effects for aversive stimuli may depend on an interaction between stimulus type and specific emotion types; for example, the time-dilating effect for visual stimuli is enhanced preferentially for disgust-inducing, relative to both sadness- and fear-inducing, pictures (Gil & Droit-Volet, 2012). In contrast, whereas angry facial expressions provoke time overestimations (Gil & Droit-Volet, 2011), facial expressions of disgust evidently do not (e.g., Droit-Volet & Meck, 2007). It should also be pointed out that threat *anticipation*, as differentiated from threat *presence*, also has the power to induce temporal overestimations (e.g., Droit-Volet, Mermillod, Cocenas-Silva, & Gil, 2010), and that the ability of angry facial expressions to induce time overestimations is observed with implicit judgments but not when attention and working memory are taxed (Gil & Droit-Volet, 2011). Importantly, studies of trait individual differences show that whereas persons with high trait anxiety show the increased lengthening of temporal perception for threatening stimuli, people who are less generally anxious may not (e.g., Bar-Haim, Kerem, Lamy, & Zakay, 2010; Tipples, 2008, 2011). In comparison, depressed persons may tend to underestimate the passage of time (e.g., Gil & Droit-Volet, 2009) whereas individuals in a state of mania may effectively be "stuck in the present" (Gruber, Cunningham, Kirland, & Hay, 2012). In summary, Droit-Volet and Gil (2009) conclude that:

> When the level of physiological activation increases, a specific clock effect occurs. The internal clock speeds up, thus causing more pulses to accumulate for the same physical unit of time. . . . When a subject is confronted with a threatening event, the internal clock runs faster . . . and the preparation for action is quicker. By modifying the perception of time, the internal clock ensures the survival of the organism in urgent situations. Consequently, the magnitude of the temporal overestimation in high-arousal conditions should be an accurate index of the basic function of certain emotions. There is thus no unique, homogeneous time but instead multiple experiences of time. Our temporal distortions directly reflect the way our brain and body adapt to these multiple times. (pp. 1944–1950)

The brain bases of our subjective sense of the passage of time are distributed and complex; Figure 3.2 illustrates the neuroanatomy of brain regions of interest frequently identified in neuroimaging studies of temporal perception. Dopaminergic pathways within the striatum appear to be critical to the process. For example, administration of cocaine or methamphetamine provokes the experience of time speeding up (Cheng, Ali, & Meck, 2007; Matell, Bateson, & Meck, 2006). In addition to the basal ganglia, studies converge on the supplementary motor area, primary

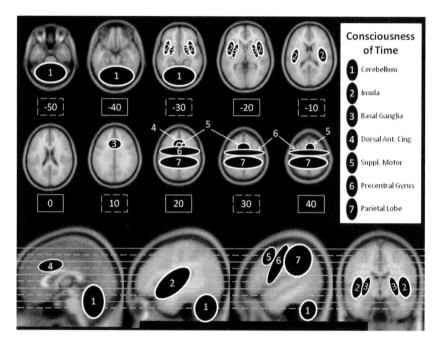

FIGURE 3.2.   The Neuroanatomy of the Consciousness of Time.

motor area, dorsal anterior cingulate, primary somatosensory cortex, parietal cortex, and cerebellum as being involved in the obviously complex neural mediation of event timing. The cerebellum is known to play a role in event timing on the order of milliseconds, whereas the former regions may contribute more directly to a timescale consistent with the subjective moment (i.e., 2–3 seconds; see reviews by Buhusi & Meck, 2005; Coull & Nobre, 2008; Grondin, 2010; Lewis & Miall, 2003; Macar et al., 2002; Meck, 2005; Rubia, 2006; Wittmann, 2009).

Kosillo and Smith (2010) review evidence suggesting that the bilateral anterior insulae also play a role in time processing but consider whether this may be due to a more general role for the anterior insula in feature discrimination. In his extensive reviews of neuroimaging studies documenting the heterogeneous set of cognitive and affective activities with which response in the anterior insula cortex has been linked, Craig (2009a, 2009b, 2010) concludes: "The only feature that is common to all of these tasks is that they engage the awareness of the subjects. Thus, in my opinion, the accumulated evidence compels the hypothesis that the anterior insula cortex engenders human awareness" (2009a, p. 65). In particular, acknowledging the strong association of insula response with emotional processing, Craig (2009a, 2009b, 2010) speculated whether the insula may partly serve to mediate subjective emotional feelings (based on bodily homeostatic representations) about the immediate present that, when compared with salient representations of events in the recent past, afford an additional basis for estimating the span of time. An implication of his model is that, when a number of significant emotional events occurs in rapid succession, subjective time perception is expected to dilate; the model suggests that such representations partly serve to guide what we perceive to be our will in action (i.e., executive behavior, choice).

The latter hypothesis is broadly consistent with the results of an exhaustive meta-analysis of human functional neuroimaging studies of insular response (Kurth, Zilles, Fox, Laird, & Eickhoff, 2010). A fourfold functional differentiation of the insula was discovered wherein sensorimotor, cognitive, chemical sensory, and socioemotional functions were predominantly mapped to bilateral middle-posterior, anterior-dorsal, right-middle, and bilateral anterior-ventral (insular pole) subregions, respectively. However, representation among all functions overlapped in the bilateral anterior-dorsal insular cortex (i.e., the "cognitive" region). The latter findings imply either that the anterior-dorsal insula acts as a multimodal convergence zone (e.g., conceivably implying the shared presence of sensorimotor, chemical sensory, and socioemotional representations in cognitive function), or that response across all these tasks somehow suggests shared task requirements in sensorimotor, cognitive, chemical sensory, and socioemotional processing (Kurth et al., 2010). Lesion studies of the insula corroborate neuroimaging findings concerning the breadth of insula involvement in multimodal representation and function (see review by Ibañez, Gleichgerrcht, & Manes, 2010).

Specifically testing the effect of emotional salience on the neural underpinnings of temporal perception, van Wassenhove, Wittmann, Craig, and Paulus (2011) conducted a neuroimaging experiment in which participants estimated whether a looming (expanding) or receding (shrinking) target was presented as longer or shorter than a series of four other stimuli. Consistent with previous findings, the true stimulus presentation duration of looming targets was overestimated (e.g., van Wassenhove, Buonomano, Shimojo, & Shams, 2008). Estimating the duration of targets was associated with greater response in the left insula, claustrum and basal ganglia, anterior cingulate cortex, and bilateral superior or middle-frontal regions. In comparison with receding targets, looming targets were also associated with greater response in the medial prefrontal cortex, posterior cingulate, and precuneus, as well as the left superior and middle-frontal cortex. The authors note that looming targets are typically understood to be more self-referential and salient (i.e., given that they are moving toward the self) as compared to receding targets, consistent with response in brain regions previously known to activate toward self-referential processing tasks (e.g., self-reference appraisal of adjectives; Northoff et al., 2006). In comparison, receding targets (relative to looming targets) were associated with greater response in the left insula, dorsal thalamus, and anterior cerebellum.

Traumatic Stress and the Dilation of Subjective Time

Psychotraumatologists have long observed phenomenological distur-bances in the subjective sense of the span of relatively brief segments of time (e.g., from minutes to hours). Specifically, during traumatic events, the consciousness of time is often reported to be altered, typically in a decelerating direction, with time seeming to move more slowly than nor-mal, thus extending the temporal sense of the subjective "now" during the traumatic event.

This observation, for example, is incorporated into the item content of the Peritraumatic Dissociative Experiences Questionnaire (P-DEQ; Mar-mar et al., 1997). For example, one of the P-DEQ items inquires whether during the traumatic event, individuals experienced a "sense that time changed . . . things seemed to be happening in slow motion." The P-DEQ is a psychometric instrument that is strongly predictive of the develop-ment of PTSD; in other words, people who endorse the experience of time dilation (in addition to other P-DEQ items) during traumatic events are more likely to develop PTSD following the traumatic event (Lens-velt-Mulders et al., 2008; Ozer, Best, Lipsey, & Weiss, 2003; van der Hart, van Ochten, van Son, Steele, & Lensvelt-Mulders, 2008; van der Velden & Wittmann, 2008), possibly through activation of brain regions associated with intrusive memory recall (Daniels et al., 2012). In addition, TRASC in relation to time are included as items in the Clinician Administered Dissociative States Scale (CADSS), a survey of acute dissociative experi-ences (e.g., items include: "Do things seem to be moving in slow motion?" "Do things seem to take much longer than you would have expected?"). We have shown that approximately one-third of individuals with PTSD, for example, report elevated CADSS scores following reminders of past traumatic events (Lanius et al., 2002, 2005). Such findings are consistent with previous research that has revealed associations between emotional arousal, the presence of aversive and distressing stimuli, and TRASC of time, as reviewed above (e.g., Droit-Volet & Meck, 2007; Droit-Volet & Gill, 2009).

Unfortunately, we are not aware of any studies that have investigated effects of altered temporal perception distinctly—that is, apart from the assessment of the broader construct of state dissociation. We recommend that future researchers conduct item-level analyses in order to ascertain the frequency with which persons experience distinctive aspects of the dissociative state, including TRASC of time. We conducted a post hoc analysis of the Lanius et al. (2002, 2005) data and found that, of those exhibiting a dissociative response (depersonalization) to trauma reminders, the majority endorsed the specific CADSS items previously noted concerning time "seeming to be moving in slow motion" and "things taking much longer than expected" (unpublished observations). In comparison, only a minority of people with PTSD who were not considered to have experienced a dissociative response to trauma reminders endorsed these items, suggesting that time dilation is a marker of a dissociative response.

Most directly, Brewin, Ma, and Colson (2013) investigated time perception in the context of state dissociative experience as induced by prolonged mirror gazing (Caputo, 2010a, 2010b). They found that, although prolonged mirror gazing failed to alter the accuracy of temporal perception at the group level, those participants who most prominently evidenced dissociative states (as measured by the CADSS) were also those most likely to exhibit altered temporal perception as assessed experimentally, although this effect was not specific to an experience of time slowing versus speeding.

It is interesting to note that the experience of time dilation has sometimes been perceived as conducive to survival by the individuals that experienced it. For example, a man who was involved in a severe motor vehicle crash, during which he was almost killed in a head-on collision with a drunk driver, noted: "I could not have reacted in a coherent way if it had not been for time slowing down. Feeling like time was moving really slowly allowed me to have the time to make all the right judgments—I was able to steer my car into the field next to the highway." Losing one's sense of time altogether can also sometimes make survival more tolerable in situations where people might be held captive for prolonged periods of time; for example, prisoners of war or political prisoners in totalitarian regimes. A woman interviewed about her experience of being held captive for nearly 2 years in Columbia stated: "Time no longer existed for me; all I focused on were different ways to escape in order to be back with my family."

However, the persistence of altered temporal perception in the aftermath of trauma can significantly interfere with a person's ability to function. For example, individuals may appear socially awkward, responding as if "out of tune," distant, detached, or "slow." This can occur over long time frames such as tens of minutes, hours, and even days. For example, "Gregory," a 62-year-old male with a history of childhood emotional and physical abuse at the hands of his father and sexual abuse by his grandmother, has often exhibited a strikingly deficient sense of temporal perception during psychotherapy sessions. Upon the closing of standard 50-minute sessions, for example, he has sometimes remarked: "Is the session over now? It feels like I have only been here for a few minutes." Speaking about such experiences, he has also noted: "I feel like I have lost all sense of time; it's like time does not exist." His drawing (Figure 3.3, also in color insert) was partly intended to convey the confusion that his deficiencies in temporal perception can create. He often notes, "It really prevents me from functioning in the world."

On an even longer timescale, on the order of weeks, months, years, and even decades, theorists have described traumatized persons as struggling with the experience of feeling emotionally numb—a state that upon careful phenomenological analysis is sometimes also suggestive of a sense of timelessness (e.g., Krystal & Krystal, 1988). Specifically, traumatized persons frequently appear fixated experientially at the time of the trauma; subjectively the experience may be something akin to a sense of timelessness, of being in an experiential vacuum or an abyss. Thus, from the time of the trauma forward, many people no longer feel as though they can fully participate in life. In the extreme case, metaphorically speaking, they may feel as though they have stopped living—ceased existing—long ago. Meaningful movement, change, growth, curiosity, and the ability to envision a future that could be different from the past and present all seem to have slowed down or come to a stop. Such experiences may more often be associated with low arousal rather than a hyperaroused state, and there-

FIGURE 3.3.   Gregory's Artwork (2010): "(1 + x)." Used with permission.

fore seem unlikely to have the same psychological meaning, and perhaps may be mediated by different neural mechanisms, when compared against the briefer episodes of time dilation described above.

The following brief selection from a transcript is included here to clinically illustrate the potential overlap between conjoint alterations in the sense of time and affect in traumatized persons. The transcript is part of a standard safe-place imagery exercise. Unfortunately, the client effectively relates that a state of emotional numbness is the only place of safety she is able to achieve from otherwise overwhelming feelings associated with the "bad things that have happened to me." The state of emotional numbness, in turn, appears to be associated with a TRASC of time.

Therapist: Where do you come to?

Client: (*Pause*) Eventually there's nothing. Just peace. (*pause*) It's sort of like an empty desert—there's no feeling, it's just emptiness, numbness, (*pause*) but it's only an image, an illusion, really there is nothing. It isn't real. (*pause*) It's as if my mind needs to see something, so it makes it there. But really it's nothingness, there's nothing here. And there's no time.

Therapist: No time?

Client: It's like time doesn't exist anymore. It's opened up. Nothing changes here. Everything stays the same.

Therapist: The desert—is it a place?

Client: It could be. Or it could be a feeling. (*pause*) It's a feeling of no feeling. It's a feeling of nothing.

Such examples suggest possible associations between time dilation, the sense of timelessness, and the experience of TRASC of emotion (e.g., emotional numbing) in traumatized persons across different orders of time (seconds, minutes, hours, and even days). For example, in the case of Elly, a survivor of the Holocaust who had been imprisoned at Dachau from ages 13 to 17, a TRASC of both timelessness and emotional numbing was partly induced by chronic starvation:

> When you are very hungry this slowness sets in. Slow motion, slow thinking—all processes of life slow down under hunger. The body doesn't want to spend an extra ounce of energy when it doesn't have to. So you walk slowly, you bend slowly, you try not to bend if you don't have to because you will have to straighten up. It is a feeling of continuous hunger, and the brain thinks of nothing but food—nothing, only food. . . . All is subdued by the hunger. Hunger—total hunger—it removes feeling, even feeling, though some remains."

Given that many traumatized persons report experiencing an alteration in their sense of time, notwithstanding general difficulties with concentration and anxiety, the practice of relatively short mindful breath meditations may be helpful not only to improve relaxation, interoceptive awareness, and orientation to the present moment, but also specifically to enhance their accuracy in temporal perception. In our view meditation practices with traumatized individuals are best kept short (e.g., 3–6 minutes, depending on the emotion regulation capacities of the individual client), given that longer periods of open-focus mindfulness meditations may occasion the occurrence of intrusive symptoms (e.g., reexperiencing).

During the in-session practice of mindfulness meditations, it is sometimes helpful for both client and clinician to meditate together. The client may close his or her eyes or keep them open (whichever feels safer); the clinician can model the client, while also periodically monitoring the client for any clear signs of distress.

Following standard procedures, instructions for mindful meditation on the breath encourage clients to maintain their attention on the present by noticing the process of their breathing, from inhalation to exhalation, with a level of pleasant curiosity and interest. The client is given the information that all minds wander and that it is common for people to find it difficult to maintain their awareness of their breathing for sustained periods. Upon becoming aware that attention has wandered, the client should covertly note (i.e., label) what it was that drew his or her attention away (e.g., a memory, a future plan, an emotion, a pain, a sound) and, after noting the source of the distraction, and without self-judging, attempt to gently let go of the source of the distraction, returning attention again toward a present awareness of breathing.

It is recommended that during the meditation a timer be used that includes interval bells. For short meditations, we typically set three interval bells within each meditation sitting, placed in equal increments from the starting and completion of the meditation, with the latter signaled, as is custom, with three consecutive bells. For example, a 4-minute (240 seconds) meditation would sound interval bells every 80 seconds, with the closing of the meditation signaled with three bells. Before beginning the meditation, the clinician should note how long the meditation will be, and the length of each interval of silence between bells. The clinician should also sound the bell and confirm that its sound is not emotionally triggering for the client; if the sound itself is found to be distressing, another one can be chosen (most meditation timer applications include this functionality). Upon the sounding of each bell, the clinician should briefly note *out loud* the bell order for the benefit of the client's time sense and expectations (e.g., "That was the first bell" . . . "That was the second bell" . . . "That was the third bell—the meditation will be complete in xx seconds with the sounding of three more bells" . . . "The meditation is now complete"). Following the meditation the "interlude" begins wherein experiences arising during and upon completion of the meditation are debriefed (e.g., "What are you aware of now?"; "What other experiences do you recall being aware of during the meditation?"; "How much time does it feel like has passed?").

In addition to the regularly cited benefits of mindfulness meditation practice for sustained concentration, interoceptive awareness, affect labeling, and orientation to the present moment, we suggest that mindfulness meditation practice likely also benefits the consciousness of time sense, particularly when conducted with interval timing. Specifically, clients learn how to gauge their subjective time relative to objective (clock) time via the interval bells. Clients tend to quickly come to anticipate the sounding of the bells, and it is self-instructive to learn whether they predict them significantly too early or late, consistent with the lengthening versus shortening of subjective time, respectively. Over time, their meditative concentration may also improve such that, with repeated practice, at the sounding of the bells, they may increasingly notice that their attention is directed toward their breathing rather than being lost in distraction. We have demonstrated preliminary validation for a scoring procedure, titled "Meditation Breath Attention Scores," based on this concept (Frewen, Evans, Maraj, Dozois, & Partridge, 2008; Frewen, Lundberg, MacKinley, & Wrath, 2011; Frewen, Unholzer, Logie-Hagan, & MacKinley, 2014).

In addition to the practice of meditation, the use of a regular watch or cell phone timer can also be helpful for clients who feel that they have a poor sense of time or who report "losing time." The client is instructed to set the timer every 15–60 minutes, as needed, at which time the client is encouraged to make a brief entry into a diary, noting what activities he or she has been engaged in at the time the alarm went off. Each time the client makes a new diary entry, it may be helpful to review previous entries from earlier in the day with the purpose of reestablishing a better sense of the passage of time. The alarm may also help the client to ground him- or herself in the present tense, thereby decreasing the individual's tendency to lose gaps of time.

Remembering versus Reliving: Flashbacks as an Altered State of Time and Episodic Autobiographical Memory

"The conscious awareness that characterizes remembering is different from other forms of conscious awareness, and different in an unmistakable manner. When you remember an event . . . you are

aware that the present experience is related to the past experience in a way that no other kind of experience is. You do not confuse it with perceiving . . . or having thoughts about what is or could be in the world. . . . Human episodic pastness does not reside in memory traces as such; it emerges as the phenomenally apprehended product of the episodic memory system, autonoetic consciousness, in ways that are as mysterious as the emergence of other kinds of consciousness from brain activity. . . . Episodic memory differs from other kinds of memory in that its operations require a self. It is the self that engages in the mental activity that is referred to as mental time travel: there can be no travel without a traveler."

—Endel Tulving (2005, p. 15)

It should go without saying that one of the defining qualities of normal waking consciousness (NWC) is that events in time are perceived to be unidirectional and forward, thus "events in the past can be remembered . . . but not changed" (LeShan, 1976, p. 88) or "relived." Seemingly somewhat in conflict with this general rule, *flashbacks*, as a psychiatric phenomenon, have been defined as quintessentially "recurrences of a memory, feeling, or perceptual experience from the past" (American Psychiatric Association, 2000, p. 823). Flashbacks characterize a TRASC in which memory and current perceptions are confused, and therefore an experience very different from normal episodic recall, as described by Tulving (2005). People who suffer from flashbacks also report that these experiences are very different from normal episodic recall. For example, one traumatized individual reported:

> "With a flashback, you are not *in* this time frame. With a normal memory you can look back at it and you know it is in the past, but with a flashback you don't know it is in the past because it is happening to you *now*. Flashbacks are much more intense because the feelings are exactly the same as what you were feeling at the time [the trauma happened]. [During a flashback] you are *living* the past, but you are in the now.

Another traumatized person described:

> "I was in a really bad car accident with my mom [in the past]— a *really* bad one. We had to be cut out. I was in the back seat; it was a left-hand turn. I was on the right- hand side of the car, behind her [mother], and I saw the car coming and hitting us. Now, when I am in cars, for example, it keeps happening. I see the car coming, and I actually physically move in the seat of the car, like I can *see* it, and I can *feel* it."

When examining the history of the recognition of flashbacks in psychiatry, one finds that the description of flashbacks as an altered state of consciousness was noted early on. These experiences were first recognized as side effects of hallucinogenic drugs. Horowitz (1969a, 1969b) characterized the phenomenology of drug-induced flashback imagery, including its typically frightening nature, intrusive quality, and its possible role in a working through of affective conflicts. He also noted the striking similarity to intrusive experiences as prompted by traumatic stress.

From the perspective of the 4-D model, flashbacks are considered constitutive of a TRASC of time, wherein past memories are experienced with a marked quality of *reliving* as distinct from *remembering* (Tulving, 2002b; Wheeler, Stuss, & Tulving, 1997). Flashbacks are differentiated from the normal recall of memories of past traumas by the fact that, when *remembering*, even if recall is intrusive and distressing, the past does not *become* the present. In contrast, *reexperiencing* (flashbacks) involves, by definition, the experience of a memory as if it is happening in the *present* tense.

It is important to point out that the disposition toward normal *remembering* versus dissociative *reexperiencing* of traumatic memories cannot be simply predicted by the severity of the traumatic event itself. For example, Elly, introduced earlier in the chapter as a survivor of the Holocaust, described his firsthand experience of a macabre scene of grievous human suffering, anguish, and despair:

> "Right at the end—about a week before liberation, the American fighter planes attacked a freight train carrying prisoners. During the attack the prisoners remained locked in the wagons while the guards ran into the woods. The planes shot up the train from one end to the other. The bullet holes were about 2 inches apart horizontally across the middle of the railway cars. A group of us were sent out to "clear out the train"— to remove the prisoners. They opened the doors and we looked inside. Aaah!—this was a terrible sight! A full train of people wounded, screaming in pain. Some of them were dead, but some were lying there bleeding, crying for water, their legs or arms cut off. We didn't have water—all we could do was carry them out— so carefully we lifted them out, crying and screaming, and we laid them on the grass and they bled to death. . . . I know I was stunned; I was stunned, like I wasn't completely there. I couldn't stop thinking about those people, feeling this pain, how they are suffering, how their life has ended, and now so shortly before the end of the war— that I should perhaps survive and these people have not made it."

As gruesome and painful a tragedy as this was, fortunately Elly, in remembering it, was able to do so from a decentered, intentioned point of view, recognizing that the event had occurred in the distant past and is not recurring again in the present. Asked specifically whether he was experiencing a flashback in telling this story, Elly replied:

> "There *was* a time when I couldn't forget . . . [but now,] no, I am telling something from long ago. I am not there. Otherwise I couldn't talk about it . . . I remember it as something that is locked away somewhere in the back (*pointing to the back of his head*), there is a corner in the brain somewhere—they will find it one day—where we put away things that we don't like to see. Like in the computer—where we have the other storage."

As a necessary symptom for the diagnosis of PTSD, past traumatic memories must be reexperienced in some form (American Psychaitric Association, 2013). Nevertheless, current PTSD diagnostic practices acknowledge that reexperiencing occurs in a variety of phenomenologically distinct forms. Thus the presence of flashbacks is coded along with intrusive memories that are devoid of a dissociative "flashback" quality, emotional or physiological signs of distress at being reminded about a past traumatic event, and nightmares concerning the event. An outcome of this classification schema, in effect, is to equate flashbacks with intrusive recall of traumatic events that do not include the experience of reliving. Moreover, the general term *reexperiencing* confuses the distinction further. Accordingly, we would recommend that all current reexperiencing symptoms of PTSD be considered forms of "distressing recall" or some similar phrasing, whereas flashbacks be differentiated from these experiences by emphasizing that they involve *reliving* rather than *remembering*. It is acknowledged that diagnostic practices were revised to explicitly clarify the dissociative nature of flashbacks in the DSM-5 criteria for PTSD (Friedman, Resick, Bryant, & Brewin, 2011), a revision supported by the 4-D model.

Despite the centrality of trauma-related flashbacks in PTSD, there have been surprisingly few specific investigations of them, in particular, as opposed to reexperiencing symptoms more broadly. Hellawell and Brewin's (2004) study compared segments of a trauma narrative that participants had indicated had been recalled as a flashback with sections that had been recalled as a "normal" memory. In their study, research participants themselves reportedly had no difficulty differentiating between flashbacks and normal trauma recall, and flashbacks were independently coded by researchers as being more detailed, involving a greater description of sensory events and motor sequences, and describing a greater experience of the primary emotions of fear, helplessness, and horror (Hellawell & Brewin, 2004). These findings are consistent with a theoretical differentiation between sensory-based and narrative encoding of trauma memories (Brewin, 2001, 2007; Brewin, Gregory, Lipton, & Burgess, 2010).

As examples, two of Hellawell and Brewin's (2004) participants described the experience of flashbacks as "like *reliving* a particular trauma—it flashes back to your mind and it feels so real" and commented that "flashbacks differ from ordinary memories of the events because of the *reality* of it all" (Hellawell & Brewin, 2004, p. 9, emphasis added). Independent blind raters observed greater movement, stasis (e.g., rigidity in arms/legs, clenched fists), vocalizations, breathing changes, evidence of autonomic nervous system changes (e.g., perspiring, flushing), facial changes (e.g., expressed emotion), and periods of ceased writing for 30 seconds or more (possibility indicative of confusion, lost focus of task-related attention, or altered state of consciousness) during flashbacks as compared to regular intrusive memories of traumatic events (Hellawell & Brewin, 2002). These findings suggest that it is useful to distinguish between flashbacks and normal traumatic recall. Specifically, flashbacks appear to have a more dissociative quality than normal (though distressing) intrusive recall of traumatic events, such as primed by trauma-related stimulus reminders.

Clinical research also suggests the importance of distinguishing traumatic memories that are experienced as flashbacks from those associated with "normal" episodic recall. Brewin and colleagues have shown that intrusive recall of traumatic life events is not specific to PTSD but occurs in a number of other psychiatric disorders, most notably depression (reviewed by Brewin et al., 2010). However, Brewin and colleagues have also shown that traumatic memories experienced by individuals with PTSD are more likely to entail dissociative reliving than are those experienced by individuals with depression (Brewin, 1998; Reynolds & Brewin, 1998; Reynolds & Brewin, 1999). This finding suggests that a distinction between flashbacks and normal intrusive recall of traumatic memories may provide one means of differentially diagnosing PTSD from depression.

However, due to the heterogeneity with which reexperiencing symptoms are recognized within the current DSM rubric, one finds that normal intrusive recall of traumatic events are much more common symptoms than are flashbacks, even in people with PTSD (Bryant, O'Donnell, Creamer, McFarlane, & Silove, 2011). Palm and colleagues' recent symptom-level study showed that whereas approximately three of every four (75%) individuals with PTSD reported the presence of unwanted memories about their trauma(s) or reported becoming upset upon being reminded of the event(s) (69%), only half (51%) reported the presence of flashbacks, defined as "suddenly acting or feeling as if the experience was happening all over again" (Palm, Strong, & MacPherson, 2009, p. 30). Accordingly, flashbacks were associated with the fifth highest item severity parameters in comparisons of the 17 DSM-IV-TR symptoms of PTSD, using methodology based on item–response theory (IRT). Betemps and colleagues also determined flashback symptoms to be associated with high clinical severity using IRT approaches (Betemps, Smith, Baker, & Rounds-Kugler, 2003), and Duke, Allen, Rozee, and Bommaritto (2008) found that flashbacks are more specific indicators of sexual assault exposure and PTSD status than are nightmares, in addition to being more strongly correlated with dissociative symptoms.

In summary, relative to the PTSD symptoms of intrusive recall and subjective upset/distress at trauma reminders, research suggests that flashbacks are less prevalent. This finding supports our hypothesis that *symptoms that typify TRASC will be observed less often in traumatized persons than symptoms representative of normal waking consciousness.* Moreover, flashbacks appear to be associated with greater clinical severity and better differentiate PTSD from trauma-related depression than does intrusive remembering.

But what is the psychological basis of our ability to differentiate past from present? As noted above, several trauma theorists have considered this question, perhaps most notably Brewin and his colleagues (e.g., Brewin, 2007, 2011; Brewin, Dalgleish, & Joseph, 1996; Brewin et al., 2010). We sketch our own current view as a testable model for understanding such phenomena in Figure 3.4 (also in color insert). We hypothesize that reliving is less probable when (1) current (particularly external) stimulus perceptions are varied and strong; (2) the sense of self is defined broadly and complexly, creating a more robust sense of self; and (3) retrieval is caused by intentional recall rather than by an external priming stimulus (i.e., a "trigger"). Accordingly, this framework suggests that in order to discourage traumatic reliving experiences one should, respectively, (1) maintain mindful sensory awareness of one's physical sense of self in the present moment (the "present self"), which may involve maintaining explicit, conscious connection with the physical environment such as through grounding skills (e.g., sensing the physical contact of one's feet with the floor beneath them); (2) build up the adaptiveness and complexity of the narrative and embodied senses of self (e.g., through encouraging self-representations such as "I am in the present," "I am resilient," "I am safe"); and (3) engage in intentional recall of traumatic events while making explicit the present context. The latter might take the form of reminding oneself that "what I'm about to remember is in the past, not the present." Intentional recall of traumatic stimuli, as such, may thereby further solidify the 'pastness' of the traumatic events.

Resourcing and strengthening the sense of self within the context of the therapeutic relationship is a particularly important aspect of overcoming reliving symptoms (Allen, 2012; Schore, 2012). Clients often have weakened and unstable senses of self as a result of past experiences of attachment trauma, prolonged childhood abuse, or other repeated traumatic experiences. Dissociative flashbacks can be distressing for both the client and for those around them, so it is important to be able to identify the common signs and symptoms of flashback experiences. These vary across clients but may include (1) staring blankly into space or lacking attention

Remembering | Reliving

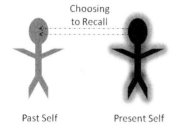

Choosing
to Recall

Past Self   Present Self

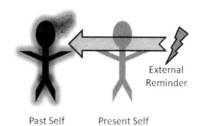

External
Reminder

Past Self   Present Self

FIGURE 3.4. Phenomenology of Remembering (NWC) versus Reliving (TRASC).

Left panel: When remembering, mental time travel and absorption in recall are partial. The sense of self resides in the present. Attention is directed, *by choice*, from present self to a past state of the self. The experience is one of being in the present and remembering the past (autonoesis). Self-awareness in the present is thus maintained; the representation of the "present self" outweighs that of the "past self." The present self, in effect, travels back to visit a past self-state. This is considered part of normal waking consciousness (NWC). *Right panel:* When reliving, mental time travel and absorption in recall occur "in full." One undergoes recall not by choice but typically as prompted by an external event highly associated with a past state of the self, which overwhelms an already weakened representation of the self in the present. As such the sense of self is as if fully residing *in* a past self-state. Attention is further directed from the point of view of this "past self," with the person's experience as if *in* the past. In effect, referring to mental time travel, "there can be no travel without a traveler" (Tulving, 2005, p. 15). Considered a trauma-related altered state of consciousness (TRASC).

(absorption); (2) sudden loss of orientation toward present environment or activities (e.g., seeming detached); (3) sudden, unprompted change in social behavior (e.g., the client yelling "Get away from me!" to an otherwise trusted friend or companion, as if referring to a previous perpetrator; sudden need to change the topic of conversation, or suddenly becoming visibly distressed or aggressive); (4) confused speech or becoming silent/mute; (5) trance-like behaviors such as repetitive rocking and/or leg bouncing; (6) sudden, seemingly unprompted need to leave current environment; and (7) alterations in presentation such as speech pattern, sophistication of language level, postural changes, or atypical behavior given previously known personality.

Particularly in the acute presence of these signs, but also simply as a regularly rehearsed intervention, the therapist may engage the client in the practice of somatic and cognitive grounding skills. In order to restore and maintain connection with the present self, it is helpful for clients to practice both mindful somatic and cognitive forms of awareness (e.g., Siegel, 2007). Somatic grounding involves becoming intentionally aware of physical sensations involving all five senses. Examples of somatic grounding techniques that clients often find helpful in overcoming acute reliving experiences (flashbacks) include:

1. Touch: "Feel your feet firmly on the ground"; "Feel the arm rests of your chair"
2. Sight: "Look at me"; "Look at my ugly coffee mug" (the use of humor is often quickly effective)
3. Smell: Use of aftershave or perfume, essential oils, scented candles (providing, of course, that these are not known triggers)
4. Taste: Use of Listerine Pocketpaks, mints, bubblegum, or fresh lemon
5. Sound: "Listen to the sound of my voice."

Encouraging clients to change their posture (e.g., changing from a sitting to a standing posture) or to perform certain simple movements can often be enough to bring back the present self (e.g., clapping hands or stamping feet are often particularly helpful, as they also create sound). In addition, cognitive grounding techniques include referring to the client by name, reorienting the client to the present time and place (e.g., "Remember that this is [month, day, year]; you are in _____ Hospital"), and providing positive encouragement such as "Remember that you are in the present; you are safe here; no one will hurt you."

In addition to standard cognitive and somatic grounding, we suggest further that the present self can be strengthened by encouraging both adaptive self-representations (e.g., "I am in the present"; "I now have choices"; "I am safe") and empowered self–other representations (e.g., "I can defend myself now—you cannot hurt me anymore"; "I am not alone anymore"). The present self can be further strengthened through (1) episodic recall of positive memories, including of times the client felt safe or competent; (2) visual imagery practices (e.g., a safe place); and (3) the application of other resources, such as the visualization of positive symbols, recitation of mantras (Korn & Leeds, 2002), or the practice of compassion-focused (*"metta,"* "loving-kindness") meditations (Hoffmann, Grossman, & Hinton, 2011). Somatic resources, such as encouraging the client to lengthen his or her spine or sit in a more upright posture, may also be helpful (Ogden, Minton, & Pain, 2006).

Once a client has sufficiently strengthened the present self and is able to regularly ground him- or herself using somatic and cognitive grounding skills, he or she can be encouraged to take part in the intentional recall and working through of past traumatic memories. Several structured methods have been described for doing so, and because these methods are well known to trauma therapists, they are not discussed in detail here. We would like to note, however, that by explicitly conveying the message that the traumatic memory is in the past, prior to engagement in traumatic memory recall, one seeks to solidify the "pastness" of the memory. For example, narrative methods frequently combine the intentional narration of traumatic experiences with structured meaning making in order to help clients understand who they have come to be as a result of what they have experienced. This understanding may allow clients to resolve feelings of shame and loss and reevaluate related experiences of the present self as inferior, bad, fragmented, or identified with the perpetrator. The strengthening of the present self is expected to facilitate the capacity for mental time travel, as in intentioned episodic recall, such that the client is able to visit his or her past without losing his or her bearings in the present. Strengthening of the present self is also expected to discourage the involuntarily reliving of the past.

Lastly, an increased capacity for mentalizing—that is, the ability to attend to and be aware of intersubjective, dyadic states of mind within and between oneself and others—has been suggested to facilitate the adaptive working through of traumatic memories. Allen and Fonagy (2006), for example, suggest that encouraging mentalizing while recalling traumatic memories provides the means for the present self to obtain increased perspective regarding traumatic events through awareness of intersubjective states of mind (e.g., "My mother was abused herself—she therefore had difficulties parenting, but she did the best she could—she did not hate me"). This increased capacity for an intersubjective perspective may further strengthen the present self and enhance the client's ability to voluntarily visit his or her past without losing connectedness with the present. The present self is thus in a stronger position ultimately to leave the past behind.

In summary, when remembering, our minds travel to the past, while at the same time holding onto the present. But without firm grounding, the present self does not travel back to the past but rather a past self effectively *becomes* or *takes the place of* the present self. In effect, there can be no travel without a traveler (Tulving, 2005, p. 15). We must firmly ground ourselves in the present to view the past with a sense of decentering and distance. One traumatized individual, who eventually reported being able to manage her flashbacks better through a more robust representation of her present self, described:

> Sometimes it's only for an instant, but for me it's like I've stepped back, sometimes decades, and sometimes it's just a brief instant when I feel like I'm right there—almost to the extent, depending on the trigger, of seeing past stuff, and then it can be gone very quickly. I have to keep really task-focused to stay out of the flashbacks. I've worked really hard at learning to not go there. One of the things I was taught through the trauma program was to refocus and kind of move on by saying "OK, you're here now." One of the traumas was a car accident, and driving is something I pretty much have to do daily. Every time I come up to a stop sign, I have to say to myself "OK, it's all right, look at everybody, everybody's good, go." But there is still the odd time when the car accident is right there.

In addition to the above quotation, note the paintings by Gregory (a trauma survivor introduced above) depicting his experience of traumatic memories early versus later on in psychotherapy (Figures 3.5 and 3.6, also in color insert). Initially, Gregory's memories occurred in the

FIGURE 3.5.   Gregory's Artwork (2011, untitled). Used with permission.

FIGURE 3.6. Gregory's Artwork (2011): "Dream II." Used with permission.

form of highly intrusive flashbacks over which he had little to no control, depicted as uncontainable and overwhelming emotional experiences pushing through a closed door which only part of him was ready to unlock.

However, with greater self-regulation and a decreased experience of internal conflict developed over the course of psychotherapy, Gregory was increasingly able to open and safely view what was behind the closed doors of his past, thereby leaving the past self in the past and opening new doors to a less traumatic present. This ability is depicted in another of his paintings, which he titled "Dream II". Gregory often uses such imagery to help him self-regulate.

Case 1: A Description of a Flashback Experience

"Tim" is a veteran medic of the Vietnam war. Herein he describes trauma-related altered sensory experiences indicative of a flashback, as well as secondary emotional responses to the flashback, as follows:

Interviewer: Have you ever felt that you were back in the past, had flashbacks, or relived a memory as if it were happening in the here and now? If so, tell me a little bit about what that's like.

Tim: Yes. The most recent time, we were at a concert at a state fair and after the concert they had a fireworks display. Ordinarily I can handle that, but this one was . . . they had some kind of display that had explosions that were going off—it seemed like it was right in front of us—and what happened for me was, as I was sitting in the seat, the explosions started going off and it sounded like really high-intensity cannon fire, and I felt like it was aimed at me.

And suddenly the scenery changed and I can only describe to you what I saw. It looked like the grounds were littered with bodies, with charred bodies, and unfortunately I was sitting in a seat and there was nowhere I could go. My first instinct was to hit the ground because that's how we handled combat situations, but because I was sitting in my seat I couldn't get down and couldn't do anything but sit there and take it. Like I say, the scenery changed, and there was this overwhelming feeling of acute loneliness, feeling as if these charred bodies that were lying all over the ground were people that were supposed to be taking care of me—in exchange for me taking care of them from a medical standpoint. It was about 45 seconds to a minute that I just was taken with panic. Extreme panic. My wife was with me, and she could tell something was going on with me. She was trying to get me to move but I was frozen, I was absolutely frozen. Then finally, at the end of the fireworks display, cannon fire went off and I was frozen for a while and from there on I went into kind of a panic attack. I felt like hitting the ground and staying on the ground, but she was able to get me out of the seat and get me moving toward the exit.

For probably about 2 hours after, the panic kept kind of hitting me in waves. While I was having the panic attacks and flashbacks, I felt like I was running out of air. It was like I couldn't breathe, it felt like I couldn't get enough air. So I was kind of panting, virtually all the way home. And all I could think about was getting home and getting calmed down somehow, getting in familiar surroundings and calmed down. And then after that I was just overcome with this intense feeling of sadness and shame. The worst feeling I had was that I couldn't help the people. First of all, their bodies were charred. But mostly because I panicked so I felt a real sense of shame. And for about 2 hours after that the numbness started to set in. It was as though every time I closed my eyes that scene would echo back on me and I was afraid to go to sleep that night because I was afraid that I would dream about it.

That flashback and the panic attack that was attached to it have really impacted me. My startle response is really elevated now. If someone comes up behind me and puts their hand on my shoulder, I will jump if I am not expecting it.

Interviewer: You said that it was like the scenery changed during the flashback. Can you tell me more about that?

Tim: When the cannon-fire-like firework thing started and when the flashback started, the only thing I could see were charred bodies all over the place. I was in battle and we were losing. Although there was no movement—it was stationary—I still had this feeling that we were being overrun.

Interviewer: Did you notice anything different about your experience of the passing of time during the flashback?

Tim: It seemed longer, because I remember in my mind wondering if it would ever end. So I guess it seemed like longer than it probably actually was. You bring up an interesting question—I should ask my wife how long I was actually noncommunicative. In other words, she couldn't talk to me, she couldn't get through to me at all. For me, it was like she wasn't even there. But I have never asked her how long that was.

Interviewer: You talked about experiencing different emotions during the flashback. Can you tell me more about that?

Tim: The thing that really hit me was this intense feeling of fear and loneliness. I felt like this was the whole world.

Interviewer: Can you tell me what do you mean when you say "the whole world"?

Tim: Meaning, this battle that was happening—like it was my whole world at that time. I had no thoughts of it ending, I had no feeling of it ending anywhere. In battles in Vietnam, I was kind of always aware of where the limits were of the conflict. I could look off to my left and look off to my right and get a feeling of how big geographically the conflict was. But this conflict didn't seem to have any boundaries. It seemed like it went on forever from a geographic standpoint.

Interviewer: You mentioned earlier having intense feelings of sadness and shame. Can you tell me a little bit more about what that was like?

Tim: It really was about having been paralyzed in that flashback and the shame seemed to come from that I couldn't act if something went down. For instance, getting back to being in Vietnam, "when something went down" meant that we came under attack, and when we came under attack, then we hit the ground and I began to scan to see if somebody got hit, so that I could get to them and start working on them [providing medical aid]. Getting back to the waves that were coming over me during this panic attack, the shame seemed to stem from knowing that during that flashback, if something came down I couldn't have helped the person. There is nothing I could have done—I was paralyzed with fear. So part of the shame was of being so terribly afraid and allowing the fear to paralyze me. That's really difficult to describe. In the military we are trained, especially in medical work, to respond. Our fear is shut down and instead our total focus is on doing our job. We can do our job during that. The shame really was coming from knowing I couldn't do my job.

From Reliving to Remembering: Working through a Past Self State via the Intentioned Recall of Traumatic Memories

In the following a woman we first met in Chapter 2 describes the phenomenological difference between her memories of past sexual assaults before versus after trauma therapy, during which she engaged in intentional recall and structured working through of her traumatic memories. These traumatic memories, previously experienced in the present tense as flashbacks, increasingly take on a quality of "pastness"; they are remembered instead of relived.

Suzy is a 48-year-old woman who was gang-raped repeatedly at school between the ages of 11 and 13. As a child, Suzy feared that her life would be at risk if she disclosed the rapes to anyone. Suzy's psychotherapy consisted primarily of working through her traumatic events utilizing narrative methods as well as eye-movement desensitization and reprocessing (EMDR). This was found to be effective in reducing her reexperiencing symptoms. Suzy described her therapeutic change as follows:

"Before I began therapy, it felt like I was always back there [in the gang-rape experiences]. I did not have words to describe the experiences. It was all in pictures, sounds, and feelings. Pictures of the gang rapes would flash in front of my eyes like a movie, but I could not find the words to describe them. And the sounds and feelings—it was terrifying. I could hear them degrading me over and over again. It was happening again. I could even feel the sensation of being kicked and raped all over again.

After I had therapy, my whole experience changed. I slowly began having fewer and fewer pictures, sounds, and feelings of the gang rapes, and I was able to start putting my experiences into words. For the first time I felt less alone with all those awful feelings because I was able to share them with someone who understood. After about 6 months of therapy, I really felt like the gang rapes were in the past for me. They will always be a really bad memory, but they were no longer intrusive. They were finally over. . . . "

Neurophenomenology of Traumatic Memory Recall

Neurophenomenologists propose that the sense of self typically implicit in human conscious experience is contextualized by referring the present moment to the immediate past and the expected future (e.g., Varela, 1999), an idea also prominent in James's (1890) writings on the subject. Intriguingly, this notion fits with the findings of neuroimaging studies, which report similarities among the functional neural underpinnings of self-referential processing (SRP), episodic memory, and prospection (i.e., imagining the future), including response within the medial prefrontal cortex (e.g., Spreng & Grady, 2010). In comparison, little is known about the neurobiology mediating our ability to differentiate past from present, presumably due to the fact that confusing these time frames occurs so infrequently in humans, thereby making it difficult to study the phenomenon experimentally. The psychopathology of PTSD, which sometimes involves this confusion, may offer a clinical model for understanding how the brain differentiates past from present, thus contributing to the neuroscientific study of the consciousness of time.

Neuroimaging studies have investigated the neural correlates of trauma memory recall in individuals with PTSD, and report the following findings: reduced response within the medial prefrontal cortex and perigenual anterior cingulate, and increased response within the dorsal anterior cingulate, right anterior insula, and amygdala (e.g., see meta-analyses by Etkin & Wager, 2007; Hayes, Hayes, & Mikedis, 2012; Patel, Spreng, Sin, & Girard, 2012; Sartory et al., 2013). However, few studies have explicitly examined whether flashbacks occur independent of general distress in response to such provocations. Given that flashbacks and state distress tend to be positively correlated (e.g., Hopper, Frewen, Sack, et al., 2007; Hopper, Frewen, van der Kolk, et al., 2007), this kind of research is difficult to accomplish. Nevertheless, research specifically examining the occurrence of flashbacks during symptom-provocation procedures has generally found that few people with PTSD experience quintessential flashbacks in response to script-driven imagery (e.g., Liberzon, Abelson, Flagel, Raz, & Young, 1999; Shin et al., 1999).

Osuch and colleagues' (2001) positron emission tomography (PET) study was specifically designed to examine the neural correlates of flashbacks. In this study, 8 of 11 participants with PTSD experienced flashbacks in varying degrees of intensity upon exposure to script-driven trauma memory reminders. Osuch et al. found that the self-reported intensity of flashbacks correlated positively with bilateral response in the insula, as well as response in somatosensory cortex, cerebellum, and brainstem, among other regions (Osuch et al., 2001).

The most direct contrast of flashbacks versus normal episodic recall of traumatic memories was conducted by Brewin, Whalley, and their colleagues (Whalley et al., 2013). These researchers presented trauma-exposed participants, who were diagnosed with PTSD, depression, or no psychiatric disorder, with select words or phrases from their own as well as other participants' trauma narratives, the latter of a nonoverlapping theme (i.e., describing the July 2005 London bombings or the December 2004 Asian tsunami). Participants' task was to identify which words were part of their own narrative. Interestingly, Whalley et al. found that only participants with PTSD identified narratives associated with flashbacks, although the number of flashback-associated stimuli that was identified per participant was not counted by the researchers. The words and phrases selected from narratives described by people with PTSD further varied in the extent to which they had been previously noted by participants to be associated with the experience of flashbacks, and participants were queried post-scan regarding the experience of flashbacks during testing, many of whom reported such experiences. Consistent with distinctions between reliving and remembering as described herein, flashbacks had been defined for participants as follows (Whalley et al., 2013):

> A type of memory that you experience as markedly different from those memories of an event that you can retrieve at will. The difference might be a marked sense of reliving of the traumatic experience(s). Some report complete reliving, whereas others report more momentary or partial reliving of perhaps just one aspect of the original experience. For some, flashback memories take them by surprise or swamp their mind. Finally, some report a sense of time-distortion and, for example, react to the flashback memory as though it was an event that was happening in the present. (p. 152)

In participants with PTSD, those trauma-related stimuli that were associated with a flashback, relative to trauma-related stimuli that were not associated with the experience of a flashback at the time of scanning, were also associated with *greater* response in the anterior cingulate cortex, dorsomedial prefrontal cortex, right supplementary motor area, bilateral insula, bilateral precentral gyrus, and bilateral supramarginal gyrus (parietal cortex). Moreover, participants with PTSD demonstrated less response in the middle and inferior temporal cortical regions during traumatic memory processing relative to individuals with depression or controls, as has been associated with remembering as experienced in NWC. Whalley et al. point out that during flashbacks, response in brain regions associated with affective and visual representations, including along the dorsal visual stream, as well as response within motor areas, suggest action motivations experienced in the possible perceived context of current visual perceptions, consistent with a "here-and-now" quality of stimulus processing.

Finally, in several previous studies published by Lanius and colleagues, participants were often prescreened in favor of including people with PTSD who report frequently occurring flashbacks (e.g., Lanius et al., 2001). We can therefore be more confident that findings regarding the neural correlates of traumatic script-driven imagery in such studies are reflective of the phenomenology of flashbacks, which have included not only deficient response in the perigenual anterior cingulate cortex and the medial prefrontal cortex but also the thalamus. We speculate that disturbance in a relatively central neural mechanism may be required in order to provoke such significant departures from NWC and reality orientation as occur in dissociative flashbacks, such as alterations in thalamocortical binding (e.g., Lanius et al., 2006; Llinás, 2001).

Summary

This chapter examined ways in which the consciousness of time can be altered by the experience of psychological trauma. Two forms of TRASC of time were reviewed: (1) time dilation and (2) the reliving of traumatic memories (i.e., flashbacks). In particular, the 4-D model asserts that the phenomenology of flashbacks should be distinguished from other forms of intrusive memories of traumatic events on the basis that it regards only the former as representing a TRASC of time and memory. To make this distinction we drew attention to the subjective difference notable between *reliving* and *remembering*; it was proposed that, during reliving, consciousness of a past self (memory) becomes stronger than consciousness of the present self (i.e., awareness of the present environment) such that the past self seems as if it *is* the present self. In contrast, during intentional recall of traumatic memories, the present self mentally time-travels back to the past self, providing the present self is sufficiently robust, while keeping one foot solidly grounded in the present; this has the phenomenological effect of remembering rather than reliving. We also reviewed results of research demonstrating that persons' sense of the span of the subjective "now" is often lengthened by traumatic events. Moreover, we discussed the possible neurobiological bases of the TRASC of time predominantly as assessed through neuroimaging. We overviewed the rationale and procedure of certain structured psychological interventions that may help normalize the TRASC of time: mindfulness meditation with interval bell timing, somatic and cognitive grounding techniques, and the intentioned recall and working through of traumatic memories. Finally, we provided several case examples of these phenomenologies as seen in clinical practice.

CHAPTER 4

Consciousness of Thought

Negative Content, Fragmented Plots, and Altered Perspective

"All psychological phenomena that are produced in the brain are not brought together in one and the same personal perception; a portion remains independent under the form of sensations or elementary images, or else is grouped more or less completely and tends to form a new system, a personality independent of the first. These two personalities are not content merely to alternate, to succeed each other; they can coexist in a way more or less complete."

—Pierre Janet (1901, p. 492–493)

"Paradoxically, the goal of dissociation is to maintain personal continuity, coherence, and integrity of the sense of self and to avoid the traumatic dissolution of selfhood. How can this be? How can the division of self-experience into relatively unlinked parts be in the service of self-integrity? . . . Self-experience originates in relatively unlinked self-states, each coherent in its own right, and the experience of being a unitary self is an acquired, developmentally adaptive illusion."

—Philip M. Bromberg (1998, p. 182)

CONSCIOUS EXPERIENCE HAS BEEN likened to a story told in the first person; in effect, consciousness seems to have a narrative structure. In this chapter we consider three ways in which the consciousness of thought can be altered in traumatized persons, specifically, in terms of (1) content, (2) structure (i.e., organization of plot), and (3) narration (i.e., perspective—first- vs. second-person perspective). Figure 4.1 highlights the dimension of thought within the 4-D model.

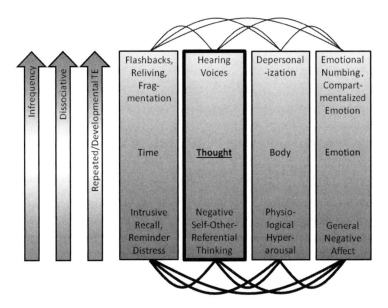

FIGURE 4.1.   The 4-D Model of the Traumatized Self Highlighting NWC Distress versus TRASC of Thought. TE = trauma exposure.

According to the 4-D model, although the content of traumatized persons' thought often differs from that of nontraumatized persons as a sign of general distress and negative affect, we consider only marked disturbances in the structure (fragmentation) and narrative perspective of thought as potentially indicative of a trauma-related altered state of consciousness (TRASC). The essential thesis of our 4-D model, as applied to the consciousness of thought, is that negative thoughts about the self—that is, consciousness of the self as comprising a list of negative concepts or "things relating to me"—are usually *not* in and of themselves constitutive of altered states of consciousness. In comparison, we do regard significant disturbances in the structure or organization of trauma narratives, as well as alterations in the *narrative perspective* of thought, as indicative of a TRASC in thought. We also briefly discuss psychotherapeutic interventions that may help alleviate disturbances in the consciousness of self-content, structure (organization), and narrative (perspective) when found to be distressing.

Narrative Consciousness: Lived Experience Like a Story

One of the defining attributes of consciousness is that it seems to be intrinsically *referential*. The referential nature of consciousness is noted in at least two ways: consciousness normally refers to (1) an object(s) and (2) a subject or agent.

The first assertion that consciousness refers to an object(s) is to say that it has content or "aboutness." In other words, consciousness is intrinsically directed at, and experientially inseparable from, some stimulus to which one's attention refers: We cannot be conscious without being conscious *of something*. This "aboutness" of consciousness is defined in phenomenology as the property of *intentionality* (Brentano, 1968; Dennett, 1987; Husserl, 1962). A basic distinction in intentional consciousness is that it is directional: whether it is referring primarily to objects outside of the conscious self's borders (object-directed, external, "primary-other content") or is referring inside, to oneself (i.e., self-directed, internal, "secondary-self content" or simply "self-consciousness"). In this way, the property of intentionality makes a very general distinction between things that are "me" versus those that are not (i.e., "not me"), or an inside world (self) versus an outside world (non-self).

The second way that consciousness is asserted to be intrinsically referential is that it necessarily refers to a subject who *is* conscious. Thus consciousness refers to an "*I*" or a conscious "being." For example, if one says "I heard this . . . " or one asks "Did you hear that?," the hearing that takes place is inherently experienced by some conscious agent or "hearer." This is basically to say that there can be no *experience* of hearing if there is no one around to hear. However, this need not cast any doubt on an objective reality existing outside the minds of conscious beings, as arguably intended by the famous thought experiment: "If a tree falls in a forest and no one is around to hear it, does it make a sound?" In comparison, the principle only asserts that the *experience* of hearing, or any other sensation, thought, or feeling, for that matter, requires a conscious agent capable of such experiences.

The idea that consciousness intrinsically requires both object and subject fits with the analogy of consciousness to a story or narrative told in the first person. At least since Aristotle, it has been recognized that the most basic structure of a story encompasses three parts: a beginning, middle, and end. Following Freytag's (1863/1900) classic five-phase plot structure, for example, the beginning provides an exposition of the character(s) and the setting of the story, describing a set of relations between one or more characters or a character and a setting. For example, one could imagine two individuals engaged in a mutually respectful, satisfying, equally financially productive and monogamous heterosexual relationship. A "rising action" then ensues, the nature of which is, effectively, to reset these relations (e.g., job loss occurs for the male and external romantic involvement occurs for the female). The rising action eventuates in a climax marking the most emotionally significant point of that resetting (e.g., the male physically and sexually assaults the female while under the influence of alcohol). A "falling action" then ensues in which the new relations among character(s) and setting are systematized (e.g., the male apologizes and is forgiven). The outcome of the falling action marks the ending and resolution of the story (e.g., as constituting the early makings of an abusive relationship). Notably, it may be meaningful to denote several mini-plots within the grander story. For example, as applied to psychotraumatology, one may conceive of the physical and sexual assault as itself comprising a beginning, middle, and end (e.g., Foa, Molnar, & Cashman, 1995), and indeed it is considered clinically and theoretically meaningful to specify "hot spots" and a "worst moment" in traumatic memories (e.g., Jelinek et al., 2010).

The analogy of consciousness to a story, or narrative, accounts for the concepts of both object and subject. On the one hand, the objects of consciousness refer to the content or what is happening in the story (i.e., what the story is about, or the plot). On the other hand, the narrative *perspective* indicates *by whom* the story is experienced (i.e., by what conscious agent[s]). In normal consciousness we experience the world in first-person perspective.

William James (1890) used the pronoun "I" to refer to the self as *subject*, that is, as a conscious *agent*. In contrast, he used the objective case of I—"me"—to refer to the self as an *object* of consciousness. In the narrative account, James's "I" refers to the narrator and his "me" refers to the plot as well as to the collection of attributes by which we tend to describe ourselves (e.g., traits, roles, preferences), the latter thus representing the self as "*experienced*." James's "I" refers to the self as the "*experiencer*."

In addition to the concepts of object and subject, however, the analogy of a story suggests a third principle of narrative consciousness: that of *structure*. Just as stories normally have a beginning, middle, and end, so too consciousness has a regular structure that creates a sense of continuity. Consciousness seems to flow in time, with present experiences linked to those of the past by way of their reference to a common agent—that is, the first-person experiencer. As such, the ongoing story of one's life is composed of the content of an ever-unfolding series of moments occurring within one's awareness. We now consider research that has investigated alterations in the content, narrative structure (organization), and narrative perspective of consciousness in traumatized persons.

Neurophenomenology of the Traumatized "Me": Alterations in First-Person Narrative Self-Content

The currently dominant phobia-based emotional processing theories of psychological trauma have encouraged interest in how traumatized people respond to threatening stimuli that are physically outside themselves.

Phobia-based models characterize traumatized persons as being chronically anxious, hypervigilant of their external environments for signs of threat, and startling at unexpected events and stimuli reminiscent of their past traumas. In sum, the focus of these explanatory models is on how traumatized people respond to the *outside world*. Neuroimaging and psychophysiological research that examines responses in traumatized persons to others' facial expressions (e.g., anger [direct threat], fear [indirect threat]: e.g., see Williams et al., 2006; Shin et al., 2005) and generally unpleasant/aversive scenes (e.g., Phan, Britton, Taylor, Fig, & Liberzon, 2006) are based in the interest of examining how they respond to external threat.

Although we agree that this description fits well for many traumatized people, we stress that an equally important but comparably neglected outcome of traumatic events regards their impact on how people respond to internal stimuli—that is, people's sense of self or "inside worlds" (Bluhm et al., 2012; Frewen, Dozois, Neufeld, Densmore, et al., 2011b). In the most straightforward sense, survey studies of PTSD participants' conscious cognition suggest that their self-referential thoughts tend to take on a negative valence.

Phenomenology of the Traumatized "Me"

To stress the significance of changes in self-content, consider the research on Foa and colleagues' Posttraumatic Cognitions Inventory, which differentiates the content of conscious thought of traumatized people with versus without PTSD (Foa, Ehlers, Clark, Tolin, & Orsillo, 1999). The psychometric properties of this survey have been examined extensively and shown to exhibit a consistent three-factor structure in a number of different cultures and languages. One of the three latent factors commonly observed in studies of item-level responses to this survey has been titled "negative cognition about the world," which includes experiences describing various anxieties about the external world that are prominent in phobia-based accounts of trauma symptoms (e.g., "The world is a dangerous place"). However, the "negative cognition about the world" factor explained only 4% of the total variance in responses collected across persons in Foa and colleagues' original research. In comparison, the first factor, labeled "negative cognitions about oneself" (e.g., "I am a weak person"), explained nearly 50% of the variance in responses, and this sizable difference has been consistently replicated in studies conducted since. In addition to negative thoughts about world and self, the third factor of the Posttraumatic Cognitions Inventory is "self-blame" (e.g., "The event happened because of the way I acted"). In sum, the lion's share of variability in responses to the Posttraumatic Cognitions Inventory can be attributed to how negatively traumatized people regard *themselves* and their roles in causing or failing to prevent traumatic experiences, rather than how threatening they tend to regard the world around them. In our survey of negative self-referential cognitions in women with PTSD related to childhood abuse, traumatized women frequently endorsed a listing of highly negative attributes as descriptions of "how they think about themselves" (e.g., "rejected," "unlovable," "despicable," "disgusting," "disgraceful"; Frewen, Dozois, Neufeld, Densmore, et al., 2011b). In other interviews, for example, a traumatized client noted: "I am broken. I am damaged. I deserve to be hurt. I will never be good enough. I deserve to die."

Whereas current diagnostic practices in psychiatry emphasize traumatic events as causes of harm or threat to the physical integrity of the self or others, symptoms of negative self-referential processing (SRP) may develop not only when the integrity of the physical bodily self is threatened or harmed but also when the adaptive content of the *self-schema* is equally wounded (e.g., Ebert & Dyck, 2004; Jobson, 2009). For example, although a randomly occurring motor vehicle accident or house fire may engender subsequent phobic fear of automobiles or flames—effectively, "negative cognitions about the world"—such events may be less likely to prompt severe negative SRP in and of themselves. However, negative SRP may correlate with anger provoked in the realization that one has been mistreated; guilt engendered in the knowledge that one may have committed a wrongdoing oneself; and shame based upon one's assumption that others conceive of one as having done something immoral or as having been fouled in character in some irrevocable way. Thus, when a person incurs extreme ridicule and rejection (e.g., a child repeatedly berated and laughed at by parents), is deprived of his or her basic dignity (e.g., a prisoner of war spat at or urinated upon, denied clothing), or is forced to participate in the harm of others (e.g., forced abuse of minors, ordered killing of someone in battle), negative SRP in the form of guilt and shame may be a more principal outcome than are even anxiety and fear. As such, we consider shame as the core affective counterpart to extreme negative self-referential cognitions (e.g., beliefs that one is "dirty," "ruined," "damaged," "no longer human," and the like; Frewen, Dozois, Neufeld, Densmore, et al., 2011b).

Friedman and colleagues' proposed revising the PTSD diagnosis to expressly acknowledge the prevalence of negative cognitive appraisals in traumatized persons (Friedman, Resick, Bryant, & Brewin, 2011). Specifically, Friedman and colleagues proposed the inclusion of "persistent and exaggerated negative expectations about one's self, others, or the world" and "persistent distorted blame of self or others about the cause or consequences of the traumatic event(s)" as diagnostically significant symptoms of PTSD (Friedman, Resick, Bryant, & Brewin, 2011, p. 759). This proposal seems consistent with the subscale structure of the Posttraumatic Cognitions Inventory.

The Traumatized "Me" and Traumatic Memory:
A Bidirectional Influence

A subject of current interest in memory research is how the content of current self-referential thought interacts with the content of memory stores. On the one hand, self-referential thought reflects the learning of past experience (i.e., memory). On the other hand, self-referential thought can influence what is remembered during memory retrieval.

In the first case, we have the simple assumption that current self-referential thought reflects the kind of life experiences one has had in the past. Thus it can be assumed that if an individual has experienced a series of successes in his or her life, he or she will be more likely to come to regard him- or herself as successful. In comparison, if an individual has experienced a series of failures, he or she will be more likely to come to regard him- or herself as a failure.

Although the influence of repetitive life events on self-referential thought seems straightforward enough, it has also been suggested that certain single, highly specific memories can be "self-defining" (e.g., Singer & Blagov 2004; Singer & Salovey, 1993). Self-defining memories are considered to have a focal influence on the content of self-referential thought and the attributes by which people characterize themselves. Perhaps particularly when occurring early in life, self-defining memories can act as the foundation upon which the later bricks of self-experience are laid. Self-defining memories are typically assessed by asking participants to note memories that (1) are remembered clearly, (2) were considered important at the time, (3) are still considered important when recollected in the present, and, most importantly, (4) help him or her understand who he or she is as a person.

Applying the concept of self-defining memories to understanding the influence of traumatic memories on traumatized person's sense of self, Sutherland and Bryant (2005) showed that, when asked to recollect self-defining memories, traumatized persons with PTSD were more likely to select memories that were traumatic in nature. In addition, Berntsen and Rubin and their colleagues have repeatedly shown, via their Centrality of Event Scale (Berntsen & Rubin, 2006, 2007), that traumatized persons who consider memories of traumatic events to be central components of their personal identity tend to experience more severe symptoms of PTSD (Berntsen & Rubin, 2006, 2007, 2008; Berntsen & Thomsen, 2005; Bernsten, Willert, & Rubin, 2003; Berntsen, Rubin, & Siegler, 2011; Boals, 2010; Pinto-Gouveia & Matos, 2011; Robinaugh, & McNally, 2010; Rubin,

Boals, & Berntsen, 2008; Rubin & Berntsen, 2004; Rubin, Berntsen, & Hutson, 2009; Schuettler & Boals, 2011; Smeets, Giesbrecht, Raymaekers, Shaw, & Merckelbach, 2010; Thomsen & Berntsen, 2008, 2009). Face-valid items from the Centrality of Event Scale for the concept of self-defining memories include survey items querying whether traumatic events have become "part of my identity," "a reference point for the way I understand myself and the world," or "a central part of my life story."

In addition to the influence of memory on self-referential thought, it is also recognized that current thought can influence which memories are most likely to be retrieved at any given moment (i.e., accessibility) and the character of memories that are retrieved (i.e., reconstruction). In particular, the *self-memory system* model developed by Conway and colleagues posits that a present "working self" (comprised of a person's current goals) biases the readiness of access to thematic contents of the "conceptual self" (essentially, a fund of schematically organized self-content knowledge), as well as the specific experiential details of autobiographical memory. The influence of the working self is usually adaptive, biasing what is activated within the semantic autobiographical knowledge base, and influencing experiential autobiographical recall so as to cohere with the working self's goals (Conway, 2005; Conway, Meares, & Standart, 2004; Conway & Pleydell-Pearce, 2000; Conway, Singer, & Tagini, 2004).

For example, if a trauma therapist defines her current working-self goal as "to help my clients," she will have ready access to concepts of herself as "benevolent" and "competent." In turn, if she should be asked in supervision to describe her recent therapy sessions, her descriptions are likely to (if unknowingly) somewhat indulge the degree to which she exhibited these virtues within the clinical hour. This tends to be the case even if she also retains, within her conceptual self-knowledge store, concepts that compete with the characterization of herself as benevolent and competent (i.e., competing memory traces would be deactivated and less readily accessible). Nevertheless, if the therapist had been told repeatedly as a child that "you are so selfish" and "you can't do anything right," her ability to exercise as a working-self goal an image of herself as benevolent and competent would itself be undermined.

Neuroimaging the Traumatized "Me"

An increasingly voluminous literature has investigated the neurophysiological processes that mediate one's sense of oneself as comprising a listing of characteristics or attributes, typically referred to in clinical psychology as the "self-schema" and what we earlier called "first-person self-contents." These studies often take the form of presenting a list of trait adjectives (e.g., "extraverted," "introverted") to individuals and explicitly asking them whether the words describe them, on certain trials, and whether they describe other people, on other trials. Pictures (e.g., scenes or objects) have also been used as stimuli and rated as to their self-relevance (Phan et al., 2003). Brain responses are recorded as people do so and are usually analyzed both as a function of task-performance (what is happening in people's brains when they actively consider whether various words or other stimuli describe them, in comparison to when they are engaged in some other task?) and as a function of the answers given (what is happening in people's brains when they are exposed to a word or other stimulus that they determine is self-descriptive, in comparison with when they encounter a stimulus that they do not consider self-descriptive?).

The first of such studies was conducted by Craik and colleagues in a report titled "Finding the Self" (Craik et al., 1999). Following a landmark review by Northoff and colleagues, these sorts of tasks have come to be collectively referred to in the social-cognitive neuroscience literature as studies of "self-referential processing (SRP)" (Northoff et al., 2006). It is now widely accepted that responses in both the anterior and posterior midline cortices, specifically the medial prefrontal cortex, adjacent perigenual anterior cingulate cortex, and posterior cingulate cortex extending into the precuneus, partly mediate the explicit evaluation of stimuli as to their self-relevance (review by Northoff et al., 2006). Meta-analyses also confirm that the temporal poles, inferior parietal lobes, and insula are also implicated in SRP (Denny, Kober, Wager, & Ochsner, 2012; Qin et al., 2012). Figure 4.2 illustrates the neuroanatomy of brain regions of interest frequently identified in neuroimaging studies of SRP.

Perhaps contrary to intuition, most individual studies have not, however, found that the task of self-reflection has an obvious "special significance" in the brain when compared with processing stimuli that are descriptive of known others (Gillihan & Farrah, 2005; Legrand & Ruby, 2009; Ochsner et al., 2005). Recent meta-analytic reviews *do* show that SRP is associated with increases in medial prefrontal cortex metabolism more than are stimuli that are familiar but not explicitly self-relevant (Denny et al., 2012; Qin & Northoff, 2011a, 2011b; Qin et al., 2012; van der Meer, Costafreda, Aleman, & David, 2010). However, most individual studies do not report this finding. In addition, the notion of a "collectivist" as opposed to "individualist" self-schema complicates any simplicity that might otherwise be assumed of a black-versus-white conceptual demarcation between *self* and *other*. For example, reflecting upon one's mother may, neurophysiologically speaking, be very similar to reflecting upon oneself if one's relationship with one's mother is close, whereas reflecting upon one's father may evoke no differences from that of considering a stranger if one's relationship with one's father was never close (e.g., Wang et al., 2012).

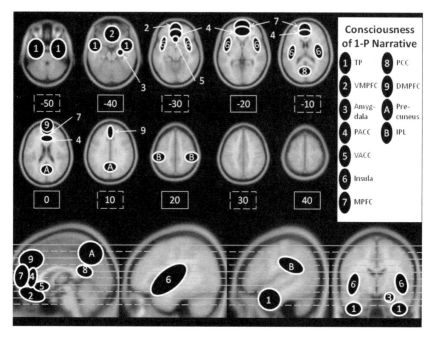

FIGURE 4.2. Neuroanatomy of Consciousness of Thought in Normal First-Person Perspective. 1-P = first-person; DMPFC = dorsomedial prefrontal cortex; IPL = inferior parietal lobe; MPFC = medial prefrontal cortex; PACC = perigenual anterior cingulate cortex; PCC = posterior cingulate cortex; TP =temporal pole; VACC = ventral anterior cingulate cortex; VMPFC = ventromedial prefrontal cortex.

A recent interest in the social-cognitive and affective neuroscience of SRP has been to compare the neural correlates of people's more positive and adaptive views of self to the more negative views often present in maladjusted individuals. Van der Meer and colleagues' framework suggests that responses in the inferior or ventral regions of the medial prefrontal cortex (including the ventral subgenual anterior cingulate) may be particularly involved in SRP that is overtly emotionally significant, whereas the superior or dorsal medial anterior cortex may mediate attentional processing that is independent of valence (van der Meer et al., 2010). Heatherton (2011) also discussed a ventral–dorsal model wherein the ventral cortex is particularly thought to underlie SRP that is negatively valenced (Moran, Macrae, Heatherton, Wyland, & Kelley, 2006). Finally, Myers-Schulz and Koenigs (2012) reviewed evidence to suggest that it may be the ventral or subgenual anterior cingulate cortex (approximately Brodmann area 25) that is particularly involved in negative SRP, whereas other regions in the ventral anteromedial prefrontal cortex may uniquely mediate processing associated with reward and associated positive affect.

Consistent with these frameworks, we recently found the neural correlates of SRP in women to vary by trait self-esteem. Individuals with lower trait self-esteem showed greater activation of the ventral anterior cingulate cortex during negative SRP, and individuals with higher self-esteem and those experiencing greater positive affect showed activation in the ventromedial and medial orbitofrontal regions during positive SRP (Frewen, Lundberg, Brimson-Théberge, & Théberge, 2012). In comparison, Lemogne and colleagues observed increasing response during SRP in the dorsal medial prefrontal cortex in both depressed individuals (Lemogne et al., 2009) and in individuals high in trait negative affect (Lemogne et al., 2011), whereas Grimm et al. (2009) found *reduced* response in the dorsal medial prefrontal cortex, anterior cingulate, and precuneus, among other regions, in depressed individuals relative to controls during a task requiring SRP of positively and negatively valenced pictures. This mixed set of results across studies seems to call into question the simplicity of a model that limits emotional aspects of SRP only to inferior regions of the medial prefrontal cortex. Unfortunately, none of the neuroimaging studies of SRP in depressed persons published to date explicitly reported on the trauma histories of research participants.

By contrast, we conducted the first two studies of explicit SRP in childhood trauma-related PTSD samples. In our first study, which did not examine effects for the emotional valence of self-descriptions, individuals with PTSD exhibited less response in the ventromedial prefrontal cortex during SRP than did controls, specifically when considering the applicability of "personal characteristics" (e.g., "I am a good friend") versus "general facts" (e.g., "Paris is the capital of France") (Bluhm et al., 2012). Our second study found a positive correlation between response in the right amygdala and positively valenced SRP in women with PTSD while viewing pictures of themselves in neutral expression while listening to positive and negative word lists (Frewen, Dozois, Neufeld, Densmore, et al., 2011b). The latter findings are consistent with other research emphasizing a role for the right amygdala in valenced SRP (Northoff et al., 2009) but opposite in laterality to the findings of Yoshimura et al. (2009), who instead found positive versus negative SRP to be associated with left and right amygdala response, respectively, in healthy controls. The idea that abnormal SRP is relevant to neuropsychological models of PTSD was also suggested by Liberzon and Martis (2006). Unfortunately, it appears that much more research is needed before we fully understand the neurophysiology of negative self-referential cognition in traumatized persons. Future work will compare performance of the *visual–verbal self–other referential processing task* in women with versus without childhood-trauma-related PTSD.

Visual–Verbal, Self–Other Referential Processing Task

Investigating how people respond to experimental stimuli that are intrinsically self-relevant (e.g., one's name, a photograph of oneself) is one way researchers study self-referential processing (SRP). Other times researchers administer stimuli that are only potentially characteristic of self (e.g., trait adjectives) and examine how people evaluate themselves in comparison with others (i.e., "other-referential processing" [ORP]). For example, as reviewed previously, researchers have investigated the psychological and neural processes mediating peoples' judgments regarding the applicability of trait adjectives such as *loved* versus *unloved* and *success* versus *failure*. In effect, such studies have examined the self in a semantic or "verbal" way. In comparison, others have examined SRP through perceptual processing, most often in the visual stream (e.g., response to facial photographs of self, akin to static mirror viewing), and typically through self-recognition judgments (e.g., is the picture of me or of someone else?; see Uddin, Iacoboni, Lange, & Keenan, 2007, for review).

However, a problem with many of these experimental designs involves the confounding of cognitive *processes* and *products* (e.g., Legrand & Ruby, 2009), or the "how" and "what" of these judgments, respectively. For example, when the words that are presented to participants are positive versus negative, most people will judge the positive words (e.g., *loved*, *successful*) as more self-descriptive than the negative words (e.g., *unloved*, *failure*). In fact, people normally judge positive words as more descriptive of themselves than others, an effect referred to as the "self-positivity bias" (review by Mezulis, Abramson, Hyde, & Hankin, 2004).

Besides overtly asking people whether stimuli are self-descriptive or self-relevant, as in questionnaire studies, experimental approaches have also been developed to study SRP and ORP indirectly, potentially assessing an *implicit* representation of self that may differ from the sense of self known explicitly. Implicit processes are often assessed by measuring participants' reaction times (RTs) to different trials that either pair self-relevant stimuli (e.g., one's name or photograph) with stimuli that are either positive/desirable or negative/undesirable (e.g., review by Zeigler-Hill & Jordan, 2010).

Nevertheless, researchers have sometimes questioned the validity of these approaches because they often fail to encourage introspection or interoception, and typically they are associated with "cold" cognitive processes rather than "hot" emotional ones (Buhrmester, Blanton, & Swann, 2011; Frewen & Lundberg, 2012). To address some of these issues, we designed a task that combines both the direct and indirect measurement of valenced verbal and visual SRP and ORP within a single methodology intended to better encourage self-reflection and to be affectively salient (see Figure 4.3); we titled our experimental procedure the *visual–verbal,*

Visual-Verbal Self-Other Referential Processing Task (VV-SORP-T)

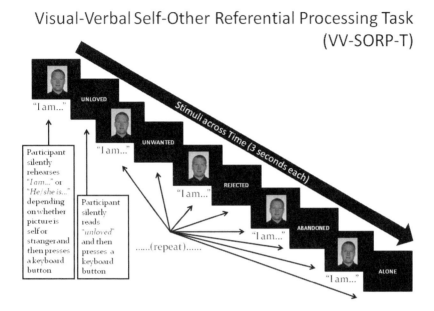

FIGURE 4.3. Sample Trial of the Visual–Verbal, Self–Other Referential Processing Task.

Participants view pictures of themselves on certain trials, and of strangers during others, intermixed between positive or negative adjectives. They press a response button after silently rehearsing "I am" or "He/she is," depending on which picture is shown, as well as after reading the words, which thereby associate the self or the other person with positive or negative traits, depending on the trial type. Participants self-monitor their affective response to the task for later report. See Frewen and Lundberg (2012; Frewen, Lundberg, et al., 2012) for further description. Reprinted from *Personality and Individual Differences*, Volume 52, Issue 4, Paul A. Frewen and Erica Lundberg, "Visual-Verbal Self/Other-Referential Processing Task: Direct vs. indirect assessment, valence, and experiential correlates," pages 509-514, March 2012, with permission from Elsevier.

self–other referential processing task (Frewen & Lundberg, 2012; Frewen, Lundberg, et al., 2012).

The Visual-Verbal-Self-Other-Referential-Processing-Task (VV-SORP-T) requires participants to view pictures of themselves during certain trials and to view pictures of strangers during others, intermixed between valenced words, therefore creating four trial types: (1) self-photograph paired with negative words (S-N), (2) self-photograph paired with positive words (S-P), (3) other photograph paired with negative words (O-N), and other photograph paired with positive words (O-P). Participants are instructed to internally rehearse the words "I am . . ." or "He/she is . . ."

when presented with the respective pictures and then read the words, creating an association between the self/other with positivity/negativity depending on the trial type (e.g., "I am . . . " *unloved* as in Figure 4.3). Participants monitor their affective responses to the task, and their degree of attention or rate of internal speech/reading speed is measured indirectly by requiring them to press a response button after rehearsing each statement.

Research so far published using the Visual-Verbal-Self-Other-Referential-Processing-Task (Frewen & Lundberg, 2012; Frewen, Lundberg, et al., 2012) has shown that healthy individuals typically report experiencing greater positive affect during S-P than O-P trials, and greater negative affect during S-N than O-N trials. In addition, participants usually are slower to press the response buttons during S-P and S-N trials than during O-P and O-N trials, which we interpreted as evidence of greater reflective processing occurring during trials specific to the self. We have also since observed, in studies yet to be submitted for publication, that self-reported affective responses to the Visual-Verbal-Self-Other-Referential-Processing-Task covary with autonomic nervous system activation as measured by heart-rate and skin conductance response. We have also since observed, in a number of studies in preparation for publication, a host of additional characteristic phenomenological responses to the Visual-Verbal-Self-Other-Referential-Processing-Task. For example:

- Both the social emotions of pride and jealousy were experienced most during O-P, whereas pity was experienced most during O-N.
- Participants experienced themselves as wanting to press response buttons most during S-N (perhaps to terminate the trials more quickly), and perceived themselves as pressing response buttons most slowly during S-P trials.
- Participants reported liking the task most during S-P trials.
- Participants experienced themselves as "agreeing" most during S-P trials, but also agreed more during S-N than O-N, while also disagreeing most during S-N.
- Participants experienced themselves as "reflecting about" and "paying more attention" during S-N relative to O-N trials, and during S-P relative to O-P trials.
- Participants perceived photographs as more attractive during S-P than S-N trials, and during O-P than O-N trials.
- Finally, we have observed several of these experiences vary by gender.

In research soon to be submitted for publication, we have also examined responses to the Visual-Verbal-Self-Other-Referential-Processing-Task from traumatized participants. Preliminary analyses suggest that traumatized persons with PTSD experience greater negative affect during both S-N and S-P trials than do nontraumatized persons, and they exhibit alterations in functional neural responses in the anterior cortical midline structures such as the medial prefrontal cortex. Open-ended experiential reports also suggest that traumatized persons often experience a number of clinically interesting phenomenological responses to the Visual-Verbal-Self-Other-Referential-Processing-Task, including increased "agreement" with S-N trials, greater tolerance for O-P than S-P trials, and a range of social emotions during ORP trials. Figure 4.4 illustrates a sampling of responses collected from women with childhood trauma-related PTSD during completion of the Visual-Verbal-Self-Other-Referential-Processing-Task.

Healing the Traumatized "Me" via
Self-Schema Reflection

A number of established general modalities as well as specific interventions exist for helping persons envision and write a more adaptive and resilient narrative for their future than has been the distressing and disorganized narrative of their past. These modalities and interventions include cognitive processing therapy, which involves the attempted restructuring of appraisals regarding external threat and internal negative self-referential cognition. This intervention has demonstrated efficacy in treating PTSD across a variety of populations, including sexual assault victims (e.g., Monson et al., 2006), combat veterans (e.g., Resick et al., 2008), and refugees (e.g., Schulz, Resick, Huber, & Griffin, 2006).

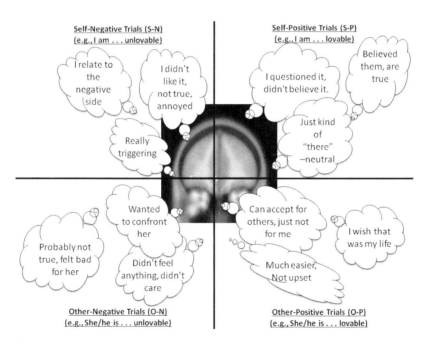

FIGURE 4.4. Examples of Phenomenological Responses to the VV-SORP-T Collected from Women with PTSD Related to Childhood Trauma Histories

Reflection upon the content and structure of a client's self-schema is indeed important in trauma therapy. We have found it useful to supplement standard cognitive restructuring techniques that are based solely in verbal dialogue with in-session paper-and-pencil exercises. For example, Figure 4.5 illustrates a "brainstorming" exercise we frequently use to identify the attributes by which clients describe themselves, as well as the association between different self-attributes and self-defining memories.

When completed over a number of sessions, the exercise can serve to chart, and contribute directly to, the adaptive restructuring of the client's "me" narrative. Therapeutic targets include increased *complexity*: that is,

Self-Schema Sheet (Brainstorming)

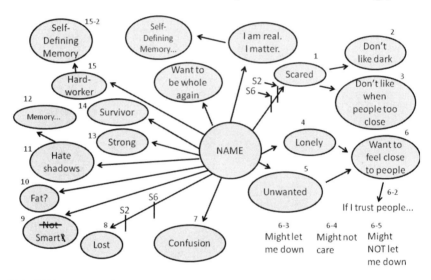

FIGURE 4.5. A Sample Reflective Exercise Involving "Brainstorming" about the Self-Schema.

It is recommended that the exercise be completed on large flip-chart paper to afford a combined verbal–visual representation of the client's self-schemas that can be easily viewed by both client and clinician. Circles are labeled with the client's self-identified characteristics. One draws a small number beside each attribute indicating the order in which it was added. Often, complexly traumatized persons will describe themselves using negative attributes before they include positive ones. Attributes may stem directly from the self (e.g., "Scared") or from other attributes (e.g., "Scared" → "Don't like dark"). Particularly central ideas that seem to represent significant new insights into the self might be labeled in their own color (e.g., "I am real. I matter."). The clinician may encourage a secondary positive reappraisal of negative attributes (e.g., as wants/needs or desire for change; e.g., "Lonely" and "Unwanted" vs. "Want to feel close to people"). The clinician seeks the client becomes able to acknowledge a more diverse and flexible sense of self than he or she was previously able to do. Increased complexity can be revealed by an increasing number of attributes noted over time, such as measured in terms of traits, roles, strengths, etc. Another therapeutic target includes increased *adaptiveness*, whereby the client is able to acknowledge a greater proportion of positive, relative to negative, attributes as self-referential than at the beginning of treatment. Please see the note to Figure 4.5 for greater elaboration regarding therapeutic procedures used in this exercise.

Figure 4.6 (also in color insert) shows a drawing by "Valerie," a childhood trauma survivor, that depicts the kinds of negative cognitions often associated with complex interpersonal trauma. Valerie presents negative SRP in the form of existential questions (e.g., "When will these scars heal for me?," "What is my true strength?," "When will these tears stop for me?"). At the same time, one can see that Valerie is experiencing an increasing sense of hope, depicted in the center of her drawing.

The Traumatized "Me" and General Negative Affect and Distress

In our view the decision to recognize negative self-referential cognition in traumatized persons as symptomatic of posttraumatic stress is highly valuable (American Psychiatric Association, 2013; Friedman, Resick, Bryant, & Brewin, 2011). Clearly, traumatized persons frequently endorse negative thoughts about themselves that are reasonably linked etiologically to the traumatic stressor (e.g., feeling guilty about the use of excessive force in combat) and traumatic relationships (e.g., early childhood maltreatment).

Nevertheless, within the 4-D model, our position is that symptoms of excess negative self-referential cognition cannot be taken at face value as an indication of a TRASC of thought. Instead it is recognized that negative self-referential thinking is dimensionally distributed in the normal popu-

---

permission to append a question mark (?) to negative attributes that the client would like to (or is willing to) question (e.g., "Fat?," "Not deserving?"). With each new viewing, the client is invited to reflect upon what has already been written, encouraging an openness to both acceptance and change, as appropriate (e.g., "Is there anything you would like to add or change?"). For example, the idea early in therapy that one is "not deserving" might be revised in a later session. It may also be meaningful to make tick marks along the length of the lines, effectively treating them as a visual analogue scale, with the left end meaning "Very Little" and the right "Very Much," to assess change in certain self-experiences (e.g., changes from sessions 2 to 6 in the feeling of being "Scared" and "Lost"). For some attributes "self-defining memories" will be relevant to note (e.g., in response to question, "Is there an early or recent memory when you especially felt, or came to know that you are, _____ [attribute], e.g., "a hard worker"?).

FIGURE 4.6. Valerie's Artwork (2013): "Not All Hope Is Lost Forever."
Used with permission.

lation; only the most narcissistic of us fail to think badly about ourselves
at least once in a while. The frequency with which one thinks negatively
about oneself is widely considered a marker for trait low self-esteem, self-
criticalness, and depressive cognition rather than a TRASC of thought (e.g.,

Hyde, Mezulis, & Abramson, 2008). Thus we suggest that cases where the contents of the conscious self-narrative are highly negative, but one fully recognizes one's thoughts as one's own (i.e. there is no disturbance in the phenomenal first-person perspective of consciousness), represent an insufficient basis for marking the presence of a TRASC of thought.

In comparison, we suggest that a change in narrative *perspective* provides stronger evidence for a TRASC of thought. Using William James's terms, an altered state of consciousness is constituted not when the "me" is traumatized (i.e., the content of thought, or what types of thought one has), but only when the "I" is traumatized as well (i.e., the form, process, or *way* in which a person consciously experiences thought is altered). The key distinction to be made here is that, in normal waking consciousness (NWC), thoughts are typically experienced as emanating from a singular "inner voice." In comparison, voice hearing entails the actual hearing of another person's speech within one's own thoughts, as if another person were talking within one's mind. We suggest that this experience constitutes a TRASC of thought. We consider these symptoms and their relation with trauma histories next.

Neurophenomenology of the Traumatized "*I*": Alterations in Narrative Voice (Perspective)

Contrary to popular belief and stereotypes encouraged by media portrayal, research suggests that hearing voices within one's head, as different from one's own egocentric thought, is *not* an extraordinarily uncommon experience within the general population. Beavan, Read, and Cartwright (2011) reviewed population-based studies of voice hearing and found that conservative, interview-based studies typically yield prevalence estimates of 1–3% within the general population (e.g., Caspi et al., 2005; Johns, Hemsley, & Kuipers, 2002; Ohayon, 2000; Tien, 1991), but much higher estimates (between 5 and 15%) are often observed when participants answer questions in self-report surveys (e.g., 8%; Shevlin, Dorahy, & Adamson, 2007). Student samples also frequently yield high estimates; for example, 39% endorsed the experience of hearing a voice speaking one's thoughts aloud in Posey and Losch's (1983) sample, an effect replicated by Barrett and Ethridge (1992). Beavan et al. (2011) point out that the true population prevalence may be underestimated, perhaps particularly in the context of interview-based studies, because assessments are typically conducted within psychiatric settings wherein participants may refrain from endorsing voice-hearing experiences for fear that they will be subsequently labeled mentally ill.

Moreover, the way in which questions about voice hearing are phrased is likely to influence endorsement rates. For example, a statement such as "I have been troubled by hearing voices in my head" may lead to lower self-endorsement rates than essentially the same question omitting the association with distress (i.e., omitting the words *troubled by*; e.g., "I've had the experience of hearing voices in my head"). This care with wording reflects the fact that most voice hearers do *not* experience their voices as distressing (Longden, Madill, & Waterman, 2012; Beavan et al., 2011). In fact, evidence suggests that only when voices are experienced with distress and personally interpreted as evidence of mental illness are they likely to be associated with psychiatric illness (e.g., Bak et al., 2005; Peters, Williams, Cooke, & Kuipers, 2011; Romme & Escher, 1989). In contrast, nonclinical voice hearers, although often exhibiting certain psychological characteristics (e.g., schizotypal traits; Sommer et al., 2010), report little or no distress or impairment associated with their voice-hearing experiences. Moreover, it is well known that some experiences of voice hearing are clearly positive (e.g., Jenner, Rutten, Beuckens, Boonstra, & Systema, 2008).

Several intensive phenomenological studies of voice hearing have been completed in recent years. Within a general community sample of voice hearers, Beavan and Read (2010) found that contact with mental health services was best predicted by voice-hearing content that was negatively valenced (e.g., "You are worthless," "No one likes you"). Consonant with this finding, Daalman and colleagues (2011) showed that the degree to which voice content subsumed negative self-referential themes was the primary predictor of whether voice-hearing persons were diagnosed with a schizophrenia spectrum disorder rather than having no diagnosis or history of mental health contact. Beavan and Read (2010) subcategorized voice content within upper-level valence categories. Voices that were considered positive were frequently characterized as providing advice/guidance, information, encouragement, comfort, or praise/compliments to the person, whereas negative voices either criticized the self or others, or encouraged the harming of self or others.

Beavan's (2011) thematic analysis of qualitative interviews with voice hearers identified five essential characteristics that could collectively establish the experience of voice hearing for most persons:

1. Valence (emotional impact, described already)
2. Highly personally meaningful content (i.e., the content of voices characterizes the individual's present state of mind, relationships, or history)
3. Assignment of the voice(s) to particular identities (e.g., often someone actually known to the person such as a family member or friend, but could be from a stranger or perceived to emanate from a spiritual force)
4. A defined relationship (i.e., the person him- or herself having a relationship with the voice that exhibits a regular structure [e.g., respectful vs. disrepectful])

5. The experiential quality of the voices seeming to be "real," even if the voices may be objectively acknowledged as not existing within the material realm.

Other research has also shown that many individuals describe having a "relationship" with their voices in which their own role often mimics their social behavior in the context of relationships with other persons (e.g., submissive persons are often found to submit to voices that are experienced as powerful and controlling; reviewed by Hayward, Berry & Ashton, 2011).

Voice Hearing and Trauma-related Disorders

Studies have also identified an association between early psychological trauma histories and voice hearing. Longden et al. (2012) reviewed the literature on the phenomenology and prevalence of voice hearing and its relationship to trauma history, PTSD, and dissociative symptoms. A consistent finding was that the prevalence of voice hearing is higher in individuals with trauma-spectrum diagnoses, including PTSD, dissociative disorders, and borderline personality disorder, as compared with people without any psychiatric diagnosis. Additionally, the prevalence of voice hearing in individuals with trauma-related disorders did not differ significantly from the prevalence of voice hearing in individuals with schizophrenia (Longden et al., 2012).

Research also associates histories of childhood abuse and neglect with symptoms of voice hearing in adults. McCarthy-Jones (2011) showed that histories of childhood sexual abuse are predictive of the presence of voice hearing in psychiatric samples. A weighted mean across seven studies revealed that approximately one of every three psychiatric patients who report experiencing voice hearing had a history of childhood sexual abuse (36%). By contrast, in those reporting a history of childhood sexual abuse, greater than half reported hearing voices (56%). The prevalence of voice hearing was also found to be two- to threefold higher in individuals with histories of childhood sexual abuse than in those without such histories. Several studies have also found childhood emotional abuse histories to be associated with voice hearing (Sommer et al., 2010; Üçok & Bikmaz, 2007), and Shevlin et al. (2007) found that the likelihood of voice hearing in a general population sample increased steeply with the number of types of childhood trauma people had experienced (neglect; sexual, physical, or emotional abuse). In Longden et al.'s (2012) view, voice hearing, although more often taken as a potential sign of psychotic thinking by both mental health professionals and the lay public, is more validly conceptualized as a sign of a dissociative process with a traumatogenic etiology.

Several studies have examined the prevalence and phenomenology of voice hearing in PTSD samples. In two samples of adolescents admitted for inpatient treatment of PTSD, Scott, Nurcombe, Jessop and their colleagues found that at least 85% endorsed hearing voices inside their heads (Jessop, Scott, & Nurcombe, 2008; Scott, Nurcombe, Sheridan, & McFarland, 2007). In their first study, the only phenomenological distinction between voices heard by adolescents with PTSD as compared with primary psychotic disorders was that the voices were more likely to be experienced as commands in the schizophrenia group (i.e., orders to perform certain tasks, make certain choices; Scott et al., 2007). In a follow-up study, Jessop et al. (2008) further explored the phenomenology of voice hearing in PTSD samples and observed themes consistent with those identified by Beavan's (2011) analysis of "realness." Specifically, all but one of the teens that were assessed believed that their voice-hearing experiences "seemed real." The participants were relatively split, however, as to whether they believed their voices represented "their own thoughts," "could be their own imagination," or considered the voice itself to be real. In the majority of the participants, voice hearing had been present for greater than 1 month, occurred at least once weekly (with approximately two of every five persons experiencing voice hearing on a daily basis), and was associated with a high degree of distress.

Two studies qualitatively explored the phenomenology of voice hearing in adults with PTSD (Anketell et al., 2010; Brewin & Patel, 2010). Both studies found that voices were regarded by persons with PTSD as manifestations of peoples' own cognition in all cases; thus by definition these experiences were not psychotic. Voices were also characterized as making the people experiencing them feel "different as a person" and were predominantly negative in affective tone (critical, intimidating, and angry). As noted above, voices were often recognized by those experiencing them as the voices of persons directly involved in their traumatic experiences (e.g., those of abusers) or could be deduced symbolically as such by informed clinicians (Anketell et al., 2010). In both studies, frequency of voice hearing was strongly correlated with a measure of trait dissociation.

An additional replicated finding is that voice hearing and other symptoms commonly taken as signs of psychosis (i.e., Schneiderian first-rank symptoms) are frequently observed in people with dissociative disorders (e.g., Putnam, 1989; Kluft, 1984, 1987; Brand, Armstrong, & Loewenstein, 2006; Ross & Keyes, 2004; Ross, Miller, Reagor, & Bjornson, 1990). Dorahy, Shannon, and colleagues (2009) examined voice hearing as a function of primary diagnosis (dissociative disorders vs. schizophrenia) and childhood trauma history and failed to identify a single indicator of the phenomenology of voice hearing that was more often observed in schizophrenia than in dissociative identity disorder (e.g., voice location as within or outside of the head, or presence of commands to perform certain actions). In comparison, individuals with dissociative disorders were more likely to experience voices before reaching adult age, were more likely to experience three or more voices, and were more likely to experience both child and adult voices (individuals with schizophrenia experienced almost exclusively adult-age voices). Additionally, individuals with dissociative disorders more often experienced two or more voices talking between themselves (with or without relation to the individual experiencing them). Honig and colleagues (1998) also showed that adults diagnosed with dissociative disorders are more likely to have experienced voice hearing prior to age 12. Besides these findings, few differences in phenomenology were documented, although it appeared that in Honig and colleagues' study, seemingly in contrast to Dorahy et al.'s findings, the experience of carrying on an internal dialogue with a voice(s) was slightly more frequently observed in persons with schizophrenia. Studies have also investigated the prevalence of voice hearing in individuals diagnosed with borderline personality disorder; such persons also frequently endorse dissociative symptoms and childhood trauma histories. Across three studies voice hearing was found to be prevalent in individuals with borderline personality disorder and was not consistently differentiated by phenomenological characteristics from voices experienced by individuals with schizophrenia (Adams & Sanders, 2011; Kingdon et al., 2010; Slotema et al., 2012).

Research often suggests traumatic stress as a common theme in the content of negatively valenced voices. As an example, Beavan and Read (2010) described one male research participant in their study who had experienced an abusive childhood and had voices that "at times when I would get physically hit or abused, sexually or emotionally, or let down, would start saying 'Go and kill that person, he's evil' . . . it was like revenge" (Beavan & Read, 2010, p. 203). Adams and Sanders (2011) observed similar findings when they examined voice content in individuals diagnosed with borderline personality disorder and with histories of childhood maltreatment. Additionally, Dissociative Experience Scale scores strongly predicted the experience of voices replaying memories of previous (presumably often traumatic) events in the samples studied by Dorahy, Shannon, et al. (2009). In a smaller sample of outpatients with varied diagnoses (schizophrenia, schizoaffective disorder, major depression, or bipolar disorder), all of whom were experiencing hallucinations or delusions at the time of the study, Reiff, Castille, Muenzenmaier, and Link (2012) observed that those with documented histories of childhood physical and sexual abuse (22 of 30 participants) were more likely to report voice hearing or delusional thinking of clear or probable thematic relevance to their past childhood traumatic experiences. Several specific content themes were identified, including fear of disclosing abuse histories.

Finally, trauma exposure may be an etiological factor for negatively valenced voice hearing. Honig et al. (1998) noted that in approximately four out of every five individuals with dissociative disorders whom they

studied, the onset of their voice hearing was subsequent to, and perceived
to be triggered by, a traumatic life event, a slightly (though not significantly) higher percentage than that observed in individuals with schizophrenia (approximately two of every three persons, 65%). Daalman and
colleagues (2012) found a high prevalence of childhood trauma histories
in adult voice hearers, independent of schizophrenia diagnosis, although
extent of maltreatment history was not significantly predictive of various
indicators of voice-hearing phenomenology. The findings led Daalman
and colleagues to posit that childhood trauma histories might predispose
individuals to experience voice hearing but might not determine the specific phenomenological types of voice hearing that people experience
(Daalman et al., 2012).

Neuroimaging Voice Hearing and Narrative Perspective

Paralleling the presently common misconception that voice hearing is
only symptomatic of people with psychotic disorders, neuroimaging studies of voice hearing have been conducted almost exclusively in individuals
with schizophrenia and related conditions (e.g., Allen, Larøi, McGuire, &
Aleman, 2008). Studies of particular interest to the neurophenomenological approach involve the characterization of neural dynamics occurring
during the acute *state* of voice hearing, as opposed to comparisons of
individuals who generally do versus do not regularly hear voices, which
fail to take account of whether or not participants actually hear voices
at the time of neurophysiological assessment (Jardri, Pouchet, Pins, &
Thomas, 2011).

The generally unpredictable nature of voice-hearing occurrences makes
state-based assessment difficult, and researchers have attempted a number
of different methods to assess their occurrence within the neuroimaging
environment. In one method the onset and offset of voice-hearing episodes are signaled entirely by participants via button press (Silbersweig et
al., 1995), whereas in another, participants are queried at regular or random intervals during a scanning procedure regarding whether voice-hearing experiences had occurred (Shergill, Brammer, Williams, Murray, &
McGuire, 2000). The combination of approaches addresses their individual limitations, the former as requiring effective self-monitoring on the
part of research participants to accurately identify the onset of voice hearing, and the latter as potentially missing the occurrence of a voice-hearing
event by not assessing for it close enough in time. Unfortunately, researchers utilizing the button-press approach have typically refrained from investigating with any detail the contents or structure of the phenomenological experience of voice-hearing occurrences in the scanner, instead only
employing a categorical "on/off" design so as to avoid tainting the psychological processes involved at time segments devoid of voice hearing.

Although an understandable strategy, the designs thereby fall short of the ideal of neurophenomenology, which calls for the relation of detailed subjective experience to objective neural data using an individual differences approach. In addition, it is not clear how specific the instructions are that are given to participants in voice-hearing experiments. Presumably participants occupy a relatively internally directed, open and receptive, yet passive, "waiting" state, paying attention to their stream of thought, and being vigilante for the possible occurrence of voice-hearing events. In such instances participants might actually be occupying a third-person narrative perspective (e.g., "Now arises an experience of voice-hearing," "No experience of voice-hearing yet!") rather than the typically more natural immersive first-person perspective on experience.

Figure 4.7 illustrates the neuroanatomy of brain regions of interest frequently identified in neuroimaging studies of voice hearing. A meta-analysis performed by Jardri et al. (2011) found five clusters of response, wherein the brains of 68 individuals with schizophrenia examined across 10 studies exhibited greater metabolism during voice hearing in comparison with periods in time during which individuals considered their voices

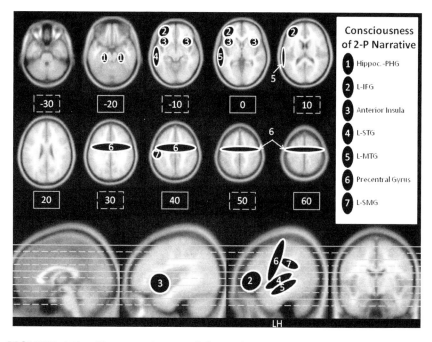

FIGURE 4.7. Neuroanatomy of Consciousness of Thought in Altered Second-Person Perspective (Voice Hearing). Hippoc.-PHG = hippocampus–parahippocampal gyrus; L-IFG = left inferior frontal gyrus; L-STG = left superior temporal gyrus; L-MTG = left middle temporal gyrus; L-SMG = left supramarginal gyrus.

absent: (1) the left inferior frontal cortex inclusive of Broca's area, the left anterior insula, and precentral gyrus; (2) the hippocampus–parahippocampal gyrus; (3) the right anterior insula and frontal operculum; (4) the left superior and middle temporal gyri (inclusive of Wernicke's area); and (5) the left supramarginal gyrus. The fact that consistent differences emerge partially serves to validate the objective "reality" of voice-hearing phenomena. Among other interpretations, the findings support the experience of voice hearing as involving brain regions mediating speech generation and production (left frontoinsular cortex, including Broca's area), auditory association (left middle and superior temporal cortex, including Wernicke's area, and the inferior parietal lobe), memory formation and retrieval (hippocampus–parahippocampal gyrus), and emotional experience (right anterior insula).

As noted previously, however, individuals with schizophrenia are not the only people who frequently experience voice hearing. Researchers have begun to investigate the degree to which the neurophysiology mediating voice-hearing experiences in individuals with versus without psychotic disorders are similar or distinct. Early evidence is suggestive of similarities, although additional studies are required to confirm initial impressions (e.g., Badcock & Hugdahl, 2012).

Specifically, the first neuroimaging study of nonpsychiatric voice hearing was conducted by Linden and colleagues (2011). Seven participants were scanned using fMRI as they reported the onset and offset of voice-hearing experiences via the button-press method. Results were contrasted with periods in which, in a different set of participants who did *not* experience voice hearing, onsets and offsets marked the beginning and end of experimenter-instructed or self-generated *imagery* of other people speaking (e.g., imagined conversation or imagined listening to a telephone message). Linden et al. needed to compare voice hearers to nonvoice hearers, rather than periods involving voice hearing versus imagery within participants who heard voices, because voice hearing occurred too frequently in their sample of voice hearers. A particular strength of the study was that Linden et al. also scanned participants' brains while they listened to audio files of actual (i.e., external) human voices.

Participants who experienced voice hearing in Linden et al.'s study (2011) showed increased metabolism in many of the brain areas previously identified as related to the experience of voice hearing in individuals with schizophrenia. These included the bilateral superior temporal sulcus (also localized in the study in response to speech sounds in the preexperiment), bilateral inferior frontal cortex (inclusive of Broca's area in the left hemisphere), bilateral auditory association cortex (inclusive of Wernicke's area in the left hemisphere), inferior parietal lobes, cerebellum, thalamus, and primary motor cortex (considered indicative of the associated button pressing). Moreover, when Linden et al. contrasted responses occurring during internal voice hearing with responses occurring during listening to actual external speech, there were no differences in the response within auditory association cortex. This finding supports the interpretation of voice hearing as involving processes common to those invoked by the hearing of actual (i.e., external) speech.

Both similarities and differences were also observed relative to non-voice hearers while the latter imagined hearing others' voices. Specifically, greater response was observed during voice hearing in the bilateral inferior parietal lobe, left middle frontal gyrus, posterior cingulate gyrus, left Heschl's gyrus (primary auditory cortex), and bilateral calcarine sulcus. Interestingly, the researchers also determined that, during volitional imagery of voices, response in the supplementary motor area preceded response in the superior temporal sulcus, during voice hearing these responses were effectively simultaneous. The result was interpreted as suggesting that the conscious *intention* of covert speech, presumably processed partly in the supplementary motor cortex, could have "arrived too late" at the auditory association cortex—the message then delivered as if without the sender address denoted "from self." On the receiving end, the auditory association cortex, not knowing the message was "self-generated," might then "think" it was sent by someone else.

Diederen and colleagues (2011) were the first to directly compare fMRI response during spontaneously occurring voice hearing in nonpsychotic persons with that occurring in individuals with a schizophrenia spectrum diagnosis. The researchers utilized conjunction analyses, which require the simultaneous observation of two effects: in this case that both psychotic and nonpsychotic voice hearers show the same brain responses during voice-hearing presence as compared with its absence. Diederen et al. showed widespread shared activation in psychotic and nonpsychotic individuals during the experience of voice hearing. Specifically, greater brain metabolism during voice hearing, relative to passive resting state, was observed in the bilateral inferior frontal gyri, insula, superior temporal gyri, supramarginal gyri, postcentral gryi, left precentral gyrus, inferior parietal lobe, superior temporal pole, and right cerebellum. Moreover, direct comparisons between groups yielded null results, which suggest that the experience of voice hearing as occurring in individuals with versus without psychotic disorders might have a similar neurophysiological basis. A follow-up study also imaged the integrity of white matter tracts, including the arcuate fasciculus, a tract that connects frontal speech areas in the left hemisphere with temporoparietal language perceptions areas (de Weijer et al., 2011). The study found that, just as was reported previously in schizophrenia (e.g., Hubl et al., 2004), the integrity of the arcuate fasciculus may be compromised in nonpsychotic voice hearers. Again, the collective findings point to the potential nonspecificity of brain-imaging abnormalities associated with schizophrenia relative to voice hearing more generally.

Voice Hearing as a Trauma-Related Altered State of Consciousness of Thought in Traumatized Persons

The clinical phenomenological studies reviewed provide solid ground for the proposal that a dissociative variant of narrative thought is frequently observed in certain traumatized persons, particularly those with complex forms of PTSD, borderline personality, and dissociative disorders. We are positing here, consistent with the population-based studies reviewed above, that consciousness in its normal form is experienced exclusively from the first-person narrative perspective in the vast majority of people. Nevertheless, many traumatized persons will experience what is often a TRASC of thought, wherein thoughts are experienced as reflecting the voices of internalized "others" that are different from the phenomenal self or ego but nevertheless are speaking to one inside one's head. Furthermore, these voices are commonly experienced as if emanating from another defined person (e.g., abuser) or entity (e.g., spirit, guide) that is associated with a particular image and semiregular set of beliefs, opinions, and character traits (Hayward et al., 2011). In traumatized persons who are experiencing distress and impairment, voice content is generally self-referential and negative in valence.

Our present interpretation of the experience of voice hearing is that it is tantamount to thoughts being experienced in the narrative perspective of second person (e.g., hearing inside or even outside your head another person saying "I hate you"), rather than in first-person perspective (e.g., having the thought "I hate myself") (see Figure 4.8; also in color insert). This is the equivalent of a change in narrative perspective. In second-person perspective a person is no longer the sole orator of his or her lived experience; another narrative voice also speaks inside his or her head. In what we consider to be a TRASC of thought, the tale of one's moment-to-moment phenomenal experience becomes shared among several speakers—a group conceivably differing in terms of interpretation (e.g., as evaluating an event as good vs. bad), emphasis (e.g., what is worthy of one's attention), affect (e.g., negative [shame, anger, sad] vs. positive), goals (e.g., what choices one should make) and sense of time (e.g. present vs. past).

It is further important to note that, in cases of dissociative identity disorder and dissociative disorder not otherwise specified, differing perspectives experienced through voice hearing are frequently not only heard but lived; that is, they are experienced as being enacted through alternate senses of agency and selfhood. For example, an individual may experience a traumatic event(s) from a second-person perspective, as if it is happening to someone else. It has long been theorized that experiencing events as such may afford trauma survivors a perceived increased ability to live

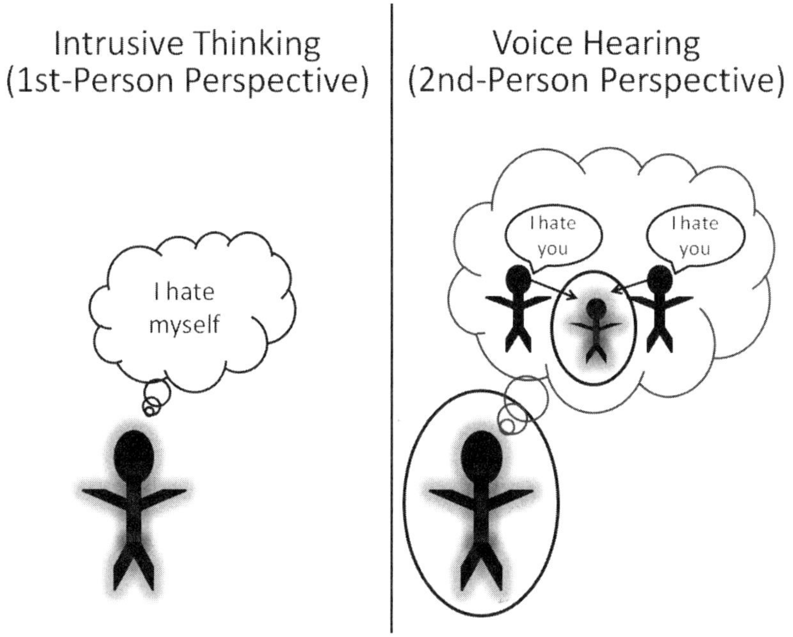

| Intrusive Thinking (1st-Person Perspective) | Voice Hearing (2nd-Person Perspective) |

FIGURE 4.8. Phenomenology of Intrusive Thinking (NWC) versus Voice Hearing (TRASC).

Left panel: INTRUSIVE THINKING—negative thoughts are experienced in first-person perspective (e.g., "I hate myself"). *Right panel:* VOICE HEARING—thoughts are experienced in second-person perspective as the personified voices of "others" (e.g., hearing a voice inside one's head saying "I hate you"). Such voices are considered different from one's own and may further be associated with other characteristics (e.g., an image).

through and endure events that would otherwise be overwhelming and unbearable. Nevertheless, the repeated division and disintegration of a person's sense of agency and identity that can occur with repeated traumatization and dissociation frequently engender problems of their own kind, particularly in cases where different aspects of self-experience conflict, thereby creating confusion, contradiction, and discord across a person's consciousness of time, thought, their body, and emotions.

A clinical example of this is provided by a 57-year-old man, "Craig," who had a long-term history of childhood sexual, physical, and emotional abuse. On two occasions Craig completed a series of social-cognitive tasks assessing empathy, mentalizing, and moral reasoning. Craig's answers to the social-cognition measures diverged so significantly across the two testing sessions as to suggest that he might have answered them from a nonsingular sense of purpose, agency, and selfhood. For example, in one set of questions Craig was presented with the ethical dilemma of being on a lifeboat that is guaranteed to sink at sea, killing him and several other passengers unless one person is thrown overboard. In this dire situation it was further suggested that a young woman has volunteered to sacrifice herself for the sake of the others on the condition that, being afraid of the actual drowning, Craig must cut her throat with his knife and throw her body into the sea. When queried regarding what he would do in this complex utilitarian dilemma (the specific question posed was: "Do you believe it is morally OK to cut the woman's throat and throw her overboard?"), Craig's personal ethical stance shifted radically from a previous response describing his adamant refusal to take the life of the woman (proposing instead an improbable solution aimed at saving many lives: "I would cut off her legs and three other pairs of legs that would weigh the same as one body, and then when we get rescued, we can all can go in for surgery and live anyway albeit without legs") to responding that he would certainly take her life ("It is the only logical thing to do"), even remarking further that he would do so without becoming emotionally involved.

Similarly, on a test assessing his ability to interpret a social faux pas, Craig identified such a significant conflict between his thoughts and emotions across repeated testing sessions as to lead him to deny that he was the author of his former responses, striking out the previous text repeatedly with his pen. Upon further questioning and reflection, Craig additionally described that he has been repeatedly told by his wife and friends that he sometimes becomes consumed by anger that he is rarely able to later recall to any significant extent. When he is able to (at least partially) recall angry episodes, however, he has noted that when in anger he feels as if it is not him experiencing the anger, but rather instead that it is someone who is more adolescent-like. This case was observed by the authors in collaboration with Dr. Margaret McKinnon and Mr. Anthony Nazarov at McMaster University.

In summary, complexly traumatized persons often experience a wrangled ensemble of negatively toned voices that are intrusive, unwanted, distressing, and beyond individuals' best efforts to silence or evade them (i.e., dyscontrol). Moreover, as a result of the often differing perspectives of the voices, an individual's experience can be severely conflicted when his or her voices disagree, sometimes causing a multitude of diverse emotional reactions to the same event (e.g., fear, anger/rage, disgust, shame). Further supporting our present argument that first-person self-referential thought and second-person voice hearing represent different psychological phenomena, the neuroimaging studies reviewed previously also suggest that the functional neuroanatomical markers attending these experiences may be largely nonoverlapping. Whereas SRP seems to be most robustly associated with response in both anterior and posterior medial structures, including the medial prefrontal cortex and cingulate gyrus, in striking contrast, voice hearing has been most robustly associated with responses in the inferolateral prefrontal cortex and primary and secondary auditory cortex. In effect, the two different experiences of thinking to oneself "I am worthless," versus hearing another person's voice in one's head saying "You are worthless," are likely to be attended by rather distinct neurophysiological markers. Neurophenomenological studies would anticipate the former experience to especially invoke response in anteromedial regions, whereas the latter would be associated with a lateral and multimodal (frontotemporal) response. In summary, the brain experiencing an internal voice saying "You are worthless" tends to look more like it would when hearing an external speaker saying "You are worthless" than it does when thinking or covertly saying to oneself "I am worthless." A neurophenomenological study directly comparing the neural correlates of self-referential thought with those of internal and external voice hearing in the same individuals, however, would provide stronger evidence for this hypothesis.

Unfortunately, neuroimaging studies have not investigated the possible traumatogenic nature of voice-hearing events in schizophrenia or healthy voice hearers, and no published studies have yet examined the neurophysiology mediating voice hearing in other trauma-related disorders. Accordingly, the immediate clinical relevance to psychotraumatology of the neuroimaging results reviewed previously concerning voice hearing in schizophrenic and nonschizophrenic samples can only be made speculatively. In order to investigate whether voices arise as a result of the same pathophysiological mechanisms in different trauma-related disorders, group comparison studies will be required in the future.

Nevertheless, we conclude that clinical and phenomenological studies suggest the potential significance of differentiating between normal (if excessive) negative cognition about self in traumatized persons from the experience of voice hearing, the latter representing a more dissociative variant of narrative consciousness. Our thesis is that, when negative self-narratives are experienced solely from the first-person perspective, one defines a normal (if distressing and upsetting) state of consciousness in the traumatized person. In comparison, when thoughts are frequently experienced from the second-person perspective as the internalized voices of others, one observes a TRASC of thought. In effect, voice hearing represents a change in the sense not only of James's "me" but also of his "I." The next section describes certain structured psychological interventions that may be helpful in reducing distress associated with voice-hearing in traumatized persons.

Psychological Treatment of Voice Hearing: Healing the Traumatized "I"

We begin this section with a quotation from "Suzy" regarding how her experience of voice hearing changed over the course of psychotherapy.

"Hearing of the voices—it was a constant droning in your head. It didn't really stop until after the dissociation stopped. It was a process. It was a matter of getting all parts of me working together. And learning to listen to what the voices had to say—not shutting them out because when I wasn't listening—when I wasn't paying attention—they got louder. But as I started to pay attention, as I started to organize things, as I listened, they became quieter. And when the dissociation stopped, it was at that time that the voices really stopped. Because the voices felt listened to. They felt heard. They felt that I was moving in the right direction. So they didn't feel as necessary. But to me those parts of me will always exist within me—they are a part of me—but if I'm doing what I need to do, then the voices are going to be quiet. It's only if I stop listening—if I stop doing the things that I need to do—then the voices are going to get loud again. So, it will be a forever thing, it doesn't just completely go away. They are a part of you—they have been with you forever and a day—they are you."

Structured approaches to trauma therapy commonly include working directly with voices. In general, voices are typically considered "parts of the self," often explicitly the internalized voices of other people with whom the client has had a relationship, or considered to be the person- ified voice of different aspects of the client him- or herself. Many clini- cians believe that, by recognizing voices as such, they can better under- stand their function. That is, on the assumption that there is a reason the voices "exist," identifying and facilitating the adaptive function of the voice may be considered a primary ingredient of therapeutic change (e.g., Schwartz, 1995).

A therapeutic exercise that can be utilized to address voices, frequently used in emotion-focused trauma therapy as developed by Paivio and Pas- cual-Leone (2010), involves empty-chair and two-chair work. In these interventions the client engages in a pseudo-conversation with different parts of him- or herself, such as may be personified by a specific voice(s), as spoken out loud in the presence of a clinician. It is critical, however, that the intervention not serve to further solidify the perceived separate- ness of the client's core self or ego from that of the voice(s), nor further reify the voice as indeed a separate "self." Instead, the intervention has as its goal increasing reflective function and insight concerning the inner conflict and distress the client is experiencing in his or her thoughts and feelings in the service of increased integration, mentalizing, and psycho- logical flexibility.

In the empty-chair intervention, the voice of an internalized "other" is temporarily made an audience. The client envisions the voice occupying a physically empty chair in the therapy office to which she speaks (e.g., communicating the way in which the voice makes her feel when a self-critical voice labels her "dirty," "ruined," "damaged," "less than human," and the like). Typically more effective, however, is a two-chair dialogue wherein the client would subsequently seat herself in the "voice's chair" and express the perspective of the voice in answer to the client's initial statements in a back-and-forth dialogue not unlike a therapeutic role play—an intervention intended to increase perspective taking, reflective function, and mentalizing.

For this intervention to be safe, organized, and therapeutic, however, it is generally accepted that the client must sufficiently exhibit "co-consciousness"; that is, be capable of "listening" to what each part of herself is expressing in each of the two chairs. The intervention is less safely conducted if there is little co-consciousness such that, for example, when the client occupies the voice's chair, she fully assumes that role as her "singular self," thereby becoming so fully absorbed in the exercise that she loses concomitant awareness of the perspective that occupied the previous chair. Ultimately, a back-and-forth conversation can be engaged, as moderated by the clinician, with the intervention always completed with the client seated in her original chair.

If moderated effectively, the intervention can bring insight and understanding into any adaptive purpose that might be served by each voice and therefore reduce the fear, anger/rage, disgust, and shame that may be experienced by one voice for another. Moreover, while continuing to exercise that purpose, the affective quality of the voice might be successfully modulated such that it becomes less distressing and demeaning. For example:

1. "It hurts my feelings when you call me a stupid slut." →
2. "I call you that because you put yourself in risky situations with men, and you disrespect yourself by being with them. It's self-abuse. It is the present now. You no longer have to engage in this type of behavior. We can use your strengths in a way that promotes healing." →
3. "Thank you for caring for my safety. But I don't think I have any strengths." →
4. "I don't agree with you. Given that you were often involved in "turning tricks" [prostitution], it seems to me like you can get through anything if you put your mind to it. What are your thoughts about that?" →
5. "I guess, if you put it that way, it makes sense." →
6. "I know you have a great fear of the unknown, which includes a fear of getting better in therapy. Could you maybe use your strength of being able to get through anything to help your whole self get better in therapy and not sabotage the treatment?" →
7. "OK, I can give that a try."

Audio-recording the intervention for later playback may be helpful, particularly when clinical judgment suggests that co-consciousness is less assured.

An intervention with similar aims to empty-chair and two-chair work is the dissociative table technique developed by George Fraser (2003). This technique has its origins in Gestalt therapy but was adapted for use with severely dissociative patients; it has also been referred to as a boardroom or conference room technique (Ross, 1988). The intervention uses the client's intrinsic capacity for self-hypnosis and begins with a safe place guided imagery exercise followed by imagining different aspects of the self sitting around a table in a safe room where each is respected equally. Communication among the different aspects of the self is then encouraged, provided that an overall sense of safety and security is established. The overarching goal of the exercise is to increase self-reflection, mentalizing, and insight in the service of the client as a whole. Treatment efficacy studies of therapeutic exercises such as the dissociative table technique are needed. The color insert section contains another painting by Gregory, inspired by the use of this therapeutic exercise; he titled the painting "Time" (Figure 4.9; also in color insert).

Finally, voice-hearing groups are also often offered as co-led group psychotherapy, the goal of which is to normalize and decrease distress associated with voice hearing, including by improving the quality of relatedness with voices. By contrast, a goal of the intervention is not necessarily to reduce the frequency of voice hearing. Unfortunately, Ruddle, Mason, and Wykes's (2011) review of the literature found little empirical support for voice-hearing groups, primarily on account of few scientifically rigorous

FIGURE 4.9.   Gregory's Artwork (2010): "Time". Used with permission.

studies having been published to date. The researchers called for a greater number of well-designed studies of efficacy, as well as greater study of therapeutic mechanisms of change.

Beyond Voice Hearing: Visual, Olfactory, and Tactile Pseudohallucinatory Experience

Studies have documented what have been termed *pseudohallucinatory* symptoms (e.g., El-Mallakh & Walker, 2010; Pierre, 2010) in as many as one-fifth to two-thirds of individuals with PTSD, depending on sampling characteristics (for reviews, see Braakman, Kortman, & van den Brink, 2009; Moskowitz & Corstens, 2007; Moskowitz, Read, Farrelly, Rudege-air, & Williams, 2009; Moskowitz, Schäfer, & Dorahy, 2008). Recognizing pseudohallucinatory features dimensionally in individuals with PTSD accords well with the high comorbidity of trauma exposure and PTSD that is observed in individuals with primary psychotic disorders (e.g., Bernard, Jackson, & Jones, 2006; Fuller, 2010; Hardy et al., 2005; Krabbendam, 2008) and the finding that trauma exposure is known to be a risk factor for primary psychotic disorders in large epidemiological studies (e.g., Shevlin, Houston, Dorahy, & Adamson, 2008). That the presence of hallucinations marks a diagnostic subtype for major depression also offers precedent for doing the same in other trauma-related disorders. Nevertheless, it is important not to confuse pseudohallucinations with the experience of flashbacks, given that the latter also commonly involve hallucinatory experience (e.g., Brewin et al., 2010; Hellawell & Brewin, 2004). It is also important to emphasize the nonpsychotic nature of the symptoms; that is, they present as frequent yet transient altered sensory perceptions that are typically associated with high stress. The term *pseudohallucinatory* is thus preferred to *pseudopsychotic* in that the latter might infer the presence of additional features of thought disorder and delusions that are *not* evident and might represent appropriate grounds for differential diagnosis with psychotic disorders (e.g., Hamner, Frueh, Ulmer, & Arana, 1999).

For example, whereas Hamner and colleagues (2000) observed equivalently clinically severe auditory hallucinations in combat veterans with PTSD and in individuals with schizophrenia, those with schizophrenia were distinguished only by blatantly delusional thinking and thought disorder. Sautter and colleagues (1999) obtained similar findings when comparing people with PTSD with pseudohallucinations and a mixed group of individuals diagnosed with schizophrenia, schizoaffective disorder, or major depression with psychotic features. In any event, the *pseudo* label prefacing each term is intended to differentiate the symptoms from bona fide signs of psychosis. By contrast, the term is not intended to denote "not real"; care should be taken to ensure that patients do not mistake use of the term, as this can be invalidating of their subjective experience. The phenomena recognized under the rubric of pseudohallucinatory features most commonly include voice hearing, as has been discussed previously, but also include other altered sensory perceptions such as transient visual, olfactory, and tactile hallucinations.

In comparison with experiences of voice hearing, the phenomenology of other types of pseudohallucinations has been less well explored in association with trauma exposure. In our own clinical assessments, conducted predominantly with women with childhood trauma-related PTSD, prototypic reports include seeing or feeling "bugs crawling" upon or beneath one's skin, seeing mice or cockroaches run across the floor, and smelling things that other people cannot, such as feces, urine, body odor, or smoke. Tactile hallucinations may also be experienced as physical numbness of certain body sensations, most often in the hands (e.g., not being able to feel one's hands, often accompanied by a feeling of detachment and disownership that one's hands are not one's own; we typically would label such symptoms as signs of depersonalization rather than pseudohallucination, however). Participants also frequently report feeling dirty from the *inside*—that is, not just on the skin but that their internal viscera have somehow been soiled or fouled. The experience is especially prominent in the case of multiple incest wherein it often seems to represent the physical, embodied counterpart to severe shame as exemplified by experiencing oneself as "dirty" and "defiled." These experiences are frequent causes of self-harm. Olfactory hallucinations typically are linked to the content of traumatic events but should be classified as such only when occurring outside of the recognized experience of a flashback. Thus, for example, participants may experience the strong scent of cigarettes or of gasoline, at times when others do not. Although these stimuli may be historically significant for them (e.g., associated with an abuser), their awareness of them in these instances may not necessarily bring about fear or reexperiencing.

In general agreement with these clinical impressions, Teicher and colleagues (1997) suggested that pseudohallucinatory-like symptoms may be evidence of limbic system and temporal lobe dysfunction in chronically traumatized persons, based on the fact that similar experiences are frequently reported by patients suffering from temporal lobe epilepsy (e.g., Teicher, Glod, Surrey, & Swett, 1993). Moreover, Teicher and colleagues have shown that pseudohallucinatory symptoms correlate with dissociative experiences and that individuals with histories of early life trauma often show nonspecific temporal lobe abnormalilites on EEG (Teicher et al., 1997). In addition to being associated with EEG temporal lobe abnormalities, dissociation has also been associated with altered activation of the temporal lobe as assessed by functional neuroimaging (e.g., Simeon et al., 2000; Lanius et al., 2002; Hopper, Frewen, van der Kolk,, et al., 2007; Reinders et al., 2006; Sar, Unal, & Ozturk, 2007; Saxe, Vasile,

Hill, Bloomingdale, & van der Kolk, et al., 1992). It is interesting to note in this regard that Penfield and Rasmussen (1950) also reported dissocia- tive (e.g., depersonalization) symptoms in response to stimulation of the superior and middle temporal gyri during neurosurgery.

Future research should further explore the association of the temporal lobe with altered sensory perceptions such as transient visual, olfactory, and tactile hallucinations in traumatized persons. Such research could have important implications for the differential diagnosis of traumatized individ- uals who often present with complex symptom pictures. Symptoms of tem- poral lobe abnormality include (1) olfactory illusions/hallucinations (e.g., smelling things that other people can't smell, such as feces, urine, rot, body odor, or smoke); (2) gustatory illusions/hallucinations (e.g., bad taste in mouth, such as a metallic taste, which may come and go for no known rea- son); (3) visual illusions/hallucinations (e.g., seeing things in one's periphe- ral vision, such as stars, bugs, mice, worms, threads); (4) illusion of move- ment (e.g., sensing movement in the peripheral vision); (5) haptic illusions/ hallucinations (e.g., feeling as though bugs are crawling on the body or that something is brushing up against the skin, such as a cobweb); (6) episodic tinnitus (e.g., ringing, buzzing, rushing, or tapping noise in the ears which comes and goes for no known reason) (Roberts et al., 1990). The following provides a clinical example of pseudohallucinations.

Case 1: "Multisensory TRASC and Pseudohallucinations in Lori"

The case of "Lori," a 48-year-old woman who described a complex history of hearing voices in addition to a host of other pseudohallucinatory expe- riences, provides an opportunity to consider the differential diagnosis of pseudohallucinatory symptomatology associated with TRASC from that associated with bona fide psychosis.

Lori presented with an extensive history of childhood sexual and physi- cal abuse, which occurred at the hands of a school janitor and several male neighbors between the ages of 4 and 18. Lori also reported that she was emotionally and physically abused and neglected by her mother. Lori was in an emotionally and physically abusive marriage at the time of assess- ment and had three adolescent/young-adult children (ages 15, 18, and 22 years). Lori was financially supported through her husband's income and her own disability payments. She had worked as a nurse until she became ill 15 years prior to the assessment. Since that time Lori has had over 50 psychiatric admissions lasting from 3 days to 6 months.

Over this period Lori was diagnosed with multiple psychiatric disorders, including schizoaffective disorder, bipolar disorder, major depression, anxiety disorder, borderline personality disorder, and schizotypal person- ality disorder. She endorsed symptoms of dysthymia throughout most of her life that were interspersed with periods of major depression lasting from several weeks to months, during which she was effectively incapacitated. Lori said that she often felt that she was on "an emotional roller-coaster," as she had no control over her emotions. In addition, she complained about intense anger that she usually directed at herself through acts of self-cutting or burning. This self-inflicted injury was not done with the intention of gaining others' attention nor as an attempt to kill herself. Rather, she hurt herself with the explicit sense that she was "bad" and "deserved punishment." She also sometimes found herself spending excessive amounts of money when she felt particularly bad about herself. However, she denied experiencing prolonged periods (more than 1 or 2 days) of increased energy or mania and denied requiring less sleep during such periods. Furthermore, she did not have a family history of bipolar disorder. Her shifts in mood occurred over the course of minutes rather than days or weeks. She was therefore not considered to have bipolar disorder. Lori further reported no present or past problems with substance abuse. She was referred to a trauma specialty clinic for diagnosis and treatment after her therapist recognized that Lori had a history of chronic, severe, unresolved trauma that seemed to be preventing her from stabilizing in the general psychiatric treatments she had been receiving before that time.

Upon assessment, Lori endorsed severe reexperiencing, avoidance, and hyperarousal symptoms consistent with a diagnosis of PTSD. She was plagued by recurrent visual, auditory, and somatosensory flashbacks during which she felt like she was reliving her past traumatic experiences. Lori also endorsed the presence of panic attacks that occurred at least twice weekly; her panic attacks were usually triggered by reminders of past abuse and were classified among the reexperiencing symptoms of PTSD accordingly. Furthermore, Lori suffered from classic signs of dissociation, for example, reporting that she would "lose time" (not be able to recall what she had done for an hour or more) several times per week, as well as sometimes fail to recognize herself when looking in mirrors.

Lori reported hearing five different voices "fighting" inside of her head on a nearly ongoing basis. She stated that one of the voices appeared to be childlike and that she could often hear the voice crying. She also reported hearing a self-critical voice that repeatedly shouted: "You are so stupid! You can't do anything right!" Yet another voice occasionally provided reassurance to Lori, in her words by "getting things done." Finally, in comparison, Lori was unable to characterize the nature of two other voices, explaining that often "things get so loud in my head that I can barely stand it." Beyond voice hearing, Lori reported additional experiences that were also considered pseudohallucinatory in nature. She saw bugs in her peripheral vision at least once a day; however, when she looked over to see the bugs more closely, they would disappear. She also often felt the sensation of bugs crawling on her skin.

Lori was administered the Structured Clinical Interview for DSM–I/II/D (SCID-I, SCID-II, SCID-D) and the Clinician-Administered PTSD Scale (CAPS) and was considered to meet criteria for five diagnoses: PTSD, major depressive disorder (recurrent), dysthymia, borderline personality disorder, and dissociative disorder not otherwise specified. In the absence of evidence of other psychotic symptoms, including delusions, thought insertion/withdrawal, thought broadcasting, or ideas of reference, and in the presence of insight into the unusual nature of her experiences, Lori was not considered to meet diagnostic criteria for a psychotic disorder. Indeed, emerging theory suggests that persons with depersonalization disorder evidence much of the phenomenology previously thought to be unique to schizophrenia (Sass, Pienkos, Nelson, & Medford, 2013). Lori further underwent an EEG, which showed no evidence of temporal lobe epilepsy.

Discontinuous Plots: The Structure of Traumatized Narratives

James's (1890) famous *stream of consciousness* described the temporal flow of thought as normally continuous and nonrandom (intelligible). As discussed in Chapter 3, rather than a disjointed series of discrete moments in time, we tend to experience events with a sense of continuity, as if seamlessly flowing through an immediate past, present, and anticipated future. Similarly, we have discussed the likening of consciousness to a story that is logically sequenced; our stories normally have an obvious beginning-middle-end structure, the endings then equally marking the beginning of the next moment or "story."

However, as reviewed below, clinical studies suggest that, in traumatized persons, traumatic memories, as well as their present day-to-day conscious experiences, not only include negative self-referential content but also often exhibit significant disorganization. The "stories" of traumatic memories, in particular, are often both experienced and told as a scattered array of sensory fragments and flashes of emotional feeling. These stories may include little background information and often lack coherence or temporal flow. Moreover, in the complexly traumatized person, life's everyday moments are often constructed quite similarly. Some traumatized persons' storied experiences are highly confused, disordered, and chaotic.

As an analogy for the structure of traumatized narrative experience, one should not picture a fallen leaf floating atop of James's gentle stream of consciousness, following an organized current to a meaningful destination. Instead we might imagine hands desperately clinging to a broken raft as it is tossed about in violent, turbulent waters. In narratives of trauma, we frequently crash against jarring waves of fear, disgust, guilt, shame, and anger. We may funnel through dark oceans of missing time, with islands of coherence and insight being few and far between. Rarely do we come to any conclusion that brings clarity or a sense of completion. With only a broken raft to hold onto, there is an ever-present risk of letting go and drowning, sinking deeper and deeper. For the complexly traumatized person, experience and traumatic memories have a certain undertow. They take hold of consciousness in a forceful way. As the memory or dissociative process takes hold, consciousness is submerged, and we are momentarily but seemingly forever without breath.

Groundbreaking studies by van der Kolk and Fisler (1995) and Foa and her colleagues (Foa, Molnar, et al., 1995) established objectively that the retelling of traumatic memories by traumatized persons with PTSD often fails to exhibit a coherent narrative structure. As determined by their Traumatic Memory Interview, 11% of the individuals evaluated by van der Kolk and Fisler were "unable to tell a coherent narrative [of their trauma] with a beginning, middle, and end" (p. 517). Furthermore, consistent with the assumption of our 4-D model that narrative disorganization is indicative of a TRASC of thought, van der Kolk and Fisler found that the tendency to be unable to provide a coherent narrative of trauma memories was moderately correlated with individual differences in trait dissociation. As observed by van der Kolk and Fisler, traumatic events were retold in a way that emphasized fragmented and disjointed sensory descriptions that were considered to mirror the format in which the traumatic memory itself may have been encoded.

Foa, Molnar, et al. (1995) similarly developed a systematic narrative coding scheme to investigate the organizational structure of traumatic memories. Their approach included coding the frequency of "fragmentation" as reflecting "lack of flow in the narrative; the coding system consisted of repetitions, unfinished thoughts and speech fillers" and "disorganized thoughts" as implying confusion or disjointed thinking (e.g., "I don't know what happened until . . . ") (p. 684). Foa and colleagues examined change in narrative structure that occurred over the course of exposure treatment. Using prolonged exposure therapy, they observed that lessened fragmentation of the trauma narrative was correlated with improved anxiety symptoms, and increased organization of the narrative was associated with improved depressive symptoms.

Many studies examining the structure of trauma narratives have been conducted since van der Kolk and Fisler's (1995) and Foa, Molnar, et al.'s (1995) landmark observations (see reviews by Brewin, 2011; O'Kearney & Perrott, 2006; Rubin, 2011). Research implementing variations on Foa and colleagues' original methodology has reliably uncovered the disorganized nature of traumatic event narratives in individuals with PTSD (Halligan, Fink, Marshall, & Vallar, 2003; Jelinek, Ranjbar, Seifert, Kellner, & Moritz, 2009; Jelinek et al., 2010; Jones, Harvey, & Brewin, 2007). Jelinek and colleagues (2009) showed that greater narrative disorganization is specific to trauma narratives and is not common to other generally unpleasant (but not traumatic) memories in individuals with PTSD, despite the fact that traumatized persons perceived both their traumatic and nontraumatic (generally unpleasant) memories to be disorganized. A follow-up report by Jelinek and colleagues (2010) further suggested that narrative disorganization is greatest during the perceived "worst moments" of the trauma narrative, concurrent with a greater sense of reliving during trauma recall (as identified by greater use of the present tense within the narrative; Jelinek et al., 2010; see also Ehlers, Hackman, & Michael, 2004).

O'Kearney and colleagues applied novel methodologies derived from autobiographical memory research and linguistics analyses to the investigation of trauma narratives (O'Kearney, Hunt, & Wallace, 2011). The first measure used by O'Kearney and colleagues was labeled "narrative cohesion" and was operationalized as the objective frequency of connections between sentences and clauses that established spatiotemporal cohesion (e.g., "*After* he hit me, I . . ."), causal cohesion (e.g., "I knew I had to do what he said *because* if I didn't . . ."), additive relations (e.g., "He held me down *and* choked me"), or comparative relations (e.g., "He said he would't hurt me, *but* . . ."). The second measure was labeled "narrative coherence" and evaluated the degree to which participants' narratives established a coherent story with a beginning, middle, and end. Narrative coherence was rated on a 6-point scale ranging from stories that were evidently so "disoriented that the listener is unable to understand" or "impoverished—consisting of too few sentences for a pattern to be recognized" to those that were more chronologically structured, integrated, and mature ("the narrative builds to a high point, dwells on it, and then resolves it") (p. 718).

In contrast with prior studies, O'Kearney et al. did not find significant differences between the narratives of traumatic versus nontraumatic negative events. However, they found that greater use of causal connectives in the trauma narrative was associated with less frequent intrusive and avoidance symptoms. O'Kearney pointed out, however, that the sample they studied had not experienced a particularly high severity or frequency of trauma exposure or symptoms. The methodologically sophisticated approach used by O'Kearney et al. should therefore be replicated in samples of participants with more chronic trauma histories and clinically significant dissociative symptoms. In addition, the researchers examined linguistic and rater measures of coherence within entire traumatic memories rather than focusing on specific "hot spots" in the narrative that might have exhibited greater disorganization.

Levine and colleagues developed the Autobiographical Interview as one way to systematically assess the structural components of episodic memory, such as the unfolding across semidiscrete moments in time (Levine, Svoboda, Hay, Winocur, & Moscovitch, 2002). This interview requires participants to select and describe an event in free form, including any and all components of the memory that can be expressed. Specific event details are then quantified from the transcribed protocol by researchers, with a particular goal to distinguish between those evident of semantic versus episodic autobiographical memory.

Semantic autobiographical memory refers to the *knowledge* that something happened, but is not associated with a phenomenological experience of it. For example, one might know that one walked to work this morning, but not have sufficient experiential clarity of the memory so as to be able to *replay* the experience again in one's mind. In comparison, *episodic autobiographical memory* is often referred to as the *feeling* and *inner experience* of knowing something happened. In other words, episodic autobiographical memory tends to involve remembering in the form of reexperiencing the memory to some extent (Tulving, 2005; but also see Chapter 3 on the consciousness of time for a discussion of the phenomenological difference between remembering and reliving). Episodic memory has been referred to as "mental time travel" back to the memory such that one experiences it again in a way that is relatively faithful to the original experience, inclusive of sensory and emotional detail (e.g., Levine, 2004; Tulving, 2005).

In order to obtain episodic autobiographical reports, clinicians and researchers administering the Autobiographical Interview are required to probe for sensory and affective detail, explaining to participants that they are "trying to get a picture of the event in my own mind." Requests for sensory detail may include perceived colors, sounds, smells, tastes, physical sensations, and how other people (if present) looked. Requests for embodied spatial details may include how one was physically positioned (e.g., standing/sitting/ kneeling/laying), including one's position in relation to others, thus taking into account the embodied perspective of the experience. Finally, requests for emotional details may include asking about what one was thinking and/or feeling at different points in time over the course of the event, and whether one has the sense that additional things had occurred but cannot be recalled. The assessing clinician-researcher also asks whether the event was experienced from a field or observer perspective. In *field* perspective, a person experiences events in the first person, as if he or she were *a part of* what was happening. In comparison, in *observer* perspective, a person experiences events as if an outside or detached observer of them, as one who is *not part of* what is happening. For our purposes, the terms *field* versus *observer* perspective fully overlap with *first-* versus *third*-person, and *centered* versus *decentered* perspectives, respectively.

We are currently using the Autobiographical Interview in a neuroimaging study examining the nature of traumatic memories in a combat-exposed military sample. The following excerpt from a participant who was encouraged to tell the story of his comrades getting hurt after being exposed to an explosion is an example of the fragmentation and disorganization of traumatic memory:

"I remember the taste and smell of the sand. I can still taste it today. The heat—it was incredible. The smell of the blood and the stretchers all over the place. The faces of my buddies—the pain they were in. We were trying to get back to the base. I can't really remember what happened then. I kept thinking about my close buddy—would he make it? And then the sand—it felt like it was all over my face."

Unfortunately, neuroimaging studies using the trauma script-driven imagery methodology have not examined in detail the narrative structure of scripts. Generally scripts are constructed so as to contain little introductory exposition, instead detailing nearly exclusively the "worst moments" and ending at the climactic points of the traumatic event. Moreover, clinicians typically narrate the scripts, likely providing a coherence of spatiotemporal and causal structure that may exceed that of the memory as it is actually encoded. Previous studies using the trauma script-driven imagery methodology have primarily investigated the nature of symptom provocation, principally with regard to emotionality and hyperarousal, and secondarily as regarding the experience of reliving (flashbacks). As such, studies have not directly addressed the neural correlates of the disorganized structure of trauma narratives; this is a much needed future research direction.

In summary, in extreme cases the fragmented nature of traumatic narratives suggests a dissociative process (van der Kolk & Fisler, 1995). Nevertheless, current evidence for the dissociative nature of narrative fragmentation remains anecdotal, for the most part. The 4-D model considers only extreme instances of narrative disorganization to be unequoivacal indicators of a TRASC of thought. Further neurophenomenological study is needed before the hypothesis can be considered substantiated.

Healing Narrative Disorganization in Traumatic Memories

Traditional cognitive-behavioral therapy and narrative therapies for PTSD may increase narrative organization via the repeated telling of trauma narratives (e.g., Foa, Molnar, et al., 1995). It may be helpful for some clients to explicitly chart timelines of any traumatic events that they experience as particularly disorganized within the context of a narrative approach to exposure therapy and meaning making. Use of a timeline forces adherence to a linear beginning-middle-end structure, and "blank spots" in memories are accordingly made explicit. Encouraging clients to indicate the occurrence of emotional "hot spots" and "worst moments" can also be helpful. More specifically, clients can be directed to imagine that they have a television remote control wand in their hand and that they can replay, pause, rewind, or play the memory in slow motion or black and white whenever they want to clarify what occurred. This technique can also sometimes bring about a greater sense of control that is often found to be therapeutic. Crucial markers of healing in trauma therapy include greater organization and less emotional dysregulation during the retelling of trauma memories. An example of this intervention is given in Figure 4.10.

In addition to creating a trauma memory timeline for specific traumatic memories, it can also be helpful to engage the client in creating a "lifeline exercise" described as part of narrative exposure therapy (Schauer, Neuner, & Elbert, 2005). This exercise involves examining all the major positive and negative life events that have occurred across a person's lifespan in chronological order. The client is encouraged to draw a line symbolizing his or her life, with the beginning (left end) of the line marking the client's birth. The client is then asked to mark each positive and negative event in chronological order with a symbol of choice; for example,

Trauma Memory Timeline

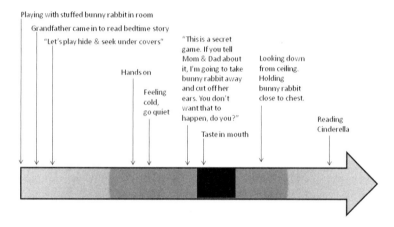

FIGURE 4.10. A Sample Reflective Exercise Involving Recall of a Trauma Narrative.

The trauma memory timeline can be used as an aid to the working through of a memory of childhood sexual abuse. Downward arrows denote the approximate points in time specifying particular moments in the overall memory. Spans of missing time in the memory are evident between the large spaces sometimes occurring between arrows. Shading of the horizontal arrow signifies emotional "hot spots" in the memory. With traditional trauma-focused exposure and narrative therapy, the "rest" of the story might be filled in, with attention to thoughts, feelings, and sensations.

a rock might be used for negative experiences and a butterfly for positive experiences. Each event is discussed as the client marks it on the "lifeline." This exercise can serve as an important tool for identifying some of the key negative and positive experiences in a client's life. Identifying positive experiences is particularly helpful for clients who have a history of prolonged childhood trauma and significant symptoms of dissociation that prevent them from being able to recall their life as an organized narrative inclusive of positive events.

Case 2: Working with Dissociative Voices to Increase Inner Security and Self-Compassion

Gregory, first introduced in Chapter 2, is a 58-year-old man who described a history of being plagued by "voices screaming inside my head." Gregory described a lifelong experience of hearing a child's voice crying inconsolably. In addition, he often reported hearing an adult voice screaming "Shut up! I hope you die!" In his mind, the voices also had accompanying images. Despite hearing these voices, Gregory showed no signs of thought disorder or delusions.

Gregory regarded the child voice to represent a child part of himself who believed that he was still living in the past, being abused by his parents and grandparents. He described this "inner child" as feeling helpless and in despair, just as he had when he was being abused as a young boy. On the other hand, Gregory reported that the adult voice expressed progressive intolerance of the child because the child exemplified a reminder of difficult past experiences. Gregory was asked whether he could visualize the adult and child communicating together to integrate each point of view, considering whether each voice might serve an adaptive purpose. He was able to do so, but initially only felt comfortable if the child and adult were "across the room from each other—not communicating." Nevertheless, engaging in this imagery exercise led to Gregory feeling significantly less inner tension over time, and he noticed that the frequency of his voice hearing decreased whenever he practiced the exercise. Moreover, with time, Gregory was able to imagine the adult and child senses of himself moving increasingly closer together and even communicating verbally. For example, he imagined the adult voice communicating to the child that "The past is over. You are safe now. Things will be OK." This coincided with the voices' decreased intrusion on Gregory, who commented: "They are no longer screaming; I feel much calmer inside."

As communication between the adult and child voices continued to progress, Gregory began to feel much more compassionate toward himself and more deserving of engaging in positive activities, including painting and spending time in the woods—two of Gregory's favorite pas-

FIGURE 4.11.   Gregory's Artwork (2009): "Adult and Child." Used with permission.

times. Gregory painted an image representing the newfound relationship between the adult and child senses of himself (Figure 4.11; also in color insert). He has noted that looking at this painting helps him feel more kindness toward himself. He often uses the picture as a coping resource in times of distress.

Summary

In this chapter we likened conscious experience to a story told in the first person. We considered three ways in which the narrative consciousness of traumatized persons can be altered: in terms of (1) content, (2) narrative perspective (i.e., first vs. second person), and (3) organization (i.e., the "plot" of the story). We reviewed studies showing that a frequent outcome of traumatic stressors involves an alteration of trauma survivors' inner worlds. Traumatized persons commonly report negative self-referential thoughts, often related to self-defining memories. Nevertheless, so long as a person's thoughts exhibit the quality of first-person narrative perspective, the 4-D model suggests that these experiences, although intrusive and distressing, are not necessarily indicative of a TRASC of thought. However, when thoughts are experienced from the second-person perspective as the personified voices of others, the 4-D model classifies a person as experiencing a TRASC of thought.

We reviewed research studies documenting that many psychologically traumatized persons experience such voices, which often seem to "address" them in ways resembling how they were treated in the past. We also reviewed the results of neuroimaging studies of SRP and voice hearing, which further suggest that the experience of first-person thinking in comparison with second-person voice hearing may emanate from distinct neurophysiological processes. In addition, we overviewed the literature examining narrative disorganization in trauma memories. It has been noted that traumatic memories and everyday experiences are often significantly disorganized in traumatized persons, which may also be considered indicative of a TRASC of thought. We briefly overviewed other pseudohallucinatory experiences commonly reported by severely traumatized persons, further indicative of TRASC, and considered the experienced division of consciousness into multiple senses of agency and selfhood as the basis of dissociative identity disorder. Finally, we considered certain structured psychological interventions that may be helpful in reducing distress and normalizing TRASC of thought in complexly traumatized persons.

CHAPTER 5

Consciousness of the Body

Depersonalization and Derealization— When the World is Strange, and the Body is Estranged

"The body keeps the score."

—Bessel van der Kolk (1994, p. 253)

"Whatever happens in your mind happens in time and in space relative to the instant in time your body is in and to the region of space occupied by your body. . . . Moreover, experiential perspective not only helps situate real objects but also helps situate ideas. . . . Ownership and agency are, likewise, entirely related to a body at a particular instant and in a particular space."

—Antonio Damasio (1999, p. 145)[1]

"The discrete out-of-body experience is the experience where subjects perceive themselves as experientially located at some other location than where they know their physical body to be . . . [while] the concepts of space, time, and location [continue to] make sense. Further, there is a feeling of having no contact with the physical body, a feeling of temporary disconnection from it."

Charles Tart (1998, p. 77)[2]

F EW WESTERN CULTURES BY now disagree that mind and body are linked within *physical* space. Our experience of mind comes out of the brain, which is of course situated within the body as a whole. Clearly there also

[1]Excerpt from *The Feeling of What Happens: Body and Emotion in the Making of Consciousness* by Antonio Damasio. Copyright © 1999 by Antonio Damasio. Reproduced by permission of Houghton Mifflin Harcourt Publishing Company. All rights reserved.

[2]Reprinted from *Journal of Near-Death Studies*, Vol. 17, Issue 2, Charles T. Tart, "Six Studies of Out-of-Body Experiences," p. 77, June 1998, with permission from Springer.

exist abstract conceptions of the self that allow for forms of experience and existence, and senses of ownership and agency, that extend beyond the physical limits of our individual bodies. Ready examples include those that broaden the concept of self via an affiliation with a social collective (e.g., family, nationality) as well as the notion central to many religions that we are fundamentally a spiritual essence, and that our consciousness will survive the death of our humanly bodies. But in keeping with biology and setting aside for now abstract psychological, social, and religious notions of the self, we cannot help but find that, in the most primordial sense, who we are is essentially bounded by our skin.

As Damasio (1999) suggests, however, physical space is not the only way wherein mind, body, and self are intertwined. Mind, body, and self are also linked within *experiential* space as well: The notion that our sense of self is *embodied* asserts that our conscious experiences are fundamentally oriented *in relation to* our bodies. Normally, our experience is revealed to us as if emanating from a place within our physical selves. Providing we, as a conscious species, tend to self-identify with our thoughts (e.g., Descartes' "I think, therefore I am"), we in turn normally claim our bodies as our own; that is, we experience a sense of ownership over our bodies. Usually it seems to us that *our minds are where our bodies are*; we consequently refer to our bodies as *me* and *mine*.

In this chapter, however, we explore ways in which the normal marriage between self-referential experience and the body can be divorced in response to psychological trauma. The phenomenological outcome of this division is that people experience themselves as separate from their bodies, and their bodies, in full or in part, as something other than themselves. Such experiences are commonly reported in chronically traumatized persons, especially during times of acute hyperarousal, hypoarousal, or affective distress; in psychiatric nomenclature these phenomena are termed *depersonalization* and *conversion* symptoms (i.e., neurological-like symptoms without known neurological origin), whereas others, including Charles Tart (1998) as quoted above, call them *out-of-body experiences*.

Figure 5.1 highlights the dimension of the consciousness of embodiment in the 4-D model. Simply put, the 4-D model asserts that distress accompanied by the disembodiment of consciousness occurs most plainly in full "out-of-body experiences" and certain other partial-bodily forms of depersonalization and conversion (e.g., limb disownership and paralysis). The 4-D model suggests that these trauma-related altered states of consciousness (TRASC) of the body should be distinguished from comparably simpler states (i.e., phenomenologically) of subjective bodily referred distress that are assumed to maintain the normal waking consciousness (NWC) of the body (i.e., forms of physiological hyper-/hypoarousal such as the embodied awareness of increased or decreased heart rate or breath-

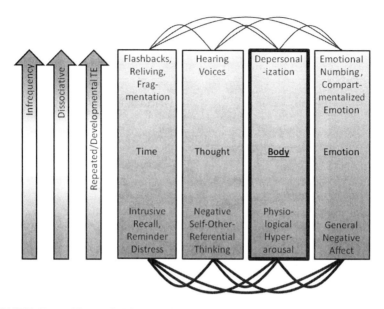

FIGURE 5.1. The 4-D Model of the Traumatized Self Highlighting NWC Distress versus TRASC of the Body. TE = trauma exposure.

ing). We also discuss psychotherapeutic exercises that may help alleviate TRASC of the body, herein primarily based on mindfulness practices, particularly the "body-scan" exercise developed within mindfulness-based stress reduction (Kabat-Zinn, 1990). Finally, we provide case examples of TRASC of the body throughout the chapter.

This chapter reviews research investigating depersonalized states wherein the sense of self and the body are experientially separated. These phenomena have only recently entered mainstream neuroscience, particularly as they have been shown to be evoked by experimental manipulations in healthy individuals via multisensory perceptual illusions and hypnotic suggestion, and research has begun to identify their neural correlates. We review neurophenomenological studies that substantiate these experiences as common outcomes of psychological trauma. We also discuss the related experience of derealization wherein the world around oneself seems strange or unreal.

Mind in Body: The Conscious Embodiment of Thought, Feeling, and Action

We have already seen that, for most of us, except perhaps the odd skeptic philosopher or enlightened Buddhist monk, conscious experience is intrinsically referential. It normally seems to us that we *own* our thoughts, feelings, and behavior. In essence, normally we perceive the existence of an "I" who is *having* each experience. We have the experience that these are *our* thoughts, feelings, and behavior—that this is *our* experience. Consciousness, as such, intrinsically couples experiential events to a sense of *self* or *ego*.

Recent experiments in normal subjects suggest that the binding between a perceiving subject and that person's conscious perceptions, as intrinsic to normal phenomenal experience, may be partly mediated by the "embodiment" of cognition and self-representation (Tsakiris, Schütz-Bosbach, & Gallagher, 2007; Tsakiris, 2010). As used here, the notion of embodiment asserts that, in a state of normal waking consciousness (NWC), the human brain is designed to have the expectation and ongoing sense that thoughts, feelings, and actions emanate from a place inside the physical self. In other words, within our experience is embedded a source signal, defined in an egocentric space: We believe that *we are where our experiences seem to come from.*

If this is true, then creating the false impression that our sensory experiences emanate from a place outside their true source should displace the sense of ourselves to the location of the illusory source. Experiments in psychology and neuroscience have indeed shown this to be the case. Altered perceptions have been induced "bottom-up," via multisensory illusions, as well as via hypnotic suggestion, which may implicate "top-down" processes.

Disembodying from the Bottom Up: Multisensory Perceptual Illusions

Probably the best-known experimental manipulation for inducing the sense of disembodiment from the bottom up is the so-called *rubber-hand illusion*. This illusion involves simultaneously rubbing a person's actual hand that is hidden from his or her view while rubbing a fake rubber hand that is fully within view: The resulting experience is that the person adopts the rubber hand as if it were his or her actual hand (Botvinick & Cohen, 1998). The rubber-hand illusion thus creates a momentary distortion in physical body schema that has been examined in detail via phenomenological and psychometric methods (Lewis & Lloyd, 2010; Longo, Schüür, Kammers, Tsakiris, & Haggard, 2008) and has been shown to impact basic physiological processing in the real hand (e.g., temperature regulation; Moseley et al., 2008). Importantly, the confusion that arises as a result of the rubber-hand illusion is therefore not merely a purely cognitive and conceptual one but one that is instead mediated from the bottom up by an embodied *felt sense*: We don't just *think* the rubber hand is ours, we *feel* it (Kikyo, Ohki, & Miyashita, 2002).

Subsequent studies demonstrate that experiences accompanying the rubber-hand illusion can also be elicited by multisensory manipulations to other body parts as well. Among the most impressive, Sforza and colleagues extended the phenomenon to self-face recognition (Sforza, Bufalari, Haggard, & Aglioti, 2010). In Sforza et al.'s experiment, participants who experienced facial tactile stimulation (paintbrush stroking the cheek) simultaneous with viewing another individual receiving the same touch were more likely to regard self–other morphed facial photographs as fully themselves and report experiences like "I felt as if the other's face was my face" (altered facial ownership, p. 152) and "It seemed as though the touch I felt was caused by the paintbrush touching the other's face" (altered referred sensation, p. 152); Sforza and colleagues referred to their illusion as *enfacement* (p. 154).

Although in the rubber-hand and enfacement illusions participants are passively oriented toward experiences, a sense of agency (perceived control over bodily actions) can also be induced over non-self (e.g., robotic) objects when object movements are synchronous with willed bodily movement. The latter was demonstrated by systematically varying (1) the relative timing, (i.e., synchronous versus asynchronous) of finger movements in the real and the rubber hand, (2) the mode of movement (active vs. passive), and (3) the manner of movement (active vs. passive). Results showed that asynchrony of movement abolished both the sense of ownership and agency. In contrast, passive movements eliminated the sense of agency but preserved the sense of ownership, whereas incongruent positioning of the rubber hand decreased the sense of ownership but left the sense of agency intact. Peoples' experience of ownership over objects as part of their physical selves, and their sense of agency in being able to enact behaviors and perform actions via the object, have therefore been suggested to be independent conscious cognitive processes (Kalckert & Ehrsson, 2012). In addition, whereas the aforementioned manipulations merely displace part of the physical self to a working equivalent non-self object, alternative manipulations can even *extend* the physical body (e.g., the stroking of two external arms simultaneous to stroking a participant's arm causes him or her to experience him- or herself as having a second right arm; Ehrsson, 2009) or *subtract from it* (e.g., the stroking of a mannequin at the position of its missing hand causes participants to experience themselves as if they too are missing the analogous limb; Schmalzl & Ehrsson, 2011a, 2011b).

Nevertheless, it is important to point out that, in none of the aforementioned illusions was the perceived physical location of the self *itself* significantly displaced. For example, participants in Sforza et al.'s (2010) enfacement experiment did *not* readily endorse statements such as "It felt as if my face were drifting towards the other's face" or "It seemed as if the touch I was feeling came from somewhere between my own face and the other's face" (p. 152). These experiences thus involve only partial or semidisembodiment; in the aforementioned experiments peoples' sense of themselves maintained connection with their body core, even if part of their body was perceived to be displaced in physical space or distorted in image or shape.

The feeling of full out-of-body experiences, however, has also been successfully induced by perceptual illusions, achieved most clearly in experiments conducted by Ehrsson (2007) and others (cf. Lenggenhager, Tadi, Metzinger, & Blanke, 2007; Lenggenhager, Mouthon, & Blanke, 2009). In Ehrsson's original experiment, participants viewed a real-time video feed of themselves from cameras placed 2 meters behind them, during which their chest was stroked with a rod by an experimenter positioned within the view of their video feed, while at the same time the experimenter stroked the camera in the would-be position of their chest if they had occupied the physical location of the camera. The subjective effect of this manipulation was for participants to experience themselves as if at the position of the cameras, thus fully displacing both their physical and subjective senses of self 2 meters behind their actual position.

A variant of this illusion, referred to as the *body-swap illusion*, causes participants to transpose their sense of self to that of a mannequin; that is, participants are able to "sense" touches applied to the body of a mannequin and consequently experience this body as if it is their own (Petkova & Ehrsson, 2008; Petkova, Knoshnevis, & Ehrsson, 2012). This illusion has been repeatedly elicited in healthy individuals through observations of the artificial body via head-mounted displays connected to video cameras placed on the mannequin's head. The camera is positioned in such a way that participants see the mannequin's body in the would-be position where they would normally see their own body, depending on head orientation. Following this visual manipulation, the body-swap illusion is induced by applying identical synchronous touches to the body of the mannequin and the participant. Alongside these experiences comes the sense of disownership of participants' actual bodies during an out-of-body illusion. Strikingly, such out-of-body illusions have proved strong enough to reduce objective physiological distress induced by threatening participants' actual bodies with a knife (Guterstam & Ehrsson, 2012). Evidently, participants come to believe that the knife, which in actuality represents a potential direct physical threat, is of less personal concern when depicted as attacking their actual self, based upon the experimentally induced faulty assumption that the person they are seeing is no longer themselves (Guterstam & Ehrsson, 2012).

Hypnotic Suggestion: Disembodying from the Top Down?

The multisensory technique of simultaneous visual and tactile stimulation utilized in the brushing methods described previously can be considered a bottom-up approach to altering the phenomenology of embodiment. This is because it is possible to change bodily felt experience by modifying participants' incoming sensations. In effect, these manipulations strikingly reveal how tactile stimulation of the body, with accompanying plausible congruent visual perception, can manipulate the mind–brain and in turn significantly alter the embodied experience of the self.

In comparison, hypnosis represents a long-established approach also widely known to be capable of evoking significant distortions in the felt sense of the embodied self. In the case of hypnosis, bodily felt experience is altered not via afferent pathways from the periphery (sensation) but instead presumably by central efferent ones (i.e., suggestion). Thus in hypnosis the mind is manipulated directly, with effects on how the body is subsequently experienced, either represented centrally only or having downstream effects on the periphery via efferent pathways that are yet to be fully understood.

The present text is not the place to review the rich yet equally controversial clinical and scientific history of hypnosis as a consciousness-altering experimental methodology or treatment; the interested reader is directed to Spiegel and Spiegel's (2004) classic text *Trance and Treatment*. In comparison, we offer a brief glance at some of the most recent literature. Specifically, it would be amiss to fail to note the renaissance occurring in hypnosis research over the last half-decade, particularly as it is increasingly recognized by the broader scientific community as a rigorous experimental methodology within cognitive neuroscience. Hypnosis is increasingly touted as providing a viable means for inducing "virtual" neurocognitive deficits in healthy subjects, in turn rendering testable models of the complex processes underlying neurological and neuropsychiatric disorders (Barnier & Oakley, 2009; Cox & Barnier, 2010; Oakley, Deeley, & Halligan, 2007; Oakley & Halligan, 2009). Theorists since Charcot have assumed that psychological processes underlying individual differences in hypnotic susceptibility, in combination with traumatic life events, provide a diathesis–stress model for the development of symptoms of psychopathology, including both psychoform and somatoform dissociation. However, it is only more recently that this model has been increasingly corroborated by neuroimaging investigations.

In particular, studies in cognitive neuroscience have specified similarities between the processes involved in dissociative symptoms, hypnotic inductions, and hypnotic alterations in sensation and perception (including response to pain). These processes seem to involve "top-down" mechanisms, primarily effected via brain regions involved in executive attention and salience detection (most notably, the dorsal anterior and dorsolateral prefrontal and dorsal cingulate cortices) and affect regulation (including ventral frontal regions) (Bell, Oakley, Halligan, & Deeley, 2012; Hoeft et al., 2012). Moreover, greater functional connectivity of the dorsolateral prefrontal and the salience network, including the dorsal anterior cingulate cortex, anterior insula, amygdala, and ventral striatum, has been associated with individuals' degree of hypnotizability (Hoeft et al., 2012).

The salience network is particularly important in detecting and integrating the most relevant somatic, autonomic, and emotional information in one's environment and thereby supraordinately motivating and guiding approach and withdrawal behaviors. In a study examining seven healthy individuals with high hypnotic susceptibility, Röder, Michal, Overbeck, van de Ven, and Linden (2007) induced experiences of depersonalization via instructions aimed at "detachment of the self from the body . . . [and] encouragement toward seeing the body from outside like in autoscopy" (p. 116). Participants' perception of pain intensity was reduced during hypnotically induced depersonalization relative to states of both waking control and hypnotically induced relaxation. Moreover, hypnotically induced depersonalization was associated with reduced response in the primary and secondary somatosensory cortex, contralateral putamen, and ipsilateral amygdala relative to a waking control state. In comparison, hypnotically induced depersonalization was associated with reduced contralateral postcentral gyrus, secondary somatosensory cortex, cingulate, and ipsilateral amygdala response relative to hypnotically induced relaxation. These findings provided evidence of the efficacy of hypnosis in altering neural response in regions known to be involved in central pain representation, somatic mapping, and emotional processing and provide further evidence for top-down control of higher cortical brain regions during hypnotic suggestion (Röder et al., 2007).

Hypnotic effects are not limited to task-oriented processes of direct relevance to the hypnotic induction. In fact, hypnotic suggestions may also modulate intrinsic neural networks examined in passive resting states, including the default-mode network (DMN; Deeley et al., 2012; Lipari et al., 2012). The DMN is one of the main intrinsic or resting-state networks in the brain and has been suggested to play an important role in self-referential processing (SRP; Greicius, Krasnow, Reiss, & Menon, 2003; Raichle, 2010; Raichle et al., 2001). Altered (i.e., reduced) metabolic connectivity between nodes of the DMN has been suggested to partly underlie the alterations in sense of self often observed in chronically traumatized individuals (Lanius, Bluhm, & Frewen, 2011). The DMN is preferentially activated when people are engaged in stimulus-independent thought (reviewed by Buckner, Andrews-Hanna, & Schacter, 2008), and it is theorized that the DMN may partly serve to consolidate, stabilize, and set the context for future information processing. A meta-analysis demonstrated that autobiographic memory recall, theory of mind (ToM; the ability to attribute mental states, including beliefs, intentions, and desires to oneself and others, as well as to understand that others have beliefs, desires, and intentions that are usually not radically different from one's own), and prospection (thinking about the future) activate the DMN (Spreng, Mar, & Kim, 2009; see also Spreng & Grady, 2010).

An increasing number of experimental studies reveal the potential of hypnotic inductions to alter the subjective experience of the embodied self. Moreover, the simplicity of the induction procedures tends to defy the often dramatic alterations in the embodiment of consciousness observed as effects of these procedures. For example, Foa and her colleagues induced significant dissociative states in both healthy participants and those with PTSD by asking them first to write up to four memories of times they felt disconnected or detached from an emotional situation in their own lives (e.g., in response to job loss, argument with spouse), followed by an incubation phase in which hypnotic suggestions were made (e.g., "Now that you're feeling detached, concentrate on this feeling. Feel it getting stronger and stronger; more and more distant. . . . Let yourself feel very disconnected, spacey, very uninvolved, very withdrawn," p. 260), followed by recitation of items taken from the Peritraumatic Dissociative Experiences Questionnaire—Clinician Rater Version (e.g., "I feel disconnected from my own body," "What's happening to me feels unreal"; Zoellner, Sacks, & Foa, 2007, p. 260). An interesting finding of the study was that people with PTSD who also had high trait dissociative symptoms were particularly susceptible to increased state dissociation following the induction. In another example, full out-of-body experiences were induced by protocols suggesting that people "move your awareness out of your body. You will move out of your body . . . and see your own body comfortably relaxing in its chair . . . you'll find your awareness can easily float from where your body is sitting" (Nash, Lynn, & Stanley, 1984, pp. 97–98).

Recent studies have examined hypnosis as a methodology for momentarily inducing psychological phenomena that mimic neuropsychiatric presentations of dissociation and conversion in healthy subjects with high trait hypnotic susceptibility (Bortolotti, Cox, & Barnier, 2012; Cox & Barnier, 2010). These studies provide a striking parallel with the psychological phenomena discussed previously as evoked by bottom-up multisensory perceptual illusions. For example, hypnotically induced mirror self-recognition deficits have been reliably induced in highly hypnotizable persons (Barnier et al., 2008). The procedure established by Barnier et al. (2008) is such that, following establishment of correct mirror self-identification, participants close their eyes and, following standard hypnotic relaxation induction procedures and entrainment to the hypnotist's suggestions, are then instructed: "In a moment, I am going to ask you to open your eyes, and when you do . . . the mirror you will see will have the properties of a normal mirror, with one major difference: The person you see in the mirror will not be you, it will be a stranger" (Barnier et al., 2008, p. 414).

A series of independent studies have since replicated Barnier et al.'s (2008) original findings that the procedure induces failed self-recognition, with highly hypnotizable participants reporting that after the induction they perceive a stranger in the mirror (Barnier, Cox, Connors, Langdon, & Coltheart, 2011; Connors, Barnier, Coltheart, Cox, & Langdon, 2012; Connors, Cox, Barnier, Langdon, & Coltheart, 2012). Importantly, evidence against a social-cognitive explanation of the accruing results in terms of experimental demand effects (e.g., participants simply "acting a role") is provided by the fact that many of the phenomenological characteristics of participants' failed recognition closely parallel those reported in neurocognitive-based clinical delusions (presumably unknown to lay participants). Specifically, participants usually reported strong conviction and maintenance of the delusion (often via secondary confabulation) despite logical challenge; exhibited specific, atypical behaviors (including referring to their reflection in the third person); and experienced significant distress at non-self-recognition in the mirror (Bortolotti et al., 2012; Cox & Barnier, 2010).

Combined partial-body (limb) disembodiment, disownership, and paralysis have also been experimentally induced by hypnosis. Halligan and colleagues examined the neural correlates of a female case of conversion disorder paralysis and compared them to neural responses in a hypnotized man. Results showed that both cases evidenced expected response in the primary motor cortex but with accompanying orbitofrontal and cingulate response (interpreted as inhibitory) when attempting but failing to initiate leg movement (Halligan, Athwal, Oakley, & Frackowiak, 2000). Moreover, a subsequent group of participants instructed to fake leg paralysis produced a different set of neural correlates, helping to discount a purely social-cognitive "actor-based" explanation for the findings (Ward, Oakley, Fackowiak, & Halligan, 2003).

Extending Halligan et al.'s findings, Rahmanovic and colleagues induced in just over half of their highly hypnotizable participants the experience of limb disownership (experience of their hand as someone else's) accompanied by, critically, loss of movement and altered perceptions (e.g., "it looks older"). The experimental procedure utilized by Rahmonovic et al. simply involved, within a hypnotized state, touching participants' nondominant arm while suggesting that the participant's arm belonged to someone else (Rahmanovic, Barnier, Cox, Langdon, & Coltheart, 2012). Investigators have also described out-of-body experiences as directly induced by (e.g., Del Prete & Tressoldi, 2005; Irwin, 1989; Nash et al., 1984; Tart, 1998; Tressoldi & Del Prete, 2007) or spontaneously occurring during (Meyerson & Gelkopf, 2004) hypnosis, as noted above, although the neurophenomological effects of these procedures require greater elaboration.

Finally, of direct relevance to the notion of the malleability of the narrative and of the autobiographical self, persons of high hypnotic susceptibility can be induced to adopt alternate identities accompanied by episodic memories that support their "new" identity (Cox & Barnier, 2009). Cox and Barnier asked participants to think of either familiar or less familiar others to whom they felt similar to or different, followed by, while hypnotized, instructions to "become this [similar or dissimilar] person" (Cox & Barnier, 2009, p. 6). More specifically, the researchers first instructed participants to engage in SRP as follows: "Think about yourself now. Pay close attention to yourself, to all of you. Pay attention to what you're like, how you feel, how old you are. Pay attention to all these different aspects of yourself, think about them. . . ." They then instructed participants to begin to become someone else, as follows: "As you sit there relaxed and hypnotized, I want you to start feeling something different. I want you to start feeling more and more like your [sister/brother/friend], more and more like [other person's name], more and more like [him/her]. I want you to start to feel more and more like that" (Cox & Barnier, 2009, p. 9). Objective cognitive and behavioral probes, including ascertainment of self-referential word lists, description of episodic memories, and an analogue to the previously described mirror self-recognition test suggested that participants had temporarily adopted an alternate identity. Many participants also found the experience to be distressing.

Interestingly, similar results were achieved in highly hypnotizable participants in the context of imagination as well (i.e., the imagination condition did not explicitly encourage participants to enter a hypnotic state). In other words, in both the hypnotic and imagination conditions, highly hypnotizable participants were more likely than low hypnotizable participants to utilize embodied visualizations (e.g., "I imagined her hands and I noticed my body being like hers; in a similar position"; "I felt like I had a space of air between my clothes and myself"; Cox & Barnier, 2009, p. 12) and other conscious and strategic psychological processes to effect a temporary alteration in their sense of identity. The findings are suggestive of the intrinsic (arguably "autosuggestive") ability on the part of highly hypnotizable people to alter the way they experience themselves. It is important to point out, however, that all of the subjective effects described were readily obtainable only by individuals who scored high in trait hypnotizability. Moreover, all of these subjective effects were easily reversed by countersuggestion.

Phenomenology of Depersonalization

Experimental studies of bottom-up and top-down mediated distortions of bodily felt experience reveal a key phenomenological property of consciousness in its normal form: consciousness seems to be situated within and bounded by the body proper. However, this body-centric representation of self, the *embodied self*, has been shown to be strikingly vulnerable to transient modification: by the simple stroking of a brush, or hypnotic suggestion alone, psychologically healthy people have been induced to experience significant alterations in the embodied experience of themselves under controlled, experimental conditions.

Blanke & Metzinger (2009) detailed a classification system for full-body illusory perceptions as observed in neurological patients with known brain damage. In their taxonomy, out-of-body experiences are defined as those wherein conscious subjectivity (i.e., the first-person perspective) is perceived to be located at a point in space different from the corporeal body, a place from which the physical body is then perceived. Out-of-body experiences are differentiated from autoscopic and heautoscopic hallucinations, wherein consciousness remains positioned within the physical body or is located simultaneously or interchangeably at both the positions of the physical and illusory (i.e., hallucinated) bodies, respectively. *Autoscopic hallucinations* are defined as perceptions of oneself as an external object, which can lead to the delusion that one has a double, whereas *heautoscopic hallucinations* involve seeing one's own body at a distance. These neurological phenomena have been associated with functional disturbances or lesions in different areas of the parietal lobe, as we discuss subsequently.

Similar to the description of out-of-body experiences as defined by Blanke and Metzinger (2009), symptoms of depersonalization represent a psychiatric disturbance defined in DSM-IV by "alterations in the perception or experience of the self so that one feels detached from, and as if one is an outside observer of, one's mental processes or body" (American Psychiatric Association, 2000, p. 530). The clinical correlates of such experiences have been recently described in large cohorts (e.g., Baker et al., 2003; review by Hunter, Sierra, & David, 2004) and found to commonly include poor response to both pharmacological and psychological intervention (e.g., see review by Simeon & Abugel, 2006). As redefined for the DSM-5, depersonalization also includes experiences of being an outside observer of the happenings of one's own mind or body as may be exemplified by perceptual alterations, altered sense of time, emotional or physical numbing, or alterations in sense of self (American Psychiatric Association, 2013, p. 302).

The significant expansion of the boundaries of the depersonalization construct implied by the revised definition used by DSM-5 is consistent with a multifactorial view of depersonalization. For example, Sierra, Baker, Medford, and David's (2005) factor analysis of a depersonalization scale indicated that depersonalization consists of at least four distinct experiences that were only weakly correlated with each other: (1) *anomalous body experience* (e.g., "feeling of being outside the body," "body feels as if it didn't belong to self"); (2) *emotional numbing* (e.g., "no emotions felt when weeping or laughing," "unable to feel affection towards family and friends"); (3) *anomalous subjective recall* (e.g., "personal memories feel as if one had not been involved in them"); and (4) *alienation from sur-roundings* (e.g., "feeling unreal or cut-off from the world," "surroundings feel detached or unreal") (p. 1527, see also: Simeon, Kozin et al., 2008; cf., Blevins, Witte, & Weathers, 2013). We prefer to reserve use of the depersonalization concept herein to the first factor identified by Sierra et al., labeled *anomalous body experience*, in better keeping with the previous DSM-IV definition and the concept of out-of-body experiences as classified in Blanke and Metzinger's taxonomy (2009). By contrast, reference to experiences of emotional or physical numbing and distorted sense of time, as contained within the DSM-5 definition, are considered to represent other dimensions in the 4-D model and are discussed in other chapters accordingly.

As noted above, altered states of embodiment may involve the body as a whole (out-of-body experience, depersonalization) or only part of the body (e.g., limb disownership or paralysis). Figure 5.2 (also in color

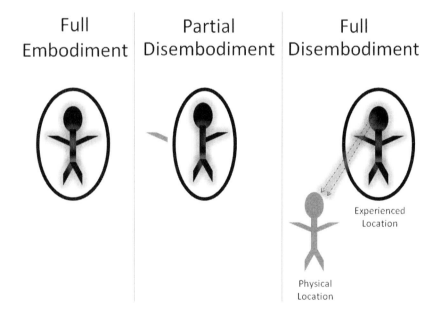

FIGURE 5.2. Phenomenology of Embodiment (NWC) versus Partial or Full Disembodiment (TRASC).

Left panel: FULL EMBODIMENT—the sense of self is associated with body-situated experience. *Middle panel:* PARTIAL DISEMBODIMENT—sense of self is associated with body-situated experience, although part of the body is experienced as "non-self" (e.g., an arm or hand is experienced as not one's own, as foreign or strange). *Right panel:* FULL DISEMBOD-IMENT—sense of self is associated with an out-of-body experience; the body as a whole is experienced as "non-self." NWC = normal waking consciousness; TRASC = trauma-related altered states of consciousness.

insert) illustrates the concepts of partial versus full disembodiment as used herein. In the figure, the experienced location of the self and consciousness are encircled and glowing; non-self objects are shown outside the ovals, as well as devoid of glow. The arm depicted in the partial disembodiment representation (center panel) may not be experienced as physically disconnected from the body, but only as if "not part of" one's body or one's self (i.e., partial body disownership). In these cases the arm may feel "strange" or "different than expected" or different from how the participant believes it "should" look and feel.

Out of Body, Out of Mind: Phenomenology of Depersonalization in Trauma-Related Disorders

Studies of embodied consciousness are relevant to the study of psychotraumatology because alterations in the conscious embodiment of self, representing a rather obvious departure from NWC, are relatively commonplace in traumatized persons. Such TRASC of the body are often experienced as highly valuable in helping individuals disconnect from their emotional experience at the time of traumatic events. For example, Suzy, a woman with a childhood trauma history introduced in previous chapters, describes her experience of depersonalization as follows:

> "For me it was like a physical separation. Here's me up here, and here's this shell down here that is being hurt and abused—but I can't feel it, I *don't* feel it, I am separate from that person, I am separate from my body now. My body is being hurt, but *I* am not being hurt. I think that is one of the things that lets you survive because it is not you; you are not experiencing the full impact of what is happening. You *are* experiencing it, but you are not experiencing the full impact."

However, if chronic symptoms of depersonalization persist in the aftermath of traumatic experience, individuals are often left feeling alienated from their surroundings, unable to fully experience affection toward their family and friends, experiencing personal memories as if they had not been involved in them, and feeling as if their body does not belong to them. For example, "Teddy," who suffered from chronic symptoms of depersonalization, noted:

> "Everything feels weird. It's hard to describe. It feels like I have to remind myself who I am. It's like I am in a dream. It feels like I have no control over what I am doing. I'm not conscious of what is happening. I'm just going through the motions. It feels like I'm trapped in a random body. I don't know who I am. I'm just this kid from London. I don't remember myself before I had depersonalization."

Another individual, "Tanaz," who suffered from chronic symptoms of partial disembodiment, noted:

> "I could not feel my feet and hands. I did not know where they were; they were not attached to me. The hands that *were* attached were not mine—to look at them was like a physical separation. They just weren't *mine*; at that point it was difficult to function because I could not feel things or I didn't have the sensations associated with my own hands."

Finally, Elly, a Holocaust survivor introduced in earlier chapters, described the experience of depersonalization this way: "There was a certain feeling of *outer worldliness*. That I am *watching myself walk*." He went on to describe the difficulties depersonalized states could create in an environment where outward bodily control was critical to survival:

> "But you also had to be very attentive, because you had to be careful. If you walk five-in-line marching, I tried not to be on the end because a guard—if you didn't walk in step—would run over and hit you— kick you in the leg—and that could break you because if you fell down and couldn't walk anymore, you were finished. That was it."

In the field of psychotraumatology the experience of clinical depersonalization has most often been studied in the form of acute responses to traumatic events, labeled *peritraumatic dissociation*. Numerous studies of peritraumatic dissociation have been conducted using the Peritraumatic Dissociative Experiences Questionnaire (P-DEQ; Marmar et al., 1997), which includes items that, upon face value, describe the characteristic symptoms of depersonalization (e.g., Item 5: "I felt as though I were a spectator watching what was happening to me, as if I were floating above the scene or observing it as an outsider." Item 6: "There were moments when my sense of my own body seemed distorted or changed. I felt disconnected from my own body"). Systematic and quantitative reviews have shown that high P-DEQ scores are significant predictors of the development of PTSD using both retrospective and prospective designs (Lensvelt-Mulders et al., 2008; Ozer et al., 2003; van der Hart et al., 2008). However, the predictive value for PTSD of peritraumatic dissociative responses is diminished when baseline indices of negative affect or other measures of clinically significant distress are controlled (Lensvelt-Mulders et al., 2008; van der Velden & Wittmann, 2008). Symptoms of peritraumatic dissociation tend to co-occur with other nondissociative signs of peritraumatic distress, including fear and other emotions (Bovin & Marx, 2011; Brunet et al., 2001; Rizvi, Kaysen, Gutner, Griffin, & Resick, 2008).

State depersonalization symptoms have also been studied experimentally in response to cues of past traumatic events, most notably through script-driven trauma imagery tasks (Frewen & Lanius, 2006a, 2006b; Lanius, Williamson, et al., 2002, 2005; Lanius, Vermetten, et al., 2010). Specifically, Lanius and colleagues observed that approximately 30% of people with chronic PTSD experience acute depersonalization upon being exposed to the trauma script-driven imagery paradigm. Consistent with Suzy's description above, the clinical utility of this phenomenological response has long been theorized to be a protective mechanism for the conscious psyche, in which mind is experienced as separated from the body so that bodily harm does not affect the psychological self. For example, one trauma survivor we interviewed reported: "I was outside my body looking down at myself. It was too overwhelming to recall the traumatic memory." Another described, during reexperiencing of a motor vehicle accident, " looking down at my own body while I was back reliving the car accident."

Researchers have also considered whether depersonalization symptoms might represent the subjective counterpart to behavioral freezing (as opposed to flight) in animals in the context of inescapable threat (i.e., tonic immobility; Abrams, Carleton, Taylor, & Asmundson, 2009; Bovin, Jager-Hyman, Gold, Marx, & Sloan, 2008; Humphreys, Sauder, Martin, & Marx, 2010; Lima et al., 2010; Marx, Forsyth, Gallup, Fusé, & Lexington, 2008; Rocha-Rego et al., 2009; Zoellner, 2008). A psychometric measure introduced previously, the Responses to Script-driven Imagery Scale (RSDI), differentiates the depersonalization (dissociative) response from that of reexperiencing and avoidance by phenomenological self-report in the context of trauma reminders (Hopper, Frewen, Sack, et al., 2007). The RSDI is predictive of differential neural responses to trauma script-driven imagery and is discussed further later (Hopper, Frewen, van der Kolk, et al., 2007).

Although studies of acute depersonalization suggest that alterations in the experience of the embodied self commonly occur both during traumatic events (peritraumatic dissociation) and during subsequent reminders of traumatic events (e.g., dissociative responses to trauma script-driven imagery), surprisingly few studies have investigated whether traumatic life events play an etiological role in more chronic clinical presentations of depersonalization. Simeon and colleagues reported elevated childhood trauma histories in clinical cases of depersonalization disorder in comparison with controls (Simeon, Gross, Guralnik, & Stein, 1997) and subsequently demonstrated the particularly salient etiological role of chronic parental emotional abuse in the development of depersonalization disorder (Simeon, Guralnik, Schmeidler, Sirof, & Knutelska, 2001; Simeon, Smith, Knutelska, & Smith, 2008). Nevertheless, in a large case series ($N =$ 204) only 14% of persons with depersonalization disorder considered traumatic events to have played a role in the development of their symptoms (Baker et al., 2003).

The Phenomenology of Derealization

Unfortunately, far less research has investigated the phenomenological basis of derealization in traumatized persons. It was recently decided that for the DSM-5, on the basis of arguments that depersonalization and derealization may be signs and symptoms of the same underlying psychopathology (e.g., Spiegel et al., 2011, 2013), derealization phenomena be classified within a combined depersonalization–derealization disorder. We believe that conceptual clarity is improved by retaining the phenomenological distinction between depersonalization and derealization as applying to a self-referential versus non-self-referential (i.e., other-, world-referential) experience, respectively. Items from the DES that capture the experience of derealization include: "Some people have the experience of feeling that other people, objects, and the world around them are not real" and "Some people sometimes feel as if they are looking at the world through a fog so that people and objects appear far away or unclear." Nevertheless, it is clear that in many phenomenal moments, experiences of depersonalization and derealization co-occur, justifying the new combined diagnosis for DSM-5.

Case 1: Outside Self and an Inside World—the Combined Experience of Depersonalization and Derealization

An example of the co-occurrence of depersonalization and derealization is described in the case of "Erica," who, in the early stages of treatment, frequently presented for psychotherapy sessions in acute states of derealization. Erica described her experiences of these instances as if finding herself in a vacuum or void, wherein an abrupt physical line bounded her personal reality from that of the outside world. Erica reported that the world around her, including her clinician, momentarily became distant, foreign, and untrustworthy. For example, Erica once described, in a state of distress: "The room is changing now . . . you're there and I'm here (*motions with hands, separating the space*) and the whole room is (*pause*) . . . I'm not *in* this room, even though I know I am [logically]—*I'm* not here. . . ."

It is diagnostically important that Erica has always demonstrated insight regarding her derealization experiences—that is, that they are a *symptom*. She knows rationally that in fact she has remained physically in the room at all times despite feeling that she was not, as in the previous quotation. Erica has also described perceptual abnormalities during such derealization experiences, including the sense that the world seems tilted on an axis about 30 degrees. She has commented before to her clinician that "right now you're on the other side, you're not real, you don't make sense."

By contrast, within this vacuum, experience is owned; it is "her" reality. Nevertheless, upon further probing, she typically occupies a partially or fully disembodied state during such episodes of derealization. For example, during the same experience of acute derealization described previously (i.e., "The room is changing . . ."), she also reported that her hands and arms felt numb and as if not belonging to her. Early in the course of psychotherapy, when experiencing states of derealization, she was often observed to rub her feet—shoeless—against the carpeted floor as a grounding behavior to feel less dissociated and distressed. When this behavior was pointed out to her in session once, she responded: "Yes, I'm doing that because my feet are going numb. And this is just (*momentary pause, reflecting*) . . . making me feel that they are *there* again."

Erica has also frequently been observed rubbing the tops of her hands in order to feel less depersonalized during times of distress; she has commented: "I'm doing this [rubbing the tops of hands] *to keep them here* [to keep her hands present and attached]. Because if I don't, they won't be here anymore. Like I'm not *here*, *here*, or *here* (*touching arms and mid-section*) [indicating that these areas of her body were experienced as if not present]."

Psychoform versus Somatoform Dissociation: Dissociations in Mind and Body

The dissociative subtype of PTSD proposed by Lanius et al. (Lanius, Vermetten, et al., 2010; Lanius et al., 2012) and overviewed in Chapter 1 has as its crux experiences of depersonalization or derealization. To briefly reiterate: The argument for recognizing a dissociative subtype emphasizes that, although certain individuals with PTSD exhibit depersonalization and derealization symptoms, *not all do*. Moreover, the subtype model asserts that distinguishing between those who do versus those who do not experience TRASC of the body is clinically meaningful. The rationale for recognizing a dissociative subtype of PTSD was threefold: (1) psychometric research suggests that dissociative versus nondissociative cases of PTSD can be distinguished independent of PTSD symptom severity; (2) subjective dissociative responses attend a set of objective psychobiological responses that are characteristically different from those of general distress experienced by other persons with PTSD; and (3) dissociative symptoms may require specific psychological treatments above and beyond standard treatment of PTSD; research support for these arguments was presented in Chapter 1. To date, the dissociative subtype of PTSD has been defined specifically in relation to symptoms of depersonalization and derealization.

In contrast, the broader concept of dissociation has historically represented a unifying, integrative construct for understanding the symptoms of "hysteria," although a distinction has been made between dissociation as predominantly *psychoform* versus *somatoform* in nature (Nijenhuis & van der Hart, 1999; van der Hart, van Dijke, van Son, & Stele, 2000). Disintegration among higher-level functions of cognition, including perception, episodic autobiographical memory, and identity are typically labeled as *psychoform* dissociation. In comparison, various conversion and somatization syndromes, typifying the phenomenon of *somatoform* dissociation, broadly include loss of voluntary control over circumscribed psychomotor behaviors and musculoskeletal systems that mimic neurological conditions (conversion), or abnormalities of other body systems (somatization) without known biomedical cause and that are presumed to be psychological in origin (i.e., due to severe stress or trauma).

Somatoform dissociation is often measured by self-reports using the Somatoform Dissociation Questionnaire (Nijenuis, Spinhoven, Van Dyck, van der Hart, & Vanderlinden, 1996), which includes items that appear to overlap with experiences of depersonalization—for example, "It is as if my body, or a part of it, has disappeared"—as well as other pseudoneurological features such as "I have an attack that resembles an epileptic seizure," "I cannot hear/see for a while [as if I am deaf/blind]," and "I'm paralyzed for a while." Clinical presentations of temporary blindness/deafness, partial or total paralysis, inability to speak, numbness, balance and coordination problems, pseudoseizures, and tremors illustrate the varied phenomena of partial disembodiments and temporary loss of neuropsychological function that occur in conversion disorders. Although symptoms of dissociation, broadly construed, are clearly endorsed with high frequency in individuals with conversion disorders (e.g., see review by Brown, Cardena, Nijenhuis, Sar, & van der Hart, 2007), relatively little research has examined the degree to which conversion symptoms and those specifically of depersonalization or derealization co-occur, and whether they might be mediated by similar or distinct psychological and neurophysiological processes.

Simeon and colleagues, however, found that symptoms of somatoform dissociation were *not* strongly endorsed by individuals with depersonalization disorder (Simeon, Smith, et al., 2008), possibly suggesting distinct etiological mechanisms. In normal populations, however, endorsements of somatoform dissociation and out-of-body experiences were strongly correlated (e.g., Irwin, 2000). Other studies also suggest that although conversion symptoms as well as other somatic signs frequently co-occur with dissociative symptoms and dissociative disorders, the association may be strongest for conversion (pseudoneurological) symptoms in comparison with other psychosomatic signs (e.g., Espirito-Santo & Pi-Abreu, 2009; Guz et al., 2004; Ozcetin et al., 2009; Sar, Akyüz, Kundakçi, Kiziltan, & Dogan, 2004).

In summary, the traumatized self involves injury to both psyche and soma. Severe interpersonal trauma, as occurs in torture, repeated domestic violence, rape, and incest, often teaches people that their bodies are not safe, are not their own, or are a place of disgust and defilement of which to be ashamed. As a result, people often seek to flee from, reject, and abandon their bodies. For example, the incest survivor may no longer wish to take ownership over his or her bodily self, believing that the flesh is irrevocably defiled. Accordingly, consciously or unconsciously, he or she rejects the bodily core, the most basic nature of him- or herself. The result seems to be the separation in consciousness of the ego from a person's bodily felt experience. What remains may be the physical sense that one is numb or "nothing," or experiences of partial or full disembodiment and detachment. In effect, people lose the bodily felt home for their subjective experiences; their minds and bodies become estranged.

The following poem was written from the embodied perspective of a trauma survivor and intended to further describe the experience of a TRASC of the body in another form of prose. The poem is titled "*I* vs. *it*" and is authored anonymously. It illustrates not only processes of depersonalization but also amnesia and recovered memory, aversive inner tension, self-harm, and suicidal ideation occurring as posttraumatic responses to repeated childhood sexual abuse.

I vs. *it*

This is what happened to it, and to me, when he abused me.
"*It*" was my body . . .

I was young when it started and didn't know what *it* was about.
I didn't know what was happening to *it*.

To him, it was his. *It* wasn't *mine* anymore.
He made it do things that I didn't want *it* to. Now he, not *I*, controlled *it*.

He was scary, so *it* became scary.
I didn't like what was happening to *it*.

Inside I was scared. But outside, *it* didn't show.

I tried to get away from him. But *it* couldn't.
So I found a way to get away from *it*.

After that, what he did stopped happening to *me*,
and started happening only to *it*.

Where he put his hands became *not me*.
Where he put his parts became *not me*.
Wherever he hurt me, became *not me*.
It wasn't *me* anymore.

I watched as it continued to be hurt. But *I* stopped feeling *it*.

Sometimes I watched from the inside, while *it* was on the outside.
Other times I watched from outside of *it*.

The more I blocked *it* out, the less I felt, and the less *it* mattered . . .

After a time, *he* went away, so I blocked *him* out too,
just as I had blocked *it* out before.

And for a time, *it* became *mine* again, and *I* was okay.

 . . . But later, when something happened to *it*, *it* reminded *me* of *him*.
I remembered that *it* had happened to *me*.

Now *he's* back in *me*.

And again *I* can't get away from *him*,
but this time I can't get away from *it* either.

It was broken, so am *I*. *It* was defiled, so am *I*. *It* feels like it was *my* fault.

I try to make *it* stop.

If I hurt *it*, I can go away. But when I come back, *he's* still there.
He's inside of *it*, so I can't get away.

I can't rid myself of *it*, so I can't rid myself of *him*.

If I make *it* kill me, will *he* finally go away?
I will make *it* all go away . . .

Source: Anonymous

Neurophenomenology of Depersonalization:
Studies in Trauma-Related Disorders

Experimental studies increasingly suggest that processing at the junction of the temporal and parietal lobes particularly within the right hemisphere (right temporoparietal junction; rTPJ) plays a significant role in mediating the embodiment of the phenomenal self. For example, Blanke and colleagues induced depersonalization via direct electrical stimulation of the rTPJ in a person undergoing brain surgery for epilepsy (Blanke, Ortigue, Landis, & Seeck, 2002; Blanke & Metzinger, 2009), and similar findings were obtained in a tinnitus patient (De Ridder, Van Laere, Dupont, Menovsky, & Van de Heyning, 2007). Tsakiris and colleagues influenced the outcome of the rubber-hand illusion via transcranial magnetic stimulation to the rTPJ (Tsakiris, Costantini, & Haggard, 2008), also demonstrating that response within the right middle insula correlated with individual differences in the intensity of the illusion (Tsakiris, Hesse, Boy, Haggard, & Fink, 2007; see also, e.g., Ehrsson, Spence, & Passingham, 2004; Ehrsson, Weich, Weiskopf, Dolan, & Passingham, 2007). A neurobiological model proposed by Tsakiris (2010) implicates the rTPJ, secondary somatosensory cortex and right posterior insula as central to the phenomenal embodiment of consciousness and selfhood. Further, research suggests involvement of anterior and posterior cortical midline structures as underpinning the cognitive–perceptual sense of body ownership (Tsakiris et al., 2010). Consistent with this, Ketay, Hamillton, Haas, and Simeon (2014) observed increased medial prefronal and anterior cingulate response during visual self-face recognition in participants with depersonalization disorder in comparison with controls. Of relevance to the design and interpretation of neuroimaging experiments, approximately one-third of healthy participants taking part in neuroimaging studies will experience at least a mild dissociative response simply as a result of being encapsulated within the scanner bore (Michal, Roder, Mayer, Lengler, & Krakow, 2005).

Figure 5.3 illustrates brain regions of interest to the consciousness of disembodiment as observed in neuroimaging studies. Consistent with roles for the medial prefrontal cortex (mPFC) and rTPJ in partly underlying our embodied sense of self, we demonstrated using fMRI that response within the mPFC and rTPJ was altered in concert with self-reported experiences of depersonalization, as prompted by trauma recall in individuals with PTSD (Hopper, Frewen, van der Kolk, et al., 2007; Lanius, Williamson et al., 2002, 2005). In addition, Lanius and colleagues (2002) observed increased response in the mPFC and rTPJ during trauma recall-induced depersonalization, in comparison with both healthy persons and individuals with PTSD who did not report symptoms of depersonalization. These results are consistent with roles for the mPFC and rTPJ in the phenomenal embodiment of conscious selfhood. Alterations in metabolic rates in the parietal cortex have also been observed in depersonalization disorder

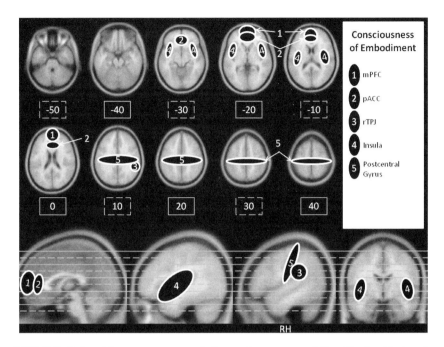

FIGURE 5.3. Neuroanatomy of Consciousness of the Body (Embodiment). mPFC = medial prefrontal cortex; PACC = perigenual anterior cingulate cortex; rTPJ = right temporoparietal junction.

during a verbal learning task (Simeon et al., 2000). Findings in psychological trauma-related depersonalization therefore corroborate some of the principal tenets of neurobiological models of the embodiment of conscious subjectivity, including involvement of the mPFC and rTPJ. Interestingly, studies even suggest that electrically stimulating over the rTPJ may resolve symptoms over depersonalization disorder patients (Jay, Sierra, Van den Eynde, Rothwell, & David, 2014; Mantovani, Simeon, Urban, Bulow, Allart, & Lisanby, 2011).

Referring particularly to the clinical phenomena of partial disembodiment, the putative role of the right insula in limb ownership and agency also requires acknowledgment. Neurological patients with anosognosia for hemiparesis/-plegia (i.e., inability to recognize, or denial of, their limb paralysis), as well as patients who experience their limbs as not belonging to them (asomatognosia) or as belonging to someone else (somatoparaphrenia), typically following stroke, commonly reveal specific damage of the right insula, relative to stroke patients without these problems (reviewed by Karnath & Baier, 2010; e.g., see Baier & Karnath, 2008). It is interesting to note that our own studies showed negative correlations between symptoms of depersonalization and activity in the right insula in people with PTSD during traumatic memory recall (Hopper, Frewen, van der Kolk, et al., 2007). Accurate recognition of the genesis of one's own movements in neuroimaging experiments with healthy controls also reveals involvement of the right insula (e.g., Farrer et al., 2003). Response in the insular cortex is often accompanied by response in the anterior cingulate cortex, which, when responding together, may be acting as part of a network that performs the important attentional function of detecting biologically relevant stimulus information in the external environment (i.e., salience detection; Menon & Uddin, 2010; Seeley et al., 2007). The anterior cingulate cortex, like the insular cortex, is known to partly represent and modulate autonomic homeostatic processes (e.g., Critchley, Melmed, Featherstone, Mathias, & Dolan, 2001, 2002; Critchley et al., 2003; Critchley, Tang, Glaser, Butterworth, & Colan, 2005). The unique yet interacting roles played by the anterior cingulate and insular cortices thus require further investigation (Craig, 2010; Medford & Critchley, 2010; Menon & Uddin, 2010).

Moreover, distinguishing the potential role of the insular cortex in disembodiment relative to its well-recognized role in general distress (e.g., anxiety; Etkin & Wager, 2007; Paulus & Stein, 2006) may prove difficult. Nevertheless, correlational analyses examining the relationship between distress related to reexperiencing symptoms versus depersonalization responses during traumatic memory recall and brain activation patterns may prove useful in this regard. For example, our own findings show that the more reexperiencing people endorse while recalling their traumatic memory, the *greater* the activation of the right insula. In contrast, the more depersonalization experienced while recalling one's traumatic memory, the *less* activation of the right insula is observed (Hopper, Frewen, van der Kolk, et al., 2007). These findings again stress the importance of the neurophenomemological method—that is, the importance of examining an individual's first-person experience and correlating it with objective measures of brain function.

Healing the Disembodied Self: Case Examples of Mindfulness, Yoga, and Somatosensory-Based Interventions

In our experience, mindfulness practices, including the practice of trauma-sensitive yoga (Emerson & Hopper, 2011), certain interventions derived from somatosensory or body-based approaches to psychotherapy (Ogden et al., 2006; Rothschild, 2003; Levine & Frederick, 1997), and components of selected empirically validated cognitive-behavioral and emotion-focused interventions are integral to healing the disembodied self. Just as trauma teaches people how to separate, flee from, and reject the bodily core of their existence, the intention of embodied mindfulness practice is to return people home to their somatic selves along with the gifts of newfound safety, compassion, honor, and respect. Although the journey of reentry into, and reclaiming of, one's body can initially be terrifying, over time, and with ongoing reassurance within the context of a therapeutic relationship, a trauma survivor's body ultimately can become a source of pleasure, pride, and joy. For some, this may be the first time they have experienced the feeling of being fully at home in their bodies. In fact, it is the somatic experience of fully embodied peace, pleasure, joy, and triumph that is one of the most salient markers of a full trauma recovery. Objective studies of the efficacy of mindfulness and somatosensory-based interventions in traumatized populations are sorely needed.

Many specific psychotherapeutic interventions share as their core goal the reembodiment of the self. In this chapter we pay particular attention to both passive and more active/exploratory practices of the mindful body scan, supplemented with somatic resource building (e.g., lengthening the spine, sitting straight) as deemed helpful to the client (Ogden et al., 2006). Practice of gentle mindful movement, as exemplified by walking meditations and simple yoga stretching, is also effective, we have found, in our clinical practices with certain clients with complex trauma, although these practices may not be considered safe or acceptable to all persons. For descriptions of the theory and practice of trauma-sensitive yoga and sensorimotor psychotherapy, we refer readers to Emerson and Hopper's (2011) and Ogden et al.'s (2006) texts, respectively. The need for systematic studies of the efficacy of these interventions in traumatized populations with PTSD and dissociative disorders is acknowledged.

Trauma-Sensitive Body Scans and Mindfulness Meditation

We have found that body-scan meditations, as popularized for Western psychology from Buddhist self-developmental practices in the Mindfulness-Based Stress Reduction program developed by Jon Kabat-Zinn (1990), can be adapted for use in the severely psychologically traumatized population toward both the assessment and healing of disembodied states. From an assessment perspective, monitoring the real-time experiential effects of embodied practices through both behavioral observations and collection of ongoing client self-report seems to be a more internally valid approach to assessing disembodied states than limiting one's assessment to asking participants about their symptoms via interview or questionnaire. This open assessment of a person's initial response to the body scan provides a roadmap for future more guided practices that may aim to more actively bring clients to a more embodied state of consciousness and sense of themselves.

As most mental health clinicians are by now familiar with, the body-scan meditation as administered in the Mindfulness-Based Stress Reduction program, and related interventions, essentially involves participants noticing the physical sensations they experience in different parts of their bodies while sitting or lying supine. The clinician guides the participant through this experiential process by traversing the gross anatomy of the body usually from inferior to superior. For example, the body scan commonly begins by instructing participants to "Allow yourself to *feel* any and all sensations in your toes, perhaps distinguishing between them and watching the flux of sensations in this region." Subsequent instructions draw participants' attention to successive areas of the body, typically moving superiorly (e.g., the feet, ankles, shins, knees, and so on). Particularly because the intervention is most often administered in groups, self-report is only rarely collected regarding what participants sensed within each part of their bodies throughout the body scan. They are largely left to become aware of and label these experiences covertly, under the assumption that the experiences will be, for the most part, relatively neutral and nondistressing; this is often not a fair assumption, by contrast, for (particularly sexually) traumatized populations, as taken up subsequently.

We have found the practice of body scans to be helpful in psychotherapy with severely traumatized persons. Essential to the practice, however, as with all psychological interventions, is to fully inform participants concerning what the body scan will generally involve and elicit their consent. Within the process of informed consent, it is important to forewarn participants that the exercise may be distressing, and to give them the opportunity to voice any specific concerns they might have about it. In particular, it is important to ask people whether particular areas of their body are especially "triggering" for them. The clinician may choose either to include or exclude these "trigger points" from the body-scan exercise. Generally, we avoid including erogenous zones in the body scan, at least in the early trials of this exercise.

In addition to the importance of conducting a thorough informed consent, we have found the following modifications to the general practice of the body scan, as otherwise typically used in other mindfulness-based interventions, to be useful to consider when conducting body scans with severely psychologically traumatized persons:

1. At participants' preference, the body scan can be completed while sitting or standing in the therapy office. We do not complete body scans with participants in a lying position as this tends to be more conducive to reexperiencing symptoms in survivors of sexual abuse. However, participants can be encouraged to practice the intervention on their own (i.e., at home) while lying in bed, first educating them about the importance of feeling safe in their body in all physical postures. The sitting versus standing positions may also vary in their potential for distress across participants. Whereas usually we conduct the body scan with participants in seated posture, completion of the exercise while standing can be a useful variant that of course represents a more physically active stance; standing may be particularly helpful when more physical stimulation might be sought in order to combat disembodied states. Similarly, when completing the body scan while sitting, the participant can be encouraged to sit

tall and slightly forward, emphasizing the embodiment of a resilient and empowered stance.

2. The body scan can be completed with participants' eyes open or closed, as they prefer. The first time participants complete the body scan, however, we recommend that they keep their eyes open throughout the exercise as they typically find that the potential for distress is greater with eyes-closed practices. In comparison, in subsequent sessions people might be encouraged to close their eyes if they feel safe to do so, because interoception is generally enhanced with eyes closed. Participants should be aware that they are free to open and close their eyes at different points during the body scan, as needed to self-regulate distress.

3. The body scan begins at a place within the participant's body that he or she identifies as the least distressing or the safest, strongest, or most confident area. If an individual is unable to identify such a location in the body, the clinician might ask him or her if beginning with the feet would be acceptable. This direction is suggested because being aware of one's feet is essential to feeling grounded in the world—the opposite of a sense of disembodiment. If the feet are a strong emotional trigger point for the client, however, another starting point is selected. In guiding the body scan, the clinician stays at this beginning place for as long as the participant needs so as to fully experience and describe whatever sensations he or she is aware of there.

4. Typically we conduct the body scan as progressing from inferior to superior in body location. If one has started the body scan somewhere near the middle of the body (e.g., abdomen, chest), this would mean scanning first the lower before the upper body. Again, as noted, this is because feeling the legs and feet can provide an experiential anchor to the world, whereas focusing first on the upper body before the legs and feet can sometimes encourage a sense of subjective detachment from the earth that may progress into a sense of experiential detachment from the bodily self as well in persons who are prone to dissociative states (i.e., depersonalization or out-of-body experience).

5. In guiding the participant's attention to the body, a sense of ownership is (at least implicitly) encouraged by referring to the participant's body in second- rather than in third-person perspective: for example, "Now, becoming aware of whatever *you* are experiencing in *your* right hand" as opposed to " . . . whatever *is* being experienced in *the* right hand," and so on.

6. In guiding the body scan the clinician should progress slowly. Again, in general, stay at the place in the body the participant is currently focused on until he or she has had sufficient time to experience and describe what he or she is aware of at that location. Progressing slowly implicitly models the expectation that a person might be able to experience or become aware

of sensations throughout his or her physical body, even if the experience is one of feeling "nothing" or of "not being able to feel" certain body parts. Moreover, progressing slowly models a relaxed state of mind, serving to contrast with states of hyperarousal, agitation, and anxiety commonly experienced by traumatized persons. A slower pace is also consistent with the message that the practice of embodied awareness sometimes takes time.

7. Encourage the participant to report any signs of distress. It is also essential for the clinician to carefully track the participant for any signs of overt discomfort during the body scan.

8. Encourage the participant to communicate out loud what he or she experiences in his or her body throughout the body scan, using the vocabulary of *physical* experience and sensation (e.g., *tightening, tingling, squeezing, tense, hot, cold*). Encourage *description* while discouraging *interpretation*; in other words, the intention of the body scan is to increase awareness of embodied consciousness, and thus attention to *what* participants are experiencing; *why* participants are experiencing whatever occurs is usually set aside during the body scan itself. However, after the body scan is completed, it is always useful to process the experience with the participant.

9. If there is a uniform absence (numbing) or dissociative detachment from literally *all* bodily sensation, we will attempt, following completion of a full body scan, to shape the experience of some healthy and safe sensation via suggestion or physical movement. For example, if participants are unable to experience *any* sensation within their body during repeated body scans, they might be encouraged to apply gentle pressure to any part of their body (i.e., with their hands) or to flex their muscles or rotate their joints (e.g., touching their fingers to their thumbs). It might also be suggested that participants imagine "sharing" a feeling that they *are* able to experience in one area of their body with another, the latter wherein they otherwise feel "nothing" or "numbness." For example, if participants report that they can feel their hands, but not their arms, imagining that the sensation experienced in their hands, *only if pleasant*, is able to spread to their wrists and forearms, thus "connecting" them through a pleasant sensation, for example, might be made.

10. Ideally, a body scan is completed throughout the body as a whole, although participants' ability to complete this exercise will vary with concentration levels and anxiety. We usually do not extend the body scan beyond 10–12 minutes.

11. Following the body scan as composed of attending to specific body parts, participants should be encouraged to experience their body as a whole, if possible, ideally facilitating an experience of embodied integra-

tion. The clinician might say: "Now, if you can, begin to be aware of your body as a whole, begin to become aware, if you can, of the entirety of your bodily self, feeling connected, together, and whole."

12. Finally, participants should be debriefed about their experiences after the body scan is completed. The clinician should inquire about any experiences participants had during the body scan that may not have been previously verbalized. The experience in its entirety is therapeutically processed during the debriefing phase to help participants develop a language for identifying and describing their feelings. If an individual has a particularly limited ability to use words to describe bodily sensations, he or she might instead draw a representation of what he or she experienced.

Case 2: Disembodiment of the Body Scan

The following transcript describes a body-scan exercise completed with Gregory, whom we have encountered several times earlier. The transcript illustrates the use of the body scan in both the assessment and treatment of TRASC of the body—in this case, partial disembodiment. At the time of the body scan, Gregory was at a stage of therapy in which he was readily processing traumatic memories and, having practiced the body-scan exercise regularly, both at home on his own and during psychotherapy sessions, Gregory was increasingly able to attend to his physical body without becoming overwhelmed with distress or experiencing marked dissociative states.

Clinician:	Should we start out with a body scan?
Gregory:	Yeah, sure.
Clinician:	So just take a position that is comfortable for you . . .
Gregory:	Do we start with the feet?
Clinician:	We started with your feet last time, but we don't have to. We can start anywhere you like.
Gregory:	Umm, no, just do it how you did it last time because that worked.
Clinician:	OK.
Gregory:	I'll just take my shoes off.
Clinician:	All right, can you focus your attention on your right foot?
Gregory:	Yup.
Clinician:	Starting with your toes, just become aware of any sensations that you may feel there . . .
Gregory:	I've got tingling in my toes.

Clinician: And then notice the sole of your foot . . .

Gregory: Yeah, I can feel the sole, I feel the bottom of my foot.

Clinician: Now just notice the top of your right foot . . .

Gregory: It's not as sensitive as the bottom, but I can feel it.

Clinician: Now moving to your right heel . . .

Gregory: Yeah, I can feel the right heel OK, it feels solid.

Clinician: And now moving up into your right ankle . . .

Gregory: Umm, not so much—it seems vaguely there—nothing solid.

Clinician: Nothing solid?

Gregory: There seems to be a bit of a gap until I reach the calf muscle.

Clinician: OK. Does your right foot feel connected to your leg?

Gregory: Partially. The top bit doesn't feel there. The top surface of the leg doesn't feel very alive.

Clinician: What happens if you move your right foot?

Gregory: I can feel the motion at the ankle, but there seems to be a part missing around the calf area, just below the calf area.

Clinician: OK. And now let's scan your left foot just for comparison, starting in with your toes . . .

Gregory: I can already feel my toes.

Clinician: And what do you notice?

Gregory: It feels totally different.

Clinician: How does it feel different?

Gregory: It just feels more solid; I don't even have to think very hard. I can feel it—right up to my knee.

Clinician: OK, and what can you feel right up to your knee?

Gregory: I can feel all the muscles all the way up to my knee.

Clinician: And does your left foot feel connected to your leg?

Gregory: Yeah, yeah, yeah, it feels very much connected. The right one still feels like a numb area.

Clinician: So now let's go back to your right foot, and slowly move from your ankle and up to your knee. Just notice what you feel . . .

Gregory: It just feels like it's a sponge; it's got a lot of holes in it, like parts are missing—it doesn't feel complete.

Clinician: And now doing the same thing with your left foot . . .

Gregory: That feels complete.

Clinician: And now starting at the right knee and slowly moving up to the hip. What do you notice?

Gregory: Umm, it doesn't feel right at all.

Clinician: What do you notice?

Gregory: A lot of numb areas. Not just on the surface, but it runs kind of deep.

Clinician: And now going on to your left leg, starting with your knee and going up to your hip, very slowly. What do you notice?

Gregory: I can feel every nerve that's there. It's just there. I can feel it.

Clinician: If you imagined making a movement with your right leg, what would that feel like?

Gregory: Imagine it or do it?

Clinician: Either or . . .

Gregory: It doesn't feel it's part of me really. No.

Clinician: And now imagining or trying the same thing with your left leg?

Gregory: (*Lifts leg, rotates, and places down again.*) Yeah, that is perfect. It is accurate and controllable.

Clinician: Accurate and controllable—how does that compare to the right side?

Gregory: It's almost like my right leg is kind of a phantom limb almost—like somebody hasn't wired it up properly—some of the nerves are correctly in place and others, umm, have been ripped out, or something is not there—it feels patchy.

Clinician: Now slowly moving into the buttocks area, first on the right . . .

Gregory: Umm, yeah, I kind of develop intense pain in that area. Uhh, yeah, that was where I was hit by my uncle.

Clinician: So that's an area that's been hurt in the past?

Gregory: Uh, yeah, absolutely.

Clinician: And how does that compare to your left buttock?

Gregory: Well, it is kind of almost the same. I can feel it, but it's not comfortable—it's sore.

Clinician: Sore—and is the pain similar to the right side or is there a difference?

Gregory: Aches more on my right at the moment, but it does switch sometimes if I had a bad nightmare about it. I'll wake up and I know that that area hurts because it's coming out in sympathy with the memory of my uncle having done that to me. So it's not numb, but it's painful.

Clinician: And is the type of pain different from side to side, or is it similar?

Gregory: It is different, yeah.

Clinician: And how is it different?

Gregory: The one on the right's sharper and on the left it's more kind of burning.

Clinician: And what happens when you notice the connection between your right upper leg and your right buttock area?

Gregory: It is like someone slid a steel plate in between my leg and my buttock—it's kind of like an area of no feeling.

Clinician: And how does that compare with the feeling in your left leg and buttock?

Gregory: The left doesn't have that. Can we move away from the buttock area because I'm getting flashbacks of being hit by my uncle?

Clinician: Yes, of course. Just remember that you're safe; you're in the present; it's 2013; no one is going to hurt you. [Grounding the client] See if you can allow that memory to pass . . . just take your time . . .

Gregory: (*After a brief moment, signaling*) I'm OK now. It's gone.

Clinician: OK. Would it be OK to continue?

Gregory: Yeah.

Clinician: OK. Bringing your attention now to your back, moving up the back slowly. So just slowly moving up your back at a pace that's comfortable for you. . . . What do you notice, first on the right side and then the left?

Gregory: I can feel my back, right the way up the spine to the base of my skull.

Clinician: And now moving to your abdomen, slowly moving up your abdomen and then your chest . . .

Gregory: Umm, the stomach is kind of there, doesn't feel complete though, umm. My chest feels a bit like a drooping flower, about to lose its petals.

Clinician: Do you feel this equally on both sides of your chest, or is there a difference between the two sides?

Gregory: The left side of my chest feels very sad.

Clinician: What would happen if you put one of your hands on the left side of your chest?

Gregory: (*Placing left hand on chest*) Yeah, I can feel it.

Clinician: What's that like?

Gregory: It's comforting.

Clinician:	And what do you notice in your body when that happens?
Gregory:	It feels more connected.
Clinician:	And feeling more connected, what happens to the drooping feeling that you alluded to earlier?
Gregory:	It kind of stops that. It's almost like it puts the brakes on it. I can feel my heart.
Clinician:	What's it like to feel your heart?
Gregory:	I can feel the pulse. It doesn't feel very happy. It feels let down.
Clinician:	What would happen if you put your other hand over the hand that's already on your chest?
Gregory:	That's [right hand] got that numb area in the wrist, so I can't really tell when it starts and finishes. It's like I've got five fingers holding the other hand, and I can feel that, and then it just disappears somewhere in my wrist, and the feeling does not come back until about halfway up my arm toward my elbow. It's just empty—it's not even there, it's almost, yeah, like transparent.
Clinician:	And how does that compare with the feeling of your left hand and arm?
Gregory:	The left side is . . . I can feel that all the way down through the shoulder.
Clinician:	What happens from the elbow to the shoulder in your right arm?
Gregory:	Umm, I can feel it's there. It feels a bit tight—that's where I had surgery, though.
Clinician:	And now let's just notice your neck . . .
Gregory:	The neck feels quite normal.
Clinician:	Front and back?
Gregory:	Yeah.
Clinician:	Sides?
Gregory:	Yeah.
Clinician:	Now slowly become aware of your face—what do you notice?
Gregory:	Contorted, umm, fragmented. It feels alien, I don't know— it's like a ball on the left temple of my head, umm, it's got pressure, it's almost a headache but not, almost like a balloon. I have had a lot of trauma in that area.
Clinician:	So another really sensitive area . . .

Gregory: Yeah, it does kind of feel like it wants to cower away and just hide.

Clinician: Remember that you are safe here. No one is going to hurt you. What if you were to put your hand over your left temple?

Gregory: (*Puts left hand on left temple*) It feels comforting. It feels better.

Clinician: And now, before ending the body scan, can you become aware of any sensations you experience at the back of your head?

Gregory: The back of my head—I can kind of feel it halfway up. The back top section seems to be missing, yeah, it's like a circle and the top is missing or something.

Clinician: Can you describe a little more what it feels like?

Gregory: Not painful or anything, it just doesn't feel like it's there—feels like it's not there.

Clinician: OK. So, reviewing, during the body scan there were a few areas of your body, at the top of the back of your head, your right wrist and forearm, and your right ankle and lower right leg, that you experienced as being absent of feelings.

Gregory: Yeah, well there are other areas which we've gone [skipped] over—the groin area is totally absent of any feelings.

Clinician: Is that an area you want to become aware of today or not? It's completely up to you.

Gregory: Umm, no, not today. Let's leave it for another day. [Note that, given Gregory's experienced separateness across different body parts, he was not encouraged to complete the body scan by experiencing his body as a whole.]

The session continued with a debriefing of Gregory's experience of the body scan, particularly focusing on processing the traumatic memory he reexperienced regarding his uncle (i.e., prompted by Gregory attending to sensations experienced in his buttocks during the body-scan exercise). The body scan, as such, was similarly used as an entry point for the processing of several other traumatic memories during other sessions. Gregory's experience of partial disembodiment, as evident in his reported experiences of the body scan, resolved over time. With continuing therapy, often including the practice of body scans, Gregory came to increasingly feel that his memories and emotions were less distressing and that his sense of self was more embodied and unified. Gregory made a drawing of himself after completing body-scan exercises at various points over the course of therapy. Figure 5.4 illustrates the disconnection Gregory expe-

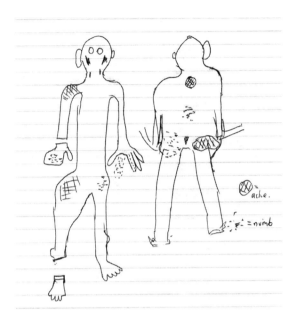

FIGURE 5.4. Gregory's Illustration of an Experience of Partial Disembodiment during a Body-Scan Exercise. *Left:* Facing forward; *Right:* facing backward. Used with permission.

rienced in his right ankle and wrist in the body scan previously described. In addition, his drawing points to areas of numbness and aching in his face, buttock region, his right shoulder, and his left index finger. It is also significant that Gregory depicted himself in this drawing without a nose or a mouth.

Case 3: A Spontaneous State of (Re-)Embodiment during Physical Exercise

"Tricia" is a middle-age woman who experienced a history of childhood abuse. Tricia had reported chronic symptoms of depersonalization in the clinical interview. At the time of the following transcript, she had only recently begun trauma-focused therapy, the latter focusing, to that date, on the learning of mindfulness-based principles, the practice of yoga, and short meditations involving attention to the breath with the goal of developing self-awareness and modulating posttraumatic responses. In this transcript Tricia describes a pleasant experience of temporary embodiment that she attributed to what she was learning in psychotherapy and to her beginning an exercise program (running).

Tricia: I'm really trying to create a transformation in my life. And part of that is through therapy. I'm working on my mental self, and my emotional self, as well as my physical self. So I'm working to get to a place where I can address those things and an environment that's conducive to transformation. And I really feel like I'm now in that place.

And one of the things is that I've never really been physically fit, or an athletic person, or a gym person, and I'm really not comfortable or happy with my physical state [body image/size] right now—I haven't been for a while—and I want to change that. So I bought a treadmill.

And I found that, after our therapy sessions, I've been reflecting on some of the stuff that came up while going on the treadmill. And so this [exercising] is something new for me. It takes an effort to do it everyday. But there is a part of me that feels like this is just such a good fit.

And so after the last session—I just found it so helpful, the imagery, and the meditations—and later that night, I was just like, really "going for it" on the treadmill, and it felt good, and I had a *really* interesting experience. For the first time I really *felt* my body. I didn't feel like I was in my head. I could really feel my body in a way that I've never felt before. So there was a moment there. It just felt good, really good.

Clinician: That sounds wonderful. And you said it felt really good. What *did* you feel? What was it like?

Tricia: I could feel my lungs breathing. And I could feel my chest expanding. And I felt the muscles in my back. And I just felt really *in my body*. And while I was on the treadmill, I was thinking through some of the stuff we had talked about [in therapy], and I was just running, and it just felt really good. *It felt like a union*—between the work I was doing here [in therapy] and the physical work I was doing on the treadmill.

Clinician: It really sounds wonderful. And the transformation you spoke of earlier—the kind of transformation that you are after in therapy—as you've said, it's one that can occur on many levels. Because if we are only in our mind, that transformation will not be as deep as if it also occurs in our body, and in our feelings—as you've said in union across all our senses of self. So that sounds like a wonderful, integrative, embodied experience of a feeling of *Here I Am*. Physical embodied awareness: Here are my lungs breathing, here is my chest expanding, here are my muscles moving. It sounds very healthy. And very alive, right?

Tricia:	Mm-umm (*nodding*).
Clinician:	A physically embodied feeling of being alive. And, as you said, in a fuller way than you usually feel, right?
Tricia:	Mm-umm (*nodding*).
Clinician:	What a wonderful experience. I'm so glad that this happened for you.
Tricia:	And I do intend for it to happen again (*smiles confidently*).

Case 4: Using Mindfulness and Somatosensory-Based Interventions to Work with a Disembodied Sense of Self

Suzy, a trauma survivor introduced in previous chapters, had been experiencing increasing depersonalization and derealization since meeting one of her previous abusers several weeks prior. When Suzy began her therapy session, she appeared very disconnected from herself and her environment while sitting on a sofa in a collapsed posture unable to make eye contact. Her therapist asked her to describe what she was feeling in her body while doing a body scan. Suzy exhibited significant difficulty expressing in words what she was feeling, noting "the words are not there. . . . " Her therapist inquired whether she would be able to draw what she was experiencing. Suzy agreed and drew a picture representing what she was feeling (see Figure 5.5, *left panel*).

The drawing depicted Suzy as experiencing both of her hands and feet as if disconnected from her trunk. In addition, Suzy depicted her brain outside of her skull, her heart in her throat, and her stomach in the location of her heart. She also portrayed her internal organs outside of her body. Moreover, Suzy depicted her eyes as spontaneously moving very rapidly in both a horizontal and vertical direction, which prevented her from being able to make eye contact with others. Finally, in her self-drawing Suzy lacks a nose, mouth, and ears.

After Suzy had completed this drawing, her therapist asked her if she would complete another body scan. Suzy noticed that looking at the drawing while doing a body scan made it much easier for her to find the words to describe what she was feeling. She began by reporting: "My insides are all jumbled up. I am not certain about my hands today. I don't think they are attached. I don't think they have been attached for quite some time." While closely examining her left hand, Suzy noted, "I am trying to feel whether they are there." Suzy continued: "My heart and stomach feel like they are in my throat. (*long pause*) I think my legs are there, but I am not sure about my feet. My feet are numb and tingly, so they may be partly there, but my hands are not there."

Suzy's therapist encouraged her to take one of her hands and notice how it feels at the point where it attaches to her arm. Suzy, while examining her left hand, noted that it felt like it did not belong to her and described that "it stops" at the wrist. Suzy continued: "I am not sure whether it is *my* hand, and that makes me nervous because I don't know whether it will hurt me, or what it will do. I think that as a child, I learned that hands are made to hurt people. And so when it does not feel like my hand, I worry that *I* will hurt people."

When the therapist inquired whether she recognized her hands, Suzy responded:

> "They look familiar, but they don't look attached. It looks like they are dangling. I have seen them before. (*long pause*) I see them when I feel disconnected. They may be the hands from another part of me. I think that maybe that part of me exists to shut down things. That part of me made it so I could not feel things. But I think sometimes that part of me has hurt me. I am not sure. That part of me carries pain. When I get overwhelmed with pain, that part of me hurts—it cuts or something. Then the mental pain goes down because now there is a different pain, a physical pain. It is like a release—for a while you can just forget about all the things in your head. There is a relief there. But then you have to deal with the cut or the burn—you are left to pick up those pieces."

Suzy's therapist encouraged her to reflect about the role of the part of her that she had just described. Suzy further related that this part of her had always functioned in a protective role. When her therapist inquired whether this part of her was functioning in the present, however, Suzy quickly responded that she was still functioning as if it were in the past; she said: "It feels like I don't have choices—I am frozen in the past."

The importance for Suzy to ground herself in the present, establishing inner safety and a sense of control across the entirety of her sense of self, was discussed. Suzy was in agreement that a goal of therapy should involve a state of being in which both her hands feel attached, she feels firmly grounded on both of her feet, and she is not regularly having out-of-body experiences. These goals were associated with the intention of increasing her sense of having, and being able to make, choices. Through a fuller sense of embodiment, she might be better able to act upon her environment, thereby experiencing a greater sense of agency and control. Suzy felt relieved to hear these therapy goals clearly articulated. Her posture became noticeably more upright and she commented that she was beginning to feel much safer.

After this intervention, Suzy again described what she was feeling in her body. She stated that things had changed significantly as a result of the intervention. She no longer felt as if her hands were detached; she examined both hands and described that they now felt firmly attached to her wrists. She also noted that her feet felt firmly grounded and that she was no longer experiencing a sensation of numbness and tingling in her feet. Suzy commented that her brain felt like it was back in her skull, her heart no longer felt like it was in her upper chest, and her stomach no longer felt like it was residing in the location of her heart. Her eyes were no longer moving horizontally or vertically, and she now demonstrated the ability to make eye contact.

When asked to make another drawing of how she depicted herself in an embodied sense, Suzy drew an image of herself that was very different from the one she drew at the beginning of the session (Figure 5.5, *right panel*). This image showed both her hands and feet fully connected to her body. Her brain, heart, stomach, and internal organs were no longer displaced. She also drew her face as including a nose and mouth, and she drew hair on her head. In this image following the body scan, she portrayed herself in karate uniform. It is noteworthy that Suzy has taken karate classes to manage overwhelming emotions and to feel an increased sense of safety within her body in the past.

FIGURE 5.5. Suzy's Illustration of Experiences of Disembodiment and (Re-)Embodiment Following a Body-Scan Exercise. Used with permission.

Case 5: Using Self-Schemas and Art Therapy to Work with a Disembodied Sense of Self

We have occasionally found that clients benefit from drawing or making a collage indicating how they view themselves at the beginning of therapy as well as at regular intervals over the course of therapy, providing that clients feel safe in doing so. Such exercises facilitate the incorporation of both verbal and nonverbal processes in self-schema work. Figure 5.6 (also in the color insert) depicts a drawing/collage completed at two different points in therapy by "Kim," a woman with significant dissociative symptoms following prolonged childhood abuse.

At the beginning of therapy, Kim depicted herself with a light line around her body to illustrate "how fragile I was and how I was rarely aware of the boundaries of my body." The "Before" drawing (*left panel*) also shows no eyes, ears, nose, or mouth. A black box covers Kim's face, which for her "symbolizes total disconnection." Moreover, no hands or feet can be observed, which Kim described as symbolizing her feeling "rarely ever grounded." Kim also described her sense of self as very fragmented, which she depicted by including several "parts of herself" within the core of her body. She describes these parts of herself as "very much separate, encapsulated."

After having engaged in trauma-focused psychotherapy using the varied approaches discussed in this text, Kim completed another collage (see Figure 5.6, color insert, *right panel*). The drawing/collage she created posttherapy shows a much clearer boundary around Kim's entire body. In addition, she depicted herself as having hands and feet as well as having a face with eyes, ears, a nose, and a mouth, communicating her newfound belief that she now "has a voice" and is feeling more grounded. She also reported feeling less fragmentation and "less chaos inside," in addition to reporting increased awareness of her emotional states. She represented these new qualities by drawing herself in a more orderly manner, the parts of herself being less encapsulated. The change between the drawings was consistent with clinical change, specifically with the significant decreases in dissociative symptoms she reported. Such clinical decreases in dissociation further coincided with fewer acts of revictimization by the client, and she was able to begin volunteering at a community mental health agency and to start to create a supportive social network.

Summary

In this chapter we examined ways in which the consciousness of embodiment, or people's sense of having, "consciously being in," owning, and belonging to a body can be altered by the experience of psychological

FIGURE 5.6. Kim's Self-Collage before and after Trauma-Focused Psychotherapy. Used with permission.

trauma. Two potential ways in which disembodiment can be provoked under experimental conditions in healthy persons were also reviewed: (1) disembodying from the bottom up, as exemplified by multisensory perceptual illusions, and (2) disembodying from the top down, through hypnotic suggestion. The neurophenomenology of partial- and full-body depersonalization in trauma-related disorders was also reviewed. In particular, the 4-D model asserts that TRASC of the body, as in experiences of depersonalization, should be distinguished from simple body-based distress (e.g., physiological hyper-/hypoarousal) as exemplary of NWC. Finally, we overviewed therapeutic exercises, in particular, variations on the body scan as used in mindfulness-based psychotherapies, as well as the use of clients' self-drawings tracking their degree of embodiment as potentially assisting them in occupying and owning a safer and more secure embodied self-state. Case examples of embodied and disembodied self-states were discussed throughout the chapter.

CHAPTER 6

Consciousness of Emotion

Feeling Too Much, and Feeling Too Little

"Is there a primal monitoring function within the brain, one that observes but is not observed? Many, including myself, believe there is no such entity. I suggest just the reverse—that there is a coherent foundational process, or "self-representation," that does not observe in the conventional sense but is observed or at least strongly "intermeshed" with various higher perceptual processes. In other words, the self-schema provides input into many sensory analyzers, and it is also strongly influenced by the primal emotional circuits. These interactions may constitute affective consciousness. This foundation process—the primordial self-schema—is not directly influenced by higher contents of consciousness, although it may be strongly and automatically modified by various other influences—by conditioned emotional "triggers," by meditation, by music, dance, and probably a variety of other rhythmic sensory-motor inputs and activities."

—Jaak Panksepp (1998, p. 309)[1]

I N THIS CHAPTER WE consider the neurophenomenology of *affective feeling*, that is, the experiential component of emotionality, as it commonly presents in traumatized persons. It is well known that people who have experienced severe trauma commonly struggle with emotion dysregulation, varying between intense states of fear, anxiety, loss, sadness, anger, guilt, and shame. From the point of view of the 4-D model, the common denominator of these emotional states is affective distress and, although often painful, intrusive, and socially disruptive, we do not consider these emotional states to be dissociative in and of themselves. Indeed all of us experience theses emotions to a varying degree within the boundaries of normal waking consciousness (NWC). As such, their presence alone is

[1]*Affective Neuroscience: The Foundations of Human and Animal Emotions* by Jaak Panksepp (1998) 135 words from p. 309. By permission of Oxford University Press, USA.

insufficient to infer the existence of a trauma-related altered state of consciousness (TRASC) of emotion.

We all have emotions, but do we all have *all* emotions? In this chapter we also consider the existence of an affective state that may be intrinsically dissociative in nature and, by definition, unavailable to NWC. Specifically, we suggest that certain presentations of emotional numbing or affective shutdown—an emotional state that is, at the same time, "*non*-emotional" or "emotionless"—exemplifies a TRASC of emotion. As such we intend to imply that the presence of marked emotional numbing, as regarded by the 4-D model, is alone sufficient to consider a person to be in a TRASC of emotion. In addition, we consider phenomenological distinctions between "*having* emotions" and "*being* an emotion" as a means of understanding other dysregulated affective states that often present in traumatized persons, as well as consider the dissociative compartmentalization of the experience of emotion, which is akin to an experience of division within the structure of selfhood along the lines of emotionality. Figure 6.1 highlights the dimension of emotion within the 4-D model.

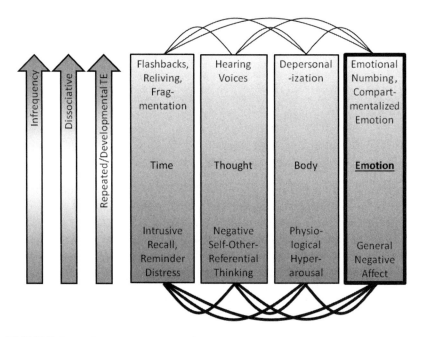

FIGURE 6.1. The 4-D Model of the Traumatized Self Highlighting NWC Distress versus TRASC of Emotion. TE = trauma exposure.

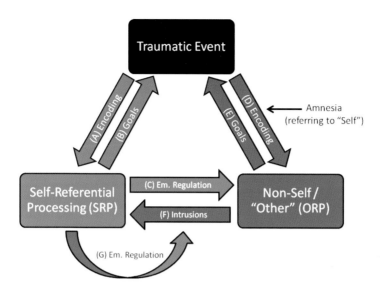

FIGURE 1.1. A (Non) Self Referential Processing Model of Dissociation.

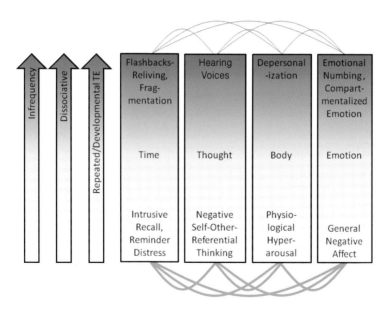

FIGURE 1.2. The 4-D Model of the Traumatized Self.

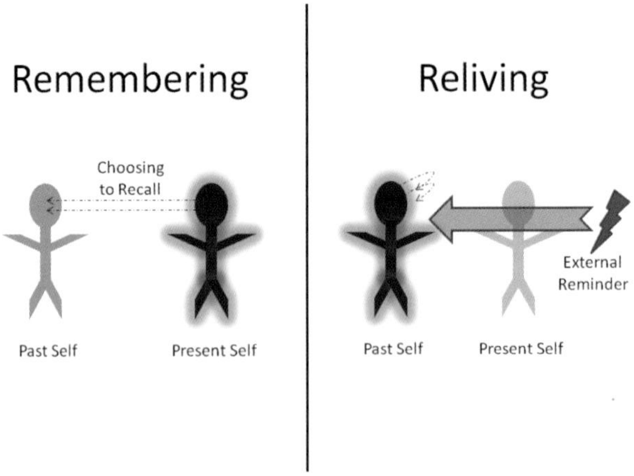

Remembering

Choosing to Recall

Past Self   Present Self

Reliving

External Reminder

Past Self   Present Self

FIGURE 3.4. Phenomenology of Remembering (NWC) versus Reliving (TRASC).

Intrusive Thinking
(1st-Person Perspective)

Voice Hearing
(2nd-Person Perspective)

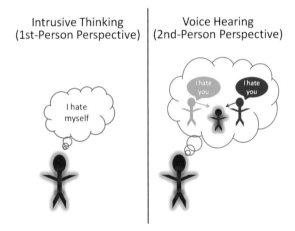

I hate myself

I hate you   I hate you

FIGURE 4.8. Phenomenology of Intrusive Thinking (NWC) versus Voice Hearing (TRASC).

Full Embodiment   Partial Disembodiment   Full Disembodiment

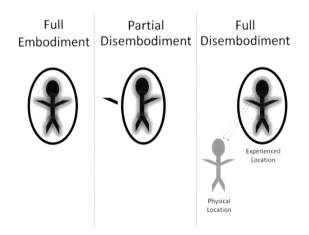

Experienced Location

Physical Location

FIGURE 5.2. Phenomenology of Embodiment (NWC) versus Partial or Full Disembodiment (TRASC).

FIGURE 6.10. Phenomenology of *Having Emotions* versus *Being an Emotion*.

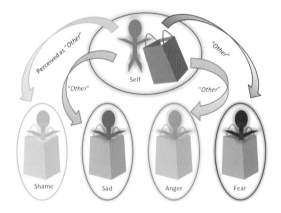

FIGURE 6.11. Phenomenology of the Compartmentalization of Emotion across Different Senses of Self.

FIGURE 6.13. Phenomenology of Emotional Numbing/Affective Shut-down.

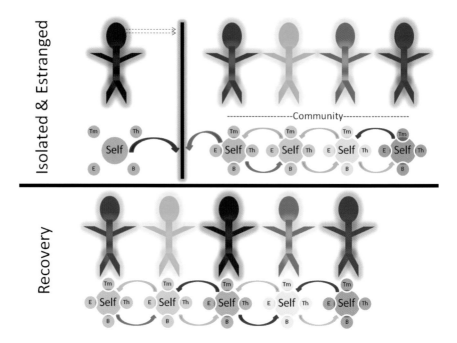

FIGURE 7.3. Social Support in Trauma Recovery.

Emotional Contagion

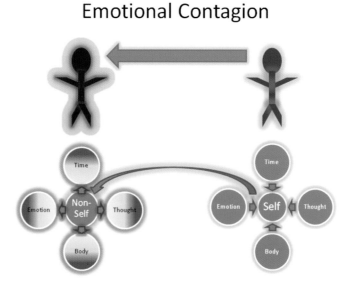

FIGURE 7.4. Emotional Contagion between the Self and the Non-Self in Terms of Time, Thought, Body, and Emotion Dimensions of Consciousness.

Mentalizing

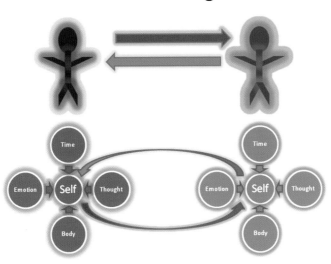

FIGURE 7.5. The Mentalizing Process of Intersubjectivity Allowing the Perceptions of Time, Thought, Body, and Emotion to Flow between Two Individuals.

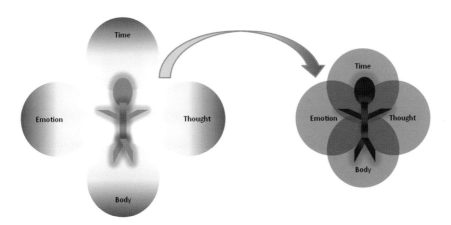

FIGURE 7.9. Integration across Dimensions of Consciousness (Time, Thought, Body, Emotion) and Emergence of a Robust Sense of Self.

FIGURE 3.3. Gregory's Artwork (2010): "(1 + x)."

FIGURE 3.5. Gregory's Artwork (2011, untitled).

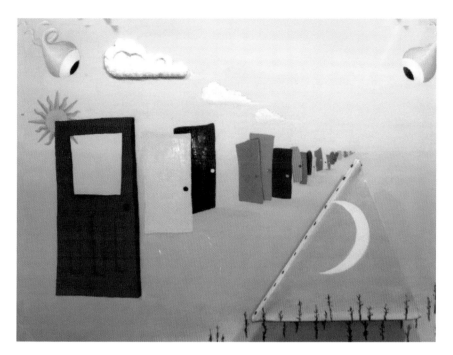

FIGURE 3.6. Gregory's Artwork (2011): "Dream II."

FIGURE 4.9. Gregory's Artwork (2010): "Time."

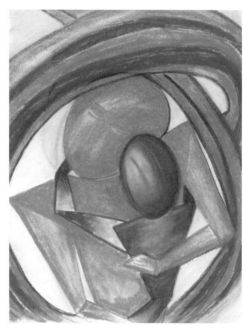

FIGURE 4.11. Gregory's Artwork (2009): "Adult and Child."

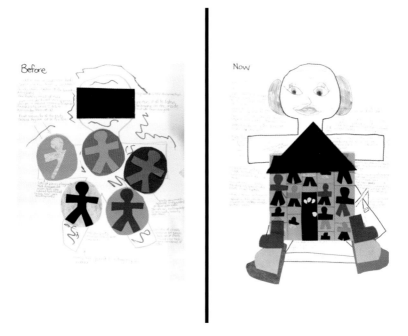

FIGURE 5.6. Kim's Self-Collage before and after Trauma-Focused Psychotherapy.

FIGURE 6.6. Stephanie's artwork (2014): "Shame—inside and out I."

FIGURE 6.14. Valerie's Artwork (2012): "It is okay to be me."

FIGURE 6.15. Mischa's Artwork (2010, untitled).

FIGURE 7.8. Jen's Artwork (2013): "Taking Space."

FIGURE 7.10. Gregory's Artwork (2010): "On a withered branch a flower blooms."

FIGURE 7.11. Janine's Artwork (2011, untitled).

Defining Distress: Classification of Emotions
and Emotional Experience

Theorists have increasingly pointed out the likely significant role played by emotional processing in the across-species evolution of consciousness (e.g., Panksepp, 1998; Izard, 2007, 2009; Panksepp & Northoff, 2009). Defining and classifying just what emotions *are*, and what affect *is*, however, are surprisingly not as simple as one might otherwise think (e.g., Izard, 2010). One dominant paradigm, termed *basic emotions theory*, hypothesizes that specific neural systems (sometimes referred to as "affect programs") are dedicated to the mediation of distinct emotional behaviors such as those consistent with universally recognized facial expressions and behaviors (e.g., anger, fear, sadness, and disgust, Ekman, 1999; e.g., fear, panic, rage, Panksepp, 1998). The principle idea behind basic emotions theory is that the brain bases for different emotions (e.g., fear vs. anger) include sets of both overlapping and nonoverlapping elements. Although evidence for the distinctiveness between emotions is notoriously weak when examined in terms of response within the autonomic nervous system of humans (Larsen, Berntson, Poehlmann, Ito, & Cacioppo, 2008), emerging empirical support is increasingly obtained for central representations as examined with functional neuroimaging (Murphy, Nimmo-Smith, & Lawrence, 2003; Phan, Wager, Taylor, & Liberzon, 2002; Vytal & Hamann, 2010; cf. Lindquist, Wager, Kober, Bliss-Moreau, & Barrett, 2012). Figure 6.2 illustrates the neuroanatomy of brain regions of interest frequently identified in neuroimaging studies of emotion.

Several theorists nevertheless cast reasoned doubt on the hypothesis that various listings of basic emotions are truly biologically distinct in the philosophical sense of "natural kinds"—that is, that categorical distinctions between basic emotions carve nature at its joints. Constructivist theorists, for example, argue that the apparent uniqueness of basic emotions may only be the product of post hoc cognitive interpretations of more rudimentary distinctions as they occur in the context of different physical and social environments. These include positivity versus negativity (pleasant vs. unpleasant/aversive), or approach versus withdrawal orientations, on the one hand, and high versus low physiological arousal, on the other (Barrett, 2006a, 2006b, 2009, 2012; Barrett & Gendreon, 2009; Feldman-Barrett & Russell, 1999; Russell, 1980, 2003, 2005, 2009; Russell & Carroll, 1999).

For example, the same high-arousal negative affective physiological state may be experienced as fear in the context of perceived vulnerability, but anger in the context of perceived dominance. These "two-factor models" of emotion are, by definition, more parsimonious than the basic emotions view, the latter dividing up emotional experiences into more discrete qualitative categories. The valence and action orientation factors categorize emotions by their experiential versus behavioral characteristics,

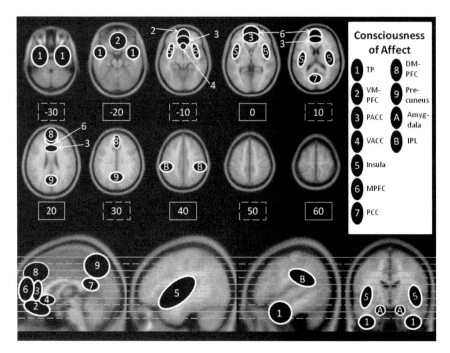

FIGURE 6.2. The Neuroanatomy of Consciousness of Emotion. DMPFC = dorsomedial prefrontal cortex; IPL = inferior parietal lobe; mPFC = medial prefrontal cortex; pACC = perigenual anterior cingulate cortex; PCC = posterior cingulate cortex; TP = temporal pole; vACC = ventral anterior cingulate cortex; vmPFC = ventromedial prefrontal cortex.

respectively, although they diverge on some specifics—for example, with respect to the categorization of anger. Anger is typically considered negative in experiential valence and categorized among other negative affects within the valence framework (e.g., with fear and sadness). By contrast, anger is typically considered forward-directed in action orientation, and thus some models classify anger among other emotions associated with forward movement, even as the latter tend to be positive in valence (e.g., with desire and wanting) (Carver & Harmon-Jones, 2009).

Much research suggests that, when persons are assessed in terms of *traits*—that is, in terms of how one usually feels—the two-factor frameworks provide a parsimonious description of individual differences in emotional experience and behavior (e.g., Cacioppo & Berntson, 1994; Cacioppo, Gardner, & Berntson, 1999; Feldman-Barrett & Russell, 1999; Russell, 1980, 2003, 2005, 2009; Russell & Carroll, 1999; Watson & Tellegen, 1985; Watson, Weise, Vaidya, & Tellegen, 1999). In broad strokes, research suggests that people who frequently endorse experiencing one or more negative affects (e.g., anxiety, sadness) are also more likely to report frequently experiencing other forms of negative affect as well (e.g., anger, shame). In other words, the frequency with which specific individuals experience specific negative emotional states is correlated. In parallel, if a person often reports experiencing one positive emotion (e.g., joy), he or she is also likely to report frequently experiencing other positive emotions as well (e.g., relaxation).

However, for some time, and in contrast with an even simpler single-factor framework that would place positive and negative affect on opposite ends of a single continuum, many theorists consider the representation of positive and negative valences to require two separate "bins" rather than only one: Positive and negative affect are considered two different *things* rather than opposite ends of a single continuum. Fundamental to this framework, early research suggested that the frequency with which a person reported experiencing positive versus negative affect was *not* strongly negatively correlated. In other words, the person who frequently experienced negative affect was not necessarily the same person who rarely experienced positive affect: These affective states did not go hand in hand quite as closely as intuition might otherwise predict (Watson & Tellegen, 1985; Watson et al., 1999).

As neurophenomenologists, however, we are primarily interested in the subjectivity of emotion *moments* as they arise in real time; that is, as affective *states* rather than affective *traits*. Measured in terms of discrete moments in time, the bipolar notions of hedonicity (i.e., valence; pleasurable vs. unpleasurable) and arousal (high vs. low, or activated vs. deactivated) may be sufficient alone as means of accounting for much of the physiological substrates of what we call affective experience (Barrett, Linquist, & Gendron, 2007; Barrett, Mesquita, Ochsner, & Gross, 2007; Feldman-Barrett & Russell, 1999; Russell, 2003, 2005, 2009; Russell & Carroll, 1999). Among many others, we had previously reasoned that a theoretical advantage of a multifactor model was the ability to represent "mixed" emotions, specifically emotional states seemingly both positive and negative in valence (Frewen, Dozois, Joanisse, & Neufeld, 2008). For example, survivors of mass murder attempts may experience both gratitude and guilt in their escape while mourning the loss of the less fortunate; without two valences, along a single-factor bipolar continuum one might have to represent the experience as somewhere within the neutral middle of an axis differentiating gratitude (e.g., contentment) and guilt (e.g., upset), while failing to represent the survivor's internal emotional conflict.

Nevertheless, it is possible that a more fine-grained temporal analysis of emotional experience would resolve the apparent conceptual conundrum of mixed emotion for bipolar models. Specifically, it may prove unreasonable to represent a mixed emotion on the order of moments (e.g., 2–3 seconds), yet different emotions may be present in vacillating fashion over the course of longer periods of time (e.g., on the order of 10s of seconds, and certainly over the course of several minutes). From this point of view, we would find it entirely unsurprising that certain college students, for example, might feel both happy and sad on their graduation day (Larsen, McGraw, & Cacioppo, 2001). Indeed an often-neglected element in scientific studies regards how emotional experience can change even over relatively brief moment-to-moment intervals (e.g., Davidson, 1998; Kirkland & Cunningham, 2012; Koval & Kuppens, 2012; Kuppens et al., 2012; Lewis, 2005). Yik, Russell, and Steiger (2011) drew researchers' attention to the fact that participants' emotional states may even change over the course of completing lengthy surveys about their emotional states, such that, for example, they may report being in a more interested, activated affective state at the beginning than by the end of the questionnaire. The next section also discusses the notion of emotional responses cued by external events (exteroception) versus internal bodily events (interoception).

Emotion on the Inside and Out:
The Internality and Externality of Emotion

Going back to Descartes and more recently to Brentano, philosophers have also characterized intentional consciousness as referring primarily either to objects defined outside the conscious self's borders (object-directed, external, primary-other content) or to consciousness of the agent who *is* conscious (i.e., self-directed, internal, secondary-self content or simply self-consciousness). In this way, the property of intentionality simultaneously makes the very general distinction between things that are "me" and those that are "not me," and between an inside world ("self") and an outside world ("not self"). The fields of social, cognitive, and affective neuroscience have increasingly acknowledged the basic distinction between an external and internal "world" in the design of neuroimaging experiments. Thus studies have probed the neural processes mediating attention directed at things outside the self, termed *exteroception*, in comparison with the processes mediating attention directed at oneself, termed either *introspection*, when consciousness reflects upon itself in an abstract, "cognitive" way (involving language, logic, and syntax), or *interoception*, when consciousness is directed toward the experience of bodily and affective feelings (see reviews by Lieberman, 2007; Phan et al., 2003; Wager, Phan, Liberzon, & Taylor, 2003).

In a now classic study that was the first to directly compare exteroception and interoception of emotional stimuli, Lane and colleagues asked participants to view both pleasant (e.g., flowers) and unpleasant (e.g., cemetery) pictures in each of two ways: (1) with an "internal focus," involving attending to and rating how they felt in response to the picture, and (2) with an "external focus," involving attending to and rating whether the scene depicted an indoor or outdoor setting (Lane, Fink, Chau, & Dolan, 1997). It is important to point out that participants did not "cognitively judge" the valence of the pictures in a neutral and detached way, but instead rated how they *felt* in response to them. When directly contrasting the two types of conscious focus, Lane and colleagues' showed that internally focusing on emotional experience was associated with increasing response within the perigenual and ventral anterior cingulate cortex, the former extending into the medial prefrontal cortex, regions to be found in the brain's anterior midline, as well as within the left insula. These brain regions have since been strongly implicated in emotional processing. In comparison, focusing on external stimuli more greatly recruited the parietal–occipital cortices bilaterally, which are less reliably implicated in emotional processing. The study therefore showed that the same visual stimuli, when consciously attended to in different ways, recruited distinct neural networks. Specifically, the internal focus was associated with regions particularly involved in emotional experiencing, whereas the external focus was associated with visual and somatosensory perceptions.

Whereas Lane and colleagues' study examined the effects of externally versus internally directed attention toward an external stimulus, other research has examined differences in emotional responding to externally versus internally *generated* emotional experience (e.g., emotions generated via response to pictures and films in comparison with recall of emotional memories and imagination of scripted vignettes, respectively). In general, results suggest that internally generated emotionality tends to be more successful (i.e., elicits emotional experiences of greater intensity) than does external stimuli (e.g., see Salas, Radovic, & Turnbull, 2012), and some researchers infer a close association between the psychological processes mediating episodic memory and imagination, on the one hand, and emotional experience, on the other (e.g., Holmes & Matthews, 2005, 2010; Holmes, Lang, & Deeprose, 2009; Holmes, Lang, & Shaw, 2009; Holmes, Matthews, Mackintosh, & Dalgleish, 2008). Meta-analyses also suggest that the brain regions involved in the internal versus external generation of emotional experience differ. For example, it has been known for some time that the amygdala tends to respond more reliably to external emotional stimuli (e.g., aversive pictures, films, and sounds) than to internal stimuli (e.g., memories, imagination; Phan et al., 2002). In addition, a recent highly unique case study of a male subject with selective ablation of the primary visual cortex, who nevertheless could imagine events visually, shows that, for example, visual imagery does not require visual perception (Bridge, Harrold, Holmes, Stokes, & Kennard, 2012).

Core Affect and the Affective Circumplex:
A Model of the Emotional Sense of Self

"Core Affect is always potentially available, although it can be focal, peripheral, or even so peripheral that it is invisible. Although . . . Core Affect can come to be directed at an Object, Core Affect per se is Object-free. That is, in pure form, it is free-floating, or non-intentional in the philosophical sense. [However,] Core Affect may be rarely experienced in this pure form (perhaps the closest cases would be drug induced), but [rather] is typically experienced embedded with other elements of consciousness as one interacts with the world. Although it is non-intentional, Core Affect is caused, and occasionally one salient event is the obvious cause. . . . But we often confront many events simultaneously, each contributing to Core Affect. As well, there are influences on Core Affect beyond awareness or even human ability to perceive. . . . Core Affect is located not in any part of the body but in the core self...which is 'me here and now.' Core self is irreflexive, first-order consciousness and thus distinct from the cognitive and narrative concept of the self. . . . Although Core affect is an ancient and non-linguistic thing, if it were translated into language, it would be 'I feel X' . . . the feelings . . . cannot be reduced to behavioural, sensory, or any other more basic elements: Core Affect is an irreducible element of consciousness."

—James Russell (2005, pp. 29–31)[1]

"The key integration step is the realization of a coherent representation of all salient conditions across all relevant systems at each immediate moment of time—a 'global emotional moment.'. . . The unified representation of all salient conditions—encoded as feelings—is in effect a representation of the entirety of the individual . . . which I refer to as 'the sentient self.' The cinemascopic model of awareness . . . is essentially a continuously updating series of global emotional moments ranging across a finite extent of present time that incorporates predictive representations based on acquired internal models. . . . Thus, a global emotional moment is the sentient self, or the neural self, at each moment of time. The essential ingredient of this model of a sentient self is the neural construct for a feeling, which represents first of all a homeostatic sensory condition in the body."

—A. D. Craig (2010, p. 569)[2]

Whereas many models describe affective experience primarily in terms of discrete "emotion episodes," as well as longer though equally pass-

[1]Originally published in Russell, J. A. (2005) "Emotion in human consciousness is reducible to core affect," *Journal of Consciousness Studies, 12*(8–10), pp. 26–42. Used with permission of Imprint Academic.
[2]Reprinted from *Brain Structure and Function*, Vol. 214, Issue 5, A. D. (Bud) Craig, "The Sentient Self," January 2010, with kind permission from Springer Science + Business Media.

ing moods, Russell's (2003) concept of *core affect* describes the affective *background* of moment-to-moment experience. According to Russell, core affect is held to be latent in all experience; it is the lens through which one experiences the world—through which all experience is felt. At the same time, however, core affect is thought to reside, usually, in the background of awareness, for the most part imperceptible unless deliberately attended to. Core affect is thought to vary across time, mirroring the ever-present change in the world around us.

The concept of *core affect* represents the moment-by-moment experience of oneself in the form of ongoing homeostatic processes generally signifying basic degrees of arousal and felt (un)pleasantness. Thus core affect construes the self as an affective background—the current core affective state acts as a screen through which future events are felt, thereby representing an affective model of selfhood, revised again and again with each passing moment. In Russell's model, core affect and Damasio's (1999) concept of "core self" are considered largely redundant, other than that core affect naturally emphasizes emotionally relevant dimensions of consciousness, whereas core self includes even more basic elements of the organism–environment relation (e.g., Russell, 2005). Again, without attending to core affect, we may be relatively unaware of how we feel, although core affect is thought to reflect the happenings of both the internal physiological milieu and external sensory world just the same. Accordingly, Russell suggests that, normally if we are asked how we are feeling, we will usually be instantly aware of the answer; this capability is theorized to be based on core affect (Russell 2003, 2005, 2009; Russell & Carroll, 1999).

Craig's (2010) concept of the affectively "sentient self" appears to significantly overlap Russell's concept of core affect. However, Craig goes further by proposing a neuroanatomical model for core affective feeling, linking this most notably to the anterior insula and particularly the right hemisphere. Craig (2002, 2005, 2010) reviews a vast amount of literature to arrive at his hypothesis that there may exist a somatotopic mapping within the insula, from posterior to anterior, over which multimodal internal body-based representations in the posterior insula are re-represented in the anterior insula as a basis for *conscious* interoception and hence *subjective feeling*. In interaction with the anterior cingulate, such representations are further thought to provide the basis for conscious affect regulation—that is, the choice and associated workings of attempts to feel differently (e.g., better) than one currently feels (e.g., Medford & Critchley, 2010). In addition, associations between representations in the insula may be communicated (partly via the cingulate) to the medial prefrontal cortex, where they may thereby influence the working of a primary node of the narrative self and thus ongoing reflective thought and evaluative judgement. This is not to say, however, that one cannot mindfully structure one's awareness in such a way as to separate feelings from thoughts, with the effect of preventing the engendering of affect-laden cognition (e.g., rumination, worry) (e.g., Farb et al., 2007).

What are the feelings of core affect *like*? As an example of a two-factor model, Russell (2003) proposes that specific states of core affect can be represented within a circumplex structure defined by two axes: pleasure (pleasantness vs. unpleasantness) and arousal (activation vs. deactivation) (see Figure 6.3). Circumplex structures model intercorrelations among variables that are encompassed within a circular space. Most circumplex models demarcate different "types" of emotional experience by their location around eight vectors (i.e., 45° increments), although Yik et al. (2011) made a strong case for recognizing at least twelve vectors. The concept of the circumplex is that, phenomenologically speaking, the likeness of any one emotional experience to another follows that of a cosine wave as one moves in equal degrees (counter)-clockwise around the circumplex (i.e., closer vs. farther apart; Yik et al., 2011). Yik and colleagues compellingly demonstrated the adequacy of a circumplex structure to account for the range of variation in the experience of most psychometric measures of emotion, mood, and personality variables currently used by researchers, at least within psychologically healthy populations.

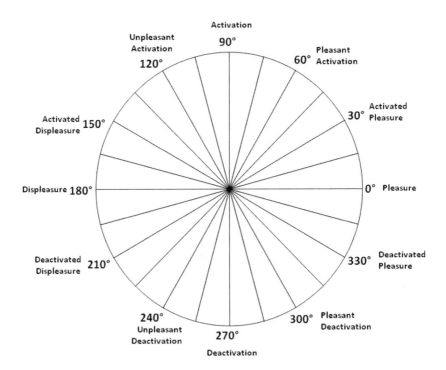

FIGURE 6.3. The Affective Circumplex. Adapted with permission from Yik, Russell, and Steiger (2011). Copyright © 2011 by the American Psychological Association. Adapted with permission. The official citation that should be used in referencing this material is Yik, M., Russell, J. A., Steiger, J. H. (2011). A 12-point circumplex structure of core affect. *Emotion, 11*(4), pages 705–31. The use of APA information does not imply endorsement by APA.

Although not explicitly considered by Yik et al. (2011), an equally striking observation of their studies was the near absence of affective measures
occupying certain 12ths of the circumplex, particularly between 75° and
105°, and between 255° and 285°—that is, referring to the vertical poles of
the circumplex and activated versus deactivated states, respectively, that
lack a strong loading on the pleasure-versus-displeasure (horizontal) axis
(e.g., see Yik et al., 2011, Figure 5). On our reading, the theoretical implications are that normal, psychologically healthy persons nearly always feel
at least somewhat good or bad; we rarely truly feel hyper- or hypoaroused
without accompanying feelings of pleasure or aversion. Our interpretation of this finding is that affective experiences between 75° and 105°, and
between 255° and 285°, akin to hyper- and hypoaroused states that lack
an accompanying strong impression of being pleasant or averse (see Figure 6.3), are very atypically experienced within NWC. Indeed, we would
suggest that such affective states hint at the presence of an altered state of
consciousness, a point to which we return later.

Thus far, a limitation relating to the external validity of Russell and
colleagues' circumplex model is the fact that, to the best of our knowledge, its ability to account for affective states associated with severe
trauma-related psychopathology has not yet been rigorously evaluated.
Based only on face validity and clinical experience, throughout this
chapter we speculate about the possible circumplex locations for several core affective experiences associated with psychological trauma.
Along with clinical examples, the circumplex model provides a simple,
intuitive guide that may assist one in considering the phenomenological
question of what experiencing trauma-related affective states might *be
like* for the traumatized person.

Trauma and the Social Emotions: Focus on Shame and Guilt

*"The majority of our patients report histories of abuse in childhood,
and many report physical or sexual abuse by intimate partners in
adult life as well. At the point of entry into treatment, the majority
easily fulfill diagnostic criteria for PTSD. . . . However, most of our
patients do not cite their PTSD symptoms as their reason for seeking
treatment. Rather, it is most commonly some breach in a relationship that acutely aggravates a profoundly damaged sense of self. In
treatment, we find repeatedly that the core issue is shame."*

—J. Herman (2011, p. 262)

Whereas emotional behavior is clearly recognized in lower and higher
animals alike, the subjective feeling or conscious component of emotionality, particularly that accompanying complex social emotions such as
pride and shame, may be an evolutionary emergence realized uniquely
in the human brain (e.g., Williamson & Allman, 2011). In addition to the
factors of pleasure–displeasure (valence), arousal–intensity (activation–

deactivation), action orientation, and internality versus externality, it has been suggested that whether emotional states occur within the context of social information processing is usefully considered. We previously defined the *sociality* dimension of emotion as referring to "the degree to which the emotional significance of a stimulus or encounter is derived within the context of social information processing or social cognition" (Frewen, Dozois, et al., 2011a, p. 375; see also Britton, Phan, et al., 2006; Britton, Taylor, Berridge, Mikels, & Liberzon, 2006; Olsson & Ochsner, 2008). Hareli and Parkinson (2008) also suggested that a heuristic division can be made between emotions that are necessarily social and those that can occur in the absence of social information processing. Social emotions were defined as those that (1) require assessment of the significance of another person's thoughts, feelings, or actions for oneself; and (2) have as their primary purpose the execution of evolutionarily significant social functions (Hareli & Parkinson, 2008). Positive social emotions include admiration, gratitude, love, compassion, and pride; negative social emotions include anger, contempt, envy, jealousy, guilt, shame, and pity. As examples, positive interpersonal events, including receiving another person's affection or praise, may bring about confidence and self-esteem in the person experiencing them (e.g., pride, Tracy & Robins, 2007; Tracy, Robins, & Tangney, 2007). In contrast, when we are rejected or experience failure, we may experience anger, sadness, or be ashamed of ourselves.

We directly compared the neural correlates of social to nonsocial emotional processing in 20 healthy women in response to the imagination of social or nonsocial emotional scripts (vignettes). The results of the study showed that imagination of scripts describing situations that frequently aroused social emotions activated brain regions previously associated with social cognition more significantly than did imagination of scripts less associated with the arousal of social emotions (Frewen, Dozois, Neufeld, Densmore, et al., 2011a). Moreover, this finding occurred irrespective of valence. More specifically, scripts that provoked feelings of self-esteem and comfort in relationships (e.g., expressed friendship and love, or an experience of being successful), as well as those that effectively encouraged the *opposite* experience (e.g., experiences of social rejection, being criticized, or failing), activated brain regions engaged by social cognition, including mentalizing: specifically, the dorsomedial prefrontal cortex, posterior cingulate cortex–precuneus, bilateral angular gyri (inclusive of the temporoparietal junction), bilateral temporal poles, and right amygdala. In comparison, imagination of solitary emotional events—for example, drowning (fear) or walking along the beach at sunrise (relaxation, pleasant)—failed to provoke these brain responses with the same magnitude. The study thus provided further validity for the distinction between social and nonsocial emotions on the basis of responses within the brain (see also, e.g., Britton, Phan, et al., 2006).

Many scholars have considered the phenomenology of the social emotion *shame* in survivors of psychological trauma. Much consideration has been devoted to the conceptual and empirical differentiation of shame from what are considered related affective states, most especially *guilt* (e.g., Blum, 2008; Kim, Thibodeau, & Jorgensen, 2011; Fletcher, 2011; Lee, Scragg, & Turner, 2001; Lewis, 1987; Nathanson, 1987, 1992; Schore, 2003a, 2003b; Tangney & Dearing, 2003; Wilson, Droždek, & Turkovic, 2006). Theoretical writings suggest that both shame and guilt arise in the context of deeming oneself at fault for a moral transgression. Nevertheless, the phenomenology of shame and guilt are thought to differ in a number of respects. For one, shame is typically considered a more intensely aversive affective state than is guilt. Moreover, shame and guilt differ in several evaluative and behavioral ways. With regard to self- versus other-focus, guilt primarily concerns self-disapproval whereas in shame, one not only disapproves of oneself but additionally believes (or has evidence) that others disapprove of oneself. In this sense, whereas guilt may be an entirely private experience, shame feels *public*. In addition, guilt and shame differ with respect to the object of blame and the past versus present focus of the affect, respectively: Guilt primarily concerns the feeling that one's *past behavior* was wrongful (i.e., "What I *did was* bad"), whereas in shame the entirety of the self is felt to be of present reproach ("Who I *am is* bad"). This distinction can be complicated by the use of the expression *ashamed of*, however, which tends to be used to refer to a particular event rather than the self in its entirety (cf. Rizvi, 2010).

Action orientation also differs between guilt and shame, with guilt primarily motivating the making of amends, and shame promoting self-concealment (e.g., keeping the event secret, hiding one's face). It has been argued that in the latter lies the key to the potential resolution of shame. Specifically, to overcome shame one must somehow tell one's story in a way that is redeeming—one seeks to reclaim one's inner sense of dignity. In addition, whereas the affective feeling of guilt may be mostly limited to a form of anxiety and the provocation of others' anger, the feeling of shame may include elements of both anxiety and disgust, and provoke disapproval and even a disgust response from others (e.g., Davey, 2011; Giner-Sorolla & Espinosa, 2011; cf. Blum, 2008; Kim, et al., 2011; Wilson et al., 2006). Blum (2008) also contrasted shame with several other socio-emotional states, including humiliation and embarrassment. According to Blum (2008), in humiliation, although one is aware that others disapprove of one, the individual may not, him- or herself, deem such judgment fair. In comparison, in a state of embarrassment, one is aware that others view one as having made a mistake, although one that lacks clear moral relevance.

In summary, shame marks the experience of being seen as bad, not just in one's own eyes, but in the eyes of others. The experience of shame is more than the experience of "I'm bad"; rather, it is the experience of "I'm bad, and I know that you know it" (Lewis, 1987; Tangney & Dearing,

2003). Shame is thus quintessentially self-conscious and social in nature. A final important point to make concerning the phenomenology of shame relates to its impact on positive affect and direct gaze. Tomkins (1995) argued that a principal function of shame is to inhibit positive emotions such as interest and enjoyment, and thus shame and positive affect are considered to be intrinsically incongruent: The experience of pride and joy are thought to be essentially impossible in the company of shame. Shame often develops out of the internalization of another person's depreciation of oneself. For example, the child who is frowned at, scolded, and told he is "a filthy, rotten, disgusting boy" may also come to view himself the same way; subsequent mistakes as an adult then recreate the shadow of this previous shame (Schore, 2003a, 2003b). The experience of shame can also have a tremendous impact on the capacity to make eye contact in an interpersonal relationship and often leads to averted gaze (Schore, 2003a, 2003b). As Jen, a patient with a long-standing history of childhood abuse and related experiences of shame, noted: "When I make eye contact with someone, then they can see me—I mean that they can see how I feel about myself—that I am not a good person." Tim, a Vietnam veteran first introduced in Chapter 3, noted: "[Eye contact] feels really scary. When I make eye contact, I feel like they're going to see a stain on my soul. I feel a sense of shame about the situation in Vietnam that I was in, and I also feel shame about some of the things that I witnessed and I didn't do anything about."

It is interesting to note that direct versus averted eye gaze has been associated with brain activation involving defensive responses and decreased social affiliation in people with PTSD related to childhood abuse, as compared to healthy individuals who show activation of brain regions associated with social cognition, including mentalizing (Steuwe, Daniels, et al., 2012). Future studies should examine the impact of shame on these brain activation patterns. In addition, therapists should continue to be mindful of the importance of allowing the traumatized individual to avert his or her gaze during the therapeutic process in order to minimize the induction of shame, including avoiding sitting directly facing the client.

Based on such research, we view certain clinical presentations of shame as relatively highly activated and unpleasant states with a hypothesized location between 120° and 150° on the affective circumplex (see Figure 6.4). This is consistent with Yik et al.'s (2010) findings for the circumplex locations of "ashamed" and "guilty" and Herman's (2011) description of subjective experiences. According to Herman (2011), shame involves:

> an initial shock and flooding with painful emotion. Shame is a relatively wordless state, in which speech and thought are inhibited. It is also an acutely self-conscious state; the person feels small, ridiculous, and exposed. There is a wish to hide characteristically expressed by covering the face with the hands. The person wishes to "sink through the floor" or "crawl in a hole and die." (p. 263)

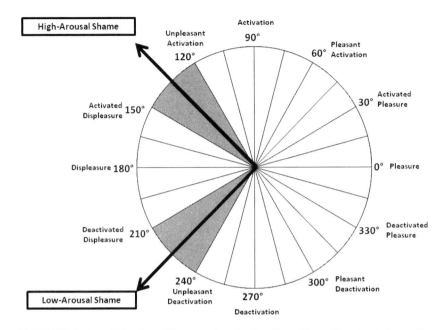

FIGURE 6.4. Affective Circumplex Indicating Hypothesized Location of High- versus Low-Arousal Shame. Adapted with permission from Yik, Russell, and Steiger (2011). Copyright © 2011 by the American Psychological Association. Adapted with permission. The official citation that should be used in referencing this material is Yik, M., Russell, J. A., Steiger, J. H. (2011). A 12-point circumplex structure of core affect. *Emotion, 11*(4), pages 705–31. The use of APA information does not imply endorsement by APA.

In addition to a high-arousal experience of shame, there is a lower-arousal dysphoric state of shame that presents as a relatively chronic condition or organization of the personality. Schore (2003a, 2003b) has suggested that, for example, the onset of blushing, a physiological response often associated with shame, may reflect a shift of balance from a dominant sympathetic to a parasympathetic autonomic response associated with more passive coping and perceived helplessness. As such, we also hypothesized an expression of shame to occur somewhere between 210° and 240° on the circumplex (see Figure 6.4).

Interestingly, functional neuroimaging studies also reveal both commonalities and differences between the brain regions mediating the experience of guilt versus shame, although the latter was not necessarily well distinguished from "embarrassment" and being "ashamed" in these studies (Michl et al., 2012; Takahashi et al., 2004). These studies are therefore unlikely to have provoked clinically significant experiences of shame as frequently observed in traumatized persons. Overall, less response was observed relative to a neutral control task for comparisons involving the experience of guilt relative to shame, consistent with the hypothesis that shame represents the stronger, more complex, and more aversive socioemotional state of the two. Relative to control tasks, reading sentences that were guilt or shame provoking was also associated with increased response within the medial prefrontal cortex, the left posterior superior temporal sulcus, and the visual cortex, thus engaging regions associated with social cognition more generally. Contrasting shame with guilt directly revealed increased response in the temporal cortex and hippocampus in two studies (Michl et al., 2012; Takahashi et al., 2004), and the dorsomedial prefrontal cortex, anterior cingulate, and right inferior frontal gyrus in the first (Michl et al., 2012), whereas contrasting guilt with shame revealed increased response in the right amygdala and insula in the study of Michl et al. (2012). Such findings are consistent with the idea that shame and guilt are more greatly associated with internalizing versus externalizing experiences and action orientations, respectively. Michl et al. also speculated that shame might be more strongly linked to biophysiological processes that vary less significantly across different cultures, as compared with guilt, the latter more greatly influenced by learned social standards.

It is important to point out that, in severely traumatized persons, shame can present not only as an acute emotional state but also as a more fundamental and enduring aspect of an individual's personality structure; in many traumatized persons the experience of shame essentially *defines who they are*. For these persons, the experience of shame runs very deep, seemingly elemental in every aspect of their being. Figures 6.6 and 6.7 illustrate "Stephanie's" experience of being permeated by feelings of shame. In addition, "Stephanie" as well as "Suzy," both survivors of severe childhood trauma, described their experiences of shame as follows:

Interviewer: Can you tell us if you experience feelings of shame? If so, can you tell us what this is like?

Stephanie: I find it [shame] very difficult to come out of. The shame is so big and so overwhelming that it becomes part of who I am . . .

Interviewer: Can you tell us if you experience feelings of shame? If so, can you tell us what this is like?

Suzy: Yes, I still have them. They have never gone away. It is hard to describe shame. Shame is like you are embarrassed of who you are and what you did. You feel guilty about what you have done and you feel badly about yourself for what you have done. There is nothing positive associated with shame.

Interviewer: What happens when you experience shame?

     Suzy: It permeates everything. It touches everything, is a piece of every emotion, every movement, it's a core part of you.

Interviewer: Would it always be there?

     Suzy: Yes, it is always there, it touches everything.

It deserves note that, in addition to fear, perpetrators will often utilize shame to keep victims in a subordinate position, limiting the likelihood of escape or rebellion. Such a relational structure is well described in historical studies of slavery, child soldiers, and of the current international commerce of prostitution and other forms of human trafficking. In severe cases the individual is *dehumanized*, that is, treated explicitly without human dignity, as less than a person; for example, being referred to and physically treated as an animal (e.g., as a dog), or referred to as an object of low value or intrinsic disgust (e.g., dirt, feces). The value of the person is severely diminished, not only in the perpetrator's eyes, but in victims' own eyes. They begin to value themselves as less than nothing; we emphasize this not only as a core *belief* but also as a *core affect*: Victims come to *feel* themselves as something vulgar and repulsive *from the inside*.

Interestingly, as relevant to the 4-D model, it has been shown that, in traumatized persons with childhood histories of abuse, dissociative symptoms were correlated with shame proneness in two studies (Dutra, Callahan, Forman, Mendelsohn, & Herman, 2008; Talbot, Talbot, & Tu, 2004). The experience of shame is also thought to be a common precursor to suicide (cf. Wiklander et al., 2012). Finally, several authors have suggested that, when a person's past traumatic experiences are more associated with an experience of shame than they are with anxiety or fear, exposure-based therapies may not be the treatment of choice. Instead, clients are perhaps better served by psychotherapies aimed at lowering self-judgmental tendencies and fostering greater self-compassion (e.g., Gilbert, 2011; Greenberg & Iwakabe, 2011). As noted previously, the experience of pride is essentially antithetical to shame, and the capacity to maintain one's personhood and a semblance of human dignity even in the face of terror and degradation, is a sure sign of resilience to trauma. In the next section Elly, a Holocaust survivor we interviewed and introduced in previous chapters, discusses the importance of maintaining one's pride and dignity as a means of survival in the Nazi death camps.

The PTSD diagnosis in DSM-5 recognizes the experience of shame in traumatized persons under the umbrella symptom "pervasive emotional states." Moreover, the presence of shame may be noted indirectly via its influence on reducing positive affect, given that a diagnostic symptom for PTSD includes "persistent inability to experience positive emotions—e.g., loving feelings" (Friedman, Resick, Bryant, & Brewin, 2011, p. 759). We discuss the concept of anhedonia, defined as a deficit and/or inability to experience positive emotions, in the section following the case of Elly. In fact, our own research shows that negative emotional states, broadly classifiable as anxiety and shame, frequently interfere with the ability to experience positive affect, therefore implicating associations between anhedonia and anxiety and shame.

Case 1: Human Pride, Dignity, and Survival

"Elly" is an 85-year-old Lithuanian Jewish man who survived the Holocaust with his father, as a prisoner of the death camp at Dachau, Germany, and his mother survived in Stutthof, Poland. Elly was in the death camp between the ages of 13 and 17, starting in Ghetto Kaunas in Lithuania for 3 years, then in Dachau for another year. We had the honor of speaking with this wise, resilient, and profoundly compassionate man, along with his beloved wife Esme, concerning his experiences as a young prisoner at Dachau as well as his life experiences since that time. Elly shares with us a life extremely well lived, an inspiring story of resilience, character, and human spirit.

> *Elly:* The most shocking experience to a person is when their life suddenly changes dramatically. That is the biggest shock. After that, the shocks maybe extend, or other terrible things happen, but the biggest shock is to suddenly become a totally different kind of human being—being a prisoner, for example, instead of a free man, or suddenly being shot at and the possibility of being killed. And that is what happened to us. We were taken from a peaceful environment—I was 13 years old when it started, I was going to school, I flew model airplanes, I was interested in science and history. . . .
>
> And the shock was suddenly to be brought into a ghetto surrounded by barbed wire—and the threat before of even coming to the ghetto was to be killed at any moment. All the major organized killing—there was killing in the streets—killing—taken out of your house and shot at in front of your door. So suddenly this terrible threat of dying—and as a young boy I worried for a long time how would I die, that was the thought for 3 years. In 1941 by August we were in the ghetto, and by October they had taken out and separated 10,000 people and killed them. And we found out later how they were killed—killed by machine guns and the bodies thrown into trenches. The worst fear was to be shot and not to be killed—to die lying with other bodies on top of you. This was the image that I tried to forget but

couldn't. This was what we lived with for those years. You had to live with courage. You had to have it—you had to just move forward. We were very fearful, I wasn't always brave. I *was* fearful—I was afraid of being shot and not being dead. These were horrible fears, horrible fears for a very long time.

Yet I knew that this could not last, and we lived in resistance. Hitler—he said he was building a state for 1,000 years—*1,000 years*—but I never believed it. I said such bitterness, such disastrous human relations that he is fostering, cannot live for long. And so I didn't believe it. I knew that the war would end with their failure. I knew it would come to an end. And so there was hope that we might survive it, though the chances were very poor. And they tried to make sure that we didn't believe it. The last commandant in Dachau—we had many commandants, all kinds of crazy people—but the last one was a particularly vicious man. He noticed that we had begun to be too happy—we were building hope—we knew that the American army was not far away, so he said: "You think that the war might end and you might be free? Forget it. We are keeping the last bullet for you! You will not make it, no matter what, so don't even think about it."

Interviewer: What helped you to keep going, Elly? To not give up or lose hope?

Elly: I knew he [the commandant] was a nothing—they hanged him later; he and 28 others from Dachau were hanged after the war. But I always looked down upon him because I did not think he ever represented a human being. We laughed at him. In fact he had one name for us— "assholes"— that was the only name he had. But we called him exactly the same. Amongst us *he* was the asshole. We had our little revenge in that we resisted. Because if you didn't resist, you died.

Interviewer: Elly, can you tell us more about how you were able to resist? And did they try to sabotage this?

Elly: They couldn't sabotage it because *we knew who we were*. An amazing example of this came from the religious ones among us—those who kept to religious rules. I was not a religious man, but there were some who didn't eat bread during Passover for 7 days, and this was an amazing thing for all of us to see—as we all were starving—and yet some wouldn't eat the bread because you can't eat [leavened] bread on the Passover. This to me was an amazing thing.

Interviewer: The resistance you were able to demonstrate, the solidarity: How was it that you were able to maintain this for so
long?

Elly: You have to, otherwise you become a slave. We were very
conscious of that—that they think we are slaves. But we are
not. We knew they are treating us like slaves, but that we
are not slaves. We are independent. We are human beings.
And I'm sure that was both conscious and unconscious, as
we did talk about it sometimes.

Though I would like to say that not all treated us poorly.
For example, I had a very good relationship with the man
(a German) who was in charge of our workshop in Dachau.
I was good with him, he liked me, he gave me extra food;
he also didn't have much, but he shared. He gave me some
of his food and he appreciated that I did the job well and
he said nice things to me. He always called me—not *Du*
[informal, *you*] but *Sie*—a polite form, and no Nazi guard
would call you *Sie*, only *Du Jude* [you Jew]. So there *were*
human relationships. It was wonderful to see a man who
was German who was treating us as equals . . . who went
out of his way to pick up some potatoes for us in the field
and bring it to us in his pockets. I mean this was an amazing thing. It was wonderful. And he saved my life—because
one time I switched on this big machine I was running and
there was a huge flame and a fire and the whole thing ran
down—and so I had stopped construction on the whole
site—thousands of people—I stopped the whole operation, for the short circuit burnt out the main transformer,
and the Nazis came running. I heard them but I couldn't
see anything as I was blinded by the light—by the flash—
and they were shouting "Sabotage! Hang him!" There was
talk about hanging me—we had hangings in the camp—but
this man said that it was not my fault, and so they left me
alone. And so this man saved my life.

He was a kind master who was good to us. Before I knew
him well, one day, the buckle on his belt broke—he had
a big square buckle with a wide belt—and his pants were
falling down. He had a problem (*smiles*). And one couldn't
even get a new buckle in the camps, and so he was com-
plaining and I said: "Give me your buckle," but he said,
"No, it can't be fixed," but I said "Give it to me," and I took
it into the workshop. And I drilled in little holes, and I put
in a nail inside, and I heated it up with solder, and then I
took coffee grinds and I painted it brown, and I gave it back

to him. And he asked, "How did you do that?," and after
that we were friends. He was good to me—he liked that
it held his pants up—a most important function (*smiles*).
So that friendship, with a man on the enemy side, it was
very valuable to maintain your humanity. It was proof that
not everybody was against you, that not the whole world
around you hates you.

Interviewer: Elly, can you tell us about what it was like to be liberated,
to be freed?

Elly: Just prior to liberation, in the last few days of the war, I
was sure I was losing my father. I saw him dying. I knew
that he was dying because I had seen so many people die.
I had carried so many dead bodies that I knew all stages of
death—from fighting it, to not caring, to giving up—and I
knew my father was in the last stages. His legs were swollen
and he couldn't get up. I had to get him his food because
he couldn't stand in line. So I knew then that he would
die—I thought within only a few days—and I was really
sad, I remember thinking *please don't go.* In the last few
days, when we knew the Americans were very close—we
knew that *all who survive will be free*—but I feared that he
won't make it. He wouldn't get up and get the food, so he
gave me his dish and said "You go and get it," and I would
encourage him, saying "They won't give it to me, you have
to," but he would say, "No, no, you get it for me, and if not I
don't care." So I stood in line and got for him the soup and
a slice of bread and brought it to him. And I think it was on
the second day, as he took the dish of soup from me, at that
moment people were shouting outside "The Americans are
here! We are free!" I said, "Father, it is over! We are free!"
and he said, "Oh, that's good—have you got the bread?"
This was *my* moment of liberation.

Interviewer: How did that feel? What was that like?

Elly: It was . . . it wasn't joy. It was just *"it's over, it's over."*
The horrible misery has finally ended in some way. So it
wasn't joy. It *was* for some—some people *were* jumping
for joy—*we were free*—but the sick ones, and all the people
lying there—from them there was no reaction. Many people lacked laughter. And I was still so afraid that my father
would die, perhaps in 2 hours. But he came through. We
were liberated on the 29th of April 1945, and had it been
2 days later, I would have lost him. He was already ready
to die, he had decided to die, but we were liberated, and
about 2 hours later he got up for the first time in 2 days

from where he was lying and he said, "So now what?", and I knew there is now hope that he will survive. I realized the change in him; I knew now that he would live. And so liberation was tied to my father living.

Interviewer: At what moment, Elly, did you begin to think of the future?

Elly: At that moment we were totally living in the present. The only question was *what will happen now*? And will they give us food? But the Americans didn't know what to do with us—they gave us 2 pounds of bully beef, though anybody who ate it, died, because we hadn't eaten for at least a year, and so the stomach couldn't take this food. They all died, they got the last stomach run and they died—so many did. And so they continued collecting bodies for weeks, a long time.

Interviewer: How does one cope, being surrounded by so much death?

Elly: Death and life had become one. They were both very similar, in the sense that you are living half dead. And so, like with the worry of my father dying, we knew you have to have the survival instinct in you, that little flame has to burn to want to live. Because otherwise, you don't. And though there *was* a kind of constant numbness, you were careful not to allow yourself to feel "I don't care what happens," because when you began to feel that, you died. We all knew that.

Interviewer: Elly, from your own personal experience, how do you think people can heal from such trauma as you have undergone?

Elly: I think people who have stress in their head from what happened to them—even when it is no longer threatening now—that leads to circular thinking, because you only keep returning to that one moment of horror, or the time of horror, or a life or few years of horror, or whatever period it was. I believe they should be helped to start doing something that is very energetic, that they have to think about, and focus on, and develop success, so that they may get satisfaction out of it.

Interviewer: The experience of mastery—a person is able to complete a task, and derive some success from it, a sense of achievement . . .

Elly: Yes. This has healing properties. Human beings feel good when they are successful even in the smallest little thing. And when they are successful, they can be proud; they have done something, it is an intellectual joy, it is not just the satisfaction of the physical. It is the intellectual satisfaction of having understood something. If you get a new insight, you get pleasure out of it, do you not? Suddenly you say: "Ah, I never thought about this before, but now I am beginning to realize something . . . "

Now, if you take a child who really suffers and you teach him how to fly, I can assure you he will not be thinking about his problem when he is flying, because he will be so completely concentrated that it will allow the other thing to step back, because he has something else to substitute for it. We can't deal all the time with the issue, because the issue keeps coming back, and so I think I was helped by really doing *other* things—like concentrating and finding success in it, which is the second stage of doing. And so I think that is very important. I think that taking you away from it, rather than only delving into it, might be another way.

Interviewer: Coming back to being liberated, at what time might you have begun to imagine another future, or begin to feel joyful again?

Elly: I know that at first there was little positive feeling. I couldn't feel it at first. And I knew that I didn't have it. Initially, first because my mother was not yet found, and I was missing her very much, but after, second, because my mind soon became totally occupied with one thought: hatred of the Germans. I have no hatred now. I truly have no hatred—I had to free myself of that. I was thinking of revenge, of anything that could be done to them, but after a while I realized that this is nonsense, I am not going to do any of this. I don't know who is guilty and you can't hate a whole people, it is ridiculous, same as the hate they had for us—*ALL JEWS*. And I remembered how as a child I had developed strong feelings of compassion for people early on. I felt so sorry for animals that were hurt. I didn't want anyone to hurt. I didn't like people being hurt. And so I forced myself to give it up, the hatred. And once I gave it up, I was able to begin to think about my own future, about myself. So I really very consciously gave up hatred as a ridiculous feeling; I liberated myself from that. And I began to think about what I would do with my life. And so after the hospital—we spent 6 months there—we weighed 70 pounds, my father and I each, we were very starved and very weak. But once I became healthy enough I began my search for work and an education to become an engineer.

I first found a workshop in the monastery where our hospital was, and I said, "I'm a metal worker, I would like to work." They said, "We don't pay" and I said, "I don't want pay, I just want to work"— and it was very helpful to me. It provided the future of doing something that succeeded, [that offered] success. They once brought in a very large lock—probably 100 years old, from one of those big doors. And the ones who were working on it—I could see they didn't know how to fix it. So I said, "Would you permit me to do that? I know how to do it." And I repaired this lock; I had to make my own spring. It was quite complicated with the workshop being somewhat primitive in fine tools, but I was able to do it right, and the lock worked again. This gave me great satisfaction, made me feel good.

And so, again, I believe that the path to improving a situation which is terrible—which occupies your mind all the time because it was so pervasive—could be possibly to push it away and remove it—no, not remove it, but push it away by achieving something: to exert control and achieve success. The success is that whatever you are doing worked. So that was my solution: I had to work, I had to study. I could not forget—and I never would—what happened. But I think that working, and studying, and being interested, and getting the joy of learning, of knowing, of doing, of success—this all was very important to me. I think it made me more or less normal.

And so, for me, life had to go on; you had to carry on. And I always liked to think about things. I am very interested in science and history and philosophy and literature and I love poetry, and all kinds of other things. And I did many things, and whatever I did I enjoyed tremendously— climbing mountains, riding horses, flying an airplane (I'm a pilot)—and becoming an engineer was very hard, I had to study hard. And I did all the other things, hunting and shooting—I learned to use a rifle—everybody had always been pointing guns at me so I thought I should learn to use one, and I learned how to shoot and I hunted crocodiles, anything. I wanted to live, I wanted to experience, and I wanted to do things. I had a lot of energy, I was energetic. And whenever an idea for an invention came to me, I would do it, I wouldn't just think about it. And I think there is some pleasure in that.

So I am very happy now. I am happy with my life. I am happy with what is happening to me, with everything else.

This was a period in life that was unreasonable, and caused by others—I didn't cause it, I didn't cause my problems, I am not guilty of it, I felt no guilt. But the joy of living, the science of investigating, of creating, of taking pride in doing good work—life is good. Things are very interesting. So I enjoy it—*just to do what you can.* So I am happy—I am a happy man. I don't know what this thing, the past, has caused me, but I don't feel any loss. It shows that, going into hell, and then coming out again, when they say "live again," *that's all you have to do—live—and I have,* and I have tried to stay happy. I know what happiness is.

Interviewer: Elly, can you tell us what happiness is to you?

Elly: Happiness is not wanting anything else, not anything more. Being satisfied with what you have totally. And for me happiness came because of love—everything else is unimportant to me—wealth, money, possessions, I don't have any such desire, only for her [Esme's] love, the only love of my life, and I feel that very strongly. I feel it is a blessing that few people have. It is total freedom, even freedom of want. I don't need anything now. And so I am happy with life. It is a real source of happiness. If I may share a German quotation, which I believe is a real fundamental truth:

Selig wer sich vor der Welt
Ohne Haß verschließt,
Einen Freund am Busen hält
Und mit dem genießt.
["Blessed is he who, without hatred,
Locks himself away from the world,
Holds his friend close to his bosom,
And enjoys life with that friend."]

(*Note*: Elly shared later that the poem was written by Goethe in a cottage in Buchenwald [Oak Forest], near Weimar, the location of a death camp—Buchenwald—a hundred years later.)

Trauma and Anhedonia: When One Can't Feel Good, and When Feeling Good Feels Bad

"Angie" is a 16-year-old woman with severe difficulties with anhedonia, the inability to experience positive affect. Angie was emotionally neglected by her parents throughout her childhood and adolescence. She believed that her parents had never loved her or showed any type of affection toward her. Angie was also repeatedly physically abused by her father when he

216 *Healing the Traumatized Self*

was drunk. Angie was hospitalized on an adolescent psychiatric unit for 18 months due to symptoms of PTSD, severe depression, and suicide risk. At admission Angie reported feeling "dead, numb, and lifeless" and experienced a loss of the experience of pleasure.

In order to help overcome Angie's feelings of numbness and deadness, she was asked whether she could identify positive memories in her past for purposeful recall and visualization. Specifically, Angie was asked whether she could recall a time in her life that she had felt loved, cared for, appreciated, or competent. Unfortunately, however, Angie could not recall a single positive memory. She was also unable to identify any positive self-attributes. When questioned whether anyone in her life had paid her a compliment, or whether she had ever excelled at anything in school that made her feel a sense of competence, Angie was not able to identify any such memories either.

With persistence, however, Angie was finally able to identify that one of the nurses on the psychiatric unit made her feel cared for and protected. Angie agreed to bring up an image of the nurse to see whether this could change her feelings of numbness and deadness. Unfortunately, the first time she visualized the image, she saw the nurse "turn around and leave" her, with this experience of perceived abandonment causing Angie to feel that she was "bad," undeserving of good feelings, and should be punished. Nevertheless, with repeated practice, and drawing the positive image of her nurse rather than internally visualizing it (an intervention Angie thought of herself), Angie slowly began to tolerate positive feelings, described initially as an ever so slight "warm and fuzzy" feeling in her abdominal region. Over time, Angie was able to identify and visualize additional positive memories, including that her grandmother had held her with affection on several occasions and that a school teacher had complimented her on her performance in math and sports. Over time Angie began to feel less emotionally "dead" and "numb," and she started to experience a greater sense of joy. She began to smile, a behavior that had not been observed by staff since her admission to the psychiatric hospital months previously. Angie also began to plan what she would do after her discharge from hospital. She reported that she felt like she was beginning to have a life worth living.

Whereas most research in the trauma field focuses on hyperarousal responses to threatening/aversive stimuli, it is also acknowledged that traumatized persons frequently exhibit deficits or *hypo*aroused responses to pleasant stimuli, such as pictures of nature, others smiling, and infants. The inability to experience positive affect in the context of stimuli and events that should normally provoke it is referred to as *anhedonia* (e.g., Kashdan, Elhai, & Frueh, 2006, 2007).

Unfortunately, relatively little experimental research has investigated anhedonia in traumatized persons. Studies have found that pleasant pictures are rated less arousing and salient by both male and female Bosnian refugees suffering from PTSD (Spahic-Mihajlovic, Crayton, & Neafsey, 2005). In men with combat-related PTSD, images of attractive women provoked less interest (as measured by viewing time; Elman et al., 2005), and both expectancy and satisfaction with winning in a Wheel-of-Fortune-like game was diminished (Hopper et al., 2008). In a neuroimaging experiment of the latter task, it was also found that reward circuitry (right nucleus accumbens, caudate, and putamen) was activated in healthy individuals both when they believed that they were about to win the game, as well as after winning in the game, whereas combat veterans with PTSD failed to show either effect (Elman et al., 2009). Also, when viewing an amusing cartoon, healthy men showed greater response in the bilateral temporal poles, implicated in social cognition, whereas traumatized men with PTSD showed a greater response in the right middle frontal cortex, possibly associated with response inhibition or negative affect (Jatzko, Schmitt, Demirakca, Weimer, & Braus, 2006).

We studied anhedonia in women with PTSD and found support for an interference of negative affect on their capacity to experience positive affect (Frewen, Dean, & Lanius, 2012; Frewen, Dozois, & Lanius, 2012; Frewen, Dozois, Neufeld, Densmore, et al., 2010). PTSD participants in the Frewen, Dozois, Neufeld, Densmore, et al. (2010) study experienced considerable negative affect, especially feelings of shame, in response to imagery of *positive* social events (e.g., being praised) and in response to positive self-referential processing (SRP; i.e., viewing one's picture while listening to lists of positive adjectives) in another experiment (Frewen, Dozois, Neufeld, Densmore, et al., 2011b).

Thus two characteristic responses to generally positive stimuli were observed in traumatized persons (DePierro, D'Andrea, & Frewen, 2014; Frewen, Dean, et al., 2012; Frewen, Dozois, et al., 2012). In the first case, individuals reported feeling affectively blunted, detached, or numb, not experiencing joy or pleasure in response to stimuli that should normally provoke such responses (e.g., receiving a compliment or gift, or the sign of another's physical affection and embrace). We referred to such responses as *hedonic deficits*, emphasizing that participants were unable to experience positive affect. In the second case, traumatized persons reported experiencing *negative* affective reactions to positive events, such as feelings of shame, anger, guilt, and unworthiness. We referred to the latter responses as *hedonic negative affective interference*, thereby emphasizing that negative feelings such as anxiety and shame were getting in the way of the individual's ability to experience positive affect.

It is further important to note that traumatic associations sometimes directly interfere with joyful responses to positive events. For example, Elly, whose German death camp experiences were discussed in the preceding section, described his recollection of the mass killings of Jewish infants and young children: "They came into the ghetto and they started to hunt for the children—they took away the children and killed them—and when the adults came home from work and found that the kids were gone—the crying that was heard all over the ghetto I could not even describe." Upon the birth of his own grandchildren, the terrible pain of the infanticide of previous generations hauntingly returned, interfering with his ability to feel joy at the time of his grandchildren's birth:

> "Grandchildren were born, *my* grandchildren. My first two were twin girls, beautiful girls. And my son came out of the hospital with these two beautiful babies in his arms and I broke out crying. Why? Why am I crying? Because I saw it—I knew what happened to those babies back there. It was the terror—the terror of knowing what happened to the babies—what they did to babies—and in this happy moment for me I totally broke up."

Despite understanding the nature of his response, in recalling this memory, Elly is painfully judgmental and ashamed, believing his feelings were unjustified:

> "It is such a horrible upsetting feeling, it is such an *unfair* feeling. Here are your grandchildren and I am crying—I can't even talk about it! It's that I want to let it go, I think it's an apparition, I think it's unfair and unreasonable and unjustified. I think it is wrong to feel that way. And I was so worried that my son would be able to see what I felt."

We hypothesize that the phenomenology of two differing core affective states each related to anhedonia can be represented on the affective circumplex (see Figure 6.5). On the basis of our research, participants' descriptions, and prior findings, we hypothesize that *hedonic deficits*, in the absence of co-occurring *hedonic negative affective interference*, should lie somewhere between a state of unpleasant deactivation and pure deactivation itself (i.e., 210°–240°). By contrast, we hypothesize that the intense state that is *hedonic negative affective interference*, based primarily in the experience of anxiety and shame, can be placed somewhere between states of activated displeasure and unpleasant activation (i.e., 120°–150°).

In our study of women with predominantly childhood-trauma-related PTSD, we further distinguished between positive events that are distinctly social (e.g., receiving a compliment, someone expressing liking)

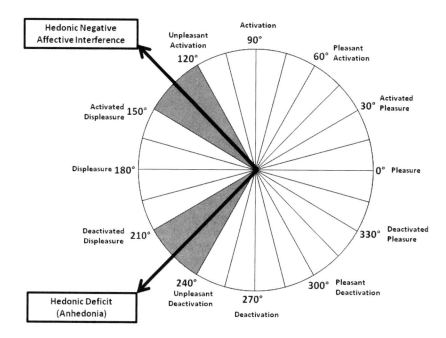

FIGURE 6.5. Affective Circumplex Indicating Hypothesized Location of Hedonic Deficit (Anhedonia) versus Hedonic Negative Affective Interference. Copyright © 2011 by the American Psychological Association. Adapted with permission. The official citation that should be used in referencing this material is Yik, M., Russell, J. A., Steiger, J. H. (2011). A 12-point circumplex structure of core affect. *Emotion, 11*(4), pages 705–31. The use of APA information does not imply endorsement by APA.

and those that are not (e.g., enjoying a pleasant walk on the beach while alone). We found that, during imagery of positive social events, traumatized women exhibited less response in the dorsomedial prefrontal cortex and left temporal pole, and as a function of increasing *hedonic negative affective interference*, showed decreasing response in the right temporoparietal junction and cerebellum. In contrast, during imagery of positive nonsocial events, traumatized women exhibited greater response in the left insula, and both hedonic deficits and negative affective interference were associated with increasing cerebellar response, but only negative affective interference was associated with increasing right middle frontal and left amygdala response. Collectively, then, our studies demonstrated alterations in brain regions associated with SRP and attention to emotion (dorsomedial prefrontal cortex), social cognition (temporal poles), embodied experience (right temporoparietal junction, cerebellum), and emotional experience (insula, amygdala, right frontal cortex) in traumatized women as they were attempting, with difficulty, to envision themselves in positive circumstances and with a positive frame of self-reference

(Frewen, Dozois, Neufeld, Densmore, et al., 2010; Frewen, Dean, et al., 2012, Frewen, Dozois, et al., 2012).

The theoretical importance of these findings is to highlight that deficits in reward circuitry may not fully account for the experience of anhedonia in all traumatized persons. Instead, experiences of *negative* affect, including anxiety and shame, accompanied by neural responses implicating higher-order emotional responding, rather than only lower-order reward circuitry, may interfere with individuals' ability to experience joy, pleasure, and healthy self-esteem in the context of positive events, such as the acknowledgment of their achievements and others' expression of relational affection toward them. If this is true, the clinical implications are important: namely, that standard psychological treatments for addressing anhedonia, such as behavioral activation (e.g., pleasant event scheduling), are unlikely to be productive in all cases. Such interventions can be expected either to have neutral or even counterproductive effects, exacerbating individuals' tendency toward anxiety and shame in the face of positive events. Instead, approaches aimed at reducing negative affective interference, such as those encouraging resource building, self-compassion, and anxiety management, may be more beneficial in such cases (Frewen, Dean, et al., 2012, Frewen, Dozois, et al., 2012; Korn & Leeds, 2002). Low self-compassion has been reliably associated with psychological problems, including affective disorders (Macbeth & Gumley, 2012), and psychological interventions explicitly aimed at developing self-compassion are being developed and validated by clinical researchers (Hoffmann et al., 2011). The next two sections describe case studies of hedonic negative affective interference in trauma survivors.

Case 2: The Feeling of Being Soiled: Hedonic Negative Affective Interference

Tim, a veteran medic of the Vietnam war, introduced in Chapter 3 with regard to his experiences of a flashback of the war (as triggered by a fireworks display at a state fair), described his experiences of hedonic negative affective experience as follows:

Interviewer: Have you had the experience of not being able to feel positive emotions, like love, joy, pleasure, or not being able to smile or laugh easily?

Tim: Yes, I have. I struggle most with what the feeling of love feels like.

Interviewer: Can you tell me more about that?

Tim: In some ways it is disabling. I can do things that I think are loving, but it seems as though there is an empty spot there.

Interviewer: Can you tell me more about that?

Tim: For instance, I encourage my wife. She belongs to a book group, and they meet once a month, and I am supportive of that. I feel like I am doing loving things when I am supportive of that, and I let her know I am glad when she has those outside activities. She gets a lot of pleasure out of her book group. Providing for that and encouraging her to do that are loving things that I do, but I struggle with . . . (*brief pause*) . . . I struggle with knowing what love *is*. At one point, I ended up going out and reading books about love, trying to figure out what love was and how I was supposed to be feeling. I found some explanations, but there is a lot of mystery about it as well. I still struggle with this. I think I have a real problem being loved—I feel uncomfortable, extremely uncomfortable. When somebody finds out that I served in Vietnam, when they say thank you, I practically turn inside out with discomfort.

Interviewer: Can you say more about what that is like?

Tim: I guess . . . almost I can say embarrassment, from a gut-level standpoint. I can feel it in my gut and my stomach and I can feel it in my head. And everything inside of me is screaming "No, no, no!" And although I have developed techniques to say "You're welcome" or at least behave appropriately, inside I still have this terrible conflict. When somebody says they appreciate anything about me, I have a terrible trouble with that. Basically it happens any time anybody says something that could be construed as loving.

Interviewer: Can you give an example of that?

Tim: I have a terrible problem with birthday presents and birthday cards. I have a problem with receiving anything. Part of that is something that has been a part of my experience since Vietnam. There is part of me that is still dwelling in unworthiness. There are a lot of thoughts and feelings connected with feeling as though my government was trying to throw me away. There are a lot of questions about that. If that happened, how can I still be worthy? Something is off balance there.

Interviewer: When did your difficulties with experiencing good feelings like love begin? Were they always there?

Tim: No. I would say before Vietnam I kind of felt the opposite. If I look back to my high school and college years, I really would say I felt valuable. I had friends in college, close friends—not so much family but a circle of friends—and I felt valued by them and I valued them [in turn]. I guess I would have to say that at that time I was able to experience both giving and receiving love. But since Vietnam it has curtailed. I no longer feel like I am a part of them. The experiences that I had in Vietnam . . . I feel very separate. Even though you can't see it, it can't be seen from the outside, I feel soiled internally and that sets me apart from the general population . . . (*brief pause*) . . . I guess what I can say is that I do have a pretty good relationship with other veterans when attending meetings. I feel very much a part of that group. But in other groups I don't feel as though I am a part of them. I feel in many ways when I am in groups like that, [that] I am incomplete. In social situations I feel like I am incomplete. Even though I can survive them, I don't like them.

Interviewer: Can you tell me more about being able to experience good feelings and relationships within the context of PTSD support groups for veterans?

Tim: There it is easier for me to experience what I will call compassion. I also feel valued in that group, and that feels good to me. But I think—and here I am in my head—I think it is because we shared that common experience of having been in combat and all of us suffering from PTSD and all the symptoms. I feel . . . as a case in point, this morning when I got there, a guy said "Here's your chair, it's got your name on it" and I took that as a compliment. I felt good about that.

Interviewer: You mentioned that in other social groups, and in other kinds of relationships, experiencing good feelings can be more difficult. For example, you have talked before [in previous interviews] about difficulties you have had when attempting to share loving feelings with your wife. Can you describe what it is like to share loving and affectionate feelings within the context of your marriage?

Tim: Well, let me start by saying that it is extremely mysterious to me. By *mysterious* I mean why I have such difficulty with it. It is a mystery. I don't know. To start out with, it is really a mystery. The second thing is that physical intimacy outside of sex is really difficult. Hugging, cuddling, stuff like that—it's a real mystery as to why it causes me discomfort. Why that is, I am not sure. If I had to take a stab at it, I would have to say it is the feeling of being soiled. That is the best word I have of describing it. Once again, it is not so much protecting myself from someone else, but it's more about protecting [my wife] from me. I feel that I am soiled inside, and if I am physically intimate, that somehow they will become soiled as well.

Interviewer: This feeling of being soiled, can you say more about what it is like for you?

Tim: It feels like the urge to break contact is extremely high, and the longer I have contact the greater the discomfort. It might start out as "OK, I am tolerating it," but little by little it becomes more and more uncomfortable until I have to pull away.

Interviewer: When you say you feel uncomfortable, can you describe where you feel that in your body?

Tim: Often times it is coming from the area of contact. For instance, if [my wife and I were] holding hands, it will kind of emanate from that point of contact and spread. It's like it moves up my arm to my chest, and I become really anxious and my anxiety level goes up and up and up. As it moves up my arm and starts down my chest, I start to become short of breath, I can't get enough air, and often times I will start sweating. So from a physiological standpoint those are the things that happen. If I had to paint a picture—if I was a person looking from the outside at myself and [my wife] holding hands—it would appear as though as time went on, that she would start to become infected so to speak. This is really difficult to dig into. It would look like the person was being negatively affected, almost as though, if I am looking at us from the outside, if she had a smile on her face and I had a frown on my face, that as an onlooker I would see her smile turn to a frown. What will invariably happen is I break contact. A part of me inside myself says "OK, I have done my duty, that's enough."

In some ways it has to do with my difficulty experiencing love, because it seems to me as though people who love each other would feel comfortable with that. And I know [my wife] feels comfortable with that. But I struggle with it, and I wonder if it would be different if I knew what love was, or more to the point, if I was able to experience love. It would seem to me that if I held hands with [my wife] and I was able to experience love, the experience would increase as opposed to becoming intolerable.

Case 3: Taming Shame and Cultivating Self-Compassion to Treat Anhedonia

Stephanie, a 62-year-old woman whom we met earlier in this chapter, was adopted at 3 months of age but felt rejected by her adoptive mother for as long as she could remember. Stephanie described: "My adoptive mother always wished that [my biological mother] would have aborted me. She repeatedly told me throughout my life how horrible, ugly, and repulsive I was. I learned to believe that I'm a mistake and I shouldn't exist."

In therapy, Stephanie came to realize that these experiences formed the basis of her feelings of shame. She remembered people often commenting on how red in the face and "off" she looked. Whenever people made such comments, Stephanie would experience a feeling of "badness" inside and thoughts such as "I am a mistake," "I should not exist," and "I want to disappear." Stephanie drew a picture of herself expressing this (Figures 6.6 and 6.7, also in the color insert). It was only after beginning therapy that Stephanie was able to identify and label such experiences as shame, and recognize that her feelings of shame were preventing her from experiencing positive feelings. For example, whenever Stephanie received a compliment from her children, grandchildren, or coworkers, she would become overwhelmed by feelings of shame, typically accompanied by the feeling of not being deserving of praise. Stephanie noted: "It was so overwhelming that I almost *became* the shame; it consumed me. It felt like my whole body was dirty and disgusting."

Stephanie worked hard in therapy to overcome her feelings of shame and, over time, she began to experience positive emotions. First she began to increase her tolerance for positive emotions by visualizing positive aspects of her life (e.g., her dog and her grandchildren). Initially, she experienced great difficulty with tolerating positive affect; unfortunately, the positive visualizations very quickly turned negative. For example, when Stephanie intentionally visualized the positive image of her dog, an intrusive image of her mother degrading her would present itself soon after. Stephanie was encouraged to visualize the positive image for relatively brief periods of time until, with practice, she was able to tolerate visualizing the image of her dog for more extended periods. She then progressed toward experiencing positive visualizations of her grandchildren. This increased capacity to tolerate positive emotional states coincided with Stephanie's feeling less inner tension and greater self-compassion. Her thoughts about being undeserving were also addressed through cognitive restructuring and the practice of interventions akin to *metta* meditations (Hofmann et al., 2011). Stephanie's symptoms of shame continued to diminish, and she became increasingly comfortable with experiencing positive affect. Coinciding with these practices, Stephanie noted that she began to feel a warm sensation in her heart whenever her grandchildren approached her. Moreover, Stephanie began to experience loving feelings whenever she held her grandchildren. She also found that she became excited whenever her dog licked her

FIGURE 6.6. Stephanie's (2014) artwork: "Shame—inside and out I." Used with permission.

FIGURE 6.7. Stephanie's (2014) artwork: "Shame—inside and out II." Used with permission.

on the face. Stephanie commented that these experiences were unimaginable before engaging in trauma therapy.

In general, taking a careful history regarding past positive associations and memories in clients' lives is an important first step in determining what experiences may be most appropriate for use in visual imagery exercises. Such experiences might include imagining feelings of safety with another individual, visualizing a past role in which one felt competent (e.g., in school or in sports), or finding comfort from being with a pet (as was helpful for Stephanie), among others. In addition, identification of resiliency traits or "resources," including those utilized in surviving previous traumatic events, can be helpful. Often a safe place (real or imagined), a positive symbol, or a mantra can be elicited (Korn & Leeds, 2002). Although clients often initially experience difficulties remembering or making positive associations, with gentle persistence most will be able to identify at least a single association from which one can broaden and build.

Positive affect tolerance can be encouraged through cognitive, behavioral, and somatic-based interventions. Positive self-statements, a cognitive intervention, can sometimes be successfully utilized to counter negative affective interference. For example, clients might produce positive counterstatements to well-rehearsed forms of negative affective interference, such as shame-based beliefs that they are undeserving of positive feelings. As positive affect tolerance grows, pleasant event scheduling and other standard approaches to encouragement of self-care can be utilized to capitalize on the client's increasing capacity for joy, pleasure, and self-regard. One example of a relatively innocuous and potentially pleasant activity is the practice of walking meditation as described in mindfulness-based therapies. At a higher level of tolerance, *metta* (or compassion-focused, "loving-kindness") meditations might be practiced, as these involve the intentional cultivation and affirmation of feelings of compassion and good will toward oneself and others (Hoffmann et al., 2011).

Finally, attention to the somatic level is unfortunately the most often neglected by psychotherapists. It is increasingly held that the capacity for positive affect is manifested on a somatic, embodied level, where it is represented in the structure and movement of the body (for detailed review, see Ogden et al., 2006; Rothschild, 2003). Lengthening of the spine, sitting in a straight rather than collapsed posture, and pushing away one's arms in order to signal a boundary are postures and movements that might encourage strength, confidence, assertiveness, and empowerment.

Alexithymia: The Feeling of "Not Knowing"

Three individuals, Erica, Stephen, and Julia, all childhood trauma survivors, were interviewed about alexithymia, the experience of difficulty identifying and describing emotional states.

Interviewer: Can you describe how you are feeling right now?

Erica: Umm, I'm just here. I think I'm sad, I don't know, I think I'm sad, I don't know.

Interviewer: How would you know if you were sad?

Erica: I don't know. I might be if I was crying, but now I'm not crying, so I don't know. Umm, I'm having a hard time today trying to figure stuff out.

Interviewer: Can you tell me about not feeling emotions?

Stephen: When I get emotions and stuff like that, I don't really feel them. I can say to someone I feel sadness because tears are welling in my eyes, but I do not know what that is really. They are just physical symptoms.

Interviewer: Have you ever felt like you don't know what you are feeling?

Julia: All the time. That's just so common. I have no idea what to . . . apparently one of my biggest problems is that I don't have any feelings or emotions or anything. I don't feel I know any of this stuff. It is like taking an exam in a class when you haven't taken the subject and you don't know any of the material. I could take it, but I am probably not going to get any of the answers right because I don't know [the material].

Interviewer: Can I ask you about your experience of some specific emotions? For example, do you often feel shame?

Julia: I'm not sure what that one is.

Interviewer: Do you know what shame is?

Julia: No, not really. I haven't quite figured it out yet.

Interviewer: What is it like when you feel threatened or afraid? Do you know this experience?

Julia: Yes, but I have no idea how to describe it.

Interviewer: Is it difficult for you to describe how it feels to be threatened or afraid?

Julia: [I have] no idea.

Researchers have described deficits in the awareness of emotions in traumatized persons primarily as indicated by assessments of alexithymia (e.g., Frewen, Dozois, Neufeld, & Lanius, 2008). The concept of *alexithymia* refers to difficulties identifying and labeling emotions (Taylor, Bagby, & Parker, 1997). This definition therefore makes use of a distinction between primary, first-order emotional experience and our second-order, reflective *meta-awareness* of such experiences (Frijda, 2005; Lambie & Marcel, 2002; Lane et al., 1997). For example, one can exhibit behavioral (e.g., crying) and psychophysiological signs (e.g., tachycardia) of emotionality of which one is not subjectively aware (Lane et al., 1997). Alternatively, as described by Erica, one can infer one's emotional experience through physiological signs such that, when these are absent, one may not know *what* one is feeling. An empirical example of such incongruence was provided by Orsillo and colleagues, who observed that individuals with PTSD exhibited a lower correspondence between self-reported affective experience and objectively coded facial affect, relative to healthy persons, in response to emotionally provocative stimuli (Wagner, Roemer, Orsillo, & Litz, 2003; cf. Luminet, Rime, Bagby, & Talyor, 2004; Orsillo, Batten, Plumb, Luterek, & Roessner, 2004).

However, other findings showing that the presence of alexithymia tends to be associated with measures of general distress (e.g., depression; Honkalampi, Hintikka, Tanskanen, Lehtonen, & Viinamaki, 2000) have historically presented somewhat of a theoretical challenge. If persons with alexithymia are not supposed to know *what* they are feeling, why is it that they often report so many negative feelings? In an influential article, Lumley (2000) hypothesized that such associations may have to do with the emotion regulatory deficits posed by an inability to identify, describe, and in turn regulate distress:

> The question has often been raised as to why alexithymic people report negative feelings, as opposed to lacking emotions or being emotionally "neutral." . . . I believe that alexithymia predisposes to a negative emotional valence. Whereas non-alexithymic people can regulate and resolve emotions stemming from stressful or conflicting events, alexithymic people fail to do so, and the negative affect remains unmodulated, yielding a chronic, yet *undifferentiated* dysphoria. (p. 52)

In addition to this point, it stands to reason that the experience of alexithymia may itself be distressing for some experiencing it. That is, not knowing what one is feeling may itself provoke anxiety and dysphoria. On a methodological note, we also previously expressed concern that some of the correlations between alexithymia and distress may be artificial, in part, due to survey item overlap (Frewen, Dozois, Neufeld, & Lanius, 2012). Specifically, some standard alexithymia questionnaires include test items that, on face value, may themselves be relatively direct measures of general distress (e.g., the item of the Toronto Alexithymia Questionnaire: "I don't know what's going on inside of me"; Bagby, Parker, & Taylor, 1994). It is possible that future studies using semistructured interviews of individuals with alexithymia will be more sensitive to such measurement problems (e.g., Toronto Alexithymia Interview; Bagby, Taylor, Parker, & Dickens, 2006). Future research is necessary to tease apart these different interpretations of the co-occurrence of alexithymia with increased distress, ideally measuring alexithymia and distress not only over lengthy periods (e.g., last week/month assessments) but instead employing measurements of affective states in real time (e.g., in response to experimental or environmental stress) using neurophenomenological and experience-sampling designs (i.e., measuring *emotion moments*).

In any case, alexithymia can be diagnosed independent of the presence versus absence of emotional distress. Accordingly, we hypothesize two placements for the experience of alexithymia within the affective circumplex (see Figure 6.8). One location, between 120° and 150°, is intended to represent an activated, highly distressing state, implying that not knowing

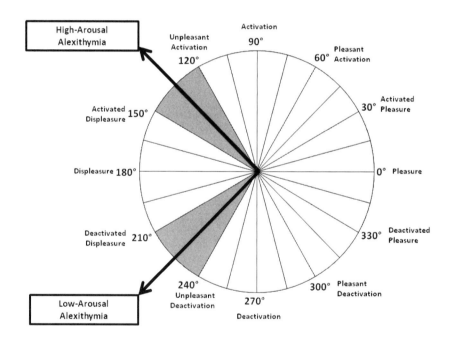

FIGURE 6.8. Affective Circumplex Indicating Hypothesized Location of Alexithymia Associated with High-Arousal Distress versus Low-Arousal Lack of Feelings (presumed to be an unpleasant affective state). Adapted with permission from Yik, Russell, and Steiger (2011). Copyright ©2011 by the American Psychological Association. Adapted with permission. The official citation that should be used in referencing this material is Yik, M., Russell, J. A., Steiger, J. H. (2011). A 12-point circumplex structure of core affect. *Emotion, 11*(4), pages 705–31. The use of APA information does not imply endorsement by APA.

what one is feeling might itself cause high distress, or that high states of distress are intrinsically difficult to identify and label (i.e., a "feeling too much" subtype of alexithymia). A second location, between 210° and 240°, represents a lower arousal, mildly unpleasant, yet for the most part "neutral" state, largely implicating the absence of feelings (i.e., a "not feeling" subtype of alexithymia).

When accompanied by distress, the interpretation of alexithymia seems relatively straightforward: The client does not know what he or she is experiencing or is unable to describe it. In fact, the interpretation of high alexithymia is more problematic when the client is not otherwise evincing obvious signs of emotional distress. In such circumstances, the question arises as to whether the individual is truly in an *emotional-less* state or is instead only unaware of, and not obviously displaying, ongoing emotionality. Over the course of recovery people often move from an inability to feel their emotions to an increasing awareness of their feelings. This shift can be associated initially with increasing distress, given that the individual is unaccustomed to experiencing feelings. It therefore may be only after traumatized persons have become acclimatized to their "new" feelings and have learned to recognize and label their emotional states that it is likely their level of distress will decrease again. Taking into account the longitudinal course of recovery from alexithymia in traumatized persons via studies of psychological treatment is therefore important, particularly given the long-held assumption that alexithymia is predictive of a poor response to psychotherapy (Ogrodniczuk, Piper, & Joyce, 2011).

The following brief transcripts of interviews with Erica and Julia illustrate these two hypothetically different clinical presentations of alexithymia. The alexithymic features described by Erica are relatively easy to interpret because they occur within the context of obvious emotional distress. Erica's experience of alexithymia is one accompanied by significant distress leading to dissociative symptoms, including derealization and detachment from feelings and emotions, matching Lumley's (2000) concept of an "undifferentiated dysphoria":

Interviewer: Have you ever had the experience of not knowing what you are feeling?

Erica: Yes, all the time. It happened to me last night. I started— and I didn't know if it was fear, anxiety, panic or . . . I tend to pace, and I just pull at my clothes, and I . . . (*visibly distressed*).

Interviewer: How are you feeling right now?

Erica: I'm almost going there again . . .

Interviewer: What are you feeling right now?

Erica: Ummm, ah . . . I don't know, I don't know what I'm feeling right now, I don't know, I don't know.

Interviewer: What's that like?

Erica: Um . . . I don't feel *real* right now, I don't feel . . . I'm going numb, my body's going numb, uh . . .

Interviewer: I'm noticing that you're rubbing your foot against the carpet . . . ?

Erica: So it has life, umm, so I can hear it [the sound of rubbing], so it makes it more real. But the rest of my body, I feel like I'm a disembodied voice right now, and I don't know where these words are coming from . . . (*pause*) . . . The less I talk, the easier it is. The more I talk the more dead I go.

Interviewer: [Erica was grounded and debriefed.]

Again, the alexithymic features described by Erica are relatively easy to interpret because they occur within the context of obvious emotional distress, exemplifying "feeling too much." In comparison, the affective state implied by Julia's answers in the next transcript is comparably less clear. Julia is asked about the experience of emotional numbing, which she endorses. Indeed she describes herself as chronically numb; her answers to the interviewer's questions suggest that, at least to her own knowledge, her subjective experiences are entirely devoid of affective feelings. In addition, Julia's reports suggest the presence of alexithymia in that she is largely unable to elaborate upon what the experience of emotional numbing *itself* is like for her, instead equating it with the whole of her existence; in Julia's words: "The numbness is not a feeling, that's just how I am." At the same time, it is not fully clear that her experience of being devoid of emotional feelings is itself a source of significant distress for Julia. In a sense she endorses not knowing what she feels (alexithymia) principally because, for the most part, she does not feel *anything*. While admitting being unfamiliar with a range of emotional experiences, Julia shows relatively little obvious distress or concern about it:

Interviewer: Have you ever had the feeling of being emotionally numb?

Julia: Yes.

Interviewer: Can tell me a little bit more about it? What is it like for you?

Julia: Ummm . . . I have absolutely no clue. It's just . . . it's nothingness. I don't know what it is.

Interviewer: Can you describe what emotional numbness is like?

Julia: I don't know. I don't know how to describe it. I know what it is to me, but I don't know how to put words to it . . . other than that you are numb. That's what it is. I don't know how to describe it other than you are numb. It *is* what it *is*.

Interviewer: Are there any other words you could use to describe the feeling of emotional numbness?

Julia: The numbness is not a feeling, that's just how I am. So how do you say how you are? You just *are* that. That's just how you are. And I am numb. I guess that is as good a word as any to describe it—it's just how I am. So how do you describe that beyond that? It's just numb—that's what it is. I don't have any more words than that to try to describe it. It's hard to say what it is.

Of significant importance to the 4-D model is the question of whether or not alexithymia can be considered a dissociative process. Research consistently shows that self-reported alexithymia and trait dissociative symptoms correlate positively, usually with small to moderate effect sizes approximating $.30 \leq r \leq .50$, in a variety of clinical samples, including in (1) individuals with depersonalization disorder (Simeon, Giesbrecht, Knutelska, Smith, & Smith, 2009); (2) individuals with severe psychopathology (e.g., Clayton, 2004; Elzinga, Bermond, & van Dyck, 2002; Glover, Lader, Walker-O'Keefe, & Goodnick, 1997; Grabe, Rainermann, Spitzer, Gänsicke, & Freyberger, 2000; Sayar & Kose, 2003; Sayar, Kose, Grabe, & Topbas, 2005; Simeon et al., 2009; Tolmunen et al., 2010; Tutkun et al., 2004); (3) outpatients with panic disorder (Kart-Ludwig et al., 2011); (4) substance-abusing and alcohol-dependent male inpatients (e.g., Evren, Cinar, & Evren, 2012; Evren et al., 2008; review by Thorberg, Young, Sullivan, & Lyvers, 2009); (5) inpatients with psychosomatic disorders (Wingenfeld et al., 2011); and (6) nonspecific treatment-seeking samples (e.g., Rosik & Soria, 2012). The symptoms have also been shown to correlate in general population samples, including in adolescents (e.g., Sayar et al., 2005; Tolmunen et al., 2010), adults (Maaranen et al., 2005; Lipsanen, Saarijärvi, & Lauerma, 2004), and undergraduates (e.g., Clayton, 2004; Elzinga et al., 2002; Irwin & Melbin-Helberg, 1997). It is important to note, however, that although correlated, factor analyses suggest that alexithymia and dissociation likely represent two distinct syndromes (e.g., Berenbaum & James, 1994; Lipsanen et al., 2004; Wise, Mann, & Sheridan, 2000). We conclude that there is insufficient evidence to suggest that the experience of alexithymia is *itself* dissociative in all cases. However, it seems that individuals who report a high frequency of dissociative experiences are also likely to be alexithymic; it is possible that the phenomenology of dissociative TRASC is itself difficult to identify and describe, leading to high endorsement of symptoms on alexithymia questionnaires.

Extant and historical theories propose alexithymia to be a deficit in the cognitive processing of emotion, with neurobiological or developmental etiology (reviews by Taylor, 2010; Taylor et al., 1997). Regarding the latter, Lane and Schwartz (1987) described a model of levels of emotional awareness, development through which is experience-dependent and particularly influenced by early relationships with caregivers. Findings showing that alexithymic characteristics are prevalent in traumatized samples (Frewen, Dozois, Neufeld, et al., 2008), including in relation with histories of childhood emotional neglect (Frewen, Lanius, et al., 2008), in addition to findings that low parental (particularly maternal) care predicts increased alexithymia (Thorberg, Young, & Sullivan, 2011), are consistent with a developmental, experience-based etiology. In our experience, repeated traumatization can have a profound effect on the development of emotional awareness. For example, a child who is being abused by a caregiver and has the impulse to escape or fight back is likely to learn quickly that escape or defense responses are futile and often only increase the risk of being harmed, leading to a sense of learned helplessness. Trauma occurring later in life can also cause people to orient away from their feelings as a means of coping. For example, Elly's wife Esme, in describing her husband, notes:

> "Elly has difficulty with feelings. He *does* have feelings that he can touch from time to time. But I would say that that was something that was lost [in Dachua]. *The turning off of feelings.* [When asked] 'How do you *feel* about that?' it is very difficult for him to say. [He can/will often say] 'I feel touched,' or 'I feel hurt,' or 'I think that that was not a right thing to do, I think that was not good.' But *the feeling itself* is very hard for him to express. To me, that was a casualty."

In addition, cognitive–affective neuroscience has begun to investigate the brain bases of individual differences in alexithymic traits. Broadly relevant to that mission, neuroscientists have increasingly emphasized the role of the right anterior insular cortex in interoceptive awareness, including during affective (particularly of unpleasant/aversive) feelings (Craig, 2002, 2003, 2009a, 2010; Lamm & Singer, 2010; Wiens, 2005). Supporting this model, Critchley and others have shown that accuracy in heartbeat detection (a measure of interoceptive awareness, during which subjects are asked to become aware of the frequency of their own heartbeat without taking their own pulse) covaries with response in the right anterior insula, which in turn is predictive of state and/or trait negative affect (Critchley, 2004; see also Pollatos, Gramann, & Schandry, 2007; Singer, Critchley, & Preuschoff, 2009). Most recently, response within the right anterior insula was confirmed in the same participants in the context of interoception (heartbeat detection) and attention to emotional experience evoked by films; both tasks also preferentially engaged the dorsomedial prefrontal cortex and cingulate cortex, relative to respective control conditions, although within nonoverlapping regions (Zaki, Davis, & Ochsner, 2012).

The dorsomedial prefrontal cortex (PFC) was found to be the brain region to respond most reliably to emotion provocation in functional neuroimaging research (Kober, Feldman-Barrett, & Joseph, 2008). Current theoretical models propose an inferior–superior division in the medial PFC, indicating particular roles for the ventromedial PFC in partly representing primary emotional response, and for the dorsomedial PFC in mediating its secondary meta-awareness (re-representation; Lambie & Marcel, 2002) and regulation partly via dorsal attentional networks (e.g., Ochsner & Gross, 2005; Lewis & Todd, 2005).

Consistent with the above findings, we observed that increasing alexithymic symptomatology in traumatized persons with PTSD predicted increasing response in the right posterior insula, yet decreasing response in the bilateral anterior insula, in response to trauma script-driven imagery (Frewen, Lanius, et al., 2008). Lessened response in the anterior insula, which is normally highly active in response to anxiety and distress in individuals with PTSD (e.g., Etkin & Wager, 2007; Hayes et al., 2012; Patel et al., 2012), could be consistent with deficient interoceptive function during affective response in more alexithymic individuals during trauma memory recall (Frewen, Lanius, et al., 2008). Increasing alexithymia was also associated with decreasing response in the perigenual anterior cingulate cortex, known to be involved in autonomic regulation and emotional processing (e.g., Critchley, 2005), but with increasing response in the posterior cingulate cortex, known to be involved in episodic memory retrieval (e.g., Nielsen, Balslev, & Hansen, 2005).

Our findings were consistent with several other neuroimaging studies of response in persons with alexithymia, which identified alterations in the functional responsiveness of the ventral and dorsal anterior cingulate cortex (Berthoz et al., 2002; Kano et al., 2003; Lane et al., 1998), ventral and dorsal medial PFC (Berthoz et al., 2002; Kano et al., 2003), right middle insula (Kano et al., 2003), and posterior cingulate cortex (Mantani, Okamoto, Shirao, Okada, & Yamawaki, 2005). Another study, notable for investigating group differences in alexithymia in a resting state, showed (among other findings) reduced connectivity of the anterior nodes of the default mode network (DMN) with the cingulate gyrus and superior frontal gyrus, and reduced connectivity of the posterior DMN with the medial PFC (Liemburg et al., 2012). The latter result—reduced connectivity between posterior and anterior nodes in the DMN—is similar to findings for individuals with PTSD observed by our group (Bluhm et al., 2009). In this regard it is further noteworthy that the individuals with PTSD studied by Bluhm et al. reported high levels of alexithymia.

Second-order cognitive reflection and intentional awareness paid toward core affective experience is thought to potentially alter the intensity of the original experience (Frijda, 2005; Izard, 1993; Lambie & Marcel, 2002; Thompson et al., 2011) or may even change its quality altogether (e.g., experiencing secondary emotions of guilt *for being* angry or emotionally numb may arise). It is also thought that people vary with respect to the level with which they are aware of their different emotional states (Lane & Schwartz, 1987). During emotional imagery, the collective findings that the dorsomedial PFC response increased with increased trait mindfulness (i.e., mindful observing; e.g., body awareness such as whether breathing slows down or speeds up), on the one hand, and decreased with increased trait emotional numbing symptoms, on the other, seem to fit a model that implicates the dorsomedial PFC in the conscious subjective experiencing of emotional responses (see Figure 6.9).

As previously noted, a meta-analysis also found that the dorsomedial PFC is the most reliably activated region of the brain in functional neuroimaging studies of emotional processing (Kober et al., 2008). The dorsomedial PFC also partly mediates social-cognitive processing (e.g., see meta-analysis by an Overwalle, 2009) and socioemotional processing more so than nonsocial emotional processing (e.g., Frewen, Dozois, Neufeld, Densmore, et al., 2011).

Notwithstanding the support for a theory of alexithymia as representing a cognitive deficit in the processing of emotion, what is implied specifically by self-report measures of alexithymia may not be clear in all cases. For example, we recently determined that nearly all of the variance in self-reported alexithymic traits in a sample of 55 women with PTSD could be accounted for by individual differences in anxiety, shame, and associated maladaptive belief sets that discouraged free emotional expression (e.g., beliefs that one would be rejected or abandoned if one communicated one's emotional feelings to others; Frewen, Dozois, Neufeld, & Lanius, 2012). In other words, such admittances tended to disqualify the theoretical assumption that self-reports of alexithymia in PTSD samples are solely explainable by developmentally or neurobiologically based deficits in emotional processing, implicating instead distress-based concerns, such as anxiety and shame, as interfering with free emotional expression in PTSD samples with childhood trauma. Nevertheless, objectively scored measures of emotional intelligence, such as the Levels of Emotional Awareness Scale (Lane, Quinlan, Schwartz, & Walker, 1990), validate that at least some traumatized persons exhibit actual deficiencies in identifying and labeling their affective states (Frewen, Lane, et al., 2008). More in-depth neurophenomenological studies of response to emotional processing tasks in a variety of trauma populations are needed to determine which effects are due simply to distress versus bona fide performance-related disturbances in emotional information processing.

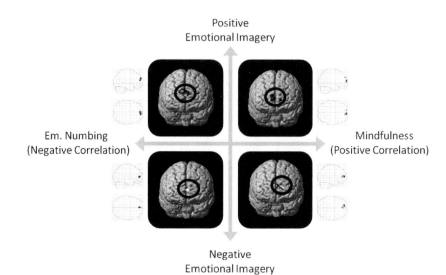

FIGURE 6.9. Association between Response in the Dorsomedial Pre-frontal Cortex during Socioemotional Imagery and Trait Emotional Numbing (Negative Correlation) and Trait Mindfulness (Positive Correlation).

Response during positive socioemotional imagery (receipt of affection/praise) is presented in upper quadrants; response during negative socio-emotional imagery (being rejected/criticized) is presented in lower quadrants. Emotional numbing symptoms were associated with *decreased* response in the dmPFC during socioemotional imagery in women with PTSD (*left quadrants*; Frewen, Dozois, Neufeld, Lane, et al., 2012). Individual differences in trait mindfulness were associated with *increased* response in the dmPFC during socioemotional imagery in healthy women (*right quadrants*; Frewen, Dozois, Neufeld, Lane, et al., 2010). Results inclusively masked for dmPFC response only. dmPFC = dorsomedial prefrontal cortex; PTSD = posttraumatic stress disorder. Reprinted from *Personality and Individual Differences*, Volume 49, Issue 5, Paul A. Frewen, David J. A. Dozois, Richard W. J. Neufeld, Richard D. Lane, Maria Densmore, Todd K. Stevens, Ruth A. Lanius, "Individual differences in trait mindfulness predict dorsomedial prefrontal and amygdala response during emotional imagery: An fMRI study" pages 479–484, October 2010, with permission from Elsevier.

We propose that helping clients identify a connection between somatic experiences and affective states can help them overcome alexithymia by creating a language for their feeling states. For example, clients can be encouraged to communicate out loud what they experience in their body while engaging in a body scan, using the vocabulary of physical experience (e.g., *tightening, tingling, squeezing, heart racing*). If clients are unable to experience *any* sensation in their body or parts of their body during repeated body scans, they might be encouraged to apply gentle pressure to any part of their body (i.e., with their hands) or flex their muscles and joints (e.g., touching their fingers to their thumbs) in order to facilitate the experience of physical sensation. Once clients are able to more easily identify physical sensations in their body, they can be encouraged to begin linking the physical sensations in their body with different feeling states. It is important to keep in mind that different clients are likely to have somewhat distinct patterns of physical sensation in their bodies as associated with specific emotional states. For example, anger for one client may be expressed through a feeling of heat throughout his or her body as well as tension in the chest and hands, whereas another client may experience anger via tension in the jaw and a feeling of tightness and squeezing in the stomach. Some clients may even find it helpful to use diagrams in order to label or draw the physical sensations they experience during different affective states. In addition, providing clients with a listing of emotion terms can be useful in educating them about emotions and assisting them in developing a vocabulary for their feeling states.

Case 4: Ending the Intergenerational Transmission of Trauma

"Katie" is a 35-year-old woman who described difficulties in emotional awareness, emotion regulation, and identity confusion. Katie presented with a long history of childhood abuse and neglect. She also experienced significant emotional numbing, which, as is typical of many trauma survivors, was expressed partly in her diminished ability to feel positive emotions in the context of close relationships. In this regard she was particularly distressed by her experience of being unable to feel and express love and affection toward her 3-year-old son, "Ben." She described her inner state: "It's like a blank. I think about my son, and I feel nothing for him. I'll be sitting there feeling confused and numb, and I wonder what I'm supposed to be feeling. It's like dead space . . . and when that happens, I have trouble using words, finding my words, I can't talk." Katie's emotional numbing and alexithymia thus significantly affected her capacity in the mothering role. Moreover, at other times Katie found that she was unable to hold Ben close because doing so reminded her of the emotional neglect and abuse she had experienced as a child. Indeed Katie often experienced flashbacks of being physically abused whenever she came into close proximity with her son. Katie felt intense guilt for not being able to experience and express loving feelings toward her son. Fortunately, to support the family, Ben frequently received respite care involving play and art therapy with other children. In this context, unfortunately, Ben was considered to be socially and emotionally withdrawn.

Katie's treatment began with an introduction to mindfulness exercises, including the body scan, with the goal of increasing her awareness of and capacity for feelings, including increasing her ability to feel warmth and tenderness toward loved ones. When Katie initially tried to engage in body scans, she reported being "completely numb" and unaware of physical sensations in her body. Katie's therapist assessed whether an adaptation of the body-scan exercise involving the self-application of gentle pressure might facilitate increasing awareness of physical sensation. Katie chose to apply pressure to her forehead with her fingertips as a body area that would likely feel safe and comfortable. She reported feeling the pressure she was applying to her forehead, but she was very hesitant to do the same at any other place in her body for fear of being overwhelmed by painful physical sensations.

Katie's boundaries and safety sensitivities were respected as she continued to practice this embodied intervention over the course of additional sessions. Ultimately she became comfortable enough to begin exploring physical sensations in other parts of her body. With increasing awareness of physical sensation throughout her body, Katie reported that her level of distress initially increased significantly. She reported not knowing what to make of "all these feelings" that she was unable to label. With reassurance and practice, however, over time Katie felt increasingly at ease with attending to her body and exercising interoceptive awareness. She also gradually learned to connect physical sensations in her body with different emotional feelings, including even, on occasion, positive ones. Katie was relieved to now be able to communicate her feelings in words and began to express her increased capacity for a range of emotions in her relationships with her son.

Katie's son likely realized, at some level, that his mother had difficulties being physically affectionate with him. For example, presumably in order to receive his mother's touch, Ben asked, "Can we play petting zoo? I will be a piggy. That way you can pet me." Katie was remorseful that she was unable to be emotionally and physically affectionate toward Ben. She tried everything she could to work through her own traumatic associations with attachment figures so that she could feel closer and be more supportive to her own son. Her therapist suggested she hold her son's hand and attempt to feel and share her love for him. Katie called this game "The Love Touch" and, fortunately, for both mother and son, over time Katie experienced increasing loving feelings and was increasingly able to hold Ben affectionately without experiencing acute PTSD symptoms. Katie noticed that as her loving feelings for and emotional availability to Ben increased, he became less withdrawn and his affect brightened. In preschool his teacher also described him as much happier and more socially interactive with other toddlers.

Trauma and Distress: Fear and Furthermore

*"Despite efforts to capture the essence of people's response to trauma,
the PTSD diagnosis does not begin to describe the complexity of how
people react to overwhelming experiences. . . . Focusing solely on
PTSD to describe what victims suffer from does not do justice to the
complexity of what actually ails them."*

—van der Kolk & McFarlane (1996, pp. 15–16)[1]

It is well known to treating clinicians that traumatized persons frequently exhibit significant problems with fear and anxiety. The scientific literature is equally replete with well-conducted systematic reviews and meta-analyses concerning the neurophysiology of fear and anxiety problems in traumatized persons (e.g., see reviews by Etkin & Wager, 2007; Hayes et al., 2012; Patel et al., 2012; Pole, 2007; Sartory et al., 2013). Clinical experience validates that traumatized persons are often on high alert, hypervigilant and apprehensive for signs of danger, especially as presenting in other people.

In comparison, far less research attention has been paid to the study of other dysregulated negative affective states that are often as equally prominent in chronically traumatized persons as is the experience of fear and anxiety. Due to this state of affairs Miller, Resick, and Keane (2009; Resick & Miller, 2009) saw it necessary to draw researchers' attention to the fact that highly traumatized individuals with PTSD often experience a multitude of dysregulated negative emotional states other than solely those of fear and anxiety. Among other symptoms of general negative affect frequently present in individuals with PTSD include anger, guilt, and shame. The multifarious nature of negative affective experiences of traumatized persons has been shown in at least three contexts: (1) peritraumatically, in response to recollections and stimulus reminders of traumatic events; (2) in response to experimental emotional stimuli; and (3) in response to questionnaires and interviews.

Referring to peritraumatic responses, it is increasingly well established that affective reactions at the time of traumatic events are typically not limited only to fear (Bovin & Marx, 2011). A prominent measure of subjective responses to acute traumatic events, for example, includes items assessing not only fear and anxiety but also other forms of nonspecific distress, including "sadness and grief," "frustration and anger," "guilt," and "shame" (Brunet et al., 2001; see also Birmes et al., 2005; Fikretoglu et al., 2006). Research also shows that when exposed to reminders of past traumatic events via the script-driven imagery procedure, reexperiencing of the traumatic event is associated not only with fear but also with numerous other emotions. For example, Lanius et al. (2001; Lanius, Williamson, et al., 2003) observed that script-driven imagery of personalized trauma narratives in individuals with PTSD often aroused the social and self-conscious emotions of shame and guilt in women exposed to childhood emotional and sexual abuse. In addition, in male combat veterans and female nurse veterans with PTSD, Shin et al. (2004) observed that the trauma script-driven imagery procedure evoked reduced happiness and increased sadness, anger, fear, disgust, surprise, guilt, and arousal, relative to imagery of neutral events. Relative to traumatized persons without PTSD, those with PTSD also experienced not only greater fear, arousal, and surprise but also more guilt (Shin et al., 2004).

Secondly, researchers have shown that individuals with PTSD often respond maladaptively to emotional stimuli other than those directly implicated in fear responses. For example, both McTeague et al. (2010) and Frewen, Dozois, Neufeld, Densmore, et al. (2010) observed elevations in self-reported negative affect in response to standardized scripts, the content of which focused on arousal of either anger or safety concerns (McTeague et al., 2010) or rejection (Frewen, Dozois, Neufeld, Densmore, et al., 2010). Studies also show a relative inability to downregulate distress in response to aversive pictures in traumatized persons with psychiatric disorders (e.g., PTSD, borderline personality disorder). This deficit coincides with decreased response in emotion regulatory regions such as the medial prefrontal cortex and anterior cingulate (Koenigsberg et al., 2009; Lang et al., 2012; New, Fan, et al., 2009; Schulze et al., 2011). Interestingly, startle potentiation and autonomic hyperarousal responses may best characterize individuals with PTSD who have experienced only single-incident traumas. In comparison, people who experienced multiple traumatic events, and particularly those who had long histories of childhood emotional, physical, or sexual abuse, differed *less* from controls in defensive-threat physiology despite reporting elevated subjective arousal (McTeague et al., 2010).

Finally, it is also increasingly well established that traumatized persons report a multitude of elevated emotional disturbances on questionnaires and in interviews. Power and Fyvie (2013), for example, found that roughly only half of 75 individuals with PTSD consecutively admitted to their clinic for treatment reported that fear or anxiety was their most disabling emotional state. Interestingly, individuals for whom fear or anxiety was *not* their most clinically significant presenting concern evidenced poorer outcomes in exposure-based treatment, prompting Power and Fyvie to consider whether subgroups of "fear-anxiety" versus "non-fear-anxiety" subtypes of PTSD should be distinguished, the latter perhaps responding better to treatments other than, or in addition to, exposure-based therapies. Symptoms of general negative affect have also been classified as either of an externalizing (e.g., anger) or internalizing (e.g., guilt, shame) nature (e.g., Miller, Grief, & Smith, 2003; Miller & Resick, 2007).

Accordingly, rather than focusing exclusively on fear and anxiety symptoms (Miller, Resick, & Keane, 2009; Resick & Miller, 2009), the diagnostic criteria for PTSD in DSM-5 explicitly recognize the heterogeneous nature of emotional responding in individuals with this disorder. Specifically, the DSM-5 diagnosis includes the symptom "pervasive negative emotional state—e.g., fear, horror, anger, guilt, or shame" (Friedman, Resick, Bryant, & Brewin, 2011, p. 759). The array of negative emotional states experienced by many traumatized persons—indeed chronic, complexly traumatized persons rarely struggle with only a single type of emotion—suggests that many trauma survivors might suffer from problems regulating core affective states (Frewen & Lanius, 2006b; Lanius, Frewen, et al., 2010); we consider emotion regulation difficulties and how they might relate to the traumatized self next.

Emotion Dysregulation and the Sense of Self: "Having" versus "Being" an Emotion

As previously noted, theorists suggest that a distinction can be made between primary, "first-order" emotional experience versus our *awareness of* our emotional experience, the latter considered a second-order re-representation of emotion (e.g., Frijda, 2005; Lambie & Marcel, 2002; Lane et al., 1997). For example, it was argued earlier that the concept of differentiating between first- and second-order representations of emotional processing provides for the case of alexithymia wherein individuals may be evidently experiencing an emotional state while nevertheless being largely unaware of it.

The implications of a first- versus second-order awareness of emotional experience may apply rather broadly. Indeed theory suggests that when one intentionally applies second-order introspective or interoceptive processes in relation to first-order core affective experience, the first-order representations are intrinsically altered (Frijda, 2005; Izard, 1993; Lambie & Marcel, 2002; Thompson et al., 2011). As arguably the first objective demonstration of this through the methods of affective neuroscience, Taylor, Phan, Decker, and Liberzon (2003) showed that rating the aversiveness of unpleasantly arousing pictures (i.e., applying a cognitive label, thus operating at the level of second-order emotional experience) increased medial PFC and anterior cingulate response, while simultaneously decreasing amygdala response, in comparison with passive viewing (i.e., first-order emotional experience).

Several studies have since replicated the effect of explicit labeling in reducing amygdala response, using variations on this experimental procedure (e.g., Lieberman et al., 2007). These studies suggest that actively engaging the will, even if only to covertly label external emotional stimuli as to their significance, can promote a higher-order level of consciousness (i.e., second-order awareness, associated with prefrontal cortical responses) relative to passively reacting to stimuli (i.e., first-order awareness, associated with limbic response, e.g., in the amygdala). Beyond simple labeling, we all know firsthand that there are many ways we can (at least try) to volitionally alter our ongoing emotional responses to events through intentionally engaging the will of second-order awareness: We may choose to eat sugar and fatty foods to comfort our feeling of loneliness, go for a walk to calm our anger, or listen to our favorite music to combat boredom. Studies in affective neuroscience are only just beginning to investigate these complex behaviors under the banner of *emotion regulation* research, briefly overviewed in Chapter 1.

One of the more well-studied emotion regulatory behaviors is *cognitive reappraisal*, which involves intentionally interpreting a stimulus or event in such a way as to influence its typical impact (Aldao et al., 2010). In neuroimaging experiments cognitive reappraisal research usually takes the form of presenting intrinsically positive and negative pictures to participants and asking them to interpret them in a positive versus negative way (e.g., if one would normally feel saddened by a picture of a woman crying, the task of cognitive reappraisal might lead one to interpret the woman's lamentation as signaling tears of joy, in turn leading one to feel not sympathy but instead perhaps to share in her delight). Studies have shown that cognitively reappraising stimuli in such a way tends to provoke response in the dorsal and ventral medial PFC, anterior cingulate cortex, bilateral middle and inferior frontal gyri, and bilateral insula, among other regions, relative to passive viewing (e.g., Diekhof, Geier, Falkai, & Gruber, 2011; Ochsner & Gross, 2005; Ochsner et al., 2002). Again, the task of cognitive reappraisal is intrinsically one involving second-order emotional processing: One's normal, automatic way of responding to emotional stimuli (first-order processing) is intentionally overcome through an attentional manipulation (second-order processing). As noted previously, in effect, the task of cognitive reappraisal involves experientially "taking a step back" from one's regular way of experiencing oneself and the world in order to willfully perceive it in a new, more adaptive way.

As noted in Chapter 1, in phenomenological terms a somewhat different approach to emotion regulation, one that even more explicitly involves "taking a step back," involves subjectively decentering, distancing, or detaching oneself from the emotional stimulus, thus taking an observer rather than field perspective (Ayduk & Kross, 2010; Fresco, Segal, et al., 2007; Fresco, Moore, et al., 2007; Kross, 2009). Such manipulations may, nevertheless, be mediated by brain mechanisms similar to those evoked by other forms of emotion regulation, including cognitive reappraisal (e.g.,

Kalisch et al., 2005; Lévesque 2003). We noted in a previous paper that instructions given to participants to distance themselves from mild electric shocks and distress associated with viewing saddening films in neuroimaging experiments are strikingly similar to the phenomenology of (at least mild) states of dissociative detachment (Frewen & Lanius, 2006b). Current research trends in studies of emotion regulation include directly comparing the neural underpinnings of different emotion regulation strategies in response to the same stimuli, such as between *cognitive reappraisal* and *suppression* (e.g., Goldin, McRae, Ramel, & Gross, 2008) and distraction (Kanske, Heissler, Schonfelder, Bongers, & Wessa, 2010; McRae et al., 2010). We again suggest that the mild decentering, distancing, or detachment facilitated by taking a second-order attentional position relative to first-order emotional experiences of distress is likely a common factor, in varying degrees, across all forms of emotion regulation. Decentering can be a healthy way to manage and tolerate forms of distress of both an internalizing and externalizing nature, so long as one does not step back "too far."

Intended as a simple phenomenological framework for applying the terminology of second- versus first-order affective experiences, we suggest the concepts of *having emotions* versus *being emotional*, respectively. The left panel of Figure 6.10 (also in color insert) illustrates the idea of *having* emotions. Here the self is conceptualized as holding a bag in which different emotional states may be temporarily contained and thus felt. Fortunately, however, the bag has a hole in the bottom of it and therefore rarely overflows: Although emotions get caught for a moment, they eventually pass through and are let go, no longer felt. The self is therefore rarely overwhelmed by the experience of "too much emotion." A key aspect of the experience of "having emotions" is that the self is not fully *identified* with the emotional experience, but rather is at least one "order" of experience removed. The self is holding the bag of first-order emotional experiences, and thus experientially aware of their weight, yet these emotional states themselves are not experienced *as* the self per se; the self is instead defined in such second-order experiences as a decentered form of attention or conscious awareness itself.

This conceptualization is consistent with the decentering practices that occur in mindfulness meditation, wherein the practitioner perceives the rising and falling of each passing "wave" of thought and emotion, just as he or she does of each passing breath, yet does not become carried away by such waves through processes of identification or attachment (e.g., Bishop et al., 2004; Brown, Ryan, & Creswell, 2007; Corcoran, Farb, Anderson, & Segal, 2010; Frewen, Evans, et al., 2008). For example, survey items from one measure of mindful decentering, intended to be completed after meditation practices as a documentation of phenomenological experiences that occurred during the meditation, include: "I experienced myself as separate from my changing thoughts and feelings" and "I was

Having Emotions

Emotion Dysregulation: *Being* an Emotion

FIGURE 6.10. Phenomenology of *Having Emotions* versus *Being an Emotion*.

Left panel: "*HAVING* EMOTIONS"—the sense of self is identified as holding a bag in which different emotional states are temporarily contained and thus felt from a decentered perspective. The self is not fully *identified* with emotional experiences; they are feelings that the self *has* rather than feelings that the self *is*. Moreover, a hole at the bottom of the bag allows emotional feelings eventually to pass through, no longer being felt. *Right panel:* "*BEING* AN EMOTION" —the self is shown *in* the bag of feelings. In such experiences, the sense of self is strongly identified with, and overwhelmed by, an emotional state. There is no attentional separation between the sense of self and the emotional feeling and therefore the emotional state cannot be regulated. Such feelings are thus "self-consuming" and may be experienced as akin to a loss of control.

aware of my thoughts and feelings without over-identifying with them" (items from the Toronto Mindfulness Questionnaire; Lau et al., 2006). In summary, through the practice of mindful decentering as an emotion regulatory practice, the self is identified with the greater ocean of attention or conscious awareness, rather than becoming fixated upon any particular "wave" of emotion, and as such is "greater than the wave."

We propose that, in contrast, the states of emotion dysregulation commonly associated with psychological trauma might be akin to something like the experience of *being an emotion*. In such experiences, the self is strongly identified with and overwhelmed by an emotional state, at least momentarily: There exists no attentional separation between the sense of self and that of the emotion. In such circumstances, the whole of attention and a person's sense of self are taken in by the wave of an emotional state, be it fear, sorrow, shame, or anger. Such feelings are therefore felt so fully that they are, at least for a moment, "self-consuming"—one experiences nothing else other than the emotional state—the sense of self effectually *is* the emotional state. Being that the self is fully identified with the emotional state and thus there is no experiential separation between self and emotion, the emotion cannot be regulated, and may be accompanied by an experience of loss of control. The loss of a sense of control and a decentered sense of self that frequently accompany states of emotion dysregulation may in turn be experienced as a transient break from one's normal state of consciousness, prompting an individual to become cognizant, only after the emotional experience has passed, of "not being myself" during the emotional episode and having lost control (see the next section), a phenomenology some theorists would label an instance of dissociation. It is important to note that extreme expressions of emotionality are often prompted by reminders of past traumatic events and, as such, are less responses to actual present circumstances as much as they are reactions to emotionally laden past experiences as if they are still taking place in the present.

The right panel of Figure 6.10 illustrates our current way of thinking about emotion dysregulation, labeled *being an emotion*. We suggest that in states of emotion dysregulation, affective feelings are something that one momentarily *is* or *becomes* rather than states that one *has*. The self is depicted *in* the bag of feeling, intended to signify an experience of the self as fully encompassed by an emotional response. In such states, the self is fused with an emotional state and therefore there is no way to put the bag down—one carries feeling not with an arm's-length separation, as one does when *having* emotions, but *as oneself*. In such instances emotions are not something we have and hold as much as something we momentarily *are*. A cardinal example of this occurs in the panic attack: In such experiences the person is fully *inside* a state of intense *inner* fear; he or she cannot get outside of it (e.g., Dalgleish & Power, 2004). We have also already discussed the fusion of a sense of self with that of shame during analogous "shame attacks": As noted earlier by Stephanie, for example, shame is "very difficult to come out of. The shame is so big and so overwhelming that it becomes part of who I am." In addition, we would contend that something similar occurs during "anger attacks" in many traumatized persons: The individual's sense of self and feelings of being in control of his or her own actions can be momentarily overwhelmed by intense anger, sometimes resulting in violence, as we see in the following section.

"Being Rage": The Compartmentalization of Anger

Erica provides a succinct description of the nature of anger in a traumatized person in this excerpt:

Interviewer: Where do you think your anger comes from? What causes you to become angry?

Erica: It's pain. That's where the anger is coming from—it's pain. Pain from everything in the past. Pain triggers the anger. And if anyone causes me to become angry, it's because they've hurt me, by making me feel something I've felt before and making me feel like I am back there. It's like I have no control over what comes out. It sometimes gets so strong that I could hurt someone.

Although studies of traumatized persons have focused mostly on the (dys)regulation of anxiety and dysphoria, many studies have also investigated the phenomenology of anger in this population. Indeed the emotional state of anger is of particular relevance to the pathology of PTSD. Not only is it well established that traumatized persons, on average, frequently experience problems with both the internalization and externalization of anger (e.g., McHugh, Forbes, Bates, Hopwood, & Creamer, 2012; Orth & Wieland, 2006), but it has additionally been shown that, whereas individuals with various anxiety disorders often report problems related to irritability and anger, research suggests that it is particularly the *perceived lack of control* over anger that distinguishes anger associated with PTSD from experiences of anger that are just as strongly associated with other anxiety disorders (Olatunji, Ciesielski, & Tolin, 2010).

Neuroimaging studies have only begun to investigate the neural bases of the controlled inhibition of anger through processes of emotion regulation. A study of individual differences in angered responses to mild social insult (i.e., rude, upset, and condescending questioning of the participant to speak louder and inquiring: "Can't you follow directions?") found that trait aggressiveness, as measured by questionnaires, was associated with increased dorsal anterior cingulate cortex (dACC) activity, envisioned by the investigators as a component of a "neural alarm system" (Denson, Pedersen, Ronquillo, & Nandy, 2009). The investigators interpreted increased dACC activity among more aggressive participants as indicative of a greater inhibitory effort on their part to overcome their natural, automatic tendency to become aggressive in the context of mild insult, provided that the dACC is associated with effortful cognitive control and error monitoring.

Along with increases in dACC activity, elicitation of angry feelings corresponded with response in the insula (associated with emotional arousal and experience), the dorsomedial PFC (associated with attention to emotion and emotional experience), and other regions known to be activated by emotional response. In a subsequent study, Denson and colleagues explicitly instructed participants to attempt to overcome any aggressive feelings that might be elicited by the same condescending tone on the part of experimenters. Findings concerning the dACC, dorsomedial PFC, and insula response during anger moments were replicated and found to further vary by between-person differences in endogenous testosterone and cortisol levels. Moreover, responses covaried more with self-reported effortful anger control than with anger intensity per se (Denson, Ronay, von Hippel, & Schira, 2013).

Finally, functional connectivity with the amygdala, widely recognized as a region of the brain involved in emotional stimulus perception, was increased with a left prefrontal control network including the orbitofrontal cortex (OFC), dorsolateral PFC, and dACC, and decreased with regions of the brainstem, following anger elicitation relative to baseline. These findings perhaps indicate increasing attempted prefrontal inhibition of the amygdala and decreasing amygdala excitation of autonomic and behavioral outputs during successful downregulation of anger; individual differences in connectivity were further found to vary by testosterone and cortisol levels (Denson et al., 2013).

Denson and colleagues' findings were consistent with another study that found that amygdala connectivity with the OFC was increased as a function of increased trait disposition toward controlling one's anger even as measured simply at rest (Fulwiler, King, & Zhang, 2012). The striking sensitivity of the brain to such minor provocations, particularly in individuals more disposed to trait anger and anger dyscontrol, is revealing. In fact, other studies have provoked anger simply by requiring participants to hear the word "No," with males who experienced greater negative affect in direct response to the verbal stimulus showing less response in the OFC, and males more disposed to control their anger exhibiting greater OFC response to hearing "No" (Alia-Klein et al., 2007).

Fabiansson, Denson, Moulds, Grisham, and Schira (2012) investigated the emotion regulation of anger in a more direct way by asking participants to recall a memory previously associated with angry feelings, followed by attempts to regulate their memory-elicited anger either through *cognitive reappraisal* ("Think about the event in a different, more objective and positive way"), *analytical rumination* ("Think about the memory in a way that brings to mind the causes and consequences of the event"), or *angry rumination* ("Think about your feelings and emotional aspects of the event") (p. 2975). Neural responding during the three different anger regulatory approaches did not differ, each showing increased response, relative to a baseline relaxation condition, in brain regions known to be involved in emotional response and control: the inferior frontal and orbitofrontal cortex, putamen, insula, and amygdala. Functional connectivity between the right inferior frontal gyrus and amygdala was found to be stronger during the analytical and angry rumination conditions relative to cognitive reappraisal.

Unfortunately, relatively few neuroimaging studies have examined the experience of anger in traumatized persons. New, Hazlett, and colleagues (2009) examined individuals with borderline personality disorder (BPD) and accompanying intermittent explosive disorder, nearly half of whom were also diagnosed with either present or past PTSD. Individuals played a game during which, on certain trials, they perceived themselves as having lost resources (money) on account of another person's action, and may choose to respond aggressively in turn by causing the loss of the other person's resources. New and colleagues noted anecdotally that their participants with BPD "describe feeling overwhelmed by anger, with no access to controlling their responses or considering the consequences of not controlling them" (New, Hazlett, et al., 2009, p. 1112). The researchers found that, during anger provocation (relative to trials in which anger was not provoked), individuals with BPD evidenced increased response in the OFC and amygdala, whereas the opposite was true of a healthy comparison group. Such responses may be indicative of both increased anger response and attempted and failed anger control. However, complicating interpretation, due to additional observation of reduced orbitofrontal metabolism in the context of control trials, the net outcome of the study was to show that individuals with BPD differed from healthy persons with respect to orbitofrontal and amygdala function mainly in the *absence* of a relatively explicit cause for anger provocation. Follow-up analyses also showed less response within the striatum, particularly in males with BPD but not specifically as a function of trial type (Perez-Rodriguez et al., 2012).

Spoont, Kuskowski, and Pardo (2010) also compared response in individuals with either intermittent explosive disorder or a personality disorder associated with aggression, with the diagnosis of PTSD again being prominent in the clinical presentation, during script-driven imagery of memories associated with feelings of anger. In comparison with the recall of neutral memories, Spoont et al. observed several group differences in several brain regions known to be involved in emotional response and control, including the OFC, amygdala, inferior frontal cortex, medial PFC, insula, caudate, and cerebellum. Additional neuroimaging studies of anger provocation in trauma-related disorders are needed.

It was argued that the concept of *being an emotion* may invoke certain dissociative elements, in particular the notion of the compartmentalization of emotionality. Specifically, during the experience of anger, a person may momentarily feel a loss of control so much so that he or she feels as if momentarily no longer him- or herself, perhaps signifying a dissociative response. Within the context of anger processing, two studies explicitly investigated correlations between individual differences in anger and dissociative symptoms in individuals with PTSD (Feeny, Zoell-ner, & Foa, 2000; Kulkarni, Porter, & Rauch, 2012). In Feeny et al.'s (2000) study of female victims of sexual ($n = 56$) or nonsexual ($n = 48$) assault, trait anger and dissociative symptoms were moderately correlated as measured 2, 4, and 12 weeks post-assault. In addition, associations between trait anger and dissociation remained significant even after controlling for PTSD symptom severity. Moreover, in Kulkarni et al.'s (2012) study of 214 male veterans, 62% of whom had been in the Vietnam war and the remaining of whom participated either in Operation Enduring Freedom or in Operation Iraqi Freedom, roughly three quarters of participants evidenced clinically significant trait anger and dissociative symptoms, and severity of trait anger again correlated moderately highly with trait dissociative symptoms. Additionally, both anger and dissociation concurrently predicted PTSD symptom severity. Feeny et al. (2000) and Kulkarni et al. (2012) therefore described anger dyscontrol and dissociative processes as complementary forms of emotional disengagement, arguably implying that, while often co-occurring, the processes underlying the expression of anger and dissociation might be relatively independent.

We certainly concur that anger problems as presenting in traumatized persons need not intrinsically imply dissociative processes. However, we also suggest another interpretation of the correlation exists: that dyscontrol over anger may itself represent a dissociative process, at least in a certain number of cases. Indeed in large samples of predominantly traumatized people with psychiatric disorders, including dissociative identity disorder, Dell and Lawson (2009) found that an "angry intrusions" factor, secondary to a general sense of self-confusion, explained the bulk of variation in response to the Multidimensional Inventory of Dissociation (MID). Consistent with this finding, a common complaint among individuals with PTSD relates to their perception of not feeling *in control over* their anger. Indeed, certain individuals with PTSD, of either sex but particularly in males, have reported that during violent fits of anger and rage, "it is as if they are no longer themselves." For example, one individual noted that, after being cut off on the road while driving, "I went into such a rage it was like I stopped thinking—I was just acting—it was like I wasn't *there* anymore." Erica has also noted: "You know, I say this out loud: I would never knowingly hurt another person. But I do. And I have. I *have* knowingly hurt other people, but I didn't, because I didn't know what was going to come out [what I was going to do or say]. If that makes sense? I don't know where these things [angry feelings] come from." In other words, persons who normally identify with a sense of self that is nonaggressive may consider, and phenomenologically *experience*, their (usually otherwise inhibited) impulses toward anger and aggression as if they are "someone else." Others, cognizant of their past impulsive acts of aggression, have even reported being "afraid of their anger," again suggesting a level of dyscontrol over it, as if their anger had a "mind of its own."

Although some might dismiss such lay expressions as mere turns of phrase, we suggest that a somewhat more literal interpretation may be warranted in at least a certain number of cases. Specifically, current understanding of anger-related emotionality includes processes of inhibition as a primary component. It is thought that a level of inhibitory self-control over anger is required in order to decrease its expression; in the absence of such inhibitory control, anger is thought, in a sense, to be left unto its own devices (Denson, DeWall, & Finkel, 2012). Emotion regulation skills are thus widely considered to be necessary in order to inhibit anger expression (DeWall, Anderson, & Bushman, 2011; Finkel et al., 2013; Roberton, Daffern, & Bucks, 2012; Wilkowski, Robinson, & Troop-Gordon, 2010). Without harboring a sense of self distinct from anger and thereby capable of regulating its expression, in severe cases of rage one may therefore experience oneself as momentarily "becoming" the state of anger, seemingly invoking, more or less subtly, a dissociative compartmentalized state of emotionality. In that state, emotion is effectively compartmentalized from one's normal sense of self and feelings of control. Beyond this, it should also be noted that, in established cases of dissociative identity disorder or dissociative disorder not otherwise specified, the compartmentalization of emotion is commonly experienced. As noted in previous chapters, individuals with these disorders experience themselves as living discrete and alternating senses of agency and selfhood that may be characterized by, among other qualities, relatively stable trait-like dispositions toward appraising, experiencing, and regulating particular emotional states. Indeed a relatively frequent first clinical presentation is to observe an individual experiencing him- or herself as "emotionally neutral" while, depending on the level of co-consciousness, acknowledging and describing what are experienced to be independent senses of self prone to the experience of discrete memories and related emotions such as anger, fear, shame, and sadness (see Figure 6.11; also in color insert).

Whether a dissociative process underlies, at least in part, the emergence of marked states of emotion dysregulation (see Figure 6.10, *right panel*) is an important theoretical question. Nevertheless, classifying all cases of apparent emotion dysregulation as intrinsically representing TRASC of emotion is not parsimonious and we would think almost certainly in error. However, we consider the more blatant alterations in sense of self that accompany compartmentalized states of emotionality in severe dissociative disorders, as depicted in Figure 6.11, to be classified by the 4-D model as plainly dissociative in nature. More research regarding the neurophenomenology of the compartmentalized experience of emotions is needed in order to scientifically evaluate differing clinical impressions regarding the degree of dissociation of emotionality in trauma-related disorders.

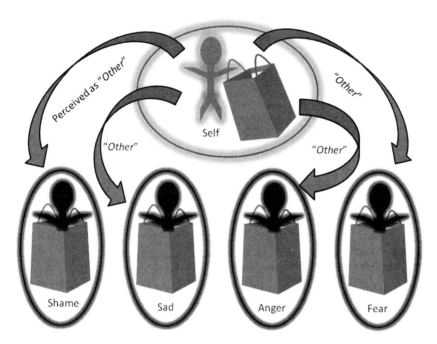

FIGURE 6.11. Phenomenology of the Compartmentalization of Emotion across Different Senses of Self.

A primary sense-of-self (*top*) is identified as typically neutral in affective state. Tendencies toward various emotional states (e.g., shame, sadness, anger, fear) are identified (from the perspective of the primary sense of self) as different senses of self.

Emotionless: Emotional Numbing and Affective Shutdown as an Intrinsic Trauma-Related Altered State of Consciousness of Emotion

"In the traumatic state, there is a psychological paralysis that starts with a virtually complete blocking of the ability to feel emotions and pain, as well as other physical sensations, and progresses to inhibition of other mental functions. The subjects themselves are able to observe and describe the blocking of affective responses—a circumstance that has led to such terms as psychic numbing, 'psychological closing off,' and 'affective anesthesia.' The paradox in the traumatic state is that the numbing and closing off are experienced as relief from the previously painful affect such as anxiety; at the same time,

they are also experienced as the first part of dying, for, along with
the affective blocking, there is a blocking of initiative and all life-
preserving cognition."

—Krystal (1988, p. 151)[1]

We have so far described a variety of affective states that frequently occur
in chronically traumatized persons: fear, anxiety, sadness, anger, guilt,
shame, anhedonia, and alexithymia. We might imagine turbulent ocean
waves to symbolize the traumatized state of emotion dysregulation (i.e.,
"pervasive emotional states"). Emotions are considered to thrash about:
Fear, shame, and anger may each rise up, one followed by the next, or all
may even crash at once. Attention, one's sense of self, and feelings of control are momentarily overwhelmed and drowned. Actions resulting from
these emotions are frequently self-destructive and may also cause social
harm. The acknowledgment of the increased variety of "pervasive negative
emotional states" that frequently occur in people with PTSD and related
disorders is a step in the right direction, addressing the hitherto undue
focus on processes specific to fear and anxiety (Friedman, Resick, Bryant,
& Brewin, 2011).

The nonspecificity of the labeled negative emotional states nevertheless remains somewhat problematic for the argument that the symptom
complaints experienced by traumatized persons might be unique. Indeed
in an influential statement Spitzer, First, and Wakefield (2007) recommended that, in order to "save PTSD from itself," symptoms of PTSD
"should be evaluated in terms of their diagnostic specificity for differentiating PTSD from other mood and anxiety disorders and that only
symptoms related to exposure to a severe trauma be retained" (p. 237).
Moreover, Spitzer and colleagues considered whether "PTSD symptom
descriptors include too many general symptoms of negative affect or general responses to negative events" (p. 237) to demarcate clear boundaries
between psychopathological outcomes from nonpathological maladjustment to general life stress. We are in agreement that this is a concern.
Neither the symptoms described by the DSM-IV diagnosis nor even those
of DSM-5 appear to signify an especially striking departure from symptoms of general distress, negative affect, and social maladjustment. This
is also arguably equally true of other trauma-related disorders, including
major depression and BPD.

In any case, as more relevant to the 4-D model, it is not parsimonious to consider such emotional states as inherently dissociative in nature.

---

[1]Republished with permission of Taylor & Francis Group LLC Books, from *Integration and Self-Healing: Affect—Trauma—Alexithymia*, by Henry Krystal, © 1988;
permission conveyed through Copyright Clearance Center, Inc.

By all accounts, these emotional states are experienced by all humans to varying degrees as part and parcel of NWC. Therefore, although we have described in phenomenological terms how these emotional states may sometimes present in a compartmentalized form, simultaneously dissociated from both one's normal sense of self and a sense of control, there is nothing *in the essence* of emotional states such as fear, anxiety, loss, sadness, anger, guilt, or shame that makes them dissociative in all or even the majority of cases. Might there exist another affective state, however, that represents a TRASC of emotion in and of itself?

Krystal wrote in detail about the prominence of emotional numbing in highly traumatized persons who were described as "without emotion," "robotic," and as if "living-dead" (Krystal, 1968, 1988). Test items from the Glover Numbing Questionnaire validate this characterization, which include experiences of "acting mechanically like a robot," "feeling dead or shut down," and feeling like "my body feels paralyzed"; Clapp & Beck, 2009; Glover et al., 1994, 1997). These characterizations contrast strikingly with the view that traumatized persons are chronically anxious and only highly emotionally reactive. In the next transcript Julia and Erica describe their experiences of emotional numbing for the interviewer.

"Interview with Julia"

Interviewer: Julia, can you give me a recent example of when you felt emotionally numb?

Julia: Probably coming into the hospital. By the elevators there were a number of people going to get on, and I don't like people being around me and I just . . . I don't know how to describe what it is. It's kind of like a wall around and everyone else is gone. Nothing touches me, sounds and smells and realizing the person is there are all gone. Just numb. It happens all the time.

"Interview with Erica"

Interviewer: The feeling of being emotionally numb . . . is that something that you've experienced?

Erica: Yes. I think that's when I lose time. I think that I just go dead . . . it's not just emotionally numb, it's physically numb. There is just nothing there, it's vacuous, it's . . . it's like I'm in a hole, I'm a lump of flesh, I'm an amoeba, I have no . . . I'm a lifeless life form, or lifeless, or not sentient or . . .I just exist, it's almost like—not even a slug. I think that a

> slug must at least have instinct—I don't even have that—an amoeba—it is the best way I can describe it. I am just existing, I don't have any other words.

Interviewer: You linked the experience to the loss of time—what is time like in the state of emotional numbing?

Erica: Time is a *"non,"* it's *"not."* I can't answer that because I'll sort of "come to," for lack of a better way of putting it, and it might be hours later. So I don't know, because I'm not aware of being aware, if I am . . .

Somewhat of a conceptual conundrum exists in the literature regarding the scope and use of the terms *emotional numbing* versus *alexithymia* and *anhedonia*, as discussed earlier in this chapter (e.g., Badura, 2003). In our view, it is useful to retain a theoretical distinction between these terms. Specifically, whereas *alexithymia* refers to not knowing *what* one is feeling, which can occur either in the presence or absence of marked distress (i.e., "feeling too much" or "feeling too little"), and *anhedonia* refers to the diminished experience of positive affect in contexts that should normally provoke it, we reserve the experience of emotional numbing for the *feeling of being* emotionally numb (e.g., Frewen, Lanius et al., 2008; Frewen, Dozois, Neufeld, & Lanius, 2012; Frewen, Dozois, Neufeld, Lane, et al., 2012). However, even as we suggest that useful conceptual distinctions are made between alexithymia, anhedonia, and the feeling of being emotionally numb, these experiences clearly *do* often go hand in hand. For example, self- or clinician-reported signs and symptoms of emotional numbing and alexithymia are correlated (e.g., Frewen, Dozois, Neufeld, Lane, et al., 2012).

Traumatized individuals commonly exhibit characteristic signs of affect dysregulation, as reviewed above. However, sometimes even more clinically prominent than discrete emotional episodes are the various affective *background* feelings these individuals commonly report, often collectively referred to as symptoms of "emotional numbing." These experiences tend to suggest that emotional numbing might represent a frequent core affective state in traumatized persons. The following untitled poem, written by a trauma survivor, gives the impression of emotional numbing as a core affective state and perhaps even a fundamental aspect of his personality structure:

> I've been numbed to the core.
> Do you see the emptiness? Do you see the hollow through my
>   eyes' door?
> You can take a look at what I've become.

You can see what I've done and where I'm gone.
So numb.
Numb to the core of my being, the core of everything, even
    the core of my existence.
Numb to the feel, touch and numb to the pain.
Numb to the thousand emotions.
Numb to the hollowness that resides in me.
So numb, I'm frozen. Frozen to my core.
What it feels like to cry tears, to me is unknown.
What it feels like to bleed, what it always felt like to want and
    need, to me is unknown?
Why do I die inside yet I feel no pain? Who, do you reside in me?
Why do you feel like my blood without which I can't live or
    survive?
So numb to the feel, what it feels like to be alive.
You know my deepest secret fear.
You know who I am even when I disappear.
I've gone a thousand miles, to be alone with my fears.
I'm living it, living my days in fear . . .
So numb to my core I can't even shed a tear.
I'm living my deepest secret fear . . .

In recent years, the concept of emotional numbing took increased prominence in the literature when a subset of PTSD symptoms were first psychometrically distinguished from cognitive and behavioral forms of avoidance by King, Leskin, King, and Weathers (1998) through factor analysis. This statistical demonstration was also predicted by earlier clinical observations (e.g., van der Kolk & McFarlane [1996, p. 12] wrote: "Despite the fact that numbing and avoidance are lumped together in the DSM-IV, numbing probably has a very different underlying pathophysiology from avoidance"). Upon close examination, emotional numbing symptoms, in their more clinically extreme cases, tend to suggest alterations in a person's sense of self, including marked social and existential disturbances. For example, among the currently recognized symptoms of PTSD include the experience of feelings of detachment or estrangement from others (American Psychiatric Association, 2013). The subjective feeling of social estrangement, also referred to as subjective *alienation*, was recently found to be the most reliable predictor of PTSD, dissociation, and depressive symptoms across three samples, in comparison with five other posttrauma appraisals studied (anger, fear, betrayal, shame, and self-blame; DePrince, Chu, & Pineda, 2011). Thus traumatized persons may report feeling distinctly "different from others," or feel that they have lost their meaning and purpose for living. In this sense, these phenomenological self-reports suggest not transient emotional episodes but instead more fundamental shifts in the way the self and consciousness are experienced.

Another helpful concept for understanding trait aspects of emotional numbing, as they are most often studied in clinical psychology and psychiatry today, is the notion of "existential feelings" as articulated by Ratcliffe (2005). Ratcliffe argues that subtle forms of existential feeling are likely implicit in all states of human consciousness, also defined as background feelings in ways seemingly very similar to Russell's (2003) concept of core affect reviewed earlier. Specifically, Ratcliffe (2005) describes existential feelings as representing "ways of finding oneself in the world . . . background orientations through which experience as a whole is structured" (p. 46). Ratcliffe gives illuminating examples of positively valenced existential feelings (e.g., feeling complete, powerful, in control, or at one with life) and negatively valenced existential feelings (e.g., feeling lost, overwhelmed, abandoned, torn, disconnected from the world, flawed and diminished, unworthy, invulnerable, unloved, empty, helpless, trapped, weighed down) (p. 45).

Ratcliffe (2005) thus similarly argues that existential feelings are embodied states that both represent and reflect the global degree of well-being and arousal of the individual at a particular moment in time. Existential feelings are therefore phenomenal subjective states, reflecting the connectedness between a person and his or her environment. Although not systematically tested, clinical experience suggests that many of the examples just listed for negatively valenced "existential feelings" describe very well the affective reports of many chronically emotionally numb traumatized persons. Moreover, although such complex existential feeling states clearly are not reducible to a discrete basic emotions view, we would suggest that most could be classified around the circumplex of core affect near the relatively deactivated negative affective state implied by 210°–240°—that is, not unlike low-arousal expressions of shame, anhedonia, and alexithymia (see Figure 6.12).

Although this chronic low-arousal presentation of emotional numbing seems to be the experience most often referred to in the PTSD literature, it can be distinguished from other putatively high- and low-arousal forms of affective shutdown often accompanying peritraumatic dissociative states—that is, affective responses that occur during traumatic events. For example, we encountered such an experience when hearing about the case study of the car accident victims in Chapter 2. Whereas the husband experienced a fight–flight (hyperaroused) response in which his primary focus involved freeing himself and his wife from their vehicle, the wife instead reported being "in shock, frozen, and numb" (hypoaroused) and that, were it not for her husband, she would not have been able to escape from the car alone. Nevertheless, it was clear that the woman's psychological state had been prompted by a stressor, and it is unclear whether her

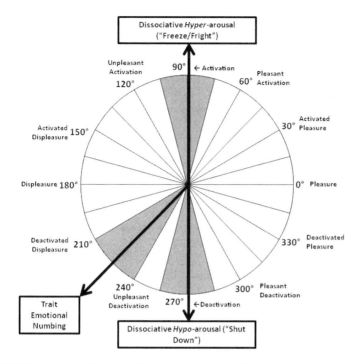

FIGURE 6.12. Affective Circumplex Indicating Hypothesized Location of Particular Expressions of Emotional Numbing. Copyright © 2011 by the American Psychological Association. Adapted with permission. The official citation that should be used in referencing this material is Yik, M., Russell, J. A., Steiger, J. H. (2011). A 12-point circumplex structure of core affect. *Emotion, 11*(4), pages 705–31. The use of APA information does not imply endorsement by APA.

state might be rightly considered an activated psychophysiological state even in the absence of obvious acceleration in her heart rate.

The use of emotional numbing as an emotion regulation strategy in fact can be every effective, necessary, and indeed is often used and explicitly taught in military settings. The self-induction of emotional numbing during prolonged stress, as is often experienced by military personnel, can mask the distressing and painful emotions as well as inner conflict created through moral dilemmas that are an everyday occurrence during deployment. Sherman (2010), for example, writes:

> Soldiers need to be hardened. They need to suck it up, not show pity or fear. The warrior ethos, today and throughout most of history, is the Stoic ethos...If [soldiers], the Stoics argue, minimize the emotions of want and distress [in chronically stressful environments],

they can learn to protect themselves from the impact of tragedy. This is how to build strong psychic armor. (p. 30)

Difficulties may occur, however, in the transition to everyday life, when the experience of emotional numbness itself can interfere with social responsibilities: "Compartmentalization . . . may be for many soldiers an involuntary response to the rage of battle and to the twin traumas of gruesome loss and [survivor's guilt]. How to integrate these experiences in the rhythm of ordinary life becomes a lifelong challenge" (Sherman, 2005, p. 98). For example, Kraft (2007) writes that a feeling of being numb came to infiltrate his relationships where it was unwelcome:

> While stationed in Iraq I imagined my children and found that, although I could picture them in my mind, I experienced genuine difficulty *feeling* them. After many long moments of searching, I sensed the actual warmth of Meg's tiny body. . . . I grew increasingly panic stricken, however, when a similar sensation of Brian eluded me. (p. 34)

Future research should focus on how one can most effectively intervene to help military personnel flexibly transition between the need to maintain a sense of emotional numbing while in battle and the desire for a healthy experience of a range of emotions within the context of family and social life.

Only one study, to our knowledge, has examined the neural correlates of the *feeling of being* emotionally numb as a predictor of neural response to emotional processing. In our study, traumatized women who endorsed survey items indicating that they frequently experience emotional numbing (e.g., "I feel like my emotions and feelings are 'frozen', 'sedated', or 'numbed out', so that I can't physically sense them"; "I feel 'cut off' from my emotions and feelings, so that I can't physically feel them, even if I try", p. 432) exhibited less response in the dorsomedial prefrontal cortex during imagery of socially relevant emotional events (e.g., receiving another person's affection or praise, or being socially rejected, excluded, or criticized; Frewen, Dozois, Neufeld, Lane, et al., 2012). Intriguingly, when healthy individuals performed the same task, individual differences in trait *mindfulness* were positively associated with response in the same brain region (Frewen, Dozois, Neufeld, Lane, et al., 2010). Figure 6.13 (also in the color insert) depicts how one might regard the more severe colorless, emotionless states of emotional numbing and affective shutdown. The self is drawn in gray, colorless, and unemotional. Furthermore, the self has relinquished his or her bag, incapable of having and holding a range of affective feelings. Such an affective state may be strongly associated with learned helplessness. Clearly, much more research is needed before we will be able to fully appreciate the neurophenomenology of the state of feeling emotionally numb.

Several studies have also examined *physical numbing* during dissociative states. As observed by Krystal (1988), physical numbing, including analgesia, often coincides with emotional numbing and therefore provides an objective marker of the latter. Analgesia and reduced pain sensitivity have been described during distressing situations in several trauma-related disorders, including BPD (Bohus, Dyer, Priebe, Kruger, & Steil, 2010; Schmahl et al., 2006, 2010; Kraus et al., 2010) and PTSD (Geuze et al., 2007; Pitman et al., 1990; but also see Mickleborough et al., 2011; Schmahl et al., 2010). Studies have typically examined this phenomenon, however, in relationship to nonsuicidal self-injury in individuals with BPD. A considerable literature suggests that individuals with BPD engage in self-injurious behavior to achieve respite from negative emotional states and in an attempt to regulate distress (reviewed by Chapman, Gratz, & Brown, 2006; Kleindienst et al., 2008; Klonsky, 2007). Other

Emotional Numbing / Affective Shut-down: The Feeling of Being *Emotionless*

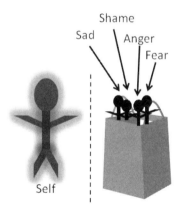

FIGURE 6.13. Phenomenology of Emotional Numbing/Affective Shutdown.

The sense of self is depicted in gray, experienced as colorless and emotionless. One experiences oneself as "cut off" and "detached from" his or her emotional feelings. Incapable of having and holding a range of emotions, the bag of feelings has been let go of, effectually discarded.

motives include satisfaction of a need for self-punishment and to obtain relief from aversive inner tension (e.g., Brown, Comtois, & Linehan, 2002; Herpertz, 1995; Kleindienst et al., 2008)—the latter often associated with states of depersonalization and derealization (Stiglmayr, Shapiro, Stieglitz, Limberger, & Bohus, 2001). In fact, significant positive correlations between pain thresholds and both dissociation and aversive inner tension have been reported (Ludäscher et al., 2007). Individuals with BPD have also been shown to use self-injurious behavior to terminate states of dissociation, including states of depersonalization and derealization (Favazza, 1998; Herpertz et al., 1995; Kleindienst et al., 2008). In turn, these dissociative states have been associated with subjective ratings of stress (Stiglmayr et al., 2008).

The neural circuitry underlying pain processing in traumatized persons and its relationship to emotion dysregulation and dissociation has also received research attention. For example, in individuals with BPD and PTSD, less response in the amygdala has been observed following a thermal pain stimulus (Geuze et al., 2010; Kraus et al., 2010; Schmahl et al., 2006), and less right amygdala response during exposure to thermal pain in individuals with PTSD was negatively predicted by trait dissociative symptoms (Mickleborough et al., 2011). The script-driven imagery paradigm has also been utilized to examine the effects of depersonalization and derealization on pain sensitivity in response to a hot thermode. Through deliberate induction of dissociative experiences, pain sensitivity was lessened during the presentation of trauma scripts when compared to neutral scripts (Ludäscher et al., 2010).

Integrative animal evolutionary models for understanding emotional numbing/shutdown as a dissociative response in the context of threat processing have been outlined by several theorists (e.g., Baldwin, 2013; Bracha, 2004; Bracha & Maser, 2008; Nijenhius, Vanderlinden, & Spinhoven, 1998; Schauer & Elbert, 2010). These models variably emphasize overt behavior and physiology rather than subjective experience as the observables requiring scientific explanation, and employ Lang, Bradley, and Cuthbert's (1997) terminology of a "defense cascade" in response to the physical closeness of the predator and degree of its impending attack. Following an orienting response to a perceived threat, a "freeze-alertness" response is often elicited when a predator remains physically distant and the organism perceives itself as potentially yet unseen. Active engagement of flight-or-fight response may occur, however, in response to obvious signals of impending attack, depending on the organism's determination regarding which (if any) of these active defensive tactics is likely to facilitate survival. However, if the organism is unable to actively defend itself in response to initial attack, or determines such efforts futile from the beginning, these models recognize a class of other behaviorally *inactive*, *immobile*, *submissive* defensive strategies variably referred to as "freeze–

fright" responses that, when prolonged, may eventuate in collapse and death feigning.

Early inactive/immobile defenses may be those most reliably associated with the subjective experiential aspects of dissociative variants of consciousness, including emotional numbing and time dilation, whereas later stages may be particularly associated with depersonalization and subsequent amnesia (i.e., poor conscious encoding of events transpiring during states of collapse and death feigning). Temporary emotional numbing/shutdown as well as collapse/death-feigning responses are therefore recognized as potentially adaptive within the context of confrontations with clearly overpowering predators. Examples occurring in modern human environments include robberies, muggings, and stranger rapes. However, when repeatedly elicited in the context of ongoing traumatic relationships, such as intimate partner violence or childhood abuse, such responses can become increasingly sensitized, amplifying an individual's self perceptions as chronically helpless. Further, these responses may preempt a selection of active defenses, when these might have successfully mitigated further violence, and further dissuade the individual from vacating the environment or the relationship for good, in cases where this might be possible (i.e., recognizing that this is often not an option available to abuse survivors, due to threats of violence or financial/caregiver dependency).

Defensive cascades may be most easily understood in the context of an example. Imagine young 6-year-old Nathan is the son of alcoholic, emotionally abusive, and physically assaultive father, Liam. Nathan has learned well to be vigilant of the signs and signals of Liam's emotional state. He is playing with his trains in the middle of the kitchen floor at about 8:00 in the evening; he has been essentially alone since coming home from school before 4:00, his grossly obese mother resigned to watching television and chain-smoking in the next room over the same period of time. Nathan orients toward the loud, revving sound of Liam's truck arriving in the driveway and freezes inside. Nathan's heart rate drops and time seems to slow as he realizes *I'm up past my bedtime*. He knows he is likely to be punished; he knows that Daddy prefers not to see him when he comes in. He knows that *I need to not be here right now*. He knows *I need to disappear*. Inside Nathan, *planning starts*: He could run for his room, but what then about the train tracks? *Daddy won't like that. Daddy hates messes. Nathan is a "stupid f--king little sh-t" whenever he makes a mess.* "Do I have enough time to put them away before Daddy comes in?" Nathan knows in this that there will be *no help from Mom*. He begins to race, frenziedly throwing the tracks into the plastic bin, but freezes again when the front door bangs open and Liam stumbles in, obviously drunk. *It's too late to run for the stairs to my bedroom*—the hallway to the stairs crosses the front door *where Daddy is*. Train tracks still clutter the kitchen floor—*out of time.* Keep still, be silent: *He hasn't seen me yet.* Quiet breathing and heart rate. *Don't cry: Maybe Daddy will go upstairs and not see me.*

But Liam approaches the kitchen for more beer in the fridge. "What the f--k is this?" In Liam: blind anger, rage. In panic, Nathan runs to his father's side in a half-embrace but with head down and gaze averted: "Daddy, I'm sorry, I . . ." "You f--king brat!" as Liam grabs a handful of Nathan's hair. Nathan is transiently aware of an embodied intention: *Go waxy and limp.* He is thrown by his hair against the kitchen table and falls. Another silent intuition from deep within: *Feel no pain.* On the floor he is repeatedly kicked in the abdomen: *Feel nothing.* The last thing Nathan remembers is that it is *best not to get up until he's gone.*

A neurophenomenological analysis of Nathan's experience is increasingly possible through defensive cascade models of dissociation (e.g., Baldwin, 2013; Bracha & Maser, 2008; Nijenhuis et al., 1998; Schauer & Elbert, 2010) that primarily focus on sympathetic and parasympathetic autonomic nervous system response. The first stage of the defense cascade involves an orienting-freezing response, occurring in the story of Nathan with his perception of the sound of Liam's arrival home in his truck from an afternoon to early evening binge at the bar: "Nathan orients toward the loud, revving sound of Liam's truck arriving in the driveway and freezes inside . . . *I need to not be here right now. I need to disappear.*" A freeze-alert response again occurs in Nathan when Liam arrives at the door: "*It's too late to run for the stairs to my bedroom*—the hallway to the stairs crosses the front door *where Daddy is.* . . . Keep still, be silent. *He hasn't seen me yet.*" Such freezing-alert responses enable Nathan to prioritize his sensory systems to the source of threat, in this case his father.

Attentive immobility further facilitates information gathering concerning signs of the potential danger and best routes for escape (e.g., Campbell, Wood, & McBride, 1997). Nathan considers that "he could run for his room, but what then about the train tracks? . . . *Daddy won't like that. Daddy hates messes.*" Pupillary dilation, a transient drop in heart rate (e.g., Bradley, Codispoti, Cuthbert, & Lang, 2001; Lang et al., 2000), motor inhibition, and focused attention likely further aid Nathan in both perceptual and cognitive processing of the environment, including Liam's likely course of action: "*Don't cry: Maybe Daddy will go upstairs and not see me.*" Further, the heightening of perceptual processing as such may be akin to an experienced sense of time dilation (i.e., the slowing down of time, as overviewed in Chapter 3): "Time seems to slow as Nathan realizes: *I'm up past my bedtime.*" The orienting-freezing response usually occurs when the distance between the organism and the predator is still considered relatively large, in Nathan's case both when Liam is still outside in his truck and again when only at the front door: "*He hasn't seen me yet.*" Such states involve heightened perceptual acuity and muscle readiness while arguably lacking a pronounced emotional element; rather than involving fear itself, the state is perhaps more akin to *preparation* for an upcoming and likely more significant level of danger and need for action mobilization. Referring specifically to the experiential characteristics of this activated state of readiness, although associated with decreased heart rate, we might hypothetically place it straight upward at 90° on the affective circumplex as a relatively *emotionless* high-arousal state.

According to defense cascade models, if the predator approaches its prey, the latter will generally attempt to flee (flight) or fight. Such stages are characterized by acute discharge of the sympathetic division of the autonomic nervous system. Activation of the locus coeruleus leads to the release of noradrenaline, facilitating increased blood supply to the heart and muscles with concomitant vasoconstriction of peripheral blood vessels. The release of endorphins centrally begins to provide analgesia as well as decreased somatosensory perception and awareness (Schauer & Elbert, 2010). As a psychophysiological state perhaps akin to a flight response, Nathan, faced with the dilemma that he cannot safely leave the mess of his toys in the kitchen, bravely "begins to race, frenziedly throwing the tracks into the plastic bin." Further, although defense cascade models note that when attempts at fleeing are unsuccessful, animals will typically resort to some form of active defense (fight), this option is unreasonable in Nathan's case and indeed simply does not occur to him.

In animals, defensive fighting would continue activation of the sympathetic nervous system, further increasing blood flow to the muscles and heart, thus increasing blood pressure and cardiac output and preparing the organism for an aggressive encounter with the predator. Increased perspiration as a means of cooling the body also often occurs and bowel mobility frequently halts due to the fact that blood flow has been redirected to the muscles and heart, sometimes occasioning the evacuation of the bowels. Nathan, knowing well that his attempting to fight his father would be entirely senseless, instead attempts an attachment behavior of proximity/affection-seeking and submissive appeasement making, running toward his father in fear, appealing, "Daddy, I'm sorry." As opposed to making eye contact and facing his father head on, however, as if expecting to be embraced, Nathan runs to the side of his father, head down and averted, thus avoiding eye contact, the latter a widely recognized signal of challenge within the animal world when occurring between conspecifics. Aversion of the head with arms partially raised would also, in theory, provide greater shielding from an anticipated blow. This attachment behavior would likely be coded as disorganized yet approach-affiliative (a "tend–befriend" strategy; Taylor et al., 2000), a response often occurring in traumatized young children, although more so in girls than in boys, at least in the context of frightened/frightening maternal caregivers (e.g., David & Lyons-Ruth, 2005). Defense cascade models of dissociation and animal threat should include, rather than only fight–flight–freeze responses, a disorganized attachment response involving affiliative approach while at the same time, guarded/shielded movement.

Unfortunately for Nathan, his attachment appeal fails to dissuade his father, eliciting violence and brutality rather than the empathic, loving, and compassionate responses for which such behaviors were evolutionarily designed. As the threat of serious physical harm escalates with the grabbing of his hair, and it is clear that he has little chance of escaping without injury, Nathan begins to exhibit what might be labeled by defense cascade models as freeze–fright and ultimately death-feigning behaviors. Thus, for example, "Nathan is transiently aware of an embodied intention: *Go waxy and limp*." He further experiences the instincts to "*feel no pain*" and to "*not to get up*." It is thought that such behaviors may foster the predator's disinterest (Miyatake et al., 2004; Pasteur, 1982; Pavlov, 1927; Moore & Amstey, 1962). In humans such a marked panic-like state is conventionally described as "scared stiff," a condition often provoked by physical restraint (e.g., Nathan is held by his hair) or other perceptions of entrapment (Marx et al., 2008; Moskowitz, 2004b).

During this stage, organisms show high levels of emotional arousal and distress yet are behaviorally unresponsive to sensory stimulation, including pain, representing the possible beginnings of functional sensory deafferentation, in humans perhaps associated with an experience of disembodiment. Functional sensory deafferentation may occur at the level of the thalamus, providing a means of modulating or shutting down overwhelming visual, auditory, somatosensory, and proprioceptive information (Schauer & Elbert, 2010). Functional sensory deafferentation may partially underlie symptoms of depersonalization and other forms of disembodiment, given that an individual's sensory, kinesthetic, and somatosensory processing (theoretically) form the coordinates upon which is based our embodied awareness of ourselves. High levels of arousal during traumatic experiences have indeed been suggested to be associated with altered thalamic sensory processing (Krystal, Bennett, Bremner, Southwick, & Charney, 1995), which can affect sensory integration at higher centers of the brain, including the frontal cortex, anterior cingulate gyrus, amygdala, and hippocampus, thereby potentiating the experience of an alteration in consciousness (i.e., dissociative symptoms; Krystal, Bremner, Southwick, & Charney, 1998). More bizarre, prolonged, catatonic-like postures that can be held for extended periods of time (even up to hours) are frequently observed during the death-feigning stage (Gallup & Rager, 1996; Marks, 1987; Ratner, 1967). Even though the organism appears dead and unresponsive from the point of view of an outside observer, the internal state of the animal may initially remain one of relatively high alert (Marx et al., 2008). Krystal (1988) noted that catatonic reactions elicited by profound helplessness were analogous to unresponsive immobility. This stage of the defense cascade is associated with coactivation of the sympathetic and parasympathetic divisions of the autonomic nervous system (Low, Lang, Smith, & Bradley, 2008), which in extremes has been associated with sudden cardiac death (Skinner, 1985, 1988).

Should the organism discover a way to escape, the state of unresponsive immobility is highly reversible and the organism can readily flee from the situation. If, by contrast, an organism continues to be confronted with the predator and no means of escape presents itself, persistence of collapse may ultimately engender a highly unresponsive and disengaged state characterized by marked emotional numbing, physical analgesia, and a lowering of the level of consciousness that is perhaps less conducive to a detailed encoding of events. This state is characterized behaviorally by flaccid immobility and subsiding of posture as well as cessation of voluntary movements and speech production (Suarez & Gallup, 1979; Porges, 1995). In such a state kinesthetic, somatosensory, and nociceptive stimuli are thought to no longer reach central processing centers in the brain, thereby leading to a relatively complete functional sensory deafferentation. Heart rate and blood pressure may further decrease due to marked inhibition of the sympathetic autonomic nervous system in conjunction with pronounced activation of the parasympathetic system.

Porges's (1995, 2011) polyvagal theory proposed the presence of two vagal systems in the brainstem medulla, which may further elucidate the underlying psychophysiological mechanism mediating this severe collapsed dissociative state. Porges suggests that a ventral vagal complex rapidly regulates cardiac output in order to facilitate ongoing prosocial engagement and disengagement with the social environment, thus providing an essential component of social bond formation. In contrast, activity of the dorsal vagal complex has been hypothesized to be associated with acute distress, causing behavioral immobilization, hypoarousal, analgesia, and severe metabolic depression. As such the latter may underlie metabolically conservative dissociative (catatonic) states that mimic death. Whereas the ventral vagal complex displays fast and transient activations, the dorsal vagal nucleus exhibits a prolonged pattern of vagal outflow, thus leading to longer-standing states perhaps experienced as highly dissociative in nature. Individuals who enter this stage of the defense cascade may require minutes to hours before returning to NWC. In this rather marked TRASC of emotion we would hypothesize that persons might be inhabiting an affective state essentially akin to 270° on the affective circumplex: that is, an *emotionless* state typified by severely low arousal in which affective feelings of negativity versus positivity are really no longer a part of the experience. In such a state an individual would seem to be momentarily "dead to the world."

Case 5: Revival from Momentarily Being Dead to the World

This case example describes emergence from a severe dissociative state in an individual who had become emotionally and physically numb and behaviorally "shutdown" and nonresponsive after the experience of a trauma reminder. The case description illustrates that repeated attempts at grounding are sometimes necessary to psychologically "revive" a person from what on the outside seems like marked states of psychophysiological shutting down in the face of stress. Moreover, it shows that a thorough knowledge of what has previously worked in grounding individuals in previous sessions, coupled with patience and trust in the process, is the mainstay of recovery from states of severe emotional numbing.

"Marie" is a 28-year-old woman who was repeatedly sexually abused by her uncle between the ages of 3 and 15 years. At the time of the present case example, Marie's psychotherapy focused on learning skills involved in mindfulness, emotion regulation, and distress tolerance. One day, Marie was at home alone watching television when she was triggered by a rape scene in a movie. This led Marie to experience an intense flashback of her own past sexual abuse by her uncle.

Much later, after the flashback episode had passed, Marie was able to describe the experience in detail. She reported smelling the alcoholic breath of her perpetrator, feeling her uncle pinning down her hands, and experiencing intense fear. She then recalled slowly starting to feel "zoned out," "numbed out," and "almost trance-like." Marie described that this feeling of numbness led her to cut her forearm, resulting in a laceration; she was hoping that the experience of pain would help her "feel alive" again. Marie's boyfriend returned home shortly after Marie had cut herself. He found her effectively in a trance-like, unresponsive state and was unable to ground her. Marie's boyfriend therefore called an ambulance, which brought Marie to the local emergency department.

Upon arriving in hospital, Marie continued to present in a trance-like state. She failed to engage in spontaneous movements and did not communicate verbally in response to questions from the medical staff. According to the emergency room physician, Marie "did not flinch" during suturing of the cut, which was performed without administration of a local anesthetic, presumably indicating marked analgesia. Marie's therapist was called to the emergency department shortly after the suturing had been completed because the emergency room staff was unable to ground Marie. The staff noted, "She is almost in a catatonic-like state."

When the therapist arrived to greet Marie in the emergency room, however, Marie did not respond verbally to her either. Marie's therapist tried to reassure her and engage her in making eye contact, saying, "Marie, look at me. You are safe here. No one will hurt you." However, these repeated efforts to reorient Marie proved unsuccessful. Marie's therapist also tried to ground Marie by encouraging her to stand up, rather than to remain seated. This simple method had been effective in previous psychotherapy sessions during which Marie had become dissociative; in this case, however, Marie was unable to follow instructions. After several failed attempts at engaging Marie in standing up, the therapist encouraged Marie to orient to the smell of vanilla perfume, a scent that Marie had often used to ground herself; unfortunately, this intervention also proved unsuccessful.

Finally, after approximately 45 minutes, the therapist recalled that Marie had previously visualized the color yellow as another way to ground herself because it signified warmth and safety for her. Luckily the therapist happened to be carrying a book with a yellow cover in her brief case. The therapist placed the book in front of Marie and encouraged her to focus on the yellow cover, stating: "You are safe here. No one is going to hurt you. You are in the present." Her therapist noticed that Marie's gaze shifted toward the yellow book cover, although she remained verbally unresponsive. Nevertheless, after focusing on the book for several minutes, Marie began to exhibit spontaneous movements for the first time since arriving in the emergency department. Shortly thereafter, she began looking at her therapist, who smiled at her. Marie was able to reciprocate the smile. Marie's therapist then reminded her that she was safe and asked her what had happened to bring her to the emergency department. Marie was finally able to speak.

At this time, Marie was able to recall and describe being triggered by the movie. She further explained that she felt completely numb while she was in the emergency room and had absolutely no experience of pain while her cut was sutured without the administration of local anesthetic. In addition, Marie reported that everything felt unreal to her. She commented that she was not able to hear her therapist until she began focusing on the yellow cover of the book. She said: "the sound came back very slowly. It was really muffled at first." She also noted a complete loss of her sense of time during the episode. After the therapist debriefed and processed what had happened with her, Marie reassured her therapist that she would be safe and that she would continue practicing grounding techniques. Marie was discharged from the emergency department and continued with her regular therapy as on outpatient.

Marie's case illustrates the repeated attempts at grounding that are sometimes necessary to "psychologically revive" traumatized individuals back to their present self. The clinician, rather than herself becoming alarmed at the clinical situation, instead continued to attempt different tactics until a stimulus and clinical stance sufficient to return Marie to NWC was found. In addition, it is worth noting that the grounding stimulus ultimately found to be effective was a *personally meaningful one*; the color yellow worked in Marie's case, but it might have been an entirely different kind of stimulus that would have worked best for another client. Providing that the most effective grounding skills can be highly patient-specific, it was the therapist's thorough knowledge of the client's prior experience as well as her relationship with the patient that proved to be the key to unlocking the dissociative barrier.

Defense cascade models of dissociation and predator threat (e.g., Schauer & Elbert, 2010) were described in the text. How can Marie's symptoms be explained by defensive cascade models of dissociation, and what dimensions of consciousness were likely altered in the aftermath of Marie's episode of reexperiencing? From Marie's description of her symptoms, it appears that she first exhibited a dissociative flashback, perceiving her uncle's sexual abuse as a current threat as opposed to only a memory from the past. Accordingly, Marie prepared to defend herself as she had previously done. Presented with the visual stimulus of impending threat (rape scene on television), Marie may have experienced a parasympathetic withdrawal response accompanied by high activation of the sympathetic division of the autonomic nervous system. During this experience, Marie's consciousness of time and memory were altered such that she relived the abuse she had suffered before at the hands of her uncle, physically feeling him pinning her down and smelling his alcoholic breath.

In order to overcome her ensuing distress and refocus her attention toward the present, Marie engaged in self-harm. Nevertheless, with time Marie began to exhibit increased signs of emotional numbness and analgesia, even to the point where she later did not experience pain when she was sutured. The ensuing state of numbness/shutdown included Marie's unresponsiveness to her environment (she later reported that she could no longer hear the sounds around her) and the absence of voluntary movement and speech production. In fact, it was noted by one of the nurses that she was in an almost "catatonic-like state." Although Marie's vital signs were not monitored during this experience, behavioral signs indicate that it would be reasonable to hypothesize that she might have exhibited a drop in heart rate and blood pressure. During an experience resembling what Schauer and Elbert (2010) labeled a flag–faint response, and one perhaps akin to an emotional state at 270° on the affective circumplex, Marie appears to have experienced marked alterations in her sense of time, body, and emotion, feeling emotionally numb.

On the Road to Recovery: Learning How to Feel

This chapter has focused on the dark side of the affective circumplex frequently inhabited by complexly traumatized persons. The traumatized self not only experiences frequent anxieties and fears but also painful social emotions (e.g., guilt, shame); a perceived inability to experience, and feel deserving of, good feelings such as love, pride, and joy (anhedonia); an inability often even to know what one is feeling (alexithymia); and variably severe *emotionless* states of acute numbing and affective shutdown, sometimes to the degree of becoming behaviorally unresponsive to their environments. It should be acknowledged, however, that with the support of an empathically attuned therapist, traumatized persons can learn to self-regulate their states of distress, decentering to come down from elevated states of *hyper*arousal, and recentering to come up from lower states of *hypo*arousal.

Ultimately, however, the therapeutic goal is not only to decrease negative affective states but also to assist the traumatized person in dwelling in the right side of the affective circumplex, that is, in variably arousing experiences of positivity such as joy, pleasure, and triumph. Some have noted that the experience of mastery, such as the overcoming of fear in psychotherapy, can partly motivate an increased sense of resilience and pride. Moreover, the client may, over time, internalize the compassionate stance of the therapist and experience self-compassion. Although such achievements do not come easily, we would suggest that treatment should be considered incomplete before clients not only experience less distress but further are able to feel a greater sense of joy, pride, triumph, and self-compassion. To end this chapter on a note of hope, we share an interview and artwork representative of survivors who have made such inroads to recovery, typified by their increased capacity for self-compassion (reduced guilt and shame), increased positive affect (reduced anhedonia), increased ability to be aware of themselves emotionally (decreased alexithymia), and increased experience of a healthy and flexible range of emotions (decreased numbing/shutdown).

As a first example, the painting by "Valerie" (Figure 6.14; also in color insert) depicts how she was hiding her true feelings behind a mask when she first began therapy (she holds a mask in her hands) often for fear of rejection and abandonment. In psychotherapy Valerie learned that by hiding her feelings, she was also effectively hiding them from herself as well. The different facial expressions at the top of her painting illustrate how Valerie learned to recognize and express different feeling states, both positive and negative, eventually helping her to realize "It is okay to be me."

As a second example, "Mischa" created a collage to represent her increased capacity to tolerate positive feelings, aided by her use of artwork. The softness and warmth inherent in this piece (Figure 6.15; also in color insert) reflects Mischa's increased ability to feel the same kinds of feelings through psychotherapy. Note the words *hope, courage, strength*, and *support* on the right middle panel.

Finally, the following interview describes the emergence of the capacity for joy and pleasure in "Jen" through trauma-focused psychotherapy, which facilitated Jen's experience of self-compassion and internal mastery.

Interviewer: Tell me about your ability to feel joy and pleasure over the course of recovery.

FIGURE 6.14. Valerie's Artwork (2012): "It is okay to be me." Used with permission.

Jen: Oh, that's been something. There was a time when I couldn't feel it at all, and there was a time that when I did feel it, I had to numb it with alcohol and drugs—it was just too painful. I did not deserve to feel good. And then there was a time where I could feel just little tiny bits of it for just a little bit of time. Over time, the bits got bigger and the time got longer, and now I have days where I'm joyful and happy, I have weeks where I'm joyful and happy, and I have months where I'm joyful and happy. I do a lot of weeping. I can just lie on my bed and it's like my eyes just weep. I try not to examine it too much—I just let it happen because I know I feel better afterwards.

FIGURE 6.15. Mischa's Artwork (2010, untitled). Used with permission.

Interviewer: Does that relate to a feeling of joy and pleasure?

Jen Yes, it does. I guess I cry tears of happiness, I guess that's what it is. My life is so much better now, so much better. And as a result, my son has benefited . . . I get so much joy from him, and I'm so thankful that I can look and listen and learn from him and enjoy him; I have the freedom to enjoy him now.

Interviewer: What does enjoyment feel like in your body?

Jen: It opens up here, it opens up here (*points to chest*), it's kind of a warm, not hot, but just slightly warm feeling. Joy feels like I can go to the washroom; my bowel movements are better than ever, and that is part of joy for me (*giggles*).

[Jennifer experienced severe constipation for years, which she associated with emotional distress.] I can feel joy because I'm looser, and it feels like I'm lighter; it feels like I'm in nature, like I'm just in nature. I can take a deep breath now. Enjoyment too, makes me open up and sometimes it just makes me ecstatic, and it makes me giggle, and it makes me feel like a child that's healthy and OK . . . I can also experience that "girl kind of joy," you know, that you have with a bunch of girlfriends. But I can experience that kind of joy even if I'm not with my girlfriends. I can think about something I've done, and that joy feels like a balloon floating free in the air. Joy inside—inside of me—feels like such a freedom, such a freedom.

Interviewer: When you feel that lightness and that loosening up of your body, does your body want to do anything?

Jen: Yes, it makes me want to dance, and sometimes I just turn on the [audio–video device] and I just dance around the basement. And sometimes it makes me just want to scream, and I have done that. I have gone to the ocean when we were in Florida, and I have just stood there and let the water lap up on my legs and screamed—not an angry scream, but just because I can, because I *can* scream.

Interviewer What is that like?

Jen: It's wonderful, it's wonderful just to scream, to be able to be opened up. I can also swallow much easier than ever before in my life. Food goes down easier, something to drink goes down easier, my own saliva goes down easier. I don't feel like everything is catching or blocking in my throat, and that's joy to be able to do that . . . It's like I'm buoyant, I'm buoyant and floating and alive, just alive. Everything is freer—my thoughts, my thoughts about myself are freer and happier and more joyous . . . It's wonderful, it's a gift, a big gift, that I hope everybody in recovery can grab a hold of . . . I think I will always cry, and it's not because I'm sad, it's because I'm free to feel emotion the way I think I'm supposed to feel it now. Even my tears are lighter, even my tears are lighter—I needed to say that, I needed to hear myself just say that: Even my tears are lighter—that's, that's recovery.

Summary

In this chapter we discussed the multitude of pervasive states of emotional distress that commonly present in complexly traumatized persons, including the social emotions of guilt, shame, and anger, anhedonia, alexithymia, and emotional numbing/affective shutdown. The latter was considered *intrinsically* a TRASC of emotion. We also discussed the nature of emotion dysregulation and the dissociative compartmentalization of emotionality. We provided case examples to illustrate the phenomenological concepts discussed, and reviewed neuroimaging studies that have investigated the neurobiological bases of alterations in affectivity in traumatized persons. The next chapter considers the process of recovery from a traumatized self as can occur in psychotherapy.

CHAPTER 7

Liberating the Traumatized Self

Resilience and Recovery

"The true value of a human being is determined primarily by the measure and the sense in which he has attained liberation from the self."

—Albert Einstein (1954/1994, p. 12)

I N THIS TEXT WE have sought to answer William James's (1902/2002, p. 136) call to "hear what the sick souls . . . have to say of the secrets of their prison-house"—that is, the prison-house of a traumatized self. In so doing we have become acquainted with some of the darkest kinds of pain and suffering a human being can endure. The Appendix contains transcriptions of additional full-length phenomenological interviews of trauma survivors who further describe their experience of trauma-related altered states of consciousness (TRASC) of time, thought, body, and emotion.

And yet, as psychotraumatologists, we know that there is hope for freedom from a traumatized self. Recovery is possible, and resilience and courage define the essence of the trauma survivor as he or she begins to heal the wounds of a traumatized past. In trauma-focused therapy, survivors work to liberate themselves from the inner captivity and isolation brought about by their own TRASC. They also become a part of something greater: a compassionate community. As such, the consciousness of the trauma survivor is unshackled and he or she breaks free of the bars that have enslaved his or her experience for so long. A world of new and unknown experience awaits him or her on the outside of this prison—a world that may have been considered unreachable by the traumatized individual before.

Fright and apprehension of the unknown often arise during this journey to freedom. The thought of entering into a therapeutic relationship can be terrifying, with the traumatized individual often expecting that the relationship with the therapist will be similar to most other relationships he or she has known: dangerous, unpredictable, and guaranteed to lead to humiliation and shame. Trust in another person is often considered inconceivable in the early stages of treatment, and the slow building of trust between the client and the therapist frequently comes about only through repeated testing of the reliability of the therapeutic relationship, as well as disruptions and repair in this relationship. Moreover, existential questions frequently arise, such as "Can I succeed in a life outside the imprisoned self? What will such a life be like? What will the unknown bring? Do I deserve a life worth living?" The road to liberation from the traumatized self is therefore frequently rocky and can feel treacherous, yet through a therapeutic alliance that provides safety, perseverance, and ongoing instillation of hope, the traumatized self can slowly learn to break free from its imprisoned state, attaining a life that is less constrained by the pain and torment imposed by TRASC.

We conclude this text by sharing our thoughts and some clinical examples regarding how healing can take place within the context of trauma-focused psychotherapy. It is our belief that TRASC can be normalized in psychotherapy, and we describe how such healing can occur over a staged approach to trauma treatment that follows the general model of trauma recovery introduced by Pierre Janet for hysteria and later elaborated on for complex PTSD (Herman, 1992b) and dissociative disorders (e.g., Putnam, 1989; Kluft, 1990). When considering a stage-oriented treatment approach, it is important to note that sometimes it can take as long or longer to undo the effects of chronic trauma as it took to create a traumatized self, with the latter for many clients beginning in infancy and yet ongoing even as they seek to enter into psychotherapy. Moreover, gains in complex trauma treatment are frequently nonlinear: There are ups and downs, and as clients learn to become more aware of themselves and their difficulties, often they will appear to worsen before getting better (e.g., Courtois & Ford, 2009; Ford & Courtois, 2013; Solomon & Siegel, 2003).

Trauma therapy, and in turn trauma recovery, begins with the establishment of safety and careful attention to the often arduous process of establishing a therapeutic relationship that is secure, trustworthy, and hope instilling. Structured interventions aimed at directly reducing TRASC, if present, and other forms of trauma-related distress are also important throughout the course of therapy. The creation of a narrative of a survivor's experiences that promotes healing, mastery, and transformation of the self, while also mourning the losses incurred as a result of traumatic events, is the mainstay of trauma treatment. Recovery must always be considered incomplete, however, until the survivor is reintegrated into a compassionate community of others who foster further resilience and the potential for continuing individual and collective growth. The latter also greatly facilitates the integrative capacity to embrace feelings of self-compassion, joy, curiosity, and triumph. Finally, following Fonagy, Allen, Bateman, Target, and their colleagues (Allen & Fonagy, 2006; Allen, Fonagy, & Bateman, 2008; Bateman & Fonagy, 2012; Fonagy & Target, 2006), we also briefly discuss the key element of treatment that they refer to as *mentalizing*, otherwise known as the client–clinician dyadic practice of *intersubjectivity*. The overarching goal of the therapeutic relationship—the most significant task and the way forward—is to form a *deeply lived experience of what a healthy relationship is*: that is, humaneness and companionship that are safe and nonthreatening, honoring of human dignity, respectful of individual autonomy, and nurturing of both self-compassion and benevolence toward others.

Security, Trust, and Hope: Initial Elements of Change

Judith Herman (1992b) systematically articulated the fundamental principles of therapeutic change in complex trauma treatment in her text *Trauma and Recovery*. Such principles of effective treatment remain largely upheld by expert therapists today (e.g., Cloitre et al., 2011; Courtois & Ford, 2009; Ford & Courtois, 2013; Solomon & Siegel, 2003). Figure 7.1 details the therapeutic processes through which the resolution of both TRASC and traumatic memories themselves can take place.

Following the standard staged-approach to trauma recovery described by Herman (1992b) and others, the first stage of trauma therapy must have as its focus the assurance of the client's safety, both within as well as outside of the therapeutic relationship. It is important to note that the latter cannot be assumed; many traumatized persons continue to experience ongoing emotional, physical, and sexual mistreatment in the context of intimate, familial, and working relationships even while undergoing psychotherapy intended to address the outcomes of traumatic events of long ago. In such contexts, the client's trauma is not over, speaking literally rather than only figuratively. Positive therapeutic outcomes cannot be reasonably expected of clients who are actively experiencing ongoing violence and abuse throughout the course of psychological treatment.

Assuring client safety therefore takes immediate precedence, but is not always easy to negotiate. The latter is particularly the case when the client fails to regard his or her current living situation as threatening or abusive, feels that he or she is deserving of the abuse, or believes that he or she is unable to leave (e.g., due to financial dependency, familial considerations, or that doing so would likely *increase* the likelihood of harm). In addition, many clients struggle with self-abusive and self-harming behaviors. In such circumstances the clinician, modeling empathic concern and explicitly

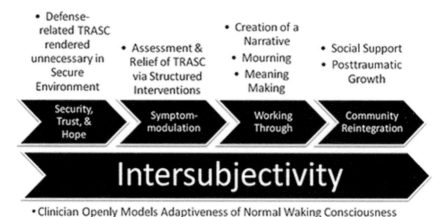

FIGURE 7.1.   Stage-Oriented Approach to Healing a Traumatized Self.

Recovering from trauma through psychotherapy is thought to require (1) the experience of security, trust, and hope within a therapeutic relationship; (2) provision of symptom relief of distress and trauma-related altered states of consciousness (TRASC) of time, thought, body and emotion; (3) processing or "working through" of traumatic memories and associated meaning making and grieving; and (4) integration into a supportive and compassionate community of others who foster further resilience and growth. Psychotherapy is understood to be an intersubjective process throughout treatment.

respectful of client autonomy, must voice his or her high valuing of the client's safety and ensure that the issue of safety continues to be addressed as foundational in the healing process. It is crucial for the therapist to stress that the first step toward recovering from the harm of past traumas is to learn how to step out of current harm's way.

Most clinicians generally regard the first step of effective therapy to be the client's nascent experience of safety and security within the therapeutic relationship itself. Complex trauma survivors will often find the therapeutic encounter to be a significant source of potential threat, at least initially, since they have frequently been abused by authority figures in the past. It is almost inevitable that such individuals expect the therapeutic relationship to become as threatening, dangerous, and humiliating as previous relationships they have encountered. Additionally, trauma survivors often worry that they will be rejected, abandoned, or fail if they should attempt to communicate their experiences to others, including those sincerely meaning to help. Moreover, fear of failure as well as fear of what life will be like as a result of effective treatment often greatly alarms traumatized individuals (e.g., "Will my therapist abandon me?"; "Can I manage living a normal life?"). As a result, repeated testing of the therapeutic relationship and ongoing rupture and repair of this relationship are often inevitable occurrences in the process of creating trust in the therapeutic alliance. Such experiences are key opportunities in which clients may learn that relational conflict can be managed in a safe fashion and eventually overcome.

Throughout this process, the individual's apprehensiveness about engaging in treatment should be normalized and acknowledged with compassion, and the therapist should inquire about what he or she could do, on an ongoing basis, to alleviate the client's anxiety about the therapeutic relationship, treatment, and fear of the unknown. Maintaining impeccable boundaries that are negotiated based on the needs of both the client and therapist is also essential in facilitating trust within the therapeutic relationship. These boundaries necessarily include a clear understanding of (1) the role of the therapist and his or her inability to engage in any form of social contact outside the therapeutic relationship; (2) the frequency and duration of sessions as well as the length of treatment; and (3) guidelines regarding crisis management that may be needed between scheduled sessions. Maintaining such boundaries will help create a predictable environment for the client, which is essential in fostering a sense of safety and trust. Creating an environment of safety and trust is of particular importance given that chronically traumatized clients often have rarely experienced predictability in their lives and in their relationships.

The clinician also seeks to develop the client's trust by honoring how far the client has already come, and the degree of current readiness for further change in the here and now, moment to moment and face to face. The clinician does not demand of the client that of which the client is currently incapable, and thus sets aside his or her expectations concerning the timeliness and trajectory over which the recovery process should take place, instead respecting the client's readiness for change, whatever it may be. At the same time, however, it is important for the therapist to have an ongoing dialogue with the client about his or her readiness to engage in treatment. Should a client not be ready to engage in treatment, it is important that this be acknowledged and the client should be respectfully encouraged to seek treatment whenever he or she has reached an increased stage of readiness. It goes without saying that many clients have endured inordinate hardship and suffering; their bravery and resilience should be honored from the first therapy session onward.

Throughout stage-oriented trauma treatment, it is essential that the clinician support the client's continued movement forward and exhibit solidarity in his or her expressed belief that the client can change and recovery is possible. The firm resoluteness of the therapist in communicating his or her belief in the client's capacity for change provides an ongoing secure base from which the client's own belief that recovery is possible may grow. Moreover, the untiring, unwavering, relentless confidence of the therapist's belief in the client can be steadying for the client, providing sustenance at times when he or she experiences self-doubt, setbacks, or even misgivings about the prospect of healing.

Relating within a therapeutic environment that fosters an experience of safety and security in the client should be considered a clinically significant intervention in its own right. Specifically, the client may have never before experienced an interpersonal encounter within which he or she has felt safe and secure. In effect, the client may be learning, for the first time, that such relationships are possible. The clinician should not underestimate the transformative power such an interpersonal experience, alone, can have for the chronically traumatized person. The experience of the therapeutic relationship may also be the first time in which the client has been treated in a humane way. Such humaneness is foundational for trauma recovery and may indeed be an important mediator of change common across different approaches to psychotherapy (Fosha, Siegel, & Solomon, 2009; Schore, 2012; Wampold, 2007, 2012).

Establishment of a safe and secure environment can also be regarded as an intervention for directly reducing the client's tendencies toward dissociation and TRASC. In particular, dissociation that was born out of the trauma survivor's need to mentally escape real threats when physical escape was not possible can slowly become less necessary within a relational context that is increasingly perceived by the client as less threatening over time. As such, formation of a therapeutic relationship that begins to instill a sense of security, trust, and hope in the client can be regarded as an interpersonal–environmental intervention often powerful enough, in and of itself, to begin to reduce some of the client's tendencies toward dissociation and TRASC.

Symptom Modulation: Increased Awareness and Relief

Interviewer: What have you found most helpful in therapy so far?

Erica: Talking to somebody who gets it. And isn't judging me. [My therapist] is the only person in the whole world who knows a lot of this stuff. [My therapist] is the person that's helped me even *realize* some of this stuff. Because I don't know what "normal" is - if there really is such a thing. I'm coming

> to the realization that *my* normal is very different from what other people would call normal. So [my therapist] is really helping me. I'm very grateful that [my therapist] found me or I found [my therapist] or whatever way you want to look at it. Very, very grateful.

Interviewer: What kinds of things have you learned in therapy?

Erica: It's helped me to see some things about myself. It's helped me to put names to certain things, too, which have made me feel less crazy. For example "dissociation": I didn't know what it was. I mean, I *did* know what it was, but I didn't know it was a "medical" thing. I knew a lot of stuff, but I guess I didn't *know* I knew it. And [my therapist] has helped me to know that yes, you did know it. If that makes sense? And I've learned some ways to better be present. Because I really didn't even know what being present *was* before. But now I've had more moments where I am aware of being present. And it doesn't always feel good—because being present can be really scary. It can be *abject terror*. But I know it's part of the process of getting better.

The acknowledged power of a secure, trusting, and hope-instilling therapeutic relationship notwithstanding, we believe it is fanciful to think that this alone will be sufficient for recovery in most cases. Supportive therapies, in our view, fall short of the status of "bona fide trauma treatments" due to their lack of an explicit focus on symptom reduction and the direct working through of past traumatic memories and grief (Benish, Imel, & Wampold, 2008). In comparison, it seems advisable that direct symptom relief of TRASC related to the client's sense of time, thought, body, and emotion be provided early in the course of the treatment, to the extent that the client is able, willing, and experientially open to such a change in his or her consciousness taking place. The experience of an early benefit of treatment in the form of immediate symptom reduction functions to bolster hope in the prospect of a deeper trauma recovery in the future, even if such a change in consciousness can itself be quite distressing, as noted by Erica above.

Directly reducing individuals' tendencies toward TRASC as defensive coping strategies prepares clients for later stages of trauma treatment that focus on the processing of traumatic memories and mourning the losses that have been incurred as a result of the trauma. Specifically, it is commonly assumed that the working through of traumatic memories and associated experiences of grief and mourning require the client to be (1) experientially present, (2) attentively focussed on the trauma narrative, (3) interoceptively regulated and aware, and (4) emotionally engaged (e.g., Jaycox, Foa, & Morral, 1998; Roemer, Litz, Orsillo, & Wagner, 2005). In contrast, dissociative responses toward TRASC, as has been argued in earlier chapters, (1) sequester clients away from an experience of the present and into flashbacks of the past; (2) confuse and disorient clients with voices of fear, doubt, or ridicule, precluding any single-minded focus on tasks at hand; (3) experientially divorce clients from their own body, interfering with their ability to fully confront their fears, own their reactions, and master them; and (4) prevent them from actually *feeling their feelings*, be they averse or pleasant in nature, instead causing them to separate from their feelings in states of emotional numbing or "affective shutdown," or become overwhelmed by them, losing awareness and insight due to the absence of self-monitoring and reflective functions.

In the case illustrations presented in previous chapters, we briefly introduced several specific interventions that clinicians often use to reduce the experience and expression of dissociative tendencies toward TRASC. In short, completion of these and other similarly structured exercises, early and throughout the course of trauma-focused psychotherapy, may aid in the phenomenological assessment and ensuing increased awareness of TRASC. Furthermore, the structured interventions can function to directly modulate (i.e., reduce) the frequency of dissociative experiences. These interventions can be practiced by the client outside of the therapy hour to obtain a more substantial benefit as affect regulation strategies. Again, such work should combat the frequency of use of TRASC as a means of coping with both everyday stressors as well as posttraumatic reminders, resulting in therapeutic gains and cultivating a greater sense of mastery in clients over experiences previously considered entirely beyond their capacity to control.

The Rebirth of the Self: Creation of a Narrative, Mourning, and Making Meaning

The focus of trauma therapy is to help clients leave the past behind through creation of an integrated life narrative that fosters resilience and, at the same time, mourns the losses brought about by traumatic life experiences. As described in Chapters 3 and 4, traumatic memories are often experienced as timeless sensory fragments that are relived rather than remembered. Moreover, traumatized individuals frequently do not have the words to describe their traumatic memories, being caught in speechless terror that cannot be communicated to others, thus perpetuating a sense of isolation and loneliness (van der Kolk & McFarlane, 1996). Intense experiences of shame that are frequently associated with traumatic memories further silence the traumatized individual and maintain a sense of detachment from the rest of the world. The resulting lack of a narrative tracing the individual's life—a narrative that is grounded in the temporal context of past, present, and future—is often fundamental to a sense of discontinuity as an entity across time, thought, body, and emotions.

It is only through confrontation of the often horrific reality of the past within a safe therapeutic environment that allows the traumatized individual to "speak the unspeakable" (Herman, 1992b) and begin to transform traumatic memories into a story that can be remembered but is not relived. As this transformation process occurs, the rebirth of a sense of self, now experienced as a more constant, continuous being across the dimensions of consciousness of time, thought, body, and emotion, emerges. As such the traumatized individual is increasingly capable of (1) leaving the past behind and living in the present, while maintaining a continuous sense of time; (2) developing a narrative in a singular voice about his or her traumatic memories in context with past, present, and future experiences; (3) experiencing an embodied sense of self that he or she can care for with self-compassion; and (4) being fully aware of and knowing his or her feelings, and having the capacity to embrace positive emotions, including happiness, joy, and triumph.

As traumatized persons begin their journey of creating a new, more adaptive life narrative, they are inevitably confronted with the enormous losses they have often incurred as a result of their traumatic experiences. Facing these losses commonly leads to mourning, often feared by the traumatized individual as insurmountable. A strong therapeutic alliance is paramount in helping the client endure the grief and sadness that frequently ensue. Respecting the pace that feels safe for the client throughout this often severely distressing stage of therapy, and being mindful that sometimes "the slower you go, the faster you get there" (Kluft, 1993, p. 146), can be beneficial in titrating the intensity of distress often involved in this work. Moreover, the idea that mourning can be viewed as a bridge that connects the past with the future can be a helpful metaphor that provides direction for the grief work often involved in trauma therapy.

For survivors of repeated trauma, it is often advantageous to focus on incidents that are particularly distressing to the individual. Herman (1992b) notes:

> For survivors of prolonged, repeated trauma, it is often impractical to approach each memory as a separate entity. There are simply too many incidents, and often similar memories have blurred together. Usually, however, a few distinct and particularly meaningful incidents stand out. Reconstruction of the trauma narrative is often based heavily upon these paradigmatic incidents, with the understanding that one episode stands for many. (p. 187)

Various methods that can be used in the creation of a trauma narrative and related mourning have been described in the literature, and a detailed review of these interventions is beyond the scope of this chapter. It is par-simonious to assume that much commonality exists between and across different specific trauma memory reprocessing interventions, although it is also reasonable to suspect that certain types of clients will respond bet-ter to, or prefer, the orientation emphasized by one particular treatment over another (Constantino, Arnkoff, Glass, Ametrano, & Smith, 2011; Nor-cross & Wampold 2011; Roth & Fonagy, 2004; Swift, Callahan, & Voll-mer, 2011). For example, some clients will respond best to interventions that are delivered in a relatively fixed, linear, and sequential form (e.g., as in an exposure-based fear heirarchy), whereas a less structured, more explorative approach (e.g., as in free association, experiential therapies, and hypnosis) may work better for others. Interventions also differ in the degree to which they utilize linguistic processes (e.g., written narratives), imagistic processes (e.g., eyes-closed imagery or hypnosis), and *rescript-ing* (i.e., attempting to re-encode the memory in a way that renders it less distressing or harmful; e.g., Arntz, 2011; Arntz, Tiesema, & Kindt, 2007; Edwards, 2007; Grunert, Weis, Smucker, & Christianson, 2007; Hack-man, 2011; Holmes, Arntz, & Smucker, 2007; Long & Quevillon, 2009; Rusch, Grunert, Mendelsohn, & Smucker, 2000; Smucker & Dancu, 1999; Smucker, Dancu, Foa, & Niederee, 1995; Smucker & Niederee, 1995; Stopa, 2011; Wheatley & Hackman, 2011; Wheatley et al., 2007; Wild & Clark, 2011).

Compassionate Community: Social Support and Prosociality

It is well established that the presence of social support after the occur-rence of traumatic events is a strong positive predictor of resilience and recovery (Brewin, Andrews, & Valentine, 2000; Ozer et al., 2003). Simple empathic acknowledgment of one's experiences by others—including not only intimate partners, close friends, and family, but also by coworkers, neighbors, law enforcement personnel, faith communities, and even the media—can sometimes be sufficient to protect the survivor against mal-adaptive outcomes (Müller, Moergeli, & Maercker, 2008; Nietlisbach & Maercker, 2009). Suzy, a trauma survivor introduced in earlier chapters, described the role friendships currently play in her recovery and how dif-ficult it was to learn to trust other people, as follows:

> "Friends are important to me. I don't have a big base of friends, I have a smaller base of friends and I know that the friends I have I can trust. They are important to me. The people that I do have in my life I can be honest with. I can tell them what's happening and not be in fear of judgment. But it takes time for me to trust someone. The guys that raped me were supposed to be my friends, so it is very difficult for me to trust people."

At the time of the same interview, Suzy was comparably disinterested in participating in an intimate relationship: "No thank you (*laughs*). That scares the hell out of me. I shut that part of me off a long time ago. It is just something I can't talk about; it terrifies me." Indeed it is well established that the presence of posttraumatic stress symptoms are associated with relationship distress between intimate partners (e.g., Lambert, Engh, Hasbun, & Holzer, 2012). However, over the course of continuing psychotherapy, Suzy had overcome her fear of intimate relationships, and at the time of this writing, is actively pursuing finding a partner. These distinctions demonstrate the different stages of readiness for new relationships at which trauma survivors can find themselves. Clients' varying readiness and desire for relationships must be treated with the utmost care, compassion, and respect by the clinician.

Beyond the roles played by immediate families, peers, and intimate relationships (i.e., social "microsystems"), socioecological models acknowledge the potential influence that exosystems (e.g., communities) and macrosystems (e.g., societies, cultures) can also play in both inciting trauma exposure as well as facilitating recovering from it (Belsky, 1980; Cicchetti & Lynch, 1993; Cicchetti & Toth, 2005; Garbarino, 1977; Harvey, 1996, 2007; Zielinski & Bradshaw, 2006). For one, group therapy for psychological trauma can be an important part of healing. Mendelsohn and colleagues (2011), authors of the *Trauma Recovery Group*, describe the healing of trauma-focused group therapy as follows:

> Participating in a group with fellow survivors can provide a powerful antidote to the shame and stigma often associated with traumas such as sexual abuse and domestic violence. The simple process of relating one's story in a safe and structured setting and recognizing one's commonalities with others who have been traumatized can be a tremendous relief for survivors who have borne the burden of silence for so many years. Experiencing the acceptance of group members who have heard the survivor's story counteracts this impaired self-reference. (p. 22)

Mendlesohn et al. (2011) also suggest that group therapy can help decrease survivors' senses of social isolation, can promote mastery and empowerment, and can serve as a basis for the modeling of healthy relationships. Clinical experience also suggests that the increased social integration and sense of support observed with recovery is often mirrored internally among those experiencing a fragmented sense of self, as in dissociative identity disorder or dissociative disorder not otherwise specified. For example, Gregory, a trauma survivor encountered in previous chapters, had described a marked sense of conflict, estrangement, and disorganization not only in his social relationships but also as experienced from within. Over the course of psychotherapy, however, Gregory experienced an increasing sense of integration and self-coherence, as depicted in his artwork (Figure 7.2; also in color insert).

Although most of the treatment literature emphasizes individual or group psychotherapy as means to trauma recovery, research in the field of community psychology shows that social action, advocacy, and support programs can also play significant roles (e.g., Harvey, 1996, 2007). Researchers have pointed out that, rather than positioned only in the role of receivers of services, a process of healing and meaning making for some individuals may entail engagement in some form of prosocial community action (Staub, 2003, 2005; Staub & Vollhardt, 2008; Vollhardt, 2009; Vollhardt & Staub, 2011). For example, many of the participants who have taken part in our research projects have reported that their primary motivation for doing so stems from their belief that increased scientific knowledge about psychological trauma and recovery may eventually serve to better protect others from suffering as they have. For example, at the conclusion of a research interview, Tim, a Vietnam veteran introduced in previous chapters, commented:

> "I am hopeful that my experience and what I have shared with you might be able to help somebody else. That's a good feeling. Because I really don't want anybody to have to go through what I have gone

FIGURE 7.2.   Gregory's Artwork (2010, untitled). Used with permission.

through in my life. I wish I could save them from having to go through that. If this is at all helpful to anybody, it's certainly worth the time we are spending."

Through acts of altruism a trauma survivor's previous sense of being alone in his or her suffering may increasingly give way to a more interdependent sense of self that is concerned not only with finding personal meaning and well-being but also with supporting the greater welfare of others. It is important to ensure, however, that such involvements signify the individual's movement forward with his or her own recovery, as opposed to only symbolizing an inability to let go of attachments to a traumatic past. Finally, turning to a faith or spiritual community in times of need can support trauma recovery in certain persons. Research suggests that, for the spiritual client, incorporating client-acceptable religious or spiritual practices as adjuncts to psychotherapy can sometimes benefit both psychological and spiritual outcomes (Worthington, Hook, Davis, & McDaniel, 2011).

Many clients have perceived themselves as forever isolated and estranged in the secrecy of their trauma. Their acceptance, welcoming, and participation in a compassionate community of others is integral to maintaining trauma recovery. Figure 7.3 (also in color insert) depicts the interpersonal experience of the traumatized person before versus after recovery. Whereas before the traumatized person may have perceived a dividing line separating him or her from others, as well as an internal division between his or her senses of time, thought, body, and emotion, in recovery the survivor begins to feel more integrated inside and safer and more secure as a part of a community of supportive others who in turn benefit from the companionship and contributions of the survivor. Through mutual engagement in relationships with others, an interdependent sense of self may emerge out of the collective members' interacting consciousnesses of time, thought, body, and emotion. The following section describes an interview with Kim, who describes, among other things, the central role that community support and participation, as well as spirituality and the practice of a faith tradition, can sometimes play in trauma recovery.

Case 1: Reaching Out Beyond the Self: Recovery as a Communal Act of Faith

Interviewer: Kim, can you tell me about recovery?

Kim: It's harder than I thought, and not what I expected. I thought that I could just wake up and be normal—bypass

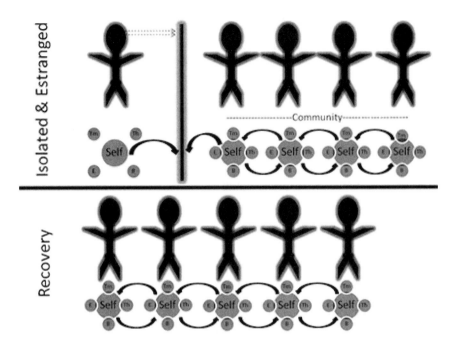

FIGURE 7.3. Social Support in Trauma Recovery.

A traumatized sense of self is experienced as not only isolated from within (in terms of a sense of self integrated across time, thought, body, and emotion), but also isolated and estranged from other people. In recovery the trauma survivor feels internally secure within a compassionate community of others. B = body; E = emotion; Th = thought; Tm = time.

thinking about everything, I guess, and not to have to struggle with not wanting to get better sometimes, thinking all that I am is "the sick one" and if that all goes away, that there won't be anything good left.

Interviewer: How have things changed for you on the road to recovery?

Kim: I have a support system now, whereas before I didn't. [Even though] I always had therapy, I would have to go home by myself, and I really didn't have anybody around me. Now I've got a strong support system that I take with me.

Interviewer: What's it like now to have a social support system?

Kim: I didn't trust it at first. It was hard. I did everything possible to try to drive them away in the beginning. It has taken a group of people that I consider generally normal, looking at me and treating me as an equal and competent and worthwhile and loveable. I'm able to look now, through their support, and say OK, well, if all these different people think that I'm OK, and that they like being around me, and they're around me not because they're getting paid to or because they have to but because they genuinely like me, maybe in the past the stuff that happened wasn't really my fault and I don't have to keep punishing myself. I think for the longest time I felt like I don't deserve any better than being maladaptive and not accomplishing anything or being punished or waking up everyday sorry that I'm alive, apologizing that I'm alive. So, that's what the support system does, and without it I don't think it's possible to recover.

Interviewer: What was it like before you had a support system?

Kim: It was awful (*voice cracks*). Very isolated. Just feeling really, really alone. I always looked after myself, but the only people I had surrounding me were people in mental institutions. And I thought that they were the only people I could ever associate with or have relationships with. And even though the nurses were there, they were there because they were getting paid. If they were nice, it was a bonus. But I didn't feel that I had anybody that actually cared about me, just because I was me, not because they had any obligation to.

I'd come out of a therapy session and I would be alone and dreading it (*voice cracks*). I would dread coming to therapy because I knew what the aftermath was going to be like—nobody to call. Without having a support system I kept going back to my parents—my abusers—because I didn't think I had anybody else. That made it way worse. But the alternative was being alone, and being degraded was what I knew, so I just kept going back to it. Now I know there is another option and it is way, way better— harder—but way, way better.

Interviewer: How about the way you view yourself—has that changed on the road to recovery?

Kim: Umm, up and down. Overall my view of myself is probably more accurate than it ever has been, just because I'm starting to see myself the way that other people see me. I still feel a lot of shame; sometimes I feel really little, and then I don't feel like *me* [child sense of self], but [in general] I see myself as more capable and competent and smart. And I don't think I'm beautiful or anything like that, but I can honestly say I'm not repulsed by myself anymore. And I see myself more as a survivor rather than a victim. Before my whole identity was "the sick one." I was everybody's project. It's a kind of "defeatism." Like, "why even try to be normal because you're never going to get there, so why bother trying?" I do feel a lot of shame still, and I know everybody says and affirms that I shouldn't, but I do anyway. And sometimes I still feel like a whore and dirty and still struggle with that.

Interviewer: What is feeling shame like for you?

Kim: It feels awful, but I feel like I deserve it. I don't want people to look at me. I have the urge to hide under tables, things like that, for no real reason, just because I don't want to be seen.

And I feel sometimes like I'm being a hypocrite, like, how can I help other people when I'm this horrible person? *If people really knew.* We can present well, and most of the people that I deal with don't know my history. But I feel like I'm being a phony because inside I feel horrible.

I'm almost 40 years old now and I haven't really lived a life—I mean, most of my life has been in mental institutions—and I figure that the people that hurt me have taken so much and, I either fight with (*crying*)—I fight with everything I can, or the alternative is to just give up, and I'm not going to let them have that over me. If I can make it easier for one more person through anything I've been through, than maybe it wasn't all for nothing. I think about my sister, and I think the only way for her to get out is if she sees me, because I can't say it's going to get better if it doesn't.

Interviewer: Tell me about hope, how have you viewed hope over time?

Kim: For the longest time I was resigned to the fact that I would always be "mental" and never have a life, never get married, never have relationships with anyone who was normal. That I'd be constantly in the hospital all the time, and that I was always going to struggle with eating. Basically I resigned myself to that I was probably going to be dead by the time I was 40, whether or not I actively did something to off [kill] myself or that my body would eventually just give out. But I eventually just made a decision that either my life has to change or I am going to off myself.

And then after a while I saw that, "OK, this is doable." It's hard but it's better than the alternative. And now I do have more hope because I see that as things come up, whereas before I wouldn't have been able to handle anything at all, now I'm able to kind of regulate it better than I used to. For me getting upset was never normal. It was an automatic shutdown. But now I can say back to myself, "OK, this is normal to be upset about this, anybody would," and you can work through it. I'm seeing that you can work through things. That there are very few things that are insurmountable. Actually, I can say that I can't think of anything that is.

Interviewer: You mentioned that you have more hope. Can you tell me what that is like, having more hope?

Kim: Umm, just a lightness . . . umm . . . in the pit it isn't dark anymore, whereas before it was just black and screaming and blood on the walls. It's not like that anymore. I guess it's not really a feeling—it's more the absence of the bad. It used to be like something was hanging down, oppressive almost, a heaviness. When I got depressed, it wasn't that I was lazy and just wanted to lie in bed—I physically felt like something was on top of me, that I just couldn't get up. Like lifting your hand to get a glass of water was work.

Interviewer: Feeling more lightness—or less heaviness—can you tell me more about what that is like?

Kim: I walk differently than I used to, which is weird. People look at me and say that I bob along. Before I would do the "thorazine shuffle" even though I was never on thorazine. Everything would just kind of hang. But now I have more bounce. You just feel like everything wants to be up; it doesn't want to be pushed down anymore. Kind of like a plant popping through the soil, just popping up so it is physically a lot different than it used to be.

Interviewer: If you were to give one message about recovery—one message that you wanted people to know—what would you say?

Kim: That it is possible. When you're right smack in the middle of it, you don't see it. I mean, I was told for years that I was smart and capable, and that it was possible, but I think the key is a support system. I think a lot of times it has to be outside your family because 9 times out of 10, they are the reason you are who you are. But finding a steady support system and working through things at your own pace. Not doing them according to what the textbook says you should be doing, or what people expect you to do, but doing what is right for you. Because if you only follow what other people tell you, rather than follow what inside you know is right, it doesn't work. It makes you frustrated and you feel like a failure, and people will start accusing you that maybe you don't want to get better bad enough. But I guess it's worth the risk of trying to get better, and seeing what the unknown is like because it's not as bad as you imagine it to be.

Interviewer: What do you think allowed you to reach out to a healthy support system?

Kim: I have a strong faith and I do believe that praying played a role. I think God did something for me because He knew that [otherwise] I was going to end up dead. I think that, through Divine intervention, and also the fact that the support system that I had was consistent, it was a conscious decision that I made. I thought I'm going to have to try to trust them. I got to the point that it was so bad that something had to change, and I knew if I didn't at least try it—try to trust even just a little bit—because I figured "What have I got to lose?" And the other thing that I thought was that they can't do anything to me that somebody hasn't done already and, it's a warped way of thinking, but, you name it, it's probably been done to me, and I'm still here, so I thought I could probably go through it again. I know that's an [odd] way of thinking, but that's what I thought. You get to the point, like an alcoholic, that you are at rock bottom—that it's either up or "6 feet under"—and that's the point that I was at.

Interviewer: Can you say more about prayer and how that helped you?

Kim: Umm, I've always had a belief in God because of the fact that I'm still here. The fact that I am still here. I mean, I've been in intensive care more than 25 times, and I'm only 37. People have just randomly shown up at my apartment when I've been unconscious—my potassium has been unregisterable in some cases—but I've prayed through it all because I believe that there is a God and that He knows what I've done, He knows what's been done to me, but He also knows the future and He knows the plans that He has for me. And so even the fact that I ended up at [a supportive community agency], it was, I believe, orchestrated by God.

Interviewer: It sounds like your faith and prayer have been incredibly important.

Kim: Yeah, without it I wouldn't be here.

Social Cognition and the Intentional Stance

As described in philosophy, the *intentional stance* is the assumption of normal waking consciousness (NWC) that other people are also conscious beings, and that their minds, brains, and bodies generally operate in ways that are essentially similar to our own. Accordingly, one normally assumes that other people also experience a sense of time, thoughts, their bodies, and emotional feelings in ways that are not radically different from our own experiences. It is upon this basis that we are capable of inferring from another person's behavior the probable qualities or contents of his or her conscious states, that is, a *theory of mind* relating to another person's actions. In other words, theory of mind refers to the phenomena of what two persons' minds tend to expect of each other, and interpret of each others' actions, both when in and outside of each others' immediate presence. It is important to point out, however, that our experience of what another person's experience "must be" always remains only a prediction; our simulated experience of another person's phenomenological state may not be an accurate representation of the other person's actual conscious experience. For example, I may experience your half smile as a sign that you like me, or that you are mocking me, and your looking away as a signal that you are thinking about something, or that you are rejecting me.

Researchers have suggested that the highly traumatized person often experiences problems with *social cognition* (Lanius et al., 2011; Nietlisbach & Maercker, 2009; Sharp, Fonagy, & Allen, 2012). In particular, they may experience significant difficulties when interpreting the meaning of others' actions (e.g., not recognizing the meaning of another person's smile), or regularly misattribute the meaning of others' affective signals and actions (e.g., believing that "your smiling means you are about to hurt me") (e.g., Frewen, Lane, et al., 2008; Nazarov et al., 2013; Nietlisbach, Maercker, Rössler, & Haker, 2010). It goes without saying that such alterations in social-cognitive processing will have a deleterious effect on the quality of traumatized persons' interpersonal relationships. For example, traumatized persons may experience great difficulty and significant fear when attempting to relate interpersonally with others. In addition, they may experience "mentalization failures," that is, trouble understanding the subjective experiences and intentions of others, often being biased to expect threat.

For example, some traumatized persons have great difficulty making eye contact with other persons, restricting their range of potential social relationships and roles. "Jen," a woman with a significant childhood history of neglect, emotional, physical, and sexual abuse, notes: "When I make eye contact with someone then they can see me; I mean that they can see how I feel about myself—that I am not a good person. Those are the things I try to hide from people. That's what I don't want them to know."

In an fMRI study we found that, upon perceiving a computerized human figure ("avatar") orienting toward the participant—that is, making direct eye contact (direct gaze), as contrasted with the figure coming into view but averting its gaze—healthy individuals activated brain areas associated with higher-order social cognition (i.e., the dorsomedial prefrontal cortex, temporoparietal junction, and temporal pole). Such responses may be associated with mentalizing (Burgess, Gilbert, & Dumontheil, 2007; Denny, Kober, Wager, & Ochsner, 2012; Gilbert et al., 2006; Gilbert, Gonen-Yaacovi, Benoit, Volle, & Burgess, 2010; van Overwalle & Baetens, 2009), facilitating effective social engagement. In comparison, traumatized persons predominantly activated regions within the brainstem (i.e., the superior colliculus, locus coeruleus, and periaquaductal gray), associated with defense responses and decreased social affiliation (Steuwe, Daniels, et al., 2012). Such findings suggest that traumatized persons, even in the context of the most basic of interpersonal encounters such as this, may be very near a flight, fight, or freeze–fright response. The extent to which these findings relate to early attachment disturbances should be addressed in future studies.

In another study, responses to the interpersonal perception task (IPT; Costanzo & Archer, 1989), an experimental procedure evaluating participants' capacity for mentalization, were compared in traumatized versus nontraumatized persons. The IPT required participants to view short videos depicting interpersonal interactions relevant to five role domains (kinship, status, competition, deception, and intimacy). Paying attention to nonverbal cues displayed by the actors, participants were required to make inferences about them—for example, deciding which of two adults, conjointly interacting with a child, is likely to be the child's responsible caregiver. Results indicated that traumatized persons exhibited deficits in theory-of-mind abilities when identifying kinship interactions, but not in the context of the other four domains. Interestingly, such deficits were moderately associated with dissociative symptoms (Nazarov et al., 2013). Future studies should investigate whether a history of role reversal in childhood is related to individuals' decreased ability to identify kinship interactions. *Role reversal* is a form of relationship disruption characterized by a parent looking to a child to meet the parent's need for comfort, parenting, intimacy, or play, and the child endeavoring to meet these needs, as opposed to the other way round.

Collectively the results of studies of altered social-cognitive processing or mentalizing in traumatized persons raise a number of important questions. For example, can repeated activation of the mentalizing system in psychotherapy improve individuals' ability to mentalize, leading to increased activation of higher brain regions associated with affiliative engagement, rather than only activation of a lower-order defensive response? And can increased function in neural networks underlying mentalizing make possible more effective use of social support along the road to recovery from trauma? Lastly, might deficits in mentalizing affect an individual's resources in the caregiving role, thereby facilitating the intergenerational transmission of trauma (i.e., the emergence of emotion regulation difficulties in the children of traumatized parents)?

The following sections contain excerpts from qualitative interviews in which several trauma survivors describe their responses to the experience of highly prevalent and elementary social signals, such as making eye contact and shaking hands with someone they have just met.

Interview 1: Suzy

Interviewer: Can you tell me what happens when you make eye contact with another person? Specifically, with an unfamiliar person you have just met?

Suzy: What would it be like? It would be uncomfortable, sometimes it is even uncomfortable when a familiar person is making eye contact with me. I get quite anxious about it. I feel that they are judging me or making some plans to do something to me. It is like I am being judged by them or that they are watching me. Eyes are a huge thing for me. I always felt that they were watching me and judging me and it didn't matter where I was, if it wasn't my parents, it was the guys who were raping me. For me there were eyes everywhere, there were eyes in the trees. I mean, I know there weren't, but for me there were eyes everywhere, and they were constantly watching me and I was constantly trying to hide myself, trying to make myself invisible. If I think someone is angry at me too, I can't look at them.

Interview 2: Stephanie

Interviewer: Can you tell me what happens when you make eye contact with another person?

Stephanie: Making direct eye contact, for the most part, I have no issue with anymore, but it's because I've had to learn it. I've had to physically and emotionally gear myself and learn to make direct eye contact. It's been a long process of retraining because, certainly as a kid, you didn't make direct eye contact—ever—that would be asking for trouble. So those are all things I've had to learn. That's what people do, that's part of the norm, and if you don't make direct eye contact, you're not calling attention to yourself. I don't want attention—that's not a good thing. To be noticed was not good. But now, I will make direct eye contact.

Interviewer: What would have happened if you made eye contact when you were young?

Stephanie: Making eye contact meant that you wanted to be noticed. Any kind of eye contact was seen as defiance, or as aggression, and it was also stating that I existed, and Mom did not want me to exist. It was not a good thing for me to exist because she didn't like me; she didn't want me. I was definitely not anything she wanted. To make any kind of eye contact was to bring attention to myself, and it would be met 99% of the time with being slugged or hit in some way. This is why I hid most of the time. Before I was probably 3 years old, I learned not to make eye contact, not to move, not to speak, and not to do anything. I learned: "Keep your eyes down all the time." You had to be very subservient. It was terror, it was way beyond fear.

Interviewer: If a person was moving forward to greet you, holding out his or her hand, what would that be like?

Stephanie: A lot of things I've learned to do have to do with what I call *stealing myself*, and that means that I will do something I may not be comfortable in doing. I may not want to do it, but I know that it is what is called for. I know it is probably what's appropriate, and then I will go ahead and I will do it. I will go ahead, and I will greet, because I know that that's what's called for. I literally *steal myself* to do those things, whether I like it or not.

Interview 3: Gregory

Gregory: I have a lot of difficulties misinterpreting facial expressions . . . I don't know why I misinterpret them, but I end up getting the wrong impression of them. Then I ask them and they say, "Oh no, you got it all wrong, I was just doing this or doing that." And then I think "Are you lying to me?" I think, "Are you lying because you are hiding something? Because I am sure I saw you show the facial expression for fear. Are you about to double-cross me, are you deceiving me because you are about to do something to me?" And then I will end up totally confused.

Interviewer: What would you experience if in a public place, another person were to make eye contact with you? What would that be like for you? What would you experience?

Gregory: I would think there is something wrong with me or I would check my body to maybe see if there is something that I am wearing or . . . something has happened to my clothing. If there was nothing wrong with that, then I would think maybe I have said something out loud and not realized I said it.

Interview 4: Valerie

Interviewer: Imagine a familiar or an unfamiliar person making eye contact with you. What happens? What would it be like?

Valerie: I shut down. Because I don't . . . I feel ashamed. Or that they are questioning why I am even alive. Or if I am even good enough for what I am doing. Or I don't belong in this existence. I start questioning myself a lot.

Interview 5: Tim

Interviewer: What would it mean to you if someone made eye contact with you?

Tim: What flashes through my mind is "don't get to know me." What's going on in here is not a happy place. That's initially my response: keep distance between. . . . If somebody saw into my eyes and saw what I took part in, they might, they might even want to beat the crap out of me for lack of a better way of putting it. It's really kind of piercing. It's almost as if they are trying to see inside of me. It's scary.

Interviewer: What would it be like if people were to see inside of you?

Tim: It feels really scary. I feel like they're going to see a kind of stain on my soul. I feel a sense of shame about being in the situation in Vietnam, and I also feel shame about some of the things that I witnessed and I didn't do anything about— case in point, watching idly while they threw a grenade in a hole with a guy and knowing full well what the outcome of that was going to be. I mean, if somebody found that out about me, they might run. . . . Previously I'd been in a PTSD group and one of the other guys in the group said that when he looked into the eyes of a person that hadn't been in Vietnam, it was kind of like looking into the eyes of a baby—they just were innocent. I have that same experience; part of me wishes that I could get that innocence back. That's something that I really wish very often.

Interviewer: Imagine that another person smiles at you. What would happen then?

Tim: Wariness. It kind of puts me on edge, part of me. . . . There is a part of me that feels good being smiled at, as opposed to being frowned or scowled at, or anything like that. But once again there is an equally powerful force that wants to keep distance. And it's not a distance that is for protecting me from them—as much as it is protecting them from me.

Connecting with Others: Intersubjectivity, Relational Consciousness, and Recovery

"At the psychobiological core of the intersubjective field is the attachment bond of emotional communication and interactive regulation."

—Allan Schore (2012, p. 75)

Interviewer: What do you hope it will be like as a result of therapy?

Erica: That I will be able to walk out the door when I want to and there won't be a thought like, "Oh, can I do it?" And not having these things happening in my head and seeing my hands shake—these things have to stop. And not having [noises] in my head. And remembering stuff. And being more aware and present. And not wondering what it's like to be everybody else, because I would be kind of the same. Because right now I think I am very different.

Interviewer: What do you think that would feel like inside?

Erica: Peace.

As articulated by Erica, many highly traumatized dissociative persons believe that they are very different from other people, specifically, that their mind–brain–body might work in ways fundamentally unlike that of others. Such a feeling may be intensely isolating; perhaps especially when experiencing TRASC, the complexly traumatized person may feel alone, foreign, and in extreme cases, even nonhuman. These individuals may perceive an unbridgeable divide as separating them from the everyday experiences of the common human being. Indeed feelings of estrangement and alienation were the trauma appraisals most reliably related to posttraumatic stress, depression, and dissociation across three (predominantly female) samples studied by DePrince and colleagues (2011). As such, experiences of dissociative TRASC, by their very nature, tend to socially isolate traumatized persons. TRASC may make it difficult for traumatized persons to *participate* in the social world that surrounds them because they may be unable to understand and identify with the normal kinds of waking conscious experiences of most others around them. Effective interpersonal interactions rely on mutually agreed upon and shared interdependent senses of time, thoughts, embodied experiences, and emotions. Effective and compassionate interpersonal relationships are possible only to the extent that persons relate to each other from a point of common reference and essential understanding, typically the NWC of time, thought, body, and emotion. In contrast, the traumatized person is frequently unable to be conscious of the present or of his or her thoughts, body, or emotions, thus lacking an integrated sense of him- or herself. Consequently, experiencing an altered sense of self, he or she is likely to experience difficulty relating with others, thus leaving him or her isolated and estranged from the common person (see Figure 7.3).

Nevertheless, at other times trauma survivors seem to take upon others' feelings too strongly, being unable to differentiate others' feelings from their own, and finding themselves overwhelmed by other people's difficulties. In this case, the lack of an integrated sense of self — resulting in an altered awareness of the present, of thoughts, of their body, and of emotions—may lead to difficulties in self–other differentiation. Specifically, traumatized individuals, lacking the intersubjective boundaries of a robust sense of self, may sometimes confuse their own experiences with that of others', the latter experienced as if momentarily their own (see Figure 7.4; also in color insert).

Indeed in research studies traumatized persons with PTSD were found to score higher than healthy persons on the "personal distress" or "empathic concern" subscales of the Interpersonal Reactivity Index (e.g., Davis, 1983), a questionnaire measure suggesting that trauma survivors may sometimes experience feelings of undue or excessive sympathy and concern for those in unfortunate circumstances, even to the extent that others' problems significantly impinge on their own ability to cope (Nietlisbach et al., 2010; Parlar et al., in press). This intersubjective process has been termed *emotional contagion* (e.g., Hatfield, Cacioppo, & Rapson, 1994). Interestingly, the neural processes that mediate emotional contagion have been found to be distinct from processes involved in mirroring nonemotional signals and in making nonemotional judgments about others. Specifically, in the mirroring of others' emotions, the ventromedial prefrontal cortex is activated in conjunction with the precuneus, temporopatietal junction, and superior temporal sulcus, whereas in mirroring of

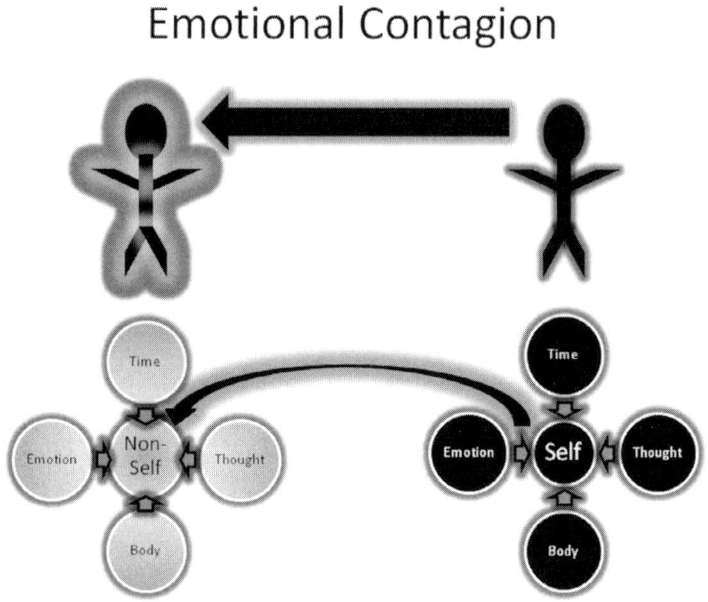

Emotional Contagion

FIGURE 7.4. Emotional Contagion between the Self and the Non-Self in Terms of Time, Thought, Body, and Emotion Dimensions of Consciousness.

The trauma survivor (*left*) does not experience a robust sense of self across his or her senses of time, thought, body, and emotion, illustrated by little white glow. In the presence of another person's emotional state (*right, black*), the survivor takes upon the other person's distress too strongly, thus overwhelming his or her own sense of self and resulting in a lowering of self–other differentiation.

non-emotional judgments the dorsolateral prefrontal cortex is activated in concert with the precuneus, temporopatietal junction, and superior temporal sulcus (Abu-Akel & Shamay-Tsoory, 2011; Nummenmaa, Hirvonen, Parkkola, Hietnen, 2008; Poletti, Enrici, & Adenzato, 2012; Wagner, Kelley, & Heatherton, 2011; Sebastian et al., 2012; Shamay-Tsoory, Aharon-Peretz, 2007; Shamay-Tsoory, Aharon-Peretz, & Perry, 2009; Shamay-Tsoory, Harari, Aharon-Peretz, & Levkovitz, 2010; Xi et al., 2011; Zaki & Ochsner, 2012). A tendency toward emotional contagion is often evident in group settings, particularly when intense emotional experiences are shared by group members. For example, "Nancy," a woman with a history of repeated emotional, sexual, and physical abuse during childhood, in response to a group member's expressing strong feelings of sadness, described: "I suddenly became really, really sad. It was very weird; it was like I did not know whether I was a separate person from 'Daniella' [the group member expressing strong feelings of sadness]." Emotional contagion can sometimes also make the trauma survivor vulnerable to being taken advantage of by others. For example, Valerie, a trauma survivor introduced in a previous chapter, has described:

> "I don't know how a normal friendship should be. I constantly feel like I am being used, or I am using them. I feel that I have to keep giving and giving just so I don't have to feel so alone. Or that they are worse off than me so I have to give more stuff. For instance, when my neighbors say that they are struggling financially with groceries, I will give them a whole bunch of canned goods and then sometimes my husband and I don't eat. And I know that we need the food. But I keep giving still or trying to give."

In this case, lacking a robust sense of self, traumatized persons frequently find themselves overwhelmed not only by their own life challenges but also unduly take upon themselves the distress and difficulties of others.

Intersubjectivity represents a fifth dimension of consciousness that refers to a phenomenological state experienced by two or more persons in the context of each others' presence. Specifically, we can think of intersubjectivity as standing for *my experience of what your experience must be, moment to moment*. Moreover, in some cases the consciousness of intersubjectivity stands for a *communal experience* between two or more people. For example, in each other's presence, irrespective of physical distance, two people may feel close or very distant, each feeling that his or her partner must feel the same. Another example is the proverbial "elephant in the room": A group of people feel anxious about something, all "know" that they are not the only one experiencing anxiety, and yet all avoid approaching or attempting to resolve the source of the anxiety. In each of these cases, although each person's experience is intrinsically private, nevertheless through intersubjectivity we have *an experience that feels public*. Intersubjective states of consciousness thus represent internal experiences of interpersonal encounters that can either be explicitly shared or kept private. Practices of open, receptive, and reflective dialogue concerning phenomenological states experienced by both client and clinician, as they arise in real time within the therapy hour, are intended to foster the client's improved understanding of both his or her own as well as other persons' experienced states of consciousness.

Trauma-related psychotherapy, for the survivor and therapist alike, requires the skillful practice of intersubjectivity—that is, the co-witnessing and dyadic regulation of consciousness between the client and clinician. Engaging processes involved in both cognitive and emotional empathising, the skilled trauma clinician, knowledgeable of the workings of the dissociative mind, first models for the client a calm, receptive, and open state of mind. The clinician, being witnessed by the client, allows the survivor access to an example of NWC that he or she might begin to internalize, thereby building a bridge for the highly dissociative individual back to a healthier and more regulated state of mind. Furthermore, through process comments, such as inquiring of the client what he or she is experiencing at significant points within psychotherapy sessions, the clinician skillfully increases the client's self-awareness of his or her own phenomenological states. Through gentle guidance and implicit suggestions, he or she may seek to modulate them directly in the direction of increased normality (NWC) and decreased distress. Figure 7.5 (also in color insert) illustrates the concept of dyadic mentalizing as it is sought as a healthy basis

Mentalizing

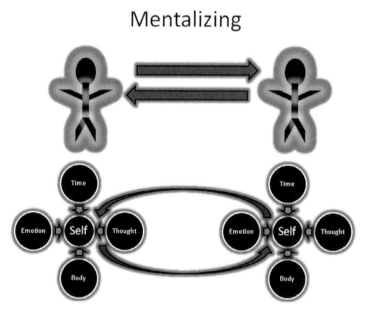

FIGURE 7.5. The Mentalizing Process of Intersubjectivity Allowing the Perceptions of Time, Thought, Body, and Emotion to Flow between Two Individuals.

Both persons (*left and right*), experience robust senses of self across the dimensions of time, thought, body, and emotion. In the presence of the other person, each person's emotional state is shared and felt, facilitating mentalizing and relational functioning, while at the same time each fully maintains his or her own sense of self, thus resulting in accurate self–other differentiation.

for intersubjectivity within psychotherapy. Allen (2012, p. 436) indeed clarifies: "The central therapeutic task is not specific to working with the content of the traumatic events, but rather involves supporting a mentalizing stance in relation to the meaning and effect of the trauma. That is, in this stance, the focus is primarily on the patient's mind, not the event. In short, a mentalizing stance emphasizes process over content."

It is thus primarily through mindful and empathic process comments that the clinician facilitates the client's increased awareness of his or her own subjective states, empowers him or her to self-soothe states of distress and increasingly integrate dimensions of consciousness. This point notwithstanding, in the context of the therapeutic working through of traumatic memories, the compassionate receptivity of the clinician, who is able to explicitly and implicitly mentalize the client's mind in his or her mind, makes possible the conjoint witnessing of the survivor's traumatic experiences, as may be necessary. This co-witnessing provides a basin within which frightening or shame-inducing experiences can now be mutually held, lessening the trauma survivor's need for dissociation and the burden of holding the experiences alone.

In sum, the traumatized self is primarily healed through participating in therapeutic relationships. In this case, subjective experiences are shared through the practice of intersubjectivity. In the case of the client–clinician relationship, the consciousness of the client as well as that of the clinician coexist within the therapy hour. Primarily through reflective dialogue and supported by the practice of specific structured interventions, the client's and clinician's states of mind, body, and brain are communicated to each other. As the client begins to feel secure enough within the therapeutic dyad, he or she will be increasingly open to examining and regulating his or her conscious states, and the clinician compassionately seeks to help him or her to do so. As such, TRASC slowly and incrementally give way to experiences of NWC. Feelings of being in the past start to recede as the client begins to make fuller contact with the experiential social present. The traumatized person begins to feel more unified inside, increasingly speaking in a more singular voice with a trusted other. He or she begins to more fully inhabit, move, and feel at home within his or her body, and thus is increasingly better able to assert him- or herself within mutually respectful relationships. In addition, he or she is more aware of him- or herself emotionally, and in greater control over states of distress.

It is important to recognize that the clinician, through his or her interactions with the client, while avoiding explicit self-disclosures, at times will communicate his or her own states of mind, body, and brain to the client, if not explicitly then at least implicitly. Therefore it is incumbent on him or her to model a healthy state of being and regulated state of consciousness that the traumatized person can begin to internalize. In this way, it is of the utmost importance that psychotraumatologists seek to develop for themselves their own inner sense of compassionate and mindful awareness (Siegel, 2010) and engage in self-care in order to continue to be empathically attuned while avoiding becoming overwhelmed or vicariously traumatized by the client's traumatic experiences.

Trauma-focused psychotherapy can be considered moving toward completion when the client (1) is experiencing more normal forms of the consciousness of time, thought, body, and emotions; (2) feels that he or she has created a life narrative and accompanying integrative sense of self that encompasses, but is greater than, the sum of his or her past traumatic experiences; and (3) is more connected within a compassionate community of supportive relationships. Figure 7.6 depicts the 4-D model of the sense of self as it presents via the conscious dimensions of time, thought, body, and emotion in a traumatized person at the beginning and upon completion of trauma-focused therapy, in a state of newfound self-recovery.

4D-Model and Sense-of-Self: From Trauma to Recovery

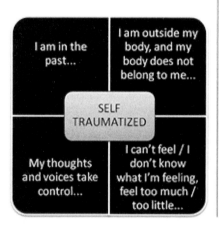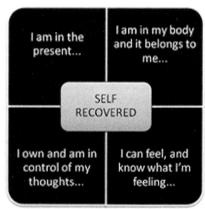

FIGURE 7.6. 4-D Model's Sense of Self from Trauma to Recovery.

Statements reflective of the 4-D model dimensions of time (*top left*), thought (*bottom left*), body (*top right*), and emotion (*bottom right*) are given in the state of a traumatized sense of self (*left panel*) versus in a state of self-recovery (*right panel*).

Intrinsic Neural Networks and the Sense of Self

Current research suggests that one of the neural networks in the brain identifiable at rest, the so-called *default mode network* (DMN) introduced previously, may be one of the primary bases of the narrative core of the self. Specifically, the DMN is thought to partly mediate an "idling state" of the brain, given that it is most active when an individual is disengaged from responding to external cognitive and behavioral events, and instead internally oriented toward stimulus-independent (and typically self-referential) thoughts and associations (e.g., reviewed by Buckner et al., 2008). The DMN can be regarded as a network of functionally interconnected brain regions, the anterior hub of which includes the medial prefrontal cortex and adjacent perigenual anterior cingulate cortex, and the posterior hub of which includes the posterior cingulate cortex and precuneus, with the anterior and posterior hubs each interacting with lateral temporoparietal cortices. As previously reviewed in Chapters 3, 4, and 6, both the anterior and posterior hubs of the DMN are involved in self-referential processing (SRP) and emotional experience. In contrast, the inferior lateral parietal cortex has been implicated in embodied cognition (reviewed in Chapter 5).

The DMN is therefore theoretically involved in each of the four dimensions of consciousness discussed by the 4-D model, perhaps as such maintaining a representation of a sense of self that is integrated across time, thought, body, and emotion. In this way, each of the four dimensions can be represented in each of the other three: (1) our subjective sense of the accumulation of time is typically marked by our passing thoughts, bodily reactions, and emotions; (2) our internal thoughts have as their primary content our memories, aspects of our present environments, future goals, somatic representations, and salient emotional associations; (3) our sense of our bodies is often colored by our sense of time, our thoughts, and our feelings; and (4) our emotions significantly influence our memories and ways of thinking, as well as engender, or are co-created by, our bodily reactions.

Moreover, we speculate that it may be somehow through the experience of a state of being in which all four dimensions of consciousness are integrated that a normal sense of human agency emerges. Specifically, we may be conscious of the sense of a now, of our thoughts, of our bodies, and of our emotions principally *so that we can act upon them*. Without awareness of a present "now," functionally each living moment may as well be already in the past. And why be aware of our thoughts if not to willfully direct them toward positive ends? Further, why be conscious of our body if not to deliberately coordinate its movement toward meaningful goals? And, finally, why be aware of our emotions if not to reflect upon or control them with good intention? In sum, upon reflection we may find that much of what makes us feel alive has to do with our impression that we can exert influence over an integrated four-dimensional sense of ourselves. We surmise that taking away the feeling of conscious agency from a person will likely render his or her experience akin to that of existential death—as indeed frequently occurs in instances of complex interpersonal and developmental trauma.

Consistent with such clinical impressions, studies examining the integrity of the DMN in individuals with PTSD related to chronic early life trauma have shown severe alterations in this neural network. Specifically, individuals with PTSD showed significantly less connectivity between the posterior and anterior hubs of the DMN; that is, between the posterior cingulate gyrus and the medial prefrontal cortex (see Figure 7.7; Bluhm et al., 2009). In fact, the DMN connectivity observed in adults with PTSD resembled that observed in children ages 7–9, possibly indicating interference with the maturation process due to the toxic effects of early life

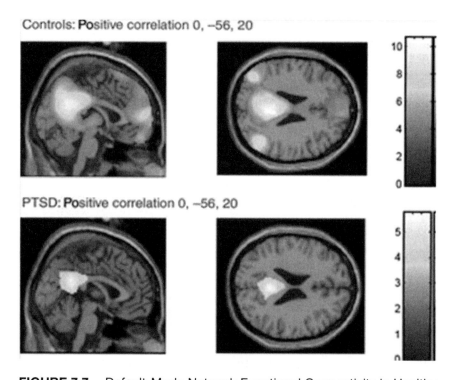

FIGURE 7.7. Default-Mode Network Functional Connectivity in Healthy Persons (*Top*) versus Traumatized Persons with PTSD (*Bottom*). Reproduced with permission from Bluhm et al. (2009). Bluhm, R. L., Williamson, P. C., Osuch, E. A., Frewen, P. A., Stevens, T. K., Boksman, K., Neufeld, R. W. J., Theberge, J., & Lanius, R. A. (2009). Alterations in default network connectivity in posttraumatic stress disorder related to early-life trauma. *Journal of Psychiatry & Neuroscience, 34,* 187–194.

stress (e.g., through the impact of stress hormones on the myelination of the corpus callosum, the fiber tract that connects the posterior cingulate cortex to the medial prefrontal cortex; Daniels, Frewen, McKinnon, & Lanius, 2011).

Research is required to investigate whether the transformation that occurs from a traumatized to a recovered sense of self through psychotherapy also normalizes or restores the DMN and other neural networks in traumatized populations. We suggest that independent of the psychotherapeutic modality, be it cognitive-behavioral, psychodynamic, mindfulness-based, hypnosis-based, or otherwise, the goal is to help the traumatized person establish a sense of self that is integrated across time, thought, body, and emotion, as well as capable of the agentic pursuit and experience of joy, pleasure, and triumph. "Anne," a woman with a complex trauma history who has since reached the final stages of recovery, describes how her sense of self changed over the course of psychotherapy. Reflecting upon her early days in treatment, she noted:

> "I was running on terror and the only way that I can describe it, in retrospect, was that it was a kind of 'animal survival psyche.' My sense of self was pretty undefined and diffuse, as if the nerve endings had no stopping place, and so without a skin or without a boundary, without the other which creates that boundary, there isn't a self."

Another trauma survivor, "Jen", experienced herself in a similar way, noting: "I consumed all space without limit and I took no space at all. No beginning with no end." In her artwork (Figure 7.8; also in color insert) note that she depicts her arms and legs as blending into the background, her sense of self as such boundless.

Toward the final stages of recovery, however, Anne described her sense of self very differently. In the following passage, note the increased sense of integration in her conscious experiences, as well as the newfound capacity for intersubjectivity, the capacity for an appreciation of other's experiences that comes about from a higher understanding of herself:

> "It just happened that, there I was, established in that universe as a separate human being, not particularly unique, sort of ordinary and with other human beings who were living their lives out too. This was all, like, miraculous, and I could only know it was miraculous in the absence of all the fear. . . . I could make eye contact, it didn't hurt anymore—because it had been physically painful to make eye contact with another human being—that just was not an issue anymore. I wouldn't jump when I was touched . . . I slowly became [able] to inhabit my body—[like] I probably felt swimming for the first time—you know, I've always been a swimmer, [though] having

FIGURE 7.8.   Jen's Artwork (2013): "Taking Space." Used with permission.

never known the pleasure of swimming, and I started to know the pleasure of swimming. I would look at myself in the mirror (*laughs*) . . . hadn't done *that* before (*laughs*) . . . I don't know that I can say too much more about it, except that in the absence of abiding terror, a self can occur. A self *does* occur, and self-in-relationship occurs, because the other comes into view: *smelled and felt and known.* And then the other is known as having their own inherent self."

Liberation through Integration:
Recovery and (Re)birth of the Self

Several writers have emphasized the curative role psychotherapy can have for SRP. For example, Kohut's (1971, 1977, 1984) seminal work in self psychology, also described in Schore (2012), stressed the fundamental role of the self in human existence. His work explored the role of psychoanalysis in four key areas: (1) the role of early relationships and their interaction with the social environment in the development of the self; (2) structuralization of the self through internalized early experiences; (3) the effects of early deficiencies in self structure on the later development of psychopathology; and (4) the role of the therapeutic relationship in the restoration of the self.

We speculate that, over the course of trauma-focused psychotherapy the four dimensions of consciousness of the traumatized person become more normalized and integrated. As in NWC, the four dimensions increasingly can be distinguished only in theory rather than in actual lived experience as they become progressively more overlapping and interdependent. The dimensions are experienced increasingly less as separate "symptoms" and correspondingly more as interconnected, regulated, and integrated states of being. As such a unitary, holistic, gestalt of experience is cultivated out of which a more integrated sense of self emerges. As is theorized to occur in recovery, Figure 7.9 (also in color insert) illustrates the emergence of a more robust and integrated phenomenological sense of self that is more fully able to experience self-compassion, joy, pleasure, and triumph.

We also would like to offer the metaphor of a tree for the self as perhaps helpful for clients to understand as a process cultivated in trauma therapy. We might envision the core of the self as the trunk of a tree, the branches as different parts of the narrative self, and the leaves or flowers of the tree as specific memories and emotions. If the trunk is not deeply rooted, it is more vulnerable to being blown away by the passing winds of emotional time. Embodiment of the core self—firmly rooting each subjective moment in the earth of the physical present, while watering the trunk with narrative and empathic support—also develops a branchlike structure capable of integrating a narrative identity that is both complex and adaptive. On each branch one fosters experiences in the present

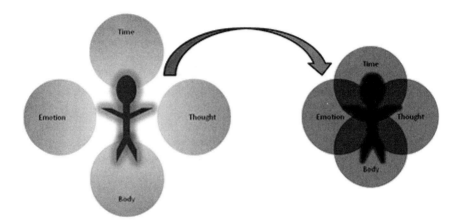

FIGURE 7.9. Integration across Dimensions of Consciousness (Time, Thought, Body, Emotion) and Emergence of a Robust Sense of Self.

In a traumatized state, a person experiences him- or herself as disintegrated across the senses of time, thought, body, and emotion, in turn resulting in a weakened experience of agency and sense of self (illustrated by gray-coloring/whitening). As a person's representations across time, thought, body, and emotion are normalized and integrated, a stronger sense of agency and sense of self emerges.

conducive to greater complexity, adaptiveness, and integration as much as one nurtures the withered, nearly broken branches of past states of self. Nevertheless, to connect the survivor with a compassionate community, one might envision one's tree as part of a deep and majestic forest. Each tree is unique and independent, standing tall above the ground, yet each are also rooted in the same fertile soil below. As part of the forest, each tree is a part of something even greater. The following drawing, created independently by a client in trauma therapy, epitomizes some of the same symbolism (Figure 7.10; also in color insert).

Self-Liberation: A Phenomenological Inquiry of What Recovery "Is Like"

We close with a transcript of an interview with Suzy, a trauma survivor from whom we have heard in earlier chapters. At the time of this writing, Suzy has been discharged from clinical care and is considered to be fully in the recovery phase of trauma treatment. She describes the process of her healing as taking place within trauma-focused psychotherapy and the community at large.

FIGURE 7.10. Gregory's Artwork (2010): "On a withered branch a flower blooms." Used with permission.

Interviewer: Tell me about recovery . . .

Suzy: Recovery is as complex as PTSD itself. Recovery doesn't happen in a straight and orderly fashion—it's not linear, it has ups and downs along the road. Sometimes you move along quite smoothly for 2 or 3 months, and then you hit a bump, or have a hiccup, and you struggle for the next 2 or 3 months. Recovery for me is like a puzzle: You're trying to find the right piece to go into the right spot, but not only do you have to find the right piece, you [also] have to find what is going to work with that piece to get it into the right spot.

So there isn't one single thing, I think, that helps with recovery. I think it's a combination of things. It's finding what works for what problem and then trying to get that piece into the puzzle. It's about finding the right piece and the right method to get the puzzle pieces in place.

You'd like it to be a very short process. You want it to be over and done with. You don't want to have the pain, you don't want to go through all the emotions. But if you don't go through those things, recovery isn't possible.

Interviewer: Can you say more about that?

Suzy: The reason that a person has PTSD, I think, is that they were unable to experience what happened at the time. But at some point you need to feel and have those experiences in order to move forward. I think the PTSD itself says, this person hasn't been able to do things they needed to do at that time, and that's what's holding them back.

Interviewer: Can you say a little more about that?

Suzy: You can't breathe, you can't tell people, you can't say how you feel because all of those things could get you into trouble. So you need to be able to go through those things and tell your side of the story—tell how you felt, experience those feelings before you can move forward. Because PTSD has you basically moving around in a circle, round and round, so it keeps you moving in a circular motion instead of forward. You can move backwards, but it definitely keeps you from moving forward.

Interviewer: What has changed for you on the road to recovery?

Suzy: What *hasn't* changed for me, I think, is a better question. It's the easier question to answer. I can't say that there is one thing that hasn't changed—*everything* has changed. I can now describe things that happened to me with words that I couldn't before. I had them as pictures but not as words, and I don't have flashbacks anymore, and I don't dissociate anymore.

Interviewer: What do you mean by "you don't dissociate anymore"?

Suzy: I don't leave my body anymore in order to be safe. And for me that's basically what dissociation is—leaving your body—it's like you've become someone else. You needed to do that as a child; it was the only way there was to survive it. The child does the best they can to survive it and the result often is some form of dissociation. You're leaving—you're actually leaving your physical body to be away from what is happening to you. And it's not anything you learn. Nobody teaches you how to dissociate, it's something that just happens—it seems like almost a natural process when you are being hurt in some way.

Interviewer: And how has that changed for you now?

Suzy:	Now I'm back in my body, and when it doesn't feel safe, I don't leave it anymore. I stay in my body. I still struggle with the emotion, but I stay in my body and deal with it. Now it feels safer for me to be *in* my body than *out* of my body. And that's a process of years of learning—that it is safer to be in my body—because if I'm in my body, I'm able to do things *with* my body. I'm able to move my body. I'm able to leave a situation if I don't like it. But before, that wasn't always a possibility or an option. It certainly wasn't as a child. But now that it *is* an option, I have the ability to remove myself from a situation that I don't like. As a child, I didn't have that ability. I didn't have that option, that choice. It would probably have been much more dangerous if I tried to leave the situation.
Interviewer:	Can you say a bit more about what's changed for you in recovery?
Suzy:	Now I feel I can experience a full range of emotions, whereas before I didn't experience them, or I denied them altogether. But now I experience a full range of emotions, and even though some emotions can still be challenging for me, it is better, I think, to experience them [than not to]. Because once you've experienced them, then you can move past them.
Interviewer:	You said that some emotions can still be challenging for you. Can you talk about which emotions are still difficult?
Suzy:	Anger is still very difficult for me; it's always been difficult for me. Anger is still a difficult emotion for me because I associate anger with abuse. My belief as a child was that if someone's angry, you could get hurt. And I still believe that, to some extent, but not to the same extent that I did before. To experience anger—it was never safe as a child—so it just became an emotion I never had. Now it's OK, it's safe for me, safer for me to have that emotion. I had to learn that I wasn't going to hurt someone the way that I was hurt—I worried about that endlessly, about hurting someone else if I felt angry. What if I hurt someone? What if I do something? What if I . . . ? Because that was the only experience I had of anger. But now I've learned that no, I'm not going to hurt somebody else; no, it's OK, nothing is going to happen to me if I'm angry.
Interviewer:	How about the experience of joy and pleasure?

Suzy: This is something that is even newer to me than experiencing my own anger. For a very long time you think that if you're feeling good, something bad is going to happen—you wait for that. You anticipate that, so you don't ever really get to feel true joy or true happiness because always in the back of your mind you're waiting for something to fall, you're waiting for something to go wrong—when will the next attack happen, what's going to happen next—you're always waiting for that. It's a childhood thing—you never knew *what* was coming next, but you knew it was coming. So you limited that ability to feel happiness or to feel joy. And you carry that through into adulthood, you carry that "Oh, something's going to go wrong, I just know it" for a very, very long time. But when you can finally get past that, and really experience true joy and true happiness, it's amazing because your life gets turned around 100%. The things that you want to do, the things that you wouldn't do before, now you do them and you don't worry about something bad happening.

Interviewer: What is it like now for you to experience joy or pleasure?

Suzy: The experience of joy or pleasure to me is the experience of an *absence of*—it's not the inclusion, I don't think, of any one thing . . . . *it's absence of fear.*

Interviewer: And what's that like?

Suzy: That I'm still trying to figure out! (*laughs*) In a way, it's very amazing because you're not always looking over your shoulder waiting for something bad to happen. In that way it's very amazing. You're able to be more in the moment, in the present time. You can enjoy what's happening in the present.

Interviewer: How does joy or pleasure feel in your body?

Suzy: It feels like sunshine in your body—that's probably the easiest way to describe it. It feels like sunshine in your body, and it's fun. Yeah, it's fun.

Interviewer: When you feel sunshine in your body, what does your body want to do?

Suzy: It wants to move. It wants to explore. It wants to have fun—sometimes it wants to dance—it wants to do many things.

Interviewer: What's that like?

Suzy: It's like a dog being left off its leash; you just want to run and have fun. So it's a freedom, it's a freedom. You couldn't *enjoy* life before, but now it's very much like a dog being let free.

Interviewer: Can you talk about what recovery means for relationships?

Suzy: That's also a new one for me. When it comes to abuse and relationships, some people will become prostitutes—it's all they know. But I went to the opposite extreme. I was fearful of touch, and I was fearful of relationships. Probably the biggest fear within a relationship was that they won't listen to me if I say no. And *can* I even say no? Certainly I couldn't as a child. And what will happen if I try to say no? Are they going to hurt me more? So that was and *is* still the biggest fear for me when thinking about relationships. So I just completely shut relationships out of my life. I didn't have them, I didn't want them. They terrified me so they were gone, they didn't exist.

Interviewer: How about now?

Suzy: Now, I'm just getting to the point that I want to have an intimate relationship. I'm exploring the possibility of having a relationship. It's taken a long time.

Interviewer: What's it like for you to think about being in a relationship now?

Suzy: There is still some fear. But now I look forward to it. I look at some of the other relationships in my life—friends and work relationships—and I'm asking myself: "Is there more to a relationship than being hurt? What will I find if I go in that direction?" So there's more of a curiosity now, there's more of a curiosity to find out. There's also fear, there's still fear of being hurt in some way, but there is definitely more of a curiosity now.

Interviewer: What is it like to be curious?

Suzy: You just want to explore. Very tentatively, you want to start. If you were an octopus, putting one tentacle out and sort of touching and seeing what happens. Then if that was OK, you want to put another one out and try to see what happens there. You want to just get a feel of things, and see what the response is to what you do. It's very tentative. That's what the curiosity is. What's going to happen if I do this? It's all those conditional things. If I do this, what's going to happen? If I do that, what's going to happen? It's sort of a tentativeness filled with curiosity.

Interviewer: What do you think is allowing you to be curious now?

Suzy: I'm safer. I feel more secure with myself, as well as from the outside world. I feel more secure. And I have more people in my life now. Part of the process in relationship building for me has been learning to have nonintimate relationships with people. And learning what's OK and what's not OK.

And learning that just about everyone had some type of difficulty in their life, some type of challenge. I think one of the big things with PTSD is you feel like nobody in the world is *like* you. No one is as defective as you are. [With recovery] you move past the point of feeling defective yourself, but you're still not sure how other people have experienced the world. And as I note more and more, I discover more and more that there really *isn't* a normal, there's no such thing as "normal life." I don't think a life absent from pain and hurt exists; I don't think that exists for anyone. I think at some point there has been pain for everyone. What the pain stems from is different for each person, but each person has experienced pain. You don't go through life without pain. So I'm learning more and more that having pain is normal, and that you need to talk to your friends, that it's OK to talk to your friends about it. And probably your friends are going to share with you things too. So there's more of a give and take in relationships.

Interviewer: How about the way you view yourself? How has that gone along the way to recovery?

Suzy: Before recovery . . . I may as well have been a piece of garbage in the trash. I hated myself, I believed I was a bad person, I believed I was a broken person, I was defective. I mean, I believed that was the reason that people hurt me— that there was something wrong with me, that I was really bad in ways that they could sense, an evil coming from me that they needed to kill. That's sort of where it started. There was certainly no positive thoughts of who I was as a person.

That has shifted over time. For the most part I don't believe I'm a bad person anymore. I believe that bad things have happened to me, but that *I'm* not a bad person. And that's a big shift. I used to believe that bad things happened because *I* was bad, but I don't believe that anymore. And I'm more willing to see some of the positives in myself. For the most part, I can now accept a compliment. And there are also a lot of social things around that teach you not to say anything good about yourself. We're [i.e., People in general are] very good at being hard on ourselves and not so good at recognizing the things we *can* do. I think that is a societal message. We are taught from a very young age, "Don't say that, don't do this, don't brag." And I think people confuse bragging with being OK with who you are. For the most part, now I feel OK with who I am, and in a strange way, many of the good parts of me come out of the bad things that happened to me.

Interviewer: Can you tell me what you mean by that?

Suzy: The person who I've become—the gentle, the kind, the caring person that people describe me as or see me as is because of what I've been through. I became those things because I didn't want to be a person who did bad things— who *wasn't* kind, who wasn't gentle, who wasn't caring about the people around them. [Because] I experienced that, I never wanted anybody else to have to experience that too. So it's because of those experiences that I made the choice to not have that happen in my life—to not be a person that caused someone else pain, to not hurt some- body else. I made that choice. It wasn't a conscious deci- sion, I don't think, but at some point it *was* a choice and I said, "No, I'm not going to hurt people."

And [my experiences have] taught me not to be judgmental of people. I find it extremely difficult to be around judg- mental people, people who can't find anything good about another person. Everybody, every person, is who they are, or where they are at that time, because of something [that has happened] in their life. And you don't know what their story is. You don't know why that person is like the way they are. So it's not up to me to judge that person, that's not my job—it's not any of our jobs. A lot of people said really negative things to me—she needs to do this, she needs to do that, she's not doing anything—but nobody took the time to sit and look at what happened to me, or they knew what happened and said "get over it." But it's not that simple. So I would never say something meaning to hurt somebody. Because I just don't think that's right.

Concluding Remarks

Although the process is arduous, the "prison-house" of the traumatized self can be unlocked and a newfound sense of self can emerge, trans- formed through the therapeutic process. The integration of a sense of self across time, thought, body, and emotion through psychotherapy eventually makes possible the full healing of a traumatized self. Through the normalization and integration across dimensions of consciousness, traumatized persons are finally freed from their past and able to experience themselves as fully conscious agents in this world. The latter allows trauma survivors to participate intersubjectively in safe, mutually beneficial, satisfying, meaningful, and compassionate social relationships, and makes possible a life that includes experiences of curiosity, joy, pleasure, and triumph.

If we have but one closing message for this book, it would be that healing and recovery are possible. Liberation and freedom from the felt imprisonment of a traumatized self are possible. The painting in Figure 7.11 (also in color insert) by Janine illustrates her experience of self-liberation and recovery from trauma. After 3 years in therapy, Janine now feels that she is able to live in the present to a much greater extent. She is also able to withstand the waves of previously overwhelming emotional states through a more resilient and embodied sense of self. Moreover, she is able to reach out toward a higher power, represented by a cloud that is reciprocating her response. The latter has helped Janine feel a greater sense of belonging and protection.

FIGURE 7.11. Janine's Artwork (2011, untitled). Used with permission.

We close by sharing the final remarks of our interview with Suzy, who, having reached and found recovery herself, speaks in hope and inspiration for other trauma survivors:

Interviewer: Before we end the interview, if you had to summarize in a few sentences, what is recovery like?

Suzy: Recovery is difficult, and recovery can be fun. You need to work at it.

Interviewer: Is recovery worth it?

Suzy: Absolutely. Now that I'm almost there, I can say that it is absolutely worth it. There *are* moments when you think . . . what the hell am I doing? But now that it's within plain view, I know that it's definitely worth it. The other thing that recovery requires is hope. You can't have recovery without hope, because if you don't feel hope, and if somebody doesn't carry hope for you, then recovery is not possible.

Interviewer: Is there anything that you would say to others who are hoping for recovery?

Suzy: Everyone has the possibility to recover. Never, *ever*, let a doctor tell you that you can't. Don't listen to those people who say you can't or that you're not doing anything, or "just get over it." Don't listen to those people. Listen to the child inside who said "I'm going to live through this" . . . because, at some point, that child made a decision to live through that. Listen to that child who said "You are going to live through this."

And if *you* can't have hope, find somebody who will carry the hope for you, until you can hold it yourself. It was many years before I found that person. And if you're a doctor, don't take that away from a person. Don't kill that in a person. Don't say "You're a noncompliant patient," "You're a difficult patient," don't say "You're not doing your best," "You're not trying." Don't do that to a person. That's a very emotional thing for me. Don't take away hope from people—as a doctor, as a therapist—never take that away from a person because you might as well kill them yourself. You are doing that much harm to a person.

Interviewer: Any final comments? On recovery?

Suzy: It's been a ride. It's been fun, it's been hard . . . but in the end, it's all worth it—*it's worth it*—every drop of blood, every tear, it's all worth it.

Appendix

Case Studies in Trauma-Related Altered States of Consciousness—a Phenomenological Inquiry into the Traumatized Self

THIS APPENDIX OVERVIEWS THE results of surveys of phenomenological experiences of direct relevance to the 4-D model of the traumatized self. Qualitative, open-ended, phenomenological interviews were conducted with five individuals (Suzy, Stephanie, Erica, Gregory, and Valerie) who were in current treatment or had recently completed treatment for psychological problems relating to severe early childhood histories of violence, abuse, and neglect as well as adult interpersonal trauma. All individuals provided written informed consent to the transcription and publication of the interviews in full for the purposes of research and teaching. Pseudonyms are used as names. The interview content underwent a small amount of editing to remove personal identifiers and to improve readability. We sometimes use italics to emphasize certain points. Otherwise the interviews can be considered essentially as original sources.

In assuming that the reader is already familiar with the main text, we offer little interpretive commentary other than a brief introduction and background: The transcriptions speak for themselves. We include, however, one or more of four symbols preceding the beginning of the participants' responses to individual questions that are intended to landmark what we consider to be descriptions specific to the four dimensions of consciousness addressed by the 4-D model: that is, the consciousness of time, thought, body, and emotion. The symbol legend is as follows: time ⌛, thought 📕, body ⚕, and emotion. 🀄

The individuals interviewed were selected because their symptom presentation was previously known to us and thought to variably illustrate the concepts described in this text, namely trauma-related altered states of the consciousness (TRASC) of time, thought, body, and emotion. All of the cases were also described in the main text to a varying extent. The cases can be considered typical of the more severe trauma-related disorders we have encountered in our clinical research program. A semistructured interview was used to guide the assessment. Questions pertained to persons' experiences of TRASC of time, thought, their body, and emotions.

The interviews take us to some of the darkest experiences a human being can endure. Nevertheless, they also illustrate the tremendous resilience, determination, and tenacity of people who have suffered through horrific violence, abuse, and neglect from very early in life. We thank the interviewees for putting words to their experiences, the kinds of experiences for which words often cannot be found.

Interview 1: Suzy

Suzy is a 48-year-old woman who grew up with an absent, alcoholic father and an emotionally neglectful mother who made it clear to Suzy that her two brothers were favored over her. Suzy was sexually abused by one of her brothers and was repeatedly gang-raped during her high school years. She spent nearly 8 years of her life hospitalized in psychiatric units. Eventually she was referred to a trauma specialty service several years prior to this interview, due to what were considered intractable symptoms of PTSD, dissociation, and depression. Suzy has since completed a lengthy stage-oriented trauma therapy; accordingly, her answers to the following questions about traumatic experiences refer primarily to past experiences. By comparison, she now reports relatively few significant symptoms of PTSD, dissociation, or depression, and has been working as a teacher for the last 2 years. She is now well along the path of recovery from a once severely traumatized self.

In our view, Suzy's interview responses demonstrate TRASC in all four forms: time, thought, body, and emotion. Suzy describes her journey of estrangement from her narrative and embodied self to the beginnings of a true capacity for, and felt deservingness of, pleasure and joy in her life.

Interviewer:

Have you ever felt that you were back in the past, had flashbacks, or relived a memory as if it were happening in the here and now?

Suzy:

Yes—flashbacks are really scary. It's like the trauma is happening all over again. You are right back there and everything is happening again, so it is very *real*; it's very scary. You experience some of the same feelings you did in the past. I know it has caused me to dissociate. You're anxiety goes up, you're heart beats faster, you're nervous, you're shaking—all of those things.

Interviewer:

One thing we are trying to understand better is whether flashbacks are different in any way from *remembering* something bad that has happened to people in the past, but knowing that it is still *in* the past...

Suzy:

Yeah, with a flashback you don't know, you are *in* that time frame, you are not in *this* time frame. So with a normal memory you can look back at it and you know it is in the past, but with a flashback you don't know it is in the past because it is happening to you *now*, and that's how it is different from a normal memory. It is much more intense as well because the feelings are exactly the same as what you were feeling in that time. If it's a normal memory, you can *look back at it*; you might have some feelings associated, but they aren't going to have the same strength and the same impact on you. *You are looking back*—you are looking at the past. But here you are *living the past* but you are [actually] in the now.

Interviewer:

What about feeling emotionally numb—have you had this experience?

Suzy:

(*Long pause*) No, I am not sure if I have ever felt emotionally numb. I suppressed everything so that I didn't feel it at the time. And if you have a flashback, you are suppressing it because you don't want to—you can't—deal with all the feelings that are coming at the same time. I think it is a little different than numbness. Numbness, to me, is you *can't* experience a feeling. When you are suppressing it, you *won't* experience a feeling because of the impact that it would have on you. It is a little different.

Interviewer:

What about feeling emptiness—have you had this feeling? And if so, can you tell us what it feels like?

Suzy:

Emptiness is a sort of helpless, hopeless feeling. It's that there is nobody there to help you. You are going through this yourself, whether it's the actual event or the "after" event. You just feel they have robbed you of everything—the people who abused you—and you have nowhere to turn or you have nowhere to go. You feel completely devoid of everything, and you don't even feel human at some points. I am not sure what it is that you *do* feel, but you don't feel like you are human. *You are a shell, with nothing in it, you are just a shell. There is nothing in there—they have taken everything that you had—they robbed you of that.*

Interviewer:

Thank you for this description of what it's like to be human and comparably with what you have been robbed of [through trauma].

Suzy:

When you are human, [although] it is not necessarily fun all the time, there are feelings, and you know that things are happening. But when you are *not* human, *there is nothing there that they haven't taken.* Essentially they have taken the life out of you. You can walk and breathe, but they have taken the important parts, the parts that are necessary, I guess to feel. And to know that *you are who you are.* They completely rob you of your identity—*they rob you of who you are.* And all that was associated with that—the highs, the lows, the hopes, the fears—all of those things are taken from you, including your identity. So you create an entirely different identity. And although I guess in some ways that [new] identity is connected to you, they are different from you. They are there for a purpose, they are there to do something for you, but at the same time *in creating that identity, it takes something away from you.* It takes away the feelings that you have, it takes away the sense of self that you had. *And if it is repeated often enough, then you completely lose that sense of who you are. So you are now an empty shell.* Everything exists within compartments that you have developed, but you are not necessarily aware that they are there, and it may take a long time before you become aware that they are. So for all intents and purposes you are walking around as an empty shell because you don't know where everything went, because it is no longer within you.

Interviewer:

Sometimes people say that they "don't know what they are feeling." Have you had such an experience?

Suzy:

Yes. You don't have the words to describe what you are feeling. Especially when the trauma happens at a young age, you just don't have those words yet, so you have everything catalogued in your mind as pictures, and you don't have the words to explain what is happening for you. It becomes really important to put words to those pictures because it makes it very difficult to explain to someone what you are going through— what you are feeling—when you don't have the words to describe them, but just a series of pictures.

Interviewer:

Is it sometimes easier to draw a picture than to describe your feelings in words?

Suzy:

For me, yes, sometimes. Yes, and sometimes drawing it helps you find what you are looking for. Because now as an adult I have a lot larger vocabulary, but sometimes you still require assistance figuring out "What is the feeling that goes with this?" Finding words can be very difficult to express what you are feeling on the inside. It's not an easy process because as a child you didn't have those words; you didn't have access to those things and certainly depending on how things are at home for a person, *there may be things that are OK to say and there may be things that are not OK to say. And if they are not OK you lose those vocabulary words.*

Interviewer:

Would you be able to give us an example of something that you might not have been allowed to talk about when you were younger?

Suzy:

We were never allowed to be angry in my house. At least, the child wasn't allowed to be angry.

Interviewer:

How about now? Is it difficult to feel anger *now*, even if perhaps by now the rules have changed?

Suzy:

Yes, there is that absolute judgment of that feeling. How could I feel that way? It is not OK for me to feel like this. I am not going to feel like this. *You are completely wanting to dismiss that feeling because it wasn't allowed before.* At some point it becomes a part of you and then it's your own unwritten rule—that you aren't allowed to be angry and that it's not OK to be angry. You have learned other things in the meantime, too, like that anger hurts people, and that when someone is angry, you are going to be hurt. So this is not a good feeling, and now *you* are going to have this feeling. It is just not going to exist for me, so, I still hate being angry. I don't like it at all, and I don't like it when I think somebody is angry at me. It frightens me still.

Interviewer:

What about not knowing what others are thinking or feeling and not being able to understand others? Have you ever had this experience?

Suzy:

No. I haven't and I will tell you why. When you are abused—at least, in my experience—you need to be very perceptive and you need to learn very early how to read other people so that you can anticipate what is coming, what will happen. This allows you even the shortest amount of time to prepare for what is coming. It allows you to prepare for the onslaught. So I am generally very perceptive about how people are feeling and what might be coming. I have had people say to me "How did you know?" I will say to someone, "It is OK to cry," and they will reply "I am not going to cry," but 5 minutes later they are crying, and they will come back to me and ask "How did you know?" I just know. I have to pay attention to what people are doing, how they are acting—the subtle changes. You have to be able to pick up on those things so that you can prepare yourself. So no, I would say it is the opposite for me. I need to be able to read people. I need to know what is going on.

Interviewer:

Thank you for explaining the difference that can exist between the difficulties a person may experience identifying his or her own feelings in comparison with being very aware of what other people are likely thinking and feeling. Did you ever have the experience that you were not able to feel positive emotions like happiness, love, joy, or pleasure, or you were not able to smile or to laugh? And if so, can you tell us about it?

Suzy:

Yes. It's getting easier, but there were times in the past when I was just devoid of anything positive, any positive emotions. The only thing you experience is darkness, everything is dark, there is nothing positive, you can't foresee anything positive, and in my darkest moment I probably never laughed at anything. It would have been a completely dark time for me—I mean, so much so that I interacted very little with the people around me. I can remember another inpatient coming up to me after a long, long time—I don't know how long I had been there—and she said, "You know, when you first came here you didn't talk to anybody, you wouldn't look at anybody, you wouldn't, you never laughed." I know, from what I have been told, that the things that I did do solely consisted of trying to die or trying to hurt myself in some way. There was absolutely no sense for me that things were going to improve, and certainly given the environment that I was in at the time, there was no reason to think that that was going to change. It is just a place of total darkness; there is no light that exists, and it is like being in a dark hole, being buried in a dark hole and you can't come out.

Interviewer:

In that kind of a state, could you let us know what you think might happen, say, for example, if someone tried to encourage you into a positive state? For example, if you were brought a vase of beautiful flowers and someone said, for example, "These are for you." What would your response be?

Suzy:

My response would probably be, "Thanks, that's nice."

Interviewer:

And what feeling would you have had inside?

Suzy:

Sadness. There have been different times when I have been work-ing with my therapist and she might say something [positive], and *she* [therapist] might feel that way, but *I* don't feel that way. *But I will let her hold onto that feeling until I can get to a space that I can feel it too.* [For example,] sometimes I know she feels hopeful, but I don't feel hopeful at all, and *so sometimes I need her to carry the feeling for me because I can't carry it myself.* I might get there, but at the time I can't carry it myself because it is not what I am feeling. *But I think there is something in knowing that someone else holds that or feels that for you,* even if you can't experience it at the time yourself. There is something in knowing that that person can hold it or feel it for you.

Certainly when I first met my therapist, I felt no hope, and I had to let her carry that because I certainly couldn't carry it. But there came a point in time in therapy that yes, I could feel hope, and *so now I could take back ownership of it.* There are still times when I can't feel something and I need her to carry it. Absolutely there have been times when I have needed somebody else to carry it until I can get there. It is important knowing that a therapist has hope for you because I have been in places where therapists tell you that what you are doing is crazy, it doesn't make sense, you are this, this, this, and this—and that offers no hope. That kind of a person is useless to me because if they have no hope for me, then I must be hopeless. And if I am already feeling that way myself, how can they help me? So it is important for a therapist, regardless of the situation, to carry some type of hope for the person because if they can't see it, then the patient certainly can't see it.

Interviewer:

You noted earlier that experiencing positive emotions has become easier for you now as compared with before. What would it be like now for you to feel positive emotions?

Suzy:

Yes, it is easier now to experience positive emotions. It can still be challenging for me, but it is easier to feel them than before. Part of that is that when you have experienced trauma, you are always expecting something bad to happen, something to go wrong. That continues with you for a very long time. Things might be going good, but you think "Oh, something is going to go wrong, something's not right, I just know it" because that was what tended to happen in the past. It could have been OK for 2 or 3 days, but then *wham* you are back to being abused, you are back to being hurt. So you are very cautious in approaching good feelings. *Can* you feel them? Absolutely. But you are cautious about them because you don't know what will happen next; you have to be very guarded. You think, *"Don't feel too good or you are going to be hurt."*

Interviewer:

Would there be a difference between feeling it and expressing it to other people?

Suzy:

Oh, you certainly wouldn't express it because if you express it, if you put it out there, you are *definitely* going to be hurt. Now it's a little different. I am OK to express, yeah, I am doing OK most of the time. There is still a bit of residual, like "If I do this, something is going to happen." But I would certainly never express it before because you don't broadcast things like that. There is always someone waiting to hurt you, be it verbally, physically, or sexually. And it probably has nothing to do with feeling good, but *at some point you have connected those two things: "I feel good, I get hurt."* You are connecting those two things.

You are considering that this is usually a child that this is happening to, so this is a childlike mind, and a child can make all kinds of connections that aren't necessarily true. But those are the connections that seem obvious to them. So you certainly don't express positive things. You might say, "No, I'm OK," but that's different than saying "I am great blah, blah, blah, blah" because you just don't do that unless you need to lie. A lot of survivors have to do this, especially if their families are being threatened or they are being threatened directly, you are going to lie for survival.

Interviewer:

Have you ever had the experience of being outside your body? If so, what was it like for you?

Suzy:

Yes. It is like watching everything from the outside. I was abused a lot in parks. So for me it was like sitting up in a tree and then watching everything from outside. When you are watching, you are watching somebody being hurt, but it is not *you* being hurt; *it is somebody else being hurt.*

You feel badly for the person there, but *it allows you some separation from exactly what is happening to you* on the ground. For me it was like a physical separation: Here's me up here, and here's this shell down here that is being hurt and abused—but I can't feel it, I don't feel it, *I am separate from that person, I am separate from my body now.* My body is being hurt but *I* am not being hurt. I think that is one of the things that let you survive because it is *not you*, you are not experiencing the full impact of what is happening. You are experiencing it—but you are not experiencing the full impact.

In the early stages you are usually not even really aware that it is happening. But I haven't been dissociating for a while now. Now, [having had therapy] the dissociation for me is mostly that I can't feel my feet and hands. I don't know where they are; they are not attached to me, the hands that are attached aren't mine, but to look at them it was like a physical separation, that they weren't my hands, they belonged to somebody else. They just weren't mine. And at that point it makes it difficult to function because you can't feel things or you don't have the sensations associated with your own hands. For me at times I feel like I am autistic because I do a lot of hand play, but what I am doing is, I am checking, like I am not sure if they are my hands. I mean, they don't look like my hands, I can't feel them, and I am trying to figure out if they are attached, and if they are not, where are my hands? And where are my feet, because these aren't mine, they belong to somebody else? *Not too long ago I realized for the first time how dangerous this can be, because you can't protect yourself when your hands are not yours.* But at the same time it was a protective mechanism you learned; when you were a child, it *did* protect you. Would it protect me as an adult? Not likely. But as a child, did it protect me? Absolutely. I wouldn't be sitting here if it had not protected me as a child. That's how I survived.

Interviewer:

Going back if we can to the experience of you being in a tree and looking down at yourself below, can you help me understand a little bit better what this is like? You described it as if you are looking down and knowing it is you but feeling at the same time that it is also *not* you—because you are in the tree. Can you say more about what this is like experientially? Can you make me a visual?

Suzy:

For me, it is different because it is not me anymore. It is just a shell. The body is just a shell there that is being hurt. The vital part is left. It doesn't look like me—it looks like someone else is being hurt because me, I'm in the tree. Is there recognition of this shell? Yes I would say there is some recognition. Is it me? I can't say that, yes, that was me because I am in the tree, so I can't be down there. You need that separation. So it can't be me there, but I know somebody is being hurt. *There is empathy there. There is sympathy with that person, but it's not me, it's no longer me. The reason I say it's a shell, because all the vital parts—the mind, everything else—is in the tree with me, so it's just a body.*

Interviewer:

Can you tell us more now about how you experience yourself when you feel it is as if you are up in a tree? How do you see yourself? What is it like?

Suzy:

When I draw it, it looks like a person, but it is probably more of a spirit than anything. But if I draw it, it is a little girl sitting up on the limb of a tree. But that's just the image, it is more of a spirit, it is more like you see in the movies, like these guardian angels floating around, that's what it is like, this person being above and watching me.

Interviewer:

And are you are safe up there?

Suzy:

Yes, I would be safe up there. *They are getting the person on the ground, but they aren't getting you.* I mean, in reality they are, but at the time that's what it looks like. For years I didn't even know that I had disconnected until I had an experience this year when I knew I became completely associated; I was completely integrated and it was a really physical experience. I became quite lightheaded and very dizzy and I knew that if I stood up, I would fall so I just sat where I was, put my head down for a bit, and after a few minutes it was like, *"OK, things are very real all of a sudden."* It felt like the sounds I was hearing were much louder. So at that point I am fully 100% in my body, and I am not sure that that had ever existed since childhood. I came in and I described it to my therapist and I knew, it was a Sunday afternoon, and I knew in that moment that that is what had happened to me. I knew 100% I was confident that that was what had happened to me. *It was a very physical experience of an integration of body, mind, and spirit and everything coming together, it was a very physical sensation for me.* And I didn't know where am I and how did I get here? So for me it was a very physical experience.

Interviewer:

What has been the effect of going through this?

Suzy:

Well, certainly initially, now *bam* all of a sudden I am in my body, and my body is experiencing all these emotions at full intensity, and it was very overwhelming. I had never experienced that full onslaught of emotion and intensity and such a variety of emotions. Everything was so intense because for the first time I was fully experiencing emotions, and it took me a while to acclimate to that; it was very scary for a while for me because I just wasn't used to it. You have to become comfortable with all of these things and there are still times for me when it can seem very overwhelming with the sheer strength of the emotions.

Interviewer:

What about seeing your environment as being very different or unreal, so that things around you become unreal for you?

Suzy:

Nothing feels real when I dissociate. Everything seems sort of foreign, like I was saying just a minute ago—with sounds all of a sudden seeming really loud. But if I am dissociated, everything feels a little farther away so it can be harder to focus on the sounds around me. I need to listen very carefully to what I am hearing if I am dissociated. Everything seems sort of dreamlike around me when I am dissociated and none of it feels real; it's like a dream going on around me and I'm just watching. The world is rotating around me and I'm right in the middle, observing and trying to follow what is going on.

Interviewer:

What would happen if in that state you would see an object, and go to it? Would you experience any connection with the object if you touched it? Would it be more or less real?

Suzy:

It's still unreal, although there might be the sense that this *must* be real. And it depends on whether my hands are attached or not. If my hands are not attached, then I cannot even really feel it, but if my hands are attached then I can at least have a tactile sense. If my hands are attached, I know that it must be real, not that it *is* real but that it must be.

Interviewer:

It sounds like a "rational understanding": Your mind telling you that it must be real, even if you don't experience a connection between touching and feeling it.

Suzy:

Seeing is different than touching. In seeing you're feeling that everything is a dream around you. But with touching there is more of a "hands-on" sort of sense.

Interviewer:

Like "more proof"?

Suzy:

I guess so, because you can feel it; my hands are attached and the object is solid, or whatever the object is, so it must be real, that's more rational. I think "this must be real" because I can feel it. If I can't feel it, though, then it is not real. But I have been working very hard to stay associated, so this has happened much recently.

Interviewer:

When you say "*to stay associated,*" can you tell us what you mean?

Suzy:

It is the opposite of *dis*sociated. I use [the term *associated*] as my opposite to *dissociated*. It means, trying to keep myself attached—keeping my hands attached, keeping my feet attached, not letting myself slip into another state. So for me being associated means that all the parts are together, and I'm the leader and in control.

Interviewer:

Is this a new experience for you, to have a feeling of being in greater control over whether you will go into dissociation?

Suzy:

I think I have understood for a while that I could control it, but there were times when I didn't want to control it because it was easier not to. It was what I knew; to me it was safer, so I would just let it slip. Once it slips, it is difficult to get back, so yes I have known for a while that I could control it. It's that "what is known." For me dissociation signified safety because that's what I did, that's what kept me safe. But it's not necessarily that conscious, it's not necessarily "OK, I'm going to dissociate [now]" and then *bang* I'm gone. It's struggling, struggling, struggling, slipping, slipping, slipping. And at some point it's "OK, I'm gone." Was I always aware that it was a choice? No, absolutely not. I wasn't for a long, long, long time. It was just something that happened. But now there are things that I can say or do to prevent dissociaton from happening.

Interviewer:

Some people have the experience of hearing voices in their head. Have you had the same experience?

Suzy:

Yes. I didn't know what they were for a long, long time. I knew I was hearing voices. It is one of the things you don't say in psychiatry. If they know that you are hearing voices, it leads to all kinds of misdiagnoses.

I didn't tell people for a long, long time in fact. But when I did eventually, they would say, oh she is schizophrenic, she is schizoaffective, schizotypal—all the misdiagnoses that go along with it. The voices were very real, I mean in my head. They were very different. They aren't voices coming from outside of my head, or from the TV or radio. And no one is just standing over here talking to me. They are in my head, and what they are is my dissociated voices, in an argument, trying to make a decision, or very upset about something. *That is what the voices are; they are the dissociated parts of me.* But nobody could ever figure that out, and by the time I entered the trauma program I had learned that you just don't talk about your voices, so I didn't mention anything for probably the first 2 years I was in the trauma program about voices.

Interviewer:

Can you tell us if you have ever had feelings of shame? If so, can you tell us what this is like?

Suzy:

 Yes, I still have them. They have never gone away. It is hard to describe shame; Shame is like you are embarrassed of who you are and what you did. You feel guilty about what you have done, and you feel badly about yourself for what you have done. There is nothing positive associated with shame.

Interviewer:

When would this feeling come up?

Suzy:

 I don't think it comes up—it permeates everything. It touches everything, is a piece of every emotion, every movement, it's a core part of you.

Interviewer:

Would it always be there?

Suzy:

 Yes, it is always there, it touches everything.

Interviewer:

You spoke earlier about a feeling of darkness. Can you tell us a little bit about what this is like?

Suzy:

 It is like walking around your house in the middle of the night and there is no light coming into the house. You can't, you don't know where you are going, you keep running into obstacles and you can't find the door. You might hit it, but you might not know what it is because you can't see it. That's exactly what it is like, wandering around in a completely black space, lots of things in it you can't see and you don't know what they are.

Interviewer:

Is the experience of darkness different from the experience of shame?

Suzy:

In some ways they are different. Shame helps to create the darkness. Generally, part of the shame was created because there is no one you can tell. They have told you that you are bad, you are no good, this was your fault, so you believe those things and you feel ashamed of yourself for the things you have done. *The shame builds to create this dark cover over everything so that you can't see light. Shame overwhelms it all, it covers it all, it creates this space where there is nothing but darkness, there is nothing good about you, there is nothing useful about you, you are no better than the trash. So the shame creates this really dark space and you can't get out,* there is never any light, because it just keeps happening. It becomes darker and darker and darker and all of a sudden it is so black, you can't see your way out. So shame is different than the darkness, because the darkness is the result of shame, and shame is the creation of the darkness.

Interviewer:

This will be the last question. We are wondering what words you would use to describe yourself. What words immediately come to mind?

Suzy:

(*Long pause*) Some of the first words are *terrified, always terrified, ashamed, sad, confused.* Some of the positive words—usually, I'm very gentle and very kind. I have a good sense of humor. In fact, I think a lot of people who have experienced trauma have a wonderful sense of humor.

Interview 2: Stephanie

Stephanie is a 62-year-old woman who was adopted at age 3. She grew up with an absent father and an emotionally and physically abusive adoptive mother who, according to Stephanie, wished that Stephanie had never been born. Stephanie was recently referred to a trauma specialty clinic for what were considered intractable symptoms of PTSD (related to childhood abuse) and depression. She currently experiences PTSD and depression symptoms with much less severity, and her descriptions also often characterize past experiences more so than current ones. Stephanie currently works as a mental health case manager with children. Her interview responses illustrate particularly well, in our view, TRASC of her body (depersonalization, out-of-body experience) and emotions. She describes clear emotional numbing and alexithymic symptomatology as well as painful experiences of shame.

Interviewer:

Have you ever felt that you are back in the past or had flashbacks of past traumatic events? Specifically, have you ever felt like you were reliving a traumatic memory as if it were happening in the here and now?

Stephanie:

Yes. Sometimes it's only for an instant, but for me it's like I've stepped back, sometimes decades, and sometimes it's just a brief instant where I feel like I'm right there—almost to the extent—depending on the trigger—of seeing past stuff, and then it can be gone very quickly. I have to keep really task-focused to stay out of the flashbacks. I've worked really hard at learning to not go there. One of the things I was taught through the trauma program was to refocus and kind of move on by saying "OK, you're here now." One of the traumas was a car accident, and driving is something I pretty much have to do daily. Every time I come up to a stop sign, I have to say to myself "OK, it's all right, look at everybody, everybody's good, go." But there are times when the car accident is right there.

Interviewer:

The next question has to do with the experience of feeling emotionally numb. Is that something you have experienced?

Stephanie:

Yeah. You say *numb*; I say *shutdown*. And for me a lot of times that's where I am. I've actually had instances where people at work ask me about what I am feeling, and I want to shout, "I don't have any feelings!" I used to have a little chart to try to figure out what I should be feeling. I might be feeling something physiologically, but I don't necessarily recognize it, and I don't necessarily have the time to flip through the little chart and try to figure it all out. It's very difficult for me to identify it—what I am feeling.

Interviewer:

What is it like for you to *feel* numb or shutdown?

Stephanie:

I would say "no man's land." For me it's not a nice place to be; it's not comfortable. I don't necessarily understand when I go into a situation that involves being with other people what I should be feeling or what's appropriate to feel at that time. I have found that I don't necessarily have the appropriate responses and so I have to be really careful. I think sometimes that part of the reason I'm shutdown is because I don't want to be inappropriate. So in order to not be inappropriate I have to have a blank slate—figure it out—OK, so what's appropriate here, what is it that I like, what's going on? I get teased a lot, certainly at work, because I wait, I watch, I listen, I figure it out, and that's how I can tell what's appropriate. It's like I don't understand what I'm feeling at all. It's almost like I don't know who I am. When I am with people, I spend a lot of my time trying to figure out what the heck is going on or what's appropriate and what's not appropriate, what I should be feeling or not feeling. It's very exhausting. I have the fear of making a mistake or being inappropriate. I tread very lightly and very carefully on pretty much every situation.

Interviewer:

Have you ever had a feeling of emptiness?

Stephanie:

What I feel when I'm feeling empty is different from what I feel when I'm numbing out or shutting down. The shutting down is usually in response to something. But the emptiness comes not from being in a situation but from having nothing to draw on. Sometimes I'll find myself just sitting and not having a clue about anything, and that is part of the feeling of emptiness. It's a different kind of shutdown. It's like you turn the lights on, but nobody's home. That's sometimes how it feels, and I have to regroup, refocus, and get task-focused—that helps deal with the void.

Interviewer:

You talked earlier about having difficulties knowing what others are thinking or feeling and not being able to understand others. Can you tell us more about that?

Stephanie:

I have that all the time. I have learned over the years to watch for all the little physical things—even how people come into a room, how they respond, how they're moving, their eyes. I've a tendency to check out the face, where are the eyes at, are they clear and bright and look like they're OK or happy or whatever? I almost do a scan—my own kind of scan.

Interviewer:

Have you had the experience of not being able to feel positive emotions, like happiness, love, joy, or pleasure, or you were not able to smile or laugh?

Stephanie:

It's extremely difficult. I can know "head wise" that something is good and positive. I can go through the scroll and know that yes, this is a really good thing, but I will be totally shutdown from the head down. Sometimes the disconnection is very great, and I have struggled with that as long as I can remember. It's probably only been in the last few years that I've actually been able to connect any of the dots there and even feel any of those [emotions]. For the longest time I would look at them on paper and I'd read about them, but I couldn't feel any of them because of the fear and the anxiety. Even with my grandkids, I can't just go and play and enjoy them because I can't connect to those emotions. It takes everything out of me.

But in the last couple of years, I have started to recognize and feel some joy. But when I experience [joy], I know it's kind of there, I know I'm feeling something, but I usually have no clue, and I can't usually put any words to it. Usually if there is any, it's because I've been able to help somebody with something—so it's tangible—I've done something and they are grateful. The experience is of being glad that I did it, I'm glad it helped them, and can see that they can change and grow and get better or whatever, but I don't like it [being joyful], so it's hard for me to experience that as a positive. I have to really work at it.

Interviewer:

Have you ever had the experience of being outside your body? If so, what was it like for you?

Stephanie:

I haven't done it in a long time, but I laugh because anytime I hear any-body talk about that, I remember years and years ago, when I was in my 30s, I was listening to the radio and they were talking about out-of-body experiences. I remember being truly mesmerized, thinking "People don't normally do this?" (*laughs*) It was just like an odd moment of, "OK, people don't normally do this." I recognized that I have to do more research; I have to start reading. I have to start figuring it out because if that's some-thing that other people don't do and it's very "out there," I need to know more about it. It was like "Wow, other people don't do that, it's not a good thing." But I don't do it as a whole anymore because I keep very focused and very grounded.

Interviewer:

What did an out-of-body experience feel like for you?

Stephanie:

It was never a bad thing, and I look back on it as a really good sur-vival skill. I really was very grateful that I was able to do that because to be in the situation and not be able to do that would have been worse. I can remember being at a shopping mall in Montreal, floating around and knowing that what was going on wasn't good. But I was OK because I was out of that—it was peaceful; it was quiet.

Interviewer:

Can you tell us more about how out-of-body experiences were a survival skill for you?

Stephanie:

Sometimes I was safe inside. I preferred to go inside. That's where I would go during the major abuse. In particular with my mother, she could pound on me all she wanted because I was not there—I was inside.

It was usually during a major physical encounter that I didn't get out of fast enough. My skills were hiding and doing other things to keep myself safe. But if I did get caught, I could go inside fairly quickly and shut everything out [so I] didn't even feel the abuse. My mother could pound on me all she wanted, but it was part of "lights on, nobody's home." You can do what you want because I'm not there, I'm inside.

In my life there were no safe people. I've heard about other people who at least had one adult they could go to, a grandmother or a neighbor, somebody. But I think a lot of the behaviors I ended up with, like going outside of my body or going inside, stem from the fact that I didn't have any "go-to person"—there was nobody. So I had to go inside or I had to go outside, because that's all I had. I didn't have anything else.

Interviewer:

Have you ever felt like people, things, or the world around you seems very unreal?

Stephanie:

If I got into situations where I was extremely overwhelmed, things would become fuzzy and unreal, and I would have to really, really focus. It was too easy to drift into that, and to allow it. And when I wasn't as well, it was almost a safety zone. You would drift in and out of it, but something would bring me back and deal with it [reality]. There were times when I didn't have the capacity to be able to deal with the here and now, so I would step back and disappear or change—I'm not sure.

Interviewer:

This next question is about hearing voices. Have you ever experienced this?

Stephanie:

I don't think so. I probably still hear my mother, but that's different in the sense that it's more a way of being than a voice. It became so ingrained that I don't have to hear anything.

Interviewer:

A way of being?

Stephanie:

I have learned that I had certain core beliefs that came strictly from what she said all those years. For example, making a mistake is a huge thing for me. When I make a mistake, it's almost like I *become* it, like *I am* a mistake. I shouldn't have been born, I wasn't wanted—all things that she taught me. I was adopted, and she [my adoptive mother] wished she could have sent me back. I was horrible, ugly, I had everything—you name it. It's a pathway that I don't like because it goes straight there—it's an old record. It's not that I hear it audibly, it is just that it goes right down a very nasty path—being unworthy, you don't deserve anything—you're garbage.

Interviewer:

Have you ever had feelings of shame?

Stephanie:

It took me a long time to figure out that what I was experiencing was shame. I'm very familiar with it now because it was part of the "I'm a mistake," part of "I shouldn't exist," part of the physical abuse. Shame also doesn't allow good feelings. I couldn't even handle somebody saying "You are doing well" or noticing that I had lost weight. I could not handle the positive; the shame didn't allow it in.

Interviewer:

Could you talk a little bit more about what the experience of shame is like for you?

Stephanie:

Usually I know I've switched into it because I can feel the shame, the intensity of it, the redness [in the face], the anxiety, the wanting to disappear, *the feeling of being bad*, the feeling of being totally unworthy and totally undeserving. It's very *physical*—it's almost like my skin is crawling, and I feel like I've got stuff all over me. I find it very difficult to come out of it. The shame is so big and so overwhelming that it becomes part of who I am.

Interview 3: Erica

Erica is a 47-year-old woman who was raised in a tumultuous household. Her father's work required the family to move, often across countries and continents, approximately every 2 years. She describes her father as physically abusive and neglectful, her mother as emotionally unstable (and diagnosed with bipolar disorder), and her younger brother as perhaps even more emotionally troubled than her (e.g., he set himself on fire on several occasions).

Erica left home at age 16. Living in impoverished and dangerous cities, Erica was no stranger to violence. She witnessed shootings and was shot at in political riots, had her life threatened at knife and gun point, and witnessed a murder by stabbing. She was sexually assaulted on numerous occasions as a young woman at knife point. Her history also includes recovering from serious drug addiction and being trafficked sexually by abusers. At present she is in the initial stages of trauma therapy. She has many coping skills. She is beginning college-level studies and is an ardent supporter of antihuman trafficking legislation.

Erica's interview illustrates the symptomatology of TRASC of her body and emotions particularly well. She describes the phenomenology of emotional numbing and its association with anhedonia, alexithymia, and depersonalization–derealization.

Interviewer:

Have you ever felt like you were back in the past? Had flashbacks or relived a memory? If yes, can you give an example?

Erica:

I was in a really bad car accident with my mom [in the past], a really bad one. We had to be cut out [of the car]. I was in the back seat; it was a left-hand turn. I was on the right-hand side of the car, behind her [mother], and I, I saw the car coming and I saw it hit us. Now, when I'm in cars, for example, it keeps happening. I see the car coming, and I actually physically move in the seat of the car, like I can see it, and I can feel it, and I can . . . it's exactly happening again—BAM! I can feel it, I can almost hear it, I can . . .

Interviewer:

What happens when the flashback is over?

Erica:

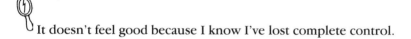 I have to figure out where I am. I guess it's almost like waking up from a nightmare—when you sit up and you go "OK. I'm at home. It's not…that wasn't real." People coming up behind me fast can do it to me easy too. If somebody gives me a fright, I'll turn around swinging, almost every time. Also if I smell a particular cologne, it takes me—*whoosh* (motions)—and that fast. *It's almost like someone sucking the soul out of somebody.* I'm sucked out of my body and I'm put somewhere else, even though my body is still standing there.

Interviewer:

What is it like to be sucked out of your body?

Erica:

It doesn't feel good because I know I've lost complete control.

Interviewer:

How about feeling emotionally numb. Have you had this experience?

It happens a lot. This may sound like a contradiction but I get days of feeling an incredible impending doom and dread, and I think that the deadness and lack of emotion is my way of dealing with it. Because if I allow myself to feel emotion, the fear will be debilitating, even though the doom already is debilitating. I go completely numb.

It's like your feet are lead. Or I'm sitting here and everything is the same. Everything is one. I'm the sofa. I'm not a person anymore. *I don't believe I exist, that degree of deadness.*

And it can feel like my hands aren't mine, and—*I'm not real.* You can look in the mirror and look at the face and your brain tells you that that is your face—but you feel like "I'm not really here." If I touch my cat, that sometimes helps bring me back out of it. She makes me a bit more real I think, and then, by actually touching her, I feel her, so I know I'm real.

Interviewer:

Can you say a little more about what it's like to feel like your hands aren't yours?

Erica:

Right now, I'm looking at my hands, and I know that they are *my* hands, but I can't really feel them. I used to sometimes burn myself with cigarettes to make me feel myself—to bring me back. I used to carve into my hand to make me recognize myself, for lack of a better way of putting it.

Interviewer:

Is there anything else that you can tell us about emotional numbness?

Erica:

It is very hard to be around other people when you are emotionally numb. I don't want to go outside those days, because I feel like people will look at me and think "She's dead. She's the walking dead." That also is one of the other many factors that can keep me inside the apartment.

Interviewer:

How about feeling empty? Have you had that experience?

Erica:

A lot. *Emptiness isn't a hole that you can see through. It's a hole inside me; there's skin on either side of the hole inside me.* It's a black hole inside me, but it's not a hole that is filled with mass. It's just flat because there's no light. The emptiness makes me feel nauseous, and that's part of when I feel impending doom. It is a feeling of no hope.

Interviewer:

How are emptiness and hopelessness related?

Erica:

If you have hope, you have things inside you that you're thinking can happen, that you can do. When you're empty, there's none of that—it is hopeless. That's when you really start having no hope for the future—there are no possibilities.

Interviewer:

How about feeling like you don't know what you are feeling? Have you had that experience?

Erica:

Yes. I put that down to anxiety. That's how I label it. It happens a lot, and I'll pace. I often pace because I don't know what's going on. I don't know what's happening. So you don't know how to deal with it. If you don't know what you are feeling, it just builds and builds and builds, and you start getting anxious about it. I'll just stand in a room and start doing circles because I don't know what to do with myself because I don't understand what I'm feeling—I don't get it.

Interviewer:

How about not knowing what others are thinking or feeling?

Erica:

I have issues understanding what they are thinking or feeling about me, but not what they're feeling about themselves. For years I've wondered whether everybody else is just like me. So I always wonder if people see themselves differently from what I see myself.

Interviewer:

How about not being able to feel positive emotions like love, happiness, joy or pleasure? Or not being able to smile or laugh?

Erica:

Yes, but it's not as debilitating or serious as the other things for me. My cat's helping bring me out of that. She's helping me feel love. I only have so many years of this life on this planet. I want to be able to enjoy them, so I'm missing out on life by not having nice feelings.

Interviewer:

When you *do* have good feelings, what do they feel like inside?

Erica:

 I don't know how to explain it. . . . I don't know what love is, but [being with my cat] feels nice. I can look at her sometimes, and she'll be doing something that will make me smile—so that's a nice feeling. So if that's love, then I'm feeling love (*smiles*).

Interviewer:

Is there anything else you want to say about feeling positive emotions like love or happiness?

Erica:

No, except that I want to feel them. I really do.

Interviewer:

You talked earlier about being outside your body. Can you describe this a little more?

Erica:

When I'm in that position, I'm not in control of my body properly. I can't be present. It makes me self-conscious. I'm wondering if people can see it, and then the shame and all of the above happens. It's like I'm sitting beside myself. When I was in the bars, I'd be on stage, and I would call it "going into character." All the girls in the bars dissociate like that, every one of them. You can watch the girls on stage, and sometimes you see them fall out of character. Then you see them get back into character, and the show goes smoothly again. Being out of body helps me get through a lot of things. But sometimes it's bad because I need to be there to deal with the situation, and I can't always bring myself back.

Interviewer:

What would it be like for you to be in an intimate relationship?

Erica:

I could not imagine it. All I can see in myself is a collection of orifices. I could not imagine ever being in an intimate relationship.

Interviewer:

The next question is about hearing voices. Is that something that you have experienced?

Erica:

 No, that's not something I have experienced.

Interview 4: Gregory

Gregory is a 59-year-old man who suffered repeated emotional and physical abuse at the hands of his father and sexual abuse at the hands of his grandmother. Unfortunately, Gregory's mother was unable to protect him from this abuse. Gregory was functioning adequately until he was assaulted by a coworker at his place of work 10 years ago. After this incident, which reminded him of the abuse he had experienced during his childhood, Gregory developed severe symptoms of PTSD, dissociation, and depression. Gregory began exhibiting dissociative symptoms, including the loss of a sense of time, chronic symptoms of depersonalization and derealization, and identity confusion. He was rarely aware of the present moment and exhibited cognitive slowing related to his dissociative symptoms. At the time of the present writing, Gregory has made tremendous progress in therapy. He is now more able to enjoy his marital relationship, his cottage in the woods, and is employed part-time, which is a source of pleasure for him. The interview with Gregory demonstrates especially well TRASC of time, body, and emotion.

Interviewer:

Have you ever felt like you were back in the past, had flashbacks or relived a memory as if it was happening in the here and now?

Gregory:

Yes.

Interviewer:

What is that like?

Gregory:

When I am feeling in the past, I can't actually realize I am reliving the past. The emotions I feel are usually quite extreme and I think they are happening to me right now in the present. But after I manage to get control of the dissociation, I realize that the feelings are recognized and are from past traumas that I had in childhood or adolescence. Then I look around for a reason why I am feeling these things but usually I can't find it, so I get even more confused—because there is nothing to pin point why I am feeling dissociated and emotionally charged.

Interviewer:

What do you mean by feeling dissociated?

Gregory:

I feel numb, and everything is very confusing. Someone will speak to me and it is like they are speaking to me in a foreign language that I do not understand. And I can be zoned out to the extent that I feel the problem is with them and not with me. That creates a lot of problems, because I will be very insistent that it is not me that has a problem at all—it is the outside world that has the problems.

Interviewer:

Can we return to the experience of reliving a memory or reliving a past event? Can you tell me a little about what it is like for you to have these experiences?

Gregory:

Normally I would get the body sensations of the past event first—kind of a feeling. If the past event has involved some sort of abuse or physical contact, like someone hitting you, I will feel numb or hot in the area that was previously affected first before I get any emotion. Then the emotion will creep in and I will try and think, "What around me has caused that?" But of course it is nothing because it is coming from the past. If I am aware enough, I will make a connection that it is coming from the past and I will be able to ground myself. But if I can't find any connection, if I don't have enough awareness that it is something that has happened in the past, I can carry on being dissociated all day.

Interviewer:

What would that feel like, being dissociated all day?

Gregory:

Like my body feels numb to touch and everything is kind of "echoey." Like if you got a cold or flu and you have these symptoms throughout the day and you might know what they are, but you can't do anything about it.

It is usually after I have been triggered, but sometimes I just don't know what triggered me. I am not aware of the trigger. If I *am* aware of the trigger I can usually effectively ground myself. But if I am not aware of the trigger, it is as if someone has just slipped it into my life without me knowing. So I don't recognize it as being something from the past, I am looking around in the present trying to find what it is that is upsetting me or disturbing me. And actually I don't find anything because it is not there. Or if I am really feeling belligerent I will blame somebody. That causes big problems at home.

Interviewer:

How about feeling emotionally numb? Is that something you have experienced?

Gregory:

Yes—feeling emotionally numb is very real. *It's almost like it is another feeling on its own.* It's like you have been living all your life with all these feelings and you know what they are. You know love and hate and sadness and the rest of them, and you can identify them, and then suddenly emotionally numb comes along and it is like a new feeling—*it is the absence of all feelings.* You don't feel *anything.* You are not even (*pause*) it's kind of like a safeguard—that someone could come up to you and say horrible things and you just look back and stare at them as though they are not even there. *It's almost like a protective shield.*

Interviewer:

How about feeling empty? Have you ever had that experience?

Gregory:

Yeah. I think I tie it down to loss of hope. You can't see beyond the next hour, let alone the next day. You can't foresee what you might be doing. It leaves you without any will to continue. You really don't *want* to continue, in fact.

Interviewer:

What triggers feelings of emptiness for you?

Gregory:

Not being wanted. Being rejected. I have been looking for work for a long time, and although I try to put the feelings of emptiness out of my mind, every time I hand in a résumé and it is not accepted, I get a small feeling of rejection and that just builds up. I am afraid it will get to a point where I might end up in hospital again. So I am afraid of that. *The emptiness is very real. It is like being hungry all the time.*

Interviewer:

Have you ever had the experience of not knowing what you are feeling?

Gregory:

Do you mean that there is a feeling there but I can't identify it?

Interviewer:

Yes.

Gregory:

That's very confusing. It's even confusing to think about it.

Interviewer:

Is that something that you have experienced?

Gregory:

I think I just lump it all into anger. If I can't understand, I think I just throw it all into the anger pot. If it is not understandable I do not want to deal with it.

Interviewer:

And then what happens?

Gregory:

It builds up. The pot fills up with confusion—so it is all confusing.

Interviewer:

And what happens then?

Gregory:

I will feel like I have had enough, and it usually ends with an aggressive outburst or something.

Interviewer:

Hmm.

Gregory:

I think I know now what you mean by not understanding what the emotion is.

Interviewer:

Not knowing what you are feeling . . .

Gregory:

It is very confusing for me to answer that. It almost feels like I want to avoid that question.

Interviewer:

What's most frightening about that question?

Gregory:

There isn't an answer. It is frightening because I feel like there is no answer. Not having an answer.

Interviewer:

And not having an answer, what makes that frightening?

Gregory:

I don't know. But I am shaking all over just thinking about this right now. It is very frightening.

Interviewer:

What did that mean in the past—not having an answer?

Gregory:

If I failed at school my father would be very angry. I don't know what the connection is—that just came right out.

Interviewer:

Just remember you are in my office and it is safe here, it is OK to not have an answer. We are human, we don't have answers to many things. Are you with me?

Gregory:

I am drifting off.

Interviewer:

Try to look at me. Breathe. Remember that you are completely safe here. You are in my office. No one is going to hurt you here. You do not have to have the answer. That is not what this is about.

Gregory:

Yes, I understand.

Interviewer:

How do you feel?

Gregory:

I am controlling it.

Interviewer:

Just remember that you are completely safe here. You are in the present. No one is going to hurt you here. (*Pause until Gregory appears less agitated.*) How are you feeling now?

Gregory:

OK. Better.

Interviewer:

Will it be OK to continue with the interview?

Gregory:

Yes.

Interviewer:

OK. The next question is about not knowing what others are thinking or not being able to understand others. Is that something you have experienced?

Gregory:

Yeah, many times.

Interviewer:

Could you tell me about what that is like?

Gregory:

Well, in the literal sense it is like someone is speaking a different language at me. But I know that can't be the case, so then I know it must be me that is wrong.

Interviewer:

What is that like? Being with another person and feeling like they are speaking another language?

Gregory:

I haven't got to the bottom of it. It's something I probably need to address more in therapy. I know there is a past connection there because I feel like a shaking child. So I know somewhere in there, there is a connecting memory.

Interviewer:

OK. Perhaps, as you say, that can be addressed more in therapy. Can you now tell me about your experience of the passage of time?

Gregory:

It gets lost. It can become one big minute. Sometimes it has no passing at all. It's almost like I have walked through a time gate or something; 3 or 4 hours can pass and it seems like a minute. But I don't appreciate that 3 or 4 hours have passed. My wife will tell me that I am zoning out. I will think that I have been looking at a picture for about 30 seconds, but she will say, "No, you have been there 10 minutes." That's probably a good example.

Interviewer:

Can you say more about what the passage of time is like for you?

Gregory:

Events unfolding in a certain order, basically. Things happen logically, normally. Like you couldn't get to that door over there without me seeing you pass in front of me and pass the table. If you suddenly appeared at that door, it would be illogical. However, if you walk to that door and I saw it to be 30 seconds but you told me you did it over a period of an hour, I might not know the difference. To me it would be 30 seconds—I wouldn't know the difference. That is an extreme case . . . but I do find that things have happened and I take it that they happened quite quickly when in actual fact they have taken a long time.

Interviewer:

What is it like to experience events unfolding like that?

Gregory:

 Well, it doesn't affect me when it is happening. I think it is normal. It is only afterwards when someone has pointed it out or I look at the clock. If the clock is right than something weird has happened, because normally it doesn't take an hour for a ball to drop from the fourth floor to the ground.

Interviewer:

If you were to compare your own internal clock to a watch or a clock on the wall, what would that be like?

Gregory:

 I would say that my clock doesn't have any hands on it.

Interviewer:

Can you tell me what you mean by that?

Gregory:

 On my clock there is no passage of time.

Interviewer:

We spoke earlier about what it is like to feel emotionally numb. Have you ever found that the feeling of emotional numbness and the passage of time are related?

Gregory:

They could be connected, but I haven't actually tested that out because when things do stop or slow down, I am not aware. So I wouldn't be inclined to test it, because I am not aware that anything is wrong. For example, I don't know how long we have been in this office—I have no idea.

Interviewer:

If you had to guess, what would you guess?

Gregory:

Two hours?

Interviewer:

It has been half an hour.

Gregory:

Even that doesn't mean anything to me, *half an hour*. Honestly, it doesn't. I don't believe I know how long a half an hour is . . . I have lost it.

Interviewer:

So when I say to you, "half an hour," what does that mean to you?

Gregory:

To me "half an hour" means, when I look at my watch now and identify what time it is now, I know 30 minutes will pass when the hand gets to 20 after. But the actual experience of how long that is—I think I've lost that.

Interviewer:

Have you had the experience of not being able to feel positive emotions, like love, happiness, joy, or pleasure? Or not being able to smile or laugh easily?

Gregory:

All of those things just seem to happen during periods of numbness. Because [otherwise] I *can* laugh and smile. But I kind of hesitate to say *love*. And I hesitate to say *fear*.

Interviewer:

Why do you hesitate?

Gregory:

Because I am not sure if I can feel those.

Interviewer:

Fear and love?

Gregory:

Yeah. My interpretation is distorted.

Interviewer:

Can you tell me more about that?

Gregory:

I think I have got the incorrect interpretation of it—love. And fear is very much tangled up with anger.

Interviewer:

Can you tell me more about love and fear, what they mean to you?

Gregory:

Well, it's like if you came up and pinched my thumb and said to me, "Oh, that's love," I would take your word for it, and then forever more associate the feeling of a pinched finger with love. I think I have got things mixed up.

Interviewer:

Have you experienced love?

Gregory:

I think I have.

Interviewer:

When you think about love, what comes to mind?

Gregory:

Someone wanting me. And all the associated actions that come with that.

Interviewer:

Such as?

Gregory:

🦋 Touching, feeling, and . . . the other person being considerate.

Interviewer:

How about fear?

Gregory:

🦋 Fear is kind of the opposite. Someone wanting to take stuff away from me. It's going to leave me empty. Fear will leave me empty. Sometimes *very* empty. Empty enough not to want to carry on anymore.

Interviewer:

What emotion gives you the most hope, making you want to go on?

Gregory:

Love.

Interviewer:

Can you say more about what feeling love is like?

Gregory:

🦋 I find that it affects everything. So it's not really just an individual emotion. It kind of gets attached to everything else. So it kind of changes everything. Even *sad* doesn't feel as sad. And painful things don't feel as painful. Stuff that demands a lot of care and attention doesn't feel as strenuous to do. So it's like a coating on top.

Interviewer:

Do you experience that in your life right now?

Gregory:

I don't.

Interviewer:

How about being outside of your body?

Gregory:

 I experience that sometimes, yeah.

Interviewer:

What's that like?

Gregory:

It's like I have grown a very long neck and I am looking down on things. *It appears things are being viewed from above—or sometimes below.*

Interviewer:

What's that like?

Gregory:

It feels very physical when that's happening. It feels like my body is being stretched and I know that I am not normal when that happens. I know that it is not normal. I am aware of it. It is not something I can skirt around. It is something so plainly obvious that I know that it is happening. It can happen when I just feel I want to get away from something.

Interviewer:

For example . . . ?

Gregory:

Situations that I am in.

Interviewer:

For example . . . ?

Gregory:

Um . . . a bad situation maybe. It doesn't always happen while a bad situation is occurring, but it very often happens after it. It feels very much out of control. It's almost like you are going up and down on a rollercoaster, that feeling of losing gravity. It's physical . . . like going up and down in an elevator. I actually feel that.

Interviewer:

How about hearing voices inside your head? Is that something you have experienced?

Gregory:

I don't get that. As far as I know, I don't get that. I sometimes talk to myself but . . . that's not hearing voices.

Interviewer:

How about feeling shame? Is that something you have experienced?

Gregory:

Occasionally I feel that. But not very often.

Interviewer:

What is feeling shame like for you?

Gregory:

Disappointment is probably the nearest thing I can think of to describe that. That would be my nearest word I can think of.

Interviewer:

How about feeling like you are frozen—is that something you have experienced?

Gregory:

Yeah, I have felt like I am frozen. That's when time actually stops still completely, and I am not. . . . That's when I am still going at normal speed and everything else is stopped. Everything else is frozen.

Interviewer:

What would that mean?

Gregory:

That's very dangerous. Something dangerous is going on and I don't know what's happening.

Interviewer:

And what is that experience like?

Gregory:

I don't feel my body. My eyes can move and my brain can think and that's it.

Interviewer:

What is it like to not feel your body?

Gregory:

There is no feeling. I don't feel it. It's completely isolated. There is no feeling at all.

Interviewer:

What words would you use to describe yourself?

Gregory:

I have to say I don't think I am a very nice person to be with. My ex-wife kept saying that to me. That's her words, not mine.

Interviewer:

We are looking for your words . . .

Gregory:

I enjoy creating things. I enjoy transforming a bunch of raw materials into something that people like. I like giving gifts to people because it makes them happy with me. I think I work pretty hard at things, [and] I don't give up very easily. I like order, but my life is continually a mess. I like geometry. Chaos has got an attraction for me. Chaos seems natural.

Interviewer:

Are there any other words that come to mind when you think about describing yourself?

Gregory:

I'm not really sure if my existence is real. I may be really good at convincing myself that my existence is reality.

Interviewer:

Can you tell me more about that?

Gregory:

What I perceive as reality might just be an elaborate dream because my dreams, or visions I have when I am apparently asleep, appear as real to me as waking up does, or . . . *sometimes if I am numb I might as well be in a dream. There is very little difference.*

Interviewer:

What's it been like to answer these questions?

Gregory:

I am hoping to get some answers for myself as we go along. I think there may have been one or two. I don't think I could have answered these questions as clearly a couple of years ago.

Interviewer:

They take a lot of reflection.

Gregory:

Yeah. I am quite aware that a few years ago I was in a constant state of dissociation, I think. When I thought I was out of dissociation, a few years ago, I was actually in a lighter state of dissociation. I considered that to be baseline, but it isn't. I know even now I am not there. I am aware of the fact that I am not there.

Interviewer:

But you are getting closer . . .

Gregory:

If I can hold down a job, I will be much better able to give that answer more consideration.

Interview 5: Valerie

Valerie is a 25-year-old woman who suffered repeated emotional, physical, and sexual abuse during her childhood at the hands of her father and uncle. She has experienced symptoms of PTSD and depression dating back to her childhood. However, these symptoms worsened after she witnessed a murder on a bus trip. Valerie also has a long history of interpersonal difficulties related to problems with assertiveness and low self-esteem. Valerie has progressed well in therapy. She has learned to regulate her intense emotional states much better. Moreover, her interpersonal relationships have ceased to be abusive. Valerie has recently begun working as a personal support worker, which has been a great source of joy for her. The interview with Valerie describes well TRASC of time and thought.

Interviewer:

Have you ever felt that you were back in the past, had flashbacks, or felt as if a memory were happening again in the here and now?

Valerie:

Yes. Almost every day.

Interviewer:

Can you tell me about what is it like to have such experiences?

Valerie:

 I feel like I am back to being a little girl and then I struggle with not understanding how a 25-year-old is supposed to respond. I could be feeling like I am back to being 14 or being 6 at any given time. Also with my neighbors not understanding the PTSD aspect, I shut down a lot, or all of a sudden I will cry a lot. A lot of the time I feel isolated because I don't know . . . I hold it in because I don't want to . . . I don't know how to express it to my husband or to my neighbors. My neighbors are kind of close-minded to what I am going through. They say, "Oh, you should just not live in the past" but yet . . . it's hard . . . it's hard because when the flare-ups—I call them *flare-ups*—when it flares up, I get—when they tell me not to live in the past, it's like they don't see the fact that it is so much of me.

Interviewer:

Can you tell me more about what it is like to experience a flashback?

Valerie:

 Feeling like a little kid.

Interviewer:

OK. And have you ever had the feeling of being emotionally numb?

Valerie:

The times that I feel emotionally numb are when my neighbors expect me to be OK after everything, and then I just sit there, and take whatever they are saying to me . . . then I become numb and afterwards I just cry because I can't, it feels like I can't show my emotions. I feel like I should take what they say to me with a grain of salt and not interpret it, but yet I don't know . . . just being numb—I don't tell even my husband or my mother-in-law what is going on. I try to pretend that I am fine and that I don't need to express. Sometimes my husband does understand the PTSD flare-ups but yet he still is not used to seeing it. And my mother-in-law, who I see almost every day, she doesn't know when there is a flare-up happening, and she tries to convince my husband to give me space and let me be OK.

Interviewer:

Is it hard for you when the people around you don't know what it is like to have PTSD?

Valerie:

Yes, especially people who say they have been through worse and have moved forward, and I have struggled so much to move forward and be OK. Sometimes I have to try hard and say I have moved forward, but yet . . . it's not so easy.

Interviewer:

Have you ever experienced the feeling of emptiness?

Valerie:

Everyday.

Interviewer:

What is it like for you to feel empty?

Valerie:

A lot of time—at any given time throughout the day—I will feel like I haven't done enough, or I am still that little person that struggles, and I feel empty—I don't want to do anything. I just hide in my bed, and hide in my apartment without answering the door. Or I will try to explain it to my mother-in-law, who is a little bit more understanding, and she tries to get my husband to understand a little more. Yet it is harder because I don't want to unload on her. So it's a tough feeling—being empty all the time. I am on depression medications and yet I am still so empty and so isolated.

Interviewer:

What about the experience of not knowing what you are feeling? Have you experienced this?

Valerie:

Everyday.

Interviewer:

Can you describe this experience—what it is like?

Valerie:

Sometimes I feel like my emotions are completely clouding my judgment. And I actually don't know if I am supposed to be happy, scared—I don't know if I should be fine being around people—and it's hard because I can't figure out what is OK, and I can't tell if I am being used by my neighbors or not. So it's tough. I don't know if I am supposed to feel happy around my neighbors, or if I should just shut down around them, because all they want from me is to move forward, and it is not so easy to do that. When I am having a bad day, they don't get it, so it is even more tough to figure out what emotion to feel around them.

Interviewer:

Have you ever had difficulty knowing what others are thinking or feeling? Not being able to understand?

Valerie:

When my neighbors try to explain how they are feeling, I try to disconnect myself so I don't take on their problems. I know they have moved forward, but I can't handle when they are struggling financially or handle them thinking that I am acting like a little girl in their eyes. And I can't explain to them that this is my state of mind, not knowing if it is a little girl or if it is me struggling with reality. Sometimes I think that they are thinking I am just an easy target for them to use, which is hard because I had to work so hard to try to be at the age of 25, and keep that maturity, yet I don't have it so easy.

Interviewer:

Can you tell me more about what it is like to have trouble understanding others?

Valerie:

I sometimes have trouble with understanding them as . . . that they are not users, they are not family members that have used me in the past. And understanding that they are only there to help me, even when they don't realize it is more trouble than good. Or I try to understand that I can't help everyone—I need to look after myself—but yet I am so used to handing out so much and I don't know how to stop.

Interviewer:

Do you sometimes have trouble experiencing positive emotions, like love, happiness, joy, or pleasure? Or that you find that you are not able to smile or laugh easily?

Valerie:

Yes.

Interviewer:

Can you describe what that is like?

Valerie:

It is hard when I am around my in-laws because I try to seem that I am OK—and that I am OK being with them, and I need their support. It's hard to explain to them that I am wanting to be away from them—I am scared to feel their love, because they have had such an impact—and being stuck in such a way of thinking. It's hard to not take away from them. It's hard. I want to help my in-laws, and feel their love, and feel normal—someone that doesn't have so many issues. But it is really hard. Or to feel happy that I am going on a trip out of town. It is hard to be OK.

Interviewer:

You mentioned that you might have problems feeling happy about going on a trip—can you tell me more about that?

Valerie:

🪴⌛ It's especially with family trips. It is scary. I enjoy it, yet I wait to see what is going to happen, because sometimes I am scared that something bad is going to happen next. I am scared that they might drop me off and not pick me up. Or they will leave me behind. I am just . . . I am not used to having two parents—even though they are my in-laws—having two parents that care enough to include me. Happiness—I am scared it is not going to last, if they see how broken I am now. Sometimes I don't know *what* to feel inside. Is it real or is it something else?

Interviewer:

Have you ever had the feeling of being outside your body?

Valerie:

🪞 Every once in a while when I . . . if my neighbors yell at me or get upset with me, I will just sit there and take it, and my body and mind won't stay, [they] will drift. I will take on what they are saying . . .

Interviewer:

What would happen then?

Valerie:

🪴🪞 For me, I cry a lot when they yell at me. And I want to separate myself, so I don't take it on emotionally, and then I try to say, "Well, they don't know the true side of me, they don't know how much damage there is, how much my PTSD *does* play a role." So I try to separate myself.

Interviewer:

What about things feeling unreal around you, like the world around you seems abnormal or is very strange?

Valerie:

Sometimes.

Interviewer:

Can you talk about what this is like?

Valerie:

Sometimes, being home alone, I don't feel like I am in the city of [residence]—I sometimes want to be in an unreal world—that way I don't get hurt so easy, or so I don't feel. But sometimes I feel lost, and I can't let go and be OK with it. And sometimes I just want to hide from the world. I can't cope. Or it's having my neighbors or my husband yell at me because I don't understand how much I need (*pause*). . . . My husband tells me I need to "grow a set," to get stronger and speak up. But yet I can't speak up so easy, and sometimes it is unreal to me for someone to say, "You need to get yourself together and be OK." And then they tell me if I don't get any better, they can put me in a hospital and it's like, they have unreal expectations of me in that sense. No matter what, they won't see how much it plagues, how much it weighs on me. The flare-ups have to do with what's going on around me. So they have a lot of unreal expectations. If I don't fill the role of what they want, then who am I really? I am not 100%. PTSD is my life. And for all the unrealistic expectations of me being this 25-year-old mature person, or being OK with everything around me, I have to wear that mask of "Yeah, I am fine" when I am not really real to myself.

Interviewer:

Have you ever heard voices inside your head?

Valerie:

Yes.

Interviewer:

Can you describe what hearing voices is like? What happens?

Valerie:

Sometimes the voices try to convince me to do self-harm, which I never act on. Or I sometimes I hear my neighbors judging me harshly. Or I will hear my mother's voice saying I failed as an independent woman if I struggle financially. Or I will hear that I am just like my father—I can't do anything right, I can't do what normal people do, I can't work a normal job without so many struggles. I hear all those voices. Or I will hear my mother-in-law's voice saying that I am no good because I cannot be independent. I can't pay for my own groceries because I depend on her, and I am only married to her son for the money. But it is not the case.

Interviewer:

Are there any other voices that you sometimes hear?

Valerie:

Child voices.

Interviewer:

Can you describe what that is like?

Valerie:

It is the little me saying that I am not taking care of myself. Or that I am no good. Those kinds of voices.

Interviewer:

Are there any other voices that you sometimes hear?

Valerie:

Sometimes my grandparents.

Interviewer:

What happens with those voices? What do you experience?

Valerie:

Basically they tell me that I am doing good, and sometimes I am doing bad because I am not as strong as I should be, or that I am too fat because I am not active enough. Or that I am just . . . tired. Just to be OK with the world when I am not.

Interviewer:

Do you experience feelings of shame?

Valerie:

 Everyday, because I can't work a job and I can't perform normal tasks. I can't cook as good as I used to, or I am not eating as well as I should. I am ashamed of smelling, because I haven't had a shower or I still stink. Or that there are people that have worked a normal job and since coming out here, I haven't worked a job. And I feel shameful because I am 25 and I should be able to work a job. I should be fine with working. I should be fine being around men. I should be fine with all these things and I am not. It is very devastating.

Interviewer:

What it is like when you feel threatened or afraid?

Valerie:

I shut down.

Interviewer:

Can you describe what this is like? What happens?

Valerie:

I try and hide. Or I will try and do something else like painting or drawing. Figure out ways to do other things.

Interviewer:

Have you ever had the feeling of being frozen in fear?

Valerie:

Sometimes. Whenever I am on a crowded bus. When my in-laws were trying to pick me up from activities because I feel if I am in a crowded spot, I don't want to move. Or sometimes I want to get out as fast as possible because I can't handle what is around. That way I am not stuck in that spot.

Interviewer:

What about your body going limp or waxy? Or feeling as if you are dead, even just for a moment?

Valerie:

Sometimes.

Interviewer:

Can you describe what you experience?

Valerie:

Sometimes it is when I am home alone and I am zoning out or my body is . . . my arm has fallen asleep, it goes completely limp, and sometimes I feel dead.

Concluding Remarks

Even though the descriptions above have taken us to some of the darkest experiences a human being can endure, they also demonstrate a remarkable capacity for resilience and recovery. Despite tremendous suffering, Suzy, Stephanie, Erica, Gregory, and Valerie persisted and persevered in the face of tremendous hardship, and all continue to work toward recovering from their traumatic events in therapy. Chapter 7 described how, partly through a stage-oriented approach to trauma-focused psychotherapy, even severe TRASC of time, thought, one's body, and emotion can be healed and restored. The recovered self is then able to more fully experience peace, joy, and pleasure in the context of meaningful interpersonal relationships.

References

Abrams, M. P., Carleton, R. N., Taylor, S., & Asmundson, G. J. G. (2009). Human tonic immobility: Measurement and correlates. *Depression and Anxiety, 26*(6), 550–556. *doi:* 10.1002/da.20462

Abu-Akel, A., & Shamay-Tsoory, S. (2011). Neuroanatomical and neurochemical bases of theory of mind. *Neuropsychologia, 49*, 2971–2984. *doi:* 10.1016/j.neuropsychologia.2011.07.012

Adams, B., & Sanders, T. (2011). Experiences of psychosis in borderline personality disorder: A qualitative analysis. *Journal of Mental Health*, *20*(4), 381-391. doi: 10.3109/09638237.2011.577846

Aldao, A., Nolen-Hoeksema, S., & Schweizer, S. (2010). Emotion-regulation strategies across psychopathology: A meta-analytic review. *Clinical Psychology Review, 30*(2), 217–237. doi: 10.1016/j.cpr.2009.11.004

Alia-Klein, N., Goldstein, R. Z., Tomasi, D., Zhang, L., Fagin-Jones, S., Telang, F., . . . Volkow, N. D. (2007). What's in a word?: No versus yes differentially engages the lateral orbitofrontal cortex. *Emotion, 7*(3), 649–659. doi: 10.1037/1528-3542.7.3.649

Allen, J. G. (2001). *Traumatic relationships and serious mental disorders*. New York, NY: Wiley.

Allen, J. G. (2012). Trauma. In A. W. Bateman & P. Fonagy (Eds.) *Handbook of mentalizing in mental health practice* (pp. 419–444). Washington, DC: American Psychiatric Publishing.

Allen, J. G., & Fonagy, P. (2006). *Handbook of mentalization-based treatment*. Chichester, West Sussex, UK: Wiley.

Allen, J. G., Fonagy, P., & Bateman, A W. (2008). *Mentalizing in clinical practice*. Washington, DC: American Psychiatric Publishing.

Allen, P., Larøi, F., McGuire, P. K., & Aleman, A. (2008). The hallucinating brain: A review of structural and functional neuroimaging studies of hallucinations. *Neuroscience and Biobehavioral Reviews. (31)*1, 175–191. doi: 10.1016/j.neubiorev.2007.07.012

American Psychiatric Association. (2000). *Diagnostic and statistical manual of mental disorders* (4th ed., text rev.). Washington, DC: Author.

American Psychiatric Association. (2013). *Diagnostic and statistical manual of mental disorders* (5th ed.). Washington, DC: Author.

Andersen, S. L., Tomada, A., Vincow, E. S., Valente, E., Polcari, A., & Teicher, M. H. (2008). Preliminary evidence for sensitive periods in the effect of childhood sexual abuse on regional brain development. *Journal of Neuropsychiatry & Clinical Neurosciences, 20*, 292–301. doi: 10.1176/appi.neuropsych.20.3.292

Anderson, M. C., Ochsner, K. N., Kuhl, B., Cooper, J. C., Robertson, E., Gabrieli, S. W., . . . Gabrieli, J. D. E. (2004). Neural systems underlying the suppression of unwanted memories. *Science, 303*, 232–235. *doi:* 10.1126/science.1089504

Angrilli, A., Cherubini, P., Pavese, A., & Manfredini, S. (1997). The influence of affective factors on time perception. *Perception & Psychophysics, 59*(6), 972–982. *doi:* 10.3758/BF03205512

Anketell, C., Dorahy, M. J., Shannon, M., Elder, R., Hamilton, G., Corry, M., . . . O'Rawe, B. (2010). An exploratory analysis of voice hearing in chronic PTSD: Potential associated mechanisms. *Journal of Trauma & Dissociation, 11*(1), 93–107. doi: 10.1080/15299730903143600

Appelhans, B. M., & Luecken, L. J. (2006). Heart rate variability as an index of regulated emotional responding. *Review of General Psychology, 10*(3), 229–240. doi: 10.1037/1089-2680.10.3.229

Arditi-Babchuk, H., Feldman, R., & Gilboa-Schechtman, E. (2009). Parasympathetic reactivity to recalled traumatic and pleasant events in trauma-exposed individuals. *Journal of Traumatic Stress, 22*(3), 254–257. doi: 10.1002/jts.20417

Arntz, A. (2011) Imagery rescripting for personality disorders. *Cognitive & Behavioral Practice, 18*(4), 466–481. doi: 10.1016/j.cbpra.2011.04.006

Arntz, A., Tiesema, M., & Kindt, M. (2007). Treatment of PTSD: A comparison of imaginal exposure with and without imagery rescripting. *Journal of Behavior Therapy & Experimental Psychiatry, 38*(4), 345–370. doi: 10.1016/j.jbtep.2007.10.006

Ayduk, Ö., & Kross, E. (2010). From a distance: Implications of spontaneous self-distancing for adaptive self-reflection. *Journal of Personality & Social Psychology, 98*(5), 809–829. doi: 0.1037/a0019205

Badcock, J. C., & Hugdahl, K. (2012). Cognitive mechanisms of auditory verbal hallucinations in psychotic and non-psychotic groups. *Neuroscience and Biobehavioural Reviews, 36*(1), 431–438. doi: 10.1016/j.neubiorev.2011.07.010

Badura, A. S. (2003). Theoretical and empirical exploration of the similarities between emotional numbing in posttraumatic stress disorder and alexithymia. *Journal of Anxiety Disorders, 17*(3), 349–360. doi:10.1016/S0887-6185(02)00201-3

Bagby, R. M., Parker, J. D. A., & Taylor, G. J. (1994). The twenty-item Toronto Alexithymia Scale: I. Item selection and cross-validation of the factor structure. *Journal of Psychosomatic Research, 38*(1), 23–32. doi: 10.1016/0022-3999(94)90005-1

Bagby, R. M., Taylor, G. J., Parker, J. D. A., & Dickens, S. E. (2006). The development of the Toronto Structured Interview for Alexithymia: Item selection, factor structure, reliability and concurrent validity. *Psychotherapy and Psychosomatics, 75*(1), 25–39. doi: 10.1159/000089224

Baier, B., & Karnath, H. O. (2008). Tight link between our sense of limb ownership and self-awareness of actions. *Stroke, 39,* 486–488. doi: 10.1161/STROKE AHA.107.495606

Bak, M., Krabbendam, L., Janssen, I., Graaf, R., Vollebergh, W., & van Os, J. (2005). Early trauma may increase the risk for psychotic experiences by impacting on emotional response and perception of control. *Acta Psychiatrica Scandinavica, 112*(5), 360–366. doi: 10.1111/j.1600-0447.2005.00646.x

Baker, D., Hunter, E., Lawrence, E., Medford, N., Patel, M., Senior, C., & David, A. S. (2003). Depersonalisation disorder: Clinical features of 204 cases. *British Journal of Psychiatry, 182*(5), 428–433. doi: 10.1192/bjp.182.5.428

Baldwin, D. V. (2013). Primitive mechanisms of trauma response: An evolutionary perspective on trauma-related disorders. *Neuroscience & Biobehavioral Reviews, 37,* 1549–1566. *doi:* 10.1016/j.neubiorev.2013.06.004

Bar-Haim, Y., Karem, A., Lamy, D., & Zakay, D. (2010). When time slows down: The influence of threat of time perception in anxiety. *Cognition & Emotion, 24* (2), 255–263. doi: 10.1080/02699930903387603

Barnier, A. J., Cox, R. E., Connors, M., Langdon, R., & Coltheart M. (2011). A stranger in the looking glass: Developing and challenging a hypnotic mirrored-self misidentification delusion. *International Journal of Clinical & Experimental Hypnosis, 59*(1), 1–26. doi: 10.1080/00207144.2011.522863

Barnier, A. J., Cox, R. E., O'Connor, A., Coltheart, M., Langdon, R., Breen, N., & Turner, M. (2008). Developing hypnotic analogues of clinical delusions: Mirrored-self misidentification. *Cognitive Neuropsychiatry, 13*(5), 406–430. doi: 10.1080/13546800802355666

Barnier, A. J., & Oakley, D. A. (2009). Hynosis and suggestion. In W. Banks (Ed.), *Encyclopedia of consciousness* (pp. 351–368). London: Academic Press.

Barrett, L. F. (2006a). Are emotions natural kinds? *Perspectives on Psychological Science, 1*, 28–58. doi: 10.1111/j.1745-6916.2006.00003.x

Barrett, L. F. (2006b). Solving the emotion paradox: Categorization and the experience of emotion. *Personality & Social Psychology Review, 10*, 20–46. doi: 10.1207/s15327957pspr1001_2

Barrett, L. F. (2009). Variety is the spice of life: A psychological construction approach to understanding variability in emotion. *Cognition & Emotion, 23*, 1284–1306. doi: 10.1080/02699930902985894

Barrett, L. F. (2012). Emotions are real. *Emotion, 12*, 413–429. doi: 10.1037/a0027555

Barrett, L. F., & Gendreon, M. (2009). Reconstructing the past: A century of ideas about emotion in psychology. *Emotion Review, 1*, 316–339. doi: 10.1177/1754073909338877

Barrett, L. F., Lindquist, K. A., Gendron, M. (2007). Language as context for the perception of emotion. *Trends in Cognitive Sciences, 11*, 327–332. doi: 10.1016/j.tics.2007.06.003

Barrett, L. F., Mesquita, B., Ochsner, K. N., & Gross, J. J. (2007). The experience of emotion. *Annual Review of Psychology, 58*, 373–403. doi: 10.1146/annurev.psych.58.110405.085709

Barrett, T. R., & Etheridge, J. B. (1992). Verbal hallucinations in normals: I. People who hear voices. *Applied Cognitive Psychology, 6*, 379–387. *doi:* 10.1002/acp.2350060503

Bateman, A. W., & Fonagy, P. (2012). *Handbook of mentalizing in mental health practice.* Washington, DC: American Psychiatric Association.

Bayne, T. (2004). Closing the gap?: Some questions for neurophenomenology. *Phenomenology and the Cognitive Sciences, 3*(4), 349–364. doi:10.1023/B:PHEN.0000048934.34397.ca

Beavan, V. (2011). Towards a definition of "hearing voices": A phenomenological approach. *Psychosis, 3*, 63–73. doi: 10.1080/17522431003615622

Beavan, V., & Read, J. (2010). Hearing voices and listening to what they say: The importance of voice content in understanding and working with distressing voices. *Journal of Nervous & Mental Disease, 198*(3), 201–205. doi: 10.1097/NMD.0b013e3181d14612

Beavan, V., Read, J., & Cartwright, C. (2011). The prevalence of voice-hearers in the general population: A literature review. *Journal of Mental Health, 20*(3), 281–292. doi: 10.3109/09638237.2011.562262

Beere, D. B. (1995). Loss of the "background": A perceptual theory of dissociation. *Dissociation, 8*, 166–174.

Beere, D. B. (2009). Dissociative perceptual reactions: The perceptual theory of dissociation. In P. F. Dell & J. A. O'Neil (Eds.) *Dissociation and the dissociative disorders: DSM-V and beyond* (pp. 209–224). NewYork: Routledge.

Bell, V., Oakley, D. A., Halligan, P. W., & Deeley, Q. (2012). Dissociation in hysteria and hypnosis: Evidence from cognitive neuroscience. *Journal of Neurology, Neurosurgery, & Psychiatry, 82*(3), 332–339. *doi:* 10.1136/jnnp.2009.199158

Belsky, J. (1980). Child maltreatment: An ecological integration. *American Psychologist, 35*, 320–335. *doi:* 10.1037/0003-066X.35.4.320

Benish, S. G., Imel, Z. E., & Wampold, B. E. (2008). The relative efficacy of bona fide psychotherapies for treating posttraumatic stress disorder: A meta-analysis of direct comparisons. *Clinical Psychology Review, 28*(5), 746–758. doi: 10.1016/j.cpr.2007.10.005

Berenbaum, H., & James, T. (1994). Correlates and retrospectively reported antecedents of alexithymia. *Psychosomatic Medicine, 56*(4), 353–359. doi: 0033-3174/94/5604-0353503.00/0

Bernard, M., Jackson, C., & Jones, C. (2006). Written emotional disclosure following first-episode psychosis: Effects on symptoms of post-traumatic stress disorder. *British Journal of Clinical Psychology, 45*(3), 403–415. doi:10.1348/014466505X68933

Bernstein, E. M., & Putnam, F. W. (1986). Development, reliability, and validity of a dissociation scale. *Journal of Nervous & Mental Disease, 174*(12), 727–735. doi: 10.1097/00005053-198612000-00004

Berntsen, D., & Rubin, D. C. (2006). Emotion and vantage point in autobiographical memory. *Cognition & Emotion, 20*(8), 1193–1215. doi: 10.1080/02699930500371190

Berntsen, D., & Rubin, D. C. (2007). When a trauma becomes a key to identity: Enhanced integration of trauma memories predicts posttraumatic stress disorder symptoms. *Applied Cognitive Psychology, 21*(4), 417–431. doi: 10.1002/acp.1290

Berntsen, D., & Rubin, D. C. (2008). The reappearance hypothesis revisited: Recurrent involuntary memories after traumatic events and in everyday life. *Memory & Cognition, 36*(2), 449–460. doi: 10.3758/MC.36.2.449

Berntsen, D., Rubin, D. C., & Siegler, I. C. (2011). Two versions of life: Emotionally negative and positive life events have different roles in the organization of life story and identity. *Emotion, 11*(5), 1190–1201. doi: 10.1037/a0024940

Berntsen, D., & Thomsen, D. K. (2005). Personal memories for remote historical events: Accuracy and clarity of flashbulb memories related to World War II. *Journal of Experimental Psychology, 134*(2), 242–257. doi: 10.1037/0096-3445.134.2.242

Berntsen, D., Willert, M., & Rubin, D. C. (2003). Splintered memories or vivid landmarks?: Qualities and organization of traumatic memories with and without PTSD. *Applied Cognitive Psychology, 17*(6), 675–693. doi: 10.1002/acp.894

Berthoz, S., Artiges, E., Van de Moortele, P.-F., Poline, J.-B., Rouquette, S., Consoli, S. M., & Martinot, J.-L. (2002). Effect of impaired recognition and expression of emotions on frontocingulate cortices: An fMRI study of men with alexithymia. *American Journal of Psychiatry, 159*, 961–967. *doi:* 10.1176/appi.ajp.159.6.961

Betemps, E. J., Smith, R. M., Baker, D. G., & Rounds-Kugler, B. A. (2003). Measurement precision of the Clinician Administered PTSD Scale (CAPS): A RASCH model analysis. *Journal of Applied Measurement, 4*(1), 59–69.

Birmes, P. J., Brunet, A., Coppin-Calmes, D., Arbus, C., Coppin, D., & Charlet, J. (2005). Symptoms of peritraumatic and acute traumatic stress among victims of an industrial disaster. *Psychiatric Services, 56*(1), 1075–1273. doi: 10.1176/appi.ps.56.1.93

Bishop, S. R., Lau, M., Shapiro, S., Carlson, L., Anderson, N. D., Carmody, J., . . . Devins, G. (2004). Mindfulness: A proposed operational definition. *Clinical Psychology: Science and Practice, 11*(3), 230–241. doi: 10.1093/clipsy/bph077

Blanke, O., & Metzinger, T. (2009). Full-body illusions and minimal phenomenal selfhood. *Trends in Cognitive Sciences, 13*(1), 7–13. doi: 10.1016/j.tics.2008.10.003

Blanke, O., Ortigue, S., Landis, T., & Seeck, M. (2002). Stimulating illusory own-body perceptions. *Nature, 419*(6904), 269–270. doi: 10.1038/419269a

Blevins, C. A., Witte, T. K., & Weathers, F. W. (2013). Factor structure of the Cambridge Depersonalization Scale in trauma-exposed college students. *Journal of Trauma and Dissociation, 14*, 288–301. doi: 10.1080/15299732.2012.729555

Bluhm, R. L., Frewen, P. A., Coupland, N. C., Densmore, M., Schore, A. N., & Lanius, R. A. (2012). Neural correlates of self-reflection in post-traumatic stress disorder. *Acta Psychiatrica Scandinavica, 125*(3), 238–246. doi: 10.1111/j.1600-0447.2011.01773.x

Bluhm, R. L., Williamson, P. C., Osuch, E. A., Frewen, P. A., Stevens, T. K., Boksman, K., ... Lanius, R. A. (2009). Alterations in default network connectivity in posttraumatic stress disorder related to early-life trauma. *Journal of Psychiatry & Neuroscience, 34*(3), 187–194.

Blum, A. (2008). Shame and guilt, misconceptions and controversies: A critical review of the literature. *Traumatology, 14*(3), 91–102. doi: 10.1177/1534765608321070

Boals, A. (2010). Events that have become central to identity: Gender differences in the Centrality of Event Scale for positive and negative events. *Applied Cognitive Psychology, 24*(1), 107–121. doi: 10.1002/acp.1548

Bohus, M., Dyer, A. S., Priebe, K., Kruger, A., & Steil, R. (2010). Dialectical behavior therapy for posttraumatic stress disorder in survivors of childhood sexual abuse. *Psychotherapy & Psychosomatic Medicine, 61*(3–4), 140–147. doi: 10.1055/s-0030-1263162

Bonanno, G. A., Noll, J. G., Putnam, F. W., O'Neill, M., & Trickett, P. (2003). Predicting the willingness to disclose childhood sexual abuse from meures of repressive coping and dissociative experiences. *Child Maltreatment, 8*, 1–17. doi: 10.1177/1077559503257066

Bortolotti, L., Cox, R., & Barnier, A. (2012). Can we recreate delusions in the laboratory? *Philosophical Psychology, 25*(1), 109–131. doi: 10.1080/09515089.2011.569909

Botvinick, M., & Cohen, J. (1998). Rubber hands "feel" touch that eyes see. *Nature, 391*(6669), 756. doi:10.1038/35784

Bovin, M. J., Jager-Hyman, S., Gold, S. D., Marx, B. P., & Sloan, D. M. (2008). Tonic immobility mediates the influence of peritraumatic fear and perceived inescapability on posttraumatic stress symptom severity among sexual assault survivors. *Journal of Traumatic Stress, 21*(4), 402–409. doi:10.1002/jts.20354

Bovin, M. J., & Marx, B. P. (2011). The importance of the peritraumatic experience in defining traumatic stress. *Psychological Bulletin, 137*(1), 47–67. doi: 10.1037/a0021353

Braakman, M. H., Kortman, F. A. M., & van den Brink, W. (2009). Validity of post-traumatic stress disorder with secondary psychotic features: A review of the evidence. *Acta Psychiatrica Scandinavica, 119*(1), 15–24. doi:10.1111/j.1600-0447.2008.01252.x

Bracha, H. S. (2004). Freeze, flight, fight, fright, faint: Adaptationist perspectives on the acute stress response spectrum. *CNS Spectrums, 9*, 679–685.

Bracha, H. S., & Maser, J. D. (2008). Anxiety and posttraumatic stress disorder in the context of human brain evolution: A role for theory in DSM-V? *Clinical Psychology: Science & Practice, 15*, 91–97. doi: 10.1111/j.1468-2850.2008.00113.x

Bradley, M. M., Codispoti, M., Cuthbert, B. N., & Lang, P. J. (2001). Emotion and motivation: I. Defensive and appetitive reactions in picture processing. *Emotion, 1*(3), 276–298. *doi:* 10.1037/1528-3542.1.3.276

Braithwaite, J. J., James, K., Dewe, H., Medford, N., Takahashi, C., & Kessler, K. (2013). Fractionating the unitary notion of dissociation: Disembodied but not embodied dissociative experiences are associated with egocentric perspective taking. *Frontiers in Human Neuroscience, 7,* 1. doi: 10.3389/fnhum.2013.00719

Brand, B. L., Armstrong, J. G., & Loewenstein, R. J. (2006). Psychological assessment of patients with dissociative identity disorder. *Psychiatric Clinics of North America, 29,* 145–168. doi: 10.1016/j.psc.2005.10.014

Brand, B. L., Lanius, R., Vermetten, E., Loewenstein, R. J., & Spiegel, D. (2012). Where are we going?: An update on assessment, treatment and neurobiological research in dissociative disorders as we move toward the DSM-5. *Journal of Trauma & Dissociation, 13,* 9–31. doi: 10.1080/15299732.2011.620687

Brand, M., Eggers, C., Reinhold, N., Fujiwara, E., Kessler, J., Heiss, W., & Markowitsch, D. (2009). Functional brain imaging in 14 patients with dissociative amnesia reveals right inferolateral prefrontal hypometabolism. *Psychiatry Research, 174*(1), 32–39. doi: 10.1016/j.pscychresns.2009.03.008

Bremner, J. D. (1999). Acute and chronic responses to psychological trauma: Where do we go from here? *American Journal of Psychiatry, 156,* 349–351.

Bremner, J. D., Krystal, J. H., Putnam, F. W., Southwick, S. M., Marmar, C., Charney, D. S., et al. (1998). Measurement of dissociative states with the Clinician-Administered Dissociative States Scale (CADSS). *Journal of Traumatic Stress, 11*(1): 125–136. doi: 10.1023/A:1024465317902

Brentano, F. C. (1968). *Psychologie vom empirischen standpunkt.* Hamburg, Germany: F. Meiner.

Brewin, C. R. (1998). Intrusive autobiographical memories in depression and post-traumatic stress disorder. *Applied Cognitive Psychology, 12*(4), 359–370. doi: 10.1002/(SICI)1099-0720(199808)12:4<359::AID-ACP573>3.0.CO;2-5

Brewin, C. R. (2001). Memory processes in post-traumatic stress disorder. *International Review of Psychiatry, 13*(3), 159–163. doi: 10.1080/09540260120074019

Brewin, C. R. (2007). Autobiographical memory for trauma: Update on four controversies. *Memory, 15*(3), 227–227. doi:10.1080/09658210701256423

Brewin, C. R. (2011). The nature and significance of memory disturbance in post-traumatic stress disorder. *Annual Review of Clinical Psychology, 7,* 203–227. doi: 10.1146/annurev-clinpsy-032210-104544

Brewin, C. R., Andrews, B., & Valentine, J. D. (2000). Meta-analysis of risk factors for posttraumatic stress disorder in trauma-exposed adults. *Journal of Consulting and Clinical Psychology, 68*(5), 748. doi: 10.1037/0022-006X.68.5.748

Brewin, C. R., Dalgleish, T., & Joseph, J. (1996). A dual representation theory of posttraumatic stress disorder. *Psychological Review, 103,* 670–686. doi: 10.1037/0033-295X.103.4.670

Brewin, C. R., Gregory, J. D., Lipton, M., & Burgess, N. (2010). Intrusive images in psychological disorders: Characteristics, neural mechanisms, and treatment implications. *Psychological Review, 117*(1), 210–232. doi:10.1037/a0018113

Brewin, C. R., Ma, B. Y. T., & Colson, J. (2013). Effects of experimentally induced dissociation on attention and memory. *Conciousness & Cognition, 22,* 315–323. doi: http://dx.doi.org/10.1016/j.concog.2012.08.005

Brewin, C. R., & Patel. (2010). Auditory pseudohallucinations in United Kingdom war veterans and civilians with posttraumatic stress disorder. *Journal of Clinical Psychiatry, 71*(4), 419–425. doi: 10.4088/JCP.09m05469blu

Bridge, H., Harrold, S., Holmes, E. A., Stokes, M., & Kennard, C. (2012). Vivid visual mental imagery in the absence of the primary visual cortex. *Journal of Neurology, 259,* 1062–1070. doi: 10.1007/s00415-011-6299-z

Briere, J. (2002). *Multiscale Dissociation Inventory (MDI)*. Lutz, FL: Psychological Assessment Resources.

Briere, J., & Runtz, M. (1987). Post-sexual abuse trauma: Data and implications for clinical practice. *Journal of Interpersonal Violence, 2,* 367–379. *doi:* 10.1177/088626058700200403

Briere, J., & Runtz, M. (1993). Childhood sexual abuse: Long-term sequelae and implications for psychological assessment. *Journal of Interpersonal Violence, 8,* 312–330. *doi:* 10.1177/088626093008003002

Briere, J., Weathers, F. W., & Runtz, M. (2005). Is dissociation a multidimensional construct?: Data from the Multiscale Dissociation Inventory. *Journal of Traumatic Stress, 18,* 221–231. doi: 10.1002/jts.20024

Britton, J., Phan, K., Taylor, S., Welsh, R., Berridge, K., & Liberzon, I. (2006). Neural correlates of social and nonsocial emotions: An fMRI study. *NeuroImage, 31*(1), 397–409. doi: 10.1016/j.neuroimage.2005.11.027

Britton, J., Taylor, S., Berridge, K., Mikels, J., & Liberzon, I. (2006). Differential subjective and psychophysiological responses to socially and nonsocially generated emotional stimuli. *Emotion, 6*(1), 150–155. doi: 10.1037/1528-3542.6.1.150

Bromberg, P. M. (1998). *Standing in the spaces*. London: Analytic Press.

Brown, K. W., Ryan, R. M., & Creswell, J. D. (2007). Mindfulness: Theoretical foundations and evidence for its salutary effects. *Psychological Inquiry, 18*(4), 211–237. doi: 10.1080/10478400701598298

Brown, M. Z., Comtois, K. A., & Linehan, M. M. (2002). Reasons for suicide attempts and nonsuicidal self-injury in women with borderline personality disorder. *Journal of Abnormal Psychology, 111*(1), 198. doi: 10.1037/0021-843X.111.1.198

Brown, R. J. (2002). The cognitive psychology of dissociative states. *Cognitive Neuropsychiatry, 7,* 221–235. *doi:* 10.1080/13546800244000085

Brown, R. J. (2004). The psychological mechanisms of medically unexplained symptoms: An integrative conceptual model. *Psychological Bulletin, 130,* 793–812. *doi:* 10.1037/0033-2909.130.5.793

Brown, R. J. (2006). Different types of "dissociation" have different psychological mechanisms. *Journal of Trauma & Dissociation, 7*(4), 7–28. doi:10.1300/J229v07n04_02

Brown, R. J., Cardena, E., Nijenhuis, E., Sar, V., & van der Hart, O. (2007). Should conversion disorder be reclassified as a dissociative disorder in DSM-V? *Psychosomatics, 48*(5), 369–378. doi: 10.1176/appi.psy.48.5.369

Brunet, A., Weiss, D. S., Metzler, T. J., Best, S. R., Neylan, T. C., Rogers, C., & Marmar, C. R. (2001). The peritraumatic distress inventory: A proposed measure of PTSD criterion A2. *American Journal of Psychiatry, 158*(9), 1480–1485. doi: 10.1176/appi.ajp.158.9.1480

Bryant, R. A., O'Connell, M. L., Creamer, M., McFarlane, A. C., & Silove, D. (2011). Posttraumatic intrusive symptoms across psychiatric disorders. *Journal of Psychiatric Research, 45,* 842-847. doi:10.1016/j.jpsychires.2010.11.012

Buckner, R. L., Andrews-Hanna, J. R., & Schacter, D. L. (2008). The brain's default network: Anatomy, function, and relevance to disease. *Annals of the New York Academy of Science, 1124,* 1–38. doi: 10.1196/annals.1440.011

Buhrmester, M. D., Blanton, H., & Swann, W. B. (2011). Implicit self-esteem: Nature, measurement, and a new way forward. *Journal of Personality and Social Psychology, 100*(2), 365–385. doi: 10.1037/a0021341

Buhusi, C. V., & Meck, W. H. (2005). What makes us tick?: Functional and neural mechanisms of interval timing. *Nature Reviews Neuroscience, 6,* 755–765. doi: 10.1038/nrn1764

Burgess, P. W., Gilbert, S. J., & Dumontheil, I. (2007). Function and localization within rostral prefrontal cortex (area 10). *Philosophical Transactions of the Royal Society of London, Series B, Biological Sciences, 362*(1481), 887–899. doi: 10.1098/rstb.2007.2095

Butler, L. D. (2004). The dissociations of everyday life. *Journal of Trauma & Dissociation, 5*, 1–11. doi: 10.1300/J229v05n02_01

Butler, L. D. (2006). Normative dissociation. *Psychiatric Clinics of North America, 29*, 45–62. doi: 10.1016./j.psc.2005.10.004

Butler, L. D., Duran, R. E. F., Jasiukaitis, P., Koopman, C., & Spiegel, D. (1996). Hynotizablity and traumatic experience: A diathesis–stress model of dissociative symptomatology. *American Journal of Psychiatry, 7*, 42–63.

Cacioppo, J. T., & Berntson, G. G. (1994). Relationship between attitudes and evaluative space: A critical review, with emphasis on the separatability of positive and negative substrates. *Psychological Bulletin, 115*, 401–423. doi: 10.1037/0033-2909.115.3.401

Cacioppo, J. T., Gardner, W. L., & Berntson, G. G. (1999). The affect system has parallel and integrative processing components: Form follows function. *Journal of Personality & Social Psychology, 76*, 839–855. doi: 10.1037/0022-3514.76.5.839

Campbell, B. A., Wood, G., & McBride, T. (1997). Origins of orienting and defense responses: An evolutionary perspective. In P. J. Lang, R. F. Simmons, & M. T. Balaban (Eds.), *Attention and orienting: Sensory and motivational processes* (pp. 41–67). Hillsdale, NJ: Erlbaum.

Caputo, G. B. (2010a). Strange-face-in-the-mirror illusion. *Perception, 39*(7), 1007. doi: 10.1068/p6466

Caputo, G. B. (2010b). Apparitional experiences of new faces and dissociation of self-identity during mirror gazing. *Perceptual and Motor Skills, 110*(3B), 1125–1138. doi: 10.2466/pms.110.C.1125-1138

Cardeña, E. (1994). The domain of dissociation. In S. J. Lynn & J. W. Rhue (Eds.), *Dissociation: Clinical and theoretical aspects* (pp. 5–31). New York, NY: Guilford Press.

Carlson, E. B., Dalenberg, C., & McDade-Montez, E. (2012). Dissociation in post-traumatic stress disorder part I: Definitions and review of research. *Psychological Trauma: Theory, Research, Practice, and Policy, 4*(5), 479–489. doi: 10.1037/a0027748

Carrick, N., & Quas, J. A. (2006). Effects of discrete emotions on young children's ability to discern fantasy and reality. *Developmental psychology, 42*(6), 1278. doi: 10.1037/0012-1649.42.6.1278

Carrick, N., Quas, J. A., & Lyon, T. (2010). Maltreated and nonmaltreated children's evaluations of emotional fantasy. *Child Abuse & Neglect, 34*, 129–134. doi: 10.1016/j.chiabu.2009.02.009

Carrick, N., & Ramirez, M. (2012). Preschoolers' fantasy–reality distinctions of emotional events. *Journal of Experimental Child Psychology, 112*, 467–483. doi: http://dx.doi.org/10.1016/j.jecp.2012.04.010

Carver, C. S., & Harmon-Jones, E. (2009). Anger is an approach-related affect: Evidence and implications. *Psychological Bulletin, 135*, 183–204. doi: 10.1037/a0013965

Caspi, Y., Gil, S., Ben-Ari, I. Z., Koren, D., Aaron-Peretz, J., & Klein, E. (2005). Memory of the traumatic event is associated with increased risk for PTSD: A retrospective study of patients with traumatic brain injury. *Journal of Loss & Trauma, 10*(4), 319–355. doi: 10.1080/15325020590956756

Chapman, A. L., Gratz, K. L., & Brown, M. Z. (2006). Solving the puzzle of deliberate self-harm: The experiential avoidance model. *Behaviour Research and Therapy, 44*(3), 371–394. 10.1016/j.brat.2005.03.005

Cheng, R.-K., Ali, Y. M., & Meck, W. H. (2007). Ketamine "unlocks" the reduced clock-speed effects of cocaine following extended training: Evidence for dopamine–glutamate interactions in timing and time perception. *Neurobiology of Learning & Memory, 88*(2), 149–159. doi: 10.1016/j.nlm.2007.04.005

Choi, J., Jeong, B., Polcari, A., Rohan, M. L., & Teicher, M. H. (2012). Reduced fractional anisotropy in the visual limbic pathway of young adults witnessing domestic violence in childhood. *NeuroImage, 59*(2), 1071–1079. doi: 10.1016/j.neuroimage.2011.09.033

Chu, J. A. (2011). *Rebuilding shattered lives: Treating complex PTSD and dissociative disorders* (2nd ed.). Hoboken, NJ: Wiley.

Cicchetti, D., & Lynch, M. (1993). Toward an ecological/transactional model of community child maltreatment: Consequences for children's development. *Psychiatry: Interpersonal & Biological Processes, 56*, 96–118.

Cicchetti, D., & Toth, S. L. (2005). Child maltreatment. *Annual Review of Clinical Psychology, 1*, 409–438. doi: 10.1146/annurev.clinpsy.1.102803.144029

Clapp, J. D., & Beck, J. G. (2009). An examination of the Glover Numbing Scale: Expanding the content validity of posttraumatic numbing. *Journal of Psychopathology & Behavioral Assessment, 31*(3), 256–263. doi:10.1007/s10862-008-9116-y

Clayton, K. (2004). The interrelatedness of disconnection: The relationship between dissociative tendencies and alexithymia. *Journal of Trauma & Dissociation, 5*(1), 77–101. doi:10.1300/J229v05n01_05

Cloitre, M., Courtois, C. A., Charuvastra, A., Carapezza, R., Stolback, B. A., & Green, B. L. (2011). Treatment of complex PTSD: Results of the ISTSS expert clinician survey on best practices. *Journal of Traumatic Stress, 24*(6), 615–627. doi: 10.1002/jts.20697

Cohen, H., Benjamin, J., Geva, A. B., Matar, M. A., Kaplan, Z., & Kotler, M. (2000). Autonomic dysregulation in panic disorder and in post-traumatic stress disorder: Application of power spectrum analysis of heart rate variability at rest and in response to recollection of trauma or panic attacks. *Psychiatry Research, 96*, 1–13. *doi:* 10.1016/S0165-1781(00)00195-5

Cohen, H., Kotler, M., Matar, M. A., Kaplan, Z., Miodowni, H., & Cassuto, Y. (1997). Power spectral analysis of heart rate variability in posttraumatic stress disorder. *Biological Psychiatry, 41*, 627–629. *doi:* 10.1016/S0006-3223(96)00525-2

Connors, M., Barnier, A., Coltheart, M., Cox, R., & Landon, R. (2012). Mirrored-self misidentification in the hypnosis labratory: Recreating the delusion from its component factors. *Cognitive Neuropsychiatry, 17*(2), 151–176. doi: 10.1080/13546805.2011.582287

Connors, M., Cox, R., Barnier, A., Langdon, R., & Coltheart, M. (2012). Mirror agnosis and the mirrored-self misidentification delusion: A hypnotic analogue. *Cognitive Neuropsychiatry, 17*(3), 197–226. doi: 10.1080/13546805.2011.582770

Constantino, M. J., Arnkoff, D. B., Glass, C. R., Ametrano, R. M., & Smith, J. Z. (2011). Expectations. *Journal of Clinical Psychology, 67*(2), 184–192. doi: 10.1002/clp.20754

Conway, M. (2005). Memory and the self. *Journal of Memory & Language, 53*(4), 594–628. doi: 10.1016/j.jml.2005.08.005

Conway, M., Meares, K., & Standart, S. (2004). Images and goals. *Memory, 12*(4), 525–531. doi: 10.1080/09658210444000151

Conway, M., & Pleydell-Pearce, C. (2000). The construction of autobiographical memories in the self-memory system. *Psychological Review, 107*(2), 261–288. doi: 10.1037/0033-295X.107.2.261

Conway, M., Singer, J., & Tagini A. (2004). The self and autobiographical memory: Correspondence and coherence. *Social Cognition, 22*(5), 491–529. doi: 10.1521/soco.22.5.491.50768

Corcoran, K. M., Farb, N., Anderson, A., & Segal, Z. V. (2010). Mindfulness and emotion regulation: Outcomes and possible mediating mechanisms. In A. M. Kring & D. M. Sloan (Eds.), *Emotion regulation and psychopathology: A transdiagnostic approach to etiology and treatment* (pp. 339–355). New York, NY: Guilford Press.

Constanzo, M., & Archer, D. (1989). Interpreting the expressive behavior of others: The Interpersonal Perception Task. *Journal of Nonverbal Behavior, 13*(4), 225–245. doi: 10.1007/BF00990295

Coull, J., & Nobre, A. (2008). Dissociating explicit timing from temporal expectation with fMRI. *Current Opinion in Neurobiology, 18*(2), 137–144. doi: 10.1016/j.conb.2008.07.011

Courtois, C. A. (2004). Complex trauma, complex reactions: Assessment and treatment. *Psychotherapy: Theory, Research, Practice, and Training, 41*, 412–425. doi: 10.1037/0033-3204.41.4.412

Courtois, C. A., & Ford, J. D. (2009). *Treating complex traumatic stress disorders: An evidence-based guide.* New York, NY: Guilford Press.

Cox, R. E., & Barnier, A. J. (2009). Selective information processing in hypnotic identity delusion: The impact of time of encoding and retrieval. *Contemporary Hypnosis, 26*(2), 65–79. doi: 10.1002/ch.358

Cox, R. E. & Barnier, A. J. (2010). Hypnotic illusions and clinical delusions: Hypnosis as a research method. *Cognitive Neuropsychiatry, 15*(1), 202–232. doi: 10.1080/13546800903319884

Craig, A. D. (2002). How do you feel? Interoception: The sense of the physiological condition of the body. *Nature Reviews Neuroscience, 3*(8), 655–666. doi:10.1038/nrn894

Craig, A. D. (2003). Interoception: The sense of the physiological condition of the body. *Current Opinion in Neurobiology, 13*, 500–505. doi 10.1016/S0959-4388(03)00090-4

Craig, A. D. (2005). Forebrain emotional aymmetry: A neuroanatomical basis? *Trends in Cognitive Sciences, 9*(12), 566–571. doi: 10.1016/j.tics.2005.10.005

Craig, A. D. (2009a). How do you feel—now?: The anterior insula and human awareness. *Nature Reviews Neuroscience, 10*(1), 59–70. doi:10.1038/nrn2555

Craig, A. D. (2009b). Emotional moments across time: A possible neural basis for time perception in the anterior insula. *Philosophical Transanctions of the Royal Society of London B, Biological Sciences, 364*, 1933–1942. doi: 10.1098/rstb.2009.0008

Craig, A. D. (2010). The sentient self. *Brain Structure & Function, 214*, 563–577. doi: 10.1007/s00429-010-0248-y

Craik, F. I., Moroz, T.-M., Moscovitch, M., Stuss, D. T., Winocur, G., Tulving, E., & Kapur, S. (1999). In search of the self: A positron emission tomography study. *Psychological Science, 10*, 26–34. doi: 10.1111/1467-9280.00102

Critchley, H. D. (2004). The human cortex responds to an interoceptive challenge. *Proceedings of the National Academy of Sciences, U. S. A., 101*, 6333–6334. doi: 10.1073/pnas.0401510101

Critchley, H. D. (2005). Neural mechanisms of autonomic, affective, and cognitive integration. *Journal of Comparative Neurology, 493*, 154–166. doi: 10.1002/cne.20749

Critchley, H. D., Matthias, C. J., Joesphs, O., O'Doherty, J., Zanini, S., Dewar, B. K., . . . Dolan, R. J. (2003). Human cingulate cortex and autonomic control: Converging neuroimaging and clinical evidence. *Brain, 126*, 2139–2152. doi: 10.1093/brain/awg216

Critchley, H. D., Melmed, R. N., Featherstone, E., Mathias, C. J., & Dolan, R. J. (2001). Brain activity during biofeedback relaxation: A functional neuroimaging investigation. *Brain, 124*, 1003–1012. doi: 10.1093/brain/124.5.1003

Critchley, H. D., Melmed, R. N., Featherstone, S., Mathias, C. J., & Dolan, R. J. (2002). Volitional control of autonomic arousal: A functional magnetic resonance imaging study. *NeuroImage, 16,* 909–919. doi: 10.1006/nimg.2002.1147

Critchley, H. D., Tang, J., Glaser, D., Butterworth, B., & Dolan, R. J. (2005). Anterior cingulate activity during error and autonomic response. *NeuroImage, 27,* 885–895. doi: 10.1016/j.neuroimage.2005.05.047

Daalman, K., Boks, M., Diederen, K., de Weijer, A., Blom, J., Kahn, R., . . . Sommer, I. (2011). The same or different?: A phenomenological comparison of auditory verbal hallucinations in healthy and psychotic individuals. *Journal of Clinical Psychiatry, 72*(3), 320–325. doi: 10.4088/JCP.09m05797yel

Daalman, K., Diederen, K. M., Derks, E. M., van Lutterveld, R., Kahn, R. S., & Sommer, I. E. (2012). Childhood trauma and auditory verbal hallucinations. *Psychological Medicine,42*(12), 1–10. doi: http://dx.doi.org/10.1017/S0033291712000761

Dalenberg, C. A., Brand, B. L., Gleaves, D.H., Dorahy, M. J., Loewenstein, R. J., Cardeña, E., . . . Spiegel, D. (2012). Comparison of the trauma and fantasy models of dissociation. *Psychological Bulletin, 138,* 550–588. doi: 10.1037/a0027447

Dalenberg, C., & Carlson, E. B. (2012). Dissociation in posttraumatic stress disorder: Part II. How theoretical models fit the empirical evidence and recommendations for modifying the diagnostic criteria for PTSD. *Psychological Trauma: Theory, Research, Practice, & Policy, 4*(6), 551–559. doi: 10.1037/a0027900

Dalenberg, C. J., & Paulson, K. (2009). The case for the study of "normal" dissociation processes. In P. F. Dell & J. A. O'Neil (Eds.) *Dissociation and the dissociative disorders: DSM-V and beyond* (pp. 145–154). New York, NY: Routledge.

Dalgleish, T., & Power, M. J. (2004). The I of the storm: Relations between self and conscious emotion experience: Comment on Lambie and Marcel (2002). *Psychological Review, 111*(3), 812–819. doi: 10.1037/0033-295X.111.3.812

Damasio, A. (1999). *The feeling of what happens: Body and emotion in the making of consciousness.* Fort Worth, TX: Harcourt College Publishers.

Daniels, J. K., Coupland, N. J., Hegadoren, K. M., Rowe, B. H., Densmore, M., Neufeld, R. W., & Lanius, R. A. (2012). Neural and behavioral correlates of peritraumatic dissociation in an acutely traumatized sample. *Journal of Clinical Psychiatry, 73*(4), 420–426. doi: 10.4088/JCP.10m06642

Daniels, J. K., Frewen, P., McKinnon, M. C., & Lanius, R. A. (2011). Default mode alterations in posttraumatic stress disorder related to early-life trauma: A developmental perspective. *Journal of Psychiatry & Neuroscience, 36,* 56–59. doi: 10.1503/jpn.100050

Davey, G. C. (2011). Disgust: The disease-avoidance emotion and its dysfunctions. *Philosophical Transactions of the Royal Society B, Biological Sciences, 366*(1583), 3453–3465. doi: 10.1098/rstb.2011.0039

David, D. H., & Lyons-Ruth, K. (2005). Differential attachment responses of male and female infants to frightening maternal behavior: Tend or befriend versus fight or flight? *Infant Mental Health Journal, 26,* 1–18. *doi:* 10.1002/imhj.20033

Davidson, R. J. (1998). Affective style and affective disorders: Perspectives from affective neuroscience. *Cognition & Emotion, 12*(3), 307–330. doi: 10.1080/026999398379628

Davis, M. H. (1983). Measuring individual differences in empathy: Evidence for a multidimensional approach. *Journal of Personality & Social Psychology, 44*(1), 113–126. doi: 10.1037/0022-3514.44.1.113

De Bellis, M. D., & Keshavan, M. S. (2003). Sex differences in brain maturation in maltreatment-related pediatric posttraumatic stress disorder. *Neuroscience & Biobehavioral Reviews, 27*(1), 103–117. doi: 10.1016/S0149-7634(03)00013-7

De Bellis, M. D., Keshavan, M. S., Frustaci, K., Shifflett, H., Iyengar, S., Beers, S. R., & Hall, J. (2002). Superior temporal gyrus volumes in maltreated children and adolescents with PTSD. *Biological Psychiatry, 51*(7), 544–552. doi:10.1016/S0006-3223(01)01374-9

De Bellis, M. D., & Kuchibhatia, M. (2006). Cerebellar volumes in pediatric maltreatment-related posttraumatic stress disorder. *Biological Psychiatry, 60*(7), 697–703. doi: 10.1016/j.biopsych.2006.04.035

de Charms, C. R. (2008). Applications of real-time fMRI. *Nature Reviews Neuroscience, 9*(9), 720–729. doi: 10.1038/nrn2414

Deeley, Q., Oakley, D. A., Toone, B., Giampietro, V., Brammer, M. J., Williams, S. C. R., & Halligan, P. W. (2012). Modulating the default mode network using hypnosis. *International Journal of Clinical & Experimental Hypnosis, 60*(2), 206–228. doi: 10.1080/00207144.2012.648070

Dell, P. F. (2001). Why the diagnostic criteria for dissociative identity disorder should be changed. *Journal of Trauma & Dissociation, 2*, 7–37. doi: 10.1097/00005053-200201000-00003

Dell, P. F. (2006a). A new model of dissociative identity disorder. *Psychiatric Clinics of North America, 29*(1), 1–28. doi: 10.1016/j.psc.2005.10.013

Dell, P. F. (2006b). The Multidimensional Inventory of Dissociation (MID): A comprehensive measure of pathological dissociation. *Journal of Trauma & Dissociation, 7*, 77–106. *doi:* 10.1300/J229v07n02_06

Dell, P. F. (2009a). The phenomena of pathological dissociation. In P. F. Dell & J. A. O'Neil (Eds.), *Dissociation and the dissociative disorders: DSM–V and beyond* (pp. 225–237). New York, NY: Routledge.

Dell, P. F. (2009b). Understanding dissociation. In P. F. Dell & J. A. O'Neil (Eds.), *Dissociation and the dissociative disorders: DSM–V and beyond* (pp. 709–826). New York, NY: Routledge.

Dell, P. F., & Lawson, D. (2009). An empirical delineation of the domain of pathological dissociation. In P. F. Dell & J. A. O'Neil (Eds.), *Dissociation and the dissociative disorders: DSM–V and beyond* (pp. 667–692). New York, NY: Routledge.

Dell, P., & O'Neil, J. A. (2009). *Dissociation and the dissociative disorders: DSM-V and beyond.* New York, NY: Routledge.

Del Prete, G., & Tressoldi, P. (2005). Anomalous cognition in hyponagogic state with OBE induction: An experimental study. *Journal of Parapsychology, 69*(2), 329–339.

den Boer, J. A., Reinders, A. A. T. S., & Glas, G. (2008). On looking inward: Revisiting the role of introspection in neuroscientific and psychiatric research. *Theory & Psychology, 18*(3), 380–403. doi:10.1177/0959354308089791

Dennett, D. C. (1987). *The intentional stance.* Cambridge, MA: MIT Press.

Denny, B. T., Kober, H., Wager, T. D., & Ochsner, K. N. (2012). A meta-analysis of functional neuroimaging studies of self- and other judgements reveals a spatial gradient for mentalizing in medial prefrontal cortex. *Journal of Cognitive Neuroscience, 24*, 1–11. doi: 10.1162/jocn_a_00233

Denson, T. F., DeWall, C. N., & Finkel, E. J. (2012). Self-control and aggression. *Current Directions in Psychological Science, 21*(1), 20–25. doi: 10.1177/0963721411429451

Denson, T. F., Pedersen, W. C., Ronquillo, J., & Nandy, A. S. (2009). The angry brain: Neural correlates of anger, angry rumination, and aggressive personality. *Journal of Cognitive Neuroscience, 21*, 734–744. *doi:* 10.1162/jocn.2009.21051

Denson, T. F., Ronay, R., von Hippel, W., & Schira, M. M. (2013). Endogenous testosterone and cortisol modulate neural responses during induced anger control. *Social Neuroscience, 8*(2), 165–177. doi: 10.1080/17470919.2012.655425

Depraz, N., Varela, F. J., & Vermersch, P. (2003). *On becoming aware: A pragmatics of experiencing.* Amsterdam, Netherlands: John Benjamins.

DePrince, A. P., Chu, A. T., & Pineda, A. S. (2011). Links between specific post-trauma appraisals and three forms of trauma-related distress. *Psychological Trauma: Theory, Research, Practice, and Policy, 3*(4), 430. doi: 10.1037/a0021576

De Ridder, D., Van Laere, K., Dupont, P., Menovsky, T., & Van de Heyning, P. (2007). Visualizing out-of-body experience in the brain. *New England Journal of Medicine, 357*(18), 1829–1833. doi: 10.1056/NEJMoa070010

DeWall, C. N., Anderson, C. A., & Bushman, B. J. (2011). The general aggression model: Theoretical extensions to violence. *Psychology of Violence, 1*, 245–258. doi: 10.1037/a0023842

de Weijer, A. D., Neggers, S. F., Diederen, K. M., Mandl, R. C., Kahn, R. S., Hulshoff Pol, H. E., & Sommer, I. E. (2011). Aberrations in the arcuate fasciculus are associated with auditory verbal hallucinations in psychotic and in non-psychotic individuals. *Human Brain Mapping, 34*(3), 626–634. doi: 10.1002/hbm.21463

Diederen, K., Daalman, K., de Weijer, A., Neggers, S., van Gastel, W., Blom, J., . . . Sommer, I. (2012). Auditory halluncinations elicit similar brain activation in psychotic and nonpsychotic individuals. *Schizophrenia Bulletin, 38*(5), 1074–1082. doi: 10.1093/schbul/sbr033

Diekhof, E. K., Geier, K., Falkai, P., & Gruber, O. (2011). Fear is only as deep as the mind allows: A coordinate-based meta-analysis of neuroimaging studies on the regulation of negative affect. *NeuroImage, 58,* 275–285. doi: 10.1016/j.neuroimage.2011.05.073

Dorahy, M. J., Shannon, C., Seagar, L., Corr, M., Stewart, K., Hanna, D., . . . Middleton, W. (2009). Auditory hallucinations in dissociative identity disorder and schizophrenia with and without a childhood trauma history: Similarities and differences. *Journal of Nervous & Mental Disease, 197*(12), 892–898. doi: 10.1097/NMD.0b013e3181c299eaXXX

Droit-Volet, S., & Gil, S. (2009). The time–emotion paradox. *Philosopical Transactions of the Royal Society B, Biological Sciences, 364*(1525), 1943–1953. doi: 10.1098/rstb.2009.0013

Droit-Volet, S., & Meck, W. H. (2007). How emotions colour our perception of time. *Trends in Cognitive Sciences, 11*(12), 504–513. doi: 10.1016/j.tics.2007.09.008

Droit-Volet, S., Mermillod, M., Cocenas-Silva, R., & Gil, S. (2010). The effect of expectancy of a threatening event on time perception in human adults. *Emotion, 10*(6), 908–914. doi: 10.1037/a0020258

Duke, L. A., Allen, D. N., Rozee, P. D., & Bommaritto, M. (2008). The sensitivity and specificity of flashbacks and nightmares to trauma. *Journal of Anxiety Disorders, 22,* 319–327. doi: 10.1016/j.janxdis.2007.03.002

Dutra, L., Bureau, J. F., Holmes, B., Lyubchik, A., & Lyons-Ruth, K. (2009). Quality of early care and childhood trauma: A prospective study of developmental pathways to dissociation. *Journal of Nervous and Mental Disease, 197*, 383–390. doi: 10.1097/NMD.0v013e3181a653b7

Dutra, L., Callahan, K., Forman, E., Mendelsohn, M., & Herman, J. (2008). Core schemas and suicidality in a chronically traumatized population. *Journal of Nervous & Mental Disease, 196*(1), 71–74. doi: 10.1097/NMD.0b013e31815fa4c1

Ebert, A., & Dyck, M. J. (2004). The experience of mental death: The core feature of complex posttraumatic stress disorder. *Clinical Psychology Review, 24*(6), 617–635. doi: 10.1016/j.cpr.2004.06.002

Edwards, D. (2007). Restructuring implicational meaning through memory-based imagery: Some historical notes. *Journal of Behavior Therapy & Experimental Psychiatry, 38*(4), 306–315. doi: 10.1016/j.jbtep.2007.10.001

Ehlers, A., Hackman, A., & Michael, T. (2004). Intrusive re-experiencing in post-traumatic stress disorder: Phenomenology, theory, and therapy. *Memory, 12*(4), 403–415. doi: 10.1080/09658210444000025

Ehrsson, H. H. (2007). The experimental induction of out-of-body experiences. *Science, 317*(5841), 1048. doi: 10.1126/science.1142175

Ehrsson, H. H. (2009). How many arms make a pair?: Perceptual illusion of having an additional limb. *Perception, 38*(2), 310–312. doi: 10.1068/p6304

Ehrsson, H. H., Spence, C., & Passingham, R. E. (2004). That's my hand! Activity in premortor cortex reflects feeling of ownership of a limb. *Science, 305*, 875–877. doi: 10.1126/science.1097011

Ehrsson, H. H., Weich, K., Weiskopf, N., Dolan, R. J., & Passingham, R. E. (2007). Threatening a rubber hand that you feel is yours elicits a cortical anxiety response. *Proceedings of the National Academy of Sciences U.S.A., 104*, 9828–9833. doi: 10.1073/pnas.0610011104

Einstein, A. (1994). *Ideas and opinions.* New York, NY: Crown. (Original work published 1954)

Ekman, P. (1999) Basic Emotions. In T. Dalgleish and T. Power (Eds.), *The Handbook of Cognition and Emotion* (pp. 45–60). Sussex, U.K.: John Wiley & Sons, Ltd.

Elman, I., Ariely, D., Mazar, N., Aharon, I., Lasko, N. B., Macklin, L., . . . Pitman, R. K. (2005). Probing reward function in post-traumatic stress disorder with beautiful facial images. *Psychiatry Research, 135*(3), 179–183. doi: 10.1016/j.psychres.2005.04.002

Elman, I., Lowen, S., Frederick, B. B., Chi, W., Becerra, L., & Pitman, R. K. (2009). Functional neuroimaging of reward circuitry responsivity to monetary gains and losses in posttraumatic stress disorder. *Biological Psychiatry, 66*(12), 1083–1090. doi: 10.1016/j.biopsych.2009.06.006

El-Mallakh, R. S., & Walker, K. L. (2010). Hallucinations, psuedohallucinations, and parahallucinations. *Psychiatry: Interpersonal and Biological Processes, 73*(1), 34–42. doi: 10.1521/psyc.2010.73.1.34

Elzinga, B. M., Bermond, B., & van Dyck, R. (2002). The relationship between dissociative proneness and alexithymia. *Psychotherapy & Psychosomatics, 71*(2), 104–111. doi: 10.1159/000049353

Emerson, D., & Hopper, E. (2011). Reconnecting mind to body. *Natural Solutions, 135*, 59–60.

Espirito-Santo, H., & Pio-Abreu, J. L. (2009). Portuguese validation of the Dissociative Experiences Scale (DES). *Journal of Trauma & Dissociation, 10*(1), 69–82. doi: 10.1080/15299730802485177

Etkin, A., & Wager, T. D. (2007). Functional neuroimaging of anxiety: A meta-analysis of emotional processing in PTSD, social anxiety disorder, and specific phobia. *American Journal of Psychiatry, 164*(10), 1476–1488. doi: 10.1176/appi.ajp.2007.070x30504

Evren, C., Cinar, O., & Evren, B. (2012). Relationship of alexithymia and dissociation with severity of borderline personality features in male substance-dependent inpatients. *Comprehensive Psychiatry, 53*, 854–859. doi: 10.1016/j.comppsych.2011.11.009

Evren, C., Sar, V., Evren, B., Semiz, U., Dalbudak, E., & Cakmak, D. (2008). Dissociation and alexithymia among men with alcoholism. *Psychiatry & Clinical Neurosciences, 62*, 40–47. doi: 10.1111/j.1440-1819.2007.01775.x

Fabiansson, E. C., Denson, T. F., Moulds, M. L., Grisham, J. R., & Schira, M. M. (2012). Don't look back in anger: Neural correlates of reappraisal, analytical rumination, and angry rumination during recall of an anger-inducing autobiographical memory. *NeuroImage, 59*(3), 2974–2981. doi: 10.1016/j.neuroimage.2011.09.078

Farb, N. A., Segal, Z. V., Mayberg, H., Bean, J., McKeon, D., Fatima, Z., & Anderson, A. K. (2007). Attending to the present: Mindfulness meditation reveals distinct neural modes of self-reference. *Social Cognitive and Affective Neuroscience*, *2*(4), 313–322. doi: 10.1093/scan/nsm030

Farrer, C., Franck, N., Georgieff, N., Frith, C. D., Decety, J., & Jeannerod, M. (2003). Modulating the experience of agency: A positron emission tomography study. *NeuroImage*, *18*(2), 324–333. doi: 10.1016/S1053-8119(02)00041-1

Favazza, A. R. (1998). The coming of age of self-mutilation. *Journal of Nervous and Mental Disease*, *186*(5), 259–268.

Feeny, N. C., Zoellner, L. A., & Foa, E. B. (2000). Anger, dissociation, and post-traumatic stress disorder among female assault victims. *Journal of Traumatic Stress*, *13*, 89–100. doi: 10.1023/A:1007725015225

Feldman-Barrett, L., & Russell, J. A. (1999). The structure of current affect: Controversies and emerging consensus. *Current Directions in Psychological Science*, *8*, 10–14. doi: 10.1111/1467-8721.00003

Fikretoglu, D., Brunet, A., Best, S., Metzler, T., Delucchi, K., Weiss, D. S., & Marmar, C. (2006). The relationship between peritraumatic distress and peritraumatic dissociation: An examination of two competing models. *Journal of Nervous and Mental Disease*, *194*(11), 853–858.

Finkel, E. J., DeWall, C. N., Slotter, E. B., McNulty, J. K., Pond, R. S., Jr., & Atkins, D. C. (2013). Using I³ theory to clarify when dispositional aggressiveness predicts intimate partner violence perpetration. *Journal of Personality & Social Psychology*, *102*(3), 533–549. doi: 10.1037/a0025651.

Fletcher, K. E. (2011). Understanding and assessing traumatic responses of guilt, shame, and anger among children, adolescents, and young adults. *Journal of Child & Adolescent Trauma*, *4*(4), 339–360. doi: 10.1080/19361521.2011.623146

Foa, E. B., Ehlers, A., Clark, D. M., Tolin, D. F., & Orsillo, S. M. (1999). The posttraumatic cognitions inventory (PTCI): Development and validation. *Psychological Assessment*, *11*(3), 303–314. doi: 10.1037/1040-3590.11.3.303

Foa, E. B., Molnar, C., & Cashman, L. (1995). Change in rape narratives during exposure therapy for posttraumatic stress disorder. *Journal of Traumatic Stress*, *8*(4), 675–690. doi: 10.1002/jts.2490080409

Foa, E. B., Riggs, D. S., & Gershuny, B. S. (1995). Arousal, numbing, and intrusion: Symptom structure of PTSD following assault. *American Journal of Psychiatry*, *152*, 116–122.

Fonagy, P., & Target, M. (2006). The mentalization-focused approach to self pathology. *Journal of Personality Disorders*, *20*, 544–576.

Ford, J. D., & Courtois, C. A. (2013). *Treatment of complex trauma: A sequenced, relationship-based approach.* New York, NY: Guilford Press.

Fosha, D., Siegel, D. J., & Solomon, M. F. (Eds.). (2009). *The healing power of emotion: Affective neuroscience, development, and clinical practice.* New York, NY: Norton.

Fraser, G. (2003). The dissociative table technique: A strategy for working with ego states in dissociative disorders and ego-state therapy. *Journal of Trauma & Dissociation*, *4*, 205–213. doi: 10.1300/J229v04n04_02

Fresco, D. M., Moore, M. T., van Dulmen, M. H. M., Segal, Z. V., Ma, S. H., Teasdale, J. D., & Williams, J. M. G. (2007). Initial psychometric properties of the Experiences Questionnaire: Validation of a self-report measure of decentering. *Behavior Therapy*, *38*, 234–246. doi: 10.1016/j.beth.2006.08.003

Fresco, D. M., Segal, Z. V., Buis, T., & Kennedy, S. (2007). Relationship of posttreatment decentering and cognitive reactivity to relatpse in major depression. *Journal of Consulting & Clinical Psychology*, *75*(3), 447–455. doi: 10.1037/0022-006X.75.3.447

Freud, S. (1961). *Civilisation and its discontents.* In J. Strachey (Ed. & Trans.), *The standard edition of the complete psychological works of Sigmund Freud* (Vol.

21, pp. 57–175). London: Hogarth Press and the Institute of Psychoanalysis. (Original work published 1930)

Frewen, P. A., Allen, S. L., Lanius, R. A., & Neufeld, R. W. J. (2012). Perceived causal relations: Novel methodology for assessing client attributions about causal associations between variables including symptoms and functional impairment. *Assessment, 19*(4), 480–493. doi: 10.1177/1073191111418297

Frewen, P. A., Dean, J. A., & Lanius, R. A. (2012). Assessment of anhedonia in psychological trauma: Development of the Hedonic Deficit and Interference Scale. *European Journal of Psychotraumatology, 3*, 8585. doi: 10.3402/ejpt. v3i0.8585

Frewen, P. A., Dozois, D. J., Joanisse, M. F., & Neufeld, R. W. (2008). Selective attention to threat versus reward: Meta-analysis and neural-network modeling of the dot-probe task. *Clinical Psychology Review, 28*(2), 307–337. doi: 10.1016/j.cpr.2007.05.006

Frewen, P. A., Dozois, D. J., & Lanius, R. A. (2012). Assessment of anhedonia in psychological trauma: Psychometric and neuroimaging perspectives. *European Journal of Psychotraumatology, 3*, 8587.. doi: 10.3402/ejpt.v3i0.8587

Frewen, P. A., Dozois, D. J. A., Neufeld, R. W. J., Densmore, M., Stevens, T. K., & Lanius, R. A. (2010). Social emotions and emotional valence during imagery in women with PTSD: Affective and neural correlates. *Psychological Trauma: Theory, Research, Practice, & Policy, 2*(2), 145–157. doi:10.1037/ a0019154

Frewen, P. A., Dozois, D. J. A., Neufeld, R. W. J., Densmore, M., Stevens, T. K., & Lanius, R. A. (2011a). Neuroimaging social emotional processing in women: FMRI study of script-driven imagery. *Social Cognitive & Affective Neuroscience, 6*(3), 375–392. doi:10.1093/scan/nsq047

Frewen, P. A., Dozois, D. J .A., Neufeld, R. W. J., Densmore, M., Stevens, T., & Lanius, R. A. (2011b). Self-referential processing in women with PTSD related to childhood abuse: Affective and neural response. *Psychological Trauma: Theory, Research, Practice, & Policy, 3*(4), 318–328. doi: 10.1037/a0021264

Frewen, P. A., Dozois, D. J. A., Neufeld, R. W. J., Lane, R. D., Densmore, M., Stevens, T. K., & Lanius, R. A. (2010). Individual differences in trait mindfulness predict dorsomedial prefrontal and amygdala response during emotional imagery: An fMRI study. *Personality & Individual Differences, 49*(5), 479–484. doi: 10.1016/j.paid.2010.05.008

Frewen, P. A., Dozois, D. J. A., Neufeld, R. W. J., Lane, R. D., Densmore, M., Stevens, T. K., & Lanius, R. A. (2012). Emotional numbing in PTSD: An fMRI study. *Journal of Clinical Psychiatry, 73*(4), 431–436. doi: 10.4088/JCP.10m06477

Frewen, P. A., Dozois, D. J. A., Neufeld, R. W. J., & Lanius, R. A. (2008). Meta-analysis of alexithymia in posttraumatic stress disorder. *Journal of Traumatic Stress, 21*(2), 243–246. doi: 10.1002/jts.20320

Frewen, P.A., Dozois, D. J. A., Neufeld, R. W. J., & Lanius, R.A. (2012). Disturbances of emotional awareness and expression in PTSD: Meta-mood, emotion regulation, mindfulness, and interference of emotional expressiveness. *Psychological Trauma: Theory, Research, Practice, & Policy, 4*(2), 152–161. doi: 10.1037/ a0023114

Frewen, P. A., Evans, E. M., Maraj, N., Dozois, D. J. A., & Partridge, K. (2008). Letting go: Mindfulness and negative automatic thinking. *Cognitive Therapy and Research, 32*(6), 758–774. doi:10.1007/s10608-007-9142-1

Frewen, P., Lane, R. D., Neufeld, R. W., Densmore, M., Stevens, T., & Lanius, R. (2008). Neural correlates of levels of emotional awareness during trauma script-imagery in posttraumatic stress disorder. *Psychosomatic Medicine, 70*(1), 27–31. doi: 10.1097/PSY.0b013e31815f66d4

Frewen, P. A., & Lanius, R. A. (2006a). Neurobiology of dissociation: Unity and disunity in mind-body-brain. *Psychiatric Clinics of North America, 29*(1), 113–128. doi:10.1016/j.psc.2005.10.016

Frewen, P. A., & Lanius, R. A. (2006b). Toward a psychobiology of posttraumatic self-dysregulation: Reexperiencing, hyperarousal, dissociation, and emotional numbing. *Annals of the New York Academy of Sciences, 1071*(1), 110–124. doi: 10.1196/annals.1364.010

Frewen, P. A., Lanius, R. A., Dozois, D. J. A., Neufeld, R. W. J., Pain, C., Hopper, J. W., . . . Stevens, T. K. (2008). Clinical and neural correlates of alexithymia in posttraumatic stress disorder. *Journal of Abnormal Psychology, 117*(1), 171–181. doi: 10.1037/0021-843X.117.1.171

Frewen, P. A., & Lundberg, E. (2012). Visual–verbal self/other–referential processing task: Direct vs. indirect assessment, valence, and experiential correlates. *Personality & Individual Differences, 52,* 509–514. doi:10.1016/j.paid.2011.11.021

Frewen, P. A., Lundberg, E., Brimson-Théberge, M. & Théberge, J. (2013). Neuroimaging self-esteem: A fMRI study of individual differences in women. *Social Cognitive and Affective Neuroscience, 8*(5), 546–555. doi: 10.1093/scan/nss032

Frewen, P. A., Lundberg, E., MacKinley, J., & Wrath, A. (2011). Assessment of response to mindfulness meditation: Meditation Breath Attention Scores in association with subjective measures of state and trait mindfulness and difficulty letting go of depressive cognition. *Mindfulness, 2*(4), 254–269. doi: 10.1007/s12671-011-0069-y

Frewen, P. A., Unholzer, F., Logie-Hagan, R. J., & MacKinley, J. D. (2014). Meditation Breath Attention Scores (MBAS): Test–retest reliability and sensitivity to repeated practice. *Mindfulness.* doi 10.1007/s12671-012-0161-y

Freytag, G. (1900). *Freytag's technique of the drama: An exposition of dramatic composition and art* (E. J. MacEwan, Trans.). Chicago, IL: Scott Foresman. (Original work published 1863)

Friedman, M., Resick, P., Bryant, R., & Brewin, C. R. (2011). Considering PTSD for DSM-5. *Depression & Anxiety, 28*(9), 750–769. doi: 10.1002/da.20767

Friedman, M., Resick, P., Bryant, R., Strain, J., Horowitz, M., & Spiegel D. (2011). Classification of trauma and stressor-related disorders in DSM-5. *Depression & Anxiety, 28*(9), 737–749. doi: 10.1002/da.20845

Frijda, N. H. (2005). Emotion experience. *Cognition & Emotion, 19,* 473–497. doi: 10.1080/02699930441000346

Fuller, P. R. (2010). Applications of trauma treatment for schizophrenia. *Journal of Aggression, Maltreatment, & Trauma, 19*(4), 450–463. doi: 10.1080/10926771003705114

Fulwiler, C. E., King, J. A., & Zhang, N. (2012). Amygdala-orbitofrontal resting-state functional connectivity is associated with trait anger. *NeuroReport, 23*(10), 606–610. doi: 10.1097/WNR.ob013e3283551cfc

Gallup, G. G. J., & Rager, D. R. (1996). Tonic immobility as a model of extreme stress of behavioral inhibition: Issues of methodology and measurement. In M. Kavaliers (Ed.), *Motor activity and movement disorders* (pp. 57–80). Totowa, NJ: Humana Press.

Garbarino, J. (1977). The human ecology of child maltreatment: A conceptual model for research. *Journal of Marriage and the Family, 39,* 721–727. *doi:* http://www.jstor.org.proxy1.lib.uwo.ca/stable/350477

Geuze, E., Westenberg, H. G., Jochims, A., de Kloet, C. S., Bohus, M., Vermetten, E., & Schmahl, C. (2007). Altered pain processing in veterans with posttraumatic stress disorder. *Archives of General Psychiatry, 64*(1), 76. doi: 10.1001/archpsyc.64.1.76

Giesbrecht, T., Jongen, E. M. M., Smulders, F. T. Y., & Merckelbach, H. (2006). Dissociation, resting EEG, and subjective sleep experiences in undergraduates. *Journal of Nervous and Mental Disease, 194*, 362–368. *doi:* 10.1097/01. nmd.0000217821.18908.bf

Gil, S., & Droit-Volet, S. (2009). Time perception, depression and sadness. *Behavioural Processes, 80*(2), 169–176. doi:10.1016/j.beproc.2008.11.012

Gil, S., & Droit-Volet, S. (2011). "Time flies in the presence of angry faces" . . . depending on the temporal task used. *Acta Psychologica, 136*(3), 354–362. doi: 10.1016/j.actpsy2010.12.010

Gil, S., & Droit-Volet, S. (2012). Emotional time distortions: The fundamental role of arousal. *Cognition & Emotion, 26*(5), 847–862. doi: 10.1080/02699931.2011.625401

Gilbert, P. (2011). Shame in psychotherapy and the role of compassion focused therapy. In R. L. Dearing & J. P. Tangney (Eds.), *Shame in the therapy hour* (pp. 325–354). Washington, DC: American Psychological Association.

Gilbert, S. J., Gonen-Yaacovi, G., Benoit, R. G., Volle, E., & Burgess, P. W. (2010). Distinct functional connectivity associated with lateral versus medial rostral prefrontal cortex: A meta-analysis. *NeuroImage, 53*(4), 1359–1367. doi: 10.1016/j.neuroimage.2010.07.032

Gilbert, S. J., Spengler, S., Simons, J. S., Steele, J. D., Lawrie, S. M., Frith, C. D., Burgess, P. W. (2006). Functional specialization within rostral prefrontal cortex (area 10): A meta-analysis. *Journal of Cognitive Neuroscience, 18*(6), 932–948. doi: 10.1162/jocn.2006.18.6.932

Gillihan, S. J., & Farah, M. J. (2005). The cognitive neuroscience of the self: Insights from functional neuroimaging of the normal brain. In T. E. Feinberg & J. P. Keenan (Eds.), *In the lost self: Pathologies of the brain and identity* (pp. 20–32). New York NY: Oxford University Press.

Giner-Sorolla, R., & Espinosa, P. (2011). Social cuing of guilt by anger and of shame by disgust. *Psychological Science, 22*(1), 49–53. doi: 10.1177/0956797610392925

Ginsburg, C. (2005). First-person experiments. *Journal of Consciousness Studies, 12*(2), 22–42.

Ginzburg, K., Koopman, C., Butler, L. D., Palesh, O., Kraemer, H. C., Classen, C. H., & Spiegel, D. (2006). Evidence for a dissociative subtype of post-traumatic stress disorder among help-seeking childhood sexual abuse survivors. *Journal of Trauma & Dissociation, 7*, 7–27. doi: 10.1300/J229v07n02_02

Glover, H., Lader, W., Walker-O'Keefe, J., & Goodnick, P. (1997). Numbing Scale scores in female psychiatric inpatients diagnosed with self-injurious behavior, dissociative identity disorder, and major depression. *Psychiatry Research, 70*(2), 115–123. doi:10.1016/S0165-1781(97)03039-4

Glover, H., Ohlde, C., Silver, S., Packard, P., Goodnick, P., & Hamlin, C. (1994). The Numbing Scale: Psychometric properties, a preliminary report. *Anxiety, 1*, 70–79.

Goldin, P. R., McRae, K., Ramel, W., & Gross, J. J. (2008). The neural bases of emotion regulation: Reappraisal and suppression of negative emotion. *Biological Psychiatry, 63*, 577–586. doi: 10.1016/j.biopsych.2007.05.031

Grabe, H. J., Rainermann, S., Spitzer, C., Gänsicke, M., & Freyberger, H. J. (2000). The relationship between dimensions of alexithymia and dissociation. *Psychotherapy & Psychosomatics, 69*(3), 128–131. doi: 10.1159/000012380

Greicius, M. D., Krasnow, B., Reiss, A. L., & Menon, V. (2003). Functional connectivity in the resting brain: A network analysis of the default mode hypothesis. *Proceedings of the National Academy of Sciences, U.S.A., 100*(1), 253–258. doi: 10.1073/pnas.0135058100

Greenberg, L. S., & Iwakabe, S. (2011). Emotion-focused therapy and shame. In

R. L. Dearing & J. P. Tangney (Eds.), *Shame in the therapy hour* (pp. 69–90). Washington, DC: American Psychological Association.

Grimm, S., Ernst, J., Boesiger, P., Schuepbach, D., Hell, D., Boeker, H., & Northoff, G. (2009). Increased self-focus in major depressive disorder is related to neural abnormalities in subcortical-cortical midline structures. *Human Brain Mapping, 30*(8), 2617–2627. doi: 10.1002/hbm.20693

Grondin, S. (2010). Timing and time perception: A review of recent behavioral and neuroscience findings and theoretical directions. *Attention, Perception, & Psychophysics, 72*(3), 561–582. doi:10.3758/APP.72.3.561

Gross, J. J. (1998). The emerging field of emotion regulation: An integrative review. *Review of General Psychology, 2*, 271–299. doi: 10.1037/1089-2680.2.3.271

Gross, J. J. (2002). Emotion regulation: Affective, cognitive, and social consequences. *Psychophysiology, 39*, 281–291. doi: 10.1017/S0048577201393198

Gross, J. J. (2013). Emotion regulation: Taking stock and moving forward. *Emotion, 13*, 359–365. doi: 10.1037/a0032135

Gross, J. J. (Ed.). (in press). *Handbook of emotion regulation* (2nd ed.). New York, NY: Guilford Press.

Gruber, J., Cunningham, W. A., Kirland, T., & Hay, A. C. (2012). Feeling stuck in the present?: Mania proneness and history associated with present-oriented time perspective. *Emotion, 12*, 13–17. doi: 10.1037/a0025062

Grunert, B. K., Weis, J. M., Smucker, M. R., & Christianson, H. F. (2007). Imagery rescripting and reprocessing therapy after failed prolonged exposure for post-traumatic stress disorder following industrial injury. *Journal of Behavior Therapy & Experimental Psychiatry, 38*(4), 317–328. doi: 10.1016/j.jbtep.2007.10.005

Guterstam, A., & Ehrsson, H. (2012). Disowning one's seen real body during an out-of-body illusion. *Consciousness & Cognition, 21*(2), 1037–1042. doi: 10.1016/j.concog.2012.01.018

Guz, H., Doganay, Z., Ozkan, A., Colak, E., Tomac, A., & Sarisoy, G. (2004). Conversion and somatization disorders: Dissociative symptoms and other characteristics. *Journal of Psychosomatic Research, 56*(3), 287–291. doi: 10.1016/S0022-3999(03)00069-2

Gyurak, A., Gross, J. J., & Etkin, A. (2011). Explicit and implicit emotion regulation: A dual-process framework. *Cognition and Emotion, 25*, 400–412. doi:10.1080/02699931.2010.544160

Hackman, A. (2011). Imagery rescripting in posttraumatic stress disorder. *Cognitive & Behavioral Practice, 18*(4), 424–432. doi: 10.1016/j.cbpra.2010.06.006

Halligan, P. W., Athwal, B. S., Oakley, D. A., & Frackowiak, R. S. J. (2000). Imaging hypnotic paralysis: Implications for conversion hysteria. *Lancet, 355*, 986–987. *doi:* 10.1016/S0140-6736(00)99019-6

Halligan, P. W., Fink, G. R., Marshall, J. C., & Vallar, G. (2003). Spatial cognition: Evidence from visual neglect. *Trends in Cognitive Sciences, 7*(3), 125–133. doi: 10.1016/S1364-6613(03)00032-9

Hamner, M. B., Frueh, B. C., Ulmer, H. G., & Arana, G. W. (1999). Psychotic features of illness severity in combat veterans with chronic posttraumatic stress disorder. *Biological Psychiatry, 45*(7), 846–852. doi: 10.1016/S0006-3223(98)00301-1

Hamner, M. B., Frueh, B. C., Ulmer, H. G., Huber, M. G., Twomey, T. J., Tyson, C., & Arana, G. W. (2000). Psychotic features in chronic posttraumatic stress disorder and schizophrenia: Comparative severity. *Journal of Nervous & Mental Disease, 188*(4), 217–221. doi: 10.1097/00005053-200004000-00004

Hardy, A., Fowler, D., Freeman, D., Smith, B., Steel, C., Evans, J., & Dunn, G. (2005). Trauma and hallucinatory experience in psychosis. *Journal of Nervous & Mental Disease, 193*(8), 501–507. doi:10.1097/01.nmd.0000172480.56308.21

Hareli, S., & Parkinson, B. (2008). What's social about social emotions? *Journal for the Theory of Social Behaviour, 38*(2), 131–156. doi: 10.1111/j.1468-5914.2008.00363.x

Harris, P. L. (2000). Understanding emotion. *Handbook of Emotions, 2*, 281–292.

Harvey, M. R. (1996). An ecological view of psychological trauma and trauma recovery. *Journal of Traumatic Stress, 9*(1), 2–23. doi: 10.1002/jts.2490090103

Harvey, M. R. (2007). Towards an ecological understanding of resilience in trauma survivors: Implications for theory, research, and practice. *Journal of Aggression, Maltreatment, & Trauma, 14*(1–2), 9–32. doi: 10.1300/J146v14n01_02

Hatfield, E., Cacioppo, J. T., & Rapson, R. L. (1994). *Emotional contagion.* New York, NY: Cambridge University Press.

Hauschildt, M., Peters, M., Moritz, S., & Jelinek, L. (2011). Heart rate variability in response to affective scenes in posttraumatic stress disorder. *Biological Psychology, 88*(2), 215–222. doi: 10.1016/j.biopsycho.2011.08.004

Hayes, J. P., Hayes, S. M., & Mikedis, A. M. (2012). Quantitative meta-analysis of neural activity in posttraumatic stress disorder. *Biology of Mood & Anxiety Disorders, 2*, 9. doi: 10.1186/2045-5380-2-9

Hayward, M., Berry, K., & Ashton, A. (2011). Applying interpersonal theories to the understanding of and therapy for auditory hallucinations: A review of the literature and directions for further research. *Clinical Psychology Review, 31*(8), 1313–1323. doi: 10.1016/j.cpr.2011.09.001

Heatherton, T. F. (2011). Self and identity: Neuroscience of self and self-regulation. *Annual Review of Psychology, 62*(1), 363–390. doi: 10.1146/annurev.psych.121208.131616

Heavey, C. L., Hurlburt, R. T., & Lefforge, N. L. (2012). Toward a phenomenology of feelings. *Emotion, 12*(4), 763–777. doi: 10.1037/a0026905.

Hellawell, S. J., & Brewin, C. R. (2002). A comparison of flashbacks and ordinary autobiographical memories of trauma: Cognitive resources and behavioural observations. *Behaviour Research & Therapy, 40*(10), 1143–1156. doi:10.1016/S0005-7967(01)00080-8

Hellawell, S. J., & Brewin, C. R. (2004). A comparison of flashbacks and ordinary autobiographical memories of trauma: Content and language. *Behaviour Research & Therapy, 42*(1), 1–12. doi:10.1016/S0005-7967(03)00088-3

Herman, J. L. (1992a). Complex PTSD: A syndrome in survivors of prolonged and repeated trauma. *Journal of Traumatic Stress, 5*(3), 377–391. doi: 10.1002/jts.2490050305

Herman, J. L. (1992b). *Trauma and recovery.* New York, NY: Basic Books.

Herman, J. L. (2011). PTSD as a shame disorder. In R. L. Dearing & J. P. Tangney (Eds.), *Shame in the therapy hour* (pp. 261–276). Washington, DC: American Psychological Association.

Herpertz, S. (1995). Self-injurious behaviour: Psychopathological and nosological characteristics in subtypes of self-injurers. *Acta Psychiatrica Scandinavica, 91*(1), 57–68. doi: 10.1111/j.1600-0447.1995.tb09743.x

Hoeft, F., Gabrieli, J. D., Whitfield-Gabrieli, S., Haas, B. W., Bammer, R., Menon, V., & Spiegel, D. (2012) Functional brain basis of hypnotizability. *Arch Gen Psychiatry. 69*(10) 1064–72.

Hoffmann, S. G., Grossman, P., & Hinton, D. E. (2011). Loving-kindness and compassion meditation: Potential for psychological interventions. *Clinical Psychology Review, 31*, 1126–1132. doi: 10.1016/j.cpr.2011.07.003

Holmes, E. A., Arntz, A., & Smucker, M. R. (2007). Imagery rescripting in cognitive behavior therapy: Images, treatment techniques and outcomes. *Journal of Behavior Therapy & Experimental Psychiatry, 38*(4), 297–305. doi: 10.1016/j.jbtep.2007.10.007

Holmes, E. A., Brown, R. J., Mansell, W., Fearon, R. P., Hunter, E. C. M., Frasquilho, F., & Oakley, D. A. (2005). Are there two qualitatively distinct forms of dissociation?: A review and some clinical implications. *Clinical Psychology Review, 25*(1), 1–23. doi: 10.1016/j.cpr.2004.08.006

Holmes, E. A., Lang, T. J., & Deeprose, C. (2009). Mental imagery and emotion in treatment across disorders: Using the example of depression. *Cognitive Behaviour Therapy, 38*(Suppl. 1), 21–28. doi: 10.1080/16506070902980729

Holmes, E. A., Lang, T. J., & Shaw, D. M. (2009). Developing interpretation bias modification as a "cognitive vaccine" for depressed mood: Imagining positive events makes you feel better than thinking about them verbally. *Journal of Abnormal Psychology, 118,* 76–88. doi: 10.1037/a0012590

Holmes, E. A., & Matthews, A. (2005). Mental imagery and emotion: A special relationship? *Emotion, 5,* 489–497. doi: 10.1037/1528-3542.5.4.489

Holmes, E. A., & Matthews, A. (2010). Mental imagery in emotion and emotional disorders. *Clinical Psychology Review, 30,* 349–362. 10.1016/j.cpr.2010.01.001

Holmes, E. A., Mathews, A., Mackintosh, B., & Dalgleish, T. (2008). The causal effect of mental imagery on emotion assessed using picture-word cues. *Emotion, 8*(3), 395. doi: 10.1037/1528-3542.8.3.395

Honig, A., Romme, M. A., Ensink, B. J., Escher, S. D., Pennings, M. H., & deVries, M. W. (1998). Auditory hallucinations: A comparison between patients and nonpatients. *Journal of Nervous & Mental Disease, 186,* 646–651. doi: 10.1097/00005053-199810000-00009

Honkalampi, K., Hintikka, J., Tanskanen, A., Lehtonen, J., & Viinamaki, V. (2000). Depression is strongly associated with alexithymia in the general population. *Journal of Psychosomatic Research, 48*(1), 99–104. doi: 10.1016/S0022-3999(99)00083-5

Hopper, J. W., Frewen, P. A., Sack, M., Lanius, R. A., & van der Kolk, B. A. (2007). The responses to script-driven imagery scale (RSDI): Assessment of state posttraumatic symptoms for psychobiological and treatment research. *Journal of Psychopathology & Behavioral Assessment, 29*(4), 249–268. doi: 10.1007/s10862-007-9046-0

Hopper, J. W., Frewen, P. A., van der Kolk, B. A., & Lanius, R. A. (2007). Neural correlates of reexperiencing, avoidance, and dissociation in PTSD: Symptom dimensions and emotion dysregulation in responses to script-driven trauma imagery. *Journal of Traumatic Stress, 20*(5), 713–725. doi: 10.1002/jts.20284

Hopper, J. W., Pitman, R. K., Su, Z., Heyman, G. M., Lasko, N. B., Macklin, M. L., . . . Elman, I. (2008). Probing reward function in posttraumatic stress disorder: Expectancy and satisfaction with monetary gains and losses. *Journal of Psychiatric Research, 42*(10), 802–807. doi: 10.1016/j.jpsychires.2007.10.008

Hopper, J. W., Spinazzola, J., Simpson, W., & van der Kolk, B. (2006). Preliminary evidence of parasympathetic influence on basal heart rate in posttraumatic stress disorder. *Journal of Psychosomatic Research, 60*(1), 83–90. doi: 10.1016/j.jpsychores.2005.06.002

Horowitz, M. J. (1969a). Flashbacks: Recurrent intrusive images after the use of LSD. *American Journal of Psychiatry, 126,* 565–569.

Horowitz, M. J. (1969b). Psychic trauma: Return of images after a stress film. *Archives of General Psychiatry, 20,* 552–559.

Hubl, D., Koenig, T., Strik, W., Federspiel, A., Kreis, R., Boesch, C., . . . Dierks, T. (2004). Pathways that make voices: White matter changes in auditory hallucinations. *Archives of General Psychiatry, 61*(7), 658–668. doi: 10.1001/archpsyc.61.7.658\

Hughes, J. W., Dennis, M. F., & Beckham, J. C. (2007). Baroreceptor sensitivity at rest and during stress in women with posttraumatic stress disorder or major depressive disorder. *Journal of Traumatic Stress, 20*(5), 667–676. doi: 10.1002.jts.20285

Humphreys, K. L., Sauder, C. L., Martin, E. K., & Marx, B. P. (2010). Tonic immobility in childhood sexual abuse survivors and its relationship to posttraumatic stress symptomatology. *Journal of Interpersonal Violence, 25*(2), 358–373. doi: 10.1177/0886260509334412

Hunter, E., Sierra, M., & David, A. (2004). The epidemiology of depersonalization and derealization: A systematic review. *Social Psychiatry and Psychiatric Epidemiology, 39*(1), 9–18. doi: 10.1007/s00127-004-0701-4

Hurlburt, R. T. (2011). *Investigating pristine inner experience: Moments of truth.* New York, NY: Cambridge.

Hurlburt, R. T., & Akhter, S. (2006). The descriptive exprience sampling method. *Phenomenology and the Cognitive Sciences, 5*(3), 271–301. doi: 10.1007/s11097-006-9024-0

Hurlburt, R. T., & Heavey, C. L. (2001). Telling what we know: Describing inner experience. *Trends in Cognitive Sciences, 5*(9), 400–403. *doi:* 10.1016/S1364-6613(00)01724-1

Hurlbert, R. T., & Heavey, C. L. (2006). The descriptive experience sampling method. In R. T. Hurlburt & C. L. Heavey (Eds.), *Exploring inner experience* (pp. 77–92). Amsterdam: John Benjamins.

Husserl, E. (1900/1901). *Logische untersuchungen.* Leipzig, Germany: Viet.

Husserl, E. (1962). *Ideas: General introduction to pure phenomenology.* New York, NY: Collier Books.

Hyde, J. S., Mezulis, A. H., & Abramson, L. Y. (2008). The ABCs of depression: Integrating affective, biological, and cognitive models to explain the emergence of the gender difference in depression. *Psychological Review, 115*(2), 291–313. doi: 10.1037/0033-295X.115.2.291

Ibañez, A., Gleichgerrcht, E., & Manes, F. (2010). Clinical effects of insular damage in humans. *Brain Structure & Function, 214,* 397–410. doi: 10.1007/s00429-010-0256-y

Irwin, H. J. (1989). Hypnotic induction of the out-of-body experience. *Australian Journal of Clinical Hypnotherapy & Hypnosis, 10,* 1–7.

Irwin, H. J. (2000). The disembodied self: An empirical study of dissociation and the out-of-body experience. *Journal of Parapsychology, 64,* 261–77.

Irwin, H. J., & Melbin-Helberg, E. B. (1997). Alexithymia and dissociative tendencies. *Journal of Clinical Psychology, 53,* 159–166. doi: 10.1002/(SICI)1097-4679(199702)53:2<159::AID-JCLP9>3.0.CO;2-O

Izard, C. E. (1993). Four systems for emotion activation: Cognitive and noncognitive processes. *Psychological Review, 100,* 68–90. doi: 10.1037/0033-295X.100.1.68

Izard, C. E. (2007). Basic emotions, natural kinds, emotion schemas, and a new paradigm. *Perspectives on Psychological Science, 2,* 260–280. doi: 10.1111/j.1745-6916.2007.00044.x

Izard, C. E. (2009). Emotion theory and research: Highlights, unanswered questions, and emerging issues. *Annual Review of Psychology, 60,* 1–25. doi: 10.1146/annurev.psych.60.110707.163539

Izard, C. E. (2010). The many meanings/aspects of emotion: Definitions, functions, activation, and regulation. *Emotion Review, 2,* 363–370. doi: 10.1177/1754073910374661

James, W. (1890). *Principles of psychology.* New York, NY: Holt.

James, W. (2002). *The varieties of religious experience: A study in human nature.* New York, NY: Routledge. (Original work published 1902)

Janet, P. (1901). *The mental state of hystericals: A study of mental stigma and mental accidents.* New York, NY: Putnam's Sons.

Jardri, R., Pouchet, A., Pins, D., & Thomas, P. (2011). Cortical activations during auditory verbal hallucinations in schizophrenia: A coordinate-based meta-analysis. *American Journal of Psychiatry, 168*(1), 73–81. doi: 10.1176/appi.ajp.2010.09101522

Jatzko, A., Schmitt, A., Demirakca, T., Weimer, E., & Braus, D. F. (2006). Disturbance in the neural circuitry underlying positive emotional processing in post-traumatic stress disorder (PTSD). *European Archives of Psychiatry and Clinical Neuroscience, 256*, 112–114. doi: 10.1007/s00406-005-0617-3

Jay, E.-L., Sierra, M., Eynde, V., Rothwell, J. C., & David, A. S. (2014). Testing a neurobiological model of depersonalization disorder using repetitive transcranial magnetic stimulation. *Brain Stimulation, 7*, 252–259. doi: 10.1016/j.brs.2013.12.002

Jaycox, L. H., Foa, E. B., & Morral, A. R. (1998). Influence of emotional engagement and habituation on exposure therapy for PTSD. *Journal of Consulting and Clinical Psychology, 66*(1), 185. doi: 10.1037/0022-006X.66.1.185

Jelinek, L., Randjbar, S., Seifert, D., Kellner, M., & Moritz, S. (2009). The organization of autobiographical and nonautobiographical memory in posttraumatic stress disorder (PTSD). *Journal of Abnormal Psychology, 118*(2), 288. doi: 10.1037/a0015633

Jelinek, L., Stockbauer, C., Randjbar, S., Kellner, M., Ehring, T., & Moritz, S. (2010). Characteristics and organizations of the worst moment of trauma memories in posttraumatic stress disorder. *Behaviour Research & Therapy, 48*(7), 680–685. doi: 10.1016/j.brat.2010.03.014

Jenner, J., Rutten, S., Beuckens, J., Boonstra, N., & Systema, S. (2008). Positive and useful auditory vocal hallucinations: Prevalence, characteristics, attributions, and implications for treatment. *Acta Psychiatrica Scandinavica, 118*(3), 238–245. doi: 10.1111/j.1600-0447.2008.01226.x

Jessop, M., Scott, J., & Nurcombe, B. (2008). Hallucinations in adolescent inpatients with post-traumatic stress disorder and schizophrenia: Similarities and differences. *Australasian Psychiatry, 16*(4), 268–272. doi: 10.1080/10398560801982580

Jobson, L. (2009). Drawing current posttraumatic stress disorder models into the cultural sphere: The development of the "threat to the conceptual self" model. *Clinical Psychology, 29*(4), 368–381. doi: 10.1016/j.cpr.2009.03.002

Johns, L., Hemsley, D., & Kuipers, E. (2002). A comparison of auditory hallucinations in a psychiatric and nonpsychiatric group. *British Journal of Clinical Psychology, 41*, 81–86.

Jones, C., Harvey, A. G., & Brewin, C. R. (2007). The organization and content of trauma memories in survivors of road traffic accidents. *Behaviour Reserach & Therapy, 45*(1), 151–162. doi: 10.1016/j.brat.2006.02.004

Kabat-Zinn, J. (1990). *Full catastrophe living: Using the wisdom of your mind to face stress, pain and illness.* New York, NY: Dell.

Kalckert, A., & Ehrsson, H. (2012). Moving a rubber hand that feels like your own: A dissociation of ownership and agency. *Frontiers in Human Neuroscience, 6*, 40–54. doi: 10.3389/fnhum.2012.00040

Kalisch, R., Wiech, K., Critchley, H. D., Seymour, B., O'Doherty, J. P., Oakley, D. A., . . . Dolan, R. J.(2005). Anxiety reduction through detachment: Subjective, physiological, and neural effects. *Journal of Cognitive Neuroscience, 17*, 874–883. doi: 10.1162/0898929054021184

Kano, M., Fukudo, S., Gyoba, J., Kamachi, M., Tagawa, M., Mochizuki, H., & Yanai, K. (2003). Specific brain processing of facial expressions in people with alexithymia: an H215O-PET study. *Brain, 126*(6), 1474–1484. doi: 10.1093/brain/awg131

Kanske, P. J., Heissler, S., Schonfelder, A., Bongers, M., & Wessa, M. (2010) How to regulate emotion?: Neural networks for reappraisal and distraction. *Cerebral Cortex, 21*(6), 1379–1388. doi: 10.1093/cercor/bhq216

Karnath, H.-O., & Baier, B. (2010). Right insula for our sense of limb ownership and self-awareness of actions. *Brain Structure & Function, 214*, 411–417. doi: 10.1007/s00429-010-0250-4

Kart-Ludwig, M., Leenen, K., Grabe, H., Jenewein, J., Nunex, Garcia, D., & Rufer, M. (2011). Alexithymia and its relationship to dissociation in patients with panic disorder. *Journal of Nervous & Mental Disease, 199*, 773–777. doi: 10.1097/NMD.0b013e822fcbfb

Kashdan, T. B., Elhai, J. D., & Frueh, B. C. (2006). Anhedonia and emotional numbing in combat veterans with PTSD. *Behaviour Research & Therapy, 44*(3), 457–467. doi: 10.1016/j.brat.2005.03.001

Kashdan, T. B., Elhai, J. D., & Frueh, B. C. (2007). Anhedonia, emotional numbing, and symptom overreporting in male veterans with PTSD. *Personality & Individual Differences, 43*(4), 725–735. doi: 10.1016/j.paid.2007.01.013

Keary, T. A., Hughes, J. W., & Palmieri, P. A. (2009). Women with posttraumatic stress disorder have larger decreases in heart rate variability during stress tasks. *International Journal of Psychophysiology, 73*(3), 257–264. doi: 10.1016/j.ijpsycho.2009.04.003

Ketay, S., Hamilton, H. K., Haas, B. W., & Simeon, D. (2014). Face processing in depersonalization: An fMRI study of the unfamiliar self. *Psychiatry Research: Neuroimaging, 222*, 107–110. doi: 10.1016/j.pscychresns.2014.02.003

Kikyo, H., Ohki, K., & Miyashita, Y. (2002). Neural correlates for feeling-of-knowing: An fMRI parametric analysis. *Neuron, 36*, 177–186. doi: 10.1016/S0896-6273(02)00939-X

Kim, S. H., Thibodeau, R., & Jorgensen, R. S. (2011). Shame, guilt, and depressive symptoms: A meta-analytic review. *Psychological Bulletin, 137*(1), 68. doi: 10.1037/a0021466

King, D. W., Leskin, G. A., King, L. A., & Weathers, F. W. (1998). Confirmatory factor analysis of the clinician-administered PTSD scale: Evidence for the dimensionality of posttraumatic stress disorder. *Psychological Assessment, 10*(2), 90–96. doi: 10.1037/1040-3590.10.2.90

Kingdon, D., Ashcroft, K., Bhandari, B., Gleeson, S., Warikoo, N., Symons, M., . . . Mahendra, R. (2010). Schizophrenia and borderline personality disorder: Similarities and differences in the experience of auditory hallucinations, paranoia, and childhood trauma. *Journal of Nervous & Mental Disease, 198*(6), 399–403. doi: 10.1097/NMD.0b013e3181e08c27

Kirkland, T., & Cunningham, W. A. (2012). Mapping emotions through time: How affective trajectories inform the language of emotion. *Emotion, 12*, 268–282. doi: 10.1037/a0024218

Kleindienst, N., Bohus, M., Ludäscher, P., Limberger, M. F., Kuenkele, K., Ebner-Priemer, U. W., & Schmahl, C. (2008). Motives for nonsuicidal self-injury among women with borderline personality disorder. *Journal of Nervous and Mental Disease, 196*(3), 230–236. doi: 10.1097/NMD.0b013e3181663026

Klonsky, E. D. (2007). The functions of deliberate self-injury: A review of the evidence. *Clinical Psychology Review, 27*(2), 226–239. doi: 10.1016/j.cpr.2006.08.002

Kluetsch, R. C., Ros, T., Théberge, J., Frewen, P. A., Calhoun, V. D., Schmahl, C., . . . Lanius, R. A. (2013). Plastic modulation of PTSD resting-state networks by EEG neurofeedback. *Acta Psychiatica Scandinavica.* doi: 10.1111/acps.12229

Kluetsch, R. C., Ros, T., Théberge, J., Frewen, P. A., Calhoun, V. D., Schmahl, C., . . . Lanius, R. A. (in press). Plastic modulation of PTSD resting-state networks by EEG neurofeedback. *Acta Psychiatica Scandinavica.*

Kluft, R. P. (1984). An introduction to multiple personality disorder. *Psychiatric Annals, 14*, 19–24.

Kluft, R. P. (1987). First-rank symptoms as a diagnostic clue to multiple personality disorder. *American Journal of Psychiatry, 144*(3), 293–298.

Kluft, R. P. (1990). Dissociation and subsequent vulnerability: A preliminary study. *Dissociation, 3,* 167–173.

Kober, H., Feldman-Barrett, L., & Joseph, J. (2008). Functional grouping and cortical–subcortical interactions in emotion: A meta-analysis of neuroimaging studies. *NeuroImage, 42*(2), 998–1031. doi: 10.1016/j.neuroimage.2008.03.059

Koenigsberg, H. W., Fan, J., Ochsner, K.N., Liu, X., Guise, K., Pizzarello, S., . . . Siever, L. J. (2009). Neural correlates of using distancing to regulate emotional responses to social situations. *Neuropsychologia, 48,* 813–1822. doi: 10.1016/j.neuropsychologia.2010.03.002

Kohut, H. (1971). *The analysis of the self.* New York, NY: International Universities Press.

Kohut, H. (1977). *The restoration of the self.* New York, NY: International Universities Press.

Kohut, H. (1984). *How does analysis cure?* Chicago: University of Chicago Press.

Koopman, C., Carrio, V., Butler, L. D., Sudhakar, S., Palmer, L., & Steiner, H. (2004). Relationships of dissociation and childhood abuse and neglect with heart rate in delinquent adolescents. *Journal of Traumatic Stress, 17*(1), 47–54. doi: 10.1023/B:JOTS.0000014676.83722.35

Korn, D. L., & Leeds, A. M. (2002). Preliminary evidence of efficacy for EMDR resource development and installation in the stabilization phase of treatment of complex posttraumatic stress disorder. *Journal of Clinical Psychology, 58*(12), 1465–1487. doi: 10.1002/jclp.10099

Kosillo, P., & Smith, A. T. (2010). The role of the human anterior insular cortex in time processing. *Brain Structure & Function, 214,* 623–628. doi: 10.1007/s00429-010-0267-8

Koval, P., & Kuppens, P. (2012). Changing emotion dynamics: Individual differences in the effect of anticipatory social stress on emotional inertia. *Emotion, 12,* 256–267. doi: 10.1037/a0024756

Krabbendam, L. (2008). Childhood psychological trauma and psychosis. *Psychological Medicine, 38*(10), 1405–1408. doi: 10.1017/S0033291708002705

Kraft, H. S. (2007). *Rule number two: Lessons I learned in a combat hospital.* Hachette Digital.

Kraus, A., Valerius, G., Seifritz, E., Ruf, M., Bremner, J. D., Bohus, M., & Schmahl, C. (2010). Script-driven imagery of self-injurious behavior in patients with borderline personality disorder: A pilot fMRI study. *Acta Psychiatrica Scandinavica, 121*(1), 41–51. doi: 10.1111/j.1600-0447.2009.01417.x

Kropotov, J. (2008). *Quantitative EEG, event-related potentials, and neurotherapy.* New York, NY: Academic Press.

Kross, E. (2009). When self becomes other: Toward an integrative understanding of the processes distinguishing adaptive self-reflection from rumination. *Annals of the New York Academy of Sciences, 1167,* 35–40. *doi:* 10.1111/j.1749-6632.2009.04545.x

Krüger, C., Bartel, P., & Fletcher, L (2011). Dissociative mental states are canonically associated with decreased temporal theta activity on spectral analysis of EEG. *Journal of Trauma and Dissociation, 14,* 473–491. doi: 10.1080/15299732.2013.769480

Krystal, H. (1968). *Massive psychic trauma.* New York, NY: International Universities Press.

Krystal, H. (1988). *Integration and self-healing: Affect, trauma, alexithymia.* Hillsdale, NJ: Analytic Press.

Krystal, J. H., Bennett, A. L., Bremner, J. D., Southwick, S. M., & Charney, D. S. (1995). Toward a cognitive neuroscience of dissociation and altered memory functions in post-traumatic stress disorder: Neurobiological and clinical consequences of stress. In M. J. Friedman, D. S. Charney, & A. Y. Deutsch (Eds.), *Normal adaptions to PTSD* (pp. 239–268). New York, NY: Raven Press.

Krystal, J. H., Bremner, J. D., Southwick, S. M., & Charney, D. S. (1998). The emerging neurobiology of dissociation: Implications for treatment of posttraumatic stress disorder. In J. D. Bremner & C. R. Marmar (Eds.), *Trauma, memory, and dissociation* (Vol. 54, pp. 321–363). Washington, DC: American Psychiatric Press.

Kulkarni, M., Porter, K. E., & Rauch, S. A. M. (2012). Anger, dissociation, and PTSD among male veterans entering into PTSD treatment. *Journal of Anxiety Disorders, 26,* 271–278. doi: 10.1016/j.janxdis.2011.12.005

Kuppens, P., Sheeber, L. B., Yap, M. B. H., Whittle, S., Simmons, J. G., & Allen, N. B. (2012). Emotional inertia prospectively predicts the onset of depressive disorder in adolescence. *Emotion, 12,* 283–289. doi: 10.1037/a0025046

Kurth, F., Zilles, K., Fox, P. T., Laird, A. R., & Eickhoff, S. (2010). A link between the systems: Functional differentiation and integration within the human insula revealed by meta-analysis. *Brain Structure & Function, 214,* 519–534. doi: 10.1007/s00429-010-0255-z

Kwako, L. E., Noll, J. G., Putnam, F. W., & Trickett, P. K. (2010). Childhood sexual abuse and attachment: An intergenerational perspective. *Clinical Child Psychology & Psychiatry, 15,* 407–422. *doi:* 10.1177/1359104510367590

LaConte, S. M. (2011). Decoding fMRI brain states in real-time. *NeuroImage, 56*(2), 440–454. doi: 10.1016/j.neuroimage.2010.06.052

Lambert, J. E., Engh, R., Hasburn, A., & Holzer, J. (2012). Impact of posttraumatic stress disorder on the relationship quality and psychological distress of intimate partners: A meta-analytic review. *Journal of Family Psychology, 26*(5), 729–737. doi: 10.1037/a0029341

Lambert, M. V., Sierra, M., Phillips, M. L., & David, A. S. (2002). The spectrum of organic depersonalization: A review plus four new cases. *Journal of Neuropsychiatry & Clinical Neuroscience, 14*(2), 141–154. *doi:* 10.1176/appi.neuropsych.14.2.141

Lambie, J. A., & Marcel, A. J. (2002). Consciousness and the varieties of emotion experience: A theoretical framework. *Psychological Review, 109*(2), 219–259. doi: 10.1037/0033-295X.109.2.219

Lamm, C., & Singer, T. (2010). The role of anterior insular cortex in social emotion. *Brain Structure & Function, 214,* 579–591. doi: 10.1007/s00429-010-0251-3

Lane, R. D., Fink, G. R., Chau, P. M., & Dolan, R. J. (1997). Neural activation during selective attention to subjective emotional responses. *NeuroReport, 8*(18), 3969–3972. doi: 10.1097/00001756-199712220-00024

Lane, R. D., Quinlan, D. M., Schwartz, G. E., & Walker, P. A. (1990). The levels Of Emotional Awareness Scale: A cognitive–developmental measure of emotion. *Journal of Personality Assessment, 55*(1–2), 124–134. doi: 10.1207/s15327752jpa5501&2_12

Lane, R. D., Reiman, E. M., Axelrod, B., Yun, L. S., Holmes, A., & Schwartz, G. E. (1998). Neural correlates of levels of emotional awareness: Evidence of an interaction between emotion and attention in the anterior cingulate cortex. *Journal of Cognitive Neuroscience, 10,* 525–535. doi: 10.1162/089892998562924

Lane, R. D., & Schwartz, G. E. (1987). Levels of emotional awareness: A cognitive–developmental theory and its application to psychopathology. *American Journal of Psychiatry.* doi: 10.1080/00223891.1990.9674052

Lang, P. J., Bradley, M. M., & Cuthbert, B. N. (1997). Motivated attention: Affect, activation, and action. In P. J. Lang, R. F. Simons, & M. Balaban (Eds.), *Attention and orienting: Sensory and motivational processes* (pp. 97–135). Mahwah, NJ: Erlbaum.

Lang, S., Kotchoubey, B., Frick, C., Spitzer, C., Grabe, H. J., & Barnow, S. (2012). Cognitive reappraisal in trauma-exposed women with borderline personality disorder. *NeuroImage, 59,* 1727–1734. doi: 10.1016/j.neuroimage.2011.08.061

Lanius, R. A., Bluhm, R. L., & Frewen, P. A. (2011). How understanding the neurobiology of complex post-traumatic stress disorder can inform clinical practice: A social cognitive and affective neuroscience approach. *Acta Psychiatrica Scandinavica, 124*(5), 331–348. doi: 10.1111/j.1600-0447.2011.01755.x

Lanius, R. A., Bluhm, R., Lanius, U., & Pain, C. (2006). A review of neuroimaging studies in PTSD: Heterogeneity of response to symptom provocation. *Journal of Psychiatric Research, 40,* 709–729. doi: 10.1016/j.jpsychires.2005.07.007

Lanius, R. A., Brand, B., Vermetten, E., Frewen, P. A., & Spiegel, D. (2012). The dissociative subtype of posttraumatic stress disorder: Rationale, clinical and neurobiological evidence, and implications. *Depression & Anxiety, 29*(8), 701–708. doi: 0.1002/da.21889

Lanius, R. A., Frewen, P. A., Vermetten, E., & Yehuda, R. (2010). Transitioning from fear conditioning to emotion and arousal regulation in PTSD. *European Journal of Psychotraumatology, 1*(1), 5467. doi: 10.3402/ejpt.v1i0.5467

Lanius, R. A., Hopper, J. W., & Menon, R. S. (2003). Individual differences in a husband and wife who devleeped PTSD after a motor vehicle accident: A functional MRI case study. *American Journal of Psychiatry, 160,* 667–669. doi: 10.1176/appi.ajp.160.4.667

Lanius, R. A., Vermetten, E., Loewenstein, R. J., Brand, B., Schmahl, C., Bremner, J. D., & Spiegel, D. (2010). Emotion modulation in PTSD: Clinical and neurobiological evidence for a dissociative subtype. *American Journal of Psychiatry, 167*(6), 640–647. doi: 10.1176/appi.ajp.2009.09081168

Lanius, R. A., Williamson, P. C., Bluhm, R. L., Densmore, M., Boksman, K., Neufeld, R. W. J., & Menon, R. S. (2005). Functional connectivity of disassociative responses in posttraumatic stress disorder: A functional magnetic resonance imaging investigation. *Biological Psychiatry, 57*(8), 873–884. doi: 10.1016/j.bio psych.2005.01.011

Lanius, R. A., Williamson, P. C., Boksman, K., Densmore, M., Gupta, M., Neufeld, R. W. J., & Menon, R. S. (2002). Brain activation during script-driven imagery induced dissociative responses in PTSD: A functional magnetic resonance imaging investigation. *Biological Psychiatry, 52*(4), 305–311. doi: 10.1016/S0006-3223(02)01367-7

Lanius, R. A., Williamson, P. C., Densmore, M., Boksman, K., Gupta, M. A., Neufeld, R. W., . . . Menon, R. S. (2001). Neural correlates of traumatic memories in posttraumatic stress disorder: A functional MRI investigation. *American Journal of Psychiatry, 158*(11), 1920–1922. doi: 10.1176/appi.ajp.158.11.1920

Lanius, R. A., Williamson, P. C., Hopper, J., Densmore, M., Boksman, K., Gupta, M. A., . . . Menon, R. S. (2003). Recall of emotional states in posttraumatic stress disorder: An fMRI investigation. *Biological Psychiatry, 53*(3), 204–210. doi: 10.1016/S0006-3223(02)01466-X

Larsen, J. T., Berntson, G. G., Poehlmann, K. M., Ito, T. A., & Cacioppo, J. T. (2008). The psychophysiology of emotion. In M. Lewis, J. M. Haviland-Jones, & L. F. Barrett (Eds.), *Handbook of emotions* (3rd ed., pp. 180–195). New York, NY: Guilford Press.

Larsen, J. T., McGraw, A. P., & Cacioppo, J. T. (2001). Can people feel happy and sad at the same time? *Journal of Personality & Social Psychology, 81,* 684–696. doi: 10.1037/0022-3514.81.4.684

Lau, M. A., Bishop, S. R., Segal, Z. V., Buis, T., Anderson, N. D., Carlson, L., & Devins, G. (2006). The Toronto Mindfulness Scale: Development and validation. *Journal of Clinical Psychology, 62*(12), 1445–1467. doi: 10.1002/jclp.20326

Laughlin, C. D., McManus, J., & d'Aquili, E. G. (1992). *Brain, symbol and experience: Toward a neurophenomenology of human consciousness.* New York, NY: Columbia University Press.

Lee, D. A., Scragg, P., & Turner, S. (2001). The role of shame and guilt in traumatic events: A clinical model of shame-based and guilt-based PTSD. *British Journal of Medical Psychology, 74*(4), 451–466. doi: 10.1348/000711201161109

Legrand, D., & Ruby, P. (2009). What is self-specific?: Theoretical investigation and critical review of neuroimaging results. *Psychological Review, 116*(1), 252–282. doi: 10.1037/a0014172

Lemogne, C., le Bastard, G., Mayberg, H., Volle, E., Bergouignan, L., Lehéricy, S., & Fossati, P. (2009). In search of the depressive self: Extended medial prefrontal network during self-referential processing in major depression. *Affective Neuroscience, 4*(3), 305–312. *doi:* 10.1093/scan/nsp008

Lemogne, C., Gorwood, P., Bergouignan, L., Pelissolo, A., Lehericy, S., Fossati, P. (2011). Negative affectivity, self-referential processing and the cortical midline structures. *Social, Cognitive, & Affective Neuroscience, 6*(4), 426–433. doi: 10.1093/scan/nsq049

Lenggenhager, B., Mouthon, M., & Blanke, O. (2009). Spatial aspects of bodily self-consciousness. *Consciousness & Cognition, 18*(1), 110–117. doi: 10.1016/j.concog.2008.11.003

Lenggenhager, B., Tadi, T., Metzinger, T., & Blanke, O. (2007). *Video ergo sum:* Manipulating bodily self-consciousness. *Science, 317*(5841), 1096–1099. doi: 10.1126/science.1143439

Lensvelt-Mulders, G., van Der Hart, O., van Ochten, J. M., van Son, M. J. M., Steele, K., & Breeman, L. (2008). Relations among peritraumatic dissociation and posttraumatic stress: A meta-analysis. *Clinical Psychology Review, 28*(7), 1138–1151. doi: 10.1016/j.cpr.2008.03.006

LeShan, L. L. (1976). *Alternate realities: The search for the full human being.* New York, NY: M. Evans.

Lévesque, J., Eugène, F., Joanette, Y., Paquette, V., Menour, B., Beaudoin, G., . . . Beauregard, M. (2003). Neural circuitry underlying voluntary suppression of sadness. *Biological Psychiatry, 53,* 502–510. doi: 10.1016/S0002-3223(03)01817-6

Levine, B. (2004). Autobiographical memory and the self in time: Brain lesion effects, fucntional neuroanatomy, and lifespan development. *Brain & Cognition, 55*(1), 54–68. doi: 10.1016/S0278-2626(03)00280-X

Levine, B., Svoboda, E., Hay, J., Winocur, G., & Moscovitch, M. (2002). Aging and autobiographical memory: Dissociating episodic from semantic retrieval. *Psychology & Aging, 17*(4), 677–689. doi: 10.1037/0882-7974.17.4.677

Levine, P. A., & Frederick, A. (1997). *Waking the tiger: Healing trauma—the innate capacity to transform overwhelming experiences.* Berkeley, CA: North Atlantic Books.

Lewis, E., & Lloyd, D. M. (2010). Embodied experience: A first-person investigation of the rubber hand illusion. *Phenomenology and the Cognitive Sciences, 9*(3), 317–339. doi: 10.1007/s11097-010-9154-2

Lewis, H. B. E. (1987). *The role of shame in symptom formation.* Hillsdale, NJ: Erlbaum.

Lewis, M. D. (2005). Bridging emotion theory and neurobiology through dynamic systems modeling. *Behavioral & Brain Sciences, 28,* 169–194. doi: 10.1017/S0140525X0500004X

Lewis, M. D., & Todd, R. (2005). Getting emotional: A neural perspective on emotion, intention, and consciousness. *Journal of Consciousness Studies, 12* (8–10), 210–235.

Lewis, P., & Miall, R. (2003). Distinct systems for automatic and cognitively controlled time measurement: Evidence from neuroimaging. *Current Opinion in Neurobiology, 13*(2), 250–255. doi: 10.1016/S0959-4388(03)00036-9

Liberzon, I., Abelson, J. L., Flagel, S. B., Raz, J., & Young, E. A. (1999). Neuroendocrine and psychophysiologic responses in PTSD: A symptom provocation study. *Neuropsychopharmacology, 21*(1), 40–50. doi: 10.1016/S0893-133X(98)00128-6

Liberzon, I., & Martis, B. (2006). Neuroimaging studies of emotional responses in PTSD. *Annals of the New York Academy of Sciences, 1071*, 87-109. doi: 10.1196/annals.1364.009

Lieberman, M. D. (2007). Social cognitive neuroscience: A review of core processes. *Annual Review of Psychology, 58*, 259–289. doi: 10.1146/annurev.psych.58.110405.085654

Lieberman, M. D., Eisenberger, N. I., Crockett, M. J., Tom, S. M., Pfeifer, J. H., & Way, B. M. (2007). Putting feelings into words: Affect labeling disrupts amygdala activity in response to affective stimuli. *Psychological Science, 18*, 421–428. doi: 10.1111/j.1467-9280.2007.01916.x

Liemburg, E. J., Swart, M., Bruggeman, R., Kortekaas, R., Knegtering, H., Curčić-Blake, B., & Aleman, A. (2012). Altered resting state connectivity of the default mode network in alexithymia. *Social Cognitive and Affective Neuroscience, 7*(6), 660–666. doi: 10.1093/scan/nss048

Lima, A. A., Fiszman, A., Marques-Portella, C., Mendlowicz, M. V., Coutinho, E. S. F., Maia, D. C. B., Figueira, I. (2010). The impact of tonic immobility reaction on the prognosis of posttraumatic stress disorder. *Journal of Psychiatric Research, 44*(4), 224–228. doi: 10.1016/j.jpsychires.2009.08.005

Linden, D. E., Thornton, K., Kuswanto, C. N., Johnston, S. J., van de Ven, V., & Jackson, M. C. (2011). The brain's voices: Comparing nonclinical auditory hallucinations and imagery. *Cerebral Cortex, 21*(2), 330–337. doi: 10.1093/cercor/bhq097

Lindquist, K. A., Wager, T. D., Kober, H., Bliss-Moreau, E., & Barrett, L. F. (2012) The brain basis of emotion: A meta-analytic review. *Behavioural & Brain Sciences, 35*, 121–202. doi: 10.1017/S0140525X11000446

Lipari, S., Baglio, F., Griffanti, L., Mendozzi, L., Garegnani, M., Motta, A., . . . Pugnetti, L. (2012). Altered and asymmetric default mode network activity in a "hypnotic virtuoso": An fMRI and EEG study. *Consciousness & Cognition, 21*(1), 393–400. doi: 10.1016/j.concog.2011.11.006

Lipsanen, T., Saarijärvi, S., & Lauerma, H. (2004). Exploring the relations between depression, somatization, dissociation, and alexithymia: Overlapping or independent constructs? *Psychopathology, 37*, 200–206. doi: 10.1159/000080132

Llinás, R. R. (2001). *I of the vortex: From neurons to self*. Cambridge, MA: MIT Press.

Long, M. E., & Quevillon, R. P. (2009). Imagery rescripting in the treatment of posttraumatic stress disorder. *Journal of Cognitive Psychotherapy, 23*(1), 67–76. doi: 10.1891/0889-8391.23.1.67

Longden, E., Madill, A., & Waterman, M. (2012). Dissociation, trauma, and the role of lived experience: Toward a new conceptualization of voice hearing. *Psychological Bulletin, 138*(1), 28–76. doi: 10.1037/a0025995

Longo, M. R., Schüür, F., Kammers, M. P. M., Tsakiris, M., & Haggard, P. (2008). What is embodiment?: A psychometric approach. *Cognition, 107*(3), 978–998. doi: 10.1016/j.cognition.2007.12.004

Low, A., Lang, P. J., Smith, J. C., & Bradley, M. M. (2008). Both predator and prey: Emotional arousal in threat and reward. *Psychological Science, 19*, 865–873. *doi:* 10.1111/j.1467-9280.2008.02170.x

Healing the Traumatized Self

Ludäscher, P., Bohus, M., Lieb, K., Philipsen, A., Jochims, A., & Schmahl, C. (2007). Elevated pain thresholds correlate with dissociation and aversive arousal in patients with borderline personality disorder. *Psychiatry research, 149*(1), 291–296. doi: 10.1016/j.psychres.2005.04.009

Ludäscher, P., Valerius, G., Stiglmayr, C., Muchnik, J., Lanius, R. A., & Schmahl, C. (2010). Pain sensitivity and neural processing during dissociative states in patients with borderline personality disorder with and without comorbid PTSD: A pilot study. *Journal of Psychiatry & Neuroscience, 35*(3), 177–184. doi: 10.1503/jpn.090022 .

Luminet, O., Rime, B., Bagby, R. M., & Taylor, G. J. (2004). A multimodal investigation of emotional responding in alexithymia. *Cognition & Emotion, 18*(6), 741–766. doi: 10.1080/02699930341000275

Lumley, M. A. (2000). Alexithymia and negative emotional conditions. *Journal of Psychosomatic Research, 49*(1), 51–54. *doi:* 10.1016/S0022-3999(00)00161-6

Lutz, A., Lachaux, J. P., Martinerie, J., & Varela, F. J. (2002). Guiding the study of brain dynamics by using first-person data: Synchrony patterns correlate with ongoing conscious states during a simple visual task. *Proceedings of the National Academy of Sciences of the United States of America, 99*(3), 1586–1591. doi: 10.1073/pnas.032658199

Lutz, A., & Thompson, E. (2003). Neurophenomenology: Integrating subjective experience and brain dynamics in the neuroscience of consciousness. *Journal of Consciousness Studies, 9–10,* 31–52.

Maaranen, P., Tanskanen, A., Honkalampi, K., Haatainen, K., Hintikka, J., & Viinamäki, H. (2005). Factors associated with pathological dissociation in the general population. *Australian and New Zealand Journal of Psychiatry, 39*(5), 387–394. doi: 10.1111/j.1440-1614.2005.01586.x

Macar, F., Lejeune, H., Bonnet, M., Ferrara, A., Pouthas, V., Vidal, F., & Maquet, P. (2002). Activation of the supplementary motor area and of attentional networks during temportal processing. *Experimental Brain Research, 142*(4), 475–485. doi: 10.1007/s00221-001-0953-0

Macbeth, A., & Gumley, A. (2012). Exploring compassion: A meta-analysis of the association between self-compassion and psychopathology. *Clinical Psychology Review, 32*(6), 545–552. doi: 10.1016/j.cpr.2012.06.003

Mantani, T., Okamoto, Y., Shirao, N., Okada, G., & Yamawaki, S. (2005). Reduced activation of posterior cingulate cortex during imagery in subjects with high degrees of alexithymia: A functional magnetic resonance imaging study. *Biological Psychiatry, 57*(9), 982–990. doi: 10.1016/j.biopsych.2005.01.047

Mantovani, A., Simeon, D., Urban, N., Bulow, P., Allart, A., & Lisanby, S. (2011). Temporo-parietal junction stimulation in the treatment of depersonalization disorder. *Psychiatry Research, 186,* 138-140. doi: 10.1016/j.psychres.2010.08.022

Marks, I. M. (1987). *Fears, phobias, and rituals: Panic, anxiety, and their disorders.* New York, NY: Oxford University Press.

Marmar, C. R., Weiss, D. S., & Metzler, T. J. (1997). The Peritraumatic Dissociative Experiences Questionnaire. In J. P. Wilson & T. M. Keane (Eds.), *Assessing psychological trauma and PTSD* (pp. 412–428). New York, NY: Guilford Press.

Martarelli, C. S., & Mast, F. W. (2013). Is it real or is it fiction?: Children's bias toward reality. *Journal of Cognition & Development, 14*(1), 141–153. doi: 10.1080/15248372.2011.638685

Marx, B. P., Forsyth, J. P., Gallup, G. G., Fusé, T., & Lexington, J. M. (2008). Tonic immobility as an evolved predator defense: Implications for sexual assault survivors. *Clinical Psychology: Science and Practice, 15*(1), 74–90. doi: 10.1111/j.1468-2850.2008.00112.x

Matell, M., Bateson, M., & Meck, W. (2006). Single-trials analyses demonstrate that increases in clock speed contribute to the methamphetamine-induced horizontal shifts in peak-interval timing functions. *Psychopharmacology, 188*(2), 201–212. doi: 10.1007/s00213-006-0489-x

Mauss, I. B., Bunge, S. A., & Gross, J. J. (2007). Automatic emotion regulation. *Social and Personality Psychology Compass, 1*, 146–167. doi: 10.1111/j.1751-9004.2007.00005.x

McCarthy-Jones, S. (2011). Voices from the storm: A critical review of quantitative studies of auditory verbal hallucinations and childhood sexual abuse. *Clinical Psychology Review, 31*(6), 983–992. doi: 10.1016/j.cpr.2011.05.004c

McHugh, T., Forbes, D., Bates, G., Hopwood, M., & Creamer, M. (2012). Anger in PTSD: Is there a need for a concept of PTSD-related posttraumatic anger? *Clinical Psychology Review, 32*, 93–104. doi: 10.1016/j.cpr.2011.07.013

McRae, K., Hughes, B., Chopra, S., Gabrieli, J. D. E., Gross, J. J., & Ochsner, K. N. (2010). The neural bases of distraction and reappraisal. *Journal of Cognitive Neuroscience, 22*(2), 248–262. doi: 10.1162/jocn.2009.21243

McTeague, L. M., Lang, P. J., Laplante, M., Cuthbert, B. N., Shumen, J. R., & Bradley, M. M. (2010). Aversive imagery in posttraumatic stress disorder: Trauma recurrence, comorbidity, and physiological reactivity. *Biological Psychiatry, 67*(4), 346–356. doi: 10.1016/j.biopsych.2009.08.023

Meck, W. (2005). Neuropsychology of timing and time perception. *Brain & Cognition, 58*(1), 1–8. doi: 10.1016/j.bandc.2004.09.004

Medford, N., & Critchley, H. D. (2010). Conjoint activity of anterior insular and anterior cingulate cortex: Awareness and response. *Brain Structure & Function, 214*, 535–549. doi: 10.1007/s00429-010-0265-x

Mendelsohn, M., Herman, J. L., Schatzow, E., Kallivayalil, D., Levitan, J., & Coco, M. (2011). *The trauma recovery group: A guide for practitioners*. New York, NY: Guilford Press.

Menon, V., & Uddin, L. Q. (2010). Saliency, switching, attention, and control: A network model of insula function. *Brain Structure & Function, 214*, 655–667. doi: 10.1007és00429-010-0262-0

Meyerson, J., & Gelkopf, M. (2004). Therapeutic utilization of spontaneous out-of-body experiences in hypnotherapy. *American Journal of Psychotherapy, 58*(1), 90–102.

Mezulis, A. H., Abramson, L. Y., Hyde, J. S., & Hankin, B. L. (2004). Is thera a universal positivity bias in attributions?: A meta-analytic review of individual, developmental, and cultural differences in the self-serving attributional bias. *Psychological Bulletin, 130*, 711–747. doi: 10.1037/0033-2909.130.5.711

Michal, M., Roder, C. H., Mayer, J., Lengler, U., & Krakow, K. (2005). Spontaneous dissociation during dunctional MRI experiments. *Journal of Psychiatric Research, 41*(1–2), 69–73. doi: 10.1016/j.jpsychires.2005.04.011

Michl, P., Meindl, T., Meister, F., Born, C., Engel, R. R., Reiser, M., & Hennig-Fast, K. (in press). Neurobiological underpinnings of shame and guilt: A pilot fMRI study. *Social Cognitive & Affective Neuroscience.* doi: 0.1093/scan/nss114

Mickleborough, M., Daniels, J. K., Coupland, N. J., Kao, R., Williamson, P. C., Lanius, U. F., . . .Lanius, R. A. (2011). Effects of trauma-related cues on pain processing in posttraumatic stress disorder: An fMRI investigation. *Journal of Psychiatry & Neuroscience, 36*(1), 6–14. doi: 10.1503/jpn.080188

Miller, M. W., Grief, J. L., & Smith, A. A. (2003). Multidimensional personality questionnaire profiles of veterans with traumatic combat exposure: Externalizing and internalizing subtypes. *Psychological Assessment, 15*(2), 205–215. doi: 10.1037/1040-3590.15.2.205

Miller, M. W., & Resick, P. A. (2007). Internalizing and externalizing subtypes in female sexual assault survivors: Implications for the understanding of complex PTSD. *Behavior Therapy, 38*(1), 58–71. doi: 10.1016/j.beth.2006.04.003

Miller, M. W., Resick, P. A., & Keane, T. M. (2009). DSM-V: Should PTSD be in a class of its own? *British Journal of Psychiatry, 194*(1), 90–90. doi:10.1192/bjp.194.1.90

Miyatake, T., Katayama, K., Takeda, Y., Nakashima, A., Sugita, A., & Mizumoto, M. (2004). Is death feigning adaptive?: Heritable variation in fitness difference of death-feigning behaviour. *Proceedings of the Royal Society of London, Series B, Biological Sciences, 271*, 2293–2296. *doi:* 10.1098/rspb.2004.2858

Monson, C. M., Schnurr, P. P., Resick, P. A., Friedman, M. J., Young-Xu, Y., & Stevens, S. P. (2006). Cognitive processing therapy for veterans with military-related posttraumatic stress disorder. *Journal of Consulting & Clinical Psychology, 74*, 898–907. doi: 10.1037/0022-006X.74.5.898

Moore, A. U., & Amstey, M. S. (1962). Tonic immobility: Differences in susceptibility of experimental and normal sheep and goats. *Science, 135*(3505), 729–730. *doi:* 10.1126/science.135.3505.729

Moran, J. M., Macrae, C. N., Heatherton, T. F., Wyland, C. L., & Kelley, W. M. (2006). Neuroanatomical evidence for distinct cognitive and affective components of self. *Journal of Cognitive Neurosicence, 8*(9), 1586–1594. doi: 10.1162/jocn.2006.18.9.1586

Moseley, G. L., Olthof, N., Venema, A., Don, S., Wijers, M., Gallace, A., & Spence, C. (2008). Psychologically induced cooling of a specific body part caused by the illusory ownership of an artificial counterpart. *Proceedings of the National Academy of Sciences of the United States of America, 105*(35), 13169–13173. doi: 10.1073/pnas.0803768105

Moser, J., Hajack, G., Simons, R., & Foa, E. (2007). Posttraumatic stress disorder symptoms in trauma-exposed college students: The role of trauma-related cognitions, gender, and negative affect. *Journal of Anxiety Disorders, 21*(8), 1039–1049. doi: 10.1016/j.janxdis.2006.10.009

Moskowitz, A. K. (2004a). Dissociation and violence: A review of the literature. *Trauma, Violence, & Abuse, 5*(1), 21–46. doi: 10.1177/1524838003259321

Moskowitz, A. K. (2004b). "Scared stiff": Catatonia as an evolutionary-based fear response. *Psychological Review, 111*(4), 984–1002. doi: 10.1037/0033-295X.111.4.984

Moskowitz, A. K., & Corstens, D. (2007). Auditory hallucinations: Psychotic symptom or dissociative experience? *Journal of Psychological Trauma, 6*(2–3), 35–63. doi: 10.1300/J513v06n02_04

Moskowitz, A. K., Read, J., Farrelly, S., Rudegeair, T., & Williams, O. (2009). Are psychotic symptoms traumatic in origin and dissociative in kind? In P. F. Dell & J. A. O'Neil (Eds.), *Dissociation and the dissociative disorders: DSM-V and beyond* (pp. 521–533). New York, NY: Routledge/Taylor & Francis.

Moskowitz, A. K., Schäfer, I., & Dorahy, M. J. (2008). *Psychosis, trauma and dissociation: Emerging perspectives on severe psychopathology.* New York, NY: Wiley-Blackwell. doi: 10.1002/9780470699652

Müller, J., Moergeli, H., & Maercker, A. (2008). Disclosure and social acknowledgment as predictors of recovery from posttraumatic stress: A longitudinal study in crime victims. *Canadian Journal of Psychiatry, 53*(3), 160–168.

Murphy, F. C., Nimmo-Smith, I., & Lawrence, A. D. (2003). Functional neuroanatomy of emotions: A meta-analysis. *Cognitive, Affective, & Behavioral Neuroscience, 3*(3), 207–233. doi: 10.3758/CABN.3.3.207

Myers-Schulz, B., & Koenigs, M. (2012). Functional anatomy of ventromedial prefrontal cortex: Implications for mood and anxiety disorders. *Molecular Psychiatry, 17*, 132–141. doi: 10.1038/mp.2011.88

Myrick, A. C., Brand, B. L., & Putnam, F. W. (2013). For better or worse: The role of revictimization and stress in the course of treatment for dissociative disorders. *Journal of Trauma & Dissociation, 14,* 375–389. doi: 10.1080/15299732.2012.736931

Nagel, T. (1974). What is it like to be a bat? *Philosophical Review, 83*(4), 435–450.

Nash, M. R., Lynn, S. J., & Stanley, S. (1984). The direct hypnotic suggestion of altered mind/body perception. *American Journal of Clinical Hypnosis, 27,* 95–102.

Nathanson, D. L. (1987). *The many faces of shame.* New York, NY: Guilford Press.

Nathanson, D. L. (1992). *Shame and pride: Affect, sex, and the birth of the self.* New York, NY: Norton.

Nazarov, A., McKinnon, M., Frewen, P. A., Parlar, M., Oremus, C., MacQueen, G., & Lanius, R. (in press). Theory of mind performance in women with posttraumatic stress disorder related to childhood abuse. *Acta Psychiatrica Scandinavia.* doi: 10.1111/acps.12142

New, A. S., Fan, J., Murrough, J. W., Liu, X., Liebman, R. E., Guise, K. G., . . . Charney, D.S. (2009). A functional magnetic resonance imaging study of deliberate emotion regulation in resilience and posttraumatic stress disorder. *Biological Psychiatry 66,* 656–664. doi: 10.1016/j.biopsych.2009.05.020

New, A. S., Hazlett, E. A., Newmark, R. E., Zhang, J., Triebwasser, J., Meyerson, D., . . . Buchsbaum, M. S. (2009). Laboratory induced aggression: A positron emission tomography study of aggressive individuals with borderline personality disorder. *Biological Psychiatry, 66,* 1107–1114. doi: 10.1016/j.biopsych.2009.07.015

Nielsen, F. Å., Balslev, D., & Hansen, L. K. (2005). Mining the posterior cingulate: Segregation between memory and pain components. *NeuroImage, 27*(3), 520–532. doi: 10.1016/j.neuroimage.2005.04.034

Nietlisbach, G., & Maercker, A. (2009). Social cognition and interpersonal impairments in trauma survivors with PTSD. *Journal of Aggression, Maltreatment, & Trauma, 18*(4), 382–402. doi: 10.1080/10926770902881489

Nietlisbach, G., Maercker, A., Rössler, W., & Haker, H. (2010). Are empathic abilities impaired in posttraumatic stress disorder? *Psychological Reports, 106,* 832–844.

Nijenhuis, E. R. S. (2013). Consciousness and self-consciousness in dissociative disorders. In V. Sinason (Ed.), *Trauma and dissociation: Conceptual, clinical and theoretical issues.* London: Routledge. Nijenhuis, E. R. S., & van der Hart, O. (1999). Forgetting and reexperiencing trauma. In J. Goodwin & R. Attias (Eds.), *Splintered reflections: Images of the body in treatment* (pp. 39–65). New York, NY: Basic Books.

Nijenhuis, E.R., Spinhoven, P., van Dyck, R., van der Hart, O., & Vanderlinden, J. (1996). The development and psychometric characteristics of the Somatoform Dissociation Questionnaire (SDQ-20). *Journal of Nervous and Mental Disease, 184,* 688-694.

Nijenhuis, E. R. S., & van der Hart, O. (2011). Dissociation in trauma: A new definition and comparison with previous formulations. *Journal of Trauma & Dissociation, 12,* 416–445. doi: 10.1080/15299732.2011.570592

Nijenhuis, E. R. S., Vanderlinden, J., & Spinhoven, P. (1998). Animal defensive reactions as a model for trauma-induced dissociative reactions. *Journal of Traumatic Stress, 11*(2), 243–260. doi: 10.1023/A:1024447003022

Noll, J. G., Trickett, P. K., Harris, W. W., & Putnam, F. W. (2009). The cumulative burden borne by offspring whose mothers were sexually abused as children. *Journal of Interpersonal Violence, 24,* 424–449. *doi:* 10.1177/0886260508317194

Norcross, J. C., & Wampold, B. E. (2011). What works for whom: Tailoring psychotherapy to the person. *Journal of Clinical Psychology, 67*(2), 127–132. doi: 10.1002/jclp.20764

Northoff, G., & Heinzel, A. (2006). First-person neuroscience: A new methodological approach for linking mental and neuronal states. *Philosophy, Ethics, & Humanities in Medicine, 1*(1), 3. doi: 10.1186/1747-5341-1-3

Northoff, G., Heinzel, A., de Greck, M., Bermpohl, F., Dobrowolny, H., & Panksepp, J. (2006). Self-referential processing in our brain: A meta-analysis of imaging studies on the self. *NeuroImage, 31*(1), 440–457. doi: 10.1016/j.neuroimage.2005.12.002

Northoff, G., Schneider, F., Rotte, M., Matthiae, C., Tempelmann, C., Wiebking, C., & Panksepp, J. (2009). Differential parametric modulation of self-relatedness and emotions in different brain regions. *Human Brain Mapping, 30*(2), 369–382. doi: 10.1002/hbm.20510

Noulhiane, M., Mella, N., Samson, S., Ragot, R., & Pouthas, V. (2007). How emotional auditory stimuli modulate time perception. *Emotion, 7*(4), 697–704. doi: 10.1037/1528-3542.7.4.697

Nummenmaa, L., Hironen, J., Parkkola, R., & Hietanen, J. K. (2008). Is emotional contagion special?: An fMRI study on neural systems for affective and cognitive empathy. *NeuroImage, 43*(3), 571–580. doi: 10.1016/j.neuroimage.2008.08.014

Oakley, D. A., Deeley, Q., & Halligan, P. W. (2007). Hypnotic depth and response to suggestion under standardized conditions and during fMRI scanning. *International Journal of Clinical and Experimental Hypnosis, 55*(1), 32–58. doi: 10.1080/00207140600995844

Oakley, D. A., & Halligan, P. W. (2009). Hypnotic suggestion and cognitive neuroscience. *Trends in Cognitive Sciences, 13*(6), 264–270. doi: 10.1016/j.tics.2009.03.004

Ochsner, K. N., & Gross, J. J. (2005). The cognitive control of emotion. *Trends in Cognitive Sciences, 9*(5), 242–249. doi: 10.1016/j.tics.2005.03.010

Ochsner, K. N., Beer, J. S., Robertson, E. R. Cooper, J.C., Gabrieli, J. D. E., Kihsltrom, J. F., & D'Esposito, M. (2005). The neural correlates of direct and reflected self-knowledge. *NeuroImage, 28*(4), 797–814. doi: 10.1016/j.neuroimage.2005.06.069

Ochsner, K. N., Bunge, S. A., Gross, J. J., & Gabrieli, J. D. E. (2002). Rethinking feelings: An fMRI study of the cognitive regulation of emotion. *Journal of Cognitive Neuroscience, 14,* 1215–1229. doi: 10.1162/089892902760807212

Ode, S., Hilmert, C. J., Desiree, J., & Robinson, M. D. (2010). Neuroticism's importance in understanding the daily life correlates of heart rate variability. *Emotion, 10*(4), 536–543. doi: 10.1037/a0018698;

Ogawa, J. R., Sroufe, L. A., Weinfield, N. S., Carlson, E. A., & Egeland, B. (1997). Development and the fragmented self: A longitudinal study of dissociative symptomatology in a non-clinical sample. *Development & Psychopathology, 9,* 855–879. *doi:* 10.1017/S0954579497001478

Ogden, P., Minton, K., & Pain, C. (2006). *Trauma and the body: A sensorimotor approach to psychotherapy.* New York, NY: Norton.

Ogrodniczuk, J. S., Piper, W. E., & Joyce, A. S. (2011). Effect of alexithymia on the process and outcome of psychotherapy: A programmatic review. *Psychiatry Research, 190*(1), 43–48. doi: 10.1016/j.psychres.2010.04.026

Ohayon, M. M. (2000). Prevalence of hallucinations and their pathological associations in the general populations. *Psychiatry Research, 97*(2–3), 153–164. doi: 10.1016/S0165-1781(00)00227-4

O'Kearney, R., Hunt, A., & Wallace, N. (2011). Integration and organization of trauma memories and posttraumatic symptoms. *Journal of Traumatic Stress, 24*(6), 716–725. doi: 10.1002/jts.20690

O'Kearney, R., & Perrott, K. (2006). Trauma narratives in posttraumatic stress disorder: A review. *Journal of Traumatic Stress, 19*(1), 81–93. doi: 10.1002/jts.20099

Olatunji, B. O., Ciesielski, B. G., & Tolin, D. F. (2010). Fear and loathing: A meta-analytic review of the specificity of anger in PTSD. *Behavior Therapy, 41*(1), 93–105. doi: 10.1016/j.beth.2009.01.004

Olsson, A., & Ochsner, K. N. (2008). The role of social cognition in emotion. *Trends in Cognitive Sciences, 12*, 65–71. doi: 10.1016/j.tics.2007.11.010

Orsillo, S. M., Batten, S. V., Plumb, J. C., Luterek, J. A., & Roessner, B. M. (2004). An experimental study of emotional responding in women with posttraumatic stress disorder related to interpersonal violence. *Journal of Traumatic Stress, 17*(3), 241–248. doi: 10.1023/B:JOTS.0000029267.61240.94

Orth, U., & Wieland, E. (2006). Anger, hostility, and posttraumatic stress disorder in trauma-exposed adults: A meta-analysis. *Journal of Consulting & Clinical Psychology, 74*(4), 698–706. doi: 10.1037/0022-006X.74.4.698

Osuch, E. A., Benson, B., Geraci, M., Podell, D., Herscovitch, P., McCann, U. D., & Post, R. M. (2001). Regional cerebral blood flow correlated with flashback intensity in patients with posttraumatic stress disorder. *Biological Psychiatry, 50*(4), 246–253. doi: 10.1016/S0006-3223(01)01107-6

Oveis, C., Cohen, A. B., Gruber, J., Shiota, M. N., Haidt, J., & Keltner, D. (2009). Resting respiratory sinus arrhythmia is associated with tonic positive emotionality. *Emotion, 9*(2), 265–270. doi: 10.1037/a0015383

Ozcetin, A., Belli, H., Ertem, U., Bahcebasi, T., Ataoglu, A., & Canan, F. (2009). Childhood trauma and dissociation in women with pseudoseizure-type conversion disorder. *Nordic Journal of Psychiatry, 63*(6), 462–468. doi: 10.3109/08039480903029728

Ozer, E. J., Best, S. R., Lipsey, T. L., & Weiss, D. S. (2003). Predictors of posttraumatic stress disorder and symptoms in adults: A meta-analysis. *Psychological Bulletin, 129*(1), 52–73. doi: 10.1037/0033-2909.129.1.52

Paivio, S. C., & Pascual-Leone, A. (2010). *Emotion-focused therapy for complex trauma: An integrative approach.* Washington, DC: American Psychological Association.

Palm, K. M., Strong, D. R., & MacPherson, L. (2009). Evaluating symptom expression as a function of a posttraumatic stress disorder severity. *Journal of Anxiety Disorders, 23*(1), 27–37. doi: 10.1016/j.janxdis.2008.03.012

Panksepp, J. (1998). *Affective neuroscience: The foundations of human and animal emotions.* New York, NY: Oxford University Press.

Panksepp, J., & Northoff, G. (2009). The trans-species core SELF: The emergence of active cultural and neuro-ecological agents through self-related processing within subcortical–cortical midline networks. *Consciousness & Cognition, 18*(1), 193–215. doi: 10.1016/j.concog.2008.03.002

Parlar, M., Frewen, P., Nazarov, A., Oremus, C., MacQueen, G., Lanius, R., & McKinnon, M. (in press). Alterations in empathic responding among women with post-traumatic stress disorder associated with childhood trauma. *Brain and Behavior.*

Pasteur, G. (1982). A classification review of mimicry systems. *Annual Review of Ecology and Systematics, 13*, 169–199.

Patel, R., Spreng, R. N., Shin, L. M., & Girard, T. A. (2012). Neurocircuitry models of posttraumatic stress disorder and beyond: A meta-analysis of functional neuroimaging studies. *Neuroscience & Biobehavioral Reviews, 36*(9), 2130–2142. doi: 10.1016/j.neubiorev.2012.06.003

Paulus, M. P., & Stein, M. B. (2006). An insular view of anxiety. *Biological Psychiatry, 60*, 383–387. doi: 10.1016/j.biopsych.2006.03.042

Pavlov, I. P. (1927). *Conditioned reflexes: An investigation of the physiological activity of the cerebral cortex.* London: Oxford University Press.

Penfield, W., & Rasmussen, T. (1950). *The cerebral cortex of man.* New York, NY: Macmillan.

Perez-Rodriguez, M. M., Hazlett, E. A., Rich, E. L., Ripoll, L. H., Weiner, D. M., Spence, N., . . . New, A. (2012). Striatal activity in borderline personality disorder with comorbid intermittent explosive disorder: Sex differences. *Journal of Psychiatric Research, 46,* 797–804. doi: 10.1016/j.jpsychires.2012.02.014

Perry, B. D., Pollard, R. A., Blakley, T. I., Baker, W. L., & Vigilante, D. (1995). Childhood trauma, the neurobiology of adaptation, and "use-dependent" development of the brain: How "states" become "traits." *Infant Mental Health Journal, 16,* 271–291. *doi:* 10.1002/1097-0355(199524)16:4<271::AID-IMH-J2280160404>3.0.CO;2-B

Peters, E. R., Williams, S. L., Cooke, M. A., & Kuipers, E. (2011). It's not what you hear, it's the way you think about it: Appraisals as determinants of affect and behavior in voice hearers. *Psychological Medicine, 42,* 1507–1514. doi: 10.1017/S0033291711002650

Petitot, J., Varela, F. J., Pachoud, B., & Roy, J. (1999). *Naturalizing phenomenology: Issues in contemporary phenomenology and cognitive science.* Stanford, CA: Stanford University Press.

Petkova, V. I., & Ehrsson, H. (2008). If I were you: Perceptual illusion of body swapping. *PLoS One, 3*(12), 1–9. doi: 10.1371/journal.pone.0003832

Petkova, V. I., Khoshnevis, M., & Ehrsson, H. H. (2011). The perspective matters!: Multisensory integration in ego-centric reference frames determines full-body ownership. *Frontiers in Psychology, 2,* 35. doi: 10.3389/fpsyg.2011.00035

Pfeifer, J. H., & Peake, S. J. (2012). Self-development: Integrating cognitive, socioemotional, and neuroimaging perspectives. *Developmental Cognitive Neuroscience, 2*(1), 55–69. doi: 10.1016/j.dcn.2011.07.012

Phan, K. L., Britton, J. C., Taylor, S. F., Fig, L. M., & Liberzon, I. (2006). Corticolimbic blood flow during nontraumatic emotional processing in posttraumatic stress disorder. *Archives of General Psychiatry, 63*(2), 184–192. doi: 10.1001/archpsyc.63.2.184

Phan, K. L., Taylor, S. F., Welsh, R. C., Decker, L. R., Noll, D. C., Nichols, T. E., . . . Liberzon, I. (2003). Activation of the medial prefrontal cortext and extended amygdala by individual ratings of emotional arousal: A fMRI study. *Biological Psychiatry, 53*(3), 211–215. doi: 10.1016/S0006-3223(02)01485-3

Phan, K. L., Wager, T., Taylor, S. F., & Liberzon, I. (2002). Functional neuroanatomy of emotion: A meta-analysis of emotion activation studies in PET and fMRI. *NeuroImage, 16*(2), 331–348. doi:10.1006/nimg.2002.1087

Pierre, J. M. (2010). Hallucinations in nonpsychotic disorders: Toward a differential diagnosis of "hearing voices." *Harvard Review of Psychiatry, 18*(1), 22–35. doi: 10.3109/10673220903523706

Pinto-Gouveia, J., & Matos, M. (2011). Can shame memories become a key to identity?: The centrality of shame memories predicts psychopathology. *Applied Cognitive Psychology, 25*(2), 281–290. doi: 10.1002/acp.1689

Pitman, R. K., Orr, S. P., Forgue, D. F., de Jong, J., & Claiborn, J. M. (1987). Psychophysiologic assessment of posttraumatic stress disorder imagery in Vietnam combat veterans. *Archives of General Psychiatry, 44,* 970–977. *doi:* 10.1037/0021-843X.99.1.49

Pitman, R. K., Orr, S. P., van der Kolk, B. A., Greenberg, M. S., Meyerhoff, J. L., & Mougey, E. H. (1990). Analgesia: A new dependent variable for the biological study of posttraumatic stress disorder. In Wolf, M.E., and Moshaim, A.D., American Psychiatric Publishing, Arlington, VA (Eds.), *Posttraumatic stress disorder: Etiology, phenomenology, and treatment* (pp. 140–147).

Pitman, R. K., Rasmusson, A. M., Koenen, K. C., Shin, L. M., Orr, S. P., Gilbertson, M. W., Liberzon, I. (2012). Biological studies of post-traumatic stress disorder. *Nature Reviews Neuroscience, 13,* 769–787. doi: 10.1038/nrn3339

Pole, N. (2007). The psychophysiology of posttraumatic stress disorder: A meta-analysis. *Psychological Bulletin, 133*(5), 725–746. doi: 10.1037/0033-2909.13.5.725

Poletti, M., Enrichi, I., & Adenzato, M. (2012). Cognitive and affective theory of mind in neurodegenerative diseases: Neuropsychological, neuroanatomical, and neurochemical levels. *Neuroscience & Biobehavioral Reviews, 36,* 2147–2164. doi: http://dx.doi.org/10.1016/j.neubiorev.2012.07.004

Pollatos, O., Gramann, K., & Schandry, R. (2007). Neural systems connecting interoceptive awareness and feelings. *Human Brain Mapping, 28*(1), 9–18. doi: 10.1002/hbm.20258

Pöppel, E. (1997). A hierarchical model of temporal perception. *Trends in Cognitive Science, 1*(2), 56–61. doi: 10.1016/S1364-6613(97)01008-5

Pöppel, E. (2004). Lost in time: A historical frame, elementary processing units and the 3-second window. *Acta Neurobiologiae Experimentalis, 64*(3), 295–301.

Pöppel, E. (2009). Pre semantically defined temporal windows for cognitve processing. *Philosophical Transactions of the Royal Society B, Biological Sciences, 364*(364), 1887–1896. doi: 10.1098/rstb.2009.0015

Porges, S. W. (1995). Orienting in a defensive world: Mammalian modifications of our evolutionary heritage: A polyvagal theory. *Psychophysiology, 32,* 301–318. *doi:* 10.1111/j.1469-8986.1995.tb01213.x

Porges, S. W. (2011). *The polyvagal theory: Neurophysiological foundations of emotions, attachment, communication, and self-regulation.* New York, NY: Norton.

Posey, T. B., & Losch, M. E. (1983). Auditory hallucinations of hearing voices in 375 normal subjects. *Imagination, Cognition, and Personality, 3*(2), 99–113. doi: 10.2190/74V5-HNXN-JEY5-DG7W

Power, M. J., & Fyvie, C. (2013). The role of emotion in PTSD: Two preliminary studies. *Behavioural and Cognitive Psychotherapy, 41*(2), 162–172. doi:10.1017/S1352465812000148

Putnam, F. W. (1989). *Diagnosis and treatment of multiple personality disorder.* New York, NY: Guilford Press.

Putnam, F. W., Helmers, K., & Trickett, P. K. (1993). Development, reliability, and validity of a child dissociation scale. *Child Abuse & Neglect, 17,* 731–741. *doi:* 10.1016/S0145-2134(08)80004-X

Putnam, F. W., & Trickett, P. K. (1987). *The psychobiological effects of child sexual abuse.* New York, NY: W. T. Grant Foundation.

Putnam, F. W., & Trickett, P. K. (1993). Child sexual abuse: A model of chronic trauma. *Psychiatry, 56,* 82–95.

Qin, P., & Northoff, G. (2011a). How is our self related to midline regions and the default-mode network? *NeuroImage, 57*(3), 1221–1233. doi: 10.1016/j.neuroimage.2011.05.028

Qin, P., & Northoff, G. (2011b). Brain imaging of the self: Conceptual, anatomical and methodological issues. *Consciousness & Cognition, 20*(1), 52–63 doi: 10.1016/j.concog.2010.09.011

Qin, P., Liu, Y., Shi, J., Wang, Y., Duncan, N. W., Gong, Q., & Northoff, G. (2012). Dissociation between anterior and posterior cortical regions during self-specificity and familiarity: A combined fMRI-meta-analytic study. *Human Brain Mapping, 33*(1), 154–164. doi: 10.1002/hbm.21201

Raichle, M. E. (2010). Two views of brain function. *Trends in Cognitive Science, 14,* 180–190. doi: 10.1016/j.tics.2010.01.008

Raichle, M. E., MacLeod, A. M., Snyder, A. Z., Powers, W. J., Gusnard, D. A., & Shulman, G. (2001). A default mode of brain function. *Proceedings of the National Academy of Sciences of the USA, 98*, 676–682. *doi:* 10.1073/pnas.98.2.676

Rahmanovic, A., Barnier, A. J., Cox, R. E., Langdon, R. A., & Coltheart, M. (2012). "That's not my arm": A hypnotic analogue of somatoparaphrenia. *Cognitive Neuropsychiatry, 17*(1), 36–63. doi: 10.1080/13546805.2011.564925

Ratcliffe, M. (2005). The feeling of being. *Journal of Consciousness Studies, 12*(8–10), 43–60.

Ratner, S. C. (1967). Comparative aspects of hypnosis. In J. E. Gordon (Ed.), *Handbook of clinical and experimental hypnosis*. New York, NY: Macmillan.

Reiff, M., Castille, D. M., Muenzenmaier, K., & Link, B. (2012). Childhood abuse and the content of adult psychotic symptoms. *Psychological Trauma: Theory, Research, Practice, and Policy, 4*(4), 356–369. doi: 10.1037/a0024203

Reinders, A. A. T. S., Nijenhuis, E. R. S., Paans, A. M. J., Korf, J., Willemsen, A. T. M., & den Boer, J. A. (2003). One brain, two selves. *NeuroImage, 20*(4), 2119–2125. doi: 10.1016/j.neuroimage.2003.08.021

Reinders, A. A. T. S., Nijenhuis, E. R. S., Quack, J., Korf, J., Haaksma, J., Paans, A. M. J., . . . den Boer, J. A. (2006). Psychobiological characteristics of dissociative identity disorder: A symptom provocation study. *Biological Psychiatry, 60*(7), 730–740. doi: 10.1016/j.biopsych.2005.12.019

Reinders, A. A. T. S., Willemsen, A. T. M., Vos, H. P., den Boer, J. A., & Nijenhuis, E. R. S. (2012). Fact or factitious?: A psychobiological study of authentic and simulated dissociative identity states. *PLoS One, 7*, e39279. *doi:* 10.1371/journal.pone.0039279

Resick, P. A., Galovski, T. E., Uhlmansiek, M. O., Scher, C. D., Clum, G. A., & Young-Xu, Y. (2008). A randomized clinical trial to dismantle components of cognitive processing therapy for posttraumatic stress disorder in female victims of interpersonal violence. *Journal of Consulting & Clinical Psychology, 76*, 243–258. doi: 10.1037/0022-006X.76.2.243

Resick, P. A., & Miller, M. W. (2009). Posttraumatic stress disorder: Anxiety or traumatic stress disorder? *Journal of Traumatic Stress, 22*(5), 384–390. doi:10.1002/jts.20437

Reynolds, M., & Brewin, C. R. (1998). Intrusive cognitions, coping strategies and emotional responses in depression, post-traumatic stress disorder and a non-clinical population. *Behaviour Research & Therapy, 36*, 135–147. *doi:* 10.1016/S0005-7967(98)00013-8

Reynolds, M., & Brewin, C. R. (1999). Intrusive memories in depression and post-traumatic stress disorder. *Behaviour Research & Therapy, 37*, 201–215. *doi:* 10.1016/S0005-7967(98)00132-6

Rizvi, S. L. (2010). Development and preliminary validation of a new measure to assess shame: The Shame Inventory. *Journal of Psychopathology and Behavioral Assessment, 32*(3), 438–447. doi: 10.1007/s10862-009-9172-y

Rizvi, S. L., Kaysen, D., Gutner, C. A., Griffin, M. G., & Resick, P. A. (2008). Beyond fear: The role of peritraumatic responses in posttraumatic stress and depressive symptoms among female crime victims. *Journal of Interpersonal Violence, 23*(6), 853–868. doi: 10.1177/0886260508314851

Roberton, T., Daffern, M., & Bucks, R. S. (2012). Emotion regulation and aggression. *Aggression and Violent Behavior, 17*(1), 72–82. doi: 10.1016/j.avb.2011.09.006

Roberts, R. J., . . . Hines, Marc E. (1990). The neuropathology of everyday life: The frequency of partial seizure symptoms among normals. *Neuropsychology, 4*(2), 65-85.

Robinaugh, D. J., & McNally, R. J. (2010). Autobiographical memory for shame or guilt provoking events: Association with psychological symptoms. *Behavior Research & Therapy, 48*(7), 646–652. doi: 10.1016/j.brat.2010.03.017

Rocha-Rego, V., Fiszman, A., Portugal, L. C., Pereira, M. G., de Oliveira, L., Mend-lowicz, M. V., . . . Volchan. E. (2009). Is tonic immobility the core sign among conventional peritraumatic signs and symptoms listed for PTSD? *Journal of Affective Disorders, 115*(1–2), 269–273. doi: 10.1016/j.jad.2008.09.005

Röder, C. H., Michal, M., Overbeck, G., van de Ven, V. G., & Linden, D. E. (2007). Pain response in depersonalization: A functional imaging study using hypnosis in healthy subjects. *Psychotherapy and Psychosomatics, 76*(2), 115–121. doi: 10.1159/000097970

Roemer, L., Litz, B. T., Orsillo, S. M., & Wagner, A. M. (2005). A preliminary investigation of the role of strategic withholding of emotions in PTSD. *Journal of Traumatic Stress, 14*(1), 149–156. doi: 10.1023/A:1007895817502

Romme, M. A., & Escher, A. D. (1989). Hearing voices. *Schizophrenia Bulletin, 15*(2), 209–216.

Ros, T., Théberge, J., Frewen, P. A., Kluetsch, R., Densmore, M., Calhoun, V. D., & Lanius, R. A. (2013). Mind over chatter: Plastic up-regulation of the fMRI salience network directly after EEG neurofeedback. *NeuroImage, 15*(65), 324–335. doi: 10.1016/j.neuroimage.2012.09.046

Rosik, C. H., & Soria, A. (2012). Spiritual well-being, dissociation, and alexithymia: Examining direct and moderating effets. *Journal of Trauma & Dissociation, 13,* 69–87. doi: 10.1080/15299732.2011.606739

Ross, C. A. (1988). *Multiple personality disorder: Diagnosis, clinical features, and treatment.* New York, NY: Wiley.

Ross, C. A., & Keyes, B. (2004). Dissociation and schizophrenia. *Journal of Trauma & Dissociation, 5*(3), 69–83. doi: 10.1300/J229v05n03_05

Ross, C. A., Miller, S. D., Reagor, P., & Bjornson, L. (1990). Structured interview data on 102 cases of multiple personality disorder from four centers. *American Journal of Psychiatry, 147*(5), 596–601.

Roth, A., & Fonagy, P. (2004). *What works for whom?: A critical review of psycho-therapy research.* (2nd ed.). New York, NY: Guilford.

Rothschild, B. (2003). *The body remembers casebook: Unifying methods and models in the treatment of trauma and PTSD.* New York, NY: Norton.

Rubia, K. (2006). The neural correlates of timing functions. In J. Glicksohn & M. S. Myslobodsky (Eds.), *Timing the future: The case for a time-based prospective memory* (pp. 213–238). River Edge, NJ: World Scientific.

Rubin, D. C. (2011). The coherence of memories for trauma: Evidence from post-traumatic stress disorder. *Consciousness & Cognition, 20*(3), 857–865. doi: 10.1016/j.concog.2010.03.018

Rubin, D. C., & Berntsen, D. C. (2004). Cultural life scripts structure recall from autobiographical memory. *Memory & Cognition, 32*(3), 427–442. doi: 10.3758/BF03195836

Rubin, D. C., Berntsen, D., & Hutson, M. (2009). The normative and the personal life: Individual differences in life scripts and life story events among USA and Danish undergraduates. *Memory, 17*(1), 54–68. doi: 10.1080/09658210802541442

Rubin, D. C., Boals, A., & Berntsen, D. (2008). Memory in posttraumatic stress disorder: Properties of voluntary and involuntary, traumatic and nontraumatic autobiographical memories in people with and without posttraumatic stress disorder symptoms. *Journal of Experimental Psychology, 137*(4), 591–614. doi: 10.1037/a0013165

Ruby, P., & Decety, J. (2001). Effect of subjective perspective taking during simulation of action: A PET investigation of agency. *Nature Neuroscience, 4*(5), 546–550. doi: 10.1038/87510

Ruby, P., & Decety J. (2003). What you believe versus what you think they believe: A neuroimaging study of conceptual perspective-taking. *European Journal of Neuroscience, 17*(11), 2475–2480. doi: 10.1046/j.1460-9568.2003.02673.x

Ruby, P., & Decety J. (2004). How would you feel versus how do you think she would feel?: A neuroimaging study of perspective-taking with social emotions. *Journal of Cognitive Neuroscience, 16*(6), 988–999. doi: 10.1162/0898929041502661

Ruddle, A., Mason, O., & Wykes, T. (2011). A review of hearing voices groups: Evidence and mechanisms of change. *Clinical Psychology Review, 31*(5), 757–766. doi: 10.1016/j.cpr.2011.03.010

Rusch, M. D., Grunert, B. K., Mendelsohn, R. A., & Smucker, M. R. (2000). Imagery rescripting for recurrent, distressing images. *Cognitive & Behavioral Practice, 7*, 173–182. doi: 10.1016/S1077-7229(00)80028-0

Russell, J. A. (1980). A circumplex model of affect. *Journal of Personality & Social Psychology, 39*, 1161–1178. doi: 10.1037/h0077714

Russell, J. A. (2003). Core affect and the psychological construction of emotion. *Psychological Review, 110*, 145–172.doi: 10.1037/0033-295X.110.1.145

Russell, J. A. (2005). Emotion in human consciousness is built on core affect. *Journal of Consciousness Studies, 12*(8–10), 26–42.

Russell, J. A. (2009). Emotion, core affect, and psychological construction. *Cognition & Emotion, 23*, 1259–1283. doi: 10.1080/02699930902809375

Russel, J. A., & Carroll, J. M. (1999). On the bipolarity of positive and negative affect. *Psychological Bulletin, 125*, 3–30. doi: 10.1037/0033-2909.125.1.3

Sack, M., Hopper, J. W., & Lamprecht, F. (2004). Low respiratory sinus arrhythmia and prolonged psychophysiological arousal in posttraumatic stress disorder: Heart rate dynamics and individual differences in arousal regulation. *Biological Psychiatry, 55*(3), 284–290. doi: 10.1016/S0006-3223(03)00677-2

Salas, C. E., Radovic, D., & Turnbull, O. H. (2012). Inside-out: Comparing internally generated and externally generated basic emotions. *Emotion, 12*, 568–578. doi: 10.1037/a0025811

Samuels, A., & Taylor, M. (1994). Children's ability to distinguish fantasy events from real-life events. *British Journal of Developmental Psychology, 12*(4), 417–427. doi: 10.1111/j.2044-835X.1994.tb00644.x

Sar, V., Akyüz, G., Kundakçi, T., Kiziltan, E., & Dogan, O. (2004). Childhood trauma, dissociation, and psychiatric comorbidity in patients with conversion disorder. *American Journal of Psychiatry, 161*(12), 2271–2276. doi: 10.1176/appi.ajp.161.12.2271

Sar, V., Unal, S. N., & Ozturk, E. (2007). Frontal and occipital perfusion changes in dissociative identity disorder. *Psychiatry Research, 156*, 217–223. *doi:* 10.1016/j.pscychresns.2006.12.017

Sartory, G., Cwik, J., Knuppertz, H., Schürholt, B., Lebens, M., Seitz, R. J., & Schulze, R. (2013). In search of the trauma memory: A meta-analysis of functional neuroimaging studies of symptom provocation in posttraumatic stress disorder (PTSD). *PLoS One, 8*(3), e58150. doi: 10.1371/journal.pone

Sautter, F. J., Brailey, K., Uddo, M. M., Hamilton, M. F., Beard, M. G., & Borges, A. H. (1999). PTSD and comorbid psychotic disorder: Comparison with veterans diagnosed with PTSD or psychotic disorder. *Journal of Traumatic Stress, 12*(1), 73–88. doi: 10.1023/A:1024794232175

Savoy, R., Frederick, B., Keuroghlian, A., & Wolk, P. (2012). Voluntary switching between identities in dissociative identity disorder: A functional MRI case study. *Cognitive Neuroscience, 3*, 112–119. *doi:* 10.1080/17588928.2012.669750

Sayar, K., & Kose, S. (2003). The relationship between alexithymia and dissociation in an adolescent sample. *Bulletin of Clinical Psychopharmacology, 13*(4), 167–173.

Sayar, K., Kose, S., Grabe, H. J., & Topbas, M. (2005). Alexithymia and dissociative tendencies in an adolescent sample from Eastern Turkey. *Psychiatry & Clinical Neurosciences, 59*(2), 127–134. doi: 10.1111/j.1440-1819.2005.01346.x

Schauer, M., & Elbert, T. (2010). Dissociation following traumatic stress. *Journal of Psychology/Zeitschrift für Psychologie, 218*(2), 109–127. doi: 10.1027/0044-3409/a000018

Schauer, M., Neuner, F., & Elbert, T. (2005). *Narrative exposure therapy: A short-term intervention for traumatic stress disorders after war, terror, or torture.* Cambridge, MA: Hofgre & Huber.

Schmahl, C., Bohus, M., Esposito, F., Treede, R. D., Di Salle, F., Greffrath, W., & Seifritz, E. (2006). Neural correlates of antinociception in borderline personality disorder. *Archives of General Psychiatry, 63*(6), 659. doi: 10.1001/archpsyc.63.6.659.

Schmahl, C., Meinzer, M., Zeuch, A., Fichter, M., Cebulla, M., Kleindienst, N., & Bohus, M. (2010). Pain sensitivity is reduced in borderline personality disorder, but not in posttraumatic stress disorder and bulimia nervosa. *World Journal of Biological Psychiatry, 11*(2, Pt. 2), 364–371. doi: 10.3109/15622970701849952

Schmalzl, L. & Ersson, H. H. (2011a). Experimental inducaiton of a percieved "telescoped" limb using a full-body illusion. *Frontiers in Human Neuroscience, 5,* 34. doi:10.3389/fnhum.2011.00034

Schmalzl, L. & Ersson, H. H. (2011b). "Pulling telescoped phantoms out of the stump": Manipulating the perceived position of phantom limbs using a full-body illusion. *Frontiers in Human Neuroscience, 5,*121. doi: 10.3389/fnhum.2011.00121

Schoenberg, P. L., Sierra, M., & David, A. S. (2012). Psychophysiological investigations in depersonalization disorder and effects of electrodermal biofeedback. *Trauma & Dissociation, 13,* 311–329. doi: 10.1080/15299732.2011.606742

Schore, A. N. (2003a). *Affect regulation and the self.* New York, NY: Norton.

Schore, A. N. (2003b). *Affect dysregulation and disorders of the self.* New York, NY: Norton.

Schore, A. N. (2012). *The science of the art of psychotherapy.* New York, NY: Norton.

Schuettler, D., & Boals, A. (2011). The path to posttraumatic growth versus posttraumatic stress disorder: Contributions of event centrality and coping. *Journal of Loss & Trauma, 16*(2), 180–194. doi: 10.1080/15325024.2010.519273

Schulz, P. M., Resick, P. A., Huber, L. C., & Griffin, M. G. (2006). The effectiveness of cognitive processing therapy for PTSD with refugees in a community setting. *Cognitive & Behavioral Practice, 13,* 322–331. 10.1016/j.cbpra.2006.04.011

Schulze, L., Domes, G., Krüger, A., Berger, C., Fleischer, M., Prehn, K., . . . Herpertz, S.C. (2011). Neuronal correlates of cognitive reappraisal in borderline patients with affective instability. *Biological Psychiatry, 69,* 564–573. doi: 10.1016/j.biopsych.2010.10.025

Schwartz, R. C. (1995). *Internal family systems therapy.* New York, NY: Guilford Press.

Scott, J. G., Nurcombe, B., Sheridan, J., & McFarland, M. (2007). Hallucinations in adolescents with post-traumatic stress disorder and psychotic disorder. *Australasian Psychiatry, 15*(1), 44–48. doi: 10.1080/10398560601083084

Sebastian, C. L., Fontaine, N. M., Bird, G., Blakemore, S. J., De Brito, S. A., McCrory, E. J., & Viding, E. (2012). Neural processing associated with cognitive and affective theory of mind in adolescents and adults. *Social Cognitive & Affective Neuroscience 7,* 53–63. *doi:* 10.1093/scan/nsr023

Seeley, W. W., Menon, W., Schatzberg, A. F., Keller, J., Glover, G. H., Kenna, H., . . . Greicius, M. D. (2007). Dissociable intrinsic connectivity networks for salience processing and executive control. *Journal of Neuroscience, 27,* 2349–2356. doi: 10.1523/jneurosci.5587-06.2007

Sforza, A., Bufalari, I., Haggard, P., & Agli200, S. M. (2010). My face in yours: Visuo-tactile facial stimulation influences sense of identity. *Social Neuroscience, 5*(2), 148–162. doi: 10.1080/17470910903205503

Shamay-Tsoory, S. G., & Aharon-Peretz, J. (2007). Dissociable prefrontal networks for cognitive and affective theory of mind: A lesion study. *Neuropsychologia, 45*(13), 3054–3067. *doi:* 10.1016/j.neuropsychologia.2007.05.021

Shamay-Tsoory, S. G., Aharon-Peretz, J., & Perry, D. (2009). Two systems for empathy: A double dissociation between emotional and cognitive empathy in inferior frontal gyrus versus ventromedial prefrontal lesions. *Brain, 132*(3), 617–627. doi: 10.1093/brain/awn279

Shamay-Tsoory, S. G., Harari, H., Aharon-Peretz, J., & Levkovitz, Y. (2010). The role of the orbitofrontal cortex in affective theory of mind deficits in criminal offenders with psychopathic tendencies. *Cortex, 46*(5), 668–677. *doi:* 10.1016/j. cortex.2009.04.008

Sharp, C., Fonagy, P., & Allen, J. G. (2012). Posttraumatic stress disorder: A social-cognitive perspective. *Clinical Psychology: Science & Practice, 19*(3), 229–240. *doi:* 10.1111/cpsp.12002

Shaw, P., Kabani, N. J., Lerch, J. P., Eckstrand, K., Lenroot, R., Gogtay, N., & Wise, S. P. (2008). Neurodevelopmental trajectories of the human cerebral cortex. *Journal of Neuroscience, 28*(14), 3586–3594. doi: 10.1523/JNEURO-SCI.5309-07.2008

Shergill, S. S., Brammer, M. J., Williams, R. M., Murray, R., & McGuire, P. (2000). Mapping auditory hallucinations in schizophrenia using functional magnetic resonance imaging. *Archives of General Psychiatry, 57,* 1033–1038. doi: 10.1001/archpsyc.57.11.1033

Sherman, N. (2005). *Stoic warriors: The ancient philosophy behind the military mind* (Vol. 1). New York, NY: Oxford University Press.

Sherman, N. (2010). *The untold war.* New York, NY: Norton.

Sheu, Y.-S., Polcari, A., Anderson, C. M., & Teicher, M. H. (2010). Harsh corporal punishment is associated with increased T2 relaxation time in dopamine-rich regions. *NeuroImage, 53*(2), 412–419. doi: 10.1016/j.neuroimage.2010.06.043

Shevlin, M., Dorahy, M., & Adamson, G. (2007). Childhood traumas and hallucinations: An analysis of the national comorbidity survey. *Journal of Psychiatric Research, 41*(3–4), 222–228. doi: 10.1016/j.jpsychires.2006.03.004

Shevlin, M., Houston, J. E., Dorahy, M. J., & Adamson, G. (2008). Cumulative traumas and psychosis: An analysis of the National Comorbidity Survey and the British Psychiatric Morbidity Survey. *Schizophrenia Bulletin, 34*(1), 193–199. doi: 10.1093/schbul/sbm069

Shin, L. M., McNally, R. J., Kosslyn, S. M., Thompson, W. L., Rauch, S. L., Alpert, N. M., & Pitman, R. K. (1999). Regional cerebral blood flow during script-driven imagery in childhood sexual abuse-related PTSD: A PET investigation. *American Journal of Psychiatry, 156*(4), 575–584.

Shin, L. M., Orr, S. P., Carson, M. A., Rauch, S. L., Macklin, M. L., Lasko, N. B., Peters, P. M., . . . Pitman, R. K. (2004). Regional cerebral blood flow in the amygdala and medial prefrontal cortex during traumatic imagery in male and female vietnam veterans with PTSD. *Archives of General Psychiatry, 61*(2), 168–176. doi: 10.1001/archpsyc.61.2.168

Shin, L. M., Wright, C. I., Cannistraro, P. A., Wedig, M. M., McMullin, K., Martis, B., . . . Rauch, S. L. (2005). A functional magnetic resonance imaging study of amygdala and medial prefrontal cortex responses to overtly presented fearful faces in posttraumatic stress disorder. *Archives of General Psychiatry, 62*(3), 273–281. doi: 10.1001/archpsyc.62.3.273

Siegel, D. J. (2007). *The mindful brain: Reflection and attunement in the cultivation of well-being.* New York, NY: Norton.

Siegel, D. J. (2010). *The mindful therapist: A clinician's guide to mindsight and neural integration.* New York, NY: Norton.

Sierra, M., Baker, D., Medford, N., & David, A. S. (2005). Unpacking the deper-sonalization syndrome: An exploratory factor analysis of the Cambridge Deper-sonalization Scale. *Psychological Medicine, 35*(10), 1523–1532. doi: 10.1017/S0033291705005325

Sierra, M., & Berrios, G. E. (1998). Depersonalization: Neurobiological perspectives. *Biological Psychiatry, 44*(9), 898–908. doi: 10.1016/S0006-3223(98)00015-8

Sierra, M., & Berrios, G. E. (2000). The Cambridge Depersonalization Scale: A new instrument for the measurement of depersonalization. Psychiatry Research, 93, 53-164.

Sierra, M., Senior, C., Dalton, J., McDonough, M., Bond, A., Phillips, M. L., David, A. S. (2002). Autonomic response in depersonalization disorder. *Archives of General Psychiatry, 59*(9), 833–838. doi: 10.1001/archpsyc.59.9.833

Sierra, M., Senior, C., Phillips, M. L., & David, A. S. (2006). Autonomic response in the perception of disgust and happiness in depersonalization disorder. *Psychiatry Research, 145*(2), 225–231. doi: 10.1016/j.psychres.2005.05.022

Silbersweig, D. A., Frith, C., Cahill, C., Holmes, A., Grootoonk, S., Seaward, J., . . . Schnoor, L. (1995). A functional neuroanatomy of hallucinations in schizophre-nia. *Nature, 378*(6553), 176–179. doi: 10.1038/378176a0

Simeon, D., & Abugel, J. (2006). *Feeling unreal: Depersonalization disorder and the loss of the self*. Oxford, UK: Oxford University Press.

Simeon, D., Giesbrecht, T., Knutelska, M., Smith, R. J., & Smith, L. M. (2009). Alexithymia, absorption, and cognitive failures in depersonalization disor-der: A comparison to posttraumatic stress disorder and healthy volunteers. *Journal of Nervous and Mental Disease, 197*(7), 492498. doi: 10.1097/NMD.0b013e3181aaef6b

Simeon, D., Gross, S., Guralnik, O., & Stein, D. J. (1997). Feeling unreal: 30 cases of DSM-III-R depersonalization disorder. *American Journal of Psychiatry, 154*(8), 1107–1113.

Simeon, D., Guralnik, O., Hazlett, E. A., Spiegel-Cohen, J., Hollander, E., & Buchs-baum, M. S. (2000). Feeling unreal: A PET study of depersonalization disor-der. *American Journal of Psychiatry, 157*(11), 17821788. doi: 10.1176/appi.ajp.157.11.1782

Simeon, D., Guralnik, O., Schmeidler, J., Sirof, B., & Knutelska, M. (2001). The role of childhood interpersonal trauma in depersonalization disorder. *American Journal of Psychiatry, 158*(7), 1027–1033. doi: 10.1176/appi.ajp.158.7.1027

Simeon, D., Kozin, D. S., Segal, K., Lerch, B., Dujour, ., & Giesbrecht, T. (2008). De-constructing depersonalization: Further evidence for symptom clusters. *Psychiatry Research, 157*, 303-306. doi:10.1016/j.psychres.2007.07.007

Simeon, D., Smith, R. J., Knutelska, M., & Smith, L. M. (2008). Somatoform disso-ciation in depersonalization disorder. *Journal of Trauma & Dissociation, 9*(3), 335–348. doi: 10.1080/15299730802139170

Simeon, D., Yehuda, R., Knutelska, M., & Schmeidler, J. (2008). Dissociation ver-sus posttraumatic stress: Cortisol and physiological correlates in adults highly exposed to the World Trade Center attack on 9/11. *Psychiatry Research, 161*(3), 325–329. doi: 10.1016/j.psychres.2008.04.021

Singer, J. A., & Blagov, P. (2004). The integrative function of narrative processing: Autobiographical memory, self-defining memories, and the life story of identity. In D. R. Beike, J. M. Lampinen, & D. A. Behrend (Eds.), *The self and memory: Evolving concepts* (pp. 117–138). New York, NY: Psychology Press.

Singer, J. A., & Salovey, P. (1993). *The remembered self: Emotion and memory in personality*. New York, NY: Maxwell Macmillan International.

Singer, T., Critchley, H. D., & Preuschoff, K. (2009). A common role of insula in felings, empathy, and uncertainty. *Trends in Cognitive Science, 13*(8), 334–340. doi: 10.1016/j.tics.2009.05.001

Skinner, J. E. (1985). Regulation of cardiac vulnerability by the cerebral defense system. *Journal of the American College of Cardiology, 5*(6 Suppl.), 88B–94B.

Skinner, J. E. (1988). Brain involvement in cardiovascular disorders. In T. Elbert, W. Langosch, A. Steptoe, & D. Vaitl (Eds.), *Behavioural medicine in cardiovascular disorders* (pp. 229–253). Chichester, UK: Wiley.

Slotema, C. W., Daalman, K., Blom, J. D., Diederen, K. M., Hoek, H. W., & Sommer, I. E. (2012). Auditory verbal hallucinations in patients with borderline personality disorder are similar to those in schizophrenia. *Psychological Medicine, 42*(9), 1873–1878. doi: 10.1017/S0033291712000165

Smeets, T., Giesbrecht, T., Raymaekers, L., Shaw, J., & Merckelback, H. (2010). Autobiographical integration of trauma memories and repressive coping predict post-traumatic stress symptoms in undergraduate students. *Clinical Psychology & Psychotherapy, 17*(3), 211–218. doi: 10.1002/cpp.644

Smith, S. D., McIver, T. A., Di Nella, M. S. J., & Crese, M. L. (2011). The effects of valence and arousal on the emotional modulation of time perception: Evidence for multiple stages of processing. *Emotion, 11*, 1305–1313. doi: 10.1037/a0026145

Smucker, M. R., & Dancu, C. V. (1999). *Cognitive behavioral treatment for adult survivors of childhood trauma: Rescripting and reprocessing.* Northvale, NJ: Jason Aronson.

Smucker, M. R., Dancu, C. V., Foa, E. B., & Niederee, J. L. (1995). Imagery rescripting: A new treatment for survivors of childhood sexual abuse suffering from posttraumatic stress. *Journal of Cognitive Psychotherapy, 9*, 3–17.

Smucker, M. R., & Niederee, J. L. (1995). Treating incest-related PTSD and pathogenic schemas through imaginal exposure and rescripting. *Cognitive Behavioral Practice, 2*, 63–93. doi: 10.1016/S1077-7229(05)80005-7

Solomon, M. F., & Siegel, D. J. (2003). *Healing trauma: Attachment, mind, body, and brain.* New York, NY: Norton.

Sommer, I. E., Daalman, K., Rietkerk, T., Diederen, K. M., Bakker, S., Wijkstra, J., & Marko P. M. (2010). Healthy individuals with auditory verbal hallucinations: Who are they? Psychiatric assessments of a selected sample of 103 subjects. *Schizophrenia Bulletin, 36*(3), 633–641. doi: 10.1093/schbul/sbn130

Spahic-Mihajlovic, A., Crayton, J. W., & Neafsey, E. J. (2005). Selective numbing and hyperarousal in male and female Bosnian refugees with PTSD. *Journal of Anxiety Disorders, 19*(4), 383–402. doi: 10.1016/j.janxdis.2004.03.004

Spiegel, D. (2012). Functional brain basis of hypnotizability. *Archives of General Psychiatry, 69*(10), 1064–1072. doi: 10.1001/archgenpsychiatry.2011.2190

Spiegel, D., & Cardeña, E. (1991). Disintegrated experience: The dissociative disorders revisted. *Journal of Abnormal Psychology, 100*, 366–378. *doi:* 10.1037/0021-843X.100.3.366

Spiegel, D., Lewis-Fernández, R., Lanius, R., Vermetten, E., Simeon, D., & Friedman, M. (2013). Dissociative disorders in DSM-5. *Annual Review of Clinical Psychology, 9*, 299–326. doi: 10.1146/annurev-clinpsy-050212-185531

Spiegel, D., Loewenstein, R. J., Lewis-Fernandez, R., Sar, V., Simeon, D., Vermetten, E., . . . Dell, P. F. (2011). Dissociative disorders in DSM-5. *Depression and Anxiety, 28*(12), 824-852. doi: 10.1002/da.20923

Spiegel, D., & Vermetten, E. (1994). Physiological correlates of hypnosis and dissociation. In D. Spiegel (Ed.), *Dissociation: Culture, mind, and body* (pp. 185–209). Washington, DC: American Psychiatric Association.

Spiegel, H., & Spiegel, D. (2004). *Trance and treatment: Clinical uses of hypnosis* (2nd ed.) Washington, DC: American Psychiatric Association.

Spiers, P. A., Schoemer, D. L., Blume, H. W., & Meslum, M. (1985). Temporolimbic epilepsy and behavior. In M.-M. Meslum (Ed.), *Principles of behavioral neurology* (pp. 289–325). Philadelphia, PA: F. A. Davis.

Spitzer, R. L., First, M. B., & Wakefield, J. C. (2007). Saving PTSD from itself in DSM-V. *Journal of Anxiety Disorders, 21*(2), 233–241. doi: 10.1016/j.janxdis.2006.09.006

Spoont, M. R., Kuskowski, M., & Pardo, J. V. (2010). Autobiographical memories of anger in violent and non-violent individuals: A script-driven imagery study. *Psychiatry Research: Neuroimaging, 183,* 225–229. doi: 10.1016/j.pscychresns.2010.06.004

Spreng, R. N., & Grady, C. L. (2010). Patterns of brain activity supporting autobiographical memory, prospection, and theory of mind, and their relationship to the default mode network. *Journal of Cognitive Neuroscience, 22*(6), 1112–1123. doi: 10.1162/jocn.2009.21282

Spreng, R. N., Mar, R. A., & Kim, A. S. (2009). The common neural basis of autobiographical memory, prospection, navigation, theory of mind, and the default mode: A quantitative meta-analysis. *Journal of Cognitive Neuroscience, 21,* 489–510. doi: 10.1162/jocn.2008.21029

Staniloiu, A., & Markowitsch, H. J. (2010). Looking at comorbidity through the glasses of neuroscientific memory research: A brain-network perspective. *Behavioral and Brain Sciences, 33,* 170–171. doi: 10.1017/S0140525X10000804

Staniloiu, A., Markowitsch, H. J., & Brand, M. (2010). Psychogenic amnesia: A malady of the constricted self. *Consciousness & Cognition, 19*(3), 778–801. doi: 10.1016/j.concog.2010.06.024

Staub, E. (2003). *The psychology of good and evil: Why children, adults and groups help and harm others.* New York, NY: Cambridge University Press.

Staub, E. (2005). The roots of goodness: The fulfillment of basic human needs and the development of caring, helping and nonaggression, inclusive caring, moral courage, active bystandership, and altruism born of suffering. In G. Carlo & C. Edwards (Eds.), *Nebraska Symposium on Motivation: Vol. 51. Moral motivation through the life span: Theory, research, applications.* Lincoln, NE: University of Nebraska Press.

Staub, E., & Vollhardt J. (2008). Altruism born of suffering: The roots of caring and helping after victimization and other trauma. *American Journal of Orthopsychiatry, 78*(3), 367–280. doi: 10.1037/a0014223

Steele, K., Dorahy, M. J., van der Hart, O., & Nijenhuis, E. R. S. (2009). Dissociation versus alterations in consciousness: Related but different concepts. In P. F. Dell & J. A. O'Neil (Eds.), *Dissociation and the dissociative disorders: DSM-5 and beyond* (pp. 155–169). New York, NY: Routledge/Taylor & Francis.

Steuwe, C., Daniels, J., Frewen, P. A., Densmore, M., Pannasch, S., Beblo, T., . . . Lanius R. (in press). Effect of direct eye contact in PTSD related to interpersonal trauma: fMRI study of activation of an innate alarm system. *Social Cognitive & Affective Neuroscience.* doi: 10.1093/scan/nss105

Steuwe, C., Lanius, R. A., & Frewen, P. A. (2012). Evidence for a dissociative sybtype of PTSD by latent profile and confirmatory factor analysis in a civilian sample. *Depression & Anxiety, 29*(8), 689–700. doi: 10.1002/da.21944

Stein, D. J., Koenen, K. C., Friedman, M. J., Hill, E., McLaughlin, K., Petukhova, M., & Kessler, R. C. (2013). Dissociation in posttraumatic stress disorder: Evidence from the World Mental Health Surveys. *Biological Psychiatry, 73,* 302–312. doi: 10.1016/j.biopsych.2012.08.022

Stiglmayr, C. E., Ebner-Priemer, U. W., Bretz, J., Behm, R., Mohuse, M., & Bohus, M. (2008). Dissociative symptoms are positively related to stress in borderline personality disorder. *Acta Psychiatrica Scandinavia, 117,* 139–147. *doi:* 10.1111/j.1600-0447.2007.01126.x

Stiglmayr, C. E., Shapiro, D. A., Stieglitz, R. D., Limberger, M. F., & Bohus, M. (2001). Experience of aversive tension and dissociation in female patients with borderline personality disorder: A controlled study. *Journal of Psychiatric Research, 35*(2), 111–118. doi: 10.1016/S0022-3956(01)00012-7

Stopa, L. (2011). Imagery rescripting across disorders: A practical guide. *Cognitive & Behavioral Practice, 18*(4), 421–423. doi: 10.1016/j.cbpra.2011.05.001

Suarez, S. D., & Gallup, G. G. (1979). Tonic immobility as a response to rape in humans: A theoretical note. *Psychological Record, 29*, 315–320.

Sutherland, K., & Bryant, R. A. (2005). Self-defining memories in post-traumatic stress disorder. *British Journal of Clinical Psychology, 44*(4), 591–598. doi: 10.1348/014466505X64081

Suvak, M. K., Walling, S. M., Iverson, K. M., Taft, C. T., & Resick, P. A. (2009). Multilevel regression analyses to investigate the relationship between two variables over time: Examining the longitudinal association between intrusion and avoidance. *Journal of Traumatic Stress, 22*(6), 622–631. doi: 10.1002/jts.20476

Swift, J. K., Callahan, J. L., & Vollmer, B. M. (2011). Preferences. *Journal of Clinical Psychology, 67*(2), 155–165. doi: 10.1002/jclp.20759

Takahashi, H., Yahata, N., Koeda, M., Matsuda, T., Asai, K., & Okubo, Y. (2004). Brain activation associated with evaluative processes of guilt and embarrassment: An fMRI study. *NeuroImage, 23*, 967–974. *doi:* 10.1016/j.neuroimage.2004.07.054

Talbot, J. A., Talbot, N. L., & Tu, X. (2004). Shame-proneness as a diathesis for dissociation in women with histories of childhood sexual abuse. *Journal of Traumatic Stress, 17*(5), 445–448. doi: 10.1023/B:JOTS.0000048959.29766.ae

Tangney, J. P., & Dearing, R. L. (2003). *Shame and guilt.* New York, NY: Guilford Press.

Tart, C. (1998). Six studies of out-of-body experiences. *Journal of Near Death Studies, 17*, 73–99.

Taylor, G. J. (2010). Affects, trauma, and mechanisms of symptom formation: A tribute to John C. Nemiah, MD (1918–2009). *Psychotherapy & Psychosomatics, 79*(6), 339–349. doi: 10.1159/000320119

Taylor, G. J., Bagby, R. M., & Parker, J. D. A. (1997). *Disorders of affect regulation: Alexithymia in medical and psychiatric illness.* Cambridge, UK: Cambridge University Press.

Taylor, S. E., Klein, L. C., Lewis, B. P., Gruenewald, T. L., Gurung, R. A., & Updegraff, J. A. (2000). Biobehavioral responses to stress in females: Tend-and-befriend, not fight-or-flight. *Psychological Review, 107*, 411–429. *doi:* 10.1037/0033-295X.107.3.411

Taylor, S. F., Phan, K. L., Decker, L. R., & Liberzon, I. (2003). Subjective rating of emotionally   salient stimuli modulates neural activity. *NeuroImage, 18*(3), 650–659. doi: 10.1016/S1053-8119(02)00051-4

Teicher, M. H., Glod, C. A., Surrey, J., & Swett, C. (1993). Early childhood abuse and limbic system ratings in adult psychiatric outpatients. *Journal of Neuropsychiatry & Clinical Neurosciences, 5*, 301–306.

Teicher, M. H., Ito, Y., Glod, C. A., Andersen, S. L., Dumont, N., & Ackerman, E. (1997). Preliminary evidence for abnormal cortical development in physically and sexually abused children using EEG coherence and MRI. *Annals of the New York Academy of Science, 821*, 160–175. doi: 10.1111/j.1749-6632.1997.tb48277.x

Teicher, M. H., Samson, J. A., Polcari, A., & McGreenery, C. E. (2006). Sticks, stones, and hurtful words: Relative effects of various forms of childhood maltreatment. *American Journal of Psychiatry, 163*, 993–1000.

Thomas, L. A., & De Bellis, M. D. (2004). Pituitary volumes in pediatric maltreatment-related posttraumatic stress disorder. *Biological Psychiatry, 55*(7), 752–758. doi: 10.1016/j.biopsych.2003.11.021

Thompson, E., & Zahavi, D. (2007). Philosophical issues: Phenomenology. In P. D.

Zelazo, M. Moscovitch, & E. Thompson (Eds.), *Cambridge handbook of consciousness studies* (pp. 67–87). New York, NY: Cambridge University Press.

Thompson, R. J., Mata, J., Jaeggi, S. M., Buschkuehl, M., Jonides, J., & Gotlib, I. H. (2011). Concurrent and prospective relations between attention to emotion and affect intensity: An experience sampling study. *Emotion, 11*, 1489–1494. doi: 10.1037/a0022822

Thomsen, D. K., & Berntsen, D. (2008). The cultural life script and life story chapters contribute to the reminiscence bump. *Memory, 16*(4), 420–435. doi: 10.1080/09658210802010497

Thomsen, D. K., & Berntsen, D. (2009). The long-term impact of emotionally stressful events on memory characteristics and life story. *Applied Cognitive Psychology, 23*(4), 579–598. doi: 10.1002/acp.1495

Thorberg, F. A., Young, R., & Sullivan, K. A. (2011). Parental bonding and alexithymia: A meta-analysis. *European Psychiatry, 26*(3), 187–193. doi: 10.1016/j.eurpsy.2010.09.010

Thorberg, F. A., Young, R., Sullivan, K. A., & Lyvers, M. (2009). Alexithymia and alcohol use disorders: A critical review. *Addictive Behaviors, 34,* 237–245. doi: 10.1016/j.addbeh.2008.10.016

Tien, A. Y. (1991). Distributions of hallucinations in the population. *Social Psychiatry & Psychiatric Epidemiology, 26*(6), 287–292. doi: 10.1007/BF00789221

Tipples, J. (2008). Negative emotionality influences the effects of emotion on time perception. *Emotion, 8*(1), 127–131. doi: 10.1037/1528-3542.8.1.127

Tipples, J. (2011). When time stands still: Fear-specific modulation of temporal bias due to threat. *Emotion, 11*, 74–80. doi: 10.1037/a0022015

Tolmunen, T., Honkalampi, K., Hintikka, J., Rissanen, M., Maaranen, P., Kylmä, J., & Laukkanen, E. (2010). Adolescent dissociation and alexithymia are distinctive but overlapping phenomena. *Psychiatry Research, 176*(1), 40–44. doi: 10.1016/j.psychres.2008.10.029

Tomkins, S. (1995). Shame-humiliation and contempt-disgust. In E. K. Sedgwick & A. Frank (Eds.), *Shame and its sisters: A Silvan Tomkins reader* (pp. 133–178). Durham, NC: Duke University Press.

Tracy, J. L., & Robins, R. W. (2007). The prototypical pride expresson: Development of a nonverbal behavior coding system. *Emotion, 7*(4), 789–801. doi: 10.1037/1528-3542.7.4.789

Tracy, J. L., Robins, R. W., & Tangney, J. P. (2007). *The self-conscious emotions: Theory and research*. New York, NY: Guilford Press.

Tressoldi, P., & Del Prete, G. (2007). ESP under hypnosis: The role of induction instructions and personality characteristics. *Journal of Parapsychology, 71*, 126–137.

Trickett, P. K., Noll, J. G., & Putnam, F. W. (2011). The impact of sexual abuse on female development: Lessons from a multigenerational, longitudinal study. *Development & Psychopathology, 23,* 453–476. http://dx.doi.org.proxy2.lib.uwo.ca/10.1017/S0954579411000174

Tsai, G. E., Condie, D., Wu, M. T., & Chang, I. W. (1999). Functional magnetic resonance imaging of personality switches in a woman with dissociative identity disorder. *Harvard Review of Psychiatry, 7,* 119–122. doi: 10.1093/hrp/7.2.119

Tsakiris, M. (2010). My body in the brain: A neurocognitive model of body-ownership. *Neuropsychologia, 48*(3), 703–712. doi: 10.1016/j.neuropsychologia.2009.09.034

Tsakiris, M., Costantini, M., & Haggard, P. (2008). The role of the right temporo-parietal junction in maintaining a coherent sense of one's body. *Neuropsychologia, 46*(12), 3014–3018. doi: 10.1016/j.neuropsychologia.2008.06.004

Tsakiris, M., Hesse, M. D., Boy, C., Haggard, P., & Fink, G. R. (2007). Neural signatures of body ownership: A sensory network for bodily self-consciousness. *Cerebral Cortex, 17,* 2235–2244. doi: 10.1093/cercor/bhl131

Tsakiris, M., Longo, M. R., & Haggard, P. (2010). Having a body versus moving your body: Neural signatures of agency and body-ownership. *Neuropsychologia, 48*(9), 2740–2749. doi: 10.1016/j.neuropsychologia.2010.05.021

Tsakiris, M., Schütz-Bosbach, S., & Gallagher, S. (2007). On agency and body-ownership: Phenomenological and neurocognitive reflections. *Consciousness & Cognition, 16*(3), 645–660. doi: 10.1016/j.concog.2007.05.012

Tulving, E. (2002a). Chronesthesia: Conscious awareness of subjective time. In D. T. Stuss & R. T. Knight (Eds.), *Principles of frontal lobe function* (pp. 311–325). New York, NY: Oxford University Press.

Tulving, E. (2002b). Episodic memory: From mind to brain. *Annual Review of Psychology, 53*(1), 1–25. doi: 10.1146/annurev.psych.53.100901.135114

Tulving, E. (2005). Episodic memory and autonoesis: Uniquely human? In H. S. Terrace & J. Metcalfe (Eds.), *The missing link in cognition* (pp. 4–56). NewYork, NY: Oxford University Press.

Tupler, L. A., & De Bellis, M. D. (2006). Segmented hippocampal volume in children and adolescents with posttraumatic stress disorder. *Biological Psychiatry, 59*(6), 523–529. doi: 10.1016/j.biopsych.2005.08.007

Tutkun, H., Savas, H. A., Zoroglu, S. S., Esgi, K., Herken, H., & Tiryaki, N. (2004). Relationship between alexithymia, dissociation and anxiety in psychiatric outpatients from Turkey. *Israel Journal of Psychiatry and Related Sciences, 41*(2), 118–124.

Üçok, A., & Bikmaz, S. (2007). The effects of childhood trauma in patients with first-episode schizophrenia. *Acta Psychiatrica Scandinavica, 116*(5), 371–377. doi: 10.1111/j.1600-0447.2007.01079.x

Uddin, L. Q., Iacoboni, M., Lange, C., & Keenan, J. P. (2007). The self and social cognition: The role of cortical midline structures and mirror neurons. *Trends in Cognitive Sciences, 11,* 153–157. doi: 10.1016/j.tics.2007.01.001

Vaitl, D., Birbaumer, N., Gruzelier, J., Jamieson, G. A., Kotchoubey, B., Kübler, A., & Weiss, T. (2005). Psychobiology of altered states of consciousness. *Psychological Bulletin, 131*(1), 98–127. doi: 10.1037/0033-2909.131.1.98

van der Hart, O., & Dorahy, M. J. (2009). History of the concept of dissociation. In P. F. Dell & J. A. O'Neil (Eds.), *Dissociation and the dissociative disorders: DSM-V and beyond* (pp. 3-28). New York, NY: Taylor & Francis.

van der Hart, O., Nijenhuis, E. R. S., & Steele, K. (2005). Dissociation: An insufficiently recognized major feature of complex posttraumatic stress disorder. *Journal of Traumatic Stress, 18*(5), 413–23. doi: 10.1002/jts.20049

van der Hart, O., Nijenhuis, E. R. S., & Steele, K. (2006). *The haunted self: Structural dissociation and the treatment of chronic traumatization.* New York, NY: Norton.

van der Hart, O., van Dijke, A., van Son, M., & Steele, K. (2000). Somatoform dissociation in truamatized World War I combat soldiers: A neglected clinical heritage. *Journal of Trauma and Dissociation, 1*(4), 33–36. doi: 10.1300/ J229v01n04_03

van der Hart, O., van Ochten, J. M., van Son, M. J. M., Steele, K., & Lensvelt-Mulders, G. (2008). Relations among peritraumatic dissociation and posttraumatic stress: A critical review. *Journal of Trauma & Dissociation, 9*(4), 481–505. doi: 10.1080/15299730802223362

van der Kolk, B. A. (1989). The compulsion to repeat the trauma: Re-enactment, revictimization, and masochism. *Psychiatric Clinics of North America, 12*(1), 389–411.

van der Kolk, B. A. (1994). The body keeps the score: Memory and the evolving psychobiology of posttraumatic stress. *Harvard Review of Psychiatry, 1*(5), 253–265. doi: 10.3109/10673229409017088

van der Kolk, B. A., & Fisler, R. (1995). Dissociation and the fragmentary nature of traumatic memories: Overview and exploratory study. *Journal of Traumatic Stress, 8*(4), 505–525. doi: 10.1007/BF02102887

van der Kolk, B. A., & McFarlane, A. (1996). The black hole of trauma. In B. A. van der Kolk, A. C. McFarlane, & L. Weisaeth (Eds.), *Traumatic stress: The overwhelming experience on mind, body, and society* (pp. 3–23). New York, NY: Guilford Press.

van der Meer, L., Costafreda, S., Aleman, A., & David, A. S. (2010). Self-reflection and the brain: A theoretical review and meta-analysis of neuroimaging studies with implications for schizophrenia. *Neuroscience and Biobehavioral Reviews, 34*(6), 935–946. doi: 10.1016/j.neubiorev.2009.12.004

van der Velden, P. G., & Wittmann, L. (2008). The independent predictive value of peritraumatic dissociation for PTSD symptomatology after type I trauma: A systematic review of prospective studies. *Clinical Psychology Review, 28*(6), 1009–1020. doi: 10.1016/j.cpr.2008.02.006

van Overwalle, F. (2009). Social cognition and the brain: A meta-analysis. *Human Brain Mapping, 30*(3), 829–858. doi: 10.1002/hbm.20547

van Overwalle, F., & Baetens, K. (2009). Understanding others' actions and goals by mirror and mentalizing systems: A meta-analysis. *NeuroImage, 48*(3), 564–584. doi: 10.1016/j.neuroimage.2009.06.009

van Wassenhove, V., Buonomano, D. V., Shimojo, S., & Shams, L. (2008). Distortions of subjective time perception within and across senses. *PLoS ONE 3,* e1437. doi: 10.1371/journal. pone.0001437

van Wassenhove, V., Wittmann, M., Craig, A. D., & Paulus, M. P. (2011). Psychological and neural mechanisms of subjective time dilation. *Frontiers in Neuroscience, 5,* 1–10. doi: 10.3389/fnins.2011.00056

Varela, F. J. (1996). Neurophenomenology: A methodological remedy for the hard problem. *Journal of Consiousness Studies, 3*(4), 330–349.

Varela, F. J. (1997). Metaphor to mechanism: Natural to disciplined. *Journal of Consciousness Studies, 4*(4), 344–346.

Varela, F. J. (1999). Present-time consciousness. *Journal of Consciousness Studies, 6*(2–3), 111–140.

Varela, F. J., & Shear, J. (1999). First-person methodologies: What, why, how? *Journal of Consciousness Studies, 6*(2–3), 1–14.

Vermetten, E., & Bremner, J. D. (2004). Functional brain imaging and the induction of traumatic recall: A cross-correlational review between neuroimaging and hypnosis. *International Journal of Clinical & Experimental Hypnosis, 52*(3), 280–312. doi: 10.1080/0020714049052352

Vermetten, E., Dorahy, M. J., & Spiegel, D. (2007). *Traumatic dissociation: Neurobiology and treatment.* Washington, DC: American Psychiatric Association.

Vollhardt, J. R. (2009). Altruism born of suffering and prosocial behavior following adverse life events: A review and conceptualization. *Social Justice Research, 22*(1), 53–97. doi: 10.1007/s11211-009-0088-1

Vollhardt, J. R., & Staub, E. (2011). Inclusive altruism born of suffering: The relationships between adversity and prosocial attitudes and behavior toward disadvantaged outgroups. *American Journal of Orthopsychiatry, 81*(3), 307–315. doi: 10.1111/j.1939-0025.2011.01099.x

Vytal, K., & Hamann, S. (2010). Neuroimaging support for discrete neural correlates of basic emotions: A voxel-based meta-analysis. *Journal of Cognitive Neuroscience, 22,* 2864–2885. doi: 10.1162/jocn.2009.21366

Waelde, L. C., Silvern, L., & Fairbank, J. A. (2005). A taxometric investigation of dissociation in Vietnam veterans. *Journal of Traumatic Stress, 18*(4), 359–369. doi: 10.1002/jts.20034

Wager, T. D., Phan, K. L., Liberzon, I., & Taylor, S. F. (2003). Valence, gender, and lateralization of functional brain anatomy in emotion: A meta-analysis of findings from neuroimaging. *NeuroImage, 19*(3), 513–531. doi:10.1016/S1053-8199(03)00078-8

Wagner, A. W., Roemer, L., Orsillo, S. M., & Litz, B. T. (2003). Emotional experiencing in women with posttraumatic stress disorder: Congruence between facial expressivity and self-report. *Journal of Traumatic Stress, 16*(1), 67–75. doi: 10.1023/A:1022015528894

Wagner, D. D., Kelley, W. M., & Heatherton, T. F. (2011). Individual differences in the spontaneous recruitment of brain regions supporting mental state understanding when viewing natural social scenes. *Cerebral Cortex, 21,* 2788–2796. doi: 10.1093/cercor/bhr074

Wallace, B. A. (2007). *Contemplative science: Where Buddhism and neuroscience converge.* New York, NY: Columbia University Press.

Wallace, B. A., & Shapiro, S. L. (2006). Mental balance and well-being: Building bridges between Buddhism and Western psychology. *American Psychologist, 61*(7), 690–701. doi: 10.1037/0003-066X.61.7.690

Waller, N. G., & Ross, C. A. (1997). The prevalence and biometric structure of pathological dissociation in the general population: Taxometric and behavior genetic findings. *Journal of Abnormal Psychology, 106*(4), 499–510. doi: 10.1037/0021-843X.106.4.499

Wampold, B. E. (2007). Psychotherapy: "The" humanistic (and effective) treatment. *American Psychologist, 62*(8), 857–873. doi: 10.1037/0003-066X.62.8.857

Wampold, B. E. (2012). Humanism as a common factor in psychotherapy. *Psychotherapy, 49*(4), 445–449. doi: 10.1037/a0027113

Wang, G., Mao, L., Ma, Y., Yang, W., Cao, J., Liu, X., . . . Han, S. (2012). Neural representations of close others in collectivistic brains. *Social Cognitive & Affective Neuroscience, 7,* 222–229. doi: 10.1093/scan/nsr002

Ward, N. S., Oakley, D. A., Frackowiak, R. S. J., & Halligan, P. W. (2003). Differential brain activations during intentionally simulated and subjectively experienced paralysis. *Cognitive Neuropsychiatry, 8*(4), 295–312. doi: 10.1080/13546800344000200

Watson, D., & Tellegen, A. (1985). Toward a consensual structure of mood. *Psychological Bulletin, 98,* 219–235. doi: 10.1037/0033-2909.98.2.219

Watson, D., Weise, D., Vaidya, J., & Tellegen, A. (1999). The two general activation systems of affect: Structural findings, evolutionary considerations, and psychobiological evidence. *Journal of Personality & Social Psychology, 76,* 820–838. doi: 10.1037/0022-3514.76.5.820

Weiskopf, N. (2012). Realtime fMRI and its application to neurofeedback. *NeuroImage, 62*(2), 682–692. doi: 10.1016/j.neuroimage.2011.10.009

Whalley, M. G., Kroes, M. C. W., Huntley, Z., Rugg, M. D., Davis, S. W., & Brewin, C. R. (2013). An fMRI investigation of posttraumatic flashbacks. *Brain & Cognition, 51,* 151–159. doi: http://dx.doi.org/10.1016/j.bandc.2012.10.002

Wheat, A. L., & Larkin, K. T. (2010). Biofeedback of heart rate variability and related physiology: A critical review. *Applied Psychophysiology and Biofeedback, 35*(3), 229–242. doi: 10.1007/s10484-010-9133-y

Wheatley, J., Brewin, C. R., Patel, T., Hackmann, A., Wells, A., Fisher, P., & Myers, S. (2007). "I'll believe it when I can see it": Imagery rescripting of intrusive sensory memories in depression. *Journal of Behavior Therapy and Experimental Psychiatry, 38*(4), 371–385. doi: 10.1016/j.jbtep.2007.08.005

Wheatley, J., & Hackman, A. (2011). Using imagery rescripting to treat major depression: Theory and practice. *Cognitive & Behavioral Practice, 18*(4), 444–453. doi: 10.1016/j.cbpra.2010.06.004

Wheeler, M. A., Stuss, D. T., & Tulving, E. (1997). Toward a theory of episodic memory: The frontal lobes and autonoetic consciousness. *Psychological Bulletin, 121*(3), 331–354. doi: 10.1037/0033-2909.121.3.331

Wittmann, M. (2009). The inner experience of time. *Philosophical Transactions of the Royal Society of London. Series B, Biological Sciences, 364*(1525), 1955–1967. doi: 10.1098/rstb.2009.0003

Wiens, S., (2005). Interoception in emotional experience. *Current Opinion in Neurology, 18*(4) 442–447. doi: 10.1097/01.wco.0000168079.92106.99

Wiklander, M., Samuelsson, M., Jokinen, J., Nilsonne, A., Wilczek, A., Rylander, G., & Asberg, M. (2012). Shame proneness in attempted suicide patients. *BMC Psychiatry, 12,* 50. doi: http://www.biomedcentral.com/1471-244X/12/50

Wild, J., & Clark, D. M. (2011). Imagery rescripting of early traumatic memories in social phobia. *Cognitive & Behavioral Practice, 18*(4), 433–443. doi: 10.1016/j.cbpra.2011.03.002

Wilkowski, B. M., Robinson, M. D., & Troop-Gordon, W. (2010). How does cognitive control reduce anger and aggression?: The role of conflict monitoring and forgiveness processes. *Journal of Personality and Social Psychology, 98*(5), 830. doi: 10.1037/a0018962

Williams, L. M., Liddell, B. J., Kemp, A. H., Bryant, R. A., Meares, R. A., Peduto, A. S., & Gordon, E. (2006). Amygdala–prefrontal dissociation of subliminal and supraliminal fear. *Human Brain Mapping, 27*(8), 651–661. doi: 10.1002/hbm.20208

Williamson, P. C., & Allman, J. M. (Eds.). (2011). *The human illnesses: Neuropsychiatric disorders and the nature of the human brain.* New York, NY: Oxford University Press.

Wilson, J. P., Droždek, B., & Turkovic, S. (2006). Posttraumatic shame and guilt. *Trauma, Violence, & Abuse, 7*(2), 122–141. doi: 10.1177/1524838005285914

Wingenfeld, K., Riedesel, K., Petrovic, Z., Philippsen, C., Meyer, B., Rose, M., . . . Spitzer, C. (2011). Impact of childhood trauma, alexithymia, dissociation, and emotion suppression on emotional Stroop task. *Journal of Psychosomatic Research, 70,* 53–58. doi: 10.1016/j.jpsychores.2010.06.003

Wise, T. N., Mann, L. S., & Sheridan, M. J. (2000). Relationship between alexithymia, dissociation, and personality in psychiatric outpatients. *Psychotherapy & Psychosomatics, 69,* 123–127. doi: 10.1159/000012379

Wittman, M. (2009). The inner experience of time. *Philosophical Transactions of the Royal Society B, Biological Sciences, 364*(1525), 1955–1967. doi: 10.1098/rstb.2009.0003

Wolf, E. J., Lunney, C. A., Miller, M. W., Resick, P. A., Friedman, M. J., & Schnurr, P. P. (2012). The dissociative subtype of PTSD: A replication and extension. *Depression & Anxiety, 29,* 679–688. doi: 10.1002/da.21946

Wolf, E. J., Miller, M., Rearon, A. F., Rybchenko, K A., Castillo, D., & Freund, R. (2012). Latent class analysis of dissociation and PTSD: Evidence for a dissociative subtype. *Archives of General Psychiatry, 69,* 698–705. doi: 10.1001/archgenpsychiatry.2011.1574

World Health Organization. (2003). The ICD-10 classification of mental and behavioural disorders: Diagnostic criteria for research. Geneva, Switzerland: Author.

Worthington, E. L., Hook, J. N., Davis, D. E., & McDaniel, M. A. (2011). Religion and spirituality. *Journal of Clinical Psychology: In Session, 67*(2), 204–214. doi: 10.1002/jclp.20760

Xi, C., Zhu, Y., Niu, C., Zhu, C., Lee, T. M. C., Tian, Y., & Wang, K. (2011). Contributions of subregions of the prefrontal cortex to the theory of mind and decision making. *Behavioural Brain Research, 221*, 587–593.

Yik, M., Russell, J. A., & Steiger, J. H. (2011). A 12-point circumplex structure of core affect. *Emotion, 11*(4), 705. doi: 10.1037/a0023980-

Yoshimura, S., Ueda, K., Suzuki, S. I., Onoda, K., Okamoto, Y., & Yamawaki, S. (2009). Self-referential processing of negative stimuli within the ventral anterior cingulate gyrus and right amygdala. *Brain and Cognition, 69*(1), 218–225. doi: 10.1016/j.bandc.2008.07.010

Zaki, J., Davis, J. I., & Ochsner, K. N. (2012). Overlapping activity in anterior insula during interoception and emotional experience. *NeuroImage, 62*, 494–499. doi: 10.1016/j.neuroimage.2012.05.012

Zaki, J., & Ochsner, K. N. (2012). The neuroscience of empathy: Progress, pitfalls and promise. *Nature Neuroscience, 15*(5), 675–680. doi: 10.1038/nn.3085

Zeigler-Hill, V., & Jordan, C. H. (2010). Two faces of self-esteem. In B. Gawronski & B. K. Payne (Eds.), *Handbook of implicit social cognition: Measurement, theory, and applications* (pp. 392–407). New York: Guilford Press.

Zielinski, D., & Bradshaw, C. (2006). Ecological influences on the sequelae of child maltreatment: A review of the literature. *Child Maltreatment, 11*(1), 49–62. doi: 10.1177/1077559505283591

Zoellner, L. A. (2008). Translational challenges with tonic immobility. *Clinical Psychology: Science and Practice, 15*(1), 98–101. doi: 10.1111/j.1468-2850.2008.00114.x

Zoellner, L. A., Sacks, M. B., & Foa, E. B. (2007). Dissociation and serenity induction. *Journal of Behavior Therapy and Experimental Psychiatry, 38*(3), 252–262. doi: 10.1016/j.jbtep.2006.06.003

Zucker, T. L., Samuelson, K. W., Muench, F., Greenberg, M. A., & Gevirtz, R. N. (2012). The effects of respiratory sinus arrhythmia biofeedback on heart rate variability and posttraumatic stress disorder symptoms: A pilot study. *Applied Psychophysiology & Biofeedback, 34*, 135–143. doi: 10.1007/s10484-009-9085-2

Index

psychotraumatology
  neurophenomenology as
    methodology for, 45–69. *see also*
    neurophenomenology
  as paradigm for consciousness studies,
    68–69
PTSD. *see* posttraumatic stress disorder
    (PTSD)
Putnam, F.W., 1, 35–36

Qin, P., 14–15
Quas, J.A., 34

rage
  "being," 246–51, 251*f*
Rahmanovie, A., 158
rape
  dissociative processing, 10–18, 11*f*
Rasmussen, T., 137
Ratcliffe, M., 256
"rational" form of consciousness, xxiii
(re-)embodiment
  during physical exercise, 183–85
reaching out beyond the self
  case example, 287–92
reaction(s)
  negative affective, 217
reaction times (RTs), 112
Read, J., 119–20, 123
readiness
  "fragmented," 57
  "steady," 57
reality
  sense of, 34
reappraisal
  cognitive, 12–14, 242, 243, 248
rebirth of self, 282
  recovery and, 309–10, 310*f*, 311*f*
recall
  anomalous subjective, 160–61
  "distressing," 86
  "normal" episodic, 87
  of trauma narrative, 144, 144*f*
  traumatic memory, 97–99
recovery, 275–319
  case example, 310–17, 318*f*
  as communal act of faith, 287–92
  connecting with others and, 298–304,
    300*f*, 302*f*, 304*f*
  goal for, xix–xx
  rebirth of self due to, 309–10, 310*f*, 311*f*
  on road to, 268–72, 270*f*, 271*f*
reembodying self
  EEG neurofeedback and, 63–66, 64*f*
reexperiencing, 57–63, 59*f*, 62*f*
  tell-tale heart–case study
    defined, 85
    in PTSD, 86
    remembering *vs.*, 85
referential consciousness, 38, 102–4

reflection
  self-schema, 115–17, 116*f*
Reiff, M., 123
Reinders, A.A.T.S., 15
relational consciousness
  connecting with others and, 298–304,
    300*f*, 302*f*, 304*f*
relationship(s)
  early, xiii
relief
  increased, 280–82
religious experiences
  James on, xxiv, xxvi
reliving
  to remembering, 96–97
  remembering *vs.*, 83–97, 89*f*, 92*f*, 93*f*
remembering
  reexperiencing *vs.*, 85
  from reliving to, 96–97
  reliving *vs.*, 83–97, 89*f*, 92*f*, 93*f*
"Remembering, Repeating and Working
    Through," x
repression
  in emotion regulation, 12–13
  Freudian, 17
Resick, P.A., 239
resilience, 275–319
respiratory sinus arrhythmia (RSA), 61
Responses to Script-driven Imagery Scale
    (RSDI), 164
responsiveness
  overmodulation of emotional, 20
reversal
  role, 294
revival from momentarily being dead to the
    world
  case example, 266–68
right temporoparietal junction (rTPJ),
    170–71, 171*f*
Röder, C.H., 156
role reversal, 294
Rozee, P.D., 87–88
RSA. *see* respiratory sinus arrhythmia (RSA)
RSDI. *see* Responses to Script-driven
    Imagery Scale (RSDI)
rTPJ. *see* right temporoparietal junction
    (rTPJ)
RTs. *see* reaction times (RTs)
Rubin, D.C., 107
Ruby, P., 14
Ruddle, A., 134–35
rumination
  analytical, 248
  angry, 248
Russell, J.A., 196, 198–201, 200*f*, 256

salience detection, 65
same event, different experience–case study
  of reexperiencing, 57–61, 59*f*
Sanders, T., 123

For details, a complete list of books in the Series, and to order online, please visit
www.tiny.cc/1zrsfw